973.9310 BAK

BAKER, RUSS

WITHDRAWN

FAMILY OF SECRETS
9781596915572 $30.00 C2009

AUG   2009

D0051032

Family of Secrets

FAMILY OF SECRETS

The Bush Dynasty,
the Powerful Forces That Put It in
the White House, and What Their
Influence Means for America

RUSS BAKER

BLOOMSBURY PRESS
New York • Berlin • London

Copyright © 2009 by Russ Baker

All rights reserved. No part of this book may be used or reproduced in any manner
whatsoever without written permission from the publisher except in the case of brief
quotations embodied in critical articles or reviews. For information address Bloomsbury
Press, 175 Fifth Avenue, New York, NY 10010.

Published by Bloomsbury Press, New York

All papers used by Bloomsbury Press are natural, recyclable products made from wood
grown in well-managed forests. The manufacturing processes conform to the environmental regulations of the country of origin.

LIBRARY OF CONGRESS CATALOGING-IN-PUBLICATION DATA

Baker, Russ, 1958-
Family of secrets : the Bush dynasty, the powerful forces that
put it in the White House, and what their influence means for
America / by Russ Baker.--1st U.S. ed.
p.   cm.
Includes bibliographical references and index
ISBN 978-1-59691-557-2 (alk. paper)
1. Bush family.   2. Bush, George W. (George Walker), 1946-   3. Bush, George W. (George
Walker), 1946---Friends and associates.   4. Bush, George, 1924-   5. Bush, George, 1924---
Friends and associates.   6. Presidents--United States--Biography.   7. United States--
Politics and government--1945-1989.   8. United States--Politics and government--1989-
9. Business and politics--United States.   I. Title.
E904.B35 2009
973.931092--dc22
[B]
2008037433

First U.S. Edition 2009

1 3 5 7 9 10 8 6 4 2

Typeset by Westchester Book Group
Printed in the United States of America by Quebecor World Fairfield

DRIFTWOOD PUBLIC LIBRARY
801 SW HWY. 101
LINCO

For my mother
and in memory of my father

Contents

Contents

Family of Secrets

CHAPTER 1

How Did Bush Happen?

The real truth of the matter is, as you and I
know, that a financial element in the larger
centers has owned the Government ever since
the days of Andrew Jackson.
 —FRANKLIN D. ROOSEVELT TO COLONEL
 EDWARD HOUSE, OCTOBER 21, 1933

History is not history unless it is the truth.
 —ABRAHAM LINCOLN

THIS IS THE TRUE STORY OF A FAMILY we thought we knew—and a country we have barely begun to comprehend.

George Bush, father and son, are vastly more complicated, and their doings are vastly more troubling, than the conventional wisdom would have it. This book reveals the story behind their story, documenting the secrets that the House of Bush has long sought to obscure.

These revelations about the Bushes lead in turn to an even more disturbing truth about the country itself. It's not just that such a clan could occupy the presidency or vice presidency for twenty of the past twenty-eight years and remain essentially unknown. It's that the methods of stealth and manipulation that powered their rise reflect a deeper ill: the American public's increasingly tenuous hold upon the levers of its own democracy.

AS HIS SECOND term came to a close, George W. Bush's approval ratings reached new lows. The prospect that Bush might go down in history as the worst president in a century, and quite possibly the worst ever, became a topic of grim speculation, even among those who had once voted for him. W. had become the lamest of lame ducks. Bush's own father, the forty-first president of the United States—along with his influential friends—watched in silent dismay.

The litany of Bush disasters was as dismally familiar as the brash one-liners that accompanied them: the failed pursuit of Osama bin Laden ("Wanted: Dead or Alive"); the bungled federal response to Katrina ("Heck-uva job, Brownie"); the mishandled occupation of Iraq ("Mission Accomplished"); the collapsed housing bubble that sent the economy sliding toward recession and millions of Americans into foreclosure ("We're creating an ownership society").

No wonder that by George W. Bush's final year in office, 81 percent of Americans told pollsters they believed the country was headed in the wrong direction. And it was becoming clearer to many that this *wrongness* was a matter not just of flawed policy decisions, but more fundamentally, of W.'s personal limitations. Which raised an obvious question—so obvious that just about everyone passed it by: How did Bush happen? Why was this particular man out of all possible aspirants encouraged and even propelled to the top?

During his meteoric career, George W. Bush has been treated as a singular if highly controversial man, an island unto himself. Many books—from the favorable *Misunderestimated* to the critical *The Bush Tragedy*—have sought to unpack, dissect, and psychoanalyze the forty-third president. Most brought some new insight, but none of the portraits seemed to fully capture the essence of the man. And as the end of his presidency neared, there was an understandable rush to move on. We had seen what happened; we were mostly appalled or, in fewer cases, ambivalent or, in fewer still, supportive. But the consensus seemed to be that whatever damage W. had wrought, his presidency was at worst some kind of aberration, a glitch in the system that could and would be patched over by his successors, who would return Washington to some semblance of representative democracy. The George W. Bush chapter would soon recede into history.

From the beginning of his first term I had doubts. There were signs of something more consequential and pervasive—well beyond the missteps, overreaching, and palace intrigues one finds in all presidential administrations. The fanatical secrecy, the proclivity for police state tactics and contempt for democratic safeguards, the blatant determination to advance the interests of those who already had so much, the efforts to politicize government services from top to bottom—these were evidence of a mind-set rarely seen in American politics. Above all, the deception at the root of the decision to invade Iraq and the disastrous occupation that followed only confirmed my feeling that the assumption of power by Bush pointed to something deeper than a callow and entitled president surrounded by enablers and Iagos with dark schemes.

In 2004, as George W. Bush headed toward reelection, I began the research that would lead to this book. I resolved to grapple with questions that went beyond the sound bites of the twenty-four-hour news cycle: What did the ascendancy of this frighteningly inadequate man signify? Could anything be learned from the George W. Bush phenomenon that would help us understand how we Americans choose our leaders and chart our collective course?

Certain things were already apparent. The Iraq War was not, and never had been, about an imminent threat to the safety of America and its allies; even Republicans like former Federal Reserve chairman Alan Greenspan were publicly acknowledging that it was mostly about oil. George W. Bush, who had run as a moderate "uniter," had in fact done everything in his power to exacerbate the divisions in our society for political gain. As a direct result of his administration's policies, the distribution of wealth in America had been further skewed toward the wealthiest fraction of Americans at the very top. An administration headed by a Republican who preached limited government with limited powers was both shrouded in secrecy and aggressively intrusive in the name of national security.

All this was generally attributed to the actions of one man, aided and abetted by a small coterie of loyal associates. Some Bush critics talked about a larger network of backers who had nurtured Bush and were benefiting from his actions. But these allusions were general and vague, and supporting facts were few. Few of the critiques succeeded in putting the Bush phenomenon in a larger context that would help people understand what forces in America had helped to bring about this state of affairs.

Seeking answers, I crisscrossed the United States, speaking with all kinds of people—Washington insiders and Texas muckrakers, old friends of Bush and dedicated foes, tycoons and typists. I interviewed scores of people familiar with the Bush family, many of whom had never spoken publicly (or in such detail) before. I read everything I could get my hands on, from popular histories to arcane treatises and self-published memoirs, along with obscure and moldering documents of every description. Old drilling records, campaign finance filings, and little-read oral history transcripts became my constant companions.

My Bush library grew to approximately five hundred books, which occupied an entire wall in my New York apartment. I reexamined the Bushes from all angles: their history, family dynamics, business dealings, the social world they inhabit, and the networks of associates, employees, and funders who were instrumental in their rise. I worked from the bottom up and the outside in—questioning neighbors and factotums, ex-girlfriends and ex-employees, and hundreds of ordinary people whose personal experiences and observations came to provide an entirely new view of this purportedly overexposed dynasty.

The more I learned, the broader my questions grew. And as my research deepened, disturbing patterns coalesced.

I came to grasp why early in his presidency, George W. Bush had sought to roll back reforms designed to provide greater access to documents that shed light on America's recent past. He seemed determined to lock the file drawers. But what did those drawers contain? Could there be clues regarding the origins of George W. Bush's most damaging policies—the rush to war in Iraq, officially sanctioned torture, CIA destruction of evidence, spying on Americans with the collusion of private corporations, head-in-the-sand dismissal of climate change, the subprime mortgage disaster, skyrocketing oil prices? Indeed there could. None of these developments looks so surprising when one considers the untold story of what came before. This book is about that secret history, and the people and institutions that created it.

BUSH'S MISTAKES—AND his biggest surely was the delusion that he could successfully lead the nation as its president—were only the most recent chapters in a story that goes back to his father and even his grandfather. Ultimately, it finds its origin in the Gilded Age of the late nineteenth century, when the so-called robber barons—whom Teddy Roosevelt called "malefactors of great wealth"—gained control of enormous industrial, transportation, and financial empires.

Although George W. Bush styled himself something of a family rebel, and the media echoed this self-serving portrayal, to a remarkable degree George W. has followed a path laid out for him by his forebears. He went to the same schools, joined the same secret societies, and benefited from similarly murky financial arrangements. He has made the same kinds of friends and surrounded himself with people closely related to those who surrounded his father, his grandfather, and even his great-grandfather. Despite all the talk about his "Oedipal" relationship to his father, the younger Bush clung closely to the trunk of the family tree.

To my surprise, I began to see that understanding George H. W. Bush (Senior, or Poppy, as his relatives and friends call him) was really the key to understanding the son—and not just in the simplistic, psychoanalytical terms to which some commentators have resorted.

For this reason, half of this book deals principally with Poppy Bush. It lays out the ways in which the father epitomizes the intersection of oil, finance, and sub rosa intelligence that has been a shadow force in our country for the last half century and more. This background is crucial to understanding George W. Bush. As Kevin Phillips so aptly noted, "Dealing separately with the administrations of George H. W. and George W.—or worse, ignoring commonalities of behavior in office—is like considering individual planets while ignoring their place within the solar system."

Building on the hidden past of George Bush the elder, I reveal how and why that most improbable national leader, George Bush the younger, was essentially cleaned up, reconditioned, and then "managed" into becoming his father's successor in the White House. Once this is understood, it becomes clear that George W., like his father, has both benefited from and faithfully served powerful interests that have remained largely hidden from the public eye and immune to public debate.

There's a paradox here: while serving forces that operate best in the shadows, the Bushes craved for themselves a place in the spotlight. To get what they wanted and to do what they felt they must, they had to live what amounts to double lives. Even as the Bushes gained fame and power, they managed to somehow avoid careful scrutiny of their actions and purposes. So adept were they at this game that they are almost never mentioned in their colleagues' writings—not Senator Prescott Bush, and not United Nations representative and Republican National Committee chairman George H. W. Bush. Although Richard Nixon makes bland reference to Poppy Bush's vice presidency and presidency in his memoirs, he does not even bother to mention that Poppy served him in two top posts and held cabinet rank. It is almost as if this clan never existed until the moment it occupied the White House.

This book fills in the gaps. It chronicles the evolution of both the Bush clan and the powerful interests it represented over the last century. In detailing how George W. Bush rose to power, it challenges the accepted wisdom with regard to a number of seminal events in recent American history. And it does so with names, dates, and sources clearly spelled out. Wherever possible, I make clear the identities of those I interviewed; virtually every informant is named.

Even some early biographers sensed that the Bushes' supposedly supporting role in history was in fact something far different. Bill Minutaglio, who wrote the first biography of George W. Bush, before he became president, shared his perceptions with me in 2004. "The Bushes, when you really begin examining them and their network, back to the founding of the country and when they set foot here, they live in the gray zone. If you think of them as part of a photograph, they're in the frame at all these watershed moments in presidential politics and at the pinnacle of finance and business power. They're right there with the Rockefellers and the Vanderbilts and the Astors, but they're not in the middle of the frame. They're off to the side in the sepia photo; they're less clear. But they are perhaps the most profound political dynasty in the history of this country."

The reason the Bushes are relevant today, even with W.'s exit from the national stage, is that the family and its colleagues and associates represent an elite that has long succeeded in subverting our democratic institutions to their own ends. And they will continue to do so unless their agenda and methods are laid bare to public scrutiny.

The story of the Bushes' rise—and fall?—is a story we ignore at our peril.

CHAPTER 2

Poppy's Secret

W HEN JOSEPH MCBRIDE CAME upon the document about George
H. W. Bush's double life, he was not looking for it. It was 1985,
and McBride, a writer for *Daily Variety*, was in a public library in
the San Bernardino Mountains, researching a book about the movie director
Frank Capra.[1] Like many good reporters, McBride took off on a "slight," if
time-consuming, tangent—spending day after day poring over reels of micro-
filmed documents related to the FBI and the JFK assassination. McBride had
been a volunteer on Kennedy's campaign, and since 1963 had been intrigued
by the unanswered questions surrounding that most singular of American
tragedies.

A particular memo caught his eye, and he leaned in for a closer look.
Practically jumping off the screen was a memorandum from FBI director J. Edgar Hoover, dated November 29, 1963. Under the subject heading "Assassination of President John F. Kennedy," Hoover reported that,
on the day after JFK's murder, the bureau had provided two individuals
with briefings. One was "Captain William Edwards of the Defense Intelligence Agency." The other: "Mr. George Bush of the Central Intelligence
Agency."[2]

To:
Director
Bureau of Intelligence and Research
Department of State

> [We have been] advised that the Department of State feels some misguided anti-Castro group might capitalize on the present situation and undertake an unauthorized raid against Cuba, believing that the assassination of President John F. Kennedy might herald a change in U.S. policy . . . [Our] sources know of no [such] plans . . . The substance of the foregoing information was orally furnished to Mr. George Bush of the Central Intelligence Agency and Captain William Edwards of the Defense Intelligence Agency.

McBride shook his head. George H. W. Bush? In the CIA in 1963? Dealing with Cubans and the JFK assassination? Could this be the same man who was now vice president of the United States? Even when Bush was named CIA director in 1976 amid much agency-bashing, his primary asset had been the fact that he was not a part of the agency during the coups, attempted coups, and murder plots in Iran, Cuba, Chile, and other hot spots, embarrassing information about which was being disclosed every day in Senate hearings.[3]

For CIA director Bush, there had been much damage to control. The decade from 1963 to 1973 had seen one confidence-shaking crisis after another. There was the Kennedy assassination and the dubious accounting of it by the Warren Commission. Then came the revelations of how the CIA had used private foundations to channel funds to organizations inside the United States, such as the National Student Association. Then came Watergate, with its penumbra of CIA operatives such as E. Howard Hunt and their shadowy misdoings. Americans were getting the sense of a kind of sanctioned underground organization, operating outside the law and yet protected by it. Then President Gerald Ford, who had ascended to that office when Richard Nixon resigned, fired William Colby, the director of the CIA, who was perceived by hard-liners as too accommodating to congressional investigators and would-be intelligence reformers.

Now Ford had named George H. W. Bush to take over the CIA. But Bush seemed wholly unqualified for such a position—especially at a time when the agency was under maximum scrutiny. He had been U.N. ambassador, Republican National Committee chairman, and then U.S. envoy to Beijing, where both Nixon and Henry Kissinger had regarded him as a lightweight and worked around him. What experience did he have in the world of intelligence and spying? How would he restore public confidence in a tarnished spy agency? No one seemed to know. Or did Gerald Ford realize something most others didn't?

Bush served at the CIA for one year, from early 1976 to early 1977. He worked quietly to reverse the Watergate-era reforms of CIA practices, moving as many operations as possible offshore and beyond any accountability. Although a short stint, it nevertheless created an image problem in 1980 when Bush ran unsuccessfully for the Republican presidential nomination against former California governor Ronald Reagan. Some critics warned of the dangerous precedent in elevating someone who had led the CIA, with its legacy of dark secrets and covert plots, blackmail and murder, to preside over the United States government.

Calling the Vice President

In 1985, when McBride found the FBI memo apparently relating to Bush's past, the reporter did not immediately follow up this curious lead. Bush was now a recently reelected vice president (a famously powerless position), and McBride himself was busy with other things. He had remarried, he continued to cover the Hollywood scene, and he had a book to finish.

By 1988, however, the true identity of "Mr. George Bush of the CIA" took on new meaning, as George H. W. Bush prepared to assume his role as Reagan's heir to the presidency. Joe McBride decided to make the leap from entertainment reportage to politics. He picked up the phone and called the White House.

"May I speak with the vice president?" he asked.

McBride had to settle for Stephen Hart, a vice presidential spokesman. Hart denied that his boss had been the man mentioned in the memo, quoting Bush directly: "I was in Houston, Texas, at the time and involved in the independent oil drilling business. And I was running for the Senate in late '63. I don't have any idea of what he's talking about." Hart concluded with this suggestion: "Must be another George Bush."

McBride found the response troubling—rather detailed for a ritual nondenial. It almost felt like a cover story that Bush was a bit too eager to trot out. He returned to Hart with more questions for Bush:

- Did you do any work with or for the CIA prior to the time you became its director?
- If so, what was the nature of your relationship with the agency, and how long did it last?

- Did you receive a briefing by a member of the FBI on anti-Castro Cuban activities in the aftermath [of] the assassination of President Kennedy?

Within half an hour, Hart called him back. The spokesman now declared that, though he had *not* spoken with Bush, he would nevertheless answer the questions himself. Hart said that the answer to the first question was no, and, therefore, the other two were moot.

Undeterred, McBride called the CIA. A spokesman for the agency, Bill Devine, responded: "This is the first time I've ever heard this . . . I'll see what I can find out and call you back."

The following day, the PR man was tersely formal and opaque: "I can neither confirm nor deny." It was the standard response the agency gave when it dealt with its sources and methods. Could the agency reveal whether there had been another George Bush in the CIA? Devine replied: "Twenty-seven years ago? I doubt that very much. In any event, we have a standard policy of not confirming that anyone is involved in the CIA."[4]

But it appears this standard policy was made to be broken. McBride's revelations appeared in the July 16, 1988, issue of the liberal magazine the *Nation*, under the headline "The Man Who Wasn't There, 'George Bush,' C.I.A. Operative." Shortly thereafter, Central Intelligence Agency spokeswoman Sharron Basso told the Associated Press that the CIA believed that "the record should be clarified." She said that the FBI document "apparently" referred to a George *William* Bush who had worked in 1963 on the night shift at the Langley, Virginia, headquarters, and that "would have been the appropriate place to have received such an FBI report." George William Bush, she said, had left the CIA in 1964 to join the Defense Intelligence Agency.

Certainly, the article caused George H. W. Bush no major headaches. By the following month, he was triumphantly accepting the GOP's presidential nomination at its New Orleans convention, unencumbered by tough questions about his past.

Meanwhile, the CIA's Basso told reporters that the agency had been unable to locate the "other" George Bush. The assertion was reported by several news outlets, with no comment about the irony of a vaunted intelligence agency—with a staff of thousands and a budget of billions—being unable to locate a former employee within American borders.

Perhaps what the CIA really needed was someone like Joseph McBride. Though not an investigative journalist, McBride had no trouble finding

George William Bush. Not only was the man findable; he was still on the U.S. government payroll. By 1988 this George Bush was working as a claims representative for the Social Security Administration. He explained to McBride that he had worked only briefly at the CIA, as a GS-5 probationary civil servant, analyzing documents and photos during the night shift. Moreover, he said, he had never received interagency briefings.

Several years later, in 1991, former *Texas Observer* editor David Armstrong would track down the other person listed on the Hoover memo, Captain William Edwards. Edwards would confirm that he had been on duty at the Defense Intelligence Agency the day in question. He said he did not remember this briefing, but that he found the memo plausible in reference to a briefing he might have received over the phone while at his desk. While he said he had no idea who the George Bush was who also was briefed, Edwards's rank and experience was certainly far above that of the night clerk George William Bush.

Shortly after McBride's article appeared in the *Nation*, the magazine ran a follow-up op-ed, in which the author provided evidence that the Central Intelligence Agency had foisted a lie on the American people.[5] The piece appeared while everyone else was focusing on Bush's coronation at the Louisiana Superdome. As with McBride's previous story, this disclosure was greeted with the equivalent of a collective media yawn. An opportunity was bungled, not only to learn about the true history of the man who would be president, but also to recognize the "George William Bush" diversion for what it was: one in a long series of calculated distractions and disinformation episodes that run through the Bush family history.

With the election only two months away, and a growing sense of urgency in some quarters, George William Bush acknowledged under oath—as part of a deposition in a lawsuit brought by a nonprofit group seeking records on Bush's past—that he was the junior officer on a three- to four-man watch shift at CIA headquarters between September 1963 and February 1964, which was on duty when Kennedy was shot.[6] "I do not recognize the contents of the memorandum as information furnished to me orally or otherwise during the time I was at the CIA," he said. "In fact, during my time at the CIA, I did not receive any oral communications from any government agency of any nature whatsoever. I did not receive any information relating to the Kennedy assassination during my time at the CIA from the FBI. Based on the above, it is my conclusion that I am not the Mr. George Bush of the Central Intelligence Agency referred to in the memorandum."

Indeed, George William Bush was so low-level that he was not even allowed to talk on the telephone or perform any substantive activities. He referred to his role as that of a "gofer." After his short probationary period, George William Bush left the agency, raising the question of whether his hiring could have been designed to provide the other George Bush with cover during a particularly sensitive period. Though that scenario appears far-fetched on first blush, such techniques are a standard part of spy tradecraft. And they can be quite successful: years later, when questions arose about the famous George Bush, there was this other nonentity, providing crucial, if flimsy, cover.

Poppy's Briny Past

Almost a decade would pass between Bush's election in 1988 and the declassification and release in 1996 of another government document that shed further light on the matter. This declassified document would help to answer some of the questions raised by the '63 Hoover memo—questions such as, "If George Herbert Walker Bush was already connected with the CIA in 1963, how far back did the relationship go?"

But yet another decade would pass before this second document would be found, *read*, and revealed to the public. Fast-forward to December 2006, on a day when JFK assassination researcher Jerry Shinley sat, as he did on so many days, glued to his computer, browsing through the digitized database of documents on the Web site of the Mary Ferrell Foundation.[7]

On that December day, Shinley came upon an internal CIA memo that mentioned George H. W. Bush. Dated November 29, 1975, it reported, in typically spare terms, the revelation that the man who was about to become the head of the CIA actually had prior ties to the agency. And the connection discussed here, unlike that unearthed by McBride, went back not to 1963, but to 1953—a full decade earlier. Writing to the chief of the spy section of the analysis and espionage agency, the chief of the "cover and commercial staff" noted:

> Through Mr. Gale Allen . . . I learned that Mr. George Bush, DCI designate, has prior knowledge of the now terminated project WUBRINY/LPDICTUM which was involved in proprietary commercial operations in Europe. He became aware of this project

through Mr. Thomas J. Devine, a former CIA Staff Employee and later, oil-wildcatting associate with Mr. Bush. Their joint activities culminated in the establishment of Zapata Oil [sic] which they eventually sold. After the sale of Zapata Oil, Mr. Bush went into politics, and Mr. Devine became a member of the investment firm of Train, Cabot and Associates, New York . . . The attached memorandum describes the close relationship between Messrs. Devine and Bush in 1967-1968 which, according to Mr. Allen, continued while Mr. Bush was our ambassador to the United Nations.

In typical fashion for the highly compartmentalized and secretive intelligence organization, the memo did not make clear how Bush knew Devine, or whether Devine was simply dropping out of the spy business to become a true entrepreneur. For Devine, who would have been about twenty-seven years old at the time, to "resign" at such a young age, so soon after the CIA had spent a great deal of time and money training him, was, at minimum, highly unusual. It would turn out, however, that Devine had a special relationship allowing him to come and go from the agency, enabling him to do other things without really leaving its employ. In fact, CIA history is littered with instances where CIA officers have tendered their "resignation" as a means of creating deniability while continuing to work closely with the agency. One such example is the colorful E. Howard Hunt, whose "resignation" in 1970 left him in a position to find work in the Nixon White House—where he promptly began a "liaison" relationship with his old bosses.[8]

Devine's role in setting up Zapata would remain hidden for more than a decade—until 1965. At that point, as Bush was extricating himself from business to devote his energies to pursuing a congressional seat, Devine's name suddenly surfaced as a member of the board of Bush's spin-off company, Zapata Offshore—almost as if it was his function to keep the operation running. To be sure, he and Bush remained joined at the hip. As indicated in the 1975 CIA memo, Bush and Devine enjoyed a "close relationship" that continued while Mr. Bush was U.S. ambassador to the United Nations nine years later. In fact, Devine even accompanied then-congressman Bush on a two-week junket to Vietnam, leaving the day after Christmas in 1967, a year before the Republicans would retake the White House. After being "out" of the CIA since 1953, Devine's top-secret security clearance required an update, though what top-secret business a freshman congressman on the Ways and Means Committee could have, requiring two weeks in Vietnam with a "businessman," was not made clear.

The writer of the above-mentioned CIA memo had appended an earlier memo from agency files, describing Thomas Devine's role in a CIA project codenamed WUBRINY. Devine was "a cleared and witting contact in the investment banking firm which houses and manages the proprietary corporation WUSALINE." (BRINY was actually a Haiti-based operation engaged by a corporation, code-named SALINE, that was wholly owned by the CIA. SALINE, like many CIA proprietaries, was in turn operating inside a "legitimate" corporation, whose employees were generally unaware of the spies in their midst.) In this case, the cover corporation was run by investment banker John Train, a sponsor and longtime enthusiast of foreign intrigues, from financing the CIA-connected literary publication the *Paris Review* to backing the Afghan rebels during the Reagan-Bush years.[9] Train was enormously well connected, and received appointments from presidents Reagan, Bush Senior, and even Bill Clinton.

Devine, like the senior George Bush, is now in his eighties and still active in business in New York. When I reached him in the winter of 2007 and told him about recently uncovered CIA memos that related both his agency connections and his longtime ties to Bush, he uttered a dry chuckle, then continued on cautiously.

"Tell me who you are working with in the family," he asked when I informed him I was working on a book about the Bushes. I explained that the book was not exactly an "authorized" biography, and therefore I was not "working" with someone in the family. Moreover, I noted, the Bushes were not known for their responsiveness to journalistic inquiries. "The family policy has been as long as George has been in office, they don't talk to media," Devine replied. But he agreed to contact the Bush family seeking clearance. "Well, the answer is, I will inquire. I have your telephone number, and I'll call you back when I've inquired."

Surprisingly enough, he did call again, two weeks later, having checked in with his old friend in Houston. He explained that he had been told by former president George H. W. Bush not to cooperate. When I spoke to him several months later, he still would not talk about anything—though he did complain that, thanks to an article I had written about him for the Real News Project (www.realnews.org), he was now listed in Wikipedia. And then he did offer a few words.

THOMAS DEVINE: Well, the notion that I put George Bush in the oil business is just nuts.

RUSS BAKER: Well, it says that in the CIA memo. I didn't make it up.

TD: That's the trouble with you guys. You believe what you read in government documents.

RB: So you think somebody put that in there deliberately and that it was untrue?

TD: I think they didn't know what they were doing . . . I wish you well, but I just broke one of the first rules in this game.

RB: And what is that?

TD: Do not complain.

In fact, Devine had little to complain about. At the time, although I was aware that he seemed to be confirming that he himself had been in the "game," I did not understand the full extent of his activities in conjunction with Bush. Nor did I understand the heightened significance of their relationship during the tumultuous events of 1963, to be discussed in subsequent chapters.

No Business like the Spy Business

Before there was an Office of Strategic Services (July 1942–October 1945) or a Central Intelligence Agency (founded in 1947), corporations and attorneys who represented international businesses often employed associates in their firms as private agents to gather data on competitors and business opportunities abroad. So it was only to be expected that many of the first OSS recruits were taken from the ranks of oil companies, Wall Street banking firms, and Ivy League universities and often equated the interests of their high-powered business partners with the national interest. Such relationships like the one between George H. W. Bush and Thomas Devine thus made perfect sense to the CIA, which was comfortable taking orders from such Wall Street icons as Henry L. Stimson, Robert A. Lovett, William "Wild Bill" Donovan, John Foster Dulles, and Allen Dulles—men who were always mindful of President Calvin Coolidge's adage that "the business of America is business."

The late Robert T. Crowley, who managed the CIA's relations with cooperative multinational corporations like Ford Motor Company and International

Telephone and Telegraph, has explained, however, that working with existing companies was not always the best way to go when the CIA was running
agents abroad. "Sometimes we would suggest someone go off on their
own," Crowley told the journalist and author Joseph Trento. "It was much
easier to simply set someone up in business like Bush and let him take
orders."[10]

The setup with Devine in the oil business provided Bush with a perfect
cover to travel abroad and, according to Crowley, identify potential CIA recruits among foreign nationals. It was a simple task for a man whose father,
Prescott, was a senior partner at the preeminent British-American investment bank Brown Brothers Harriman.

Understanding the role of Brown Brothers Harriman is central to understanding the Bush legacy and the vast, if underappreciated, influence of the
Bushes' immediate circle. At Yale, in 1916, Prescott Bush had become close
friends with his classmate Roland "Bunny" Harriman, heir, along with his older
brother, W. Averell Harriman, to E. H. Harriman's vast railroad, shipping,
mining, and banking empire. Both Harrimans, like Prescott Bush, were initi-
ates of the Yale secret society Skull and Bones. After graduation, Prescott took
a job offer from a Skull and Bones elder in St. Louis, where he soon married
the daughter of the prominent St. Louis stockbroker George Herbert Walker.
Shortly after that, G. H. Walker was hired by the Harrimans to come to New
York and build a new investment banking empire for the family.

Perhaps to forestall charges of obvious nepotism, Prescott spent several
years working for other firms before joining W. A. Harriman in 1926. One
year after the stock market crash of 1929, W. A. Harriman merged with Brown
Brothers, a white-shoe banking partnership whose Wall Street operation dated
to 1843, and whose roots went back decades earlier to cotton mills in England.
The oldest and largest partnership bank in the United States, Brown Brothers
Harriman has never been widely known outside Wall Street and Washington,
yet it remains extremely influential in the closely connected worlds of finance
and politics.

The firm's real power lies in its ability to meld moneymaking with policy—
in particular, foreign policy advantageous to the interests of its clients. On
June 7, 1922, the *Nation* published an editorial titled "The Republic of Brown
Brothers." It attacked the "new imperialism" of the United States in Central
America and the Caribbean, a concomitant in good part of the "dollar diplo-
macy" promoted by Secretary of State Philander C. Knox during President
Taft's administration. The editorial asserted that over the past dozen years, the

American government had reduced Haiti, Santo Domingo (later known as the Dominican Republic), and Nicaragua "to the status of colonies with at most a degree of rather fictitious self-government." The United States had "forced ruinous loans, making 'free and sovereign' republics the creatures of New York banks." In effect, the U.S. government had been "agents for these bankers, using American Marines when necessary to impose their will." But according to Brown Brothers Harriman's in-house history, *Partners in Banking*, it was the other way around—the firm was doing the U.S. government a favor.[11]

Earlier partners in the Brown Brothers bank in England had served in governments in that country, and the firm's influence in the United States was perhaps even greater. Brown Brothers Harriman was resolutely bipartisan, and partners moved effortlessly from Wall Street to Washington and back through a steadily revolving door. Prescott and some others were Republicans, while Democrat Averell Harriman built a formidable career for himself in government service, at high levels and in every conceivable capacity, for presidents from FDR to Lyndon Johnson. Partner Robert Lovett, yet another Bonesman in the firm, worked directly as one of Henry Stimson's "wise men" on foreign policy before being named secretary of defense by President Truman.

The Brown Brothers Harriman group was to a person rabidly Anglophilic. Indeed, the Bushes have long touted their distant familial ties to the House of Windsor.[12] And like the once-great British Empire, the sun never set on the operations of the banking firm. Thus it was that the vanquishing of the German Empire in World War I presented abundant opportunities to invest throughout Europe, and led to extensive financial relationships in German-influenced areas. As a result of this, Prescott Bush and Brown Brothers would have some assets seized by the U.S. government for continuing to do business with the most powerful German industrialists at a time when those men were financing the Nazi Party and the rise of Adolf Hitler.[13]

By the time George H. W. Bush founded his own company, Zapata Petroleum, it was not difficult to line up backers with long-standing ties to industrial espionage activities. One was Clark Estates Inc., a trust benefiting the descendants of a founder of what would become known as the Singer sewing machine company. By setting up British factories in 1868, Singer earned the distinction of being perhaps the world's first multinational corporation. Clark Estates was a ground-floor investor in Zapata in 1953.[14]

Clark Estates and Zapata had the same legal representation: Winthrop, Stimson, Putnam & Roberts, the old law firm of former secretary of war and Bonesman Henry Stimson.

"Poppy" Bush's own role with intelligence appears to date back as early as the Second World War, when he joined the Navy at age eighteen.[15] On arrival at his training base in Norfolk, Virginia, in the fall of 1942, Bush was trained not only as a pilot of a torpedo bomber but also as a photographic officer, responsible for crucial, highly sensitive aerial surveillance. On his way to his ship, the USS *San Jacinto*, Bush stopped off in Pearl Harbor for meetings with military intelligence officers assigned to the Joint Intelligence Center for the Pacific Ocean Areas (JICPOA).

After mastering the technique of operating the handheld K-20 aerial camera and film processing, Bush recruited and trained other pilots and crewmen. His own flight team became part bomber unit, part spy unit. The information they obtained about the Japanese navy, as well as crucial intelligence on Japanese land-based defenses, was forwarded to the U.S. Navy's intelligence center at Pearl Harbor and to the Marine Corps for use in planning amphibious landings in order to reduce casualties.

The so-called Operation Snapshot was so hush-hush that, under naval regulations in effect at the time, even revealing its name would lead to court-martial. According to a book by Robert Stinnett, a fellow flier, Admiral Marc Mitscher hit the "bulkhead" when he saw that Bush's team had filed a report in which they actually referred by name to their top-secret project. The three people above Bush in his command chain were made to take razor blades to the pages of the report and remove the forbidden language.[16]

The lesson was apparently not lost on Bush. From that moment forward, as every Bush researcher has learned, Bush's life would honor the principle: no names, no paper trail, no fingerprints. If you wanted to know what Bush had done, you had to have the patience of a sleuth yourself.

A Changing Story

The enveloping fog extends even to Poppy Bush's most sterling political symbol: his record as a war hero.

On September 2, 1944, the plane he was piloting was hit by Japanese fire during a bombing run over Chichi Jima, a small island in the Pacific. Bush successfully parachuted to the ocean surface, where he was rescued. His two crew members perished.

A documentary film about the rescue was aired as part of a 1984 Republican Convention tribute to Vice President Bush. And on September 2, 1984, forty years to the day of his doomed bombing mission, a ceremony was held at the Norfolk Naval Station, complete with a Navy band and an encomium from Navy Secretary John Lehman. Bush's war service, Lehman declared, was the beginning of a career "which went on to mark some of the most remarkable achievements in the annals of American politics."[17]

The real story turns out to be far more complicated. In particular, there are two unresolved issues: What did Bush know of his crew members' fate? And how badly was his plane hit at the moment when he decided to bail out? These are not merely hypothetical: as the pilot, Bush's decision to ditch the craft would have doomed anyone still on board. Navy regulations dictate that officers who are thought to have abandoned crew members could be court-martialed.

On board with Bush that day were Radioman Second Class John Delaney, situated below in the plane's belly, and, directly behind Bush, the turret gunner Lieutenant Junior Grade William Gardiner "Ted" White. Bush would claim in an early 1980s interview with author Doug Wead that he had seen at least one parachute leaving the plane. In 2002 he told the author James Bradley that he had not known the fate of either of his crew members. After Bradley had finished conducting an interview with Bush for his book *Flyboys: A True Story of Courage*, the former president turned to the author and asked if he had any information on the fate of his two crewmen.

"It still plagues me if I gave those guys enough time to get out," Bush said.

Bradley would later write in his book: "No one knew exactly what had happened to Ted and John that day, only that both of them died."[18]

Yet Poppy has offered multiple conflicting versions of the episode. In a letter to his parents following his rescue, Poppy asserted that after the plane was hit, he had ordered his crew members to parachute out. He was uncertain what happened next, he claimed, due to the smoke that filled the cockpit: "They didn't answer at all, but I looked around and couldn't see Ted in the turret so I assumed he had gone below to get his chute fastened on."

Another version surfaced in the 1980s, when his staff decided that Bush had previously been too modest and now needed to acknowledge his heroism.

They hooked him up with a writer, Doug Wead, who prepared the book *George Bush: Man of Integrity*. In that book, which got little attention, Poppy says:

> I looked back and saw that my rear gunner [White] was out. He had been machine-gunned to death right where he was.[19]

There also exists a tape of Bush being interviewed by Wead, as part of a set of interviews the author conducted with famous figures, including Jimmy Carter and former Israeli leader Menachem Begin. On that tape, Bush can be heard to refer clearly to White, and to mention that he saw that White was very much in the plane before bailing out:

> One of them jumped out and his parachute streamed. They had fighter planes over us and they could see the chute open, and *the other one . . . he was killed in the plane.* You can see, [in] a torpedo bomber, the pilot is separate from the crew, but *you can look over and see the turret, and he was just slumped over.* [emphasis mine]

Another claim of Poppy's would later be challenged: that his plane was effectively crippled. In *Looking Forward*, a 1988 campaign book coauthored by Bush and campaign staffer Victor Gold, Poppy writes: "The flak was the heaviest I'd ever flown into . . . Suddenly there was a jolt, as if a massive fist had crunched into the belly of the plane. Smoke poured into the cockpit, and I could see flames rippling across the crease of the wing, edging toward the fuel tanks."

Not so, said Chester Mierzejewski, the tail gunner in the plane directly ahead of Bush's. Mierzejewski came forward to challenge Bush after noticing inconsistencies in public accounts of Bush's mission that day. He was struck by how all the versions differed from what he saw. Mierzejewski had the best and most unobstructed view, and could see directly into Bush's cockpit. A nonpolitical man who had been Bush's partner in shipboard bridge games, Mierzejewski wrote a personal letter to the vice president in March 1988, stating that his memory of that day was "entirely different" from what Bush had been saying in television interviews. Bush, an assiduous letter writer, never responded, so Mierzejewski took his story to the *New York Post* in August 1988. The *Post* quoted the tail gunner as saying that only Bush himself had bailed out and that Bush's plane was never on fire. "No smoke came out of his cockpit when he opened his canopy to bail out . . . I think he could have saved those lives if they were alive. I don't know that they were, but at least they had a chance if he had attempted a water landing."

In interviews with other papers over the next few days, Mierzejewski, also a recipient of a Distinguished Flying Cross, would say that he was inclined to give Bush the benefit of the doubt until he realized the extent of the inconsistencies.[20]

Perhaps this problem with story discrepancies, a problem that would resurface time and again in Poppy's life, so often it became a virtual theme, explains why Poppy Bush never penned a comprehensive autobiography.[21] There were too many secrets, too many different stories to keep straight.

More than half a century later, when he was seventy-two years old, Poppy again began parachuting out of planes, ostensibly as a birthday celebration. He would continue this show of bravado and virility into his eighties. "The reasons behind this are strictly personal," Jim McGrath, Bush's assistant, said when the 1997 jump was announced. "It has to do with World War Two. When it happens, we'll explain it." But when the time came, no satisfying explanation emerged. Poppy treated his skydive as a novelty and a thrill—and never clarified what happened on September 2, 1944.

CHAPTER 3

Viva Zapata

I N 1945, WITH THE END OF THE WAR, George H. W. "Poppy" Bush entered Yale University. The CIA recruited heavily at all of the Ivy League
schools in those days, with the New Haven campus the standout.
"Yale has always been the agency's biggest feeder," recalled CIA officer
Osborne Day (class of '43). "In my Yale class alone there were thirty-five
guys in the agency."[1] Bush's father, Prescott, was on the university's board,
and the school was crawling with faculty serving as recruiters for the intelligence services.[2] Most notable was Norman Holmes Pearson, a professor of American studies who had headed wartime counterintelligence in
London and was instrumental in setting up systems after the war for recruitment and vetting of potential agents.[3]

The school's secret societies helped to make it a happy hunting ground.
Journalist Alexandra Robbins, who wrote a book-length study of Skull and
Bones, describes how these groups serve as a "social pyramid, because the
process successively narrowed down the elite of a class."[4] Yale's society boys
were the cream of the crop, and could keep secrets to boot. And no secret society was more suited to the spy establishment than Skull and Bones, for
which Poppy Bush, like his father, was tapped in his junior year. Established
in 1832, Skull and Bones is the oldest secret society at Yale, and thus at least
theoretically entrusted its membership with a more comprehensive body of
secrets than any other campus group. Bones alumni would appear throughout the public and private history of both wartime and peacetime intelligence; names such as William Bundy, William Sloane Coffin Jr., Richard
Drain, and Evan Galbraith would be associated with the fledgling CIA. And

these spies would regularly return to the Skull and Bones tomb, writes Robbins, where "they would speak openly about things they shouldn't have spoken about."[5] Famous spies would also emerge from other Yale secret societies and from the general campus population.[6]

Bush and his friends weren't quite the Edward Wilson character portrayed in the 2006 movie *The Good Shepherd*, which shows a Yale poetry student and Skull and Bones member being wooed at every turn by the Office of Strategic Services. But they weren't far off.[7]

One of the OSS recruiters was James Burnham, a philosophy instructor and covert operations adviser whose catches included a young Connecticut oil scion named William F. Buckley Jr. in 1950. He introduced the future conservative intellectual to a CIA officer and fellow Yale alumnus named E. Howard Hunt. The latter was already on a career trajectory that would include a supporting role in the toppling of Guatemala's democratically elected president in 1954, more central participation in the Bay of Pigs invasion in 1961, and Watergate in 1972. Buckley, who was inducted into Skull and Bones and finished Yale shortly after Bush, went to work in the CIA's Mexico City station under Hunt, something Buckley did not acknowledge until 2005, though their friendship had long been recognized.[8]

When Bush entered Yale, the university was welcoming back countless veterans of the OSS to its faculty. Sherman Kent, a member of the research and analysis division of the OSS, played a major role in the pipeline. Bush, with naval intelligence work already under his belt by the time he arrived at Yale, would have been seen as a particularly prime candidate for recruitment.

Bush's Proving Ground

Out of Yale, Bush went directly into the employ of Dresser Industries, a peculiar, family-connected firm providing essential services to the oil industry. Dresser has never received the scrutiny it deserves. Between the lines of its official story can be discerned an alternate version that could suggest a corporate double life.

For roughly the first half century of its existence, the S. R. Dresser Manufacturing Company had been a small, solid, unexceptional outfit. By the late 1920s, the children of founder Solomon Dresser wanted to liquidate the company in order to finance their high-society lifestyle. They found eager

buyers in Prescott Bush's Yale friends Roland and W. Averell Harriman—
the sons of railroad tycoon E. H. Harriman—who had only recently set up a
merchant bank to assist wealthy families in such endeavors. At the time,
Dresser's principal assets consisted of two very valuable patents in the rapidly expanding oil industry. One was for a packer that made it much easier
to remove oil from the ground; the other was for a coupler that made long-
range natural gas pipelines feasible. Instead of controlling the oil, Dresser's
strategy was to control the technology that made drilling possible. W. A.
Harriman and Company, which had brought Prescott Bush aboard two
years earlier, purchased Dresser in 1928.

Prescott Bush and his partners installed an old friend, H. Neil Mallon, at
the helm. Mallon's primary credential was that he was "one of them." Like
Prescott Bush, Mallon was from Ohio, and his family seems both to have
known the Bushes and to have had its own set of powerful connections. He
was Yale, and he was Skull and Bones, so he could be trusted.

A quiet, modest, balding man, Mallon remained a bachelor until his six-
ties and became essentially a chosen member of the Bush family. Poppy
would name his third son Neil Mallon Bush, after this "favorite uncle." Evidence of the special relationship appears in a November 23, 1944, letter En-
sign George H. W. Bush sent from the aircraft carrier *San Jacinto* to his
parents:

> Here is something which pleased me. Today I got a package of
> Xmas presents from Neil Mallon. There were some books, a knife
> set, couple of games, picture frame and some little soap pills. A
> fine present and it made me very happy. I shall write Neil this
> afternoon—he has always been such a good friend to us children,
> hasn't he?

Hiring decisions by the Bonesmen at the Harriman firm were presented
as jolly and distinctly informal, with club and family being prime qualifications. The way one Harriman partner, Knight Woolley, a Yale and Bones con-
frere of Prescott Bush's, tells it, Mallon simply wandered into their offices at
the precise moment they were deciding who should run the newly acquired
Dresser.[9] Mallon was flush from a recent six-month mountaineering holiday
in the Swiss Alps when he stopped in for a visit.[10] Roland Harriman turned
and pointed at Mallon, then uttered the words, "Dresser! Dresser!" upon
which Mallon was escorted into the office of Prescott's father-in-law, George

Herbert Walker, then president of Harriman and Company, for a pro forma job interview. Walker promptly installed Mallon at Dresser's helm. Mallon had been a factory manager at the giant Continental Can Company, but had no oil, gas, or CEO experience. He was a trusted insider, however, in a group that prized loyalty and secrecy. He was what Prescott's grandson George W. Bush would come to euphemistically refer to in his letters of introduction for friends and colleagues as "a good man." And, as Poppy's brother William Henry Trotter "Bucky" Bush put it, Mallon "could charm the fangs off a snake."[11]

Under Mallon, the company underwent an astonishing transformation.[12] As World War II approached, Dresser began expanding, gobbling up one militarily strategic manufacturer after another. While Dresser was still engaged in the mundane manufacture of drill bits, drilling mud, and other products useful to the oil industry, it was also moving closer to the heart of the rapidly growing military-industrial sector as a defense contractor and subcontractor. It also assembled a board that would epitomize the cozy relationships between titans of industry, finance, media, government, military, and intelligence—and the revolving door between those sectors.[13]

Prescott Bush himself remained on the board for two decades, but he was more than a mere director. "I was Neil Mallon's chief adviser and consultant in connection with every move that he made," Prescott asserted in an oral history.[14]

Have Briefcase, Will Travel

After graduating from Yale in 1948, Poppy headed out to visit "Uncle Neil" at Dresser headquarters, which were then in Cleveland. Mallon dispatched the inexperienced Yale grad and Navy vet, with his wife, Barbara, and first-born, George W., in tow, to Odessa, the remote West Texas boomtown that, with neighboring Midland, was rapidly becoming the center of the oil extraction business.

Oil was certainly a strategic business. A resource required in abundance to fuel the modern navy, army, and air force, oil had driven the engine of World War II. With the end of hostilities, America still had plenty of petroleum, but the demands of the war had exhausted many oil fields.

As President Roosevelt's secretary of the interior and later his petroleum administrator for war, Harold Ickes had warned in 1943, "If there should be a World War III it would have to be fought with someone else's petroleum, because the United States wouldn't have it." He elegantly laid out the challenge: "America's crown, symbolizing supremacy as the oil empire of the world, is sliding down over one eye . . . We should have available oil in different parts of the world . . . The time to get going is now."[15] Ickes's eye was then on Saudi Arabia, the only place in the Middle East that had huge untapped oil pools under the control of an American oil company, the Rockefellers' Standard Oil of California.

If the young George H. W. Bush understood anything about the larger game, and his expected role in it, he and his wife, Barbara, certainly did not let on to the neighbors in those early days in dusty West Texas. "They didn't want *anything* from their parents," recalls Valta Ree Casselman, who lived next door to the Bushes in Odessa and frequently babysat while Barbara was at bridge games. "[Barbara] told me, he wanted to make it on his own." Yet there was something that his father had that Poppy very much wanted: connections, without which the young family would have been adrift on an unfriendly sea. "George was paid well," says Casselman. "He was paid a lot more than my husband"—who, she notes, as a warehouseman, was technically at a higher-level job than Bush. Whether Bush took his advantages for granted is not clear, though in their memoirs, he and Barbara characterize themselves as living lives of modest privation.[16]

Poppy's initial jobs included sweeping out warehouses and painting machinery used for oil drilling, but he was soon asked to handle more challenging tasks. In 1948, at precisely the time that the United States was encouraging Communist Yugoslavia's Marshal Tito in his split with Moscow, one of Poppy's assignments as an employee of Dresser's International Derrick and Equipment Company (Ideco) subsidiary was to squire around town a man he described as a potential client from the Balkan country. In his memoir, Poppy tells us nothing about the substance of the visit, but does regale us with tales from the culture gap:[17]

> It was during the peak of the season of '48, my first autumn as an Ideco trainee, that Bill Nelson gave me my first real sales assignment . . . "Dallas is sending over a customer," Bill said glumly after hanging up the phone one morning . . . "Not just a foreigner but a damn communist."

His guest arrived with a Yugoslav-English dictionary. Bush showed him Ideco's inventory, then he and Barbara took the man to a rowdy Odessa-Midland football game:

> Our guest put his hands to his ears, then shook his head. This wasn't the sport called football that he'd grown up with back in Belgrade.

Bush does not say whether he made the sale. Coincidentally or not, however, around that same time, the National Security Council was preparing papers on Yugoslavia titled "Economic Relations Between the U.S. and Yugoslavia" and "U.S. Policy Toward the Conflict Between the USSR and Yugoslavia."[18]

Finally, there is the not-surprising fact that Dresser was well-known in the right circles as providing handy cover to CIA operatives. Three former CIA officials, one a former Bonesman, confirmed the arrangement to author Joseph Trento.[19] Dresser's global sales and acquisition efforts provided excuses for travel and technical inquiries virtually anywhere.

Continuing his whirlwind "training," Dresser transferred Bush to California, where the company had begun acquiring subsidiaries in 1940. Poppy has never written or spoken publicly in any depth about the California period of his career. He has made only brief references to work on the assembly line at Dresser's Pacific Pump Works in the Los Angeles suburb of Huntington Park and sales chores for other companies owned by Dresser. In later years, when criticized for his anti-union stands, he would pull out a union card, which he claimed came from his membership in the United Steelworkers Union.[20] Why Bush joined the Steelworkers (and attended their meetings) is something of a mystery, since that union was not operating inside Pacific Pump Works.

To be sure, the company was not just pumping water out of the ground anymore. During World War II, Pacific Pump became, like Dresser, an important cog in the war machine. The firm supplied hydraulic-actuating assemblies for airplane landing gear, wing flaps, and bomb doors, and even provided crucial parts for the top-secret process that produced the atomic bombs dropped on Hiroshima and Nagasaki.[21]

While in California training for Dresser, Poppy, the pregnant Barbara, and little George W. were constantly on the go, with at least five residences in a period of nine months—Huntington Park, Bakersfield, Whittier, Ventura, and Compton. Poppy was often absent, according to Barbara, even from their brief-tenure outposts. Was he truly a Willy Loman, peddling drill bits, dragging a pregnant wife and a one-year-old child with him? Or was he doing something else? Although "ordinary" scions often toil briefly at the bottom, Bush was no ordinary scion.

Bush would so effectively obscure his life that even some of his best friends seemed to know little about what he was actually doing—though they may have intuited it. Roderick Hills, a longtime friend of Bush's, said in a 1991 interview that Bush probably would have been happiest as a career intelligence officer.[22] And another longtime Bush associate told a reporter anonymously that Poppy's own accounts of various periods in his life "are often off 10 to 30 percent . . . there is a certain reserve, even secretiveness."[23]

From Dallas, with Love

In 1950, during the time that Poppy Bush had squired a Yugoslav Communist around the oil fields for Dresser Industries, the cold war got hot in an unexpected quarter when North Korean Communist forces launched an invasion of the south. Their attack had not been even vaguely anticipated in the National Intelligence Estimate—from the fledgling CIA—which had arrived on the president's desk just six days before. Heads rolled, and in the ensuing shake-up, Allen Dulles became deputy director in charge of clandestine operations, which included both spying and proactive covert operations. For the Bushes, who had a decades-long personal and business relationship to the Dulles family, this was certainly an interesting development.

The Dulles and Bush clans had long mixed over business, politics, and friendship, and the corollary to all three—intelligence. Even as far back as World War I, while Dulles's uncle served as secretary of state, Prescott's father, Samuel Bush, oversaw small arms manufacturing for the War Industries Board, and young Allen played a crucial role in the fledgling intelligence services' operations in Europe. Later, the families interacted regularly as the Bush clan plied their trade in investment banking and the Dulleses in the law.

In 1950, Dresser was completing a corporate relocation to Dallas, which besides being an oil capital was rapidly becoming a center of the defense industry and its military-industrial-energy elite. Though a virtual unknown on his arrival, Neil Mallon quickly set about bringing the conservative titans of Dallas society together in a new local chapter of the nonprofit Council on World Affairs, in whose Cleveland branch he had been active. Started in 1918, the World Affairs Councils of America were a localized equivalent of the Rockefeller-backed Council on Foreign Relations, the presidency of which Allen Dulles had just resigned to take his post at the CIA.

A September 1951 organizing meeting at Mallon's home featured a group with suggestive connections and affiliations. It included Fred Florence, the founder of the Republic National Bank, whose Dallas office tower was a covert repository for CIA-connected ventures; T. E. Braniff, a pioneer of the airline industry and member of the Knights of Malta, an exclusive, conservative, Vatican-connected order with longtime intelligence ties; Fred Wooten, an official of the First National Bank of Dallas, which would employ Poppy Bush in the years between his tenure as CIA director and vice president; and Colonel Robert G. Storey, later named as liaison between Texas law enforcement and the Warren Commission investigating the assassination of President Kennedy.

Another attendee was General Robert J. Smith, who as a colonel in World War II had played a role in the earliest cold war operations, including the secret 1944 transport of Nazi intelligence agents. At the time of Mallon's house meeting, Smith, a Texan, was deputy chairman of a little-known Washington entity called the National Security Resources Board.[24] Among its principal concerns was the establishment of adequate supplies of strategic resources, oil in particular. Smith's presence at the Dallas meeting suggests that the creation of Mallon's Dallas Council on World Affairs may have had some kind of sanction at the highest levels.

Soon, the group moved even closer to the center of power. General Dwight Eisenhower had been courted by both major political parties but had responded to entreaties from a GOP group that included the Rockefellers and Prescott Bush, as well as Allen and John Foster Dulles. (As attorneys, the Dulleses had done business with Prescott Bush and Brown Brothers Harriman for years.) With Ike the Republican nominee, they all scrambled for seats on his train. The Dulleses were key advisers. Prescott Bush was backing Ike and mounting what would be a successful race for a Senate seat from Connecticut. Prescott's son George H. W. Bush was not left out. He became the Midland County chairman of the Eisenhower-Nixon campaigns in both 1952 and 1956. With the West Texas city at the center of the oil boom, young George functioned as a crucial link between the Eastern Establishment, the next Republican administration, and Midland's oil-based new wealth.

Following Ike's decisive victory, the Dulles brothers obtained effective control of foreign policy: John Foster became Ike's secretary of state, and Allen the director of the Central Intelligence Agency. The rest of the administration was filled with Bush allies, including national security adviser Gordon Gray, a close friend of Prescott's, and Treasury Secretary Robert B. Anderson, a sometime member of the Dresser Industries board.

Eisenhower, with no track record in civilian government and little enthusiasm for the daily grind, was only too happy to leave many of the operational decisions to these others. Even the normally hypercautious Prescott, who frequently golfed with the new president, would admit to this. In an oral history interview conducted by Columbia University, the interviewer asked Prescott about trade policy:

> INTERVIEWER: Had the president laid down any guidelines for the course of action?
> PRESCOTT BUSH: No, he did not . . . I don't think he knew much about [the policy]. After all, why should he? He'd been a military man all his life, and he was turning to a group of congressmen and businessmen.[25]

Some of those businessmen taking it upon themselves to help chart the course were from the Dallas group. Shortly after Ike took office, Mallon's Council on World Affairs announced its intention to send fifteen members on a three-month world tour, for meetings with what the group characterized as "responsible" political and business leaders. Shortly after the group returned, Dulles came to visit with the Dallas council chapter. An October 28, 1953, letter from Mallon to Dulles reveals nothing about the director's objective in visiting Dallas—but does comment on the fact that Dulles and his wife, Clover, were made "honorary Texans" and presented with cowboy hats.

The true power wielded by the duo of Prescott Bush and Neil Mallon is revealed in a round of correspondence where the two virtually demanded a high-level Washington job for a friend: the oilman and adventurer Tom

Slick.[26] Slick sat on the Dresser Industries board but was best known for his esoteric explorations, including searches for Bigfoot and the Loch Ness Monster. Loren Coleman, an anthropologist and retired professor who wrote two books on Slick, asserts that the explorer was actually a longtime CIA operative who used his adventure travel as cover for his spy work.[27]

At the time, the CIA was in the process of creating plausible deniability as it began what would be a series of efforts to topple "unfriendly" regimes around the world, including those in Guatemala and Iran. Since the CIA's charter severely constrained the domestic side of covert operations, agents created a host of entities to serve as middlemen to support rebels in countries targeted for regime change. During the early days of Dresser in Dallas—and of Zapata Petroleum—Dulles was just beginning to experiment with "off the books" operations. Eventually, by the seventies and eighties, when Poppy Bush ran the CIA and coordinated covert operations as vice president, hundreds, perhaps thousands, of such entities had been created.

The Bushes were apparently so good at keeping people guessing that otherwise savvy intelligence operatives misperceived the actual roles of both Prescott and Poppy. Captain William R. Corson, for example, was convinced that Allen Dulles was using Poppy as a "business-cover asset" as part of an elaborate chess game with his old friend Prescott Bush—who by then was in charge of monitoring Dulles's CIA for the U.S. Senate. Corson believed that Dulles had recruited Poppy without Prescott's knowledge.

The theory was based on an awareness that Poppy (and his siblings) had never gotten over their fear and awe of their forbidding father, who stood six feet four, drank heavily, and stood in watchful judgment over his children. Poppy was said to virtually cower in his father's presence. "George's insecurities were clay to someone like Dulles," said Corson.[28] Dulles convinced Poppy, Corson said, that "he could contribute to his country as well as get help from the CIA for his overseas business activities. Of course it was all nonsense. Dulles could care less about helping the kid. It really was a tool to help give him a wedge with Prescott if he needed it."

Corson was a member of a military covert operations team that answered directly to President Eisenhower. He recalled a time in 1955 when Senator Prescott Bush visited him in Hong Kong as part of an inquiry into a botched U.S. effort to kill the Chinese premier Zhou En-lai at an international conference by poisoning his rice bowl with a slow-acting toxin.[29]

While enjoying a round of golf together at Victoria Island's Shek O Golf

Club course overlooking the South China Sea, Prescott pressed Corson, who knew the CIA director well, about the relationship between Dulles and Dulles's own son. "He wanted to know how the [Dulles] son got along with his father," Corson recalled. "I told him he hated his father."[30] Corson asserted that this surprised Prescott.

Corson, who would later work personally for Dulles, said he warned Prescott about Dulles's Machiavellian tactics. Specifically, he said that it would not be beyond the calculating director to try to recruit George into intelligence work as a way of exerting leverage over Prescott and his Senate colleagues. "He just shook his head and laughed . . . He disparaged George."

Most likely, Prescott was putting on a show for Corson. After all, by that time Poppy was already very much part of the team. Nevertheless, his complicated relationship with his father would both create tension and foster a lifelong quest for approval that would be mirrored in the relationship between Poppy and his own son George W. Bush.

A Hunch, a Dream, and a Whole Lotta Moolah

In 1953, as Dulles was building his global machine, Poppy Bush launched his own enterprise, with help from Dulles, Mallon, and Poppy's maternal uncle Herbert Walker. The importance of this strategic alliance and others like it in setting Poppy on his professional path would be deliberately blurred.

The "official" version of Poppy's life, disseminated again and again to credulous journalists and authors, portrays Bush as a young fellow who rejected the easy path to Wall Street, pointed a red Studebaker into the sun, and struck out on his own for the West Texas oil fields. Here's a typical account, offered to the historian Herbert Parmet by Bush's elder brother, Prescott Bush Jr.: "[Poppy] met a bunch of fellows in the Navy from the West and the Southwest, and they talked a lot about the oil industry and the opportunities there and everything else, and that's what made up his mind that he wanted to go out there and see what he could do in the oil industry."[31]

Such accounts failed to note that the Bush family had long been connected at the very top of the oil industry, through ties to the Rockefellers and their Standard Oil of New Jersey and its large Texan subsidiary, Humble Oil.[32] But a future political career necessitated a more modest start—albeit one benefiting from considerable outside assists. It was a template closely followed years later by Poppy's eldest son.

Poppy's first venture involved convincing a local landman by the name of John Overbey to partner with him. The landman business was sharp-elbowed; it involved obtaining oil field intelligence, then convincing landowners to sell the drilling rights on their property. Overbey handled the real estate end; Poppy raised the cash.

Bush got money from Uncle Herbie (George Herbert Walker Jr., Skull and Bones, 1927), an investment banker. Uncle Herbie also was instrumental in bringing in others, including Eugene Meyer, a Yale graduate and owner of the influential *Washington Post*. Meyer's investments were handled by Brown Brothers Harriman.[33] Meyer was one of many media titans, such as Prescott's good friend and fellow Bonesman Henry Luce, founder of *Time* magazine, and William Paley of CBS (on whose board Prescott sat), who shared an interest in intelligence. In a 1977 *Rolling Stone* article, Carl Bernstein, famed for breaking the Watergate story in the *Washington Post*, states that both Luce and Paley cooperated regularly with the CIA, and even mentions his own paper's history with the agency, though he does not fully probe the *Post*'s intelligence connections. "Information about Agency dealings with the *Washington Post* newspaper is extremely sketchy," he concludes.[34]

For Poppy, well-connected investors like Meyer weren't hard to come by. Though start-ups are risky, there were incentives. For one thing, income tax rates for the rich back then were so high—90 percent in some cases—that losses could be recouped almost dollar for dollar in taxes saved. For another, when you invested in a young Poppy Bush, you got the older, more influential Prescott in the bargain. And the extended Bush clan truly represented a kind of private-public business combine. For example, within months of Prescott being named to the Joint Congressional Committee on Atomic Energy, Uncle Herbie formed a partnership to invest in commercial nuclear energy businesses.[35]

The news business, the policy business, and the intelligence business had a lot in common: they were all about who you knew and what you knew. In fact, so was the oil business. The Bushes' skill at cultivating connections was evident in 1953, when Poppy joined forces with a couple of brothers from Tulsa, Hugh and Bill Liedtke, to form Zapata Petroleum. The Liedtkes' contacts were nearly as interesting as the Bushes', with strands leading to, among others, the millionaire former bootlegger Joseph P. Kennedy and Ray Kravis, the father of the famed corporate raider Henry Kravis. Based on a "hunch" of Hugh Liedtke's, the company drilled 127 consecutive "wet" holes, and the firm's stock exploded from seven cents a share to twenty-three dollars a share.

There is no dispute that the Liedtkes handled much of the operational side of the company. But the accounts of the Bush-Liedtke partnership leave out something quite significant. As documented in chapter 11, the Liedtkes would later involve themselves in political operations with Poppy Bush that would contribute to the demise of Richard M. Nixon.

Pirates of the Caribbean

Zapata Offshore, which provided perfect cover for activities in a host of hot spots around the world, may have been the brightest stone in Allen Dulles's crown. On April 10, 1953, exactly two weeks after Zapata Offshore's land-based sister, Zapata Petroleum, was launched,[36] Neil Mallon wrote to CIA director Dulles about an upcoming meeting at D.C.'s Carlton Hotel. "In addition to Bob Johnson, I have invited a close personal friend, Prescott Bush. We want to talk to them about our Pilot Project in the Caribbean and have you listen in."[37]

The letter was written in a kind of code-speak. Prescott Bush was well known to Dulles, as was his close relationship to Mallon and the fact that he was a sitting United States senator. He had brought Mallon and Dulles together, and the two had become close friends, visiting each other, exchanging gifts, and sending notes on important family vacations.

Mallon would play a crucial role for Dulles by introducing him to the powerful new-moneyed oil elites in Dallas that would, along with a separate group in Houston, become the leading funders of off-the-books covert operations in Latin America. They would commence with efforts to overthrow Latin American and Caribbean leaders in the 1950s. The efforts would continue, under Poppy Bush, with Iran-contra in the 1980s.

What was the "pilot project" to which Mallon referred? Very likely it was Zapata Offshore, launched by Poppy in 1954, just as the U.S. government, under an administration dominated by the Dulles-Bush circles, began auctioning offshore mineral rights. The funding, again, came courtesy of Uncle Herbie, who organized a stock issue.

In 1958, Zapata Offshore's drilling rig *Scorpion* was moved from the Gulf of Mexico to Cay Sal Bank, the most remote group of islands in the Bahamas and just fifty-four miles north of Isabela, Cuba.[38] The island had been re-cently leased to oilman Howard Hughes, who had his own long-standing CIA ties, as well as his own "private CIA."[39] Hughes would even lend his ship to the CIA to dredge for a Soviet submarine.[40]

By most appearances, a number of CIA-connected entities were involved in the operation. Zapata leased the *Scorpion* to Standard Oil of California and to Gulf Oil. CIA director Dulles had previously served as Gulf's counsel for Latin America. The same year that Gulf leased Bush's platform, CIA veteran Kermit "Kim" Roosevelt joined Gulf's board. This was the same Kermit Roosevelt who had overseen the CIA's successful 1953 coup against the democratically elected Iranian prime minister Mohammad Mossadegh, after Mossadegh began nationalizing Anglo-American oil concessions. It looked like the Bush-CIA group was preparing for operations in the Caribbean basin.

The offshore platforms had a specific purpose. "George Bush would be given a list of names of Cuban oil workers we would want placed in jobs," said one official connected to Operation Mongoose, the program to overthrow Castro. "The oil platforms he dealt in were perfect for training the Cubans in raids on their homeland."[41]

The importance of this early Bush connection with Cuba should not be ignored in assessing his connections to contemporaneous events. For example, it sheds light on the 1963 memo from J. Edgar Hoover discovered by reporter Joseph McBride. The memo, which mentioned a briefing about Cuban activity in the wake of the JFK assassination, had been given to "George Bush of the CIA." Years later, many figures from the Bay of Pigs operation would resurface in key positions in administrations in which Poppy Bush held high posts, and during his own presidency.[42] Others would show up in off-the-books operations run by Poppy's friends and associates.[43]

George H. W. Bush did not, however, limit himself to the Caribbean. This period of his life was characterized by frenetic travel to all corners of the world, though Zapata had only a handful of rigs. The pattern would continue through his entire career. He set up operations for Zapata Offshore in the Gulf of Mexico, the Persian Gulf, Trinidad, Borneo, and Medellín, Colombia. Clients included the Kuwait Shell Petroleum Development Company, which began his close association with the Kuwaiti elite.

Facing Fidel

That a lot of what was labeled "national security" work was largely about money—making it, protecting it—was fairly transparent. Through the story of the Bushes and their circle runs a thread of entitlement to resources in other countries, and anger and disbelief when others challenged that claim.

Upon coming to power in 1959, Fidel Castro began to expropriate the massive properties of large foreign (chiefly American) companies. The impact fell heavily on American corporations that had massive agricultural and mineral operations on the fertile island, including Brown Brothers Harriman, whose extensive holdings included the two-hundred-thousand-acre Punta Alegre beet sugar plantation.[44] After Castro took power, the Eisenhower administration began a boycott of Cuban sugar, which is a crucial component of the island's economy. The Cubans in turn became increasingly dependent on the USSR as supplier of goods and protector.

Poppy swung into gear the same year that Castro began nationalizing those properties. He severed his ties to the Liedtkes by buying out their stake in Zapata Offshore, and then moved its operations to Houston—which, unlike the remote Midland-Odessa area, had access to the Caribbean through the Houston Ship Channel.[45] Meanwhile, back in Washington, after extensive planning, the Bay of Pigs project began with Eisenhower's approval on March 17, 1960.

For anyone who asked about the origins of Zapata Petroleum's name, Bush had a good story. A theater in downtown Midland happened to be showing the Marlon Brando film, *Viva Zapata!,* a biography of Emiliano Zapata, the Mexican revolutionary. Bush would claim that the partners had a flash that Zapata represented the image of independence their oil company was seeking. Ironically enough, General Zapata had fought for land redistribution on behalf of peasants, with resulting losses for precisely the kinds of people who staked Bush's companies.

Moreover, Bush and his friends were hardly "independents." To the contrary, they were connected to some of the wealthiest and most powerful people in the country, who owned enormous expanses of land throughout Latin America and elsewhere—exactly the kind of people Zapata loathed. The key thing—and possibly Bush's telegraphed message—was that Emiliano Zapata gained international repute for one thing: overthrowing a government.

Beyond providing a staging area for Cuban rebels, Zapata Offshore appears to have served as a paymaster. "We had to pay off politicians in Mexico, Guatemala, Costa Rica, and elsewhere," said John Sherwood, chief of CIA anti-Castro operations in the early 1960s. "Bush's company was used as a conduit for these funds under the guise of oil business contracts . . . The major breakthrough was when we were able, through Bush, to place people in PEMEX—the big Mexican national oil operation."[46]

Bush's Mexican Connection

The complicated PEMEX affair began in 1960, when Zapata Offshore offered a lucrative secret partnership to a competing Mexican drilling equipment company, Perforaciones Marinas del Golfe, or Permargo. George H. W. Bush did not want this relationship exposed, even decades later. When investigative reporter Jonathan Kwitny tried to document Bush's precise involvement with Permargo for a 1988 article, he was told by an SEC spokeswoman that Zapata filings from 1960 to 1966 had been "inadvertently destroyed" several months after Bush became vice president.[47]

Bush's Mexican counterpart in this arm's-length relationship, Jorge Diaz Serrano, was ultimately sentenced to ten years' imprisonment for defrauding the Mexican people of fifty-eight million dollars. Diaz Serrano later admitted to remaining a personal friend of Bush and visiting the vice president in Washington shortly before his fraud conviction in Mexico.[48] He told Kwitny that Poppy Bush's interest in the oil business seemed limited: "In those days, I remember very clearly, he was a very young chap and when we were talking business with him at his office, he spent more time on the telephone talking about politics than paying attention to the drilling affairs." As in other respects, father would be mirrored by son, as George W. Bush, too, would become well-known in the oil business for his preference for anything but the task at hand.

Evidence that Zapata Offshore was more than just Poppy Bush's oil company surfaced in the years that followed. Bush increasingly spent his time on politics, and others were brought in to transform the company into a larger entity that could more credibly run global operations. According to former Zapata executive Bob Gow:

> After George lost his first bid for public office . . . we had a num-
> ber of discussions with a man named Bill Clements, who was
> president of a company named Sedco . . . I was very surprised to
> become aware during some of those discussions that George did
> not really care if Bill Clements was to be head of a combined com-
> pany of Zapata and Sedco. I believe he would have been happy to
> have Bill Clements assume that role . . . George's real interest was
> in politics.[49]

(Clements did not take over Zapata, but the two companies did enter into a joint venture in the Persian Gulf. Clements became deputy defense secretary under Nixon, and then governor of Texas, where he gave a job to an eager new arrival to the state named Karl Rove.)

Bush's reward for all his troubles may have come in 1965, when one of the company's rigs was ostensibly lost in Hurricane Betsy. For the first time in its history, the insurance giant Lloyds of London paid out an oil-platform disaster claim without physical evidence. Zapata received eight million dollars for a rig that had cost only three million.[50]

The fate of the rig remains a mystery. "The platform was stable at the time," recalled Vincent "Buddy" Bounds, the last man evacuated from it. "I remember we were taken off just before dark . . . I was surprised to hear it disappeared without a trace; it was awfully big."[51] Poppy's brother Bucky recalled the fears expressed by Zapata Offshore staff that it would be impossible for an insurance claim to be paid because of the absence of any wreckage. But Poppy himself was calm, reassuring his people that "everything is going to be all right."[52]

In February 1966, Poppy left Zapata to run for Congress. Members of his circle stepped in at the offshore company to ensure continuity. One of them was Poppy's former aide William Stamps Farish III, who also began managing Poppy's assets in a blind trust. Farish fit in nicely. He was heir to an oil fortune, and his family went way back with the Bushes. In 2001, he was named ambassador to Britain by George W. Bush.[53]

The financials of Zapata, like those of latter-day Enron, were almost impossible to understand. This appears to have been by design. A bit of this can be gleaned from the words of the company's former executive Bob Gow, another in a small army of Bush loyalists who show up repeatedly in the family story—and by extension the nation's.

Resetting the Sales

Bob Gow may be the only person in American history to be employed by one future president (Poppy Bush—at Zapata) and to later employ another (George W.—at Gow's post-Zapata agricultural mini-conglomerate Stratford of Texas).

In 2006, I traveled to Mexico, to the western Yucatán, and met with Gow on his bamboo plantation not far from the Mayan ruins at Uxmal. I also obtained Gow's self-published memoirs, the five hundred pages of which include much about Zapata, bamboo, beeswax, and catfish, but manage to say little about the Bushes and their doings. Gow did, however, admit that he did some spying for the CIA.

Gow was a member of the country's mostly invisible elites. The family was certainly well connected. His grandfather's company played a role in the building of the Boston subway. His father was called to Washington in World War II and rose rapidly in the war-mobilization hierarchy. (His role was similar role to that of Samuel Bush in the First World War.) After the war, the Gows returned to Massachusetts, where Bob attended Groton. His roommate was Ray Walker, a cousin of George H. W. Bush.

Bob Gow and Ray Walker would room together again at Yale, and both would be inducted into the 1955 class of Skull and Bones (along with David McCullough, the noted biographer of Harry Truman and John Adams). Ray Walker eventually became a psychotherapist in Vermont and a quiet critic of Bush-Walker politics and values. Gow, however, was captivated, and served increasingly as a soldier for the Bush clan.

Gow's recruitment by the Bushes illustrates the kind of opportunities that come to those of the "right sort" and possessed of the appropriate discretion. By his own account, Gow was plodding along in an unremarkable career at the Norton Company, a grinding-wheel firm run by his father. Then, out of the blue, he received a call from Ray Walker's father, George Herbert Walker Jr., a.k.a. Poppy's "Uncle Herbie." Uncle Herbie, as a key figure behind Zapata, believed that Gow was exactly the person for a new venture, Champlain-Zapata, a partnership to manufacture machines for molding expandable polystyrene.

Gow possessed no apparent qualifications for the job, but Herbie insisted he was just right for it. Gow's memoir recounts the company's efforts to produce four different products, all without success. These included a plastic box for packaging berries that was canceled when Gow realized the box caused the berries to rot faster. This, Gow would drolly note, taught him to "think outside the box."

By investing in a risky polystyrene enterprise at a time when the parent company was not doing well, and entrusting it to the inexperienced Gow, Poppy Bush and his uncle revealed a fundamental illogic that seems to have run through the entire venture. In reality, not much could be said about Gow's business abilities besides the fact that he was an amiable fellow and a "good man"—Scottish roots, Yale, Skull and Bones, old-line WASPy family, longtime Bush ties. He could be trusted to put the best spin on things and keep his mouth shut. (Even his former roommate Ray Walker laughed when asked whether Gow could have been seen as formidable.)

In 1961, Gow, still struggling at Champlain-Zapata, got another call from Uncle Herbie Walker. This time the latter proposed a promotion: Gow would go to Texas to work as an executive for Poppy at Zapata Offshore, with attractive stock options. "Even though I was perhaps less qualified to be a Financial Vice President than I was to do any of the other jobs, Herbie, particularly, convinced me I could do it . . . George [was] very persuasive that I should come to Houston," he writes.

An embodiment of the Peter principle, in which individuals rise to the limits of their competence and then go higher, Gow continued to be promoted. "When I first arrived at Zapata Offshore, the man who had been the controller of the company quit . . . George suggested that I might be able to run all the accounting, controllership and financial functions with the assistance of two ladies who made the entries in the accounting department. Neither of these ladies had a great understanding of why they were making their entries. I had only taken one accounting course at Yale . . . I really did not know what a financial vice president of a company was supposed to do."[54]

Even when Poppy Bush ran things, there was something fishy going on— literally. "When George Bush was head of Zapata," Gow says in his memoir, "I had proposed to him that it would be useful for us to diversify into other profitable areas in the ocean. One of these might be the raising of fish. George made an arrangement with Texas A&M University to give us the use of a biological facility that A&M had on Galveston Bay. I was given the additional duty of Director of Marine Biological Research."

The tone of the venture is suggested in this anecdote from Gow:

> One day, George came into my office and asked me to make a presentation for a bank loan where Zapata Offshore would borrow

$5,200,000, more than its entire net worth at the time . . . I went to the bank, made the presentation, and was told that we could have the loan. I then went back . . . and told George that the loan had been approved. He was very surprised. What he had meant for me to do was to prepare the presentation and then he and I would go to the bank together . . . This rig, which was eventually christened "The Maverick," was lost in a storm some years later.

And this:

Many people have asked me what it was like to work for George [H. W.] Bush. George was a good boss to work for . . . He always wanted us officers of the company to be going to lunch with important people.

Gow portrays Bush as traveling constantly when he was Zapata chief, and far from connected when on premises. "George had an opportunistic style of management," writes Gow. "He kept his options open much longer than other bosses I had worked for . . . I would ask George where, as a company, we were trying to get. He would often answer something to the effect that we would have to see what opportunities turned up."

Though Gow has little to say in his book about the company's underlying operations or Poppy's role in them, he proudly notes Zapata's complex web of foreign ventures. In all probability, the foreign operations had dual functions. Since Zapata was set up with guidance from Neil Mallon, it is likely that the overseas undertakings were modeled in part on Dresser's. According to the in-house history of Dresser, one of the company's bolder moves was a then-innovative tax strategy that involved a separate company in the tiny European principality of Liechtenstein. "A considerable [benefit] was the fact that no American taxes had to be paid on international earnings until the money was returned to the United States."[55] That is, *if* the money was ever returned to the United States. And there was another characteristic of funds that were not repatriated: they were out of sight of federal authorities. There was no effective way to know where they went ultimately, or for what purposes.

That was Dresser. Now, Zapata, according to Gow: "Zapata, at that time, consisted of a number of foreign corporations incorporated in each country where our rigs operated . . . It was largely the brainchild of the tax department

at Arthur Andersen and the tax lawyers at Baker and Botts . . . Until the
profits were brought back to the United States, it was not necessary at that
time to pay U.S. taxes on them. Because of the way Zapata operated around
the world, it seemed as though it never would be necessary to pay taxes . . .
As time passed and Zapata worked in many other countries, Zapata's cash . . .
was in the accounts of a large number (dozens and dozens) of companies
located in almost all the countries around the world where Zapata had ever
drilled."[56]

Whether Zapata was partially designed for laundering money for covert
or clandestine operations may never be known. But one thing is certain: spy
work depends, as much as anything, on a large flow of funds for keeping
foreign palms greased. It is an enormously expensive business, and it requires layers and layers of ostensibly unconnected cutouts for the millions
to flow properly and without detection.

So WHAT, EXACTLY, was Zapata? Was it CIA? Gow won't say. Although in his
memoirs he freely admits that he served the CIA later on, he strives mightily to avoid extensive discussion of the Bush clan.

Shortly before my visit with him concluded, and as we finished a deli-
cious lunch of the tilapia Gow was raising nearby, I asked him about the
mention in his memoirs (which Gow said he had assumed only his family
and friends would read) about doing work for the Central Intelligence
Agency in Guatemala, in the early seventies. This was the time frame in
which George W. Bush worked for Gow as a trainee and traveled on business to Guatemala.

> RUSS BAKER: You tell the story about when you were in
>   Guatemala . . .
> BOB GOW: Yeah.
> RB: . . . and you did some work for the agency.
> BG: Yeah. Well, I did all the things that I said I did there—I guess I
>   said I did, in there.
> RB: You did?
> BG: Uh-huh. I went off and investigated regions of the country.
> RB: For them?
> BG: Yeah.

RB: Did you find anything interesting?
BG: No.

Then I asked Gow about allegations that Zapata Offshore had played a role in the Bay of Pigs invasion: "Any comments on those?"

Gow hesitated a moment, smiled just a bit, and then replied, "No."

CHAPTER 4

Where Was Poppy?

G EORGE H. W. BUSH MAY BE ONE OF the few Americans of his generation who cannot recall exactly where he was when John F. Kennedy was shot in Dallas on November 22, 1963.

At times he has said that he was "somewhere in Texas."[1] Bush was indeed "somewhere" in Texas. And he had every reason to remember. At the time, Bush was the thirty-nine-year-old chairman of the Harris County (Houston) Republican Party and an outspoken critic of the president. He was also actively campaigning for a seat in the U.S. Senate at exactly the time Kennedy was assassinated right in Bush's own state. The story behind Bush's apparent evasiveness is complicated. Yet it is crucial to an understanding not just of the Bush family, but also of a tragic chapter in the nation's history.

A Reasonable Question

The two and a half years leading up to November 22, 1963, had been tumultuous ones. The Bay of Pigs invasion of 1961, designed to dislodge Fidel Castro and his Cuban revolution from its headquarters ninety miles off the Florida Keys, was an embarrassing foreign policy failure. Certainly in terms of lives lost and men captured, it was also a human disaster. But within the ruling American elite it was seen primarily as a jolt to the old boys' network—a humiliating debacle, and a rebuke of the supposedly infallible CIA. For John Kennedy it also represented an opportunity. He had been impressed with the

CIA at first, and depended on its counterinsurgency against Communists and nationalists in the third world. But the Bay of Pigs disaster gave him pause. Whatever Kennedy's own role in the invasion fiasco, it had been planned on Dwight Eisenhower's watch. Kennedy had been asked to green-light it shortly after taking office, and in retrospect he felt the agency had deceived him in several key respects.

The most critical involved Cubans' true feelings toward Castro. The CIA had predicted that the island populace would rise up to support the invaders. When this did not happen, the agency, Air Force, Army, and Navy all put pressure on the young president to authorize the open use of U.S. armed forces. In effect they wanted to turn a supposed effort of armed Cuban "exiles" to reclaim their homeland into a full-fledged U.S. invasion. But Kennedy would not go along. The success of the operation had been predicated on something—a popular uprising—that hadn't happened, and Kennedy concluded it would be foolish to get in deeper.

Following the disaster, CIA director Allen Dulles mounted a counteroffensive against criticism of the agency. Dulles denied that the plan had been dependent on a popular insurrection. Just weeks after the calamity, he offered this account on *Meet the Press*: "I wouldn't say we expected a popular uprising. We were expecting something else to happen in Cuba ... something that didn't materialize."[2] For his part, Kennedy was furious at Dulles for this self-serving explanation. He also was deeply frustrated about the CIA's poor intelligence and suspected that the CIA had sought to force him into an invasion from the very beginning.

The president told his advisers he wanted to "splinter the CIA into a thousand pieces and scatter it to the winds."[3] Within weeks of the invasion disaster, Washington was speculating on Dulles's departure. By autumn, he was gone, along with his lieutenants Charles Cabell and Richard Bissell. But in the end, it was not the CIA but rather John F. Kennedy who was destroyed.

THE ASSASSINATION OF JFK has fathered a thousand theories, and nearly as many books and studies. Through it all, no consensus has emerged. Most "respectable" academics, journalists, and news organizations don't want to get near the matter, lest they be labeled conspiracy nuts. Most Americans harbor an overwhelming psychic resistance to what retired UC Berkeley professor and author Peter Dale Scott has called the "deep politics" surrounding the assassination.[4] Few of us care to contemplate the awful prospect that the forces we depend upon for security and order could themselves be subverted.

When the Kennedy assassination *is* mentioned, the inquiry tends to focus on the almost impossible task of determining who fired how many shots and from where. This obsession with the gun or guns bypasses the more basic— and therefore more dangerous—questions: Who wanted Kennedy dead, and why? And what did they hope to gain?

A Firing Offense

The years since the first assassination investigation was hastily concluded in September 1964 have not been kind to the Warren Commission. Subsequent inquiries have found the commission's process, and the resulting report, horrendously flawed. And there are lingering questions about the very origins of the commission. First, all the members were appointed by Kennedy's successor, Lyndon B. Johnson, who was—stark as this may sound—a chief beneficiary of the assassination, having immediately replaced the dead president to become the thirty-sixth president of the United States.

The commission's chairman was the presiding chief justice of the Supreme Court. Earl Warren was the perfect choice because he was seen by the public as an honest, incorruptible man of substance. Warren's involvement gave the commission a certain credibility and convinced major newspapers like the *New York Times* to continue supporting the commission report over the years.

Many have credited Warren, who initially resisted LBJ's call to service, with an altruistic motive for finally acquiescing and leading the panel to the conclusions it reached. Not so LBJ.

As Johnson explained in a taped telephone conversation with Senator Richard Russell, himself reluctant to join the panel:

> Warren told me he wouldn't do it under any circumstances . . . He came down here and told me *no*—twice. And I just pulled out what [FBI director] Hoover told me about a little incident in Mexico City . . . And he started crying and he said, "I won't turn you down. I'll just do whatever you say."[5]

In other words, Johnson, who gained the presidency he had long sought with JFK's death, installed as head of the investigating commission a man whom he apparently blackmailed into taking the position.

Allen Dulles, the member who asked the most questions, would have been himself considered a prime suspect by any standard police methodology.[6] Dulles had resigned under pressure from Kennedy. Moreover, he was expert not only in assassinations but also in deception and camouflage.

Dulles's animus toward Kennedy was never overt, but it was incontrovertible. In ousting him, Kennedy was showing the door to a man who had spent his entire adult life in spy work. Behind the pipe-smoking, professorial mien, Allen Dulles *was* a ruthless, calculating man with blood on his hands. Certainly, the veteran master spy, director since 1953, could not have expected to stay on under Kennedy indefinitely. But to be forced out after what seemed to him a glorious decade of covert operations (including successful coups in Guatemala and Iran)—and on account of what he considered Kennedy's failure of nerve regarding the Bay of Pigs invasion—must have been galling. Dulles was, according to his subordinate E. Howard Hunt, a "remarkable man whose long career of government service had been destroyed unjustly by men who were laboring unceasingly to preserve their own public images."[7]

Among those infuriated with the Kennedys was none other than Dulles's good friend Senator Prescott Bush. In 1961, when Dulles brought his successor, John McCone, to a dinner at Prescott's home, the senator recalled that he "tried to make a pleasant evening of it, but I was rather sick at heart, and angry too, for it was the Kennedy's [sic] that brot [sic] about the [Bay of Pigs] fiasco."

He expressed this anger in a condolence letter to Allen Dulles's widow in 1969, discovered among Dulles's papers at Princeton University. Prescott's next line is particularly memorable: "I have never forgiven them."[8] The expression of such lingering resentment, six years after JFK's death, was doubly chilling because it came just months after a second Kennedy, Robert, had been gunned down under mysterious circumstances, once again by a seemingly unstable lone gunman.

Poppy's New Zeal

In the spring of 1962, about six months after Dulles's departure from the Kennedy administration, both Prescott Bush and his son Poppy made some considerable and rather abrupt changes to their lives. Prescott Bush, having already begun his reelection campaign and opened his headquarters, surprised virtually everyone by reversing himself and announcing that he would not seek a new term after all. The reason he gave was that he was tired and physically not well enough to endure another six years. This decision struck people as curious, in part because Prescott so clearly loved his life in Washington, and in part because he would turn out to be physically robust for a number of years afterward, and would even express his deep regret at having chosen to leave the Senate. Whatever took him away from Washington seems to have been pressing.

Just as Prescott was leaving the political arena, his son was entering it at high speed. Poppy, who until then had been barely involved with local Houston politics, suddenly became consumed with them. Conventional accounts treat Bush's new interest as simply the next step in the life of an ambitious man, but for the Bush family, there was an almost inexplicable urgency. At a Washington political gathering, Prescott pulled aside the Harris County (Houston) GOP chairman, James Bertron, and demanded that Bertron find a place in his organization for Poppy. "Senator," replied Bertron, "I'm trying. We're all trying."[9]

This pressure quickly paid off. In the fall of 1962, Poppy was named finance cochair of the Harris County Republican Party, a position which likely entailed visiting wealthy oilmen and asking them for money. Just few months later, in early 1963, James Bertron abruptly announced his intention to retire and move to Florida, and Poppy announced his intention to succeed him. A party activist who had expressed his desire for the position suddenly abandoned his candidacy, and Bush won the position by acclamation. Now he had a plausible reason not only to be visiting with wealthy oilmen, but also to be building an operational team, ostensibly for political purposes.

Poppy on the Go

That summer of 1963, right in the middle of his move out of the oil business into politics, Poppy Bush embarked on a busy itinerary of foreign business travel for Zapata Offshore. The trip seemed ambitious, especially when one considers the realistic opportunities for a firm with just a few rigs.[10]

Upon his return, Poppy's new lust for political power hit warp speed: now he had decided to seek a U.S. Senate seat. In less than a year he had gone from uninvolved to finance cochair to county chairman to U.S. Senate hopeful. As a businessman engaged in offshore drilling, Poppy Bush had little reason to be traveling extensively throughout Texas. As Harris County chairman, Poppy had Houston as his bailiwick. But as a Senate candidate, he had every reason to be seen all over the Lone Star State.

Bush's political work, like his oil work, may have been cover for intelligence activity. But there were political objectives as well, ones that conflicted with those of John Kennedy. In deciding to run for U.S. Senate, Poppy was playing a key role in the Republican effort to unyoke the conservative South from the Democratic wagon it had pulled to victory in 1960. Jack and Bobby Kennedy, meanwhile, were busy strategizing exactly how to prevent that— and this was going to be a crucial battle, given JFK's wafer-thin victory in the previous election. Two states in particular would be battlegrounds: Florida and Texas. In theory, a candidate like Poppy Bush, with his family connections to Wall Street, could be a strong fund-raiser and perhaps contribute to a substantially increased Republican turnout in 1964, even if Bush himself was not elected. To head off this larger threat, it was clear to Kennedy's political advisers that Jack would have to campaign in Texas, along with Florida. Kennedy was interested in revoking the oil depletion allowance, a decision that would have meant steep losses for Texas oilmen, and he continued voicing his support for civil rights, always a contentious issue in the South.[11]

As a candidate for statewide office, Poppy Bush was on the go in the fall of 1963, moving around Texas and spending time in Dallas, where he opened a headquarters.

Another Memory Lapse

Jack Kennedy's death in Dallas on November 22, 1963, was one of the most tragically memorable moments in the lives of those who lived through it. So Poppy Bush's inability or unwillingness to say where he was on that day is extremely odd, to say the least.

His haziness became an issue a quarter century after the assassination— when there emerged yet another good reason for Bush to have recalled that day vividly. On Thursday, August 25, 1988, about six weeks after the *Nation* published Joseph McBride's piece on "George Bush of the CIA"—and just a week after George H. W. Bush accepted the Republican presidential nomination—a short article appeared in the *San Francisco Examiner*, with the intriguing headline: "Documents: Bush Blew Whistle on Rival in JFK Slaying."

The article began like this:

> A man who identified himself as George H. W. Bush phoned the
> FBI in Houston a few hours after President John F. Kennedy's as-
> sassination in Dallas to report that a right-wing Young Republican
> had "been talking of killing the president," FBI documents show.

The FBI, the article goes on to say, promptly followed up on Bush's tip and interviewed the Young Republican, a man by the name of James Milton Parrott. Parrott claimed he had never threatened Kennedy, and his mother declared that he had been at home with her in Houston all day.

The author of this story, the *Examiner*'s Miguel Acoca, had been unable to reach Parrott but noted that the FBI report on Bush's call listed the address of the tipster as 5525 Briar, Houston, Texas—the address of the man who was now, in 1988, vice president of the United States.[12]

Like Bush, Acoca, a Panamanian, had graduated from Yale. He spent the early 1960s in the Miami area working for *Life* magazine, where dinners at his Coconut Grove apartment were typically populated by Cuban émigrés and CIA officers managing the war against Castro. While still in Miami, Acoca became interested in the group running the CIA's JM/WAVE Cuban operations station in the area, and developed a growing obsession with as-sassinations in general, and JFK's in particular.[13]

Acoca had placed a call to Bush's office once he discovered that the vice president had been the tipster back on November 22, 1963. His call brought a familiar response:

> Bush's press office at first said the vice president hadn't made the
> call and challenged the authenticity of the FBI reports. Then, sev-
> eral days later, an aide said Bush "does not recall" making the call.[14]

Acoca's story about Bush didn't get much attention, running on page A-11 of the *Examiner*. The media reaction was similar to that which greeted journalist Joseph McBride's earlier revelations: next to nothing. A few news-papers picked up the *Examiner* piece off the Hearst wire, but not a single paper bothered to assign reporters to follow up.

Thus, neither of two vexing questions—whether George Bush had been a CIA operative in 1963, and whether he had called the FBI on November 22 with purported information related to the JFK assassination—became is-sues for Bush in 1988 as he sailed into the White House.

By the fall of 1992, though, things were growing uncomfortable for Pres-ident Bush. Arkansas governor Bill Clinton's challenge was gaining momen-tum, the economy was in the doldrums, and now an initiative from Congress and the public posed a new dilemma for Poppy. Oliver Stone's *JFK*, released in December 1991, had aroused public interest and helped prod Congress to unanimously pass the President John F. Kennedy Assassination Records Collection Act of 1992. It required each federal agency to collect and forward all records about the JFK assassination to the National Archives, which would then make them available to the American people.

THE 1988 ACOCA article that caused so little stir had been based on a brief FBI summary of Bush's tip about Parrott. But there was a longer, more de-tailed memo in the archives, waiting to be unearthed and released.

President George H. W. Bush now found himself in the awkward posi-tion of potentially outing himself. Should he veto the politically popular JFK Act just days before voters would go to the polls to choose between him and his surging challenger, Bill Clinton? Bush, with little enthusiasm, signed the bill—though, in a move that his son George W. Bush would use without restraint, Poppy issued a "signing statement" that essentially attached con-ditions, asserting unilateral executive authority to withhold records on the basis of several concerns, including national security. Still, Poppy couldn't claim national security about everything, certainly not about documents that some already knew to exist, especially documents that had his own name on them.

Whether he knew it or not, with his signature, Poppy was moving the more detailed "Parrott memo" toward the light of day. In fact, government records show that the complete FBI memo from December 22, 1963, lay-ing out the particulars of Bush's call to the agency, was finally declassified in 1993, along with thousands of other papers—by the Clinton adminis-tration.

That memo, reporting the call that had come in on the day of the assassination to Special Agent Graham W. Kitchel of the Houston FBI bureau, contained some important new identifying information and other details:

> At 1:45 p.m. Mr. GEORGE H.W. BUSH, President of the Zapata Off-shore Drilling Company, Houston, Texas, residence 5525 Briar, Houston, telephonically furnished the following information to writer by long distance telephone call from Tyler, Texas.
>
> BUSH stated that he wanted to be kept confidential but wanted to furnish hearsay that he recalled hearing in recent weeks, the day and source unknown. He stated that one JAMES PARROTT has been talking of killing the president when he comes to Houston.
>
> BUSH stated that PARROTT is possibly a student at the University of Houston and is active in political matters in this area. He stated that he felt MRS FAWLEY, telephone number SU 2-5239, or ARLINE SMITH, telephone number JA 9-9194 of the Harris County Republican Party Headquarters would be able to furnish additional information regarding the identity of PARROTT.
>
> BUSH stated that he was proceeding to Dallas, Texas, would remain in the Sheraton-Dallas Hotel and return to his residence on 11-23-63. His office telephone number is CA 2-0395.

The memo contained several intriguing details, but no news organization picked up on them. Indeed, no one paid any heed to the whereabouts of Poppy Bush at the time of the JFK assassination—except Barbara Bush. In 1994, three decades after Poppy began not remembering where he was on November 22, 1963, it was suddenly Barbara who remembered.

Barbara's Hair-Raising Day

In the art of propaganda, and in the daily business of public relations, a cardinal rule is that if a problem emerges, it must be managed immediately. The trick is to quickly acknowledge and gain control of the new material, mitigating the damage by redirecting it in a beneficial way. This is known in tradecraft as "block and bridge."

Thus it was that the first and only Bush family acknowledgment of where Poppy Bush was on that red-letter day came in classic form—from the wife, in the most innocuous swathing. The venue was her 1994 book, *Barbara Bush: A Memoir*, which was published ten months after the document's declassification. Deep in that book, mostly a compendium of narrow-gauge, self-serving recollections, there it was: not just a recollection of the assassination, but the reproduction of an actual letter written by Barbara on the very day, at the very *moment*, that Kennedy was shot. The letter has plenty of details, but it omits one important personal item from that day: Poppy's call to the FBI; perhaps Poppy did not mention it to her?

Barbara begins to describe that fateful day on page 59 of her memoirs:

> On November 22, 1963, George and I were in the middle of a several-city swing. I was getting my hair done in Tyler, Texas, working on a letter home. Here are some excerpts:

The following is how the excerpts appear in the book, ellipses and all.

> Dearest Family,
> Wednesday I took Doris Ulmer out for lunch. They were here from England and they had been so nice to George in Greece. That night we went to. . . .
>   I am writing this at the Beauty Parlor and the radio says that the President has been shot. Oh Texas—my Texas—my God—let's hope it's not true. I am sick at heart as we all are. Yes, the story is true and the Governor also. How hateful some people are.
>   . . . Since the Beauty Parlor the President has died. We are once again on a plane. This time a commercial plane. Poppy picked me up at the beauty parlor—we went right to the airport, flew to Ft. Worth and dropped Mr. Zeppo off (we were on his plane) and flew back to Dallas. We had to circle the field while the second presidential plane took off. Immediately Pop got tickets back to Houston and here we are flying home. We are sick at heart. The tales the radio reporters tell of Jackie Kennedy are the bravest I've ever heard. The rumors are flying about that horrid assassin. We are hoping that it is not some far right nut, but a "commie" nut. You understand that we know they are both nuts, but just hope that it is not a Texan and not an American at all.

I am amazed by the rapid-fire thinking and planning that has already been done. L.B.J. has been the president for some time now—2 hours at least and it is only 4:30.

My dearest love to you all,
Bar[15]

The Tyler story is borne out by the personal recollections of Aubrey Irby, then vice president of the local Kiwanis Club (and later president of Kiwanis International during Bush's vice presidency).[16] As Irby explained to the author Kitty Kelley, Bush had been waiting to deliver a luncheon speech to his organization—to one hundred men gathered at Tyler's Blackstone Hotel.

"I remember it was a beautiful fall day," recalled Aubrey Irby, the former Kiwanis vice president. "George had just started to give his speech when Smitty, the head bellhop, tapped me on the shoulder to say that President Kennedy had been shot. I gave the news to the president of the club, Wendell Cherry, and he leaned over to tell George that wires from Dallas confirmed President Kennedy had been assassinated.

"George stopped his speech and told the audience what had happened. 'In view of the President's death,' he said, 'I consider it inappropriate to continue with a political speech at this time. Thank you very much for your attention." Then he sat down.

"I thought that was rather magnanimous of him to say and then to sit down, but I'm a Republican, of course, and I was all for George Bush. Kennedy, who was bigger than life then, represented extremely opposite views from Bush on everything."[17]

In a 2007 interview with me, Irby described George H. W. Bush at the time of the news as matter-of-fact and supremely well composed.[18] It was not unlike his own son's composure in another moment of crisis, when, after being told about the 9/11 attacks, he calmly returned to reading "The Pet Goat" to a class of Florida second graders. As for Barbara, she miraculously found herself in the unique position of actually writing a very long letter that began while Kennedy was alive, captured the first news of the assassination, and then concluded with confirmation of his death. She, like Poppy, showed impressive composure and focus.

A Lunch with Doris—But Where Were Al and Poppy?

Barbara's curious role as recording secretary to history-in-the-making was interesting enough that one would expect the letter to have surfaced well before 1994. Yet, until it appeared in Barbara's memoirs, it was not even known to exist. Meanwhile, the original letter itself has not turned up. Thus, many questions remain—questions that I hoped to pose to Poppy and Barbara, who declined to be interviewed for this book.

The excerpted letter warrants careful scrutiny, especially because of all the perplexing particulars. The note begins with a dull thud—a bland mention of a lunch with a "Doris Ulmer." No Ulmer appears in any of the Bushes' other books, which list hundreds of family friends, well-known and completely obscure. Therefore, presumably only very close Bush relatives, such as her children, would know who Doris Ulmer was or would even conceivably wish to learn of Barbara lunching with her. No one else would understand that George had even been in Greece on the occasion Barbara mentions when the Ulmers were said to be so nice to him—nor would anyone else know in what way they were so nice to him.

And yet, the style and comments in the assassination portion of the letter—"we are hoping that it is not some far right nut but a 'commie' nut"—are odd things to write to children.

It's not clear from Barbara's memoirs who the recipients of the letter were. She says "Dearest Family" and that it was "a letter home." But those of her children who were at home were all ten years old or younger. The eldest, George W., was away at prep school in New England. Also, it would seem odd to write "a letter home" if you were only gone from home for several days of an in-state campaign swing—you would likely be back before the letter arrived. And she signed it "Bar," not the typical identifier in a letter to young children.

So the "letter home" more logically would have been to her *other* home, that is, to her parents living in the house she had left nearly two decades before. But that scenario really doesn't make much sense either. Her mother had died in a 1949 auto accident, and her father had remarried. Barbara was known not to be especially close to her family during a period of many years and had not attended her mother's funeral. Was "love to you all" intended for her father and stepmother? Her siblings had also long since left the nest, but perhaps she circulated correspondence among them. Besides, how did Barbara happen upon such a letter that she had purportedly written thirty years earlier? Had she kept a copy and recently discovered it? Had relatives unearthed it?

Whether or not the letter was an authentic contemporaneous document, one can assume that many of the particulars of that day were in the letter because they were true and verifiable. Hence, they are of interest here.

Poppy's call to the FBI about Parrott being the potential assassin obviously did nothing to assist the FBI in any meaningful way. Perhaps the call *was* made out of a genuine desire to be helpful. Perhaps. But it clearly did something else: It established in government investigative files that, at the time of the assassination in Dallas, Poppy and Barbara were in Tyler, Texas. (These were things that Poppy had good reason to want established, as we'll see later.)

The notion that there was more to the phone call than simple altruism and patriotism can be found in an examination of the most seemingly insipid of matters—such as Barbara Bush's lunch with Doris Ulmer.

Although there were numerous Doris Ulmers in the United States at the time, only one matches the description of an old friend who had helped Poppy when Poppy visited Greece, and who was in 1963 a resident of London: Mrs. Alfred C. Ulmer Jr.

Al Ulmer is sometimes described as having filled the positions of "attaché" and "first secretary" at the U.S. embassy in Athens from the late forties through the midfifties. Yet a memorial tribute to him in the alumni publication of his alma mater, Princeton, scores higher on the candor meter, describing his life in the wartime OSS and the CIA.[19] Ulmer was a good friend and confidant of CIA director Allen Dulles.[20] He embodied the attitude that nobody could tell the CIA what to do—nobody: "We went all over the world and we did what we wanted," Ulmer later recalled. "God, we had fun."[21] He also managed coups.[22]

When JFK forced Dulles out of the CIA following the Bay of Pigs debacle, Ulmer left as well. He went to work for the Greek shipping magnate Stavros Niarchos. That Ulmer had not fully left the espionage racket is suggested in part by Niarchos's own long history with the CIA, which he assisted with many covert operations.[23] In fact, the company Ulmer ran, Niarchos London, Ltd., was itself a CIA proprietary according to author Peter Evans, who knew Niarchos personally.[24] Niarchos would in turn be introduced into Poppy Bush's immediate circle, buying Oak Tree Farm, a prime Kentucky horse-breeding property, and leasing it to the manager of Poppy Bush's financial affairs, William Stamps Farish III.

By 1963, Poppy Bush seems to have known Ulmer for at least a decade. The reference in Barbara's letter to the Ulmers being "so nice" to Poppy when Poppy visited Greece likely referred to the early 1950s, when Al Ulmer was station chief in Athens and Poppy Bush was beginning his frenetic world travels, ostensibly on behalf of his modestly sized Midland oil company.

Apparently, the relationship had continued, because records at the George H. W. Bush Presidential Library in College Station, Texas, show Bush stopping off to see Ulmer in London in the summer of 1963—as part of Bush's self-described "world tour." (Poppy would make another in 1965, and again visit with Ulmer.)

Ulmer also had another connection to Bush—via Robert Maheu. The Zapata Offshore drilling rig that Poppy Bush had positioned near Cuba in 1958 was located off Cay Sal island, which was leased by Howard Hughes. At the time, Hughes employed Maheu as his private spook. A former FBI man whose private security firm sometimes fronted for the CIA on unauthorized operations, Maheu was, in turn, an old friend of Ulmer's. The two had worked together on cooking up the military revolt against Indonesian president Sukarno in 1958—and even attempted to use an actor to portray Sukarno in a pornographic home movie with a female Soviet agent.[25] Maheu was later involved in a series of failed plots, commencing in 1960, that involved recruiting the Mafia for a hit on Fidel Castro. In all such things, one finds a certain circularity.

Mr. Zeppa's Plane

Besides Doris Ulmer, the other person Barbara mentioned in her letter is "Mr. Zeppo"—the man who had lent them his plane on November 22. As with so many other clues in documents concerning Poppy Bush, this one appears a dead end, until one realizes that the name has been slightly misspelled. There was in fact no Mr. Zeppo, but there was a man, since deceased, by the name of Zeppa. Joe Zeppa founded the Tyler-based Delta Drilling Company, which became one of the world's largest contract oil drillers, with operations around the globe.

Joe Zeppa, as the story goes, was an Italian immigrant who came to America and set out as a young man for the oil fields. But, as with the Bush story, it turns out there is more to it. Before he got to Texas, Giuseppe (Joe) Zeppa, who emigrated from northern Italy at the age of twelve, came to New York, where his older brother, Carlo (Charlie), was living and working as a waiter. Charlie's wife worked as the personal maid to a wealthy lady, Mrs. George H. Church. Mr. Church worked for the Wall Street law firm of Shearman & Sterling as head of its trust department, which handled, among other clients, the estate of William G. Rockefeller (John D. Rockefeller's nephew, a major investor in the railroad that employed Samuel Bush, and a director of the Harrimans' Union Pacific Railroad) and Standard Oil magnate Henry H. Rogers. The Churches had no children and eagerly embraced young Joe Zeppa. They got him a job as a stockboy at Shearman & Sterling, and he quickly moved up in the firm, eventually becoming an accountant.[26]

Zeppa, probably one of the only Italians on Wall Street at the time, pronounced himself a Republican, and had himself baptized and joined the Calvary Baptist Church, a favorite of the Rockefellers, who were prominent and ardent donors to Baptist institutions and causes. When Zeppa went off to World War I, Mr. Shearman sent O. Henry books to the young man in France.

With this kind of support network, Zeppa had a personal history that was less rags to riches than something akin to Poppy Bush's experience of the world and how it works.

By the time Poppy came to Tyler to speak to the Kiwanis, Joe Zeppa was a good man to know. One of his sons, Chris, had previously served as the county Republican chairman, and Joe Zeppa himself owned and lived in the Blackstone Hotel, the site of Bush's Kiwanis speech.

Barbara, in her letter, notes the use of Zeppa's plane to leave Tyler early in the afternoon on November 22. What she does not mention is that, in all probability, she and Poppy had also arrived on Zeppa's plane. The very fact that Zeppa lent his plane to Poppy is surprising, according to Zeppa's son Keating, who was on company business in Argentina at the time. "Joe Zeppa was not a great one for having an actual active hand in a political campaign," he told me, adding: "He was not one to say, 'Here, I'll send the plane after you.' If Joe Zeppa were going in a given direction and a politician wanted to go along, that was fine with him." When told that the plane bypassed Dallas's downtown Love Field, dropped Zeppa off at Fort Worth's municipal airport, and then backtracked to Dallas, Keating Zeppa said that was not something that his father ordinarily would have done.[27]

Though the movements of Zeppa's plane on the afternoon of November 22 once it left Tyler are intriguing, much more important is where it came from on the morning of November 22: Dallas.

The following facts have never been recounted by Poppy Bush nor have they appeared in any articles or books—and Barbara herself says nothing about this. On the evening of November 21, 1963, Poppy Bush spoke to a gathering of the American Association of Oil Drilling Contractors (AAODC) at the Sheraton Hotel in Dallas. Since Zeppa himself was a former president of AAODC, it is likely that he attended that gathering. It is also likely that both Zeppa and the Bushes actually spent the night in Dallas—and that they were in Dallas the next morning: the day that Kennedy was assassinated.

This brings us to the vexing question of Poppy's motive in calling the FBI at 1:45 P.M. on November 22, to identify James Parrott as a possible suspect in the president's murder, and to mention that he, George H. W. Bush, happened to be in Tyler, Texas. He told the FBI that he expected to spend the night of November 22 at the Sheraton Hotel in Dallas—but instead, after flying to Dallas on Zeppa's plane, he left again almost immediately on a commercial flight to Houston. Why state that he expected to spend the night at the Dallas Sheraton if he was not planning to stay? Perhaps this was to create a little confusion, to blur the fact that he had *already* stayed at the hotel—the night before. Anyone inquiring would learn that Bush was in Tyler at the time of the assassination and *planned* to stay in Dallas afterward, but canceled his plan following JFK's death.

A Tip from Poppy

As curious as all that is, nothing is quite so odd as the object of Bush's patriotic duty. Nobody seems to have believed that James Parrott had the capability—or even the inclination—to assassinate Kennedy. Bush acknowledged in the tip-off call that he had no personal knowledge of anything. He passed the buck to others who supposedly knew more about the threat and about Parrott—though what those others knew, if anything, has never emerged, until now.

During the period Bush ran the Harris County Republican organization, it had no more than a handful of employees. Among those were the two women he had mentioned to the FBI as potential sources on Parrott's alleged threat ("Mrs. Fawley" and "Arline Smith"), and a sole male—by the name of Kearney Reynolds. Though Bush made no mention of Reynolds, he was in fact the one who was most closely connected to Parrott.

Shortly after receiving Bush's call, the FBI dispatched agents to the Parrott house. At the time, Parrott was away, but according to a bureau report, his mother provided an alibi—likely in a motherly attempt to protect her son—which Parrott himself would later refute in his own explanation of the day's events.[28]

> She advised [James Parrott] had been home all day helping her care for her son Gary Wayne Parrott whom they brought home from the hospital yesterday. [Mrs. Parrott's other son could not help, because he was in jail.]

She also mentioned another person who could provide an alibi.

> Mrs. Parrott advised that shortly after 1:00 P.M. a Mr. Reynolds came by their home to advise them of the death of President Kennedy, and talked to her son James Parrott about painting some signs at Republican Headquarters on Waugh Drive.

In reality, both Reynolds and James Parrott put the visit between 1:30 and 1:45 P.M. The president's death became public at 1:38 P.M. central time, when CBS anchorman Walter Cronkite read an Associated Press news flash. Poppy Bush's call to the FBI followed seven minutes later.

Sometime later that day, agents interviewed Parrott himself. Parrott stated that he had never made any threats against Kennedy and that he had no knowledge of the assassination beyond what he had learned in news accounts. He indicated the extent of his dissent: picketing members of the Kennedy administration when they came to town. In a 1993 interview, Parrott stated that Reynolds had come to his home to ask him to paint some signs for the Republican headquarters—and informed him of the president's death. Parrott also provided the FBI with Reynolds' first name and said that both were members of the Young Republicans.

The following day, agents interviewed Kearney Reynolds.

> On November 23, 1963, Mr. Kearney Reynolds, 233 Red Ripple Road, advised he is a salaried employee of the Harris County Republican Party. He advised at approximately 1:30 P.M., November 22, 1963, he went to the home of James Parrott, 1711 Park, and

talked to Parrott for a few minutes. He advised he could vouch for Parrott's presence at 1711 Park between 1:30 P.M. and 1:45 P.M. on November 22, 1963.

What is so remarkable about all this is that at the precise moment when Poppy was calling the FBI with his "tip" about a possible suspect about whom he could offer few details, Poppy's own assistant was at the suspect's home, transacting business with him on behalf of Poppy. Clearly Parrott was far better known to Poppy than he let on. Why was Reynolds supposed to go to Parrott's house at this time? The net effect was that Reynolds bailed Parrott out, by providing him with an alibi. Thus, Parrott became Poppy's alibi, and Poppy's assistant became Parrott's. Everyone was taken care of. While the point was to generate two separate alibis, drawing attention to their interconnectedness was problematic. Because when the full picture emerges, the entire affair appears as a ruse to create a paper trail clearing Poppy, should that become necessary. Parrott was merely a distraction and a minor casualty, albeit a person who ought not face lasting consequences or attract undue attention.

(Recent efforts to speak with Parrott were unsuccessful. All telephone numbers associated with the Parrott family, including James Parrott, his mother, brother, nieces, and nephews are disconnected, and no current information on any of them is readily obtainable.)

In 2007, I interviewed Kearney Reynolds. In the interview—which did not initially touch on the FBI report—Reynolds exhibited an excellent memory for detail and extensive knowledge from that period, as the Republicans challenged the Democratic monopoly in Texas politics. He described the politics of the period, Bush's chairmanship, and the operation of the Republican headquarters—which he said Bush had relocated into an old house in the Montrose section of Houston, a property that Reynolds said the staff dubbed "the Haunted House."[29]

With prompting, Reynolds confirmed that, due to the temporary absence of an executive director, he was the only full-time male employee, along with a secretary and perhaps a receptionist. He coordinated precinct chairpersons and other volunteers, and thus was the main person to have contact with people like Parrott.

I asked him if he had heard or read of Bush's call from Tyler to the FBI regarding a threat to Kennedy. Reynolds said he was unaware of it. However, he did then offer, almost as an afterthought, his recollection, not of visiting

Parrott that day, but of being asked to accompany Parrott down to the offices of the Secret Service:

> There was a young man who came around headquarters . . . and somebody said that he had made a threat against Kennedy and this was, I believe, this came up after the assassination . . . The end result was, it was suggested that I contact the Secret Service, the local Secret Service, and I accompanied this young man . . . And we went down, and this was kind of a strange kid, mild-mannered, quiet, kind of seemed to be living in another world, and I took him down one day, escorted him down there.

At that point in our conversation, I shared with Reynolds the details of the FBI report (including Parrott's name), which stated explicitly that Reynolds had actually visited Parrott at home at around 1:30 P.M. on November 22, or precisely the time that Poppy Bush was calling the FBI.

> Well I never went to the guy's house because, as I remember, the little episode that I mentioned—as I recall, I met him at the headquarters, and we went on downtown to the Secret Service office.[30]

Asked why he would even be accompanying a man whom he said he did not know well—and whom his own boss believed to have threatened the life of the president—to the Secret Service office, Reynolds replied that he did not know, but only perhaps because Bush himself was out of town: "I worked a great deal with the volunteers and the precinct chairman, and probably on a face-to-face, name-to-name basis, probably knew more of them than almost anybody else."

At that point, Reynolds said his memory had been refreshed. "I knew him by name and sight . . . It was just sort of a casual [acquaintance] within the context of working at the headquarters." Reynolds mentioned that many of the volunteers were women, so presumably Parrott stood out.

After I read him a portion of the FBI memo, more recollections came back.

"I seem to remember that some of this did brew up before the Kennedy assassination . . . Kennedy came to Houston, I think on a Thursday night, and he was assassinated on Friday morning."

Reynolds says he was asked to attend an event Thursday night at the home of a party activist named Marjorie Arsht.

"There was some kind of little social-political thing at her house, and I was asked to be there and watch Parrott, which I think I did. And again this is conditional because my memory is just not that good. Now, but I do remember the following day or the day after or whatever after the assassination, that somebody called me and asked if I was with Parrott that night or whatever, and I answered yes. I think I remember that."

I asked him why they wanted him to watch Parrott.

"I don't know," said Reynolds hesitantly. "He was just—he wasn't your everyday campus guy. He just seemed kind of distant and remote—quiet, polite, soft spoken, but didn't talk much and just seemed distant. Now who or to what extent other people talked to him or perceived him to be a little on the edge, I don't know."

He went on to describe people who would come into the headquarters and rant for two hours on some pet topic, like a return to the gold standard, and why you might want to keep an eye on such a person. But then he agreed that Parrott was not such a person.

In fact, as the FBI report reveals, he was quite harmless—barely able to fend for himself. He had only a seventh grade education, had been discharged from the Air Force by a psychiatrist, gone into sign-painting, lived with his mother, and apparently volunteered regularly with the Harris County GOP quietly and without incident.

Until the Bush phone call.

No Harm Done

The cumulative result was that Poppy was listed in government files as having been in Tyler on November 22, 1963—while Parrott faced no long-term consequences for having been secretly accused.

In the aforementioned 1993 interview, Parrott would insist that for many years he had been unaware that it was Bush who had made the accusation against him. He also noted that he had actually gone on to work for Bush's unsuccessful presidential reelection campaign in 1992.[31] In an article covering the frenzied GOP-convention podium attacks on the Clinton-Gore team over family values, Parrott is described as passing out flyers saying, "No queers or baby killing," while wearing a plastic shield over his face, explaining that it was protection against the AIDS virus.[32]

As time passed, Parrott increasingly told a story that meshed with Bush's, inflating his own significance along the lines of what the Bush forces were putting out. "It was mainly a rumor put out by those trying to neutralize us," he said in the 1993 interview, claiming that he and other conservatives were in the middle of a bitter struggle with Bush and other "moderates" over the need to go after those suspected of Communist activities.

That said, the notion that Parrott was active in any sort of aggressive rightist circles seems either untrue or irrelevant to what actually happened on November 22. More likely, Parrott was simply set up, his right-wing ideology used as a red herring by Poppy to legitimate his phone call. After all, if Parrott did not have an ideological motivation to kill Kennedy, why would he be considered a threat?

Another curiosity: either the FBI agent who took Bush's call, or Bush himself, misspelled the surnames of the two supposed witnesses whom Bush said would know more about Parrott. To be sure, if the phone numbers provided for them in the memo were correct, the FBI would be able to find them. But years later, researchers who tried had difficulty figuring out who those people were—or how to track them down. In fact, only extensive cross-referencing reveals that "Mrs. Fawley" is actually a Mrs. *Thawley*. And "Arline Smith" turns out to be *Aleene* Smith.

These were either mistakes or deliberate errors; in any case, it is reminiscent of the way Barbara Bush mangled their friend Mr. Zeppa's name in her letter. George Bush knew both of these women well. Nancy Brelsford Thawley was vice chair of the Harris County Republican Party, and Aleene Smith was a well-known Texas Republican activist who worked for Bush at Zapata Offshore; both women remained with Bush for many years thereafter, accompanying him to Washington. Bush should have at least known how to spell their names.

The background of the FBI agent is also of note. Graham Kitchel was unusually close to J. Edgar Hoover, and his record is full not only of commendations from the head of the vast organization but also of personal notes, including a get-well card in 1963 from Hoover after Kitchel underwent surgery. In addition, in a 1990s interview, Kitchel's brother George, an offshore oil engineer, explained that he, George Kitchel, was an old friend of George H. W. Bush.

In summary, then, Bush called in a pointless tip about an innocent fellow to an FBI agent whom he knew, and whom he knew could be counted on to file a report on this tip—out of what may have been hundreds of calls, some of them not even worthy of documenting. And, after a cursory investigation, the tip was confirmed as useless. But the call itself was hardly without value. It established for the record, if anyone asked, that Poppy Bush was not in Dallas when Kennedy was shot. By pointing to a seemingly harmless man who lived with his mother, Bush appeared to establish his own Pollyannaish ignorance of the larger plot.

While Parrott had eyewitnesses to his being in Houston before, after, and *at the time of* a shooting that took place 240 miles away, Bush had Kiwanis eyewitnesses to where he was at around 12:30, the time of the shooting and the scheduled time of his luncheon speech.

The big mystery, of course, is the call to the FBI. Bush clearly made the call; Parrott clearly was never any threat. Therefore, Poppy Bush was willing to divert the investigative resources of the FBI on one of the busiest days in its history. Beyond that are the baffling particulars: Why did Bush have one of his people visit Parrott's house almost exactly as Poppy was fingering Parrott as a possible suspect? And why was Bush so determined to establish his presence in Tyler that day—and to document, as it were, his concern for Kennedy's well-being? Why was Parrott so unperturbed to have been falsely accused by Poppy Bush?

The answer may lie in Poppy's mention to the FBI that he would be traveling next from Tyler to Dallas, and that he would be staying at the Sheraton. This was, in fact, akin to a magician's trick—drawing the audience's attention slightly from the real action. In truth, Poppy had *already been* at the Sheraton in Dallas—the night before, speaking to the AAODC convention. By telling the FBI that he was *planning to* go there, he created a misleading paper trail suggesting that his stay in Dallas was many hours after Kennedy's shooting, rather than a few hours before.

In fact, although he did travel from Tyler to Dallas, he stayed only briefly, did not stay at the Sheraton this time, and went right back to Houston. The Parrott call served no purpose besides manufacturing a reason to create a government record of his presence in Tyler and his plan to go to Dallas later on the 22nd. Once Parrott had served, however unwittingly, his purpose, there was no reason for him to suffer—hence, Reynolds's visit to Parrott's house around the time of the assassination, which effectively created an alibi clearing Parrott. In other words, no harm done.

As for the reference to the Ulmers in Barbara's letter, why risk introducing so controversial a person? Like Bush's use of Joe Zeppa's plane, it helped establish that Bush had in fact spent time with Al Ulmer. Better to include Ulmer's wife's name (but not his) and Zeppa's name (misspelled) so that should a rare hardy investigator bother to figure out the sequence of events, Bush could claim that he obviously had nothing to hide—after all, there it was (in a way) in Barbara's letter.

In fact, Poppy Bush had good reason to obfuscate the details of his relationships and his conduct because they would, at minimum, lead to further inquiry at a time when an investigation into the death of a president was—or should have been—open-ended. The secrets themselves, and the urgency of keeping them hidden, would become a principal rationale in the family's political efforts. And, as we shall see, they go a long way toward explaining the unprecedented information lockdown and seeming paranoia of the George W. Bush administration—whose earliest acts included an effort to put his father's records under lock and key forever.

CHAPTER 5

Oswald's Friend

IN 1976, MORE THAN A DECADE AFTER the assassination of President John F. Kennedy, a letter arrived at the CIA, addressed to its director, the Hon. George Bush. The letter was from a desperate-sounding man in Dallas, who spoke regretfully of having been indiscreet in talking about Lee Harvey Oswald and begged Poppy for help:

> Maybe you will be able to bring a solution into the hopeless situation I find myself in. My wife and I find ourselves surrounded by some vigilantes; our phone bugged; and we are being followed everywhere. Either FBI is involved in this or they do not want to accept my complaints. We are driven to insanity by this situation . . . I tried to write, stupidly and unsuccessfully, about Lee H. Oswald and must have angered a lot of people . . . Could you do something to remove this net around us? This will be my last request for help and I will not annoy you any more.

The writer signed himself "G. de Mohrenschildt."[1]

The CIA staff assumed the letter writer to be a crank. Just to be sure, however, they asked their boss: Did he by any chance know a man named de Mohrenschildt?

Bush responded by memo, seemingly self-typed: "I do know this man DeMohrenschildt. I first men [sic] him in the early 40'3 [sic]. He was an uncle to my Andover roommate. Later he surfaced in Dallas (50's maybe) . . . Then he surfaced when Oswald shot to prominence. He knew

Oswald before the assassination of Pres. Kennedy. I don't recall his role in all this."

Not recall? Once again, Poppy Bush was having memory problems. And not about trivial matters. George de Mohrenschildt was not just the uncle of a roommate, but a longtime personal associate. Yet Poppy could not recall—or more precisely, claimed not to recall—the nature of de Mohrenschildt's relationship with the man believed to have assassinated the thirty-fifth president.

This would have been an unusual lapse on anyone's part. But for the head of an American spy agency to exhibit such a blasé attitude, in such an important matter, was over the edge. At that very moment, several federal investigations were looking into CIA abuses—including the agency's role in assassinations of foreign leaders. These investigators were heading toward what would become a reopened inquiry into Kennedy's death. Could it be that the lapse was not casual, and the acknowledgment of a distant relationship was a way to forestall inquiry into a closer one?

Writing back to his old friend, Poppy assured de Mohrenschildt that his fears were entirely unfounded. Yet half a year later, de Mohrenschildt was dead. The cause was officially determined to be suicide with a shotgun. Investigators combing through de Mohrenschildt's effects came upon his tattered address book, largely full of entries made in the 1950s. Among them, though apparently eliciting no further inquiries on the part of the police, was an old entry for the current CIA director, with the Midland address where he had lived in the early days of Zapata:

BUSH, GEORGE H. W. (POPPY), 1412 W. OHIO ALSO ZAPATA PETROLEUM, MIDLAND.

When Poppy told his staff that his old friend de Mohrenschildt "knew Oswald," that was an understatement. From 1962 through the spring of 1963, de Mohrenschildt was by far the principal influence on Oswald, the older man who guided every step of his life. De Mohrenschildt had helped Oswald find jobs and apartments, had taken him to meetings and social gatherings, and generally had assisted with the most minute aspects of life for Lee Oswald, his Russian wife, Marina, and their baby.

De Mohrenschildt's relationship with Oswald has tantalized and perplexed investigators and researchers for decades. In 1964, de Mohrenschildt and his wife Jeanne testified to the Warren Commission, which spent more time with them than any other witness—possibly excepting Oswald's widow, Marina. The commission, though, focused on George de Mohrenschildt as a colorful, if eccentric, character, steering away every time de Mohrenschildt recounted yet another name from a staggering list of influential friends and associates. In the end, the commission simply concluded in its final report that these must all be coincidences and nothing more. The de Mohrenschildts, the commission said, apparently had nothing to do with the assassination.

Even the Warren Commission counsel who questioned George de Mohrenschildt appeared to acknowledge that the Russian émigré was what might euphemistically be called an "international businessman." For most of his adult life, de Mohrenschildt had traveled the world ostensibly seeking business opportunities involving a variety of natural resources—some, such as oil and uranium, of great strategic value. The timing of his overseas ventures was remarkable. Invariably, when he was passing through town, a covert or even overt operation appeared to be unfolding—an invasion, a coup, that sort of thing. For example, in 1961, as exiled Cubans and their CIA support team prepared for the Bay of Pigs invasion in Guatemala, George de Mohrenschildt and his wife passed through Guatemala City on what they told friends was a months-long walking tour of the Central American isthmus. On another occasion, the de Mohrenschildts appeared in Mexico on oil business just as a Soviet leader arrived on a similar mission— and even happened to meet the Communist official. In a third instance, they landed in Haiti shortly before an unsuccessful coup against its president that had U.S. fingerprints on it.

The press was briefly intrigued by de Mohrenschildt, and especially by the fact that he knew both the assassin and the assassinated. Reported the Associated Press:

> A Russian-born society figure was a friend both of the family of President Kennedy and his assassin, Lee Harvey Oswald. A series of strange coincidences providing the only known link between the two families before Oswald fired the shot killing Mr. Kennedy in Dallas a year ago was described in testimony before the Warren Commission by George S. de Mohrenschildt.[2]

He was actually much more intriguing—and mystifying. As Norman Mailer noted in his book *Oswald's Tale*, de Mohrenschildt possessed "an eclecticism that made him delight in presenting himself as right-wing, left-wing, a moralist, an immoralist, an aristocrat, a nihilist, a snob, an atheist, a Republican, a Kennedy lover, a desegregationist, an intimate of oil tycoons, a bohemian, and a socialite, plus a quondam Nazi apologist, once a year."[3]

During all these examinations, and notwithstanding de Mohrenschildt's offhand recitation of scores of friends and colleagues, obscure and recognizable, he scrupulously never once mentioned that he knew Poppy Bush. Nor did investigators uncover the fact that in the spring of 1963, immediately after his final communication with Oswald, de Mohrenschildt had traveled to New York and Washington for meetings with CIA and military intelligence officials. He even had met with a top aide to Vice President Johnson. And the commission certainly did not learn that one meeting in New York included Thomas Devine, then Poppy Bush's business colleague in Zapata Offshore, who was doing double duty for the CIA.

Had the Warren Commission's investigators comprehensively explored the matter, they would have found a phenomenal and baroque backstory that contextualizes de Mohrenschildt within the extended petroleum-intelligence orbit in which the Bushes operated.

Back in Baku

The de Mohrenschildts were major players in the global oil business since the beginning of the twentieth century, and their paths crossed with the Rockefellers and other key pillars of the petroleum establishment. George de Mohrenschildt's uncle and father ran the Swedish Nobel Brothers Oil Company's operations in Baku, in Russian Azerbaijan on the southwestern coast of the Caspian Sea. This was no small matter. In the early days of the twentieth century, the region held roughly half of the world's known oil supply. By the start of World War I, every major oil interest in the world, including the Rockefellers' Standard Oil, was scrambling for a piece of Baku's treasure or intriguing to suppress its competitive potential. (Today, ninety years later, they are at it again.)

In 1915, the czar's government dispatched a second uncle of George de Mohrenschildt, the handsome young diplomat Ferdinand von Mohrenschildt,[4] to Washington to plead for American intervention in the war—an intervention that might rescue the czarist forces then being crushed by the invading German army. President Woodrow Wilson had been reelected partly on the basis of having kept America out of the war. But as with all leaders, he was surrounded by men with their own agendas. A relatively close-knit group embodying the nexus of private capital and intelligence-gathering inhabited the highest levels of the Wilson administration. Secretary of State Robert Lansing was the uncle of a young diplomat-spy by the name of Allen Dulles. Wilson's closest adviser, "Colonel" Edward House, was a Texan and an ally of the ancestors of James A. Baker III, who would become Poppy Bush's top lieutenant. Czarist Russia then owed fifty million dollars to a Rockefeller-headed syndicate. Keeping an eye on such matters was the U.S. ambassador to Russia, a close friend of George Herbert Walker's from St. Louis.[5]

Once the United States did enter the war, Prescott Bush's father, Samuel Bush, was put in charge of small arms production. The Percy Rockefeller–headed Remington Arms Company got the lion's share of the U.S. contracts. It sold millions of dollars worth of rifles to czarist forces, while it also profited handsomely from deals with the Germans.[6]

In 1917, Ferdinand von Mohrenschildt's mission to bring America into the world war was successful on a number of levels. Newspaper clippings of the time show him to be an instant hit on the Newport, Rhode Island, millionaires' circuit. He was often in the company of Mrs. J. Borden Harriman, of the family then befriending Prescott Bush and about to hire Prescott's future father-in-law, George Herbert Walker.[7] Not long after that, Ferdinand married the step-granddaughter of President Woodrow Wilson.

In quick succession, the United States entered World War I, and the newlywed Ferdinand unexpectedly died. The von Mohrenschildt family fled Russia along with the rest of the aristocracy. Emanuel Nobel sold half of the Baku holdings to Standard Oil of New Jersey, with John D. Rockefeller Jr. personally authorizing the payment of $11.5 million.[8] Over the next couple of decades, members of the defeated White Russian movement, which opposed the Bolsheviks and fought the Red Army from the 1917 October Revolution until 1923, would find shelter in the United States, a country that shared the anti-Communist movement's ideological sentiments.

Refugees from a Revolution

In 1920, Ferdinand's nephew Dimitri von Mohrenschildt, the older brother of George, arrived in the United States and entered Yale University. His admission was likely smoothed by the connections of the Harriman family, which soon persuaded the Bolshevik Russian government to allow them to reactivate the Baku oil fields. At that point, the Harriman operation was being directed by the brilliant international moneyman George Herbert Walker, the grandfather of Poppy Bush.

The Soviets had expropriated the assets of the Russian ruling class, not least the oil fields. Though ultimately willing to cooperate with some Western companies, the Communists had created an army of angry White Russian opponents, who vowed to exact revenge and regain their holdings. This group, trading on an American fascination with titles, was soon ensconced in (and often intermarried with) the East Coast establishment. The New York newspapers of the day were full of reports of dinners and teas hosted by Prince This and Count That at the top Manhattan hotels.

Dimitri von Mohrenschildt plunged into this milieu.[9] After graduating from Yale, he was offered a position teaching the young scions of the new oil aristocracy at the exclusive Loomis School near Hartford, Connecticut, where John D. Rockefeller III was a student (and his brother Winthrop soon would be). There, Dimitri became friendly with Roland and Winifred "Betty" Cartwright Holhan Hooker, who were prominent local citizens. Roland Hooker was enormously well connected; his father had been the mayor of Hartford, his family members were close friends of the Bouviers' (Jackie Kennedy's father's family), and his sister was married to Prince Melikov, a former officer in the Imperial Russian Army.

While Dimitri von Mohrenschildt clearly enjoyed the high-society glamour, in reality his life was heading underground. Dimitri's lengthy covert résumé would include serving in the Office of Strategic Services wartime spy agency and later cofounding Radio Free Europe and Radio Liberty. In 1941, Dimitri also founded a magazine, the *Russian Review*, and later became a professor at Dartmouth.

When the Hooker marriage unraveled, Dimitri began seeing Betty Hooker. In the summer of 1936, immigration records show that Dimitri traveled to Europe, followed a week later by Betty Hooker with her young daughter and adolescent son.

Betty's son, Edward Gordon Hooker, entered prep school at Phillips Academy in Andover, Massachusetts. There, he shared a small cottage with George H. W. "Poppy" Bush. Bush and Hooker became inseparable. They worked together on *Pot Pourri*, the student yearbook, whose photos show a handsome young Poppy Bush and an even more handsome Hooker. The friendship would continue in 1942, when both Bush and Hooker, barely eighteen, enlisted in the Navy and served as pilots in the Pacific. Afterward, they would be together at Yale. When Hooker married, Poppy Bush served as an usher. The relationship between Bush and Hooker lasted for three decades, until 1967, when Hooker died of an apparent heart attack.[10] He was just forty-three. Six years after Hooker's death, Poppy Bush would serve as surrogate father, giving away Hooker's daughter at her wedding to Ames Braga, scion of a Castro-expropriated Cuban sugar dynasty.

The relationship couldn't have been much closer. Yet Bush never mentions Hooker in his memoirs or published recollections, even though he finds room for scores of more marginal figures. Certainly his family was aware of Hooker.

Poppy's prep school living arrangements would have mattered to Prescott Bush. The Bush clan is famously gregarious, and like many wealthy families, it puts great stock in the establishment of social networks that translate into influence and advantage. Prescott took a strong interest in meeting his children's friends and the friends' parents, as expressed in family correspondence and memoirs. Moreover, as a prominent Connecticut family with deep colonial roots, the Hookers would have had great appeal for Prescott Bush, an up-and-coming Connecticut resident with political aspirations and a great interest in the genealogy of America's upper classes.

In 1937, Betty Hooker and Dimitri von Mohrenschildt married. By then, Dimitri had been hired by Henry Luce as a stringer for *Time* magazine. Prescott would likely have been keen to know his son's roommate's stepfather—this intriguing Russian anti-Communist aristocrat, with a background in the oil business and a degree from Yale, working for Prescott's Skull and Bones friend Luce.

Meanwhile, Dimitri's younger brother, George, had been living with their family in exile in Poland, where he finished high school and then joined a military academy and the cavalry. In May 1938, George arrived from Europe and moved in with his brother and new sister-in-law in their Park Avenue apartment. Young George de Mohrenschildt came to America armed with the doctoral dissertation that reflected the future trajectory of his life: "The Economic Influence of the United States on Latin America."[11] The oil south of the border was certainly of interest to Wall Street figures such as Prescott Bush and his colleagues, who were deeply involved in financing petroleum exploration in new areas.

The Imperial Horse Guards

The White Russian émigrés in the United States were motivated by both ideology and economics to serve as shock troops in the growing cold war conflict being managed by Prescott's friends and associates. No one understood this better than Allen Dulles, the Wall Street lawyer, diplomat, and spymaster-in-ascension. Even in the period between the two world wars, Dulles was already molding Russian émigrés into intelligence operatives. He moved back and forth between government service and Wall Street lawyering with the firm Sullivan and Cromwell, whose clients included United Fruit and Brown Brothers Harriman. The latter was at that time led by Averell and Roland Harriman and Prescott Bush.

Whether in government or out, Dulles's interests and associates were largely the same.[12] He seemed to enjoy the clandestine work more than the legal work. As Peter Grose notes in *Gentleman Spy: The Life of Allen Dulles*, he worked during the 1940 presidential campaign to bring Russian, Polish, and Czechoslovak émigrés into the Republican camp. "Allen's double life those first months after Pearl Harbor [in 1941] had specific purpose, of course," Grose observes. "The mysterious émigrés he was cultivating in New York were potential assets for an intelligence network to penetrate Nazi Germany."[13]

Dimitri von Mohrenschildt was a star player in this game on a somewhat exalted level. He found sponsorship for a role as an academic and publisher specializing in anti-Bolshevik materials, and later became involved in more ambitious propaganda work with Radio Liberty and Radio Free Europe. Younger brother George was more willing to get his hands dirty. He took a job in the New York offices of a French perfume company called Chevalier Garde, named for the czar's most elite troops, the Imperial Horse Guards. His bosses were powerful czarist Russian émigrés, well connected at the highest levels of Manhattan society, who worked during World War II in army intelligence and the OSS.[14] One of them, Prince Serge Obolensky, had escaped Soviet Russia after a year of hiding and became a much-married New York society figure whose wives included Alice Astor. His brother-in-law Vincent Astor was secretly asked by FDR in 1940 to set up civilian espionage offices in Manhattan at Rockefeller Center. Astor was soon joined in this effort by Allen Dulles.

The next stop for George de Mohrenschildt was a home furnishings company. His boss there was a high-ranking French intelligence official, and together they monitored and blocked attempts by the Axis war machine to procure badly needed petroleum supplies in the Americas. Young de Mohrenschildt then traveled to the Southwest, where he exhibited still more impressive connections. Ostensibly there to work on oil derricks, he landed a meeting with the chairman of the board of Humble Oil, the Texas subsidiary of Standard Oil of New Jersey, predecessor to Exxon.

The jobs kept becoming more interesting. By the midforties, de Mohrenschildt was working in Venezuela for Pantepec Oil, the firm of William F. Buckley's family. Pantepec later had abundant connections with the newly created CIA and was deeply involved in foreign intrigue for decades.[15] The Buckley boys, like the Bushes, had been in Skull and Bones, and Bill Buckley, whose conservative intellectual magazine *National Review* was often politically helpful to Poppy Bush, would in later years admit to a stint working for the CIA himself.

George de Mohrenschildt's foreign trips—and some of his domestic wanderings as well—drew the interest of various American law enforcement agencies. These incidents appear to have been deliberate provocations, such as his working on "sketches" outside a U.S. Coast Guard station. In many of these cases de Mohrenschildt would be briefly questioned or investigated, the result of which was a dossier not unlike that of Lee Harvey Oswald's. These files were full of declared doubts about his loyalties and speculation at various times that he might be a Russian, Japanese, French, or German spy. A classic opportunist, he might have been any or all of these. But he also could have simply been an American spy who was creating a cover story.

The Cold War Comes to Dallas

In the ensuing years, George de Mohrenschildt bounced frenetically around every corner of the burgeoning energy landscape. In 1950, together with Poppy Bush's old friend and former roommate Eddie Hooker, he launched a modest oil investment firm, Hooker and de Mohrenschildt, with "offices in New York, Denver, and Abilene." At this time West Texas was the center of a new boom. Poppy Bush was working there in his role as a trainee for Neil Mallon's Dresser Industries. Meanwhile, a vastly more ambitious enterprise was afoot in Dallas, where Mallon relocated Dresser Industries in 1950. At that time, Dallas was still a relatively modest-size city, but growing rapidly.

Once primarily a banking center for wealthy cotton farmers, it had become a center of petroleum finance and home to the new breed of superrich independent oilmen. With help from House Speaker Sam Rayburn and Senate Majority Leader Lyndon Johnson, Dallas had attracted a number of defense contractors, which made it a growing hub of the nation's military-industrial complex.

By the early fifties, Dallas contained a small and close-knit community of Russian émigrés, perhaps thirty in all. They were drawn together by business interests, an anti-Communist worldview, and participation in a new church they had founded, though many were not religious. Almost every week they attended social gatherings at one another's homes. George de Mohrenschildt developed ties with the most important of them.

The man who would be considered the "godfather" of the émigré community was Paul Raigorodsky, a former czarist Russian cavalry officer who had fought against the Red Army. After the Bolshevik victory, Raigorodsky came to the United States with the help of the Red Cross and the YMCA. Like many of the other émigrés, he married into American society at a high level: his new father-in-law had set up the Dallas Federal Reserve Bank. Before long, he was on the oil and military track, with important assignments in war and peace, including some from powerful figures in the Bush-Dresser orbit. Some accounts have him serving in the OSS, the forerunner of the CIA. He also became an acknowledged friend of FBI director J. Edgar Hoover. Raigorodsky was a director of the Tolstoy Foundation, a U.S.-government-funded organization that assisted Russian exiles.

The second most influential man in the Russian émigré community was George Bouhe, an oil accountant. In the 1920s, while a high school student in Petrograd, Bouhe had worked for the American Relief Administration (ARA), a spy-cover charity that provided food aid to the Russian population via branch offices set up by American executives in various Russian cities.[16] Bouhe's supervisors, impressed with his work, urged him to come to the United States. He crossed a river into Finland in the middle of the night and traveled to New York, where he went to work for the Rockefellers' Chase Bank. Then he moved to Dallas, where he became the bookkeeper for Lewis W. MacNaughton, a partner in the highly influential petroleum geology consulting firm DeGolyer and MacNaughton and a board member of Dresser Industries.

Bouhe and Raigorodsky both would befriend de Mohrenschildt and remain in close contact with him during 1962 and 1963. The Russian community as a whole bonded naturally with the city's right-wing oilmen and bankers, and all clustered together under the remarkable leadership of Poppy Bush's "uncle," Neil Mallon. In 1951, Mallon launched the Dallas Council on World Affairs. Under this umbrella, Mallon brought together many of Dallas's most powerful citizens, from oilmen and titans of the burgeoning military-contracting industry to German scientists who had fled the wreckage of Hitler's Germany to help fashion weapons against the Communist threat.

George de Mohrenschildt moved to Dallas in 1952, established himself as a consulting geologist, and was quickly accepted into the city's ruling elite. He joined the powerful Dallas Petroleum Club and became a regular at Council on World Affairs meetings.[17] Many of the figures involved in those two entities also showed up on the boards of other influential local groups. One was the Texas chapter of the Crusade for Freedom, a private conduit for laundered money to be sent to "freedom fighters."

The roots of Crusade for Freedom date to 1949. Senator Herbert Lehman of New York, son of a founder of Lehman Brothers, together with a group of associates established the National Committee for a Free Europe Inc. Backed by Secretary of State Dean Acheson (Yale '43, Scroll and Key), this group spawned a subsidiary, the Crusade for Freedom, with General Lucius Clay, which proceeded to launch a series of gigantic annual fund-raising campaigns.

One of the first events it funded was a nationwide radio address by General Dwight D. Eisenhower, urging Americans to support it. The money raised went to entities connected with Radio Free Europe and Radio Liberty, which were centers of anti-Communist propaganda, and consequently home to many former Nazis and Nazi collaborators. At the direction of Washington, these entities laundered U.S. government funds (including monies from the CIA) for use by Eastern European insurgents. This was a forebear of later CIA money-laundering operations, including Iran-contra, in which Poppy Bush played a hidden but significant role. Among the European immigrants who were deeply involved in these operations were Dimitri von and George de Mohrenschildt.

Members of the Texas Crusade for Freedom would become a who's who of Texans connected to the events surrounding the assassination of John F. Kennedy. In addition to Neil Mallon, members included Raigorodsky, MacNaughton, Everette DeGolyer, and Dallas mayor Earle Cabell, brother of Charles Cabell, who was Allen Dulles's deputy CIA director. Another member was D. Harold Byrd, who owned the building in downtown Dallas that would become known as the Texas School Book Depository. Still another was E. M. "Ted" Dealey, publisher of the *Dallas Morning News*, who was a harsh critic of Kennedy.[18]

It was a dense web, and its links went to the heart of the intelligence establishment. Neil Mallon had a direct pipeline to Allen Dulles. Prescott Bush noted in a letter around this time that Mallon was "well known to Allen Dulles, and has tried to be helpful to him in the CIA, especially in the procurement of individuals to serve in that important agency."[19]

MEANWHILE, GEORGE DE MOHRENSCHILDT, thrice-married bon vivant, finally met his match, literally and figuratively in 1957 when he became involved with Jeanne LeGon, who would become his fourth wife.[20] Like George, Jeanne was Russian, and she had come to the United States and settled in New York City in the same year he did. In one of many extraordinary coincidences, they claimed to have lived next door to each other yet did not meet until years later. Jeanne had been born Eugenia Fomenko in 1914 in Harbin, China, near the Russian border, to Russian parents. Her father, Mikhail L. Fomenko, had run the Far Eastern Railroad for the Chinese government until it sold the railroad to the Russian Communist government in 1925.

Fomenko had needed scouts and informants to keep him up-to-date about his competitors and about regional intrigues. Jeanne's subsequent secret work in America—and that of her brother Sergei—may have emerged from that milieu. She would later tell the Warren Commission that she and her first husband, Robert LeGon, had fled Manchuria when it was under Japanese control because they feared that he would be killed due to his knowledge of a secret Japanese airfield he had worked on. Eventually, they made their way to New York, where brother Sergei was working on the top-secret Manhattan Project with J. Robert Oppenheimer.

In 1953 Jeanne and Robert joined the Russian elite's move to Dallas. Her first job there was as a designer with Nardis Sportswear, which was owned by Bernard L. "Benny" Gold a tough-talking Russian-born Jew who had started out as a Brooklyn cabdriver and ended up as a titan of the Dallas fashion scene. By 1950, splashy Dallas fashions were all the rage, gobbled up by stores all over the United States, and Nardis was the top of the heap.

The store shipped goods out on planes via Slick Airways, owned by the oilman and world-renowned explorer Tom Slick, a Dresser Industries board member and good friend of Prescott Bush. Benny Gold knew everyone; he was president of the Dallas Fashion Center and threw huge parties. When Jeanne first arrived in town, Benny Gold put her up in his mansion.

Gold was an intriguing figure. He joined all the anti-Communist groups as well as Neil Mallon's Dallas Council of World Affairs. He employed people who would prove to have tantalizing connections. While Jeanne designed clothing, her coworker Abraham Zapruder cut the patterns and material. A decade later, Zapruder, by then the owner of his own company, would become world famous for his breathtaking home-movie footage of the Kennedy assassination.

Cuba Sí, Cuba No

During the 1950s, as petroleum reserves in the Southwest declined, oilmen there were looking to the southern hemisphere for new opportunities. George de Mohrenschildt, who always seemed to move at the behest of people of higher rank than himself, turned to Cuba. He later told the Warren Commission that he left the Buckleys' Pantepec Oil back in 1946 after a falling-out with a company vice president. Yet by 1950 he was working with his former boss, Pantepec president Warren Smith, on the latter's new firm called the Cuban-Venezuelan Oil Voting Trust Company (CVOVT). In passing, de Mohrenschildt mentioned to the commission that the CVOVT had managed to obtain leases covering nearly half of Cuba. He appears to have been telling the truth, but Warren Commission counsel Albert E. Jenner Jr. did not find this remarkable fact interesting.[21]

This showed that de Mohrenschildt was no rogue operator or bohemian—as Jenner repeatedly sought to characterize him. Rather he was at the center of a major corporate effort, involving many of America's largest institutions. Through connections in the Batista regime, the CVOVT had managed to corner exclusive exploration rights to millions of acres on the island. Like all foreign businesses operating in Cuba, it had to work through the dictator's American intermediaries, notably the mobster Meyer Lansky, who was de facto representative of American "interests" on the island.[22]

The CVOVT never amounted to much besides promising reports and modest production.[23] Still it became a Wall Street darling. Though now almost completely forgotten, on many days in the mid-1950s, it was one of the four or five most actively traded issues on the American Stock Exchange. By November 30, 1956, the *New York Times* had this announcement:

> The Cuban Stanolind Oil Company, an affiliate of the Standard Oil Company (Indiana), has signed an agreement with the Cuban-Venezuelan Oil Voting Trust and Trans-Cuba Oil Company for the development of an additional 3,000,000 acres in Cuba. This is in addition to the original agreement covering 12,000,000 acres. Stanolind has agreed to start drilling within 120 days and maintain a one-rig continuous drilling program [for] three years.[24]

This was apparently a big deal for companies like Stanolind, which had no foreign production at all until it went into Cuba. But the CVOVT was about a lot more than just Cuba. According to its filings, it was formed in Havana in 1950 "to assure continuity of management and stability of policy for shareholders of twenty-four oil companies in South America."[25] That is, it was some kind of holding company with a focus on "stability" in Latin American countries, which could reasonably be assumed to refer to creating conditions of political stability favorable to the exploration activities.

The Empire Trust Company, a New York–based bastion of power and wealth, appears to have played a key role in the financing of the Cuban venture. A short item in the *New York Times* of May 14, 1956, noted:

> Election of Charles Leslie Rice, a vice president of the Empire Trust Company of New York, as a voting trustee of the Cuban-Venezuelan Oil Voting Trust, was announced over the week-end.

Empire Trust's John Loeb had a network of associates that amounted to "something very like a private CIA," wrote Stephen Birmingham in *Our Crowd: The Great Jewish Families of New York*.[26] Empire worked hard to protect its foreign investments and especially its stake in the defense contractor General Dynamics. Empire entrusted its affairs in Texas to Baker Botts, the law firm of James Baker's family.[27] Besides Rice, another Empire Trust director was Lewis MacNaughton, a Dresser Industries board member from 1959 to 1967. MacNaughton was the employer of George Bouhe, the Russian émigré who would later introduce George de Mohrenschildt to Lee Harvey Oswald. Perhaps the most curious of the Empire Trust figures was Jack Crichton, a longtime company vice president who joined Empire in August 1953 and remained through 1962.[28]

Crichton, who had been hired soon after leaving the military in 1946 by oil industry wunderkind Everette DeGolyer, quickly became a go-to guy for numerous powerful interests seeking a foothold in the energy arena. He started and ran a baffling array of companies, which tended to change names frequently. These operated largely below the radar, and fronted for some of North America's biggest names, including the Bronfmans (Seagram's liquor), the Du Ponts, and the Kuhn-Loeb family of financiers. According to his former lawyer, Crichton traveled to the Middle East on oil-related intelligence business. On behalf of prominent interests, he was involved with George de Mohrenschildt in his oil exploration venture in pre-Castro Cuba. In a 2001 oral history, Crichton volunteered that he was a friend of George de Mohrenschildt's: "I liked George. He was a nice guy."[29]

By 1956, in addition to his other duties, Crichton started a military intelligence reserve unit on the side.[30] On the day of Kennedy's assassination, as will be elaborated upon in chapter 7, he would arrange for a member of the Dallas Russian community to rush to Marina Oswald's side and provide translations for investigators—which were far from literal translations of her Russian words and had the effect of implicating her husband in Kennedy's death. Shortly after the assassination, Crichton would become the GOP nominee for governor of Texas in a race against the incumbent John Connally, who had recovered from his wounds of November 22. On the same ticket was the Republican nominee for the United States Senate, Poppy Bush.

Unfortunately for the rich and powerful behind the Cuban oil venture in the 1950s, just as the possibility of extracting vast wealth from that small island drew increasing interest from Wall Street, Fidel Castro's revolution was gaining strength. At the same time, what look to have been intelligence operations under oil industry cover were moving into position, as Poppy Bush began moving his rigs to Howard Hughes's Cay Sal Bank in the Bahamas.

On January 1, 1959, Fulgencio Batista fled Cuba, and the next day Castro's army marched into Havana.

On November 22, 1959, the *New York Times* reported that the new Cuban government had approved a law that would reduce the size of claims for oil exploration and halt large-scale explorations by private companies. These claims were now limited to twenty thousand acres, a major setback for companies such as CVOVT, with its fifteen million acres.[31]

According to the *Times*, big foreign oil companies had already spent more than thirty million dollars looking for oil over the preceding twelve years. The article cited petroleum industry sources speculating that nationalization of the refining industry was soon to come. The government also imposed a 60 percent royalty on oil production, believed to be the highest anywhere. Standard Oil of New Jersey had, according to the article, invested thirty-five million dollars in a Cuban refinery, and other companies had invested comparable sums.[32]

Among other things, the new law put an end to the go-go days of the Cuban-Venezuelan Oil Voting Trust stock. That story was summed up neatly in William A. Doyle's syndicated advice column, "The Daily Investor," on August 14, 1961:

> Q. I bought some shares of Cuban-Venezuelan Oil Voting Trust a couple of years ago. This stock was listed on the American Stock Exchange but I never see it quoted there any more. What's the trouble?

> A. The trouble is spelled C-a-s-t-r-o. When that bearded dictator took over the government in Cuba, he started kicking American investors smack in the pocketbook. The Cuban-Venezuelan Oil Voting Trust story is somewhat involved. But its chief cause of grief came when the Communist-oriented Cuban government refused to extend its concession to explore for oil. That just about wrecked this outfit. The stock's price dropped. You won't find the shares quoted on the American Stock Exchange, because this stock was de-listed from that exchange, as of Dec. 1, 1960. Technically, it is still possible to buy and sell these shares in the over-the-counter market. But you'll be lucky if you can get 10 cents a share.[33]

Brown Brothers Harriman also had a stake in Cuban affairs that went back at least to the 1920s. Its affiliate, the Punta Alegre Sugar Corporation, controlled more than two hundred thousand acres in the province of Camagüey.[34] Officials of the firm served on the board of Punta Alegre up to the moment that Castro expropriated its land—and even afterward, as the sugar company began moving its remaining assets to the United States.

The CIA's Allen Dulles responded quickly to developments on the island.

He created the Cuban Task Force, with teams in charge of clandestine operations, psychological warfare, and economic and diplomatic pressure. Out of these emerged Operation 40, an elite group of Cuban exiles who, after specialized training, were to infiltrate Cuba and deal a mortal blow to the revolution, including the assassination of its principal leaders.

The chief of the task force was Tracy Barnes, a Yale graduate and Dulles's wartime OSS comrade who was related to the Rockefeller clan by marriage. More than a decade earlier, Barnes's first CIA job had been as deputy director of the Psychological Strategy Board, a little-known entity that explored everything from the use of psychotropic drugs as truth serum to the possibility of engineering unwitting assassins, i.e., Manchurian candidates. Later, he worked on the successful 1954 operation to overthrow the democratically elected president of Guatemala, Jacobo Arbenz. Barnes had received propaganda support from David Atlee Phillips and E. Howard Hunt, including the distribution of faked photographs purporting to show the mutilated bodies of Arbenz opponents.

Phillips and Hunt would be hounded by allegations that they had been present in Dallas on November 22, 1963. Both men consistently denied it. But according to his son St. John Hunt, E. Howard began confessing knowledge of a plot against Kennedy near the end of his life and named Phillips as one of the participants.[35]

Hunt and Phillips attended the first meeting of the Cuban Task Force, held January 18, 1960, in Barnes's office. Barnes spoke at length on the objectives. He explained that Air Force General Charles Cabell, a Texan (and brother of Dallas's mayor), would be in charge of air cover for an invasion, and that Vice President Richard Nixon, whose brief included some national security areas, was the administration's Cuba "case officer."

In his memoirs, former Cuban intelligence official Fabian Escalante asserted that Nixon had met with an important group of Texas businessmen to arrange outside funding for the operation. Escalante, whose service was vaunted for its U.S. spy network, claimed that the Texas group was headed by George H. W. Bush and Jack Crichton. Escalante's assertion cannot be easily dismissed: Crichton's role in covert operations, about which extensive new information is provided in chapter 7, was little understood at the time Escalante published his memoirs.[36]

In March 1960, the Eisenhower administration signed off on a plan to equip and train Cuban exiles, and drills soon began in Florida and Guatemala. One of Dulles's top three aides, the covert operations chief Richard M. Bissell

(Yale '32), was made director. Around this time, George de Mohrenschildt happened to take a business trip to Mexico City, where the CIA station was deeply involved in the coming attractions.

By the fall of 1962, when de Mohrenschildt was devoting much of his time to squiring Lee Harvey Oswald, he had gained entrée to the crème de la crème of the petroleum world. One longtime buddy of his and of Poppy Bush's, offshore drilling expert George Kitchel, would tell the FBI in 1964 that de Mohrenschildt counted among his good friends the oil tycoons Clint Murchison, H. L. Hunt, John Mecom, and Sid Richardson. Other commission testimony revealed that in the couple of years prior to the Kennedy assassination, de Mohrenschildt had traveled frequently from Dallas to Houston, where he visited with figures such as George Brown of Brown and Root, the construction and military contracting giant that helped launch LBJ's career, and Jean de Menil of Schlumberger, the huge oil services firm.

Several of these men had even sent de Mohrenschildt abroad on business; one could be forgiven for wondering if these trips were in fact what the CIA calls "commercial cover." George Brown had dispatched him to Mexico, where his mission seemed to be heading off a Mexican government oil deal with the Soviet deputy premier Anastas Mikoyan, who arrived at the same time.[37] Murchison dispatched him to Haiti on several occasions. In 1958, he went to Yugoslavia on what was said to be business for Mecom—whose foundation, the San Jacinto Fund, was later identified as a CIA funding conduit.

The Warren Commission knew at least pieces of all this. Yet in 1964, after two and a half days of testimony by George de Mohrenschildt and his wife Jeanne, the commission would conclude that George was essentially an eccentric if well-connected figure whose life encompassed a series of strange coincidences.

CHAPTER 6

The Hit

THE EVIDENCE WAS MOUNTING THAT Poppy Bush was not the genial bumbler the public remembered—the bland fellow in the turtleneck who drove a golf cart around Kennebunkport and could never make up his mind.

Apparently Poppy had secrets, and he kept them well. It seems that he had been involved in intelligence work for much of his adult life. He had been in and around hot spots of covert action. And in the fall of 1963, he had for some unfathomable reason been worried that someone would discover he had been in Dallas on the evening of November 21 and seemingly the morning of November 22.

As far as I knew, he had attended the oilmen's meeting and then left for Tyler. Why hide that fact?

One obvious reason is that no one with any political ambition would want to be associated in the public's mind with the events in Dallas on November 22, 1963. But in that case, what does it say about Poppy that his first instinct was to create an elaborate cover story to airbrush away an inconvenient fact?

It is theoretically possible, of course, that there was something totally apart from the assassination he didn't want known. But given his documented intelligence ties and the fact that figures close to him were connected to the event, the likelihood that his attempt to distance himself from Dallas on November 22 was unrelated to the tragedy of that day seems low.

In the absence of any plausible alternative explanation, I found the possibility that George H. W. Bush himself was somehow linked to the events in Dallas worth pursuing, as a working hypothesis at least. Among the material

I had to consider was that memo from J. Edgar Hoover referring to a brief-ing given to "George Bush of the CIA" on the day after the assassination. I also had to take into account the visit from England that week by Al Ulmer, the CIA coup expert—and that Ulmer had spent time with Poppy. There were still more disturbing facts, perhaps all coincidental, which I gathered and which will be presented below and in the next chapter.

Still, I was unsure how to proceed. I was well aware of the perils of even touching the assassination topic, and as a journalist with a reputation to protect, I naturally had reservations. I wasn't eager to be dismissed as gullible or self-aggrandizing or downright wacky—as I know so often hap-pens to people (sometimes justifiably) who tackle such topics, unless they advance the conventional wisdom or simply point to the "unsolved myster-ies" that haunt historians. But I knew I should not, and really could not, ig-nore what I was finding.

So I stepped back. Examining the circle around Bush, I could see it was full of people who had grievances—personal, political, or economic—against Kennedy, and whether or not they wanted him out of the way, who clearly were advantaged by his death.

After the Bay of Pigs disaster, JFK had been blunt about his feelings to-ward the intelligence elite that had concocted the Cuban scheme. "I've got to do something about those CIA bastards," he had raged.[1] Heads had rolled, and Allen Dulles, the Bushes' close friend, was still smarting over his firing. So was Charles Cabell, the brother of Dallas mayor Earle Cabell and the CIA's deputy director of operations during the Bay of Pigs invasion; Kennedy deep-sixed his career. Also holding a grudge against the Kennedys was Prescott Bush, who was furious at both JFK and RFK for sacking his close friend Dulles. And there were many others.

The downside of dissembling is that it invites curiosity and the inevitable question: What exactly is the dissembler trying to hide? Poppy Bush went to such lengths, even raising distracting suspicions about a regular volunteer for his Harris County Republican organization and frequent presence in its offices, that I felt there had to be more to the story. In Poppy's book-length collection of correspondence, *All the Best, George Bush*, there are no letters in the relevant time frame even mentioning the JFK assassination. Remarkably for a Texan, and an aspiring Texan politician, of that era, Bush has apparently never written anything about the assassination. This applies even to his ane-mic memoir, *Looking Forward*, in which he mentions Kennedy's visit to Dal-las but not what happened to him there.[2] Once I began to piece together the

scattered clues to what might be the true narrative, I realized that Poppy's resort to crafty evasions and multilayered cover stories in this incident seemed
to fit a pattern in his life. Over and over, those seeking to nail down the facts
about George H. W. Bush's doings encounter what might be characterized as
a sustained fuzziness; what appear at first glance to be unexceptionable details turn out, on closer examination, to be potentially important facts that
slip away into confusion and deniability. Little is ever what it seems.

To get a better idea of what happened on November 22 requires a detour,
not so much away from Poppy but rather into the spider's web of connections around him. We start with motive.

BY THE FALL of 1963, the Kennedy brothers had made enough enemies to
fill an old hotel full of suspects in an Agatha Christie mystery.

There were the many powerful figures under investigation by RFK's Justice Department, and untold numbers of movers and shakers who felt
slighted or humiliated by other Kennedy maneuvers. Jack's insistence on
Allen Dulles's resignation following the Bay of Pigs debacle was in effect a
declaration of independence from the Wall Street intelligence nexus that
had pretty much had its way in the previous administration. Like FDR, JFK
was considered a traitor to his own class. Also like FDR, he had the charm
and political savvy to get away with it. With his wealthy scoundrel of a father
in his corner, he could not be bought or controlled.

And of course there was the Mafia, which was desperately attempting to
recoup its huge losses after Castro shut down their casinos and exiled or im-
prisoned leading mafiosi. After Castro announced in December 1959 that
he was a Communist, the CIA recognized its newly found common cause
with the underworld and solicited the services of several mobsters, in what
became the notorious CIA-Mafia plots to assassinate Castro. According to
numerous public and private investigations, those plots spun out of control
and might have evolved into a plot against JFK. There was motive aplenty:
Attorney General Robert Kennedy relentlessly pursued the mob-tied Team-
sters boss Jimmy Hoffa and a long list of underworld figures.

Then, too, many prominent people nursed more private grievances. For
one thing, Jack Kennedy could not keep his pants on. He thought nothing
of romancing the wives and girlfriends of the powerful. The FBI tracked
many affairs during JFK's brief time in office, but then J. Edgar Hoover was
no fan of the Kennedys either.

And there were the Cuban exiles who blamed the failure of the Bay of Pigs invasion on President Kennedy rather than on its overseer, the CIA's Allen Dulles.

Kennedy Hangs Tough

Kennedy had campaigned on promises to increase the military's conventional arms budget in order to fight guerrilla wars. But he became increasingly wary of the nation's war machine, especially after the Cuban missile crisis. During those tense days, as the nation seemed to drift toward nuclear confrontation, and his military advisers pushed for a preemptive first strike against the missile sites in Cuba, Kennedy had turned to his adviser Arthur M. Schlesinger Jr. and said, "The military are mad."[3] He preferred a negotiated solution for getting the missiles out of Cuba, and he and Khrushchev eventually reached one. This gained them worldwide praise, but it exacerbated tensions for both men with hard-liners in their own countries.

President Kennedy was aware that the Pentagon was deeply concerned about his policies. After reading *Seven Days in May*, a novel about a coup by U.S. armed forces against a president seen as an appeaser, he convinced John Frankenheimer to make it into a movie.[4] JFK even offered the director a prime shooting location outside the White House—despite vociferous objections from the Pentagon.[5] "Kennedy wanted *Seven Days in May* made as a warning to the generals," said Arthur Schlesinger.[6]

President Kennedy also alienated critics over Indochina. Historians still debate JFK's long-term plans regarding troop levels there, but he clearly worried about a looming quagmire. Here, too, the lessons of the Bay of Pigs applied: the United States could not win without the support of the local populace. Anti-Communist hawks were skeptical of Kennedy's motives. Some even issued preemptive warnings: "If Jack turns soft on communism, *Time* will cut his throat," said Henry Luce, the magazine's publisher, and a friend of Prescott Bush and fellow Bonesman.[7]

Kennedy's economic policies were drawing additional heat. In Latin America, for example, he antagonized American businessmen, including Nelson Rockefeller, when he interfered with their oil and mineral development plans in Brazil's vast Amazon basin.[8] "Those robbing bastards," JFK told Walter Heller, chairman of the Council of Economic Advisers, when Heller mentioned the oil and gas industry. "I'm going to murder them!"[9]

On June 10, 1963, in a speech at American University in Washington, D.C., the president took a direct shot at the military-industrial complex by announcing support for the Limited Nuclear Test Ban Treaty, which prohibited aboveground and underwater nuclear weapons tests. Kennedy had been stunned to learn of the human cost of radioactive fallout. "You mean it's the rain out there?" he had asked a nuclear adviser while watching rain fall outside the Oval Office.

"Yes, Mr. President," the official had answered.

But the nuclear arms race was another bonanza for business—uranium mining operations in particular. These constituted a growing share of earnings for the oil exploration and resource extraction industry.[10] (Decades later, the George W. Bush–Dick Cheney administration would pull the United States out of the treaty regime that had begun with the Test Ban Treaty. This would be just one of many instances in which the younger Bush fulfilled objectives long harbored by Kennedy's right-wing enemies.)

Texas had been the center of the uranium-mining industry since the 1920s. After World War II, defense contractors had expanded rapidly there as well, especially in Dallas. The place was thick with people who had serious problems with the Kennedy administration, in terms of both ideology and business interests. It was a combustible mix.

Old Boys, New Money

In the early 1960s, Dallas was not the shining example of administrative efficiency its boosters sought to project. It was more like New Orleans—spectacularly corrupt, and with forceful elements, from the genteel to the unwashed, jockeying for power. The police force included KKK members and habitués of gangster redoubts such as Jack Ruby's Carousel Club.[11] Yet Dallas also was a growing bastion of new money and corporate clout, a center of the domestic oil industry, along with a heavy clustering of defense contractors and military bases.

Texas was in a sense a feisty breakaway republic with a complicit colony of transplants from the Eastern Establishment. Texas oil riches and Eastern entitlement, combined with the mix of intelligence and defense, gave rise to an atmosphere of intrigue. The established energy giants had long relied on corporate covert operations to help maintain their far-flung oil empires. Now independent producers and refiners were getting into this game as well; and the mind-set tended to spill over into politics. A 1964 *New York Times* article reported on a group of businessmen who had formed "an invisible government . . . [that ran] Dallas without an electoral mandate." The group was powerful and confident enough that it essentially advertised the fact that anyone seeking project approval should come to it, rather than the official government agencies. Politically, the members of this new establishment "begin with the very conservative and range rightward," the *Times* added.[12]

The Kennedys understood the political importance of Dallas, and of Texas in general. They chose Lyndon Johnson, a fierce competitor for the nomination in 1960, to be Jack's vice president because they needed Southern, in particular Texan, votes. After the election they appointed Texans like John Connally, a lawyer representing oil interests, to be secretary of the Navy, and George McGhee, the son-in-law of Everette DeGolyer, the legendary oil industry figure, as deputy secretary of state. But political accommodation does not necessarily bring affection. Dallas still was not a friendly place for JFK.

Prominent within the group of transplants from the Eastern Establishment was Poppy Bush. As the son of a powerful Connecticut senator, he was unusually well connected, and both ingratiating and indefatigable. While Prescott Bush and Allen Dulles remained anchored in the East, Poppy and "Uncle" Neil Mallon had done well in Houston and Dallas, respectively. Mallon nurtured the de facto power structure emerging in Dallas, most of which worked out of one particular Dallas high-rise, the Republic National Bank Building. A Kennedy rally would not have attracted many people from there, and not for reasons of ideology alone.

If Jack Kennedy angered people accustomed to being treated with deference by mere officeholders, his brother Bobby turned them apoplectic. Where Jack was charming, Bobby was blunt. Where Jack was cautious, Bobby was aggressive. Bobby's innumerable investigations into fraud and corruption among military contractors, politicians, and corporate eminences—including a Greek shipping magnate named Aristotle Onassis—made many enemies. His determination to take on organized crime angered FBI director Hoover, who had long-standing friendships with mob associates and enjoyed spending time at resorts and racetracks in the company of these individuals.[13] Hoover routinely bypassed the Kennedys and dealt with Vice President Johnson instead. In fact, the Kennedys were hoping that after the 1964 election, they would have the clout to finally retire Hoover, who had headed the FBI since its inception four decades before.

Allowance for Greed

President Kennedy demonstrated his willingness to buck big money during the "steel crisis" of April 1962, when he forced a price rollback by sending FBI agents into corporate offices.[14] But Kennedy's gutsiest—and arguably his most dangerous—domestic initiative was his administration's crusade against the oil depletion allowance, the tax break that swelled uncounted oil fortunes. It gave oil companies a large and automatic deduction, regardless of their actual costs, as compensation for dwindling assets in the ground. Robert Kennedy instructed the FBI to issue questionnaires, asking the oil companies for specific production and sales data.

The oil industry—in particular, the more financially vulnerable Dallas-based independents—did not welcome this intrusion. The trade publication *Oil and Gas Journal* charged that RFK was setting up a "battleground [on which] business and government will collide." FBI director Hoover expressed his own reservations, especially about the use of his agents to gather information in the matter. Hoover's close relationship with the oil industry was part of the oil-intelligence link he shared with Dulles and the CIA. Industry big shots weren't just sources; they were clients and friends. And Hoover's FBI was known for returning favors.

One of Hoover's good friends, the ultrarich Texas oilman Clint Murchison Sr., was among the most aggressive players in the depletion allowance dispute. Murchison had been exposed as far back as the early 1950s—in Luce's *Time* magazine no less—as epitomizing the absurdity of this giveaway to the rich and powerful.[15] Another strong defender of the allowance was Democratic senator Robert Kerr of Oklahoma, the multimillionaire owner of the Kerr-McGee oil company. So friendly was he with his Republican colleague Prescott Bush that when Poppy Bush was starting up his Zapata Offshore operation, Kerr offered some of his own executives to help. Several of them even left Kerr's company to become Bush's top executives.

Kerr today is almost completely forgotten, except perhaps in his native Oklahoma. But he was for decades one of the most powerful men in American politics. He played a significant role in the career of Harry S Truman, with whom he shared early roots as a fellow Freemason and member of the militaristic American Legion.[16] Although the former haberdasher would publicly exhibit some independence, he often buckled privately to Kerr and his like-minded friends. One example was Truman's decision to create the nation's first true peacetime spy apparatus, which eventually became the Central Intelligence Agency.

Kerr-McGee was also the nation's leading producer of uranium, and profited handsomely from the arms race.[17] Even among a cutthroat Washington crowd, Robert Kerr's vicious side stood out—and he did not much like the Kennedys. As an old friend and mentor to LBJ, Kerr had been so angry on learning that Johnson had accepted the number-two spot under Jack Kennedy that he was ready to start shooting. Wheeling on Johnson, his wife, Lady Bird, and Johnson aide Bobby Baker, Kerr yelled: "Get me my .38. I'm gonna kill every damn one of you. I can't believe that my three best friends would betray me."[18]

Jack vs. Lyndon

Lyndon Johnson shared in the prevailing oil belt enmity toward Kennedy. In fact, he was the one person in the White House the oilmen trusted. The Kennedys, for their part, had never liked LBJ—he had run hard against Jack in the 1960 primaries. They asked him to be Jack's running mate for political purposes alone. Within a year of the inauguration, there was already talk of dumping him in 1964. RFK, in particular, detested Johnson, and the feeling was mutual. RFK's investigations of military contractors in Texas increasingly pointed toward a network of corruption that might well lead back to LBJ himself. According to presidential historian Robert Dallek, RFK "closely followed the Justice Department's investigation, including inquiries into Johnson's possible part in Baker's corrupt dealings. Despite wrongdoing on Baker's part that would eventually send him to prison, Johnson believed that Bobby Kennedy instigated the investigation in hopes of finding something that could knock him off the ticket in 1964."[19]

LBJ had numerous connections with the Bushes. One came through Poppy's business partners Hugh and William Liedtke, who probably knew LBJ even before they knew Bush. While in law school in Austin, the Liedtkes had rented the servants' quarters of Johnson's home. (At the time, the main house was occupied by future Democratic governor John Connally, a protégé of Johnson's.[20]) Another connection came through Senator Prescott Bush, whose conservative Republican values often dovetailed with those of Johnson during the years when LBJ served as the Democrats' majority leader. After Johnson ascended to the presidency, he and newly elected congressman

Poppy Bush were often allies on such issues as the oil depletion allowance and the war in Vietnam.

The Texas Raj, as it has been called, was a tight and ingrown world. Denizens sat on one another's boards, fraternized in each other's clubs, and intermarried within a small circle, with most of the ceremonies being held in the same handful of churches. Whether one was nominally a Democrat or Republican did not much matter. They all shared an enthusiasm for the anything-goes capitalism that had made them rich, and a deep aversion to what was known in the local dialect as "government inference." That meant anything the government did—such as environmental rules or antitrust investigations—that did not constitute a favor or bestowal.

The man who perhaps loomed largest in this world is also among the least well known. His name was Everette DeGolyer, and he and his son-in-law George McGhee represented, to a unique degree, the ongoing influence that the oil industry has had on the White House, irrespective of the occupant. They were also allies of the Bushes. In addition to his consulting firm DeGolyer-MacNaughton, DeGolyer founded Geophysical Service Inc., which later became Texas Instruments, and was a pioneer in technologies that became central to the industry, such as aerial exploration and the use of seismographic equipment in prospecting. His career spanned the terms of eight American presidents, many of whom he knew; he was also on close terms with many Anglo-European oil figures and leaders of the Arab world. He sat on the board of Dresser Industries for many years, and, as we shall see in chapter 13, played a central role in cementing the U.S.-Saudi oil relationship. Until he died in 1956, DeGolyer was the man you went to if you wanted to get into the oil and gas game. The intelligence agencies sought him out as well.

DeGolyer's son-in-law, the husky and voluble George McGhee, was the son of a bank president from Waco, with a career trajectory similar to Poppy Bush's: Phi Beta Kappa, Rhodes scholarship (offered but not accepted in Poppy's case), and naval service in the Pacific, followed by work in Washington on the War Production Board. McGhee also sat on the board of James and William Buckley's family firm, Pantepec Oil, which employed George de Mohrenschildt, whom McGhee knew personally. Both McGhee and de Mohrenschildt were active in Neil Mallon's Dallas Council on World Affairs. After the war, McGhee served as assistant secretary of state for Near East affairs.

"The Middle East had the one greatest capacity of oil in the world and was extremely valuable," McGhee said in an oral history interview. "When I was assistant secretary of state, I dealt with this issue."[21] In 1951 he spent eighty hours at the bedside of Iran's prime minister Mohammed Mossadegh in an attempt to mediate the terms of ownership for the Anglo-Iranian Oil Company.[22] Two years after their unsuccessful talks, Mossadegh was overthrown in a CIA-led coup. Time and again, McGhee "was on the front lines in the early crises that defined the Cold War," according to Daniel Yergin, author of *The Prize: The Epic Quest for Oil, Money and Power*.

McGhee became a protégé of Senator Lyndon B. Johnson, even serving in 1959 as chairman of the Dallas County LBJ for President Club. When LBJ became vice president, he oversaw McGhee's appointment as undersecretary of state for political affairs. McGhee's elevation to one of the top posts in the State Department particularly annoyed Robert Kennedy, who managed to get him reassigned as ambassador to West Germany. McGhee "was useless," said RFK. "In every conversation you had with him, you couldn't possibly understand what he was saying."[23] Needless to say, McGhee did not become a member of the Bobby Kennedy fan club.

In many respects, Bobby became the lightning rod for the hostility that Jack deflected with his charm. Bobby did not shrink from the role of enforcer. For as long as Jack remained president—and in 1963 a second term seemed likely—Bobby would have the sheriff's badge. And even worse was the prospect that the Kennedys could become a dynasty. After Jack there might be Bobby; and after Bobby, Ted. It was not an appealing prospect to the Bushes and their circle; and it is only stating the obvious to observe that this was not a group to suffer setbacks with a fatalistic shrug.

The Kennedy administration struck at the heart of the Southern establishment's growing wealth and power. Not only did it attack the oil depletion allowance, but its support of the civil rights movement threatened to undermine the cheap labor that supported Southern industry. Yet in the space of five years, Jack and Bobby Kennedy were dead, and the prospect of a Kennedy political dynasty had been snuffed out. Instead, within a dozen years of Bobby Kennedy's assassination, a new conservative dynasty was beginning to emerge: the House of Bush.

That the president of the United States, not to mention a senator and presidential candidate, could be assassinated by domestic enemies does not sit easily in the American mind. We want to believe in our institutions and in the order they embody. It is unnerving to even consider the possibility that the most powerful among us might deem themselves exempt from the rules in such a fundamental way. Yet, the leaders of these same institutions have frequently seen nothing wrong with assassinating leaders in other countries, even democratically elected ones. The CIA condoned, connived at, or indeed took an active role in assassination plots and coups against figures as varied as Guatemala's Arbenz, the Dominican Republic's Trujillo, Congo's Lumumba, Chile's Allende, Cuba's Castro, Indonesia's Sukarno, Iran's Mossadegh, and Vietnam's Diem. Is it that difficult to believe that those who viewed assassination as a policy tool would use it at home, where the sense of grievance and the threat to their interests was even greater?

One of the assassination enthusiasts, at least where foreign leaders were concerned, was George McGhee, who served the State Department in two places ruled by leaders who became targets: Patrice Lumumba and Rafael Trujillo. As the *Washington Post* wrote in McGhee's obituary: "In the early 1960s, as undersecretary for political affairs, Dr. McGhee was dispatched to Congo and the Dominican Republic when the instability of civil wars and unaccountable governments threatened to destabilize the peace."[24] Some years before McGhee's death, a JFK assassination researcher asked him in writing if he had had a role in Trujillo's death. McGhee wrote back that while he had not, the assassination "was not a problem for me."[25]

Prepping a Patsy?

For a nation traumatized by the death of John F. Kennedy, the notion that a rootless and disturbed individual could murder the president was troubling enough—but far less troubling to contemplate than the alternative possibility, that the assassination was part of a larger plot. The arrest and subsequent murder of Lee Harvey Oswald provided, in today's jargon, a grim kind of "closure" for the public, one elaborately ratified by the Warren Commission. To probe into the nexus of interests that benefited from Kennedy's death and its connection to the events of November 22—well, that would be the opposite of closure. The figure of Oswald, the lone gunman, was a highly questionable fit with the evidence, but neatly fulfilled the psychological needs of the country.

The conventional account goes like this: Oswald, an unstable person who hates the United States, begins showing an interest in Communism and seeks haven in the Soviet Union, where he works in a factory and marries a Russian woman, Marina. Disillusioned by his experience in the "workers' paradise," he returns with Marina to the Dallas–Fort Worth area and descends into a spiral of anger and irrationality. He experiments with myriad political causes, buys a rifle, and travels to New Orleans, where he expresses sympathy for Castro's Cuba and consorts with a bewildering array of flamboyant and disreputable figures. He returns to the Dallas area, takes a job along the route of a planned motorcade for President Kennedy, and as Kennedy passes, shoots him. Oswald is later captured, and almost immediately is killed by Jack Ruby, a local nightclub owner with ties to mobsters actively involved in CIA-Mafia plots to assassinate Castro.

Yet even as the Warren Commission was endorsing that scenario, doubts were arising. The lawyer Mark Lane, onetime New Orleans district attorney Jim Garrison, and historian David Kaiser all spent years challenging the Oswald-as-lone-assassin theory. The House Select Committee on Assassinations convened in 1976 and concluded three years later that a conspiracy was likely. Oliver Stone's blockbuster *JFK* film—which chronicles Garrison's court battle against the Warren Commission's findings—led to the formation of the U.S. Assassination Records Review Board.

When Lee Harvey Oswald told the press after his first interrogation, "I am a patsy," many dismissed it as the predictable disclaimer of the guilty. But what if it were true? What if Lee Harvey Oswald really had been set up as the fall guy to deflect attention from the real plotters? Most other "lone nuts" who have killed presidents or celebrities have proudly claimed responsibility for their crime, not tried to blame others.

If any group of plotters *were* setting up Lee Harvey Oswald, they would want him to appear as both darkly mysterious and an obvious suspect. They might run elaborate tracks across Oswald's path, to generate false leads and a thick fog of misinformation. Who would be better qualified to do this than an expert in the game—that is, someone with experience in intelligence and covert operations?

Peter Dale Scott, a retired UC Berkeley professor, has documented that Oswald may well have believed that he was working at least indirectly for a U.S. government agency, perhaps related to the investigation of trafficking in unregistered guns. In his book *Deep Politics and the Death of JFK*, Scott shows how Oswald's activities, starting with his return to the United States from Russia in 1962, closely tracked specific objectives of the FBI and the Bureau of Alcohol, Tobacco and Firearms (ATF). Though Texas laws in 1963 allowed untraceable over-the-counter firearms purchases, Oswald went to the seemingly unnecessary step of ordering his guns through interstate mail, which required identification and left a paper trail. Moreover, the two guns he ordered through the mail were both from companies being investigated by the ATF as well as the Senate.[26] At the time, the ATF was housed within the Treasury Department, not the Justice Department, and thus was beyond the immediate jurisdiction of President Kennedy's brother.

If Oswald were connected to the government in any way, he would not have been high-level. Like many foot soldiers in the intelligence wars, he would not necessarily have known precisely whom he was working for, or why. Rather, he could well have thought he was on one mission while he was actually being used for another. If that were so, it might not have been until the assassination and his arrest that he finally grasped the situation. In that case, his words at his arrest might have been the most candid statement in the whole affair.

ALL THIS MIGHT seem a mere exercise in speculation, but certain facts are clear: Oswald was a young man who craved guidance and purpose. His father died before he was born, and he lived for a spell in an orphanage until his mother remarried (briefly) and reclaimed him at the age of three. Not surprisingly, he seemed eager to find a father figure, escape from his dominating mother, and establish some stability in a peripatetic life that included nineteen moves before the age of seventeen.

His was an upbringing that can often lead to the military, and at thirteen, Oswald became a cadet in the Louisiana Civil Air Patrol (CAP). According to Collin B. Hamer Jr., who served as cadet adjutant of CAP's Moisant Squadron in 1957, and later headed the City Archives collection of the Louisiana Public Library, Oswald was a student of one David Ferrie—a protégé of New Orleans mob boss Carlos Marcello. A number of Oswald's fellow cadets told the House Select Committee on Assassinations the same thing.[27] Oswald and Ferrie can also be seen together in a group photograph from a 1955 CAP training camp.

The Civil Air Patrol was a national volunteer auxiliary to the military. Founded during World War II as a civilian organization, it played a role in safeguarding the American coastline from German U-boats and was eventually shifted to peacetime duties such as disaster relief. Its founders included two Rockefeller brothers and D. Harold Byrd, the right-wing Texas businessman and lifelong friend of LBJ's, who owned the building that would later house the offices and warehouse facilities of the Texas School Book Depository in Dallas.

The Civil Air Patrol was very much perceived as a bulwark of the cold war. A profile of the organization in the May 1956 *National Geographic* magazine noted that in the event of a nuclear attack, "CAP would support Civil Defense with the aerial damage surveys, radio communication, evacuation of injured, and airlift of food and medical supplies . . . [and] radiation monitoring."[28] It's not hard to imagine that the impressionable young cadets might have been targets for recruiting into the clandestine services.

No one should be surprised to learn that the United States ran a fake defector program during the cold war—such intrigue is a staple in the spy-versus-spy world.[29] By 1957, Oswald appeared to be good Soviet bait. During a three-year stint in the Marine Corps, he had been briefly stationed in Japan at Atsugi air base, from which the CIA launched supersecret U-2 spy planes over the USSR. After his return to the United States, he subscribed to the Communist Party newspaper. Soon thereafter, he was on his way to the Soviet Union as a would-be defector.

It was in the fall of 1959 that Oswald boarded a freighter bound for Europe. After stops in France, England, and Sweden, he traveled to Helsinki, Finland, where he obtained a visa valid for a six-day visit to the Soviet Union. On October 16 he arrived in Moscow. He visited the U.S. embassy there to dramatically renounce his U.S. citizenship and proclaim to the inevitable Soviet-installed microphones that he would give radar secrets to the USSR. Then he moved on to Minsk. In 1961, he met the attractive young pharmacist Marina Prusakova at a Palace of Culture dance and married her just six weeks later. Marina lived with her uncle, who was a colonel in the Soviet Interior Ministry security service; Oswald's marriage to her only added a frisson of intrigue to his profile, raising eyebrows all around. It has certainly been cited as further evidence that he was operating for the Soviet cause.

In any case, the Soviets themselves apparently never quite trusted him. In Minsk he was constantly monitored by the authorities. Later, seemingly disillusioned by what he had seen of the grim reality behind the Soviets' stirring propaganda, he would beg the United States to let him come home.

In fact, Oswald decided early on that he really didn't want to be in the Soviet Union at all. As George Bouhe, a member of Dallas's White Russian community who spent a lot of time with Oswald, would tell the Warren Commission:

[T]he man came to the American Embassy in Moscow asking for the permit to return to his native land. It took 2 years or something to process that application . . . I felt that whatever investigating agency of the United States, whether it is Secret Service, CIA, or anybody else concerned with repatriation with such a suspicious character, took their good little time of 2 years to process his return back to the United States. [He said], "Damn it, I don't know why it took them so long to get on the horse."[30]

The Escort Service

On July 28, 1960, CIA director Allen Dulles, wearing a full business suit, arrived at vice presidential nominee Lyndon Johnson's Texas ranch to administer a top-secret briefing on national security.[31] Such a briefing may have been customary at that time, but the soon-to-be vice president had his own sphere of influence as well—and as the former majority leader, an existing relationship with Dulles. And as would be proven later, he had no compunction about keeping his boss out of the loop.

Allen Dulles's interest in Texas seems to have picked up shortly after he left the Kennedy administration. In December 1961, he contacted a colleague still with the CIA to request contact information for agency officers based in Houston.[32] After the JFK assassination, Johnson would bring Dulles back into government—first as a member of the Warren Commission investigating Kennedy's death and then as a member of the Gilpatric Committee, a group of advisers on the proliferation of nuclear weapons.[33]

Since 1961, LBJ had aligned himself with the Joint Chiefs of Staff on a policy JFK was resisting—namely, their desire to send U.S. combat troops to Asia. As a result, Vice President Johnson and his military aide Howard Burris were provided a steady stream of Vietnam intelligence reports that were denied to the president.[34]

About the same time that Dulles was contacting his ex-colleagues in Texas, George de Mohrenschildt was invited to lunch by J. Walton Moore, the local CIA man in Dallas.[35] The Domestic Contacts Service (DCS), for which Moore worked, was the CIA branch that routinely debriefed Americans returning from abroad, including from "Iron Curtain" nations.[36]

According to Edward Jay Epstein, author of several books on the Kennedy assassination, just before de Mohrenschildt died, he described to Epstein his meeting with Moore. De Mohrenschildt said it had taken place in late 1961—which would have been about a half year before Oswald returned to the United States.

> Moore purposefully steered the conversation in a new direction, the city of Minsk, where, as Moore seemed to know even before he told him, De Mohrenschildt had spent his childhood. Moore then told him about an ex-American Marine who had worked in an electronics factory in Minsk for the past year and in whom there was "interest," since he was returning to the Dallas area. Although no specific requests were made by Moore, De Mohrenschildt gathered that he would be appreciative to learn more about this unusual ex-Marine's activities in Minsk.
>
> In the summer of 1962, De Mohrenschildt heard more about this defector. One of Moore's associates handed him the address of Lee Harvey Oswald in nearby Fort Worth and then suggested that De Mohrenschildt might like to meet him. He added, as if it was an inducement, that this ex-Marine had returned from Minsk with a pretty Soviet wife.[37]

De Mohrenschildt and Moore had met a number of times prior to that, first in 1957 following a lengthy stay by de Mohrenschildt in Yugoslavia, and again after other de Mohrenschildt trips. This pattern raises the question of whether there was a formal reporting relationship between the two at the time de Mohrenschildt was asked to keep an eye on Oswald.

De Mohrenschildt and Oswald are not known to have met until several months following Oswald's return to the United States. The fact that de Mohrenschildt was neither the first nor the last person to spend significant time with Oswald in the interval between his return to the United States and the assassination served as de Mohrenschildt's basis for suggesting that he himself could not have been involved in a plot. But that argument seriously underestimates the subtlety of the people who conceive and execute such plots.

Such people would of course have known that in 1962, when Oswald returned to the United States, there was no better milieu in which to "sheepdip" him than the Russian émigré community of the Dallas–Fort Worth area. He had spent some of his formative years locally. The émigrés generally were comfortable with the cold war world of cloak-and-dagger and eager to help in anything represented as an anti-Soviet cause. Collecting information on Lee Harvey Oswald—including, if necessary, appearing to befriend him—would have seemed unexceptional.

When de Mohrenschildt and Oswald finally did meet, in October 1962, they must have seemed an odd pair. De Mohrenschildt was bull-chested and middle-aged—an anti-Communist, White Russian, aristocratic bon vivant. Oswald, by contrast, was skinny, taciturn, allegedly leftist, and twenty-two years old, from a broken lower-middle-class home. His wife, Marina, was the allegedly apolitical niece of a colonel in the Soviet secret police. Yet, despite their differences, the de Mohrenschildts and Oswalds soon became inseparable.

George and Jeanne de Mohrenschildt were constantly in and out of the Oswald household, making introductions and offering help in finding housing, child care, marriage counseling, social introductions, and more. A State Department document relates one such example. "Mrs. de Mohrenschildt took Mrs. Oswald in her car from Fort Worth to Dallas for dental treatment, a week or two after they first met Oswald," it says. "According to Mr. and Mrs. De Mohrenschildt, they were interested in the Oswalds solely in [sic] helping them as 'unfortunate people.' "[38] The de Mohrenschildts were devoted to the Oswalds to a truly remarkable extent; never before had they been known to take such an interest in managing the details of other people's lives. And certainly not people as contentious and purportedly "difficult" as the Oswalds. Neither Lee nor Marina was easy to be around—and neither exhibited much gratitude. It certainly appeared a labor of obligation rather than of love.

A Legend in the Making

More than anything, George de Mohrenschildt helped Lee Harvey Oswald secure employment. Apparently with Oswald's full cooperation, he subjected the returnee to a kind of reverse laundering. With each pass through the machine, another layer of soil stuck to him. An improbable sequence of jobs and living arrangements made Oswald seem more and more unstable—not unlike the classic misfits who throughout history have attempted to assassinate national leaders. And because Oswald was involved in such a range of activities in so short a time (less than a year and a half), investigators would later find it difficult to follow all the twists and turns.

DRIFTWOOD PUBLIC LIBRARY
801 SW HWY. 101
LINCOLN CITY, OREGON 97367

Under de Mohrenschildt's tutelage, "Agent Oswald," having clawed his way out of the Soviet Union, began dropping hints everywhere that he was a Communist stooge. As Bouhe would tell the Warren Commission: "Oswald had a little table in his apartment on Mercedes Street in Fort Worth. I cannot remember the exact names, but certainly Karl Marx, Lenin and his works, and similar things which I do not remember. And I positively, being aghast at such an assortment, flipped over the first two-three pages, and I think in two out of three I saw the stamp of the Fort Worth Public Library."[39]

Oswald worked for a spell at a mapmaking company that handled classified work, including military diagrams of Cuba. The owner would later explain that a friend had asked him to hire Oswald. The de Mohrenschildts also took Oswald to anti-Castro meetings in Dallas. This was a prelude to the next step in Oswald's reverse laundering, a move to New Orleans, where he behaved in a bizarre manner. At various points he appeared to be pro-Castro and then either anti-Castro *or* a pro-Castro person infiltrating anti-Castro groups.

And there was even Oswald's purported trip in September 1963 to Mexico City, where he supposedly visited the Cuban and Soviet embassies in attempts to acquire travel visas. Most researchers now believe that this was an impostor pretending to be Oswald—which itself seems to establish a larger plot.

The picture became still murkier when FBI agents were ordered—by some unknown higher-up—to keep an eye on Oswald. Their intrusive inquiries with his employers created yet more static, and helped ensure that Oswald's tenure at each of these jobs was brief.

More than half a year before the assassination, on April 10, 1963, someone shot a rifle through the Dallas window of right-wing firebrand General Edwin A. Walker. Marina Oswald later told the Warren Commission that the shooter had been her husband, an assertion with which she seemed palpably uncomfortable. She described how, a few days after she heard about the Walker shooting, George de Mohrenschildt had climbed the stairs of their house, calling out, "Lee, how did you miss General Walker?" For his part, de Mohrenschildt insisted that he had not actually known whether his friend was the triggerman; he shrugged off his role in the incident as an ill-timed "joke."

Shortly after this, de Mohrenschildt handed Oswald off to yet another person, Ruth Paine, a Quaker housewife who would even chauffeur Marina from Dallas to New Orleans and back. By passing Oswald along to Paine, de

Mohrenschildt could truthfully assert that he had been neither the first person in contact with Oswald upon his return from Russia nor the final person in his life before the assassination. That Paine's mother-in-law, Ruth Forbes Paine, was a close friend of one Mary Bancroft, former OSS spy and the mistress at varying times of both Allen Dulles and Henry Luce, was probably not known to Dulles's fellow Warren Commission members. One wonders what they would have made of this connection, certainly an indirect one yet suggestive nevertheless.

If someone really was "setting up" Oswald, getting him out of Dallas to New Orleans would have been a brilliant stroke. It diverted attention from Dallas and onto a steamy locale with an irresistible cast of characters—the mob-connected ex-G-man Guy Banister, the flamboyant businessman Clay Shaw, and the lecherous gay pilot David Ferrie, to name just a few. Evidence of this is the ample number of books devoted to Oswald's New Orleans period. Compared with the cast from the Big Easy, Texans like de Mohrenschildt, Poppy Bush, and Jack Crichton would have seemed white-bread respectable. Various middlemen even arranged for Oswald to be in the public eye while in New Orleans—on a radio debate, handing out leaflets, involved in a scuffle that made it onto TV. This opera buffa would later be portrayed as the spontaneous doings of a confused (or incredibly devious) twenty-two-year-old.

The Haitian Laundromat

The next individual to take a trip through a reverse laundry was de Mohrenschildt himself. Given his connections to prominent people, in particular Poppy Bush, if de Mohrenschildt *was* involved in a plot, it would be especially important to create a benign explanation for his interactions with Oswald. And more important, it would be necessary to demonstrate that taking care of Oswald was not de Mohrenschildt's principal occupation at the time. In other words, de Mohrenschildt would have needed his own "legend," as a cover story is known in the spy trade. The facts—as they have been presented thus far—may suggest that de Mohrenschildt himself was something of a pawn, steering Oswald but unaware of the larger picture or of Oswald's fate. However, further material, which will be presented below and in chapter 12, suggests a greater degree of knowledge on de Mohrenschildt's part.

That a cover was created for de Mohrenschildt—indeed an oversize umbrella that could encompass all the powerful people he knew—is suggested by a series of events that began right when de Mohrenschildt first met Oswald in October 1962.

On October 19, de Mohrenschildt wrote to George McGhee at the State Department, offering a slide show of the "walking tour" of Latin America that had taken him—coincidentally, of course—near a CIA training camp in Guatemala just before the Bay of Pigs invasion. De Mohrenschildt indicated in his letter that if the government was not interested in his Guatemalan experiences, he might just forward the material to some European friends who thought the Soviet Union was a place "where there is a great demand for travelogues and adventure stories."[40]

Anyone finding this document in government records would naturally assume that de Mohrenschildt was some kind of freelancer of intelligence, if a seemingly goofy one, obviously neither loyal to the United States government nor in its employ. The document would also provide a cover explanation for contacts between de Mohrenschildt and McGhee, mentioned earlier in this chapter as one who intensely disliked the Kennedys and who would be moved out of the State Department by a disrespectful Bobby Kennedy.

On February 16, 1963, de Mohrenschildt wrote to JFK personally, again offering his travelogue. He went out of his way to say that he had also discussed the travelogue with McGhee.[41]

In April, 1963, de Mohrenschildt traveled to the East Coast for a series of meetings that, while supposedly secret, were nevertheless strikingly well documented. Thus, if anyone were to realize that de Mohrenschildt had important connections, those connections would appear to relate to the business transacted on the East Coast, and not to Oswald. Everyone associated with de Mohrenschildt would have a good explanation for why they knew everyone else. And, to make it more confusing still, this cover story would be layered over another one that was even more intriguing, and that would itself lead to a dead end.

Allen Dulles once called CIA documents "hieroglyphics." Like the old lion surrounded by his adoring cubs, Dulles used to expound on such elements of tradecraft to his fellow Warren Commission members. On one occasion, he told them that no one would be able to grasp an intelligence memo except for those involved in its creation and their colleagues.

This creates endless, perhaps deliberate, obstructions for someone trying to piece together the story of the Kennedy assassination. When Thomas J. Devine, Poppy Bush's business partner and a former CIA agent, coyly suggested to me that the problem with journalists like myself is that "you believe what you read in government documents," he was referring to such deeply coded disinformation. Devine's warning about CIA documents is especially interesting in light of the way two agency reports from April 1963 portray Devine himself. Both describe preparations for, and then a meeting with, George de Mohrenschildt as he comes to New York from Dallas and then moves offstage to Haiti. At first glance, the documents seem routine. Here's what they purport to say:

On April 25, 1963, at three thirty in the afternoon, a CIA operative code-named WUBRINY/1 held a meeting in the library of the Knickerbocker Club, one of New York City's most exclusive men's clubs, on East Sixty-second Street, just off Fifth Avenue.[42] There were two others present. One was C. Frank Stone III, chief of operations for the European section of the CIA's clandestine wing. The other was M. Clemard Joseph Charles, the general manager of the Banque Commerciale D'Haiti.

This "contact report" was declassified in 1998 but went unnoticed at the time. The purpose of the 1963 meeting, it said, was to prepare for the impending arrival from Dallas of George de Mohrenschildt, who is described as a business contact of a Haitian banker identified as "Mr. Charles," i.e., Clemard Charles. De Mohrenschildt was coming to New York to discuss mineral concessions in Haiti and the establishment of a sisal plantation there, the report goes on to say. It mentions nothing about de Mohrenschildt's vast intelligence connections and makes only passing reference to his dealings in other natural resources such as oil and uranium. Nor is there mention of his long-standing ties to George H. W. Bush, nor of the fact that he periodically provided briefings to intelligence agencies on his return from trips abroad, as other government records show.[43]

Nevertheless, talking about sisal fit de Mohrenschildt's normal cover: traveling in pursuit of strategic resources. Sisal was used in the manufacture of rope—a critical supply on naval and commercial vessels. Haiti was a good choice because it was of strategic importance to the United States as a point close to Cuba and therefore perfect for monitoring Castro and launching covert operations at the island. And de Mohrenschildt was perfect because he had a prior history with Haiti, having traveled there during the fifties, ostensibly to conduct business on behalf of various powerful oilmen.

The second document describes de Mohrenschildt's arrival the next afternoon, at the New York offices of the investment banking firm of Train Cabot, inside an entity code-named SALINE.[44] This was in fact the covering organization for operation WUBRINY, and WUBRINY's chief agent and operator, WUBRINY/1—who was none other than Thomas Devine.[45] (In a 2008 interview, Devine declined to say whether he was involved with WUBRINY, but in a separate 2008 interview, retired CIA officer Gale Allen told me he remembers both WUBRINY and Devine.)[46] According to WUBRINY/1's report to his superiors, when de Mohrenschildt mentioned his work on behalf of a particular small oil company, he "looked around the room and over his shoulder and said that 'my connection with this is, of course, confidential.'"

Were this CIA report to pass into the hands of, say, a congressional committee, the staffer likely would skim it and move on. Nothing much seems to be happening. Indeed, one almost has the impression that the CIA officer and de Mohrenschildt were performing a piece of theater, with de Mohrenschildt hamming it up a bit with the over-the-shoulder glance. Or perhaps the officer made that up to enhance the overall effect, which is to establish distance between the agency and this supposed sisal investor.

De Mohrenschildt comes off as a bit of a rube, fooled by the CIA man's cover and believing that a legitimate business deal is on the table. The CIA document casts its own operative, the author of the memo, as dubious of de Mohrenschildt and his motives—and in no way involved with him. The result is a paper trail that acknowledges contact with the man who was also Oswald's mentor, but in a totally different context, and in a way that permits complete deniability of the Oswald connection.

The Potomac Two-Step

De Mohrenschildt had just spent the last half year in almost constant contact with Lee Harvey Oswald, who had recently returned from several years in Soviet Russia. De Mohrenschildt had done so, moreover, at the CIA's request, or so he claimed. It seems unlikely that the sole topic of the New York meeting with WUBRINY/1 would have been sisal in Haiti. Nevertheless, in the minds of these people, sisal was apparently enough to hang a legend on. Now there was a documented and apparently benign reason that Thomas Devine (and by implication, Devine's longtime associate George H. W. Bush) knew a man about to be under fierce scrutiny for his own ties to the alleged killer of the president of the United States.

In case the "sisal" document of April 1963 was not enough, de Mohrenschildt next traveled to Washington, D.C., where he and his friend Mr.
Charles met with other government figures, ostensibly to talk about sisal.
Here the story gains a more intriguing layer—namely, the suggestion that
de Mohrenschildt's real purpose was to secure U.S. government backing for
a coup d'état against the Haitian dictator François "Papa Doc" Duvalier. De
Mohrenschildt and Charles appear to have obtained an audience with none
other than Howard Burris, military adviser to Vice President Lyndon Johnson, with the prospect of meeting LBJ himself.[47]

As noted in correspondence dated April 18, 1963:

> Dear Mr. Mohrenschildt:
>   Your letter has come in the Vice President's absence from the
> office . . . I would like to suggest that you see Colonel Howard Bur-
> ris, Air Force Aide to the Vice President, when you come to Wash-
> ington. Should Mr. Johnson happen to have any office hours here
> during your stay, we will be happy to see if a mutually convenient
> time can be found for you to meet . . . With warm wishes, Sincerely,
> Walter Jenkins, Administrative Assistant to the Vice President.[48]

The Haitian coup therefore could have been intended as the operative
story to explain why Oswald's mentor de Mohrenschildt was interacting
with powerful U.S. government figures in the period prior to the JFK assassination. The new story was introduced in 1978 testimony to the House Select Committee on Assassinations. The witness was Dorothe Matlack,
assistant director of the Army Office of Intelligence, who explained that she
had also met with de Mohrenschildt and that he raised the idea of the U.S.
government playing a role in the coup. "I knew the Texan [de Mohren-
schildt] wasn't there to sell hemp," Matlack said.[49]

This story would have been a clever one, since indeed an examination of
de Mohrenschildt's past, as noted earlier, shows him periodically in the en-
virons of unfolding coups. Yet Matlack's testimony served still another
purpose—besides justifying de Mohrenschildt's presence in meetings with
LBJ's adviser and with a CIA operative tied to Poppy Bush, it also justified
any ties that would emerge between de Mohrenschildt and Army Intelligence.[50] That last point, as we shall see, is especially critical, because Army
Intelligence figures show up in key roles before, at the time of, and in the
immediate aftermath of the assassination.

Indeed, Matlack's story would have rung true. De Mohrenschildt appears to have persuaded the Haitian Mr. Charles that he would be able to secure approval for the coup, and that Charles would be installed to replace Duvalier. It seems that de Mohrenschildt may have been directed to travel earlier to Haiti to persuade Charles to participate in the New York and Washington meetings—because he took a brief earlier trip to the island in March.

What passed for the feeble beginnings of a coup attempt did in fact occur in Haiti, soon after de Mohrenschildt arrived on the island. But it didn't succeed, and perhaps wasn't intended to. De Mohrenschildt and his circle had no apparent problem with Papa Doc, even if the Kennedys did. Duvalier, who was generally considered a friend by many elements in the U.S. military and intelligence establishment, did not suffer greatly. De Mohrenschildt's "friend" Clemard Charles wasn't so fortunate. The Haitian dictator jailed him for approximately a decade. Thus, Charles himself may have been another unwitting pawn.

Whether or not by design, the Haiti story served as the ultimate cover. It explained why de Mohrenschildt would know all these powerful people, and did so in the context of a supposed plot to depose a hated foreign leader.

Let's play the tape again: De Mohrenschildt travels to the East Coast in the spring of 1963, on a mission that takes his story away from Poppy Bush, Jack Crichton, and others in the Texas intelligence network. His trail leads instead outside the United States, to geopolitical intrigue that is totally unrelated to Lee Harvey Oswald, the Soviet Union, or what was happening in Dallas. Even if disclosed, this new story would cause no great upset to the American people. Removing Duvalier and promoting democracy in the hemisphere were aims of the revered Kennedy himself.

It might seem impossibly convoluted. But in the shadow world of covert operations, it would be business as usual.

There even was cover for the Domestic Operations division, a CIA program that was, on its face, problematical under the agency's charter from Congress, which forbade its participation in any domestic surveillance or police operations directed at the American public. The domestic division maintained an entire floor at 1750 Pennsylvania Avenue, near the White House.[51] Among its operatives, according to his own testimony before Congress, was Dulles's friend E. Howard Hunt, previously associated with the coup in Guatemala and the Bay of Pigs invasion, and subsequently convicted in Watergate.[52]

Within hours after Devine met with de Mohrenschildt at the Knickerbocker Club, a Domestic Operations case officer in Washington was creating the legend that the domestic division, like WUBRINY, had no idea who de Mohrenschildt really was. The officer, Gale Allen, requested an "expedite check" of this supposedly unknown character. He got back a report from 1958 when de Mohrenschildt had returned from Yugoslavia and briefed J. Walton Moore of the CIA's Dallas office. This way, if de Mohrenschildt later claimed he knew Moore, it could be attributed to this innocuous 1958 briefing rather than the 1961 lunch to talk about Oswald.

To anyone who tried to follow this trail, it would appear that Domestic Operations was unfamiliar with George de Mohrenschildt. Were investigators to dig a bit further and happen upon the reports from WUBRINY, they would learn that George de Mohrenschildt was a self-aggrandizing entrepreneur with a taste for intrigue. Dig still further, and they would learn that he was a friend of a Haitian banker who had been eager to foster a coup d'état against the evil President Duvalier. Each layer of this plausible cover story would lead the investigator further from the truth.

They even provided cover for the powerful oilmen who sponsored de Mohrenschildt's travels to hot spots, ostensibly to represent their business interests. The Warren Commission reviewed some correspondence that shows meetings between de Mohrenschildt and these oilmen. In every case, the letters purport to relate to sisal, though some of the letters are suggestive of an unspoken alternative agenda. For example, one 1962 letter, to de Mohrenschildt's Dallas White Russian community "godfather" Paul Raigorodsky from the oilman Jean de Menil, who himself provided weapons to Cuban exiles, thanks the Russian for sending de Mohrenschildt around, and refers to some idea of de Mohrenschildt's as not being "very well cooked" but does find it "slightly visionary."[53] It is hard to see sisal planting as even slightly visionary.

Yet this was indeed de Mohrenschildt's cover, and it proved effective. There were numerous assassination inquiries in the 1970s, all in response to the failings of the Warren Commission. But none came close to penetrating the layered accounts I have just described. In fact, they did not even sniff the trail.

The Book Cover

One thing seems indisputable. By the time the de Mohrenschildts left the United States for Haiti in May 1963, Lee Harvey Oswald had been turned into a man with multiple personas, all of them capable of killing Kennedy. Oswald hated Kennedy either because he—Oswald—admired Castro or because he was anti-Castro. Perhaps Oswald was angry at Kennedy over the Bay of Pigs fiasco, or else he just liked to take potshots at important people. He was fond of guns, a bit violent, and even sometimes beat up his wife. He was a potential time bomb with a short fuse.

There was something in the lurid saga of Oswald to fit almost any theory, and therefore to confirm none. Whether Oswald was complicit or not in the process, his background and activities had been so muddied that no one would ever figure him out. Or settle for sure whose side he had been on. Or determine whether he was acting on his own or taking orders when he fired at Kennedy—if in fact he did.

Five months after de Mohrenschildt left for Haiti, Oswald obtained a job in a building along what barely six weeks later would be the Kennedy parade route. That building would become known as the Texas School Book Depository. In the years since, there has been endless debate over which weapon fired the fatal shots, whether it was Oswald who fired them, where the shots came from, ad infinitum. There has been not enough attention paid to the building itself and how Oswald happened to be there.

Some theories contend that Oswald—or anyone who might have been directing him—could not have known that the motorcade would pass by the Book Depository at the time he took the job there. But there were only two possible routes through downtown to JFK's destination, the Dallas Trade Mart, and the Book Depository building stood on one of them. If someone wanted to put Oswald along the route, he could have arranged for Oswald to secure a job in the Book Depository building, then selected the route that passed by there. Officially, the decision to reroute the motorcade from Main Street to Elm, in front of the Book Depository building, was made only a week before the event—by two Secret Service agents. But that does not mean that a determination of the final route was not made much earlier by someone who could share the information with Oswald or someone connected with him.[54]

In any case, if it was Oswald's intention to kill JFK from the Book Depository, he on his own could not possibly have known what the route would be at the time he obtained his job in the building. Only an insider involved with shaping JFK's trip could have had any confidence that the Depository building would be on the ultimate route of the motorcade. The Trade Mart was already known to be the likely venue of Kennedy's Dallas luncheon speech, but according to the Secret Service, even if an alternative venue was chosen, there would be a high probability that a presidential parade would still pass right by the Book Depository. J. Lee Rankin, a general counsel for the Warren Commission, said that "to anticipate that this particular location would be a prime location for anything like this . . . is reasonable in light of our conversations with the Secret Service."[55]

The process that resulted in Oswald's hiring at the Book Depository is yet another facet of the story that has gotten short shrift. Usually his presence in the building is portrayed as an accident of fate. Yet recall that the owner of the building was one D. Harold Byrd, a right-wing oilman, founder of the Civil Air Patrol, avid Kennedy hater—and a friend of both Clint Murchison and George de Mohrenschildt. This all could be coincidence, but surely it is the kind of coincidence that invites a few more questions.

Yet when I began researching Byrd, I was stunned to find that his name did not even appear in the vast majority of books by Kennedy assassination authorities, nor was he even interviewed by the Warren Commission. I found further that not only had Byrd employed de Mohrenschildt at his Three States Oil and Gas Co. during the 1950s, but that the connection went deeper still. Documents I studied show that in September 1962, just weeks before he began to squire Oswald, George de Mohrenschildt incorporated a charity ostensibly devoted to the study of cystic fibrosis—and put D. Harold Byrd's wife on the board.[56] Mrs. Byrd's role on the charity board would have created a convenient excuse for de Mohrenschildt to have been interacting with her husband during this period. Other board members included Paul Raigorodsky, J. Edgar Hoover's good friend and the White Russian community's godfather.

On May 24, 1963, in Dallas, the U.S. Air Force presented to D. Harold Byrd its Scroll of Appreciation for his work with the Civil Air Patrol (where Oswald was a cadet). Among the Air Force generals he counted as friends was Charles Cabell, Allen Dulles's CIA deputy director, key Bay of Pigs figure, and brother of Dallas mayor Earle Cabell, also a good friend of Byrd's.[57]

So how did Oswald end up working at this building that belonged to a friend of de Mohrenschildt's? The most widely accepted explanation is that Oswald got the job indirectly—via Ruth Paine, the new "friend" who had come to him through the efforts of the de Mohrenschildts, and who was providing a home for Oswald's wife, Marina, and their daughter. Paine purportedly heard about the Book Depository from a neighbor, one Linnie Mae Randle, whose brother already worked there.[58]

But missing from these accounts is that the neighbor's brother had obtained *his* job there just slightly ahead of Oswald. Moreover, the brother had moved from a small Texas town to Dallas shortly beforehand. Given what we now know about George de Mohrenschildt's close relationship with Byrd, owner of the Book Depository building, and the chain of events that followed, it is plausible that Oswald's hiring could have been deliberately orchestrated through this chain to obscure the underlying direct connection.

Then there is the intelligence background of Paine's family, which was in addition to her mother-in-law's ties to Dulles's girlfriend. There was more to this simple Quaker housewife than meets the eye. When Marina Oswald was asked by the Orleans Parish grand jury why she had cut off contact with Ruth Paine after the assassination, she said: "I was advised by the Secret Service not to be connected with her, seems like she was . . . not connected . . . she was sympathizing with the CIA. She wrote letters over there and they told me for my own reputation, to stay away."[59]

Is it possible that the brother was hired as a player—or in spycraft parlance, a "cut-out"—who could "refer" Oswald to a job in this particular building? This might seem speculative, but other pieces of the puzzle do point in that direction. I was surprised to learn, for example, that the building was almost completely devoid of tenants until about six months before the assassination.[60] I was even more surprised to learn that the very name, Texas School Book Depository, is misleading. It sounds like a building where the state of Texas kept schoolbooks. But in fact, Texas School Book Depository was the name of a private company, which had operated out of another location before it moved into the building on Dealey Plaza in the spring of 1963. Until then, the structure was known as the Sexton Building.[61]

The officers of the Book Depository Company were—like Byrd, Murchison, and their core group—outspoken critics of Kennedy, and also major military buffs. Its president turned out to be one Jack Cason, who was also the long-time head of the local American Legion post, a leading forum for hard-line military views. The company, like all publishers and distributors of books that shaped the perceptions of young Americans—of all Americans—was of keen interest to the propaganda machinery of the U.S. government, and the intelligence community. Allen Dulles was even a member of the advisory board of Scholastic Magazines, whose publications were distributed to schoolchildren throughout the country.

These operations at least seem to offer a plausible explanation of why a man like Cason, affluent and socially connected, deeply involved in anti-Communist and military-themed activities, might choose to bypass more traditional pursuits such as oil and banking in favor of the textbook distribution business. The CIA was deeply involved, abroad and at home, in creating and distributing literature that would promote democratic Western values in the cold war battle for hearts and minds. As the Senate's Church Committee would note: "In 1967 alone, the CIA published or subsidized over 200 books, ranging from books on African safaris . . . to a competitor to Mao's little red book, which was entitled *Quotations from Chairman Liu.*" One such book, produced by the Domestic Operations division—the one that was monitoring Oswald—told the story of "a young student from a developing country who had studied in a communist country." According to the CIA, that book "had a high impact in the United States."[62]

The important point here is that a division of the CIA was producing general nonfiction books, and it would not be inconceivable that it was also interested in the textbooks distributed by companies such as the Texas School Book Depository.

Allen Dulles even infiltrated that paragon of objectivity the *Encyclopaedia Britannica*, whitewashing the agency's Bay of Pigs fiasco in an article in the 1963 *Book of the Year.*[63]

It is worth noting that D. Harold Byrd, a big-game hunter, decided to take his first-ever foreign safari—to Africa—during this period. That removed him from Dallas precisely when the assassination took place. Besides Byrd's far-right politics, his founding role in the Civil Air Patrol, and his ties to de Mohrenschildt, he evidently rejoiced in Kennedy's assassination—as suggested by the macabre fact that he arranged for the window from which Oswald purportedly fired the fatal shots to be removed and set up at his home.[64]

Dulles Does Dallas

As far as we know, on November 22, 1963, George de Mohrenschildt was far away from Dallas too, managing his "business ventures" in Haiti. According to the record, de Mohrenschildt and Oswald had no contact during the prior six months. It was this hiatus, and de Mohrenschildt's physical absence from the United States, that enabled the Warren Commission to discount his otherwise glaring relationships with Oswald and Oswald's pre-assassination "handlers" in Dallas. Not to mention his many links to members of the Texas Raj, who were noted for their anti-Kennedy animus and extensive ties to the national intelligence apparatus.

One curious matter concerns some communications about de Mohrenschildt in June 1963, between the Republic National Bank in Dallas and Brown Brothers Harriman in New York—where ex-senator Prescott Bush had just resumed work as a senior partner. The date is important because it is just after de Mohrenschildt leaves for Haiti. The communications, revealed in an FBI agent's report of 1964, appear odd. As it is presented, a confidential client of Brown Brothers, "a firm dealing in the import and export of fibers," had made a credit inquiry "concerning George de Mohrenschildt." Brown Brothers had replied that it knew nothing of him, but forwarded the inquiry to Republic National Bank, whose "report was favorable concerning de Mohrenschildt's credit." Why this confidential client would ask a bank in New York about a man based in Texas—and this bank in particular—is not made clear. The thread, or fiber, tying this mini-episode to the larger unfolding drama is sisal. It gave yet more prominent people—including top officials at Republic National Bank and Prescott Bush at Brown Brothers Harriman—the same cover story it provided to everyone else: if anyone discovered that they had been dealing with de Mohrenschildt, they could claim that their sole motive was to make money off Haitian sisal.[65]

The coincidences mount. After his dismissal as director of the CIA, Allen Dulles had written a book called *The Craft of Intelligence*—with the assistance of E. Howard Hunt. As might be expected, it was hardly a tell-all exposé. Reviewers were generally unimpressed, especially with the innocuous anecdotes. "It is a book that could as well have been written from an outside, as from an inside, view," wrote one critic.[66] The book did, however, give Dulles a reason to remain in the public eye—including a visit to Dallas in late October 1963. Although excerpts had been published, most notably in *Harper's*, starting at the beginning of the year, *The Craft of Intelligence* was held for release until the fall. Dulles appears to have made no book-related appearances outside the Washington–New York corridor except for Dallas, to which he traveled at the invitation of Neil Mallon to speak at the Council on World Affairs.[67] The Dallas Council would certainly be a receptive audience. After all, it had been conceived, in Mallon's own words, along "the guidelines of central intelligence."

THIS GIVES US Dulles in Dallas, scant weeks before the assassination; Al Ulmer, the foreign-based CIA coup expert, in Texas and visiting with Poppy

Bush; E. Howard Hunt, top Dulles operative and covert operations specialist, said by his own son to have been in Dallas; and Poppy Bush in Dallas—
until he leaves town either the night before or on the very day of the
assassination and places his covering alibi phone call from Tyler, Texas.[68]
Oswald's all-too-public "friend" George de Mohrenschildt is safely off on important business in Haiti, and D. Harold Byrd is off on a safari. Again, this scenario may mean nothing. It all may just be coincidence. But the confluences
among this cast of characters are at the very least remarkable. It does not take
a hypercharged imagination to construe a larger story of which they might be
part, or to wonder why these people might have gone to such lengths to create
"deniability" concerning any connections to the events in Dallas—unless they
had a connection.

Another salient fact is that, on the day of the assassination, Deputy Police Chief George L. Lumpkin was driving the pilot car of Kennedy's motorcade, a quarter mile ahead of JFK's vehicle.[69] Lumpkin was a friend of
Jack Crichton, Poppy Bush's GOP colleague. Like Crichton, moreover, he
was a member of an Army Intelligence Reserve unit. (Lumpkin would
later tell the House Select Committee on Assassinations that he had been
consulted by the Secret Service on motorcade security, and his input had
eliminated an alternative route.)[70] In the car with Lumpkin was another
Army officer, Lieutenant Colonel George Whitmeyer, commander of all
Army Reserve units in East Texas, who happened to be Jack Crichton's
boss in the Reserve.

Although Whitmeyer was not on the police list of those approved to ride
in the pilot car, he had insisted that he be in the vehicle and remained there
until the shooting. The only recorded stop made by the pilot car was directly
in front of the Depository building. Lumpkin stopped briefly there and
spoke to a policeman handling traffic at the corner of Houston and Elm.

To the right of the motorcade, in front of the grassy knoll, stood Abraham
Zapruder with his camera, ready to capture the 8-millimeter short film that
would make his name famous.

The Zapruder film would be cited vigorously by both critics and supporters of the Warren Commission's conclusions. As of late 2008, the latest
attempt to back up the lone gunman theory was historian Max Holland's
twelve-years-in-the-making study of the assassination. Citing the Zapruder
film, Holland argues that a careful study of it shows that Oswald actually
fired the first shot earlier than previously calculated. This allows, according
to Holland, enough time for Oswald to have gotten the second and third

shots off before the car sped up. He says this new theory establishes that Oswald could have done it—and therefore indeed did do it, and did it alone. "If I restore faith in the Warren Commission," Holland told the *Washington Post*, which published a highly sympathetic profile of the author, "I'll put to rest some of the disturbing questions people have had."[71]

Zapruder is widely characterized as an innocent bystander, simply an onlooker who happened to capture historic footage that would dominate the evidentiary debate. Innocent he may well have been, but hardly unknown in Dallas intelligence circles.

It turns out that the short, bald recorder of history was also a former colleague of Mrs. de Mohrenschildt, who worked with her at Nardis when she first moved to Dallas. Zapruder also sat on the board of Neil Mallon's Dallas Council on World Affairs. Like numerous figures in this story, he had a propensity for groups built on loyalty and secrecy, having attained the status of thirty-second-degree Freemason. The film he would make on November 22 would soon be purchased by Henry Luce, a Skull and Bones colleague of Prescott Bush and a devotee of intelligence—whose wife, Clare Booth Luce, had personally funded efforts to overthrow Castro.[72] Henry Luce had warned that JFK would be punished if he went soft on Communism. After quickly purchasing the original Zapruder film, Luce's *Life* magazine kept it in lockdown until New Orleans D.A. Jim Garrison successfully subpoenaed it in 1969.

At the moment that Kennedy's car passed the Stemmons Freeway sign on Elm Street, a man standing in front of the grassy knoll opened an umbrella and pumped it repeatedly above his head. Even the House Select Committee on Assassinations found this strange, given that it was a gloriously sunny day. Next to him was a man with a dark complexion who appeared to be speaking on a walkie-talkie shortly after shots were fired.[73]

In 1978, one Louis Steven Witt came forward to identify himself as the "Umbrella Man."[74] A self-described "conservative-type fellow," Witt claimed that he had opened his umbrella repeatedly because a colleague had told him that the gesture would annoy the president.[75] He did not elaborate on *why* anyone would have thought this.[76] In his testimony before the House Select Committee on Assassinations, he lamented that "if the Guinness Book of World Records had a category for people who were at the wrong place at the wrong time, doing the wrong thing, I would be No. 1 in that position, without even a close runner-up."[77] He also claimed to have no recollection of the dark-complexioned man, though photos show the two men speaking. Witt's curious and seemingly choreographed umbrella opening remains another question mark on a day full of perplexing coincidences.

Where Was Poppy? Part II

If indeed it can be established that Oswald was being guided to his destiny—either because he would become the shooter or because he would be framed for the shooting—then whoever was running him, and whoever was controlling Oswald's controller, were integral parts of a plot.

By now, we have enough information to show, fairly conclusively, that Oswald was being managed by Poppy's old friend de Mohrenschildt. We also have others connected with Poppy closely associated with the events of November 22. And we have Poppy creating an alibi for himself.

Details on who fired the gun, whose gun it was, and how many shots were fired from where remain relevant, but become of secondary importance. The central question is the story that lies behind these details.

In summation, here's just some of the new, relevant information:

- Poppy Bush was closely tied to key members of the intelligence community including the deposed CIA head with a known grudge against JFK; he was also tied to Texas oligarchs who hated Kennedy's politics and whose wealth was directly threatened by Kennedy; this network was part of the military/intelligence elite with a history of using assassination as an instrument of policy.

- Poppy Bush was in Dallas on November 21 and most likely the morning of November 22. He hid that fact, he lied about knowing where he was, then he created an alibi based on a lead he knew was false. And he never acknowledged the closeness of his relationship with Oswald's handler George de Mohrenschildt.

- Poppy's business partner Thomas Devine met with de Mohrenschildt during that period, on behalf of the CIA.

- Poppy's eventual Texas running mate in the 1964 election, Jack Crichton, was connected to the military intelligence figures who led Kennedy's motorcade.

- Crichton and D. Harold Byrd, owner of the Texas School Book Depository building, were both connected to de Mohrenschildt—and directly to each other through oil-business dealings.

- Byrd brought in the tenant that hired Oswald shortly before the assassination.

- Oswald got his job in the building through a friend of de Mohrenschildt's with her own intelligence connections—including family ties to Allen Dulles.

Even Jack Ruby's slaying of Oswald fits the larger pattern seen here—one in which Oswald is indeed a "patsy"—a pawn in a deadly game who would never be permitted to say what he knew.[78]

Ruby himself practically admitted as much. After his trial, he made a statement to reporters as to his motives in shooting Oswald, and essentially admitted to a conspiracy.

> RUBY: Everything pertaining to what's happening has never come to the surface. The world will never know the true facts, of what occurred, my motives. The people had, that had so much to gain and had such an ulterior motive for putting me in the position I'm in, will never let the true facts come above board to the world.
> REPORTER: Are these people in very high positions, Jack?
> RUBY: Yes.[79]

As WITH SO many events in his life, Poppy had been very careful about November 22, 1963. Thanks to the Kiwanis lunch, Barbara's letter, and the Parrott phone call, he could reasonably claim to have been "out of the loop," even while people he knew certainly appear to have very much been in it—or far too close for comfort. In any case, as we shall see in the next chapter, there was still more to the story.

CHAPTER 7

After Camelot

Iᴀ Poppy Bush was busy on November 22, 1963, so was his friend Jack Crichton. Bush's fellow GOP candidate was a key figure in a web of military intelligence figures with deep connections to the Dallas Police Department—and, as previously noted, to the pilot car of JFK's motorcade.

Crichton came back into the picture within hours of Kennedy's death and the subsequent arrest of Lee Harvey Oswald, when a peculiar cordon sanitaire went up around Marina Oswald. The first to her side was Republican activist and precinct chairman Ilya Mamantov, a vociferous anti-Communist who frequently lectured in Dallas on the dangers of the Red menace. When investigators arrived, Mamantov stepped in as interpreter and embellished Marina's comments to establish in no uncertain terms that the "leftist" Lee Harvey Oswald had been the gunman—the lone gunman—who killed the president.[1]

It is interesting of course that the Dallas police would let an outsider—in particular, a right-wing Russian émigré—handle the delicate interpreting task. Asked by the Warren Commission how this happened, Mamantov said that he had received a phone call from Deputy Police Chief George Lumpkin. After a moment's thought, Mamantov then remembered that just preceding Lumpkin's call he had heard from Jack Crichton. It was Crichton who had put the Dallas Police Department together with Mamantov and ensured his place at Marina Oswald's side at this crucial moment.

Despite this revelation, Crichton almost completely escaped scrutiny. The Warren Commission never interviewed him. Yet, as much as anyone, Crichton embodied a confluence of interests within the oil-intelligence-military nexus. And he was closely connected to Poppy in their mutual efforts to advance the then-small Texas Republican Party, culminating in their acceptance of the two top positions on the state's Republican ticket in 1964.

During World War II, Crichton had served in the Office of Strategic Services, the predecessor to the CIA. Postwar, he began working for the company of petroleum czar Everette DeGolyer and was soon connected in petromilitary circles at the highest levels. A review of hundreds of corporate documents and newspaper articles shows that when Crichton left De-Golyer's firm in the early fifties he became involved in an almost incomprehensible web of companies with overlapping boards and ties to DeGolyer. Many of them were backed by some of North America's most powerful families, including the Du Ponts of Delaware and the Bronfmans, owners of the liquor giant Seagram.

Crichton was so plugged into the Dallas power structure that one of his company directors was Clint Murchison Sr., king of the oil depletion allowance, and another was D. Harold Byrd, owner of the Texas School Book Depository building.[2]

A typical example of this corporate cronyism came in 1952, when Crichton was part of a syndicate—including Murchison, DeGolyer, and the Du Ponts—that used connections in the fascist Franco regime to acquire rare drilling rights in Spain. The operation was handled by Delta Drilling, which was owned by Joe Zeppa of Tyler, Texas—the man who transported Poppy Bush from Tyler to Dallas on November 22, 1963.

It was in 1956 that the bayou-bred Crichton started up his own spy unit, the 488th Military Intelligence Detachment. He would serve as the intelligence unit's only commander through November 22, 1963, continuing until he retired from the 488th in 1967, at which time he was awarded the Legion of Merit and cited for "exceptionally outstanding service."

Gimme Shelter

Besides his oil work and his spy work, the disarmingly folksy Crichton wore a third hat. He was an early and central figure in an important Dallas institution that is virtually forgotten today: the city's Civil Defense organization. Launched in the early 1950s as cold war hysteria grew, it was a centerpiece of a kind of officially sanctioned panic response that, like the response to September 11, 2001, had a potential to serve other agendas.

So avid and extensive was the Dallas civil defense effort that the conservative radio commentator Paul Harvey singled it out for special praise in his syndicated column in September 1960: "The Communists, since 1917, have sold Communism to more people than have been told about Christ after 2,000 years," Harvey wrote, a sentiment common in rightist circles of the era. "But they got their converts one at a time. You and I can 'convert' two others to become militant Americans this week . . . That's precisely the nature of the counterattack that has been mounted in Dallas."[3]

Early in 1961, Crichton was the moving force behind a cold war readiness program called "Know Your Enemy," which focused on the Communist intention to destroy the American way of life. In October 1961, Dallas mayor Earle Cabell introduced a short documentary *Communist Encirclement— 1961*. Afterward, the *Dallas Morning News* wrote that the Channel 8 switchboard was "flooded . . . with calls from viewers lauding the program, which deals frankly with Communist infiltration." So great was the sense of alarm that at the 1961 Texas State Fair in Dallas, 350 people per hour made their way through an exhibitor's bomb shelter.[4]

On April 1, 1962, Dallas Civil Defense, with Crichton heading its intelligence component, opened an elaborate underground command post under the patio of the Dallas Health and Science Museum.[5] Because it was intended for "continuity-of-government" operations during an attack, it was fully equipped with communications equipment. With this shelter in operation on November 22, 1963, it was possible for someone based there to communicate with police and other emergency services. There is no indication that the Warren Commission or any other investigative body or even JFK assassination researchers looked into this facility or the police and Army Intelligence figures associated with it.

On November 22, Crichton suggested Mamantov to the police department as the ideal person to interpret for Marina. His basis for knowing this was that in his role in military intelligence he maintained surveillance of Russians in Dallas, working closely in this regard with the police department.

Marina's statements through Mamantov would play a crucial role in starting a chain of events that could have led to a U.S. missile strike on Cuba. In the hours following Kennedy's assassination, the Dallas Police Department passed along information purportedly gleaned from Marina Oswald that suggested possible ties between her husband and the government of Cuba. Though the information would turn out to be wrong, it was quickly passed to Army Intelligence, which then passed it along to the U.S. Strike Command at MacDill Air Force Base in Florida, the unit that would have directed an attack on the island had someone ordered it in those chaotic first hours after Kennedy's death. That this sequence of events took place is confirmed by the original Army cable from military intelligence in Texas, declassified a decade later. What is not clear is how close matters ever got to zero hour.[6]

A key element in this tangled tale is the little-appreciated overlap between the Dallas Police Department and Army Intelligence. As Crichton, who has since died, would reveal in a little-noticed oral history in 2001, there were "about a hundred men in that unit and about forty or fifty of them were from the Dallas Police Department."[7] Thus, Crichton was a crucial figure linking many seemingly disparate elements: military intelligence, local police, the GOP, the White Russians, the oil community, George de Mohrenschildt, and Poppy Bush.

The Poppy and Jack Show

In the fall of 1963, about two months before JFK's assassination, the two political neophytes Jack Crichton and George H. W. Bush both decided to mount GOP races for statewide office. The following year, they would head the Texas GOP's ticket, with Crichton the nominee for governor and Bush for U.S. Senate. Both used the same lawyer, Pat Holloway, who worked out of the Republic National Bank Building. The man who recruited them as candidates, state GOP chairman Peter O'Donnell, would several years later be forced by newspaper revelations to admit that his family foundation was a conduit for CIA funds.[8]

Thus, in November 1963, Bush and Crichton were essentially working in tandem. Given that alliance, Poppy would need to explain not only where he was on November 22 and why he tried so hard to hide that, but also what he knew about Crichton's activities that day and about Crichton's Army Intelligence colleagues in the pilot car of the motorcade.

In his oral history, Crichton couches his relationship with Bush in benign and casual terms. He says that he and Poppy "spoke from the same podiums and got to be fairly good acquaintances." Their appearances on behalf of the Texas Republican Party evolved into a private friendship that continued over the years. "When he was head of the CIA, I called him one day and I said, 'George, I'm coming to Washington, would you have time to play tennis?' And he said 'Yeah.' He said, 'How would you like to play at the White House?' And I said 'Man, that'd be a real deal.' So he said, 'Well, I'll have you a partner.' "[9]

A Crime of Commission

The Warren Commission's official mandate had been to conduct "a thorough and independent investigation" of the assassination.[10] However, along with subsequent investigative bodies, it failed to assemble, much less connect, even the most obvious of dots. Virtually everybody on the commission was a friend of Nixon's or LBJ's—or both. The members shared another characteristic: they were, almost without exception, from the conservative establishment and definitely not Kennedy admirers who would have gone to any length to find the truth about JFK's death. Along with Allen Dulles, members included Republican congressman Gerald Ford and John J. McCloy, a top operative for the Rockefeller family. No doubt coincidentally, McCloy had been best man at the wedding of Henry Brunie, head of Empire Trust, which employed Jack Crichton and invested in de Mohrenschildt's Cuban oil project.

Transcripts of the panel discussions produce a sense that the commission members and investigators were either incredibly naïve or else walking on eggshells.[11] At an early executive session, Earl Warren told his colleagues, "We can rely upon the reports of the various agencies . . . the FBI, the Secret Service, and others." But commission member Senator Richard Russell, a conservative Georgia Democrat who headed the Armed Services Committee on which his friend Prescott Bush had served, made at least a brief stand. "I hope," he said, "that you'll get someone with a most skeptical nature, sort of a devil's advocate, who would take this FBI report and this CIA report and go through it and analyze every soft spot and contradiction in it, just as if he were prosecuting them."

Many were already wondering whether CIA personnel might themselves know something about the assassination and how helpful they would be to the investigation. In one executive session, Russell turned to Dulles and expressed his doubts about Dulles's compatriots: "I think you've got more faith in them [the CIA] than I have. I think they'll doctor anything they hand to us."[12]

During the commission's investigation, Dulles and his colleagues some-times traveled to Dallas, especially to hear witnesses who could not come to Washington. When they did, they set up their temporary conference room in the boardroom of the Republic National Bank. The decision to do so is re-vealing, if nothing else than of a striking lack of concern for appearances. The Republic National Bank board was wired into the heart of the anti-Kennedy elite. The bank building itself stood out from other Dallas towers as an important symbol: the headquarters of Dresser Industries and of a number of corporations, law firms, and trusts connected with the Central Intelligence Agency, as well as being the building in which de Mohren-schildt himself had had offices.[13]

A Fascinating Tan

Members of the commission were often absent during testimony. But George de Mohrenschildt's appearance caused a stir.[14] Among those present were Dulles, Ford, McCloy, and two commission attorneys. As de Mohren-schildt would recall in an early draft of his unpublished memoirs:

> The late Allen W. Dulles, former head of CIA, and a scholarly look-ing man, was there. He was, by the way, a friend of Mrs. Hugh Auchincloss [Jackie Kennedy's mother] and he came over to talk to us amicably . . . What amazed me, looking backward at my testi-mony, was that whatever good I said about Lee Harvey Oswald seemed to be taken with a grain of salt as if the decision regarding his guilt had already been formed.[15]

Commission assistant counsel Albert E. Jenner Jr. was the staffer who conducted the interrogations of George and Jeanne de Mohrenschildt, which lasted two and a half days. As he did with several other key witnesses, Jenner had private conversations with George de Mohrenschildt both inside and outside the hearing room. Perhaps to ensure that he would not be ac-cused of something underhanded, he went out of his way to state the fact of those outside consultations for the record.[16] Aside from asking de Mohren-schildt, on the record, to verify that everything they had discussed privately was reiterated in the public session, Jenner never made clear what the subject matter of those private conversations was.

The transcript of the de Mohrenschildts' testimony runs 165 pages.[17] It reveals George to be a remarkably interesting, dynamic character, whose life resembled that of a fictional adventurer. But numerous points of his testimony, especially relating to his background and connections, cried out for further scrutiny. Instead, Jenner consistently demonstrated that he was either incompetent or deliberately incurious when it came to learning anything useful about de Mohrenschildt.

To wit, here is an exchange between Jenner and de Mohrenschildt, in Washington, on April 22, 1964, with a historian, Dr. Alfred Goldberg, present. Jenner, who had already read extensive FBI reports on de Mohrenschildt, could be forceful when he wanted answers. But most of his moves were away from substance. He seemed determined to reach the commission's conclusion that de Mohrenschildt was a "highly individualistic person of varied interests," and nothing more. In fact, Jenner stonewalled so assiduously that even de Mohrenschildt registered amazement:

> MR. JENNER: You are 6'1", are you not?
>
> MR. DE MOHRENSCHILDT: Yes.
>
> MR. JENNER: And now you weigh, I would say, about 195?
>
> MR. DE MOHRENSCHILDT: That is right.
>
> MR. JENNER: Back in those days you weighed around 180.
>
> MR. DE MOHRENSCHILDT: That is right.
>
> MR. JENNER: You are athletically inclined?
>
> MR. DE MOHRENSCHILDT: That is right.
>
> MR. JENNER: And you have dark hair.
>
> MR. DE MOHRENSCHILDT: No gray hairs yet.
>
> MR. JENNER: And you have a tanned—you are quite tanned, are you not?
>
> MR. DE MOHRENSCHILDT: Yes, sir.
>
> MR. JENNER: And you are an outdoorsman?
>
> MR. DE MOHRENSCHILDT: Yes. I have to tell you—I never expected you to ask me such questions.

Why was Jenner even on the commission staff? Chairman Warren offered an oblique justification for his hiring that perhaps was more revealing than the chief justice intended. He was a "lawyer's lawyer," Warren said, and a "businessman's lawyer" who had gotten good marks from a couple of unnamed individuals. Commission member John McCloy timidly inquired whether they shouldn't hire people with deep experience in criminal investigations. "I have a feeling that maybe somebody who is dealing with government or federal criminal matters would be useful in this thing." Warren then implied that this was unnecessary because the attorney general (Robert Kennedy) and FBI director (J. Edgar Hoover) would be involved, totally ignoring the strong personal stakes of both officials in the outcome—and the strong animosity between them. Allen Dulles said little during this discussion of Jenner.

Company Man

Albert Jenner was truly a curious choice for the commission staff. He was fundamentally a creature of the anti-Kennedy milieu—a corporate lawyer whose principal work was defending large companies against government trust-busting (which came under the aegis of the slain president's brother Robert). His partner specialized in trust accounts on behalf of the super-rich. Jenner's most important client was Chicago financier Henry Crown, who was the principal shareholder in General Dynamics, then the nation's largest defense contractor and a major employer in the Fort Worth area. At the time of the commission hearings, General Dynamics was struggling to recover from legal and financial problems under the new leadership of Roger Lewis, who had been assistant secretary of the Air Force in the midfifties. Lewis also was a former executive vice president at Pan American Airways, the CIA-connected company on whose board sat Prescott Bush.[18]

At the time of the assassination, Secretary of the Navy Fred Korth was under investigation for corruption in the awarding of a seven-billion-dollar contract for a fighter jet, the TFX, to General Dynamics' Fort Worth facility. Korth was a Texan, named to the post by JFK at LBJ's request, to replace another Texas friend of LBJ's, John Connally, when Connally resigned to run for governor. Just a few months before his appointment, Korth had authorized the bank he headed to make a loan to General Dynamics. Then, as secretary, he overruled the Pentagon's Source Selection Board, which had recommended the contract go instead to Boeing. In November 1963, Korth resigned when it became known that he was soliciting business for his bank on Navy Department stationery.[19]

Korth and his family were friends of the Bushes. Penne Korth, his daughter-in-law, would become cochair of Poppy Bush's inaugural in 1989 and be named by him as ambassador to Mauritius.[20]

The bottom line is that the Warren Commission did not assign a seasoned criminal investigator to figure out de Mohrenschildt's relationship with Oswald and his larger circle of connections. Instead, they turned the job over to a man whose principal experience and loyalties were firmly planted in the very circles most antagonistic to Kennedy.

THE WARREN COMMISSION had been pressed to wrap up its inquiries quickly and neatly. But George de Mohrenschildt, whose wife described him as a man who didn't know how to shut up, was not always a compliant witness. Commission transcripts contain some tantalizing admissions, which, in the hands of a determined truth-seeker, would have led to important revelations. But whenever de Mohrenschildt let something slip, Jenner would quickly push it aside. He'd even mix up dates, thus creating a hopelessly jumbled chronology of the de Mohrenschildts' lives.

Among the leads Jenner did not pursue was one from George Bouhe, the Russian community leader who had served as Oswald's first handler before passing him on to de Mohrenschildt. In his own testimony, Bouhe told Jenner that he had been wary of Oswald at first. He said he had even worried about attending an initial welcome dinner for the Oswalds thrown by Peter Paul Gregory, Oswald's first White Russian contact on returning from the USSR.[21] So Bouhe called a lawyer friend, Max Clark, who happened to be married to a Russian princess, to ask his advice. "And after a couple of days, I don't remember exactly Mr. Clark's answer, but there were words to the effect that since he was processed through the proper channels, apparently there is nothing wrong, but you have to be careful. I think these were the words. Then I accepted the invitation for dinner."

Jenner did not pursue what this reference to "proper channels" meant. And he did not then ask for more information on Max Clark. Not that he was likely to have needed the answer. Max Clark had previously been head of security for General Dynamics, Jenner's top client, and was aware of the Kennedy administration's ongoing investigation of the company.

My Dinner with Mrs. Auchincloss

When the Warren Commission released transcripts of its interview with George de Mohrenschildt, the Associated Press remarked on the "strange coincidences," particularly that de Mohrenschildt was a friend of both Lee Harvey Oswald and the "family of President Kennedy." The latter assertion was not quite accurate. In fact, he was a friend of the family of President Kennedy's *wife*.

De Mohrenschildt had known Jackie's family since the late 1930s. During the summer following his arrival in the United States, he, his brother, and his sister-in-law, along with Poppy's Andover roommate Edward Hooker, headed for the Hooker summer cottage in Bellport, Long Island.[22] In Bellport they had some houseguests: Janet Bouvier and her daughter, the future Jacqueline Kennedy. A long-lasting friendship ensured. Jackie grew up calling de Mohrenschildt "Uncle George" and would sit on his knee. According to some accounts, de Mohrenschildt was at one point engaged to Jackie's aunt Michelle.

"We were very close friends," de Mohrenschildt explained to Jenner. "We saw each other every day. I met Jackie then, when she was a little girl. Her sister, who was still in the cradle practically. We were also very close friends of Jack Bouvier's sister, and his father."

This revelation seemed not to interest Jenner, who snapped, "Well, bring yourself along."

Though Jenner did not find the Jackie Kennedy coincidences even remotely interesting, her own mother did. After the assassination, when de Mohrenschildt wrote Mrs. Auchincloss, offering his condolences, she wrote back: "It seems extraordinary to me, that you knew Oswald and that you knew Jackie as a child. It is certainly a very strange world."[23]

So close were de Mohrenschildt and Jackie's family that even after the assassination, Oswald's friend was still welcome in the Auchincloss home. Indeed, immediately after their Warren Commission depositions concluded, George and Jeanne de Mohrenschildt had dinner with Mrs. Auchincloss and her current husband, Hugh. There, de Mohrenschildt would later recall, "The overwhelming opinion was that Lee was the sole assassin . . . I tried to reason—to no avail."[24]

Jeanne de Mohrenschildt added her recollections of that evening: "Well, the one thing struck me [was that] Mrs. Auchincloss . . . didn't want any investigation, she didn't want to know who killed Jack, why and what for. All she kept telling me was that Jack is dead and nothing will bring him back . . . I couldn't possibly understand how the person, a woman, being so close to the man that was so . . . killed so horribly, having no interest whatsoever to continue the investigation and finding a person who did it."

This story should be taken with a grain of salt. The de Mohrenschildts might have been self-serving in casting themselves as more interested than Jackie's mother in getting at the truth. Still, if they accurately characterized her preferences, Mrs. Auchincloss's lack of interest in getting to the bottom of things is striking. In any case, at the end of the dinner, according to the de Mohrenschildts, Janet Auchincloss informed the couple that, because of the awkward circumstances, Jackie never wanted to see them again. No reason was given. Did Jackie believe that the de Mohrenschildts knew something, or were even in some way involved? Or was she just concerned for appearances?

Regardless, the simple fact that de Mohrenschildt knew Jackie *and* was the central figure in the life of the man believed to have assassinated Jackie's husband surely deserved more attention. That the Kennedy marriage had never been as happy as the public was given to believe, that it had deteriorated badly in the last few years, and that Jackie had gone off, over White House objections, to spend time on the yacht of Greek shipping magnate Aristotle Onassis—these did not necessarily add up to anything meaningful. That Onassis, who was seriously at odds with Bobby Kennedy, had nearly entered into a Haitian investment venture with George de Mohrenschildt may have been no more than coincidence.[25] Nor does the Bush-Hooker-Bouvier-de Mohrenschildt interweave mean anything in and of itself. But a credible investigation into the assassination of a president would necessarily have probed more deeply into all these matters. Yet a credible investigation is precisely what the Warren Commission wasn't.

There is yet another piece still to this maddening puzzle. It turns out that at least one other guest joined the Auchincloss–de Mohrenschildt dinner that night following the commission depositions: Allen Dulles.[26]

Poppy's Moment

Although the mysteries behind the Kennedy assassination were not resolved by the Warren Commission, the rest of the world began to move on. Certainly, Poppy did. Though he lost the 1964 Senate election—as did his friend Jack Crichton the governor's race—Poppy had helped set in motion events that would get him to Washington in two short years. Bush wanted to carve out a new congressional district from that of Representative Albert Thomas, a New Deal Democrat who had played a key role in bringing NASA's Space Center to Houston. By the time of Kennedy's assassination, Thomas was showing signs of early senility. A key reason for President Kennedy's visit to Texas that fateful week was to attend an event honoring Thomas, and generally to boost Democratic prospects for 1964.

In a watershed moment, Poppy and the GOP won a lawsuit they had filed in the fall of 1963 to force the state of Texas to redraw its gerrymandered congressional districts.[27] This victory would play an important role in the state's gradual shift from the Democratic to the Republican column, which would affect the balance of power in American politics for decades to come. Moreover, it would pave the way for Poppy's election to the House of Representatives, and later his son's political rise.[28]

One specific result of Poppy Bush's suit was the drawing of a "super-Republican" district tailor-made for him.[29] Many of the people who lived there were East Coast transplants like Poppy himself, Ivy League graduates for whom tennis and martinis were a more natural choice than horseshoes and tequila. Poppy had done especially well in that area in his Senate race. So in 1966, Poppy sold his shares in Zapata Offshore, left the company in the hands of trusted associates, ran hard, won, and headed for Washington.

There's a Spy in the House

Congress was a great place for a spy—even better, in some ways, than the CIA. Congressmen were expected to travel the world, looking into matters of interest to the United States. In December 1967, less than a year after Bush was sworn in, he was off to Indochina, with his CIA partner Thomas Devine in tow. It was Christmas break, a time when congressmen often make overseas trips, but Bush and Devine did not have a typical agenda. Correspondence indicates that having arrived in Vietnam, Bush and Devine hastily canceled an appointment with the U.S. ambassador in favor of other, unstated activities.[30]

For the CIA, the hot item at the time was the so-called Phoenix Program, a secret plan to imprison and "neutralize" suspected Vietcong. This was being rolled out at precisely the moment that Poppy and Devine arrived "in country." By the time CIA director William Colby admitted to the program in July 1971, more than twenty thousand people had been killed—many of them possibly innocent, officials later concluded. One person involved in Phoenix's early stages was Felix Rodriguez, a Cuban exile and CIA operative. Rodriguez would go on to become a great friend of Poppy Bush's, even visiting him in the White House.

If J. Edgar Hoover's 1963 memo was correct in mentioning "George Bush of the CIA" as an intermediary with Cuban exiles, the coincidence of Rodriguez's activities in Vietnam with that of Bush's visit raises questions as to how the two were connected. In 1970 Rodriguez joined the CIA front company Air America, which allegedly played a role in trafficking heroin from Laos to the United States. The Laotian operation was led by Donald Gregg, who would later serve as national security adviser during Poppy Bush's presidency.

When Bush and Devine traveled to Vietnam the day after Christmas 1967, Devine was in his new CIA capacity, operating under commercial cover.[31] Handwritten notes from the trip show that Poppy was especially interested in the Phoenix Program, which he referred to by the euphemism "pacification."

The two remained in Vietnam until January 11, 1968. Whatever information they were seeking, they left just in time. Only three weeks after the freshman congressman from Texas and his CIA sidekick departed Saigon, the North Vietnamese and Vietcong launched the massive Tet Offensive.

Poppy and Lyndon

Meanwhile, the Kennedy assassination had put into the White House Lyndon Baines Johnson, who had a long-standing but little-known relationship with the Bush family. This dates back at least to 1953, when Prescott Bush joined Johnson in the U.S. Senate. Johnson was the powerful majority leader and Prescott had his own pipeline to the highest levels at the Eisenhower White House. That same year, Poppy Bush started Zapata Petroleum with Hugh and William Liedtke, who as law students at the University of Texas several years earlier had rented LBJ's guesthouse. Later, Bush became close with LBJ's chief financiers, George and Herman Brown, the founders of the construction giant Brown and Root (which later became part of Halliburton).

Pat Holloway, former attorney to both Poppy Bush and Jack Crichton, re-counted to me an incident involving LBJ that had greatly disturbed him. This was around one P.M. on November 22, 1963, just as Kennedy was be-ing pronounced dead. Holloway was heading home from the office and was passing through the reception area. The switchboard operator excitedly noted that she was patching the vice president through from Parkland Hos-pital to Holloway's boss, firm senior partner Waddy Bullion, who was LBJ's personal tax lawyer. The operator invited Holloway to listen in. LBJ was talk-ing "not about a conspiracy or about the tragedy," Holloway recalled. "I heard him say: 'Oh, I gotta get rid of my goddamn Halliburton stock.' Lyn-don Johnson was talking about the consequences of his political problems with his Halliburton stock at a time when the president had been officially declared dead. And that pissed me off . . . It really made me furious."[32]

There are many other examples of LBJ's apparent unconcern after the as-sassination, though none so immediate. For instance, on the evening of No-vember 25, LBJ and Martin Luther King talked, and LBJ said, "It's just an impossible period—we've got a budget coming up." That morning, he told Joe Alsop that "the President must not inject himself into, uh, local killings," to which Alsop immediately replied, "I agree with that, but in this case it does happen to be the killing of the President." Also on the same day LBJ told Hoover, "We can't be checking up on every shooting scrape in the country."[33]

By 1964, with LBJ in the White House and Poppy Bush the Texas GOP nominee for U.S. Senate, their relationship was highly cordial. An intrigu-ing, if oblique, note from LBJ's assistant Leslie Carpenter to Walter Jenkins, a top LBJ adviser, dated August 14, 1964, referred to Poppy: "Some one may like to know that George Bush was in town today for the day . . . [Bush] also had a press conference. During it, he carefully refrained from saying any-thing critical of the President."[34] LBJ has also been plausibly characterized as secretly rooting for Bush to beat the liberal Democratic candidate for Sen-ate, Ralph Yarborough, whom LBJ disliked greatly; since the Democrats held a solid two-thirds majority in the Senate, LBJ knew that his party could af-ford to lose the seat.

In any case, while in Washington, Poppy had a warm relationship with Johnson, notwithstanding Bush's persistent attacks on the Democratic Party, especially back in Texas.

One of the more peculiar relationships in an already bizarre enterprise resulted from Bush's choice of a surrogate to run Zapata Offshore's office in

Medellín, Colombia. To begin with, there was the question of why a small, unprofitable company needed such far-flung outposts. Why, in particular, did it need one in Medellín, 150 miles from any offshore drilling locale—a city whose very name would later become synonymous with the cocaine trade? Bush's choice to represent Zapata in Colombia was Judge Manuel B. Bravo, of Zapata County, Texas.[35]

Judge Bravo's singular claim to fame was his role in Lyndon Johnson's fraud-ridden election to the U.S. Senate in 1948. As reports of an extraordinarily close race came in on election night, Bravo continually revised upward the Johnson count from Zapata County's Ballot Box 3, until LBJ was assured victory. A federal investigation led to a trial, but by that time the ballots from Box 13 in Jim Wells County had conveniently disappeared from the judge's office. The lack of evidence effectively ended Johnson's peril. Johnson won by eighty-seven votes.[36]

In 1967, President Johnson sent Poppy a note wishing him a happy birthday. The following year, LBJ's decision not to seek reelection paved the way for Richard Nixon's ascent to the presidency—and Nixon's steady sponsorship of Poppy Bush's own ascent to power. When Nixon was inaugurated in 1969, Bush took the unusual step of leaving the GOP festivities to see LBJ off at the airport. Soon thereafter, he was a guest at the LBJ ranch. There is no public record of what the two men talked about.

CERTAINLY, IT HAD been a tumultuous few years for America, and busy ones for Poppy. His astonishing ability to carry on parallel lives, one visible, one deeply hidden, continued undiminished. But soon, there would be an understudy: his namesake, George W. Bush.

CHAPTER 8

Wings for W.

THE REPLACEMENT OF JOHN F. KENNEDY with Lyndon Baines Johnson was certainly good for the Texans close to both LBJ and Poppy Bush. The Houston-based Brown and Root company, for example, joined a consortium that won a $380 million ($2.5 billion in current dollars) no-bid contract to build Navy facilities in South Vietnam.

The problem was that all this war-making required fresh cannon fodder, and Poppy wasn't about to let eldest son George W. Bush be part of that.

W., as friends call him, was not only Poppy's namesake; he was in many respects a chip off the old block, if a more rough-edged one. In fact, his adolescence and young adulthood mirrored Poppy's to a remarkable extent—same prep school, same university, same fraternity and secret society. The acting-out and the pranks, emphasized so strongly in conventional biographies, had all been within the boundaries of the acceptable for someone of his station—summed up in the proverbial "sowing of wild oats." Indeed, his grandfather Prescott quite outshone him in that regard. His grandfather's exploits ranged from purportedly stealing the skull of Geronimo to falsely claiming to his parents that as a World War I artillery officer, he had saved the lives of the top military commanders of the United States, Britain, and France. In a letter home, Prescott claimed that during a battlefield tour for the trio, he deflected an incoming shell with his bolo knife—and said that for this he had been recommended for the three nations' highest honors.[1] His parents proudly arranged for a front-page story in the local Columbus, Ohio, newspaper, only to face the deep embarrassment of learning that it had all been a joke. Measured by this yardstick, George W.'s own high jinks were clearly par for the family course.

Indeed, W. was essentially a dutiful son, dedicated to the family and its ethos. He worked hard to meet his father's standards. Even W.'s summer jobs had been an apprenticeship in the Bush family business, broadly speaking. In 1962 he was a messenger for the Baker Botts law firm, and in 1963 he spent the summer laboring for Poppy's pal John Greenway at his Quarter Circle XX Ranch in northern Arizona. By the following summer, he was ready to work on Dad's Senate campaign. One was never too young to be exposed to the family trade: his father had even taken him as a young boy on business trips, including a visit to Zapata Offshore's branch office in Medellín, Colombia. On one such trip, W. met the Gammells, a Scottish banking family that had helped bankroll Poppy's early ventures. (Poppy's ties to the Gammell clan would prove so enduring that half a century later— as we shall see in chapter 21—a Gammell would help President George W. Bush forge a relationship with British prime minister Tony Blair that would pave the way for agreement on the invasion of Iraq.)

Like his father, W. from an early age lived a life full of carefully guarded secrets and sub rosa intrigues—essentially a double life, populated with faithful old boys, strange mishaps, and the recurrent need for incomplete reminiscences, disinformation, and dissembling. Above all, father and son share a code of loyalty worthy of a Sicilian Mafia clan. "The Bushes are loyal to each other to the hilt," one family friend observed. "You make one of them mad, you make all of them mad."[2] Poppy and W. have been much closer over the years than is widely understood. The fact of this closeness is in itself crucial to understanding how and why W. was propelled to the top, and what shaped the views that led him to do what he did as president.

One of the first notes of intrigue concerns his sudden announcement, January 1, 1967, of his engagement to Cathryn Wolfman—a beautiful blonde from Houston whom Bush had met at a party when he was at Yale and she was attending Smith College (Barbara's alma mater). Following a sledding accident, Wolfman had returned to Houston to recuperate and transferred to Rice University. The engagement announcement, which appeared in a local newspaper after Wolfman had returned to Houston, was not followed up by anything concrete. No specific wedding date was set, and the whole thing seems to have petered out. "We grew apart," W. told the *Houston Chronicle*.[3] Like so many events in W.'s life, this seemingly simple matter is clouded by multiple accounts and vagueness. W.'s parents appear to have disapproved for personal reasons. "[Barbara Bush] couldn't abide the fact that Cathryn's stepfather was Jewish," onetime Bush family friend Cody

Shearer told the author Kitty Kelley. " 'There'll be no Jews in our family,' she said."[4] W. later claimed that after being deployed to basic training, he never spent time with Wolfman again.

What is not widely known is that within two years of her engagement to George W. Bush, Wolfman was offered and accepted a job with the Central Intelligence Agency as an economic analyst in the North Vietnamese section, and after graduation she moved to Washington. In a 2006 interview at her home in Palo Alto, California, Wolfman[5] told me that, since she was offered the CIA position while still a Rice student, she had always assumed her recruitment by the agency that Poppy would later head was merely a coincidence.[6] Wolfman had no reason to know of Poppy's history of CIA activities (documented in earlier chapters) or his extensive personal connections within the agency. Perhaps it was a coincidence, but several people I interviewed told me how Poppy liked to arrange favorable outcomes for those who had to be erased from the Bush family album.

Whether or not Poppy Bush helped ease Cathryn Wolfman out of his son's life, he almost surely helped a more acceptable woman in. Once Wolfman was gone, W. began dating Tina Cassini, the daughter of Oleg Cassini, George de Mohrenschildt's good friend and Jackie Kennedy's fashion designer, and a White Russian.[7] "Mr. Bush knew exactly what he was doing," W.'s friend Doug Hannah recalled about Poppy. "He would set up guys and girls that he thought belonged together. He even set up his own brother Jonathan with the daughter of a stockbroker, tried his damnedest to get that working. Mr. Bush would set people up, get them dates, give them money to go out and have a good time, and just revel in his abilities to put those things together."[8]

By the mid-1960s, Poppy had settled into the operational persona that would characterize his adult life. The elder Bush was a master intriguer. He reveled in knowing everyone's business, in doing favors and then calling them in. He kept tabs on his growing network of personal contacts through a massive system of index cards, and he kept this network alive and growing through small kindnesses, ingratiating notes, and the thousands of Christmas cards he sent each year.

The old intelligence hand generally knew about everything—including, of course, the bigger challenges in his children's lives. And no bigger challenge faced W. than the prospect of military service. The family knew that after he graduated from Yale in the spring of 1968, he would lose his draft deferment. As a single man, he faced almost certain deployment to Vietnam.

But as Poppy and his fellow politicians knew only too well, Vietnam was a charnel house. Even those who supported the war generally weren't eager for their own sons to go—especially not eldest sons carrying both their first and last names. On the other hand, evading military service was tricky for a Bush scion because the men in the family were all hawks. Grandfather Prescott Bush, the World War I vet, had been a supporter of military force in Vietnam. Poppy, the World War II vet, had championed the Vietnam cause in his losing Senate campaign of 1964; he had even endorsed the use of nuclear weapons.[9] Two years later, after winning a congressional seat from a wealthy part of Houston, he supported Lyndon Johnson's escalation of the conflict. And during W.'s final college Christmas break, right at the time that the younger Bush was confronting his own military future, his father happened to be in Vietnam, ostensibly on a congressional fact-finding mission and to show support for the troops.

What made W.'s position even more awkward was that he had personally supported the war while studying on the Yale campus, where the antiwar movement was dominant. Now he was boxed in. He certainly could not become a draft dodger, and if he ever hoped to follow his family forebears into elective office, he would need a requisite show of bravery and patriotism. At the very least he would have to avoid the appearance of cowardice and hypocrisy. He also could not escape the looming shadow of his father, who had enlisted at age eighteen; and the views of the Republican base, which skewed heavily toward veterans and military-minded voters.

One way out was the National Guard, which in those days offered what amounted to safe service: you could claim to have done your duty without much risk or inconvenience. Many young men volunteered to be called by the Guard, but only a lucky few were chosen. Fortunately, the deck was notably stacked in Texas, where the Guard was highly politicized. The solution was therefore obvious: obtain a berth in the Guard, even it meant jumping to the front of the long waiting list of candidates. But there were also serious risks to a high-profile political family—if the patriarch was revealed to have pulled strings to keep his son out of Vietnam.

The family's calculated leveraging of power and manipulation of connections for favorable treatment, as well as its relentless efforts to hide what had been done, constitute the larger story behind W.'s avoidance of Vietnam service. The real story has been obscured through a cover-up carefully orchestrated and sustained for more than three decades. The striking success of this disinformation campaign is a sobering demonstration of the effectiveness of propaganda management techniques more commonly associated with the cold war.

As a result, the particulars of W.'s military service remain only vaguely understood by the public. No authoritative explanation has been provided for how Bush got into the National Guard, much less what he did while he was there, or whether he served his obligatory term as opposed to skipping out on his commitment. The public has been left with a gnawing sense that something had gone deeply wrong—something that went to the very core of Bush's character. The fog of uncertainty surrounding Bush's Guard service seems especially remarkable when one considers that military force was the signature of W.'s presidency. The truth behind the fog reveals a great deal not just about W. himself, but also about class and privilege in America and about the relationship of the media to the ruling elite.

These things matter not only in a symbolic way. Had the true story been told earlier, the history of Bush's eight-year presidency might have been substantially different—indeed there likely would have been no such presidency—and thousands of American fighting men and women might still be alive, along with untold numbers of Iraqis.

The Champagne Unit

George W. Bush has always claimed that he got into the Guard like anyone else—he applied, qualified, and was admitted. Specifically, Bush claims that during his 1967 Christmas break, he heard that there might be openings in the Houston-based 147th Fighter Wing of the Texas Air National Guard. According to W., he talked with the unit's commander, Lieutenant Colonel Walter "Buck" Staudt, who confirmed that there were positions available for pilots.[10]

In fact, there was no shortage of pilots. Tom Hail, a historian for the Texas National Guard, was asked in the late 1990s to prepare a special museum display on then-governor Bush's Guard service. He discovered records establishing that while there were two empty slots at the time, there were also two other pilots ready to fill those slots.[11] More generally, there were thousands of eager applicants on Guard waiting lists nationwide—and many of the applicants to the 147th were considerably more qualified than Bush.

But there are qualifications, and then there are *qualifications*. The 147th

was known locally as the "champagne unit" because of its high-society ros-
ter. Among its members were scions of great wealth and privilege—a
grandson of the oil billionaire H. L. Hunt, the sons of Texas senator Lloyd
Bentsen and governor John Connally, and an heir to the Houston-based
Sakowitz department store fortune. Clint Murchison Jr., owner of the Dallas
Cowboys, had gotten seven of his players out of Vietnam service and into
the unit. Most of the members didn't even fly, but rather served in support
capacities, according to former naval fighter pilot Bill White, who later
spent years as a business partner to Jim Bath, a Guardsman who served as
the 147th's spokesman. "They created a bunch of slots," White told me,
"[like] 'finance officer,' that didn't really exist, just to create a home for these
guys, the politicians' kids."[12] For W., being admitted to the 147th was like
getting into Yale as a legacy.

Years later, Ben Barnes, who was Speaker of the Texas House of Representatives in 1968, would publicly admit that he had helped Bush gain ad-
mittance to the Texas Air National Guard. Barnes would tell the story to Dan
Rather on *60 Minutes II* in 2004. What Barnes did not mention was that a
childhood friend of Bush's had been working as his secretary at the time he
helped Bush. Nor did he note that the woman's boyfriend would go on to become one of the most important figures in Bush's life—the man who would
lead the fund-raising for all of W.'s campaigns. Indeed, everyone involved
would take care to hide this early web of connections—though it will be detailed in chapter 20.

Clearly, favoritism in admission was the norm for the 147th Fighter Wing,
but special treatment for George W. Bush didn't end there. The Guard also
took the unusual step of arranging special flight training for W. Typically, the
Guard sought to piggyback off the regular military services by enrolling
trained Air Force pilots who had flown jets in combat or in overseas support
capacities and were now happy to join Guard units to make a little extra
money. Yet U.S. taxpayers paid over one million dollars to train George W.
Bush to fly, as though he would be going overseas—when those in charge had
to have known that he would not.

The fact that George W. Bush—who had never flown a plane and had no
officer training—was brought into the Guard as a pilot was something of an
anomaly to begin with. He stuck out during his flight training at Moody Air
Force Base in Georgia as the only Guardsman among some two hundred
Air Force pilots. On top of that, he had scored a dismal 25 percent on his initial pilot aptitude tests—a score that later prompted Bush to say, with his

typical self-deprecating humor, "They could sense I would be one of the great pilots of all time."[13]

W. was so wired that he did not even have to bother with standard requirements, essentially becoming an officer by fiat. In a show of truly extraordinary favoritism, W. had been granted an unusual direct commission as a second lieutenant. "I've never heard of that," said Guard historian Tom Hail. "Generally they did that for doctors only, mostly because we needed extra flight surgeons."[14] Ordinarily, to obtain a second lieutenant's rank, one would need to attend officer training school, pull eighteen prior months of military service, or have eight semesters of ROTC. Bush had done none of these.

The Top Gun

Hardly any accounts of George W. Bush's life explain what role, if any, his father played in his youthful adventures. Given what we know about the meddling by powerful parents of other luminaries, such as the Kennedys, this is a striking omission. Because of it, one has a sense that the father was absent throughout and that W. was making good (or bad) on his own.

Fostering this impression was consistent with Poppy's no-fingerprints modus operandi. In reality, though, officials in W.'s Guard unit knew exactly who the new recruit's father was. Several months after Bush received his commission, his commanding officer, Lieutenant Colonel Staudt, had the ceremony reenacted so that he could be photographed with W. and his congressman father. Even Mrs. Staudt crowded into the photo. A year later, when a round of congressional base-closing decisions threatened Ellington Field, where the 147th was located, Congressman George H. W. Bush helped keep it open.

No sooner had W. obtained these unusual perquisites on his way in than he got permission to opt out: at least temporarily. Following six weeks of basic training at Lackland Air Force Base in San Antonio, W. took an extraordinary two-month leave to work on the Senate campaign of Florida congressman Edward Gurney, which was being run by Poppy Bush's lieutenant Jimmy Allison.[15] Along with Texas, Florida was a crucial part of Nixon's Southern strategy, and Poppy poured an army of Allisons and Bushes into the mix.

Only after Gurney was elected, in November, did W. move on to Moody

Air Force Base near Valdosta, Georgia, where he would be taught to fly a plane. For nearly a year, W. took lessons in a basic commercial Cessna, as most beginners do, and learned about jets on a simulator. Then he returned to the Houston area and Ellington Field, for the far more daunting task of learning to fly a real fighter jet.

SHORTLY AFTER HIS return from Georgia, in November 1969, while drinking at the bar of the officers' club, Bush cast his eye on Inge Honneus, a striking Danish émigré.[16] As Honneus would recount to me in a 2006 interview, she had come to the United States to work for NASA in Florida and had a short-lived marriage to an American. She had just transferred to the Houston area, where she worked for the LTV Corporation, a subcontractor for NASA's LBJ Space Center, which was about five miles south of Ellington Field.[17] Honneus's account of her experiences with Bush—which is, to be sure, one woman's side of the story—has not been previously published. There seems to be little doubt that Honneus was in Houston and around Bush's base in that period, as attested by a clipping from a local newspaper showing her at a party surrounded by Air Force officers.

Honneus's story makes a striking contrast to the oddly bland, published interviews with Houston society women who described their interactions with Bush in those days. Most portray W. as a decent, polite man who would never have pushed himself on a woman. In one instance, a self-described former girlfriend was struck by the fact that Bush always brought a male friend along on dates.

As Honneus tells it, the night they met at the officers' club, W. looked sharp in his officers' whites and tried to make himself even more appealing by pretending he was in the Air Force. "He proceeded to tell me that he was a pilot, his father was a senator [sic], and blah blah blah," Honneus recalled. "I wasn't that impressed. It just seemed that he thought he could do anything, be anything, say anything, because his father was a senator . . . Then he ran after me for about three or four months. I wouldn't really give him the time of day. He pretty much wined and dined me, we got to be friends, and later on in life I realized he'd lied to me about being an officer in the Air Force."

Although Bush pursued her relentlessly, she kept rebuffing his advances. She was going through a divorce, had a four-year-old daughter, and just was not interested in a romance. "I was doing quite well for myself . . . I felt that, next time I have a relationship with anybody, it'd better be a little bit more stable than the relationship I'd had with my daughter's father."

Still, Bush was charming and persistent, and they soon fell into what Honneus characterized as a nonintimate friendship. Typically, she said, he would pick her up in his sporty dark-green Datsun 240, and they would drive around Houston while he got things off his chest. Honneus remembered Bush predicting that, because his parents made things so easy for him, he would never amount to anything.

Honneus said W. once, briefly, took her to his parents' house, where she remembered meeting a brother. She also recalled that W. seemed reluctant to introduce her to his relatives since she wasn't from an affluent or prominent family.

Things abruptly intensified between the two. At eleven o'clock one night, there was a knock on her door. Standing there, clad in his flight suit, was George W. Bush. He told Inge he couldn't live without her. She let him in, quickly excusing herself to put on something more presentable than a nightgown. When she returned a few minutes later, she got quite a shock. There, on her couch, was W. in all his primal glory: Bush-naked from head to toe. Whether she was allured, or simply worn down by his full-frontal advances, Honneus let Bush spend the night. He left at six A.M. and promised to call the next day.

After three or four days without word, Honneus asked her girlfriends whether any of them had seen him. One suggested that she visit the officers' club that evening to quiz his buddies there.

As she described this encounter to me, Honneus searched for the right words. "Do you remember the movie *Top Gun*—they were standing at the bar, all in their white coats, looking absolutely gorgeous, and Tom Cruise was like the center of attention? Well, that was George! He was standing with his back to me, laughing and joking and drinking with his buddies, and I'm thinking, 'Oh my God, there's George. Why didn't he call me?' I run over there, young of course, young and excited. I tap him on the shoulder, and I say, 'George, where have you been?' And he turned around, looked at me and said: '*Who . . . are . . . you?*'

"And everybody laughed. They thought it was so funny. 'Who are you?'—straight to my face. I don't know what my response was, other than I was gone out of Texas the next day. Never to return." Literally. Honneus was so devastated that within twenty-four hours, she had left the state for good, moving to California, where she is now a software engineer.

Though Honneus told me she didn't consider herself overly sensitive, what she found so troubling was the complete disconnect between Bush's assiduous five-month courtship and his abrupt and cruel public rejection of her once he had achieved his goal. She was reticent to go into greater detail regarding her night with Bush, but she did say that soon after it, she felt ill and went to the doctor. The result, she said, was a miscarriage.[18] Because she never spoke again with Bush, he would not learn the outcome of his exertions.

WHILE GEORGE W. BUSH was thus occupied, the Bushes, father and son, were being showered with favorable publicity. W.'s return to Houston from flight training in Georgia in November 1969 had come at a convenient time for Poppy, who was embarking on his second run for the U.S. Senate. As eldest son, W. was naturally expected to do his part. In March 1970, with the Republican primary less than two months away, Poppy Bush's campaign office began directing a barrage of press releases at local media outlets. At the same time, another press release reached media outlets from the Texas National Guard, touting George Walker Bush as "one member of the younger generation'[who] doesn't get his kicks from pot or hashish or speed. Oh, he gets high, all right, but not from narcotics."[19] The press release, delivered to the Houston dailies, went on to describe Bush's first solo flight and the thrill he got from his jet engine's afterburners.

Weekend Warrior

In June 1970, after George W. had completed his jet pilot training in Houston, his full-time obligation with the Guard gave way to the part-time status commonly referred to as "weekend warrior." For many, this meant time to go back to work. For W., it meant more time for water volleyball and alcoholic refreshment. Again jumping the line, he rented a place at the Chateaux Dijon, an exclusive apartment complex with 353 castle-motif dwellings. It was a famous playground for the children of Houston's upper crust, and as with the 147th Guard unit, you had to know someone to get in.

Other members and alumni of the 147th Fighter Wing lived at the Chateaux. And many good buddies who did not live there, like Bush's friend Jim Bath, were constantly stopping by. "The scene around the pool was awe inspiring," Bath once told an interviewer.[20] "Lots and lots of great-looking girls and people barbecuing and drinking beers." At Chateaux Dijon, W. would come in contact with many figures who would later play significant roles in his life. Fellow Midlander and future wife Laura Welch lived nearby in the complex, although both Laura and George have consistently maintained that they never met during that period.

W. and his closest peers belonged to something called the Master's Club. It included nearly one hundred bachelors who enjoyed wearing tuxedos and smoking cigars and who held a fancy-dress dance once a year. The club and its dances provided what Jim Woodson, the club's organizer, called "a controlled atmosphere. You knew who was dancing next to you."[21] The exclusivity ensured that only a certain kind of person got close to these young knights, and that nothing would come back to haunt them as they assumed their places in society.

In later years, when reporters raised questions about Bush's past behavior, his campaign sought to convey the impression that his oft-cited misdeeds during these years centered on excessive drink. Inge Honneus said Bush drank quite a bit, but added that he was not exceptional in this regard: "That was our social niche. You know, we didn't go to church on Sundays; we went to barbecues and had beer. I would say he drank about as much as anybody else drank [back then]. And you've got to understand something too: It was NASA, the space program—everybody drank. Everybody drank and drove. It was the thing to do."

Bush has generally hedged on the question of drug use. Asked about it during his first presidential campaign, W. insisted that he could have passed the same background screening his father underwent before Poppy's inauguration in 1989, which certifies no illegal drug use during the fifteen preceding years. This evasive answer certainly left open the possibility that he used illegal drugs *prior* to 1974.[22]

Some sources who are now pillars of Houston society claim to remember W. indulging in cocaine, but because none will go on the record this cannot be considered reliable. Yet there is little doubt that the upright voters who would later support W. politically would have been mightily displeased by the moral atmosphere at Chateaux Dijon. Even Laura Welch reportedly enjoyed a good time, which in those days often meant smoking marijuana. Kitty Kelley quotes Robert Nash, an Austin friend of many of Laura's Southern Methodist University peers, as recalling that Laura partook of pot.[23]

One pastime that definitely appealed to many in Bush's circle was political campaigning. Texas politician Lloyd Bentsen's two sons served in Bush's

Guard unit, and one was a neighbor of Bush's. After Poppy Bush announced his intention to run for Senate in 1970, the Bentsen boys' father announced that he too would seek the seat—as a Democrat. The contest provided much excitement for the privileged denizens of Chateaux Dijon. W. frequently served as surrogate speaker for his father. His friend and neighbor Robert Chandler took a campaign staff position, and Jim Bath frequently had strategy lunches with Poppy. Before the polls closed on election day—and before it was known that the elder Bentsen had defeated the elder Bush—a press release from the Texas Guard announced the promotions of George W. Bush and Lloyd Bentsen III to the rank of first lieutenant.[24] It seemed as if the brass was hedging its bets: promote them both, and the Guard would win either way.

With the end of the campaign, Bush had little to occupy his time besides the Chateaux's attractive young ladies. For six months, he had been dating Robin Lowman, one of the best-looking women in the complex.[25] What exactly transpired between Bush and Lowman would become the subject of extensive reporting by several journalists, working for publications that ranged from the New York Times and Vanity Fair to the National Enquirer. Like many of the more potentially radioactive stories about the Bushes, none of these ever saw print.

One magazine was ready to publish an article in 2004 but pulled it after the public uproar following the 60 Minutes II debacle over Bush's Guard record. The reasons the others did not run the story varied, but ranged from the reticence of the publisher to a generalized sense that such a story had a high risk factor for retribution, both from the candidate's staff and from a public intrigued yet repulsed by coverage of such topics—especially in the aftermath of the Monica Lewinsky saga.

Nevertheless, four reporters who worked on these articles had been persuaded about the fundamental truth of the underlying story; they shared their experiences and detailed source notes with me. Their cumulative narrative—which in certain respects has echoes of the story Inge Honneus told me about her own Bush experience—is as follows:

Michele Perry, who was dating W.'s friend Robert Chandler in early 1971, claimed to have been present in his apartment one day when he received a panicked phone call from George W. Bush. Perry heard Chandler say, "Calm down. We can take care of it." She soon learned what W. was so worked up about: Lowman was pregnant. Chandler then sprang into action, calling a doctor friend of his to arrange an abortion.

Lowman was taken to Houston's Twelve Oaks Hospital (now the Bayou City Medical Center), where a surgeon friend of Chandler's attended to her. Since abortion was illegal in Texas, and would be until *Roe v. Wade* was decided two years later, the doctor diagnosed a miscarriage, which would then necessitate a procedure called a D&C—often a euphemism for an early-term abortion. Perry and Chandler visited Lowman at the hospital after the procedure, and had to break the news that W. himself would not be coming there to see her.[26]

In reporting this story, one news organization obtained a tape in which Perry calls Lowman and tries to get her to confirm the matter. In the taped call, Lowman confirms that she had been dating Bush, and admits to going into the hospital in that period for a procedure. However, she insisted that it was not an abortion but a "D&C." In the call, Lowman mentions that after the procedure she never saw Bush again.

The doctor, who declined to confirm or deny to journalists whether he performed the procedure—as would be standard practice to protect patient confidentiality—donated a thousand dollars to Bush in 2000 and two thousand dollars, the maximum, in 2004. Chandler also declined to confirm or deny the story. My efforts to speak with Lowman were unsuccessful.

One journalist got a chance to raise the matter, at least obliquely, with Bush himself. During the 2000 campaign, *New York Times* reporter Jo Thomas, who had explored the abortion story, mentioned Lowman's name to Bush while interviewing him on the campaign plane on June 28, 2000, during a flight from Cleveland to Austin in the company of her editor, Jim Roberts, and Bush's communications director, Karen Hughes. In a 2004 meeting at her home in Syracuse, New York, Thomas, who was by then serving as associate chancellor of Syracuse University, consented to provide me with a detailed account of that Bush interview, including notes and a tape. In the conversation, Thomas can be heard reciting a list of the names of women whom Bush knew and was said to have dated. Bush briefly acknowledges knowing each one. Then she mentions Lowman by name, says that she had called her, and begins to explain what transpired: "She just said . . ." Bush cuts her off, midsentence, and artfully poses his own question to Thomas, putting her on the defensive. It is clear that the subject is out of bounds, and Lowman is never mentioned again. "When I read Robin Lowman's name, his face shattered," Thomas recalled.[27]

The story has a certain resonance primarily because Bush's political success was predicated in part on appealing to those who oppose a woman's right to an abortion. As president, Bush promulgated tough new policies that withheld U.S. funds not only to programs and countries that permitted abortions, but even to those that advocated contraception as opposed to abstinence. Moreover, his appointments to the Supreme Court put the panel on the verge of reversing *Roe v. Wade*. Like his insistence on long prison sentences for first-time drug offenders and his support for military action, his own behavior in regard to sexual responsibility and abortion could be considered relevant—and revealing.

ALTHOUGH THE ELDER Bush's name never comes up in reference to this episode or its resolution, he knew the players, including Chandler, quite well. Not surprisingly, he seems to have stepped in to assume what would be an increasingly common role: cleaning up after his son in a dicey situation. Soon after the alleged Lowman incident, W. was yanked from his beloved pleasure dome and moved into a garage apartment behind the house of family friends in a sedate residential neighborhood of Houston. There, he was given a roommate who could keep an eye on him: Don Ensenat, a Louisiana native and Delta Kappa Epsilon brother. After graduating from Yale, Ensenat had worked on Poppy's 1970 campaign. Later, he would be rewarded for his services with an appointment by President George H. W. Bush as ambassador to Brunei, and by President George W. Bush as the United States chief of protocol.

George W. not only needed looking after; he needed to be kept occupied. He grudgingly reported for work at Stratford of Texas, a global agricultural conglomerate run by Bob Gow, Poppy Bush's former lieutenant. Gow would tell reporters that Bush had shown up on his own, but a friend of Gow's remembers otherwise. David Klausmeyer told me in a 2006 interview at his Houston home, "I knew why he was there. His dad got him the job."[28]

Stratford was located in the Tenneco Building in the heart of Houston's financial and oil center. It was a small outfit, with about a dozen employees on the management team. "That's when I first met George W. Bush," recalled Klausmeyer, a consultant who worked in the office. "He was a trainee, more or less. He was killing time." Actually it was one of W.'s longer stints of employment. But if his duties were a mystery, so too was his abrupt departure.

In later conversations with reporters, Bush would dismiss his tenure at Stratford as an inconsequential, "stupid coat-and-tie job" that he quit, after less than a year, out of boredom.[29] Reporters generally took the assertion at face value. In fact, Stratford—and Bush's time there—deserves a second look.

Like Zapata, Stratford had a complex financial structure and unprofitable foreign operations. While working there, George W. was exposed to a range of international assignments, in places like Jamaica and Guatemala, that he has never spoken about. Years later, when W. was a presidential candidate, he would be accused of lacking foreign policy credentials, with the evidence being that he had apparently never even traveled abroad. He could have countered these accusations by drawing attention to the trips he undertook while working for Stratford, but he chose not to—a curious omission unless he did not want anyone looking into these trips.

Trouble in the Cockpit

Whatever the true reason for his departure from the full-time Stratford job and his return to leisure-filled unemployment, during this same period something went wrong with his part-time career as a military pilot.

Records show that in early 1972, W. began having difficulties in the cockpit. His flight logs from that year show that he was ordered to return to a two-pilot training plane—the very sort from which he had graduated two years before. This was after he had logged more than two hundred hours in his single-seat jet fighter—a remarkable comedown for the unit's onetime poster boy. Although reported by the Associated Press in 2004 after it obtained the records in a long-running lawsuit, this revelation never gained traction with the media.

According to the flight logs, Bush's friend Jim Bath, a former Air Force pilot, went up with him on some of these retraining flights, perhaps to boost his confidence. But even this friendly assistance does not seem to have helped. Back in his own F-102, Bush on one occasion needed three passes before he could make a landing. Even in a flight simulator, it took multiple attempts before he succeeded in landing his virtual plane.[30]

Because fighter jets fly in tight formation, Bush's difficulties were everyone's problems. That may explain why, on April 16, 1972, he flew for the last time. And soon he was gone altogether from the unit and the state. In military records, his departure was explained as due to a career opportunity— W. had landed a management position with the U.S. senatorial campaign of

Winton "Red" Blount, Nixon's postmaster general and a friend of Poppy's. As his Texas Air National Guard supervisors, presumably relying on what Bush told them, would write in a report the following year: "A civilian occupation made it necessary for him to move to Montgomery, Alabama."

Whistling Dixie

By the time George W. Bush arrived in Montgomery, Blount's run for the U.S. Senate was well under way. The campaign manager was Poppy's longtime aide Jimmy Allison; he and his wife, Linda, had been in Alabama since the beginning of the year.[31] Nevertheless, a seemingly significant position was created for W. As the *Washington Post* noted in a February 2004 profile, "Although a relative newcomer to political campaigns, Bush was given a title—assistant campaign manager—and responsibility . . . He was charged with developing county organizations, particularly in the hilly northern part of the state, and he impressed people with his energy."[32]

In fact, the campaign had three other individuals whose responsibilities entailed coordinating county organizations—with each responsible for one third of the state. What this left for Bush to "coordinate" is hard to say. He was designated as a sort of liaison between Allison and other campaign staff, but his responsibilities remained rather vague. According to several campaign staffers with whom I spoke, Bush worked irregularly, showing up late much of the time, often well into the afternoon. His specific duties ranged from affixing bumper stickers to transporting boxes of literature for a campaign known from the start to be a losing cause.[33]

Indeed, W. had not even chosen to go to Alabama. He had been ordered to go by his father. Linda Allison, Jimmy's widow, would later describe to me how sometime in the late spring of 1972 her husband received a phone call from Poppy, who was then the U.S. ambassador to the United Nations. "Big George called Jimmy and said, 'He's killing us in Houston. Take him down there and let him work on that campaign.' The tenor was, 'Georgie is in and out of trouble seven days a week down here, and would you take him up there with you?' "[34]

This scenario tracks with other evidence. W. had cleared out of Houston so fast that several of his friends said they didn't even recall knowing that he was leaving town. Bush had asked permission from his Guard superiors to do "equivalent duty" in Alabama, and he did apply to join an Alabama

Guard unit. The unit he chose, the Montgomery-based 9921st Air Reserve Squadron, was weak tea compared with the 147th Fighter Wing in Texas, and it was certainly an unusual choice for a pilot. It was, in fact, a postal unit that met but one night a month; the rumor was that it would soon be shut down altogether. As the unit's head, Colonel Reese H. Bricken, later put it: "We had no airplanes. We had no pilots. We had no nothing."[35]

Unfortunately for Bush, the Air Reserve Personnel Center in Denver nixed the transfer.[36] Bush would eventually get a more appropriate assignment, the 187th Tactical Reconnaissance unit, located at Montgomery's Dannelly Field Air Guard Station. His acceptance into the 187th is a documented fact. Beyond that, Bush's military service simply vanishes into the fog. Despite the efforts of journalists and investigators throughout his presidency, the military has been unable to locate records documenting his complete service.

In 2000, it would be a Republican and Bush supporter, former Dannelly commander Ret. General William Turnipseed, who would put W. in the hot seat by telling the media: "I'm dead-certain he didn't show up."[37] Bush claimed to remember performing his Guard duty as required while in Alabama, but no credible records or eyewitnesses ever emerged to back him up. Indeed, in 2004, former members of the Alabama National Guard ran repeated notices in the Guard publication *Interceptor Magazine* soliciting any evidence of Bush's presence with the 187th. None was forthcoming; the posted rewards were never claimed.

Despite W.'s lackluster performance on the Blount campaign, the local press took a shine to him from the start. An August 11, 1972, *Montgomery Independent* society column noted the arrival in Alabama of the campaign's "coordinator"—"young, personable George Bush, 26." The next and only mention in the *Independent* describes the election-night party at the Whitley Hotel. Among those holding forth on the dance floor was "handsome, bright, young George Bush, son of the U.S. Ambassador to the United Nations." It was apparently quite a party. Two eyewitnesses described to me a drunken Bush screaming at police officers. "He was down in the parking lot, just railing on these cops," recalled one. "I couldn't believe they didn't throw him in jail."[38]

Young Bush enjoyed regaling associates with accounts of his drinking exploits. Blount's nephew, C. Murphy Archibald, remembers W. telling one particular story "what seemed like a hundred times . . . He would laugh uproariously as though there was something funny about this. To me, that was

pretty memorable, because here he is, a number of years out of college, talking about this to people he doesn't know. He just struck me as a guy who really had an idea of himself as very much a child of privilege, that he wasn't
operating by the same rules."[39] W. also enjoyed recounting his adventures at
Yale—how he got stopped by police officers there "all the time" for driving
drunk but always got off when they learned who he was.

Two unconnected acquaintances of a well-known male Montgomery socialite, now deceased, recounted to me a story told to them by the socialite.
In this account, the man had been partying with Bush at the Montgomery
Country Club, combining drinking with illicit drugs. The socialite had told
them that when the two made a brief stop at W.'s cottage so he could change
clothes, Bush complained about the brightness, climbed up on a table, and
smashed the chandelier with a baseball bat. Indeed, the family that rented
Bush the cottage told me that he left extensive damage, including a
smashed chandelier, and that he ignored two bills they sent him. The total
came to about nine hundred dollars, a considerable sum in 1972.

A Guarded Assessment

The scenario in which W. fled Texas because he was having flying problems
was confirmed to me when I spoke with Janet Linke. She is the widow of
Jan Peter Linke, an Air Force pilot who had been flying an F-102 for the
Florida Air National Guard and was brought in to take Bush's place in the
147th Fighter Wing. In a 2004 interview, Mrs. Linke told me of a conversation that she and her husband had with Bush's commanding officer, not
long after they arrived at Ellington. According to Linke, "[Bush] was muck-
ing up bad. [Lieutenant Colonel Jerry] Killian told us he just became afraid
to fly." Linke also recalled that Killian told them Bush "was having trouble
landing, and that possibly there was a drinking problem involved in that."[40]

Even at the time, Janet Linke realized that Killian meant something out
of the ordinary. She knew from personal experience that drinking was commonplace among pilots during that period. Within a year after her husband
took Bush's place, Jan Peter Linke died when his car went off a road and
plunged into a lake. Authorities concluded that Linke had been drinking
and fell asleep at the wheel. This left Janet Linke a twenty-seven-year-old
widow with a three-year-old son. Another member of the unit, Dr. Richard
Mayo, said of drinking among the pilots: "I think we all did, yeah. There's a

great correlation between fighter pilots and alcohol. I mean, beer call was mandatory."[41]

In summary: W. left his Houston Guard unit under a cloud, then apparently failed to show up for equivalent duty in Alabama. In Montgomery, his drunken exploits as a campaign staffer were known among the staff and others, but in print he was described as a prince. And while all this was going on, his father, named to head the national Republican Party at the end of 1972, finally seemed on an upward track commensurate with his ambitions. Clearly, the problems with his eldest son could not be allowed to thwart those ambitions.

X-Ray Optional

After Blount's defeat in early November 1972, W. packed up and returned to Texas. But he did not report back to his unit at Ellington as he was required to do.

That December, the Bush annual holiday gathering was held in Washington, D.C., where Poppy was taking over the helm of the embattled Republican Party. The GOP was then in the midst of the Watergate affair, with new revelations unfolding daily. According to a story that has become a staple in the media narrative, W. had an altercation with his father around this time. Supposedly, W. had taken his younger brother Marvin to visit the Allisons—who had a house in the capital from the time Jimmy had worked at the Republican National Committee. After leaving the Allisons' house, W. drove home drunk and managed to mow down some garbage cans in the process. In a scene beloved of the media, when the father tried to confront his son, W. challenged him to a fight, "mano a mano."[42]

The story leaves a vivid impression of a rebellious young man who was beyond his family's control—a part the legendary James Dean might have played. In reality, W. may have been out of control and under the influence of alcohol, but the proverbial acorn never strayed far from the tree. During the preceding six months, while apparently failing to perform his Guard duty, W. had been in regular contact with his parents. He and his father had been together at the GOP convention in August 1972 in Miami; in October at his grandfather Prescott's funeral in Connecticut and at the parents' apartment at the Waldorf Towers in New York City; and finally for this extended visit over the 1972–73 holidays.

Of course the incoming chairman of the Republican Party could ill afford any embarrassment concerning his son's military service. So the stories of W.'s antagonism toward Poppy were useful in this regard. If the young rebel had indeed acted independently of his father, then the latter was off the hook for what had happened. I could find no evidence that Poppy has ever been pressed to say what he knew about these matters, and he declined interview requests relating to his son during W.'s presidency.

From their holiday gathering in Washington, the Bush clan repaired for New Year's 1973 to their winter home on Florida's exclusive Hobe Sound. There they were joined by the Allisons. W. continued to show a lack of maturity. One day, as his mother attempted to drive several miles to the country club where she and Mrs. Allison were to join their husbands, "Georgie," twenty-six years old, drove in front of them in another car, keeping at a crawl the entire distance, and forcing his mother's vehicle to stall numerous times. "Bar[bara] was *grim*," Mrs. Allison recalled.[43]

Such juvenile behavior could be tolerated, however. What really needed attention was W.'s vanishing act from the Guard. Poppy Bush, an expert in making problems go away, apparently took matters into his own hands.

From Florida, W. did not head directly back to Texas. Instead, he stopped off in Alabama—a state where he no longer resided—and did two things. First, he visited a dentist at Dannelly Air Force Base for a routine X-ray, thereby generating paperwork that could be presented to the press three decades later as evidence of his Alabama military service. The White House would portray the visit as an exam. But in a 2004 interview, the dentist who had seen Bush, Dr. John Andrew Harris, told me that his clinic did not even do actual dental work. Bush, he said, was merely there to have his teeth charted for identification purposes in case of death. This is especially odd, since by the time of Bush's visit, the nonresident of Alabama was no longer flying at all, seemingly negating the entire purpose of the exam.[44]

On that same quick stop in Montgomery, W. called a young, former Blount campaign staffer, invited her to dinner, showed up wearing his military uniform, and announced that he was in town for "guard training." Decades later, during W.'s 2004 reelection campaign against John Kerry, who had served with distinction in Vietnam, Bush's staff was pressed to explain the gap in his military service. The White House released the record of the dental exam and referred phone calls to the young Blount staffer. The American media, for the most part, accepted these two items as proof that Bush had fulfilled his service obligation.

Very Private Public Service

Having "fixed" his military service problem in Alabama, W. went back to Texas, where he attempted to secure his missing service credits. But his superiors did not want him back. This was a serious hitch. It would be nine months before W. could be packed off to Harvard Business School, and there were untold ways in which the prodigal son could get himself into trouble in Houston. So another solution was found: unlikely as it may sound, George W. enrolled as a "counselor" in an inner-city youth program.

Professional United Leadership League, or PULL, was an attractive place to park W. for a spell. He was an avid sports fan, and PULL was all about sports. Its front men were two retired Houston Oilers football players, John L. White and Ernie Ladd. They recruited a pantheon of local sports greats who mentored neighborhood kids. PULL was not only acceptable to the Bushes; it was virtually a creation of Poppy's. Several years earlier, Poppy had hit upon the idea to help generate African American support in his senatorial race. He donated much of the start-up money for PULL in 1970, then served as the organization's honorary chairman.[45]

U.S. News & World Report would state in 1999 that Bush senior had arranged for W. to serve at PULL because he "hoped to expose the footloose son to 'real life.' "[46] In a video shown at the 2000 Republican Convention, Bush's stint at PULL was touted as emblematic of Bush's "compassionate conservatism." "Well, a wonderful man named John White asked me to come and work with him in a project in the Third Ward of Houston," Bush says in the video. "If we don't help others, if we don't step up and lead, who will?"

But the evidence points in a rather different direction. Ten days before W.'s reelection in 2004, Knight Ridder published a little-noticed story by reporter Meg Laughlin that was based on conversations with former PULL employees who had reluctantly agreed to talk. "We didn't know what kind of trouble he'd been in, only that he'd done something that required him to put in the time," said Althia Turner, White's administrative assistant. "George had to sign in and out. I remember his signature was a hurried cursive, but he wasn't an employee. He was not a volunteer either," she said. "John said he had to keep track of George's hours because George had to put in a lot of hours because he was in trouble."[47]

Others echoed those observations. Former Houston Oilers player Willie Frazier, who was a PULL summer volunteer in 1973, said, "John said he was doing a favor for George's father because an arrangement had to be made for the son to be there." The impression was that Poppy had arranged for W. to work at PULL as some kind of "restitution." Fred Maura, a close friend of White's, put it this way, referring to W. as "43," for the forty-third president, and his father as "41," for the forty-first president: "John didn't say what kind of trouble 43 was in—just that he had done something and he [John] made a deal to take him in as a favor to 41 to get some funding."

Maura's claim tracks with the recollections of Jack Gazelle, who worked at a city of Houston office that distributed federal revenue-sharing grants. Gazelle told me he remembers returning from an extended summer leave to be told that "George Bush Jr." was in the office doing research into obtaining grants from the Nixon administration for PULL.[48] Gazelle said that Bush didn't seem to want to be recognized, and that when he said hello, W. simply ignored him.[49]

Although George W. describes this period as one of full-time work counseling children, some of his putative colleagues don't remember it that way. Jimmy Wynn, the former Houston Astros baseball star, told me in a 2004 interview that the gregarious Bush was popular with the kids. But rather than working intensively counseling individual kids, Wynn said, W. addressed large assemblies of PULL participants from time to time.[50]

In any case, Bush has insisted that he worked at PULL full time from early 1973 until he left for Harvard in the fall. Yet that's also the period when he claims to have put in long hours at Ellington Field. His payroll records show him being credited with a surge in Guard duty during the summer—when those inner-city kids were out of school and needed PULL the most. For example, Bush is recorded as being on base for seventeen out of the twenty-two weekdays in July. This suggests an urgent need to add hours to his service in order to qualify for an honorable discharge. Yet Bush couldn't possibly have been in two places at the same time—and eyewitness accounts suggest that he may not have been on base at all.

The White House has released Bush's recollections of his 1973 Texas Guard duty that cite "paper shuffling" and "odds and ends" in the flight operations office. It was the kind of job that would have enabled the lively jokester ample time to socialize. As Bush told the *Texas Monthly* in 1994, "What I was good at was getting to know people."

Yet none of his Guard friends have been willing or able to confirm without ambiguity that Bush returned to the Texas unit after Alabama. This raises questions regarding the legitimacy of the payroll records released by the White House, which show Bush being paid for so many days of service from late 1972 until the middle of 1973. In one sense, it was Alabama all over again: the gregarious, in-your-face George W. Bush somehow managed to be invisible on two military bases over a period of seventeen months.

Indeed, W.'s superior officers at Ellington would sign papers saying that he had "not been observed" between May 1, 1972, and April 30, 1973. And no paperwork about alternative service in Alabama was ever produced or forwarded to the Texas Air National Guard as required by regulations. The lack of any documented service would raise questions back at Denver's Air Reserve Personnel Center, the same folks who had told Bush he could not hide out in a do-nothing postal unit. The center wrote the Texas Air National Guard asking for an explanation of Bush's disappearance and received this cryptic response: "Report for this period not available for administrative reasons."

Just about all the evidence suggests that George W. Bush went AWOL from National Guard duty in May 1972 and never returned, thus skipping out on two years of a six-year military obligation. Ever diligent, Bush's political fixers would later produce those payroll records that supposedly documented a brief, intense flurry of activity in the late fall of 1972 and again in late May through July 1973, i.e., after the period during which W.'s superiors filed a report that he was a no-show. The only evidence that such activity ever took place is a machine-generated form called a 526, unsigned and undated.[51] W.'s 526 includes not only "points" for actual duty, but also something called "gratuitous points," which a Guardsman is awarded even while on inactive status. Under even the most generous interpretation, this looks an awful lot like some superior officers protecting their posteriors—and W.'s.

Bush's Guard mates have been almost unfailingly supportive of whatever accounts the Bush team has put out over the years—with a rare exception. In a 2002 telephone interview with USA Today, Dean Roome, Bush's flying foursome partner and briefly his roommate during jet training in 1970, admitted that the final two years of Bush's Guard service were troubled. "You wonder if you know who George Bush is," Roome told the newspaper. "I think he digressed after a while. In the first half, he was gung-ho . . . Where George failed was to fulfill his obligation as a pilot. It was an irrational time in his life."[52]

It might have been irrational. It was certainly illegal. And in cases other than Bush's, the consequences could be severe. According to Jim Moore, an

Austin reporter who researched Bush's military service extensively, even the slightest infraction brought swift retribution. "I distinctly remember talking to a [Guard] company commander in Lubbock . . . who told me that if anyone was even 10 minutes late for a drill or any kind of duty, they were in trouble," Moore told me. "If they didn't show up at all, he either sent someone from the base or called the cops. In one case he told me about, one of his guys was ten minutes late for a second time and he sent MPs to the guy's house and they dragged him out of bed when he was having sex with his wife . . . I spoke to a lot of people about this and you generally did not screw up and miss Guard drills because if you did most [commanding officers] simply made you eligible for the draft."[53] In other words, one wrong move and you were headed to sunny Vietnam.

Boots in Harvard Yard

At this point in his life, George W. Bush was by no means a likely candidate for Harvard Business School. Even taking into account the value of connections, Harvard's decision to admit W. inevitably raises eyebrows. How he got into this bastion of excellence has never been made clear, though Harvard's willingness to accommodate the Bush clan would take on new meaning thirteen years later, when the university committed a sizable chunk of its endowment to prop up an oil company on whose board W. sat—a subject discussed in chapter 16.

Regarding the Harvard admission, once again the Bush family story is that W. did it on his own. The carefully constructed tale, routinely offered to and accepted by most journalists and biographers, is that W. sprang the news over Christmas 1972 when he and his father were purportedly at each other's throats. As usual, one can find inconsistencies in the accounts. In one version, brother Marvin seeks to inject calm at a tense moment by giving his father the good news of George's acceptance at Harvard. In another version, it is Jeb who announces the surprising development.[54] No matter, George tells his father: I have no intention of going; I just wanted to prove that I could get in without your help.

Yet in his 2000 campaign book, *A Charge to Keep*, Bush implies that he applied to Harvard Business School not in the fall of 1972, as the above story suggests, but in the spring of 1973 while he was working at PULL. If that account is correct, it would mean he both applied and was accepted after the normal application deadline. Either way, it is unlikely (though not impossible) that the son of the head of the national Republican Party would get into Harvard without his father's knowledge. This is especially so given W.'s lack of either compelling qualifications or a direct family legacy at Harvard.

In the end, of course, he did attend Harvard. He arrived in Cambridge decked out in his cowboy boots and Air National Guard flight jacket. What he didn't do was sign up as required with an Air Force Reserve unit in Massachusetts and serve out his original military obligation through the middle of 1974. Instead, he hung out on campus, spit chewing tobacco, and forged important links with figures who would play significant roles in his upward mobility and soon-to-be-growing prosperity.

CHAPTER 9

The Nixonian Bushes

I N EARLY 1969, THE NEWLY ELECTED Richard M. Nixon took one of his first acts as president: he arranged a date for his twenty-three-year-old daughter, Tricia, with George W. Bush. Not only that, he even dispatched a White House jet, at taxpayers' expense, to pick up young Bush at Moody Air Force Base in Georgia, in order to bring him back to Washington.

This would not be the only time that Nixon would bestow special favors upon the Bush family. Six months earlier, as the GOP presidential candidate, he had seriously considered Poppy as a potential running mate, even though the latter was just a freshman congressman. Two years after W.'s date with Tricia, following Poppy's second unsuccessful bid for the U.S. Senate, Nixon named him his ambassador to the United Nations. And two years later, with President Nixon's nod, Poppy served a stint as chairman of the Republican Party. It was a quick rise from relative obscurity to the highest level of national politics—and all with Nixon's help.

Taped conversations reveal that Nixon considered Poppy Bush a lightweight.[1] Nevertheless, he repeatedly pushed Poppy ahead, often over people who were much more qualified. This put the elder Bush on the upper rungs of the ladder to the presidency. In all probability, had Nixon not so favored Poppy, he never would have reached the top. And had Poppy Bush not been president, his son George W. Bush almost certainly would not have either. In no small way, Richard Nixon helped to create the Bush presidential dynasty.

What disposed Nixon so positively toward the Bushes? A little-known fact, certainly missing from the many splendid biographies of the thirty-seventh president, is the likely role of Poppy Bush's father, Prescott, in launching Nixon's own political career.

Beyond that, the depth and complexity of the ongoing relationship between Nixon and the Bushes, a relationship that spanned nearly three decades, has somehow eluded most historians. An index search of the name Bush in the major Nixon biographies—including even those published after George H. W. Bush rose to the presidency—finds at most a handful of mentions, and in some cases, none at all.

The long overlooked Nixon-Bush story is a tale filled with plots and counterplots, power lust and ego trips, trust and betrayal, strategic alliances and rude revenge. It has a kind of mythic circularity: the elite Bush clan created the "populist" Nixon so that a President Nixon could later play a major role in creating a Bush political dynasty. And finally, the trusted Bushes, having gotten where they wanted, could play a role in Nixon's fall.

GENERALLY, RICHARD NIXON was known to be a wary and suspicious man. It is commonly assumed that he was paranoid, but Nixon had good reasons to feel apprehensive. One was probably the worry that someone would unearth the extent to which this self-styled outsider from Whittier, California, had sold his soul to the same Eastern Establishment that he publicly (and even privately) reviled. At the same time, he knew that those elites felt the same about him. They tolerated him as long as he was useful, which he was—until he got to the top. Then the trouble started.

Obeisance

When Poppy Bush arrived in Washington after the 1966 elections, he was immediately positioned to help large moneyed interests, and by so doing improve his own political fortunes. His father, still influential, had twisted arms to get him a coveted seat on the House Ways and Means Committee, which writes all tax legislation. The committee was the gatekeeper against attempts to eliminate the oil depletion allowance, and Bush's assignment there was no small feat. No freshman of either party had gotten on since 1904.[2] But former senator Prescott Bush had personally called the committee chairman. Then he got GOP minority leader Gerald Ford—a Warren Commission member and later vice president and president—to make the request himself.[3]

It was a lot of voltage, but the rewards were worth the effort. Poppy now would be a go-to rep for the oil industry, which could provide Nixon with the Texas financial juice he would need to win the Republican nomination in 1968. Bush was also now a crucial link to an alliance that was forming between Eastern bankers, Texas oilmen, and intelligence operatives.

Indeed, Texans and Bush friends dominated the Nixon presidential campaign. For fund-raising, Poppy recruited Bill Liedtke, his old friend and former Zapata Petroleum partner, who became Nixon's highest-producing regional campaign finance chairman. Poppy's ally, Texas senator John Tower, endorsed Nixon shortly before the 1968 GOP convention and was put in charge of Nixon's "key issues committee." Once Nixon's nomination was secured, Poppy and Prescott worked their networks furiously, and within days some of the most influential members of the Republican Party sent letters to Nixon urging him to choose Poppy as his running mate. The names must have given Nixon pause—the CEOs of Chase Manhattan Bank, Tiffany & Co., J. P. Stevens and Co., and on and on. Not surprisingly, executives of Pennzoil and Brown Brothers Harriman were among the petitioners.[4]

Thomas Dewey, éminence grise of the GOP, also pushed for Poppy. Nixon put Bush's name on a short list. But as he glimpsed the prize in the distance, he began to assert his independence. To the surprise of almost everyone, he selected as his running mate Spiro Agnew, Maryland's blunt and combative governor, who had backed Nixon opponent Nelson Rockefeller, the "limousine liberal," in the primaries. Agnew seemed to offer two things. One, he could be the attack dog who enabled Nixon to assume the role of statesman that he craved. And two, there was little chance that he would outshine the insecure man under whom he would be serving. (Poppy Bush would adopt a variation on this same strategy in 1988 when he selected as his running mate Senator Dan Quayle, who was handsome but inexperienced, and would be ridiculed for his gaffes and general awkwardness.)

After Nixon tapped Agnew, Prescott Bush, writing to his old friend Tom Dewey, registered his disappointment in a measured manner: "I fear that Nixon has made a serious error here," Prescott wrote. "He had a chance to do something smart, to give the ticket a lift, and he cast it aside."[5] Actually

Prescott was seething; he hadn't felt this betrayed since John Kennedy fired his friend Allen Dulles as CIA director. As for the Bush children, they had learned years earlier to fear the wrath of their stern, imposing father. "Remember Teddy Roosevelt's 'Speak softly and carry a big stick'?" Poppy once said. "My dad spoke *loudly* and carried the same big stick."[6]

But beyond political expediency, Prescott may have had good reason to expect Nixon to follow "suggestions" from the GOP establishment—a reason rooted in the earliest days of Nixon's political career.

Nixon's Big Break

In Nixon's carefully crafted creation story, his 1945 decision to enter politics was triggered when the young Navy veteran, working on the East Coast, received a request from an old family friend, a hometown banker named Herman Perry. Would he fly back to Los Angeles and speak with a group of local businessmen looking for a candidate to oppose Democratic congressman Jerry Voorhis?[7] They felt he was too liberal, and too close to labor unions.[8]

The businessmen who summoned Nixon are usually characterized as Rotary Club types—a furniture dealer, a bank manager, an auto dealer, a printing salesman. In reality, these men were essentially fronts for far more powerful interests. Principal among Nixon's bigger backers was the arch-conservative Chandler family, owners of the *Los Angeles Times*. Nixon himself acknowledged his debt to the Chandlers in correspondence. "I often said to friends that I would never have gone to Washington in the first place had it not been for the Times," he wrote.[9] Though best known as publishers, the Chandlers had built their fortune on railroads, still the preferred vehicle for shipping oil, and held wide and diverse interests.

Yet Voorhis appears to have recognized that forces even more powerful than the Chandler clan were opposing him. As he wrote in an unpublished manuscript, "The Nixon campaign was a creature of big Eastern financial interests . . . the Bank of America, the big private utilities, the major oil companies." He was hardly a dispassionate observer, but on this point the record bears him out. Nixon partisans would claim that "not a penny" of oil money found its way into his campaign. Perhaps. But a representative of Standard Oil, Willard Larson, was present at that Los Angeles meeting in which Nixon was selected as the favored candidate to run against Voorhis.[10]

Representative Voorhis had caused a stir at the outset of World War II when he exposed a secret government contract that allowed Standard Oil to drill for free on public lands in Central California's Elk Hills. But the establishment's quarrel with Voorhis was about more than oil. While no anticapitalist radical, Voorhis had a deep antipathy for corporate excesses and malfeasance. And he was not afraid of the big guys. He investigated one industry after another—insurance, real estate, investment banking. He fought for antitrust regulation of the insurance industry, and he warned against the "cancerous superstructure of monopolies and cartels."[11] He also was an articulate voice calling for fundamental reforms in banking.

He knew Wall Street was gunning for him. In his memoir, *Confessions of a Congressman*, Voorhis recalled:

> The 12th District campaign of 1946 got started along in the fall of 1945, more than a year before the election. There was, of course, opposition to me in the district. There always had been. Nor was there any valid reason for me to think I lived a charmed political life. But there were special factors in the campaign of 1946, factors bigger and more powerful than either my opponent or myself. And they were on his side.
>
> In October 1945, *the representative of a large New York financial house* [emphasis mine] made a trip to California. All the reasons for his trip I, of course, do not know. But I do know that he called on a number of influential people in Southern California. And I know he "bawled them out." For what? For permitting Jerry Voorhis, whom he described as "one of the most dangerous men in Washington," to continue to represent a part of the state of California in the House of Representatives. This gentleman's reasons for thinking me so "dangerous" obviously had to do with my views and work against monopoly and for changes in the monetary system.[12]

It is not clear whether Voorhis knew the exact identity of the man. Nor is it clear whether Voorhis knew that his nemesis, the Chandler family, had for several years been in business with Dresser Industries. The latter had begun moving into Southern California during the war, snapping up local companies both to secure immediate defense contracts and in anticipation of lucrative postwar opportunities. One of these companies, Pacific Pump

Works, which manufactured water pumps, later produced components for the atomic bomb. The Chandlers were majority shareholders in Pacific Pump when Dresser acquired the company, and so gained a seat on the Dresser board, along with such Dresser stalwarts as Prescott Bush.

But there was even more of a Bush connection to the movers and shakers behind Nixon's entry into politics. In October 1945, the same month in which that "representative of a large New York financial house" was in town searching for a candidate to oppose Voorhis, Dresser Industries was launching a particularly relevant California project. The company was just completing its purchase of yet another local company, the drill bit manufacturer Security Engineering, which was located in Whittier, Nixon's hometown.[13] The combined evidence, both from that period and from the subsequent relationships, suggests that Voorhis's Eastern banking representative may have been none other than Prescott Bush himself. If so, that would explain Nixon's sense of indebtedness to the Bush family, something he never acknowledged in so many words but clearly demonstrated in so many actions during his career.

A Quick but Bumpy Ascent

In his first race for public office in 1946, Nixon went after the incumbent Voorhis with a vengeance. It was a campaign that helped put the term "Red baiting" into the political lexicon. After his victory, Nixon continued to ride the anti-Communist theme to national prominence.

Following two terms in the House, Nixon moved up to the Senate in the 1950 election. By 1952, he was being foisted on a reluctant Dwight Eisenhower as a vice presidential candidate by Wall Street friends and allies of Brown Brothers Harriman.

But the further Nixon rose, the more he resented the arrogance of his Eastern elite handlers. Though he would continue to serve them diligently throughout his career, his anger festered—perhaps in part over frustration with the extent to which he was beholden.

Meanwhile, George H. W. Bush, not yet thirty years old and a relative newcomer to West Texas, was named chair of the Eisenhower-Nixon campaign in Midland County. For someone with political ambitions of his own, it was an enviable assignment, and Poppy threw himself into it. When a heckler interrupted a welcoming ceremony for Eisenhower's vice presidential running mate, Poppy rushed at the man, grabbed his anti-Nixon sign, and tore it to bits.

Nixon himself would demonstrate a more effective response to criticism. His storied "Checkers speech," answering charges that he had accepted political donations under the table, was a masterful appeal to middle-class sensibilities, with a maudlin self-pity that went up to the edge but not over.[14] Telegrams of support came pouring in to Republican headquarters; and one of the first politicians to write was the silver-haired U.S. senator from Connecticut, Prescott Bush:

> No fair-minded person who heard Senator Nixon bare his heart and soul to the American people Tuesday night could fail to hold him in high respect. I have felt all along that the charges against Dick Nixon were a dirty smear attempt to hurt him and the Republican ticket . . . [These smears] will boomerang in his favor. Nixon is absolutely honest, fearless and courageous. I'm proud of him.[15]

Nixon saved his political skin that night, but money problems would continue to plague him. This increased his seething resentment of Jack Kennedy, who never had to grovel for money (and who was smooth and handsome to boot). As anyone who knew Nixon, including the Bushes, must have realized, his dependence on the financial resources of others constituted a vulnerability. That vulnerability would later lead to his undoing. The essence of Nixon's relationship with the Bushes, as with other key backers, was that they had the wherewithal and he didn't. And since money was behind the relationship that made Nixon, it was only fitting that when Watergate undid him, it was to a large extent money—as we shall see in chapters 10 and 11—that was behind his downfall.

Symbiotic Relationship

During the Eisenhower years, the Texas oil industry really took off. Poppy was now part of a "swarm of young Ivy Leaguers," as *Fortune* magazine put it, who had "descended on an isolated west Texas oil town—Midland—and created a most unlikely outpost of the working rich."[16] Central to these ambitions was continued congressional support for the oil depletion allowance, which greatly reduced taxes on income derived from the production of oil. The allowance was first enacted in 1913 as part of the original income tax. At first it was a 5 percent deduction but by 1926 it had grown to 27.5 percent. This was a time when Washington was "wading shoulder-deep in oil," the *New Republic* reported. "In the hotels, on the streets, at the dinner tables, the sole subject of discussion is oil. Congress has abandoned all other business."[17]

Following the discovery of the giant East Texas oil fields in 1931, there was nothing Texas oilmen fought for more vigorously than their depletion allowance.[18] From its inception to the late 1960s, the oil depletion allowance had cost taxpayers an estimated $140 billion in lost revenue.[19] Nixon supported the allowance in 1946, while Voorhis opposed it. Six years later, General Dwight D. Eisenhower supported it, and he got the oilmen's blessings—and substantial contributions as well.[20]

The Bushes backed Nixon passionately in his 1960 presidential campaign against John F. Kennedy. After Nixon lost—and then lost again when he ran for governor of California two years later—the oil lobby began to look for another horse. Poppy Bush saw his opening. He knew which way the political winds were blowing: toward an ultraconservatism based on new wealth, in particular the wealth of independent oilmen.

In 1964 the Bushes gave their support to presidential candidate Barry Goldwater, even though this meant turning against their longtime allies, the Rockefellers. One can only speculate as to their motives, though Prescott Bush's puritanical streak may have played a role. Goldwater's opponent, Nelson Rockefeller, recently divorced, had decided in 1958 to wed Margaretta "Happy" Murphy, an even more recently divorced mother of four. Prescott delivered Rockefeller a public tongue lashing that *Time* called "the most wrathful any politician had suffered in recent memory."[21] This may have been just a convenient target. As political historian Rick Perlstein put it, conservatives genuinely preferred Goldwater, "and welcomed the remarriage as an excuse to cut loose from someone they were never excited about in the first place."[22]

Goldwater's success in snatching the 1964 Republican nomination from Rockefeller changed the ideological dynamics of the Grand Old Party. Even though Goldwater lost the presidential race, the party would never be the same. So-called movement conservatives managed to build an uneasy alliance between social issue ground troops and the corporate libertarians who finance the party. The ever-nimble Bushes managed to straddle both camps.

Political ambition ran in the Bush family. According to his mother, Prescott had wanted to be president and regretted not getting into politics sooner. The lesson was not lost on Poppy. If he wanted to be president, he would have to take the long view and get started early. An alliance with Richard Nixon could be useful. Nixon would vouch for his rightward bona fides, and thereby make moot the patrician residues of Yale that still clung to him.

Nixon Presidency, 1969

As for Nixon, he understood only too well the perils he faced. With his paranoid tendencies, he worried constantly about where the next challenge would come from. Robert Dallek's biography *Nixon and Kissinger: Partners in Power* describes Nixon as "an introspective man whose inner demons both lifted him up and brought him down." When he looked at George Bush—a handsome, patrician Yale man with no worries about money—he likely saw another version of Jack Kennedy, which for him was not a recommendation.

But people were nagging Nixon, people he couldn't ignore—all the more so once he locked up the nomination in 1968. "As your finance chairman in Texas," wrote Bill Liedtke, "I am committed, and will back you up whatever you decide [about a running mate]. However . . . George Bush, in spite of his short service in the House, could help you win. George has appeal to young people and can get them fired up. He's got plenty of energy. Lastly, Dick, he's a loyal kind of guy and would support you to the hilt."[23]

Instead Nixon chose a running mate who was less capable and ambitious, and consequentially, less threatening. Having angered both Prescott and Poppy with his choice of Agnew, he knew that he would need to make amends to them and their allies.

Outside the small circle of longtime Nixon loyalists, the Bush group seems to have fared better than any other party faction in Nixon's first administration. Bill Clements, Poppy's friend and sometime oil drilling partner, became deputy secretary of defense, a position that involved securing oil for the U.S. military.[24] Bush's ex-business partner Bill Liedtke of Pennzoil (formerly Zapata Petroleum), the prodigious Nixon fund-raiser, successfully recommended former Baker Botts lawyers for positions on the Federal Power Commission.[25] The FPC made crucial decisions affecting the natural gas industry, including one that directly benefited Pennzoil.[26]

For his chief political adviser, Nixon chose Harry S. Dent of South Carolina, the architect of his "Southern strategy," which had centered on wooing conservative Democrats to the Republican cause. Poppy Bush's election from Texas's Seventh Congressional District had benefited greatly from this strategy. As his top aide, Dent chose Tom Lias, who had run the candidate selection process for the Republican Congressional Campaign Committee during that election cycle. These men, especially Lias, are little known today. But they would play crucial roles in the process that would lead ultimately to Nixon's resignation.

Meanwhile, to head the Republican National Committee (RNC), Nixon picked Rogers Morton, a congressman from Kentucky, who had been his convention floor manager. Morton, a Yale graduate, was an old friend of the Bushes who had served with Poppy on the Ways and Means Committee.[27] Morton in turn named as his deputy chairman Jimmy Allison, Poppy's longtime friend, administrative assistant, and former campaign manager. Because at the time the RNC chairmanship was a part-time position and Morton was busy on Capitol Hill, Allison was the de facto day-to-day manager of the Republican Party. This was a huge step up for Allison, and quite a triumph for the Bushes. In a phrase, they had the place wired.

Once in the Oval Office, some presidents have warmed to the public aspects of their role. FDR, Kennedy, Reagan, and Clinton come to mind. Others retreat into a kind of self-imposed exile. They cut themselves off from outside advice and effectively hunker down against attack. That was the case with Nixon, whose reclusive tendencies were abetted by his national security adviser, Henry Kissinger.

As a longtime protégé of the Rockefeller family, Kissinger was suspect on both the left and right. Movement conservatives in particular feared that the Rockefellers had a grand global design that included accommodation, rather than confrontation, with the Russians and Chinese. Nixon would become embroiled in this growing dispute within the Republican Party, between the two factions known as the "traders" and the "warriors."

The traders were the Eastern Establishment internationalists who supported free trade, arguing that it would prevent another world war. They generally had a sense of noblesse oblige that translated into the "corporate liberalism" of a Nelson Rockefeller, then New York governor, who believed that ameliorative social programs for the needy were the price of a healthy business climate. The warriors, on the other hand, generally represented new money from the Southwest and Southern California. Although they lacked experience in foreign policy, they resented having to take backseats to their Eastern rivals, especially when it came to the increasingly important task of securing oil and mineral resources in such places as Southeast Asia.

Personally, Nixon felt more comfortable with the warriors. But especially in his first term, he worked to accommodate both sides, while he and Kissinger fashioned foreign policy themselves, in a way that bypassed the Pentagon, the CIA, and even the State Department. He wasn't about to let the "the striped-pants faggots on Foggy Bottom" tell him what to do, he said, and that included the Yalies at the CIA.[28] As his secretary of state Nixon chose his old friend William Rogers, with whom he had worked on the Alger Hiss spy case. Rogers knew little about foreign policy, but Nixon considered that a good thing, because Rogers would keep quiet and do as he was told. "Few Secretaries of State can have been selected because of their President's confidence in their ignorance of foreign policy," Kissinger wryly observed.[29]

However, this determined effort to conduct foreign policy in secret and exclude the entities normally charged with that function caused growing alarm, particularly within the military and the defense industry.[30] Eventually, the Nixon administration would discover that the military had its own powerful "back channel." That apparatus, little recalled today, was the equivalent of a spy ring inside the Nixon White House. Its operatives passed top-secret documents from the National Security Council to the Joint Chiefs of Staff without Nixon's knowledge. On discovering what seemed to him not only disloyalty but also borderline treason, Nixon expressed his fury to aides, who convinced him that the only option was to handle the matter quietly.[31]

The First Challenge

Despite his earlier attempts to keep the peace among the party's factions, Nixon was soon embroiled in a series of power struggles. Perhaps the most important concerned the oil depletion allowance, as members of Congress in 1969 launched new attempts to rein in the costly giveaway. Representative George H. W. Bush was the industry's Horatio at the bridge—or perhaps its George Wallace. "In an era when civil rights became the great moral issue that galvanized liberals," observed Bush biographer Herbert S. Parmet, "the targeted oil depletion allowance was not far behind."[32]

Poppy had barely completed his first term in the House. But he had an urgent task. President Nixon was under pressure to support a reduction in the depletion allowance, and some signals were emerging from the administration that he might do just that. Poppy, joined by Senator Tower, flew to Nixon's vacation home in California to help save the day. The trip was apparently a success. Nixon affirmed his intention to block the reform efforts.[33] Bush later wrote Nixon's treasury secretary, David Kennedy, to thank him for reversing an earlier statement hinting that the White House might cave in to popular pressure for reform, adding: "I was also appreciative of your telling how I bled and died for the oil industry."[34]

The moment passed, but protecting the allowance remained uppermost in the minds of independent oilmen—and Nixon was not proving sufficiently stalwart on the matter. The White House sent political operative Jack Gleason out to West Texas to calm flaring tempers. "Harry [Dent] sent me down to Midland, to the Midland Petroleum Club, to talk to them about the depletion allowance," Gleason told me in a 2008 interview.[35] Gleason had trouble understanding the complex issue, so he was not clear on precisely what the oilmen were mad about. "Almost got lynched and run out of town . . . It was a very ugly scene. Fortunately one guy . . . saved my ass, or otherwise I'd still be buried somewhere at the Petroleum Club."

A battle to control the soul of the president, not unusual in any administration, was under way. While the conservative, hawkish independent oilmen thought he was insufficiently loyal to their cause, the Rockefeller Republicans felt the same from their side. Writing in the *Dallas Morning News*, Robert Baskin noted fears among the Eastern corporate elite that Nixon was being dominated by the right wing.[36] A few months later Baskin further underlined the point in an article headlined "Divisiveness Within GOP Rising." In truth, Nixon's reign was a highly complicated one, far from doctrinaire, with issues handled on a case-by-case basis. Thus, Attorney General John Mitchell could say the administration was against busing but for desegregation. Nixon himself could complain about people in his administration being too tough on corporations, yet his Justice Department aggressively pursued antitrust actions that angered industry. While waging the Vietnam War, Nixon held secret peace talks with the North Vietnamese Communists. He also produced a series of liberal-leaning reforms, including creating the Environmental Protection Agency and the Occupational Safety and Health Administration. And Nixon implemented the first major affirmative action program. But some of his Supreme Court nominees leaned far to the right, and Nixon and his attorney general championed tough law-and-order tactics against political protesters and dissidents.[37] His presidency was a mixed bag, meaning no one was entirely happy, and everyone perceived someone else as having the inside track.

Thus, the July 1969 *Dallas Morning News* article describing moderates as fearful of the influence of a cabal of conservatives—a cabal that included such names as Tower, Morton, Dent, and Allison. What was left unsaid was that all these people were in the Bush camp. If nothing else, it was a testament to Poppy's dexterity: the embodiment of blue-blooded Wall Street interests had morphed into a champion of the radical, upstart Southwest.

Bush's Run for the Money: The 1970 Campaign

As early as the 1968 GOP convention, Nixon had tried to keep the Bush family close but not too close. He assured Poppy that he would support him in another Senate bid, and Poppy took that seriously. By January 1969, even before Nixon's inauguration, Poppy's administrative aide Jimmy Allison was back in Houston to lay the groundwork for another campaign. (After several months in Houston, Allison would return to D.C. as deputy director of the Republican Party.) There was no mistaking Poppy's ultimate goal, though—and "ultimate" in Poppy's mind did not mean that far in the future. As his brother Jonathan commented, "It was a long shot but he wanted to get into position to run for President."[38]

Nixon's support for Poppy's Senate bid made sense strategically for the Republicans, and besides, he had little choice. As congressman, Bush had supported him unfailingly, backing even the president's most unpopular policies, from the continuation of the Vietnam War to the Supreme Court nomination of Judge G. Harrold Carswell, a purported racist.

Nixon knew that in running for the Senate, Bush risked giving up a safe House seat and his powerful position on the Ways and Means Committee, which was so crucial to the oil industry. To sweeten the pot, Nixon told Poppy that if he won, he'd be in the running for the VP slot in 1972, replacing Agnew; if Bush lost, Nixon would try to find him a desirable cabinet position.[39]

Bush's prospects seemed bright in 1970. His presumptive Democratic opponent, Senator Ralph Yarborough, was an unreconstructed liberal populist in an increasingly conservative, buttoned-down state. Then disaster struck. Former congressman Lloyd Bentsen Jr. entered the Democratic primary—and he was even more conservative than Bush. In a summer

1970 newspaper column, Bush family friend William F. Buckley lamented Bentsen's entry, praised Bush as "genuinely talented on the platform and in the ways of the world," and quoted Rogers Morton that Poppy was the only one of his generation of GOP figures who could "go all the way to the top."

Bush raised enormous amounts of money and campaigned relentlessly. But for a second time he fell short. This was particularly hard for the competitive Poppy, whose father had become U.S. senator from Connecticut without even bothering to run for the House. He was disconsolate and confessed to his old friend Robert Mosbacher, "I feel like Custer."[40]

President Nixon offered pro forma condolences. "I am sure . . . that you will not allow this defeat to discourage you in your efforts to continue to provide leadership for our party and the nation," he wrote in a cable on November 5, 1970, right after the election.[41]

Bush waited for a more tangible form of consolation, and then waited some more. When a friend tipped him off that Treasury Secretary David Kennedy was leaving, Bush called Nixon and made a modest pitch for a job—not of secretary but of *undersecretary*.[42] Poppy knew too little about finance to assume the top post. Besides, it was the undersecretary who dealt specifically with issues of concern to oil interests.

Nixon's response came as a shock. His new treasury secretary would be John Connally, the Texas governor and conservative Democrat who had just helped defeat Bush by throwing his weight behind Lloyd Bentsen. Connally would most certainly not want Bush on his staff—not that Bush would have wanted to serve under him anyway. And even if Connally had been willing, it was unlikely that Nixon would okay having two Texans in top Treasury Department posts. For Nixon's part, he wanted at least one Democrat in his cabinet, to create a perception of bipartisanship, and also help his Southern strategy in the 1972 campaign. He also greatly admired the confident, handsome Connally. But the move must have raised suspicions in Bush's mind about which candidate Nixon really had wanted to win the Texas Senate race.

Bush's suspicions were on target. It would subsequently be shown that Nixon often secretly backed conservative Democrats, especially Southern hard-liners like Senator James Eastland of Mississippi, who would support his policies while staying out of Republican internecine squabbling.[43]

Now, with the Connally business, Bush was livid. This is what he got for his loyalty to Nixon? John Tower put it this way: "He was out of work, and he wanted a job. As a defeated senatorial candidate, he hoped and fully expected to get a major job in the Administration. Yet the Administration seemed to be paying more attention to the very Democrat who had put him on the job market. What gives?"[44]

It was the kind of political snub that could not—and perhaps would not—be easily forgotten. Nixon had already disappointed Poppy by choosing Spiro Agnew over him as a running mate. Now this.

But Poppy was nothing if not resilient. Once again, he suggested a job to Nixon: ambassador to the United Nations. The case he made shows a keen grasp of Nixon's neurosis and class envy, and a willingness to exploit it. There was a "dirth [sic] of Nixon advocacy in New York City," where the U.N. was based, Bush wrote the president, noting that he was well suited to "fill that need in New York social circles."[45]

Nixon complied. Parmet described the meeting where the matter was settled:

> Bush did most of the talking. He told the president that he pre-
> ferred going to New York as ambassador to the United Nations . . .
> He and Barbara could . . . become invaluable . . . Nothing in the
> record of the session indicates any discussion of global factors, or,
> for that matter, US relationships with that world body.[46]

The inexperienced Poppy was again being offered something for which he was ill-prepared—an important diplomatic post at a time of global turmoil. Among the hot-button issues on which he was expected to hold forth were the China-Taiwan dispute, Vietnam, and the Middle East conflict. Some of his closest friends were astonished. Congressman Lud Ashley, an old chum from his Skull and Bones days, put it this way: "George, what the fuck do you know about world affairs?" To which Poppy replied, "You ask me that in ten days."[47]

In private, neither Nixon nor his top adviser on foreign affairs, Henry Kissinger, thought much of Bush's capacities. On April 27, 1971, several months after Poppy's appointment, Nixon raised the possibility of sending Poppy on a secret diplomatic mission to China.

PRESIDENT NIXON: How about [UN Ambassador George H.W.] Bush?

KISSINGER: Absolutely not, he is too soft and not sophisticated enough.

PRESIDENT NIXON: I thought of that myself.[48]

In a 1992 letter to Herbert Parmet, Nixon claimed that he had made the U.N. appointment because Bush "not only had the diplomatic skills to be an effective ambassador, but also because it would be helpful to him in the future to have this significant foreign-policy experience."[49] Although Bush was an amiable fellow, it is a stretch to believe that either the first or the second part of that statement fully conveyed Nixon's true motives. But one thing was clear: Nixon did not feel he could leave Poppy entirely out in the cold.

Not only did Nixon appoint Poppy to the U.N.; he also upgraded the post to that of full ambassador, a title previously conferred only upon envoys to foreign states. He even made Bush a member of his cabinet. This was most unusual, but it put Bush in a unique position: although he traveled to Washington regularly for cabinet meetings, he was "a Washington outsider" by dint of his being based in New York. Whatever Nixon's ultimate purpose in continuing to mollify him, these decisions clearly worked to Poppy's advantage. When the Watergate scandal erupted, nobody thought to include George H. W. Bush in the circle of blame. He was literally out of sight, out of mind. But not necessarily out of the loop.

CHAPTER 10

Downing Nixon, Part I: The Setup

Who Will Rid Me of This Troublesome Priest?
—ASCRIBED TO HENRY II

O N JUNE 17, 1972, A GROUP OF BURGLARS, carrying electronic surveillance equipment, was arrested inside the Democratic National Committee offices at 2650 Virginia Avenue, NW, in Washington, D.C., the Watergate building complex. The men were quickly identified as having ties to the Nixon reelection campaign and to the White House.

Though at the time the incident got little attention, it would snowball into one of the biggest crises in American political history, define Richard Nixon forever, and drive him out of the White House.

Most historical accounts judge Nixon responsible in some way for the Watergate burglary—or at least for an effort to cover it up. And many people believe Nixon got what he deserved.

But like other epic events, Watergate turns out to be an entirely different story than the one we thought we knew.

Hanky-Panky, Cuban-Style

Almost no one has better expressed reasons to doubt Nixon's involvement than Nixon himself. In his memoirs, Nixon described how he learned about the burglary while vacationing in Florida, from the morning newspaper. He recalled his reaction at the time:

> It sounded preposterous. Cubans in surgical gloves bugging the
> DNC! I dismissed it as some sort of prank . . . The whole thing

made so little sense. Why, I wondered. Why then? Why in such a blundering way ... Anyone who knew anything about politics would know that a national committee headquarters was a useless place to go for inside information on a presidential campaign. The whole thing was so senseless and bungled that it almost looked like some kind of a setup.[1]

Nixon was actually suggesting not just a setup, but one intended to harm *him.*

Perhaps because anything he might say would seem transparently self-serving, this claim received little attention and has been largely forgotten.

NOTWITHSTANDING NIXON'S INITIAL reaction to the news of the break-in, less than a week later he suddenly learned more—and this gave him much to ponder.

On June 23, Nixon's chief of staff, H. R. "Bob" Haldeman, came into the Oval Office to give the president an update on a variety of topics, including the investigation of the break-in. Haldeman had just been briefed by John Dean, who had gotten his information from FBI investigators.

> HALDEMAN: ... The FBI agents who are working the case, at this point, feel that's what it is. This is CIA. ...

Nixon's response would show that he had already realized this:

> NIXON: Of course, this is a, this is a [E. Howard] Hunt [operation, and exposure of it] will uncover a lot of things. You open that scab there's a hell of a lot of things and that we just feel that it would be very detrimental to have this thing go any further. This involves these Cubans, Hunt, and a lot of hanky-panky that we have nothing to do with ourselves ... This will open the whole Bay of Pigs thing ...

Of course, it is important to remember that Nixon knew every word he uttered was being recorded. Like his predecessors Kennedy and Johnson, he had decided to install a taping system so that he could maintain a record of his administration. He was, in a way, dictating a file memo for future historians.

But that doesn't make everything he said untrue. While Nixon undoubtedly spun some things, he still had to communicate with his subordinates, and the tape was rolling while he was trying to run the country. Those were actual meetings and real conversations, tape or no tape. And though the result was 3,700 hours of White House tape recordings, Nixon evinced merely sporadic consciousness of the fact that the tape was rolling. Only after his counsel John Dean defected to the prosecutors did Nixon appear to be tailoring his words.

Nixon's memoirs, combined with the tape of June 23, make clear that Nixon recognized certain things about the implementation of the burglary. The caper was carried out by pros, yet paradoxically was amateurish, easily detected—an instigation of the crime more easily pinned on someone else. A break-in at Democratic Party headquarters: On whom would that be blamed? Well, who was running against a Democrat for reelection that fall? Why, Richard Nixon of course. Nixon, who frequently exhibited a grim and self-pitying awareness of how he generally was portrayed, might have grasped how this would play out publicly. Dick Nixon: ruthless, paranoid, vengeful—*Tricky Dick*. Wouldn't this burglary be just the kind of thing that *that* Dick Nixon—the "liberal media's" version of him—would do? Nixon's opponent, George McGovern, made this charge repeatedly during the 1972 campaign.

Though Nixon would sweep the election, it would become increasingly apparent to him that, where Watergate was concerned, the jury was stacked. The path was set. Someone had him in a corner.

But who?

Many people, including those within Nixon's own base of support, were not happy with him—even from early in his administration. As Haldeman noted in his diary, one month after the inauguration in 1969:

> Also got cranking on the political problem. [President's] obviously concerned about reports (especially Buchanan's) that conservatives and the South are unhappy. Also he's annoyed by constant right-wing bitching, with never a positive alternative. Ordered me to assemble a political group and really hit them to start defending us, including Buchanan . . . [and political specialist Harry] Dent.[2]

There would be growing anger in the Pentagon about Nixon and Kissinger's secret attempts to secure agreements with China and the Soviet Union without consulting the military. And there were the oilmen, who found Nixon wasn't solid enough on their most basic concerns, such as the oil depletion allowance and oil import quotas.

As for the burglary crew, Nixon recognized them instantly, because he knew what they represented. While serving as vice president, Nixon had overseen some covert operations and served as the "action officer" for the planning of the Bay of Pigs, of which these men were hard-boiled veterans.[3] They had been out to overthrow Fidel Castro, and if possible, to kill him.

Nixon had another problem. These pros were connected to the CIA, and as we shall see, Nixon was not getting along well with the agency.

ONE OF THE main reasons we fundamentally misunderstand Watergate is that the guardians of the historical record focused only on selected parts of Nixon's taped conversations, out of context. Consider a widely cited portion of a June 23 meeting tape, which would become known forever as the "smoking gun" conversation:

> HALDEMAN: The way to handle this now is for us to have [CIA
>   deputy director Vernon] Walters call [FBI interim director] Pat
>   Gray and just say, "Stay the hell out of this . . . this is ah, busi-
>   ness here we don't want you to go any further on it."
> NIXON: Um hum.

Short excerpts like this seem especially damning. This one sounds right off the bat like a cover-up—Nixon using the CIA to suppress an FBI investigation into the break-in.

But these utterances take on a different meaning when considered with other, less publicized parts of the same conversation. A prime example: Haldeman went on to tell Nixon that Pat Gray, the acting FBI director, had called CIA director Richard Helms and said, "I think we've run right into the middle of a CIA covert operation."

Although the first excerpt above sounds like a discussion of a cover-up, when we consider the information about the CIA involvement, it begins to seem as if Nixon is not colluding. He may well have been refusing to take the rap for something he had not authorized—and certainly not for something that smelled so blatantly like a trap. Nixon would have understood that if the FBI were to conduct a full investigation and conclude that the break-in was indeed an illegal operation of the CIA, it would all be blamed squarely on the man who supposedly had ultimate authority over both agencies—him. And doubly so, since between the burglars and their supervisors were ties not just to the CIA but also directly back to Nixon's reelection committee and the White House itself.

Yet, however concerned Nixon certainly must have been at this moment, he played it cool. He concurred with the advice that his chief of staff was passing along from the counsel John Dean, which was to press the CIA to clean up its own mess.

If the CIA was involved, then the agency would have to ask the FBI to back off. The CIA itself would have to invoke its perennial escape clause— say that national security was at stake.

This must have sounded to Nixon like the best way to deal with a vexing and shadowy situation. He had no way of knowing that, two years later, his conversation with Haldeman would be publicly revealed and construed as that of a man in control of a plot, rather than the target of one.

Sniffing Around the Bay of Pigs

How could Nixon have so quickly gotten a fix on the Watergate crew? He might have recognized that the involvement of this particular group of Cubans, together with E. Howard Hunt—and the evidence tying them back to the White House—was in part a message to him. One of the group leaders, G. Gordon Liddy, would even refer to the team as a bunch of "professional killers." Indeed, several of this Bay of Pigs circle had gone to Vietnam to participate in the assassination-oriented Phoenix Program; as noted in chapter 7, Poppy Bush and his colleague, CIA operative Thomas Devine, had been in Vietnam at the peak of Phoenix, and Bush had ties to at least some from this émigré group.

So Nixon recognized this tough gang, but this time, they weren't focused on Fidel Castro; they were focused on Dick Nixon.

Hunt was a familiar figure from the CIA old guard. A near contemporary of Poppy Bush's at Yale, Hunt had, as noted in earlier chapters, gone on to star in numerous agency foreign coup operations, including in Guatemala. He had worked closely with Cuban émigrés and had been in sensitive positions at the time John F. Kennedy was murdered and Lee Harvey Oswald named the lone assassin. Moreover, Hunt had been a staunch loyalist of Allen Dulles, whom Kennedy had ousted over the failed Bay of Pigs invasion; he allegedly even collaborated on Dulles's 1963 book, *The Craft of Intelligence*.[4] Hunt was one connected fellow, and his presence in an operation of this sort, particularly with veterans of the Cuba invasion, was not something to pass over lightly.

Nixon had further basis for viewing the events of Watergate with special trepidation. From the moment he entered office until the day, five and a half years later, when he was forced to resign, Nixon and the CIA had been at war. Over what? Over records dating back to the Kennedy administration and even earlier.

Nixon had many reasons to be interested in the events of the early 1960s. As noted, he had been the "action officer" for the planning of the Bay of Pigs and the attempt to overthrow Castro. But even more interestingly, Nixon had, by coincidence, been in Dallas on November 22, 1963, and had left the city just hours before the man he barely lost to in 1960 had been gunned down.

FIVE YEARS AFTER the Kennedy assassination, as Richard Nixon himself assumed the presidency, one of his first and keenest instincts was to try to learn more about these monumental events of the past decade.

Both of Nixon's chief aides, Bob Haldeman and John Ehrlichman, noted in their memoirs that the president seemed obsessed with what he called the "Bay of Pigs thing." Both were convinced that when Nixon used the phrase, it was shorthand for something bigger and more disturbing. Nixon did not tell even those closest to him what he meant.

When Nixon referred to the Bay of Pigs, he could certainly have been using it as a euphemism, because any way one thought about it, it spelled trouble. The Bay of Pigs invasion itself had been a kind of setup of another president. JFK had made clear that he would not allow U.S. military forces to be used against Castro. When the invasion by U.S.-backed Cuban exiles failed, the CIA and the U.S. military hoped this would force Kennedy to launch an all-out invasion. Instead, he balked, and blamed Dulles and his associates for the botched enterprise, and, to their astonishment, forced them out of the agency. As noted in chapter 4, these were the roots of the hatred felt by Hunt, Dulles, and the Bush family toward Kennedy.

Nixon was keenly aware that Kennedy's battle with powerful internal elements had preceded JFK's demise. After all, governments everywhere have historically faced the reality that the apparatus of state security might have the chief of state in its gun sights—and that it certainly possesses the ability to act.

Moreover, Richard Nixon was a curious fellow. Within days of taking office in 1969, Nixon had begun conducting an investigation of his own regarding the turbulent and little-understood days leading up to the end of the Kennedy administration. He had ordered Ehrlichman, the White House counsel, to instruct CIA director Helms to hand over the relevant files, which surely amounted to thousands and thousands of documents. Six months later, Ehrlichman confided to Haldeman that the agency had failed to produce any of the files.

"Those bastards in Langley are holding back something," a frustrated Ehrlichman told Haldeman. "They just dig their heels in and say the President can't have it. Period. Imagine that. The Commander-in-Chief wants to see a document and the spooks say he can't have it . . . From the way they're protecting it, it must be pure dynamite."[5]

Nixon himself then summoned Helms, who also refused to help. Helms would later recall that Nixon "asked me for some information about the Bay of Pigs and I think about the Diem episode in Vietnam and maybe something about Trujillo in the Dominican Republic"—all events involving the violent removal of foreign heads of state.[6]

Fidel Castro had managed to survive not only the Bay of Pigs but also multiple later assassination attempts. Diem and Trujillo were not so fortunate. And President Kennedy, who made a lot of Cuban enemies after the botched Bay of Pigs operations, had also succumbed to an assassin's bullet. This was a legacy that might well seize the attention of one of Kennedy's successors.

The explosiveness of the mysterious "Bay of Pigs thing" became abundantly apparent on June 23, 1972, the day Nixon instructed Haldeman to tell CIA director Helms to rein in the FBI's Watergate investigation. Recalled Haldeman:

> Then I played Nixon's trump card. "The President asked me to tell you this entire affair may be connected to the Bay of Pigs, and if it opens up, the Bay of Pigs might be blown . . ."

Turmoil in the room, Helms gripping the arms of his chair, leaning forward and shouting, "The Bay of Pigs had nothing to do with this. I have no concern about the Bay of Pigs." . . . I was absolutely shocked by Helms' violent reaction. Again I wondered, *what was such dynamite* in the Bay of Pigs story?[7]

Nixon made clear to his top aides that he was not only obsessed with the CIA's murky past, but also its present. He seemed downright paranoid about the agency, periodically suggesting to his aides that covert operatives lurked everywhere. And indeed, as we shall see, they did.

In all likelihood, the practice of filling the White House with intelligence operatives was not limited to the Nixon administration, but an ongoing effort. To the intelligence community, the White House was no different than other civil institutions it actively penetrated. Presidents were viewed less as elected leaders to be served than as temporary occupants to be closely monitored, subtly guided, and where necessary, given a shove.

If the CIA was in fact trying to implicate Nixon in Watergate (and, as we shall see, in other illegal and troubling covert operations), the goal might have been to create the impression that the agency was joined at the hip with Nixon in all things. Then, if Nixon were to pursue the CIA's possible role in the assassination of Kennedy, the agency could simply claim that Nixon himself knew about these illegal acts, or was somehow complicit in them.

A Little Exposure Never Hurts

Something had been gnawing at Nixon since November 22, 1963. Why had he ended up in Dallas the very day the man who he believed had stolen the presidency from him was shot? Nixon had been asked to go there just a few weeks before, for the rather banal purpose of an appearance at a Pepsi-Cola corporate meeting—coinciding with a national soda pop bottlers' convention. The potential implications could not have been lost on this most shrewd and suspicious man.

Nixon was no shrinking violet in Dallas. He called a press conference in his hotel suite on November 21, the day before Kennedy's murder, criticizing Kennedy's policies on civil rights and foreign relations but also urging Texans to show courtesy to the president during his visit.

More significantly, he declared his belief that Kennedy was going to re-place Vice President Johnson with a new running mate in 1964. This was an especially incendiary thing to say, since the whole reason for Kennedy's visit was to cement his links to Texas Democrats, help bridge a gap between the populist and conservative wings of the state party, and highlight his part-nership with Johnson. Nixon's comment was hot enough that it gained a place in the early edition of the November 22 *Dallas Morning News*, under the headline "Nixon Predicts JFK May Drop Johnson."[8]

This was likely to get the attention of Johnson, who would be in the mo-torcade that day—and of conservatives generally, the bottlers included, whom Johnson had addressed as keynote speaker at their convention earlier in the week.

Nixon had finished his business and left the city by 9:05 on the morning of the twenty-second, several hours before Kennedy was shot. He learned of the event on his arrival back in New York City. Like most people, he no doubt was shocked and perhaps a bit alarmed. Many people, Nixon in-cluded, believed that Kennedy had stolen the presidential election in 1960 by fixing vote counts in Texas and Illinois.

At the very least, the appearance of Nixon's November 21 press confer-ence remarks in the newspaper just hours before Kennedy's death was a stark reminder of the large and diverse group of enemies, in and out of pol-itics, that JFK had accumulated.

Certainly, Nixon himself was sensitive to the notion that his appearance in Dallas had somehow contributed to Kennedy's bloody fate. According to one account, Nixon learned of the assassination while in a taxi cab en route from the airport. He claimed at the time and in his memoirs that he was calm, but his adviser Stephen Hess remembered it differently. Hess was the first person in Nixon's circle to see him that day in New York, and he re-called that "his reaction appeared to me to be, 'There but for the Grace of God go I.' He was very shaken."[9]

As Hess later told political reporter Jules Witcover: "He had the morning paper, which he made a great effort to show me, reporting he had held a press conference in Dallas and made a statement that you can disagree with a person without being discourteous to him or interfering with him. He tried to make the point that he had tried to prevent it . . . It was his way of saying, 'Look, I didn't fuel this thing.' "[10]

Nixon's presence in Dallas on November 22, 1963, along with LBJ's—and Poppy Bush's quieter presence on the periphery—created a rather remarkable situation. Three future presidents of the United States were all present in a single American city on the day when their predecessor was assassinated there. Within days, a fourth—Gerald Ford—would be asked by LBJ to join the Warren Commission investigating the event.

Bottled Up

Nixon's unfortunate timing resulted from a series of events that seem, in retrospect, almost to have benefited from a guiding hand. In mid-1963, friends had persuaded him that his long-term prospects required a move from California, where he had lost the 1962 race for the governorship. Now that he was a two-time loser, Nixon's best hope, they counseled, was to find a position in New York that would pay him handsomely, and let him politick and keep himself in the public eye. His friend Donald Kendall, the longtime head of Pepsi's international operations, offered to make him chairman of the international division.[11] But the consensus was that a law firm job would suit him better, so he joined the firm of Mudge, Stern, Baldwin, and Todd. Kendall sweetened the deal by throwing the law firm Pepsi's lucrative legal business. In September, Kendall himself was promoted to head the entire Pepsi company.

On November 1, President Ngo Dinh Diem of South Vietnam, a corrupt anti-Communist, was overthrown and assassinated. On November 7, Nixon wrote to GOP strategist Robert Humphreys, expressing outrage over Diem's death and blaming the Kennedy administration. "Our heavy-handed complicity in his murder can only have the effect of striking terror in the hearts of leaders of other nations who presumably are our friends."[12]

Historians disagree on what exactly Kennedy knew about Diem's death, though Kennedy registered shock at the news—just as he had when Patrice Lumumba, the Congolese independence leader, was assassinated in 1961. Kennedy realized that he could be blamed. Later on, it would be established by the Senate Intelligence Committee that the CIA had been attempting to kill Lumumba.

Also of interest is a little-noticed comment made by President Lyndon Johnson in 1966, caught by his own recording equipment, in which he declared about Diem: "We killed him. We all got together and got a goddamn bunch of thugs and assassinated him."[13] It is not clear whom he meant by "we."

Kendall asked Nixon to accompany him to Dallas for the Pepsi corporate gathering coinciding with the bottlers' convention in late November. The convention was an important annual event for Pepsi, and so would have been on Kendall's schedule for a while, though the necessity of Nixon's presence is less apparent. And with LBJ as keynote speaker, and appearances by Miss USA, Yogi Berra, and Joan Crawford, Nixon, the two-time loser, did not even appear at the convention.

For his part, Nixon seems to have agreed to go because it was an opportunity to share the limelight surrounding Kennedy's visit. And since Nixon was traveling as a representative of Pepsi, and flying on its corporate plane—something noted in the news coverage—Kendall was getting double duty out of Nixon's play for media attention. That was something Kendall understood well.

Donald Kendall was, like Nixon and Poppy Bush, a World War II Navy vet who had served in the Pacific. But instead of politics, he had gone into the business world, joining the Pepsi-Cola company and rising quickly through the ranks. Like Nixon and Bush, he was enormously ambitious. And in his oversight of Pepsi operations abroad, he also shared something else with them: a deep concern about Communist encroachment—which was just about everywhere. Plus Kendall had a passion for covert operations.

Kendall's particular reason for being interested in Cuba was sugar, for many years a key ingredient of Pepsi-Cola. Cuba was the world's leading supplier; and Castro's expropriations, and the resulting U.S. embargo, had caused chaos in the soft drink industry. (It also had affected the fortunes of Wall Street firms such as Brown Brothers Harriman, which, as noted in chapter 3, had extensive sugar holdings on the island.)

Indeed, articles from the Dallas papers anticipating the bottlers' convention talked openly about all these problems with Cuba. One of the articles, titled "Little Relief Seen for Sugar Problem," explains the pressure felt by soft drink bottlers in light of a crisis concerning high sugar prices. The president of a major New York–based sugar company is quoted explaining why the crisis had not yet been averted: "The government probably thought the Castro regime might be eliminated."[14]

It is in this context that we consider a June 1963 letter from Nixon to Kendall, then still running Pepsi's foreign operations. A researcher working for me found it in Nixon's presidential library archives; it appears to be previously unpublished.

Dear Don:

In view of our discussion yesterday morning with regard to Cuba, I thought you might like to see a copy of the speech I made before the American Society of Newspaper Editors in which I directed remarks toward this problem.

When I return from Europe I am looking forward to having a chance to get a further fill-in with regard to your experiences on the Bay of Pigs incident.

Dick

The letter rings a little odd. Nixon and Kendall were close, and more than two years had passed since the Bay of Pigs; it was unlikely that this would be the first chance Nixon got to discuss the subject with his friend. Furthermore, Kendall is not known to have had any "experiences" in relation to the invasion. In a 2008 interview, Kendall, by then eighty-seven years old but still maintaining an office at Pepsi and seeming vigorous, said that he could not recall the letter nor provide an explanation for it.

Given this, the use of the phrase in the letter appears to be some form of euphemism between friends, a sort of discreet wink. Nixon, the former coordinator of covert operations under Ike, clearly knew that Kendall was more than a soda pop man. Nixon's experiences representing Pepsi instilled in him a lasting—and not altogether favorable—impression of what he acidly termed "the sugar lobby." Haldeman got the message that treading carefully was wise. Some of his notes are intriguing in this respect. He urges special counsel Charles Colson:

0900 Cols[on]—re idea of getting pol. commitments—
Sugar people are richest & most ruthless
before we commit—shld put screws on
& get quid pro quo
ie Fl[anigan]—always go to Sugar lobby or oil etc.
before we give them anything[15]

The CIA also knew the soft drink industry well. The agency used bottling plants, including those run by Pepsi, Coca-Cola, and other companies, for both cover and intelligence. Moreover, the local bottling franchises tended to be given to crucial figures in each country, with ties to the military and the ruling elites. It was not just bottlers that played such a role; there were marketing monopolies for all kinds of products, from cars to sewing machines, given out on recommendations of the CIA.

Kendall was a close friend of the Bush family and a fellow resident of Greenwich, Connecticut. In 1988, he would serve in the crucial position of finance chairman for Poppy Bush's successful run for the presidency. His support for the Bushes included donating to George W. Bush's 1978 Midland congressional campaign.

And as noted by the *New York Times*, Kendall was identified with the successful effort to overthrow the elected democratic socialist president of Chile, Salvador Allende.[16]

As the *Times* would report in July 1976:

> One of Mr. Kendall's great passions is international trade, and his interest in foreign affairs won him a footnote in a 1975 interim report of a Senate Select Committee. The report was called "Alleged Assassination Plots Involving Foreign Leaders," and discussed in part the assassination of Salvador Allende Gossens, the Marxist Chilean president who was killed in 1973.
>
> The report stated that Mr. Kendall had requested in 1970 that Augustin Edwards, who was publisher of the Chilean newspaper El Mercurio, as well as a Pepsi bottler in Chile, meet with high Nixon Administration officials to report on the political situation in Chile. (Pepsi bottling operations were later expropriated by the regime.) That meeting, which included Mr. Kendall, Mr. Edwards, Henry Kissinger and John N. Mitchell, was indeed held, and later the same day, Mr. Nixon met with Dr. Kissinger and Richard Helms, Director of the Central Intelligence Agency. Mr. Helms later testified that President Nixon had ordered at the follow-up meeting that Chile was to be saved from Allende "and he didn't care much how." Mr. Kendall says he sees nothing sinister, or for that matter even controversial, in his action.

LIKE MANY ON the right, quite a few bottlers regarded the Kennedy administration's policy toward Castro's Cuba as dangerously soft. Declassified FBI files show that, after Kennedy's death, one man contacted the FBI regarding threatening remarks that his brother, a bottler, had made in reference to the president. Another convention attendee was identified in FBI reports as having had a drink with Jack Ruby, the assassin of Lee Harvey Oswald, on the night of November 21.[17]

Though unhappy with Kennedy, these independent businessmen clearly wanted to hear what Johnson had to say, which is why the Texas-born vice president was the convention's keynote speaker.

By some estimates, the convention included close to eight thousand bottlers—so many, in fact, that it had taken over Dallas's largest venue, the new Market Hall. This meant that when Kennedy's trip planners determined where he would speak on November 22, one of the very few sufficiently large and central venues had long since been taken. The Dallas Trade Mart thereby became the most likely location for Kennedy's speech, with the route through downtown to the Trade Mart, past the Texas School Book Depository, as the most likely for the presidential motorcade.

In fact, the Trade Mart was secured by that most unlikely group of "friends" of JFK, the Dallas Citizens Council, whose members' views were described by the *New York Times* as "very conservative and range rightward." The council had cosponsored the luncheon as a putative peace offering to JFK.[18] Indeed, it seems that JFK's itinerary in Dallas was circumscribed by the bottlers and the Citizens Council.

The mere fact that eight thousand strangers had poured into Dallas in the days before JFK's arrival should presumably have been of interest, yet the Warren Commission ignored the event altogether.

Another interesting thing about the bottlers' convention is that the Army Reserves volunteered to help facilitate an unusual extracurricular activity. As noted in chapters 6 and 7, Poppy Bush's friend Jack Crichton was head of a local Army Intelligence unit. Associates of Crichton's who were involved with the Army Reserves had managed to get into the pilot car of Kennedy's procession, with one as the driver. Crichton would also provide the interpreter for Marina Oswald after her husband's arrest as the prime suspect in Kennedy's murder.

According to a short item in the *Dallas Morning News* the day before Kennedy was shot, members of the Dallas unit of the 90th Artillery Division of the Army Reserve would be providing trucks and drivers to transport two hundred orphans to a livestock arena for a rodeo sponsored by the bottlers' group. This was to take place at nine P.M. on the night before Kennedy's arrival. The arena was at Fair Park, near the site under which Crichton's Dallas Civil Defense maintained its underground emergency bunker and communications facility. Putting aside the Dickensian aspect of moving orphans in

Army trucks within an affluent American city, this raises some questions about the reason for this odd maneuver. Whatever the true purpose of a small platoon of Army vehicles being permitted to move about Dallas on purportedly unrelated civilian business as the president's arrival was imminent, it appears investigators never considered this incident worthy of a closer look.

Cumulatively, the bottlers' convention was responsible for a number of curious circumstances that may be said to have some relevance to the events surrounding Kennedy's death:

- The convention brought Nixon to Dallas.
- It brought eight thousand strangers to Dallas.
- It sent army vehicles into action on city streets the night before the assassination.
- Its early reservation of one large venue helped determine Kennedy's ultimate destination and thus the motorcade route.

In any event, as Nixon's adviser Stephen Hess has recounted, the former vice president emerged deeply shaken about the timing of his Dallas visit. It served to remind him that if he ever occupied the Oval Office, he too could be vulnerable and targeted—by the very same players. And his presence in this incriminating spot was suggestive of wheels within wheels, to which he of all people would have been alert. Were these intrigues what fueled President Nixon's obsession with the CIA and its cloak-and-dagger activities in the Kennedy era? This little-noted tug-of-war, a struggle over both current policy and past history, would become an ongoing theme throughout Nixon's term in office.

The Loyalist in Chief

At one time, Poppy Bush had worked hard to position himself as Richard Nixon's most loyal servant. An example appeared in a 1971 profile of Poppy in his role as Nixon's United Nations ambassador. Under the banner headline "Bush Working Overtime," the *Dallas Morning News* of September 19, 1971, portrayed the ambassador as poised at the center of world affairs. Leaning forward at his desk, a large globe next to him, his lean face bearing a look of calm intensity, George H. W. Bush looked almost presidential.

The reporter for the Texas paper picked up on that. But he was equally struck by Poppy's devotion to the sitting president. Ambassador Bush, he noted, "is loyal—some say to a fault—to President Nixon, and frequently quotes him in conversation."

It was the image Poppy wanted to convey. Even when the reporter asked for his own views, he quickly deferred. "I like to think of myself as a pragmatist, but I have learned to defy being labeled," Bush said. "What I can say is that I am a strong supporter of the President."

Of course, when someone defies being labeled, it gives him extraordinary flexibility to move in different circles, to collect information, to spin on a dime—in short, to behave a lot like a covert intelligence officer.

The image of Poppy as the ultimate loyalist was one he would project for three more years—right up to the final days of the Nixon presidency. Not even Nixon, who was famously distrustful, seemed to doubt it. After winning the 1972 election in the midst of the Watergate scandal, Nixon decided to hedge his bets and clean house.

Planning to fire all but his most trusted aides, Nixon instructed Ehrlichman to "eliminate everyone except George Bush. Bush will do anything for our cause."[19] This trust endured to the end of Nixon's presidency.

If indeed Bush was ever a Nixon loyalist, he certainly flipped the moment the tide turned. This new stance emerged with the 1974 public release of the transcript of Nixon's smoking gun conversation with Haldeman. As Bush would record in his diary after Nixon's final cabinet meeting, the taped conversation was irrefutable proof that "Nixon lied about his knowledge of the cover-up of the Watergate scandal . . . I felt betrayed by his lie . . . I want to make damn clear the lie is something we can't support."

Added Poppy: "This era of tawdry, shabby lack of morality has got to end."[20]

THIS PURPORTED DIARY entry was most likely part of Poppy's perennial alibi trail. It could have been Bush family tradecraft, something like Barbara's Tyler, Texas, hair salon letter from November 22, 1963—always intended for public view. Perhaps the most revealing part is the point at which Bush summarizes the content of the smoking gun conversation. Poppy selectively paraphrases a tiny part of that session, making it look as if Nixon had ordered Haldeman (as Bush put it) to "block the FBI's investigation of the Watergate break-in." This, Poppy asserted, "was proof [that] the President had been involved, at least in the cover-up."

What Poppy omitted were two key things: that it was actually John Dean's suggestion, not Nixon's, to block the investigation—and that the CIA was at the center of the intrigue to begin with.

Watergate's Unknown Prelude

The series of scandals that undid Richard Nixon's presidency are principally identified with the 1972 burglary at the Democratic party offices in the Watergate complex. But one could argue that Watergate—and Nixon's downfall—really began in late 1969, during Nixon's first year in office, with a phone call from a man almost no one today has heard of.

An independent oilman named John M. King dialed in to offer ideas for improving Nixon's hold over Congress. Former White House staffer Jack Gleason remembered the episode: "[King] called one day in '69 and said, 'You know, we have to start planning for 1970.'"

King's call suggested he was principally concerned about helping Nixon, but in retrospect, there may have been more at stake. For one thing, King was a member of the fraternity of independent oilmen who were growing increasingly unhappy with Nixon. As we saw in the last chapter, the oil barons were up in arms over threats to the oil depletion allowance, convinced that Nixon was not solidly enough in their corner. But they had other gripes. As Haldeman noted in a diary entry in December 1969: "Big problem persists on oil import quotas. Have to make some decision, and can't win. If we do what we should, and what the task force recommends, we'd apparently end up losing at least a couple of senate seats, including George Bush in Texas. Trying to figure out a way to duck the whole thing and shift it to Congress."[21]

On a more personal level, King was mired in problems. The Denver-based King had assembled a global empire with oil drilling and mining operations in a hundred countries; he was known for a high-flying lifestyle and a gift for leveraging connections. He even had two Apollo astronauts on his board. In 1968, King had donated $750,000 to Nixon, and as a big donor, his calls always got attention. But King was, according to a *Time* magazine article of the period, something of a huckster. By late 1969, his empire was on the verge of collapse. In the end, he would face jail and ruin.

Perhaps he was looking to secure intervention from the White House. Perhaps it was just general business insurance. Or perhaps he was speaking on behalf of his fellow independent oilmen.

In any event, King's pitch sounded like a good idea. He was proposing that the Nixon White House funnel money from big GOP donors directly to Senate and House candidates of its choice, rather than following the customary method: letting the Republican Party determine the recipients. To do this without provoking the wrath of the GOP establishment, King suggested it be kept under wraps.

This idea appealed to the White House brass, and soon, a special operation was being convened.

"As it matured, we had a couple of meetings with Ehrlichman and Haldeman and went over some of the ground rules," said Gleason. Haldeman brought the bare bones of the idea to Nixon, who thought it sounded fine.[22] Anything that involved secrecy and centralized White House control was likely to find a receptive ear. Gleason's recollection is confirmed by a notation in Haldeman's diary of December 11: "I had meeting with [Maurice] Stans, Dent, and Gleason about setting up our own funding for backing the good candidates in hot races. A little tricky to handle outside the RNC but looks pretty good."[23]

The White House political unit assigned the job of organizing and running the new fund to its operative Gleason, an experienced GOP fundraiser. Gleason was instructed by his boss, Harry Dent, to find an office for the operation. When he suggested renting space in one of those prefurnished office suites that come with secretarial and other services, he was told that this would be too expensive.

That struck Gleason as odd, since it would not have cost much more and would have been a pittance in relation to the large sums that would be raised. But he followed his orders and rented something cheaper and more discreet. Dent directed him to a townhouse on Nineteenth Street, in a residential area near Dupont Circle. The space was not just in a townhouse but in the *basement* of a townhouse. And not only that, it was in the back of the basement. Reporters would later describe it as a "townhouse basement back room"—an arrangement guaranteed to raise eyebrows if ever discovered.

The way in which the funds were to be handled also struck Gleason as unnecessarily complicated, and even furtive. While donors could simply—and legally—have written a single check to each candidate's campaign committee, they were instructed instead to break up their donations into a number of smaller checks.[24] The checks were then routed through the townhouse, where Gleason would pick them up and deposit them in a "Jack Gleason, Agent" account at American Security and Trust Bank. Gleason then would convert the amounts into cashier's checks and send them on to the respective campaign committees, often further breaking each donation up into smaller ones and spreading them over more than one campaign committee of each candidate.

The ostensible reason for these complex arrangements was to enable the White House to control the money. The actual effect, however, was to create the impression of something illicit, such as a money-laundering operation aimed at hiding the identities of the donors.[25]

Somewhere along the way Gleason began to detect an odor stronger than that of quotidian campaign operations. What seemed suspect to him was not that Nixon would help Republican candidates—that was how things worked. What bothered him were the operational details. Many seemed positively harebrained, the kind of things with which no president should be associated. But Gleason just figured that Richard Nixon, or his subordinates, had a blind spot when it came to appearances of impropriety.

Deep-Sixing Nixon

Late in the election season, Gleason's superiors told him to add a new component to the Townhouse Operation. Gleason found this new development particularly disturbing. It was called the "Sixes Project." Launched in October 1970, when the midterm elections were almost over, it provided an extra personal donation of six thousand dollars to each of thirteen Senate candidates—in cash.

Gleason's job was simple enough: get on a plane, fly out to meet each of the candidates, and personally hand over an envelope of cash. He was to add a personal message: "Here's a gift from Dick and Pat." And he was to keep meticulous receipts, noting who received the cash and the date of the transaction.

Gleason was not happy about his role as dispenser of envelopes full of cash. As he told me in a 2008 interview,

> Of all the silly things I've ever been asked to do in this life, traveling around with six thousand dollars to give the guy and say, "This is from Dick and Pat," was colossally bad . . . Now you crank me up, leave a paper trail a mile long and a mile wide of flight tickets, hotel reservations, rental cars, everything, and have me traipsing

all over the country giving these guys six thousand dollars in cash, [and besides], the six thousand doesn't matter, doesn't get you any-where. If we give you a quarter of a million, what's another six thousand? . . . The six thousand dollars itself was a disconnect, be-cause everything else was largely done to keep the whole thing un-der wraps.[26]

In those days, the campaign finance laws, most of which were at the state level, were limited and rarely enforced. Reporting requirements were thin, but those candidates who wanted to abide by the law made sure to report any cash they received to their respective campaign committees. That posed a challenge for a candidate caught in a grueling nonstop schedule, who was handed an envelope of cash. It would be easy enough to forget to report it, whether deliberately or accidentally.

Even back in 1973, Gleason could come to only one conclusion. When special prosecutors in the Watergate investigation later grilled him about the Townhouse Operation, he told them as much. "The purpose of these contributions was to set up possible blackmail for these candidates later on."[27] However, at that point Gleason assumed that the sponsors of the blackmail were Nixon loyalists—perhaps even authorized by the president himself.

Alarmed at this arrangement, and cognizant that he might be generating myriad campaign law violations, Gleason asked the White House for a legal analysis. But despite multiple requests, he never got it. Finally, he asked for a letter stating that nothing he was being asked to do was illegal. (That letter, Gleason later explained, would somehow disappear before it could arrive at the offices of the Watergate prosecutors.)

Since the six-thousand-dollar donations were ostensibly generated by "Dick and Pat," one could easily surmise that Richard Nixon, or those under his authority, were indeed out to get something on Republican candidates. Once they took the cash, the recipients would have to do as he wanted, or else risk exposure. As Assistant Special Prosecutor Charles Ruff wrote to his boss: "It has been our guess that [the Nixon White House] hoped to gain some leverage over these candidates by placing cash in their hands which they might not report."[28]

Had this become known, Nixon would have had trouble explaining it. Few would have believed that such a scheme could have been run under White House auspices without Nixon's approval. And yet that seems to have been the case. In fact, Nixon's name rarely appears in the Townhouse files of Watergate prosecutors—for whom the evidence of Nixon's wrongdoing would have been the ultimate prize.

Even the complex and calculating Charles Colson, who served as special counsel to the president in 1970, admitted to prosecutors that Nixon was not involved. Colson said that he had sat in on a Townhouse planning meeting and later briefed the president about "political prospects in that race"—but "did not recall that the fundraising aspects were discussed with the President."[29]

John Mitchell, who was attorney general before he resigned in 1972 to head up Nixon's reelection campaign, attended a meeting for "substantial contributors" and later told prosecutors that "the President stopped by, but was not present during discussions of campaign finances." Mitchell himself denied participation in or knowledge of the Townhouse plan.[30] Even Herb Kalmbach, Nixon's personal lawyer, seems to have been involved only in the most benign part of the operation: the legal solicitation of funds from wealthy donors.[31] Of course, all this could be about denials and deniability—but as we shall see, it apparently was not.

Meet John Dean

At the time Townhouse was becoming operational, the position of counsel to the president opened up. John Ehrlichman, Nixon's trusted aide, was moving to head up domestic affairs, and Ehrlichman was looking for someone to replace him—a smart lawyer and good detail man who was also loyal to the president. The man who came on board on July 27, 1970, was John Wesley Dean III.

Dean arrived at 1600 Pennsylvania Avenue just as President Nixon was trying to figure out how to deal with massive street demonstrations against the Vietnam War. A month before, a White House staffer named Tom Huston had drawn up a plan to spy on the demonstrators through electronic surveillance, recruitment of campus informants, and surreptitious entry into offices and meeting places.

In hindsight, this sounds especially odious, and it was, but at the time, and from the vantage point of the administration and its supporters in the "silent majority," America was besieged. The general atmosphere in the country and the domestic violence, actual and hinted, surrounding the Vietnam War debate, felt like chaos was descending. Even so, Attorney General John Mitchell shot down the notorious "Huston Plan." John Dean, however, took an immediate interest in some of the proposals.

Although his official duties centered on giving the president legal advice—often on arcane technical matters—Dean was considered a junior staffer and had virtually no contact with Nixon. Nevertheless, the White House neophyte quickly began taking on for himself the far edgier and dubious mantle of political intelligence guru.[32]

Among the bits of intelligence Dean collected were the details of the Townhouse Operation. In November 1970, following the midterm elections, Jack Gleason turned over all his files to the White House, where Haldeman had them delivered to Dean. Watergate investigators would later discover that "Haldeman also gave Dean several little notebooks which pertained to the 1970 fundraising."[33] Those little notebooks would have told Dean who the donors were, how much they gave, and the identity of the recipients.[34]

Shortly after the files ended up in Dean's hands, the media began receiving—perhaps coincidentally—leaks about the Townhouse Operation. One of the first reports was an AP article with no byline that appeared in the *New York Times* on December 27, 1970. It said that seven ambassadors had received their positions as rewards for their contributions to the Townhouse Operation: "Mr. Jack Gleason left the staff of a White House political operative, Harry Dent, this fall to run the fundraising campaign from a basement back office in a Washington townhouse." And there it was: Gleason caught up in something that sounded sinister, complete with the townhouse basement back office, all purportedly on behalf of Richard Nixon.

IN FEBRUARY 1972, someone cranked Townhouse back up again. Jim Polk, an investigative reporter at the *Washington Star* with an impressive track record on campaign finance matters, got more information about the fund from "inside sources."

Polk published an article headlined "Obscure Lawyer Raises Millions for Nixon." It sounded even more disturbing than the previous one. Polk's article did two things: it introduced the public to Nixon's personal lawyer Kalmbach and it provided many new details about the Townhouse fund.

> A little-known lawyer in Newport Beach, Calif., has raised millions of dollars in campaign contributions as an unpublicized fund-raiser ... [and] as Nixon's personal agent ... to collect campaign checks from Republican donors ... Kalmbach helped to raise nearly $3 million in covert campaign money ... The checks were sent through a townhouse basement used by former Nixon political aide Jack A. Gleason. But the operation was run from inside the White House by presidential assistant H.R. (Bob) Haldeman ... Only a portion of this money has shown up on public records. The rest of the campaign checks have been funneled through dummy committees.

When I spoke to Polk in 2008, not surprisingly, he no longer recalled the identity of his source. But whoever had leaked this story to him was no friend of Nixon's. Yet if it was intended to provoke further interest, it failed. Someone had attempted to light a fuse with Townhouse, but it did not ignite.

Just four months later, however, another fuse was lit. And this one would burn on and on.

The Brazen Burglary

If Townhouse was engineered to discredit Nixon, it had one potential flaw. The wrongdoing involved technical financial matters that reporters might find daunting. Watergate, on the other hand, was inherently sexy; it had all the elements of the crime drama it became. The break-in was brazen and easily grasped, and carried out in such a manner as to just about guarantee both failure and discovery. It also involved a cast of characters that neither reporters nor television cameras could resist (as the Watergate hearings later would demonstrate). It was like a made-for-TV movie: burglars in business suits, living in a fancy suite near the scene of the crime; Cuban expatriates; documents in pockets leading to the White House. Even Nixon had to interrupt his reelection campaign to confront it.

But the burglars didn't appear to take anything, so what was the intended crime? Breaking and entering—for what purpose?

As with the JFK assassination, theories abound. The burglars were found with bugging equipment. But that made little sense; Nixon didn't have much to worry about from his presumed Democratic opponent, George McGovern. The risks of a bugging operation far outweighed any conceivable gains. And if Nixon had really wanted inside dope on the McGovern campaign, which he hardly needed, he could have sent teams into McGovern's headquarters up on Capitol Hill, or to Miami, where the Democrats would hold their convention.

If, on the other hand, the intent was to fire the public imagination, the Watergate complex was far better—and Washington itself a necessary locale if the national press was to stay with the story week after week.

With all this in mind, Nixon's observation in his memoirs that "the whole thing was so senseless and bungled that it almost looked like some kind of a setup" seems on the mark.

If the Cubans were really trying to do the job, their supervisors were guilty of malpractice. They might as well have called the D.C. police to reserve an interrogation room.

The flubs were so obvious it was as if they were the work of amateurs—which it was not. Burglary team member James McCord left tape *horizontally* over a lock, so that it could be spotted, as it was, by a security guard when the door was closed. If he had taped the lock *vertically*, it would have been invisible to a passerby. And if the intent was to pull off a real burglary, there was no need for tape anyway—as the burglars were already inside. Even so, after the security guard discovered and removed the tape, McCord put it right back.

The entire operation reflected poor judgment. An experienced burglar would have known not to carry any sort of identification, and certainly not identification that led back to the boss. How elementary is that? Among the incriminating materials found on the Watergate burglars was a check with White House consultant E. Howard Hunt's signature on it—and Hunt's phone number at the White House, in addition to checks drawn on Mexican bank accounts. Despite the obvious risks, the burglars were also instructed by Hunt to register at the Watergate Hotel, and to keep their room keys in their pockets during the mission. These keys led investigators straight back to an array of incriminating evidence, not the least damaging of which was a suitcase containing the burglars' ID cards. Everything pointed back to CREEP and the White House.

The most interesting thing was that the materials identified the burglars as connected not just to the White House, but to the CIA as well. And not just to the CIA, but to a group within the CIA that had been active during the controversial period that included the Bay of Pigs invasion and the assassination of JFK.

Hunt, whose status in the CIA was described earlier, was a high-ranking (GS-15) officer and a member of the "Plumbers," a White House special investigations unit ostensibly dedicated to stopping government leaks to the media. As discussed in chapter 6, Hunt had been a key player in the coup in Guatemala and the Bay of Pigs invasion, in addition to working very closely with Allen Dulles himself. As noted previously, Dulles was in Dallas shortly before November 22.

And Hunt had been there on the very day of the assassination, according to an account confirmed in 1978 by James Angleton, the longtime CIA counterintelligence chief. Angleton, clearly concerned that investigations would uncover Hunt's presence in Dallas anyway, went so far as to alert a reporter and a House Committee to Hunt's being in the city that day, and then opined that Hunt had been involved in unauthorized activities while there; "Some very odd things were going on that were out of our control."[35]

Watergate burglar and electronic surveillance expert James McCord, like Hunt, had also been a GS-15 agent, serving for over a decade in the CIA's Office of Security. Around the time of the Kennedy assassination, he began working with anti-Castro Cubans on a possible future invasion of the island. Allen Dulles once introduced McCord to an Air Force colonel, saying, "This man is the best man we have." Regarding Nixon, McCord dismissed him to a colleague as not a team player, not "one of us."[36]

In a long-standing tradition, both Hunt and McCord had officially "resigned" from the agency prior to the Watergate time frame. But their continued involvement in CIA-related cover operations suggested otherwise. Indeed, as noted earlier in the book, many figures, including Poppy Bush's oil business colleague Thomas J. Devine, officially took retirement prior to participating in seemingly independent operations in which deniability was crucial.

Though Hunt claimed to have cut his CIA ties, he actually went out of his way to draw attention to those ties while working in the Nixon White House. He ostentatiously ordered a limousine to drive him from the White House out to CIA headquarters in Langley, Virginia. It was as though he was trying to broadcast the notion that Nixon was working closely with the agency—with which, as we now know, the president was in reality battling.

After Hunt's alleged retirement, he was employed at the Mullen Company, a public relations firm that served as a CIA cover. In a 1973 memo, Charles Colson recounted a meeting he'd just had with Senate Republican minority leader Howard Baker. Charles Colson wrote, "Baker said that the Mullen Company was a CIA front, that [Hunt's] job with the Mullen Company was arranged by [CIA director] Helms personally." Baker also informed Colson that, during Hunt's time at the Mullen Company, his pay had been adjusted to the exact salary he would have been making had he stayed at the spy agency.[37]

Eugenio Martinez, one of the anti-Castro Cuban burglars, was another CIA operative in the break-in crew. Indeed, he was the one member of the team who remained actively on the CIA payroll, filing regular reports on the activities of the team to his Miami case officer. Then there was Bernard L. Barker, who first worked as an FBI informant before being turned over to the CIA during the run-up to the Bay of Pigs.[38] Frank Sturgis, too, had CIA connections. Martinez, Barker, and Sturgis had worked with Hunt and McCord on the Second Naval Guerrilla operation.

So Nixon, who had been trying to see the CIA's file on the Bay of Pigs, was now staring at a burglary purportedly carried out in his name by veterans of the same "Bay of Pigs thing" with strong CIA ties. It was like a flashing billboard warning. CIA professionals, Cuban exiles, all tied to the events of 1961 through 1963, suddenly appearing in the limelight and tying themselves and their criminal activity to the president.

Layers and Layers

If most of us ever knew, we have probably long since forgotten that before the June 1972 Watergate break-in, there was another Watergate break-in by the same crew. With this earlier one, though, they were careful to avoid detection and were not caught. At that time, they installed listening devices. The second burglary, the one that seemingly was designed for detection, and designed to be traced back to the Nixon White House, ostensibly revolved around removing listening devices installed earlier—and therefore drawing attention *to* the devices and the surveillance.

The conclusion one would likely draw from their being caught red-handed is that Dick Nixon is up to yet another manifestation of his twisted and illegal inclinations. And what were they listening to? Purportedly, DNC personnel were arranging for "dates" for distinguished visitors with a call-girl ring. The ring was operating from down the street, not far from where the bugs were being monitored. The conclusion is that Nixon was perhaps trying to sexually blackmail the Democrats. It got more and more objectionable.[39]

But the fact is that no evidence shows Nixon wanting to sexually blackmail Democrats, nor wanting to install bugs at the DNC, nor wanting to order a burglary to remove the bugs. Yet somebody else clearly had a good imagination, and a talent for executing a script that was magnificently inculpatory of someone who would appear to deserve removal from the highest office in the land.

EVENTUALLY, AMERICANS WOULD learn that the Watergate break-ins were not the first such operation that made Nixon look bad, and not the first coordinated by Hunt and featuring Cuban veterans of the Bay of Pigs invasion. Back in September 1971, the team hit the Beverly Hills office of Dr. Lewis Fielding, the psychiatrist of Daniel Ellsberg, the whistle-blower who leaked the explosive Pentagon Papers to the *New York Times*.[40] First, though, Nixon, who was initially indifferent over the leak, was persuaded to take on the *Times* for publishing the documents, a posture that would position him as a foe of public disclosure. It also escalated his already adversarial relationship with the news media—a relationship that would become a severe disadvantage to Nixon as the Watergate "revelations" began to emerge. Nixon was also persuaded to authorize the formation of a leak-busting White House group, which was soon dubbed "the Plumbers." Soon, purportedly operating on Nixon's behalf—but without his actual approval—the Hunt team broke into Dr. Fielding's office, having been told to photograph Ellsberg's patient files.

However, as with Watergate, the burglary appears to have had an ulterior motive. Senator Baker, ranking Republican on the Senate Watergate Committee, learned of this, according to White House special counsel Charles Colson, when Baker interviewed the Cuban émigré Eugenio Martinez, who participated in the burglaries of both Fielding's office and the DNC office in Watergate:

> Baker told me of his interview with Martinez who said that there were no patient records in Dr. Fielding's office, that he, Martinez,

DRIFTWOOD PUBLIC LIBRARY
801 SW HWY. 101
LINCOLN CITY, OREGON 97367

was very disappointed when they found nothing there, but Hunt on the other hand seemed very pleased and as a matter of fact broke out a bottle of champagne when the three men returned from the job. Martinez says that he has participated in three hundred or four hundred similar CIA operations, that this was clearly a 'cover' operation with no intention of ever finding anything.[41]

In fact, though the burglars were ostensibly seeking records while on a covert mission, they did not act like people who wished to avoid discovery. In addition to smashing the windows and prying open the front door with a crowbar, the burglars proceeded to vandalize the office, scattering papers, pills, and files across the floor. The result was to ensure the generation of a crime report, establishing a record of the burglary. The break-in would not become public knowledge until John Dean dramatically revealed it two years later—and implicitly tied Nixon to it by citing the involvement of Egil Krogh, the man in charge of Nixon's so-called Plumbers unit.[42]

Dean and his lawyers showed far greater enthusiasm for pursuing the Beverly Hills break-in than even the prosecutors. As Renata Adler wrote in the *New Yorker*: "Dean's attorney, Charles Shaffer, practically had to spell it out to [the prosecutors] that they would be taking part in an obstruction of justice themselves if they did not pass the information on."[43]

Like Watergate, the Fielding office break-in was on its face a very bad idea that was not approved by Nixon but certain to deeply embarrass him and damage his public standing when it was disclosed. The principal accomplishment of the break-in was to portray Nixon as a man who had no decency at all—purportedly even stooping to obtain private psychiatric records of a supposed foe. This was almost guaranteed to provoke public revulsion.

THE NOTION THAT a group surrounding the president could be working to do him in might sound preposterous to most of us. But not to veterans of America's clandestine operations, where the goal abroad has often been to do just that. And Nixon was a perfect target: solitary, taciturn, with few friends, and not many more people he trusted. Because of this, he had to hire virtual strangers in the White House, and as a result, the place was teeming with schemers. Nixon was too distrustful, and yet not distrustful enough. It was supremely ironic. Nixon, ridiculed for his irrational hatred

DRIFTWOOD PUBLIC LIBRARY
801 SW HWY 101
LINCOLN CITY, OREGON 97367

and "paranoia" toward the Eastern Establishment, may in the end have been done in by forces controlled by that very establishment. Of course, it was nothing less than that level of power to remove presidents, plural, one after the other if necessary.

Among the myriad plots was the so-called Moorer-Radford affair, cited in chapter 9, in which the military actually was spying on Nixon and stealing classified documents in an attempt to gain inside information, influence policy, and perhaps even unseat the president.[44]

That Nixon could actually have been the victim of Watergate, and not the perpetrator, will not sit well with many, especially those with a professional stake in Nixon's guilt. Yet three of the most thoroughly reported books on Watergate from the past three decades have come to the same conclusion: that Nixon and/or his top aides were indeed set up. Each of these books takes a completely different approach, focuses on different aspects, and relies on essentially different sets of facts and sources. These are 1984's *Secret Agenda*, by former *Harper's* magazine Washington editor Jim Hougan; 1991's *Silent Coup*, by Len Colodny and Robert Gettlin; and 2008's *The Strong Man*, by James Rosen.

Rosen's *The Strong Man: John Mitchell and the Secrets of Watergate* is a biography of Nixon's close friend, attorney general, and campaign chief, the highest-ranking official ever to be sentenced to prison. The book, on which Rosen labored for seventeen years, is based on sources not previously interviewed and also on unprecedented access to documents generated by the Senate Watergate Committee and Watergate special prosecutors. Rosen asserts that the Watergate operation was authorized behind Mitchell's back by his subordinate Jeb Magruder and by John Dean and was deliberately sabotaged in its execution by burglar and former CIA officer James McCord. As Rosen puts it:

> Mitchell knew he had been set up. In later years, his mind reeled at the singular confluence of amazing characters that produced Watergate—Dean, Magruder, Liddy, Helms, Hunt, McCord, Martinez—and reckoned himself and the president, neither of whom enjoyed foreknowledge of the Watergate break-in, victims in the affair. "The more I got into this," Mitchell said in June 1987, "the more I see how these sons of bitches have not only done Nixon in but they've done *me* in."[45]

Rosen also writes:

> The [Watergate] tapes unmasked Nixon not as the take-charge boss
> of a criminal conspiracy but rather as an aging and confused politi-
> cian lost in a welter of detail, unable to distinguish his Magruders
> from his Strachans, uncertain who knew what and when, what
> each player had told the grand jury, whose testimony was direct,
> whose hearsay.

My independent research takes the argument one step further, and the
facts in a completely new direction. It leads to an even more disturbing conclusion as to what was really going on, and why.

Woodward at His Post

The accepted narrative of Nixon as the villain of Watergate is based largely on
the work of Bob Woodward and Carl Bernstein. They both were young reporters on the *Washington Post*'s Metro desk when the story fell into their laps.
When it was over, they were household names. Woodward in particular would
go on to become the nation's most visible investigative journalist, and indeed
the iconic representation of that genre. The work of "Woodstein" would play a
key role in enhancing the franchise of the *Post* itself. Yet this oeuvre—in particular the role of Woodward—has become somewhat suspect among those
who have taken a second and third look—including *Columbia Journalism
Review* contributing editor Steve Weinberg, in a November/December 1991
article.

Woodward did not fit the profile of the typical daily print reporter. Young,
midwestern, Republican, he attended Yale on an ROTC scholarship and
then spent five years in the Navy. He had begun with a top-secret security
clearance on board the USS *Wright*, specializing in communications, including with the White House.[46]

His commanding officer was Rear Admiral Robert O. Welander, who
would later be implicated in the military spy ring in the Nixon White
House, mentioned in chapter 9. According to *Silent Coup*, an exhaustive
study of the military espionage scandal, Woodward then arrived in Washington, where he worked on the staff of Admiral Thomas Moorer, chief of naval
operations, again as a communications officer, this time one who provided

briefings and documents to top brass in the White House on national security matters. According to this account, in 1969–70, Woodward frequently walked through the basement offices of the White House West Wing with documents from Admiral Moorer to General Alexander Haig, who served under Henry Kissinger.

In a 2008 interview, Woodward categorically denied having any intelligence connections. He also denied having worked in the White House or providing briefings there. "It's a matter of record in the Navy what I did, what I didn't do," Woodward said. "And this Navy Intelligence, Haig and so forth, you know, I'd be more than happy to acknowledge it if it's true. It just isn't. Can you accept that?"

Journalist Len Colodny, however, has produced audiotapes of interviews by his *Silent Coup* coauthor, Robert Gettlin, with Admiral Moorer, former defense secretary Melvin Laird, Pentagon spokesman Jerry Friedheim—and even with Woodward's own father, Al—speaking about Bob's White House service.[47]

At a minimum, Woodward's entry into journalism received a valuable outside assist, according to an account provided by Harry Rosenfeld, a retired *Post* editor, to the *Saratogian* newspaper in 2004:

> Bob had come to us on very high recommendations from someone in the White House. He had been an intelligence officer in the Navy and had served in the Pentagon. He had not been exposed to any newspaper. We gave him a tryout because he was so highly recommended. We customarily didn't do that. We wanted to see some clips, and he had none of that. We tried him out, and after a week or two I asked my deputy, "What's with this guy?" And he said well, he's a very bright guy but he doesn't know how to put the paper in the typewriter. But he was bright, there was that intensity about him and his willingness, and he acted maturely. So we decided because he had come so highly recommended and he had shown certain strengths that we would help get him a job at the *Montgomery County Sentinel*.[48]

In 2008, some time after I spoke to Woodward, I reached Rosenfeld. He said he did not recall telling the *Saratogian* that Woodward had been hired on the advice of someone in the White House. He did, however, tell me that he remembered that Woodward had been recommended by Paul Ignatius, the *Post*'s president. Prior to taking over the *Post*'s presidency, Ignatius had been Navy secretary for President Johnson.

In a 2008 interview, Ignatius told me it was possible that he had a hand in at least recommending Woodward. "It's possible that somebody asked me about him, and it's possible that I gave him a recommendation," Ignatius said. "I don't remember initiating anything, but I can't say I didn't." I asked Ignatius how a top Pentagon administrator such as himself would even have known of a lowly lieutenant, such as Woodward was back in those days, and Ignatius said he did not recall.[49]

In September 1971, after one year of training at the Maryland-based *Sentinel*, Woodward was hired at the *Washington Post*. The *Post* itself is steeped in intelligence connections. The paper's owner, the Graham family, were, as noted in chapter 3, aficionados of the apparatus, good friends of top spies, and friends also of Prescott Bush. They even helped fund Poppy Bush's earliest business venture. Editor Ben Bradlee was himself a Yale graduate who, like Woodward, had spent time in naval intelligence during World War II.[50] (As noted earlier, Poppy Bush had also been associated with naval intelligence during World War II: prior to beginning his work with the CIA, he had been involved with top-secret aerial reconnaissance photography.)

Woodward demonstrated his proclivity for clandestine sources a month before the Watergate break-in, in his coverage of the shooting and serious wounding of presidential candidate George Wallace at a shopping center in Washington's Maryland suburbs. A lone gunman, Arthur Bremer, would be convicted. Woodward impressed his editors with his tenacity on the case, and his contacts. As noted in a journalistic case study published by Columbia University:

> At the time, according to [*Post* editors Barry] Sussman and [Harry] Rosenfeld, Woodward said he had "a friend" who might be able to help. Woodward says his "friend" filled him in on Bremer's background and revealed that Bremer had also been stalking other presidential candidates.[51]

As to Woodward's initial introduction to the newspaper, nobody seems to have questioned whether a recommendation from someone in the White House would be an appropriate reason for the *Post* to hire a reporter. Nor does anyone from the *Post* appear to have put a rather obvious two and two together, and noted that Woodward made quick work of bringing down the president, and therefore wondered who at the White House recommended Woodward in the first place—and with what motivation.

Others, however, were more curious. After Charles Colson met with Senator Howard Baker and his staff—including future senator Fred Thompson— he recounted the session in a previously unpublished memo to file:

> The CIA has been unable to determine whether Bob Woodward was employed by the agency. The agency claims to be having difficulty checking personnel files. Thompson says that he believes the delay merely means that they don't want to admit that Woodward was in the agency. Thompson wrote a lengthy memo to Baker last week complaining about the CIA's non-cooperation, the fact that they were supplying material piecemeal and had been very uncooperative. The memo went into the CIA relationship with the press, specifically Woodward. Senator Baker sent the memo directly to [CIA Director] Colby with a cover note and within a matter of a few hours, Woodward called Baker and was incensed over the memo. It had been immediately leaked to him.[52]

Woodward's good connections would help generate a series of exclusive-access interviews that would result in rapidly produced bestselling books. One was *Veil: The Secret Wars of the CIA, 1981–1987,* a controversial book that relied in part, Woodward claimed, on a deathbed interview—not recorded—with former CIA director William Casey. The 543-page book, which came out as Poppy Bush was seeking the presidency, contained no substantive mentions of any role on the part of Bush in these "secret wars," though Bush was both vice president with a portfolio for covert ops *and* a former CIA director.

Asked how it was possible to leave Bush out of such a detailed account of covert operations during his vice presidency, Woodward replied, "Bush was, well, I don't think he was— What was it he said at the time? *I was out of the loop?*" Woodward went on to be blessed with unique access to George W. Bush—a president who did not grant a single interview to America's top newspaper, the *New York Times,* for nearly half his administration—and the automatic smash bestsellers that guaranteed.[53] Woodward would also distinguish himself for knowing about the administration's role in leaking the identity of CIA undercover officer Valerie Plame but not writing or saying anything about it, despite an ongoing investigation and media tempest. When this was revealed, Woodward issued an apology to the *Post*.

To ITS CREDIT, the *Washington Post* in these years had other staffers doing some of the best reporting on the intelligence establishment. Perhaps the most revealing work came prior to Nixon's tenure, while Woodward was still doing his naval service. In a multipart, front-page series by Richard Harwood in early 1967, the paper began reporting the extent to which the CIA had penetrated civil institutions not just abroad, but at home as well. "It was not enough for the United States to arm its allies, to strengthen governmental institutions, or to finance the industrial establishment through economic and military programs," Harwood wrote. "Intellectuals, students, educators, trade unionists, journalists and professional men had to be reached directly through their private concerns."[54] *Journalists too.* Even Carl Bernstein later wrote about the remarkable extent of the CIA's penetration of newsrooms, detailing numerous examples, in a 1977 *Rolling Stone* article. As for the *Post* itself, Bernstein wrote:

> When *Newsweek* was purchased by the Washington Post Company, publisher Philip L. Graham was informed by Agency officials that the CIA occasionally used the magazine for cover purposes, according to CIA sources. "It was widely known that Phil Graham was somebody you could get help from," said a former deputy director of the Agency. "Frank Wisner dealt with him." Wisner, deputy director of the CIA from 1950 until shortly before his suicide in 1965, was the Agency's premier orchestrator of "black" operations, including many in which journalists were involved. Wisner liked to boast of his "mighty Wurlitzer," a wondrous propaganda instrument he built, and played, with help from the press. Phil Graham was probably Wisner's closest friend. But Graham, who committed suicide in 1963, apparently knew little of the specifics of any cover arrangements with *Newsweek*, CIA sources said.
>
> In 1965–66, an accredited *Newsweek* stringer in the Far East was in fact a CIA contract employee earning an annual salary of $10,000 from the Agency, according to Robert T. Wood, then a CIA officer in the Hong Kong station. Some *Newsweek* correspondents

and stringers continued to maintain covert ties with the Agency into the 1970s, CIA sources said.

Information about Agency dealings with the *Washington Post* newspaper is extremely sketchy. According to CIA officials, some *Post* stringers have been CIA employees, but these officials say they do not know if anyone in the *Post* management was aware of the arrangements.[55]

When the Watergate burglary story broke, Bob Woodward got the assignment, in part, his editor Barry Sussman recalled, because he never seemed to leave the building. "I worked the police beat all night," Woodward said in an interview with authors Tom Rosenstiel and Amy S. Mitchell, "and then I'd go home—I had an apartment five blocks from the Post—and sleep for a while. I'd show up in the newsroom around 10 or 11 [in the morning] and work all day too. People complained I was working too hard."[56] So when the bulletin came in, Woodward was there. The result was a front-page account revealing that E. Howard Hunt's name appeared in the address book of one of the burglars and that a check signed by Hunt had been found in the pocket of another burglar, who was Cuban. It went further: Hunt, Woodward reported, worked as a consultant to White House counsel Charles Colson.

Thus, Woodward played a key role in tying the burglars to Nixon.

Woodward would later explain in *All the President's Men* (coauthored with Bernstein) that to find out more about Hunt, he had "called an old friend and sometimes source who worked for the federal government." His friend did not like to be contacted at this office and "said hurriedly that the break-in case was going to 'heat up,' but he couldn't explain and hung up." Thus began Woodward's relationship with Deep Throat,[57] that mysterious source who, Woodward would later report, served in the executive branch of government and had access to information in the White House and CREEP.[58]

Based on tips from Deep Throat, Woodward and Bernstein began to "follow the money," writing stories in September and October 1972 on a political "slush fund" linked to CREEP. One story reported that the fund had financed the bugging of the Democratic Party's Watergate headquarters as well as other intelligence-gathering activities.[59] While Nixon coasted to a landslide victory over the liberal Democrat George McGovern, the story seemed to go on hiatus. But just briefly.

Poppy Enters, Stage Right

If someone did want to undermine the president from outside the White House, he couldn't have found a better perch than the chairmanship of the Republican Party.

Right after the election, Poppy Bush, again utilizing his pull with Nixon, had persuaded the president to bring him back from his cushy U.N. post and install him at the Republican National Committee. This put him at the very epicenter of the nationwide Republican elite that would ultimately determine whether Nixon would stay or go.

As chairman of the RNC, Poppy was expected to be the president's chief advocate, especially to the party faithful. He would travel widely, interact with big donors and party activists. If anyone would have their finger on the pulse of the loyalist base, it was Poppy. He would have a good sense of what would keep supporters in line, and conversely, what might convince them to abandon ship.

But Poppy was unique among RNC chairmen over the years in that he had convinced Nixon to let him maintain an official presence at the White House. Just as Nixon had permitted him to participate in cabinet meetings as U.N. ambassador, he now continued to extend that privilege while Poppy ran the RNC. This was unprecedented for someone in such an overtly partisan position.

Here was a man closely connected to the CIA, as we have seen, now both running the Republican Party and sitting in on cabinet deliberations. An intelligence officer couldn't have asked for a better perch. Moreover, this put him in the catbird seat just as Watergate began heating up.

But Poppy was even more wired into Nixonworld. When he came to the RNC, he hired Harry Dent and Tom Lias, the top officials of Nixon's Political Affairs office, which had established the Townhouse Operation. Dent was the architect of Nixon's Southern strategy, with which Poppy Bush and his backers were closely allied. Lias had ties to Poppy from before working in the White House. He had been a top organizer for the Republican Congressional Campaign Committee, strategizing how to elect people like Poppy to formerly Democratic seats in the South.

After Poppy came to Washington, the two often socialized. According to Pierre Ausloos, stepfather of Lias's daughter, and a friend of the family, "On weekends, Bush would always invite [Lias] for a barbecue party at his house here in Washington."[60] Ausloos also remembers that during the 1968 Republican convention, Lias's daughter's babysitter was Poppy's son, George W. Bush.

Thus, at the time Dent and Lias were installed in the White House Political Affairs office, they were already close with Bush. Indeed, right after the 1970 election and the termination of the Townhouse Operation, Bush took Lias with him to New York, where Lias served as a top aide on Poppy's United Nations staff. The U.N. choice struck people who knew Lias as odd. Lias had no relevant qualifications or knowledge for the U.N. post, just as Poppy himself didn't.[61]

Poppy's decision, once he moved to the RNC, to hire both Lias and Dent—the two men supervising Jack Gleason's Townhouse Operation—is surely significant.

Meanwhile, Poppy Bush and his team had already been in contact with John Dean.

In a brief 2008 conversation, in which a prickly Dean sought to control the conditions of the interview, I asked him whether he had any dealings with Bush. "I think there are some phone calls on my phone logs, but I never met with him personally," he said.

Indeed, phone logs show that on June 24, 1971, Ambassador Bush called Dean, and on December 6, 1971, Tom Lias of Ambassador Bush's office called. The logs show other calls from Lias as well. It is not clear—nor did Dean volunteer an opinion—why Bush and Lias would have been calling him at all.[62]

Slumming in Greenwich

When the Senate created a committee to investigate Watergate, there was no guarantee that anything would come of it. The perpetrators—the burglars and their supervisors, Hunt and Liddy—were going on trial, and it was uncertain whether the hearings would produce any further insights. Moreover, the committee featured four rather somnolent Democrats and three Republicans, two of them staunch Nixon loyalists.[63]

This left only one wild card: Lowell Weicker, a liberal Republican from Connecticut.

A freshman, and an independent one, Weicker was not disposed to knee-jerk defense of Nixon. Furthermore, he saw himself as a crusader. At six feet six, Weicker was imposing, considered basically well-intentioned, a little naïve, and in love with publicity. He had gotten his political start in the Bush hometown of Greenwich, Connecticut; and like the Bushes, he was heir to a family fortune, in his case from two grandfathers who owned the Squibb pharmaceutical company.

But there the similarities ended. Weicker chose for his base Greenwich's Third Voting District, which consisted almost entirely of working-class Italians. "Just decent, hard-working, down-to-basics families." Weicker would say. "Had I been raised as a typical Republican in the salons of Fairfield County, discussing international issues at teas and cocktail parties, I know my career would have been a short one once off the Greenwich electoral scene."[64] In 1960, Weicker aligned himself with Albert Morano, a congressional candidate opposed by the Bush family. Now the Bushes saw Weicker as a traitor to his class. Over the years, Weicker and Bush would generally maintain a cool but civil relationship, driven by political expediency.[65]

"I think he was viewed as an outsider from day one, and it was a perspective he relished," said Townhouse operative Jack Gleason, who got to know Weicker so well he served as best man when Weicker married for a second time. "Because he always used to joke about 'the Round Hill boys out to get me again' every time he was up for reelection."[66]

Weicker had arrived in Washington in 1968, following his election to the House of Representatives. Given the past, this would have made him a not-very-welcome colleague of Poppy Bush. And Poppy probably was not enthused when, after only two years in the House, Weicker was elected to Prescott Bush's old Senate seat—in the same year Poppy lost his *second* Senate bid. Weicker's star was rising faster than Poppy's—and in the Bush home state to boot. It must have rankled.

Still, Weicker's least endearing qualities—his considerable ambition, love of publicity, and penchant for self-aggrandizement—would shortly prove useful in at least one respect: as a champion of the "truth" on the Senate Select Committee on Presidential Campaign Activities, commonly known as the Watergate Committee. The same Republican maverick who had no qualms about challenging his party's leadership in Connecticut would soon debut his maverick persona on the national stage.

In his memoirs, Weicker writes that he was given the Watergate Committee assignment because he was one of only two Republicans who volunteered and that his interest in "campaign financing" and dwindling faith in the democratic process spurred his personal interest.[67] Interestingly, the other Republican volunteer, stalwart conservative Edward J. Gurney of Florida, had won his seat with the help of Bush's top political lieutenant, Jimmy Allison—and eldest son George W. Bush, who took the extraordinary step of securing a leave from his National Guard unit in 1968, when he had barely begun his military training. The other Republican on the committee was Minority Leader Howard Baker, a moderate. Weicker was the only Republican on the committee with the inclination to prove his independence from the party and openly challenge the president.

By the spring of 1973, six defendants had been sentenced in the DNC burglary, and the Watergate hearings were due to begin.[68] There was now an opportunity for Nixon to put the whole Watergate affair behind him, without mortal damage to his presidency. Weicker, however, already saw his role as an honest broker, and he criticized Nixon's attempts at tamping down the matter. "I think the national interest is achieved by opening, not closing, the White House doors," he said. He added that he would vote in favor of subpoenas for White House officials to appear before the committee.[69]

Poppy Bush apparently agreed. On March 20, the day after Weicker's remarks, Poppy went to see Nixon at the Oval Office. In his usual oblique way, ascribing his advice to others, he urged Nixon to send John Dean to testify.

> BUSH: We're getting hit a little bit, Mr. President . . . It's building, and the mail's getting heavier . . .
> NIXON: What do you think you can do about it? . . . We've got hearings coming up. The hearings will make it worse.
> BUSH: . . . I was speaking with the executives at the Bull Elephants[70] . . . The guy said to me, . . . *why doesn't the President send Dean?* . . . The disclosure is what they're calling for.
> NIXON: We are cooperating . . . They don't want any cooperation. They aren't interested in getting the facts. They're only interested in [political gains?] . . . I wish there were an answer to Watergate, but I just don't know any . . . I don't know a damn thing to do.[71] [emphasis added]

John Ehrlichman remembers that meeting well, as noted in his memoirs. "Bush argued that the only way to blunt the current onslaught in the newspapers and on television was for the president to be totally forthcoming—to tell everything he knew about all aspects of Watergate."[72]

This was a significant moment, where Poppy demonstrates a possible connection to and interest in Dean. It was a sort of specific advice that warrants attention, because it is an indication that the outsider Bush is unusually well informed about who knows what inside the White House—and encourages Nixon to let Dean begin confessing his knowledge. When I asked Dean in 2008 why he thought Poppy Bush was suggesting he testify, he said he had no idea.

Nixon resisted Poppy's advice to have Dean testify because, Nixon maintained, there was no White House staff involvement in Watergate, and therefore Dean's testimony would serve only to break executive privilege, once and for all. "The president can't run his office by having particularly his lawyer go up and testify," Nixon told Poppy.[73]

If Poppy Bush seemed to have unusually good intelligence as to what was happening in the Oval Office, it might have had something to do with a good friend of his who was right in there with Nixon and Dean during the most critical days of Watergate. Richard A. Moore, a lawyer who served as a kind of elder statesman off of whom Nixon and Mitchell could bounce ideas, was, like Poppy, an alumnus of Andover, Yale, and Skull and Bones. Moore served as special assistant to the chief of military intelligence during World War II and is believed to have transitioned to civilian intelligence after the war. Over the years, Moore was practically a member of the extended Bush clan, exchanging intimate notes with Poppy and even joining family dinners.

Moore shows up in background roles on a number of Nixon tapes, and phone logs show a flurry of phone calls between Moore and Dean, especially in the final weeks before Dean turned on Nixon. In a little-reported taped telephone conversation from March 16, Dean tells Nixon that he and Moore are working on a Watergate report; he also mentions that he and Moore drive home together. On March 20, in an Oval Office meeting featuring Nixon, Dean, and Moore—just prior to Nixon's meeting with Poppy Bush—Moore can be heard typing the report in the background.

Dean would later write that the term "cancer" as used in his famous "cancer on the presidency" briefing had been suggested by Moore—who though a close Nixon adviser in these sensitive days, managed to emerge from Watergate obscure and unscathed. His Watergate testimony did not support Dean, but he tended to be ambiguous. As *Time* magazine noted on July 23, 1973, "The Moore testimony was certainly not evidence that the President had had prior knowledge of the Plumbers' felonious break-in. But it seemingly betrayed a curious nonchalance on the President's part toward questionable activities by White House staffers."

Later, with Nixon departing and Ford preparing to become president, Moore urged Ford to make Poppy Bush his vice president, arguing that Bush had strong economic credentials. Moore specifically cited Poppy's ties to Wall Street through his father and grandfather, "both highly respected investment bankers in New York." Moore would go on to work on all of Poppy Bush's presidential campaigns. including his unsuccessful 1980 bid, and would in 1989 be named by Poppy as his ambassador to Ireland.

Repeat After Me

Immediately after Poppy tried to convince Nixon to send Dean to testify, Dean himself telephoned the president. Dean asked to urgently meet the following morning and carefully explained to Nixon that there were important details of which the president was unaware and that he would tell him about these things—but did not yet tell him:

> DEAN: I think that one thing that we have to continue to do, and particularly right now, is to *examine the broadest, broadest implications of this whole thing, and, you know, maybe about thirty minutes of just my recitations to you of facts* so that you operate from the same facts that everybody else has.
> NIXON: Right.
> DEAN: I don't think—*we have never really done that.* It has been sort of bits and pieces. Just paint the *whole picture for you,* the soft spots, the potential problem areas . . . [74] [emphasis added]

In other words, Dean was admitting, nine months into the scandal, that he knew quite a bit about Watergate that he had never revealed to the president. Now Dean planned to clue him in.

Nixon then inquired about the progress on a public statement Dean was to be preparing—and was made to understand that the statement was going to try to avoid specifics, i.e., employ a common practice, stonewalling:

> NIXON: And so you are coming up, then with the idea of just a stonewall then? Is that—

DEAN: That's right.

NIXON: Is that what you come down with?

DEAN: Stonewall, with lots of noises that we are always willing to
cooperate, but no one is asking us for anything.

Nixon went on to pressure Dean to issue a statement to the cabinet explaining, in very general terms, the White House's willingness to cooperate in any
investigations. Without going into detail, Nixon wanted to publicly defend the
innocence of White House officials whom he believed were innocent:

NIXON: I just want a general—

DEAN: An all-around statement.

NIXON: That's right. Try just something general. Like "I have
checked into this matter; I can categorically, based on my investigation, the following: Haldeman is not involved in this, that
and the other thing. Mr. Colson did not do this; Mr. So-and-so
did not do this. Mr. Blank did not do this." Right down the line,
taking the most glaring things. If there are any further questions, please let me know. See?

DEAN: Uh huh, I think we can do that.[75]

But Dean apparently didn't intend to "do that." He was seemingly waiting
for the right moment to create the right effect—and that moment would not
come until he had jumped the wall to the other side and become the key witness for the prosecution.

In Haldeman's diary entry of the same day, he observes that Nixon wants
to come clean, but that Dean is warning him not to:

[The president] feels strongly that we've got to say something to get
ourselves away from looking like we're completely on the defensive and on a cover-up basis. If we . . . are going to volunteer
to send written statements . . . we might as well do the statements
now and get them publicized and get our answers out. *The problem is that Dean feels this runs too many leads out.* [emphasis added]

Thus, according to this account, Nixon was interested in facing his problems. This included, it appears, telling what they knew—Nixon's version, in
any case.

And John Dean was urging Nixon not to do that. To make that case, Dean was feeding Nixon's paranoia. In other words, Dean seemed to be saying: *Too many leads out. Let me control this process.*

In response to a combination of events—Weicker's call for more disclosure, Bush's intervention with Nixon aimed at forcing Dean to testify, and Dean's own insistence that there was more to the story—Nixon met with Dean the next day. That conversation, together with the smoking gun episode, would help seal Nixon's fate.

ON THE MORNING OF MARCH 21, Nixon's White House counsel stepped into the Oval Office and proceeded to deliver a speech that would make Dean famous for the rest of his life. He would dramatically warn the president of a "cancer on the presidency" soon to become inoperable. This speech, which would shortly become Dean's principal evidence against Nixon, may have been carefully calculated based on Dean's awareness that the conversations were being taped. (Dean would later say he *suspected* he was being taped, but as we shall see, he may have known for certain.)

In fact, for this dramatic moment, Dean had begun performing dress rehearsals some eight days earlier. This is borne out by earlier taped conversations—ones whose very existence has been largely suppressed in published accounts. In these earlier tapes, we hear Dean beginning to tell Nixon about White House knowledge related to Watergate. (Most of these tapes are excluded from what is generally considered the authoritative compendium of transcripts, *Abuse of Power: The New Nixon Tapes*, by Stanley Kutler, who told me in a 2008 interview that he considers himself a close friend of John Dean.)[76]

In one unpublicized taped conversation, from March 13, Dean told Nixon that Haldeman's aide Gordon Strachan had foreknowledge of the break-in, was already lying about it in interviews, and would continue to do so before a grand jury. The Watergate prosecutors, for whom Dean was a crucial witness, had the March 13 tape, but did not enter it into evidence.

> DEAN: Well, Chapin didn't know anything about the Watergate, and—
> NIXON: You don't think so?
> DEAN: No. Absolutely not.

NIXON: Did Strachan?

DEAN: Yes.

NIXON: He knew?

DEAN: Yes.

NIXON: About the Watergate?

DEAN: Yes.

NIXON: Well, then, Bob knew. He probably told Bob, then. He may not have. He may not have.

DEAN: He was, he was judicious in what he, in what he relayed, and, uh, but Strachan is as tough as nails. I—

NIXON: What'll he say? Just go in and say he didn't know?

DEAN: He'll go in and stonewall it and say, "I don't know anything about what you are talking about." He has already done it twice, as you know, in interviews.[77]

This is significant since Strachan, a junior staff member, was essentially reporting to Dean—a fact that Dean failed to point out to Nixon. Although Strachan was Haldeman's aide, when it came to matters like these, he would, at Dean's request, deal directly with Dean. "As to the subject of political intelligence-gathering," Strachan told the Senate Watergate Committee, "John Dean was designated as the White House contact for the Committee to Re-elect the President." Thus, if Strachan knew anything about Watergate, even after the fact it seems to have been because Dean included him in the flow of "intelligence."[78]

ON MARCH 17, IN ANOTHER tape generally excluded from accounts of Watergate, Dean told Nixon about the Ellsberg break-in. He also provided a long list of people who he felt might have "vulnerabilities" concerning Watergate, and included himself in that list.

NIXON: Now, you were saying too, ah, what really, ah, where the, this thing leads, I mean in terms of the vulnerabilities and so forth. It's your view the vulnerables are basically Mitchell, Colson, Haldeman, indirectly, possibly directly, and of course, the second level is, as far as the White House is concerned, Chapin.

DEAN: And I'd say Dean, to a degree.

NIXON: You? Why?

DEAN: Well, because I've been all over this thing like a blanket.

NIXON: I know, I know, but you know all about it, but you didn't, you were in it after the deed was done.

DEAN: That's correct, that I have no foreknowledge . . .

NIXON: Here's the whole point, here's the whole point. My point is that your problem is you, you have no problem. All the others that have participated in the God-damned thing, and therefore are potentially subject to criminal liability. You're not. That's the difference.[79]

In the heavily publicized "cancer" speech of March 21, Dean essentially reiterated what he had told Nixon previously, if in more detail. But he added an important element—one which would cause Nixon serious problems when the "cancer" tape was played for the public: a request for one million dollars in "hush money" for the burglars. Informed by Dean of a "continual blackmail operation by Hunt and Liddy and the Cubans," Nixon asked how much money they needed. Dean responded, "These people are going to cost a million dollars over the next two years." There is debate as to whether Nixon actually agreed with Dean's suggestion to pay money or merely ruminated over it. He never did pay the money.

Dean's behavior did not appear to be that of a lawyer seeking to protect his client, let alone advice appropriate to the conduct of the presidency.

CHAPTER 11

Downing Nixon, Part II: The Execution

I F, AS IT APPEARS, WATERGATE WAS INDEED a setup, it was a fairly elaborate covert operation, with three parts: 1) creating the crime, 2) implicating Nixon by making him appear to be knowledgeable and complicit in a cover-up, and 3) ensuring that an aggressive effort would be mounted to use the "facts" of the case to prosecute Nixon and force him from office. The third area is where Lowell Weicker was absolutely indispensable.

The very day after Dean went to see Nixon to deliver his "cancer on the presidency" speech, Weicker, preparing for the hearings, received a visitor.

According to Weicker's memoir, the visitor was Ed DeBolt, a Republican national committeeman from California. "DeBolt opened my eyes wide," Weicker writes, "In sum, what he said was that many people in California politics considered Nixon to be a 'chronic gutter fighter.' If that had reached the East, I didn't know about it."[1]

As presented in the memoir, this visit played a major role in convincing Weicker that Watergate might be more serious than he had understood—and that it would have been in character for Nixon himself to have sanctioned the break-ins.

At a minimum, Weicker comes across as oddly sheltered, having missed a good two decades of acclaimed Herblock cartoons characterizing Nixon as a gutter fighter, beginning with a 1954 comic showing him crawling out of a sewer. Indeed, by 1973 Nixon had been widely represented as a political smear artist.

In fact, the DeBolt-Weicker story turns out to be more complicated than the senator indicates in his memoir. In a 2008 interview, DeBolt told me that it was actually Weicker who called and summoned him, and that Weicker knew DeBolt was not merely a party activist from California, but a Washington insider. During the 1972 campaign, DeBolt had been one of the Nixon campaign's key operatives.[2] By the time Weicker called him, in March 1973, DeBolt was a high-ranking staffer for the party—on the payroll at Poppy Bush's RNC.

"He called me up one day—he knew where I was because he had my phone number at the RNC—and he asked if I would come see him for a few minutes," recalled DeBolt, who served as the RNC's deputy chairman for research and campaigns. They met in the Senate cafeteria.

DeBolt said that he characterized Nixon to Weicker as a complicated individual, a mix of good and bad: "I liked [Nixon] . . . He was very, very smart, and he really cared about me and the staff; he just didn't show it . . . I would see this man who knew so much but he was more insecure than my puppy. So, I always felt sorry for him. I just think he got in over his head."

The most curious aspect of DeBolt's interaction with Weicker was that when he responded to the senator's summons, he found him sitting with a prepared list of detailed questions, based on information that only someone high up in the White House or RNC could have known about DeBolt.[3] "I don't remember volunteering a whole lot of stuff. He had a list in front of him, of questions, and he was going down the list and checking them off. He was clearly asking questions that his staff had put together . . ."

In Weicker's memoir, he suggests that DeBolt's purported revelation about Nixon's "gutter fighter" reputation, caused him to spring into action. One thing he did, according to DeBolt, was to enter a part of DeBolt's comments into the committee records.

After DeBolt's visit, the senator excitedly called his staff and met with them over the weekend. His press secretary, Dick McGowan, started to devote "enormous amounts of time" to the scandal. McGowan, who, intriguingly, would himself later go to work for Poppy Bush, would turn Weicker's office into what he called "a gold mine" of information. At times, reporters were stumbling over each other as they waited for their daily handout. Many of the "exclusives" that appeared in the media were from the Weicker team's own investigation.[4]

ON MARCH 29, barely nine days after he had met with Nixon and recommended having Dean testify, Poppy called the White House with an even more urgent request. As recounted in Haldeman's diaries, the purpose of Bush's call was to get the president to start talking about Watergate publicly:

> George Bush just called. *It [i.e., disclosure] must be from the President* at the President's earliest possible convenience. This is the most urgent request he has ever made of the President . . . This is an outgrowth of conversations he's had with Gerry Ford and Bryce Harlow . . . He doesn't necessarily have solutions but feels that this political advice . . . is of the utmost urgency.[5] [emphasis added]

Poppy Bush was almost frantic to get Nixon's ear—again claiming to be carrying input from influential Republicans. And his message was always the same: it's urgent that you confess White House misdeeds.

DeBolt, who worked at the RNC from 1971 to 1973, said he found Bush's presence at the party's helm bizarre. "I wondered how in the heck Bush got to be RNC chairman," he said. "He had been a flop in everything he had done, and he had nobody at the RNC who was rooting for him—nobody. [The order to install Bush] came directly from Nixon, and we always wondered about that."

And who had the best access to intelligence overall in and between the FBI, the White House, the RNC, and the reelection campaign? One guess. "Dean got copies of every single report," DeBolt recalled. "We were led to believe that Dean was keeping us out of trouble; he was checking on stuff, for Nixon."

OVER AT THE Capitol, on April 10, 1973, Weicker received another visitor. It was Jack Gleason, previously of the Townhouse Operation, who was no longer associated with the White House. He came now with words of caution. Someone—Gleason cannot recall who—on the White House staff, figuring he would pass along the information to Weicker, had told Gleason that the senator was going to be implicated for allegedly accepting a Townhouse-transferred campaign donation and not reporting it.[6]

Based on the tip from Gleason, who himself still assumed that Townhouse had been authorized from the very top, Weicker said that he concluded Nixon was trying to set him up. Sometime later, he contacted the special prosecutor's office and urged that it investigate Townhouse.

Even if Gleason was, as he asserts, trying to do the right thing, someone inside the White House was using essentially the same information for a different purpose: seemingly not to frame Weicker but rather to anger him. Or to give Weicker the impetus to set that moldy would-be scandal, Townhouse, back in play.

Cranking up the volume further, a few days after Gleason's visit, an anonymous source inside the White House tipped off reporters about illegalities in the 1970 Weicker campaign and suggested that the reporters talk to Gleason. The goal seems to have been to make Gleason the fall guy, but more important, to further prime the pumps for the revival of Townhouse in the news.

MEANWHILE, JOHN DEAN took the step that would land him in the history books: he publicly switched sides.

Ostensibly operating solely in his own interests, Dean broke with Nixon, purportedly because he worried about facing possible prosecution and hoped to secure a deal for himself. This defection enabled Dean to become the virtual guide for both prosecutors and senatorial committee members. When he became the witness for the prosecution, Dean brought with him the noose with which to hang Nixon. Now he would "tell all" about the things Nixon "had done"—creating the charge that would ultimately drive the president from office. Dean informed the special prosecutors that Nixon was involved in a cover-up. He also told them about the break-in at Ellsberg's psychiatrist's office. And he kept on talking.

Will the Real John Dean Please Stand Up?

To this day, thanks in part to his bestselling book, *Blind Ambition*, John Dean lives in memory as an ambitious and self-absorbed young lawyer who got caught up in Nixon's scheming and then, from some combination of self-preservation and guilt, blew the whistle. As a result, Dean became something of a hero on the left—and years later an MSNBC pundit and outspoken critic of the George W. Bush administration.[7] He even wrote a bestselling critique of W. called *Worse Than Watergate*.

But the widely accepted characterization of Dean as a misguided underling whose ambitions led him to participate for a period in Nixon's depraved schemes does not comport well with the actual facts of his life. John Wesley Dean III was wired—and sponsored—from the get-go.

Dean was the son of an affluent Ohio family, and his early years were shaped by military values—including following orders—*not* doing one's own thing. He graduated from Staunton Military Academy in Virginia, where he roomed with Barry Goldwater Jr., and became lifelong friends with the Goldwater family, which had close ties to the Bushes. (Barry Goldwater Jr. was in the wedding party in 1972 when Dean married his second wife, Maureen. And Barry Goldwater Sr. would play a crucial role in pushing Nixon out by publicly calling for him to go—an important signal from a party elder.)

Dean attended two colleges in the Midwest before coming to Washington. There he married Karla Hennings, the daughter of a recently deceased Democratic senator from Missouri, and met Robert McCandless, who was married to Karla's sister. McCandless was from the oil-rich state of Oklahoma and had learned the ways of the Capitol on the staff of Senator Robert Kerr, the Oklahoma oilman and friend of the Bushes who was long regarded—after Texas's Speaker, Sam Rayburn—as the power behind Lyndon Johnson's rise.[8]

After graduating from Georgetown Law School, Dean took a job with a Washington law firm. He was soon accused of conflict of interest violations because he had allegedly been negotiating his own private deal relating to a broadcast license for a new television station after being assigned to prepare an identical application for a client.[9] The firm fired him for this transgression, and despairing of being hired by another law office, he turned to his brother-in-law for advice. McCandless suggested that he find another job fast, before his status as unemployed became too apparent, and preferably a job where his firing might not come up.

Dean used his connections to a Republican member of the House Judiciary Committee to get a job as the committee's chief minority counsel. William McCulloch, a representative from Ohio who was Dean's boss on the Judiciary Committee, said of him: "He was an able young man, but he was in a hell of a hurry." When a National Commission on the Reform of Federal Criminal Law was created in 1967, Dean was appointed associate director. In 1968, Dean volunteered to write position papers on crime for the Nixon campaign. After the inauguration, he got a job with Deputy Attorney General Richard Kleindienst, an Arizonan and protégé of Barry Goldwater; presumably Dean's longtime friendship with Barry Jr. did not hurt.[10] Among other things, his government work dealt with antiwar demonstrations and wiretapping laws.

In little over a year, in July 1970, when John Ehrlichman became the president's chief domestic adviser, and his job as the president's lawyer opened up, Dean moved in. It had been a dizzyingly steep climb, from ousted law firm associate to counsel to the president of the United States in four short years.

Egil, or "Evil," Krogh?

How exactly did John Dean get onto the White House staff? He was brought on by Egil "Bud" Krogh Jr. Friends of Krogh dubbed him "Evil Krogh," as a joke, insisting that it was the exact opposite of a man of formidable rectitude. In fact, Krogh was a complex figure.

A longtime friend of John Ehrlichman's and a former member of his Seattle law firm, Krogh brought into the White House not just Dean but also Gordon Liddy. And he approved the break-in at Ellsberg's psychiatrist's office—an act whose exposure would seriously damage Nixon.

Although Dean joined the president's staff in July 1970, records show Krogh trying to get him into the White House, even on a piecemeal basis, months earlier. As early as March 2, Krogh arranged daily White House access for the outsider. A memo dated March 2 says: "John Dean . . . will be coming to the White House every day until approximately November 1970. I would appreciate your issuing him a White House pass for that reason . . . Bud Krogh." On March 24, Krogh shifted gears, including Dean on a list of four people he was recommending for "personnel recruitment." It is not clear how Krogh knew Dean or why he became so determined to bring Dean into the White House—or whether he was told to do so. "He has been one of my closest confidants in developing Congressional strategy," Krogh wrote to Haldeman. Krogh ultimately got Dean hired without a background check.[11]

Krogh had begun his work for Nixon by helping with the inauguration, then was made an adviser on the District of Columbia. Quickly, though, he maneuvered himself into far heavier fare. He became liaison to the FBI and the Bureau of Narcotics and Dangerous Drugs (BNDD), a precursor to the DEA. And soon he went even deeper. "We sent [him] . . . to work with the BNDD and the CIA to try and buy off some of the heroin labs in the Golden Triangle," Ehrlichman said.[12] Charles Colson confirmed to Len Colodny that Krogh was "carrying large amounts of money over to Southeast Asia to pay off some of the drug lords. That had to be Agency work."[13] Colson also wrote: "What I remember is that there was a CIA contact, that Krogh dealt with...The CIA liaison to the White House, by the way, also dealt with Hunt all through the Watergate period—one of the very suspicious and unexplored aspects of the CIA's involvement."[14]

Krogh had been a student of University of Washington law professor Roy Prosterman, an expert in the design of agrarian reforms intended to blunt Communist incursions. Prosterman designed the "Vietnam pacification program," which had aspects of land redistribution but became best known for its association with the Phoenix Program, an operation in which thousands were assassinated.[15] Krogh traveled to Vietnam prior to Nixon's election, ostensibly to assess land reform programs in association with Prosterman. Under Nixon, though Krogh's White House job involved domestic policy, he went back to Vietnam for the BNDD, purportedly to address the growing drug addiction of American troops.[16] The BNDD also sent John Dean to the Philippines, and that's where he was when the Watergate break-in took place. Dean's wife Maureen got a job in 1971 with the BNDD, organizing the new National Commission on Marihuana and Drug Abuse despite what Maureen describes in her memoirs as a lack of relevant experience.[17]

Krogh served four and a half months in prison for his role in the Ellsberg job, went back to legal practice, and now lectures on legal ethics.

Intelligence Czar

John Dean seemed to love the role of intelligence czar. As private investigator turned White House gumshoe Jack Caulfield would recall, "I saw a desire [on the part of Dean] to take greater chances as [Dean] saw the potential rewards. And the key to the ball game was intelligence—who was going to get it and who was going to provide it. Dean saw that and played the game heartily . . . I was getting my instructions from Dean . . ."[18]

What made Dean so successful was his ability to protect himself legally and otherwise, and to disassociate himself personally from those very intelligence activities. When, on March 21, 1973, he famously told Nixon that there was a "cancer on the presidency," he began his description of the whole Watergate episode to the president by putting the onus on Haldeman, rather than himself, as the person who originated White House intelligence operations.

DEAN: It started with an instruction to me *from Bob Haldeman* to
see if we couldn't set up a perfectly legitimate campaign intelligence operation over at the Re-Election Committee. [emphasis
added]

NIXON: Hm-hmm.

Next, Dean denied any involvement in intelligence and claimed he decided to rely on someone else:

DEAN: Not being in this business, I turned to somebody who had
been in this business, Jack Caulfield.

Eventually, Dean continued, G. Gordon Liddy, counsel to the Committee
to Re-elect the President, was assigned responsibility as in-house expert on
intelligence operations because he "had an intelligence background from
the FBI."

So, Dean added, "Liddy was told to put together this plan, you know, how
he would run an intelligence operation."[19]

Was told by whom? Dean doesn't say, but according to Liddy, he "was
told" by Dean himself.[20]

Thanks to post-Watergate reporting by several journalists and authors—
reporting that failed to gain wide circulation or was aggressively attacked by
Dean and others with a vested interest in controlling the story—we now
know the following:

- In November 1971, it was Dean who actually recruited two private
  eyes to do a walk-through of Watergate.[21] Jack Caulfield, a former
  New York City cop, relayed the order to Tony Ulasewicz, who had
  worked for Nixon in the past. "Dean wants you to check out the offices of the DNC."[22] Ulasewicz complied and simply walked through
  the offices as a visitor, casing out the location of desks, who sat
  where, and any other useful information.
- In January 1972, it was Dean who encouraged Liddy, counsel to the
  Committee to Re-Elect the President, to set up a "really first class
  intelligence operation," which led to Operation Gemstone, an intri-
  cate plan consisting of several potential clandestine operations,
  each one named after a precious stone. These included eavesdropping on—and infiltration of—Democratic campaigns. Liddy recalls

in his autobiography, *Will*, that it was Dean who "encouraged him to think bigger" because previous intelligence operations had been "inadequate." Liddy, at Dean's prodding, incorporated eavesdropping on—and infiltration of—Democratic campaigns.[23]

- In April 1972, it was Dean—not Mitchell or Haldeman—who was reportedly the instigator of the break-in at the DNC. Dean ordered Jeb Magruder to ask Liddy: "Do you think you can get into Watergate?"[24] Magruder belatedly admitted this to reporters Len Colodny and Robert Gettlin: "The first plan [for a break-in] had been initiated by Dean," he told them.[25]
- In June 1972, according to an account offered by Robert F. Bennett— E. Howard Hunt's boss at the CIA front Mullen Company and himself later a U.S. senator—it was Dean who offered Hunt hush money during the Watergate cover-up. Nowhere in the literature of Watergate has it been suggested that President Nixon knew anything about such an offer by Dean to Hunt so early in the game.[26]

On June 23, 1972, Dean prompted what became the key evidence of a "cover-up" by Nixon: the so-called smoking gun tape. Dean told Haldeman that money found on one of the burglars had been traced to a Mexican-Texan money trail and "our problem now is to stop the FBI from opening up a whole lot of other things."[27] In other words, Dean convinced Haldeman to discuss the cessation of an investigation, a piece of lawyerly advice that would become part of Haldeman and Nixon's infamous smoking gun conversation leading to charges of obstruction of justice and cover-up.

Ironically, if anyone was blocking (and monitoring) the investigation, it was John Dean. When FBI director Pat Gray refused to curtail his investigation into the money trail, Dean insisted on sitting in on every one of the FBI's witness interviews of White House staff. Gray, in his memoirs, concluded that Dean was central to "hatching the plot that would eventually drive Nixon from office."[28]

CAREFULLY REVIEWING THE ACCUMULATED facts, it appears that Poppy Bush and John Dean were not serving Richard Nixon's interests at all. Far from advising the president and advancing his interests, they appear to have been skillfully engineering a series of crucial events whose only outcome could be devastating for Nixon—and then audaciously urged him to take responsibility for those very events.

J. Anthony Lukas, in a 1976 review of Dean's book *Blind Ambition* for the *New York Times Book Review*, wrote: "Dean was one of the sleaziest White House operatives, a compulsively ambitious striver who pandered to his superiors' worst impulses, largely engineered the cover-up of their activities, turned informer just in time to plea bargain for himself, got sprung from prison after serving only four months and then signed a contract to write this book."[29]

Neighbors and Friends

In the spring of 1973, as Dean began cooperating with prosecutors, Weicker decided he wanted to meet Dean. In his memoirs, the senator describes the origins of their strategic alliance this way: "Through one of those loose Washington connections—an associate of mine who knew an associate of Dean's lawyer—I began trying to set up a meeting with Dean. Like everyone else in Washington, I had lots of questions for him."[30]

That Weicker had to go through intermediaries seems strange, because all he had to do was open his front door. Sometime in the spring of 1973—records do not reveal whether it was before or shortly after their first meeting—John Dean and Lowell Weicker became neighbors, living in townhouses in Alexandria, Virginia, across the street from each other.[31] (In 1974, when Dean wanted to move to California but was having trouble selling his house, Weicker bought it.)

Nevertheless, two weeks before the Watergate Committee hearings were scheduled to start, about the beginning of May, the lawyers arranged a meeting between Dean and Weicker at the Rockville, Maryland, home of Dean's lawyer Charles Shaffer.

The moment Dean got Weicker's ear, he went way beyond simply telling Weicker what he knew. He was laying it on triple thick—being unnecessarily dramatic, as if to ensure that Weicker "got it." The senator would have to be wearing industrial-strength earplugs and blinders not to.

During the meeting, according to Weicker's memoirs, Dean dramatically (and quite unnecessarily) pulled Weicker into another room to "speak privately." "Are you sure you are able to handle the dirt the White House is planning to hit you with?" Dean asked. Weicker listened carefully.

"Are you worried about the White House being able to accuse you of improper campaign contributions?" Dean continued. "They have every intention of using the material as blackmail."[32] Dean was referring to the Townhouse money, and he was letting the senator know that he knew Weicker was a recipient. If this was an effort by Dean to inflame Weicker even further, it succeeded. Weicker, who had already been warned by Jack Gleason, was now snorting with anger at Nixon.

As ODD A coincidence as Dean's ending up living across the street from Weicker was his legal representation in this period.

In his memoir, *Blind Ambition*, Dean says that he contacted an outside lawyer for advice and that the man happened to refer Dean to Charles Shaffer, with whom Dean was already acquainted: "I had met Charlie once, on a duck-hunting trip to the Eastern Shore of Maryland, many years earlier."

As a young lawyer, Shaffer had worked on the staff of the Warren Commission. This made him yet another of a growing list of people associated with the JFK scenario or "investigation" who show up in Watergate.

Dean's cocounsel was Robert McCandless, who had been his brother-in-law while both had been married to sisters. McCandless was the mentor who had guided Dean when he got in trouble with his law firm and rebounded with a job on Capitol Hill.

After Watergate, McCandless would partner with Bernard Fensterwald, who had represented former CIA officer and Watergate burglar James McCord—the one whose botched door-taping ensured that the burglars were discovered. Fensterwald would make an unsuccessful attempt to become chief counsel of the House committee investigating assassinations; his bid was adamantly opposed by the committee's vice chairman, Representative Henry Gonzalez, sponsor of the first resolution calling for an assassination inquiry.[33] At the time he became cocounsel for Dean, McCandless resigned from the law firm Burwell, Hansen and McCandless, which handled the business of several CIA proprietaries, seemingly independent firms that were actually run by, and for the benefit of, the agency. His firm's CIA ties are cited, among other places, in a book coauthored by former CIA officer Philip Agee.[34]

Some years after representing Dean, McCandless went on to represent Haiti's military junta.[35] McCandless has denied having CIA connections.

Hays Gorey, a special correspondent for *Time*, was invited into a Dean strategy session with his lawyers, and soon wrote impressed dispatches about the earnest convert. Gorey wrote: "His youthful appearance showing no sign of ordeals past or to come . . . John W. Dean III exudes confidence like a Dale Carnegie graduate. He is clear of eye, strong of voice, steady of hand. His self-assurance may be justified, for Dean is the only major Watergate witness who is both able and willing to tell a lot."[36]

SOON, WEICKER AND Dean were the best of friends, sharing walks, even dinner. As Jack Gleason put it, "Weicker was Dean's drinking buddy." Through his weeks of preparation, Weicker seemed thrilled at the prospect of having such an exciting witness as Dean. And when Dean took the witness stand at the Senate Watergate hearings, in late June 1973, he was eager to be helpful. His first day of testimony had been devoted mostly to reciting a 245-page "opening statement." As he would later reflect in *Blind Ambition*, "The squealer's fear was still very much on my mind . . . I realized . . . how difficult it would be to give a convincing account of my motivation."

Never arrogant, often humble, always appearing to be sincere, Washington's "Golden Boy," as the press quickly dubbed the fair-haired whistle-blower, was highly conscious of his image. At times Dean would take a deep breath before answering a question, he wrote, "to make it look as if I were thinking."

One of the questions made him particularly nervous. It came from Senator Herman Talmadge: "Now, after all those facts were available to you, why did you not, as counsel to the President, go in at that time and tell him what was happening?"

"Senator," Dean responded, "I did not have access to the President." Dean quickly gauged that this was a weak response, and shifted tack. "I was never presumptuous enough to try to pound on the door to get in."

Talmadge was still incredulous.

Dean, feeling suddenly vulnerable, tried blaming the access problem on a remote, inaccessible president; and when that didn't work, he shifted blame onto the president's aides, claiming he'd been told his reporting channel was to Haldeman and Ehrlichman. And when that didn't work, he tried "another angle." He actually blamed himself. "Senator, I was participating in the cover-up at that time."[37]

That worked. During the break, McCandless told him that that one sentence went a long way to winning the senators' confidence.

When Weicker took center stage, the first thing out of his mouth was a speech alluding to a plot against him. In his memoirs, Dean would attribute the outburst to what he had earlier sprung on Weicker at that meeting in Shaffer's house, "when I informed him of a White House strategy to 'neutralize' him . . . with Jack Gleason's 1970 Town House Operation." Dean concluded that Weicker was "still piqued about what I had told him."

The hearings were going well, and Dean now suggested something that might make them go even better. "I might also add," he said, "that in my possession is . . . a memorandum that was requested of me, to prepare a means to attack the enemies of the White House. There was also maintained what was called an 'enemies list' which was rather extensive and continually updated."

Weicker asked for copies. Dean said he would supply them.

"The press went crazy over the enemies list," Dean later recalled.[38]

The Burning Bush

Finally, it was time for the man behind the curtain to take his bow. The man was George H. W. Bush.

But first, a bit of anonymous leaking. On July 11, someone informed the *Washington Post* that Senator Lowell Weicker was a recipient of money from the murky-sounding Townhouse fund. Weicker, as expected, went bananas. On July 12, the senator was quoted in the *Washington Post* as admitting having received the money, but indignantly asserting that he had done nothing wrong and that he had properly reported the money.

That evening, Weicker took a call. It was RNC chair Poppy Bush on the line. Poppy thought Weicker might like to know that he, Poppy, had in his possession some receipts from Townhouse—including some relating to Weicker.

Actually, Poppy confided, he too was on the list. He seemed to be suggesting: *We're in this together.*

Then the chairman of the Republican Party put an odd question to the freshman senator: "What should I do with the receipts?" Bush asked. "Burn them?"[39]

Now Weicker knew the game: the White House was setting him up. "Destroying potential evidence is a criminal offense," Weicker would later write in his memoirs.[40] Here, he felt sure, was the head of the Republican Party, calling for his boss, Richard Nixon, trying to knock out the man who represented the biggest threat to the president.

Outraged, Weicker told Bush that under no circumstances should he even *think* about burning any documents. Then Weicker got in touch with a federal prosecutor.

Bush denied the story, but Weicker stands by it to this day.

As head of the Republican Party, Bush should have taken the receipts to the party's lawyer months earlier, when Gleason had turned them over, and asked for advice, thereby invoking lawyer-client privilege.

Though Weicker says he knew a trap when he saw one, and told Bush so, he saw a fake trap—the one he was supposed to see. And he did exactly what was expected. Had Weicker thought it through, he would have realized that this rash act by Bush hardly served Nixon's interest. It was too obvious, too aggressive, and too certain to provoke ire. If Bush was looking out for Nixon, he was doing so in an awfully reckless fashion, especially for a man noted for his prudence. He was making Lowell Weicker mad, not just at him but also at the president. And what had been for Watergate investigator Weicker an opportunistic crusade with an edge of authentic outrage over Republican abuses in the White House was now becoming personal. Now Weicker's own political survival was at stake.[41] Now it was Nixon or him.

As the nation's eyes fixed on the televised hearings, Lowell Weicker emerged as a veritable bulldog against Richard Nixon. In the course of two months, and with help from John Dean, he revealed that Nixon had an enemies' list, that the White House was trying to embarrass the senator with false Townhouse fund allegations, that Nixon was connected to both the Watergate and Ellsberg break-ins, that Nixon was a participant in a cover-up.

Weicker made an emotional speech during one of the hearings about how the Nixon administration had "done its level best to subvert the [Watergate] committee hearings."[42] He stated that Republicans were appalled by "these illegal, unconstitutional and gross acts." Republicans, he insisted, "do not cover up . . ."[43] He received cheers and applause. Weicker was riding high.

It was one of the defining moments of his life. Indeed, when I called him in 2008 and tried to share with him what I had discovered about the true background of Watergate, he wouldn't hear of it. "You are talking to somebody that, having spent a major portion of his political career and life on this investigation, I really don't like to be told by other people what was going on," Weicker told me.[44]

Butterfield: The Icing on the Cake

The man who actually came bearing the knife with which Richard Nixon would commit political hara-kiri was not Bush or Dean or Weicker or Hunt. It was an obscure figure named Alexander Butterfield, a Nixon aide who supervised White House internal security, which included working closely with the Secret Service and coordinating the installation of Nixon's secret taping system.

At first Alexander Butterfield seemed hesitant when he sat down with staff members of the Watergate Committee on July 13. "I was hoping you fellows wouldn't ask me about that," he purportedly said when questioned about the possible existence of such a White House taping system. Then he proceeded to describe it in detail.

Nixon wanted to tape conversations for the historical record. Butterfield obliged and found technicians to install tiny voice-activated microphones.[45] "Everything was taped," he told his astonished listeners, "as long as the President was in attendance."[46]

Within days of Butterfield's revelations, this previously obscure White House security officer became another Watergate hero, a man who followed his conscience. As *New York Times* contributor A. Robert Smith wrote two years later, "It was Friday the 13th and Butterfield had put the Senate investigators on the trail of the 'smoking pistol'—hard evidence of impeachable behavior, preserved on tape—that would force the President to resign."

Why had Butterfield done it? In the *Times*, Smith wrote that "Butterfield's testimony was . . . remarkable for a man who, in 20 years of military service, had been taught to follow orders rather than pursue higher ideals."[47]

The thrust of the *Times* piece was that Butterfield had changed. But there were hints that there might be more to it—that Butterfield might still be following orders, just not ones from the commander in chief.

Buried toward the end of the article was brief mention of allegations that Butterfield had been in the CIA, followed by Butterfield's denial. Butterfield said that his only contact with the CIA had been when he was in the Air Force. From 1964 to 1967, as military aide to Defense Secretary Robert McNamara, he had been in charge of "rehabilitating" Cuban survivors of the Bay of Pigs invasion—the same work that various sources have said Hunt and McCord performed. Yet left unmentioned was the involvement of just such Cuban survivors in Watergate, and in Nixon's downfall.

Years later, Butterfield admitted that immediately prior to joining the White House staff he had worked as the military's "CIA liaison" in Australia.[48] Moreover, while Butterfield claimed that Haldeman had offered him the White House job, Haldeman was quite emphatic in recalling that Butterfield had written to him asking for a position. If Haldeman was right about this too, then it adds to the list of people with CIA connections—notably Hunt, Dean, McCord, and Poppy Bush—who had pushed hard to get into Nixon's inner sanctum.

Butterfield and the tapes had come to the committee's attention courtesy of two people: Woodward of the *Washington Post*, who suggested they look into Butterfield; and Dean, who mentioned in his opening statement that he thought his conversations were being taped.

The person who first directed Congress's attention to the smoking gun conversation, on March 14, 1973, was General Vernon Walters, CIA deputy director.

It looks a bit like a CIA layer cake, with Butterfield as the icing.

THE BEST LAID plans require contingencies. If a group was setting out to steer the Watergate affair in a particular direction, it would have been advisable to make sure that nothing went wrong.

One thing that could have gone wrong was that the Watergate Committee staff might figure out that a group of CIA-connected figures with ties to the Bay of Pigs and the events of November 22, 1963, was setting Nixon up.

The person who was most potentially problematic in that regard was Carmine Bellino, the Senate committee's chief investigator. An old associate of the Kennedys, he had been around the block a few times—and if anything smelling of 1963 surfaced, he would be most likely to follow it up.[49]

So it is interesting to note that one of the few overt measures Poppy Bush took as RNC chairman during Watergate was to attack Carmine Bellino. In this, he relied on hearsay from others—much as he had in claiming that the Bull Elephants wanted Dean to testify—and years earlier in telephoning in the "threat" to President Kennedy supposedly represented by James Parrott in 1963.[50]

During this same eventful month of July 1973, George Bush issued a long statement demanding an investigation into whether Bellino had ordered electronic surveillance of the Republicans in 1960. "This matter," Bush announced in a press conference on July 24, 1973, "is serious enough to concern the Senate Watergate Committee, and particularly since its chief investigator is the subject of the charges."[51]

Three days after Bush's press conference, twenty-two Republican senators signed a letter to Senator Sam Ervin, chair of the Senate Watergate Committee, urging that the committee investigate Bush's charges and that Bellino be suspended. The Republicans had chosen their target well, and Ervin had no choice but to comply. The Bellino flap took up a lot of the Watergate Committee's time. It also neutralized Bellino, who never had a chance to fully defend himself or to dig deeper.

Committee chairman Sam Ervin would later state, with a hint of bitterness, "One can but admire the zeal exhibited by the RNC and its journalistic allies in their desperate efforts to invent a red herring to drag across the trail which leads to the truth of Watergate."[52]

In fact, it was Ervin himself who had snapped at the herring. He mistakenly assumed that Poppy's mission was to ardently defend Richard Nixon. What he missed was what everybody missed: that Watergate was actually not a Nixon operation at all, but a deep, deep covert operation *against* Nixon— seeking to protect the prerogatives and secrets of a group accountable to no one.

The Little Man on the Cake

If Poppy was the blushing bride of this enterprise, his groom atop the cake would be a surprising figure: the tough, no-nonsense Watergate prosecutor Leon Jaworski.

Jaworski entered the Nixon chase in October 1973, after Haig helped persuade Nixon to force out the independent counsel Archibald Cox, yet another ill-advised act that turned public opinion against Nixon and suggested his guilt.[53] A survey of books on Watergate shows that little attention was paid to Jaworski's background, or, especially, to how he came to be prosecutor.

Jaworski was a conservative Texas Democrat who had actually backed Nixon in 1968. As a young man, he had served as legal counsel to some of Houston's most powerful figures—oil and cotton kings so influential they had the ear of presidents like Franklin Roosevelt. Perhaps these connections helped him obtain an important post in World War II: prosecutor at the Nuremberg war crimes tribunal. This activity earned him a top-secret clearance that for some reason was never relinquished after the end of the war. As will be discussed in chapter 16, prosecutions of war criminals both in Asia and in Europe were not simply lofty and symbolic pursuits of justice. They were intelligence exercises, in which powerful figures from the losing side could be made to reveal valuable information, ranging from the locations of billions of dollars of war loot to the country's scientific and military technology advances.

After the war, Jaworski returned to his Houston law practice and became a close friend of, and lawyer for, Lyndon Johnson. Jaworski and Johnson's professional and personal relationship would prove mutually beneficial. In his memoir, Jaworski said that his good friend LBJ "had a boundless capacity for hard work . . . Lyndon was a man of extra dimensions, who thought bigger, laughed louder, and got mad faster than most men. He had the ability . . . to make people move, jump, change their minds."[54]

When JFK was assassinated, Jaworski, along with a friend, Southern Methodist University law school dean Robert Storey, another Nuremberg prosecutor, quickly launched a Texas-based investigation of the assassination under the auspices of Texas attorney general Waggoner Carr. When Earl Warren was asked to convene a national commission of inquiry, he told the Texans that no independent Texas-based investigation could be allowed, principally because it would be viewed with suspicion. He also said that the Texans could not work for the Warren Commission. But he agreed to a compromise: the Texans could handle the Texas end of the investigation for the commission, and could have one of their number present at every commission hearing. Thus, Jaworski and his friends were monitoring all proceedings, including those at which Bush's old friend and Oswald's mentor George de Mohrenschildt testified.

Jaworski's own memoir, oddly titled *Confession and Avoidance*, is in itself an elaborate exercise in self-clearance. The book, published in 1979 during a period of renewed interest in the Kennedy assassination, belittles Oswald's mother for asserting that she believes her son was framed—and portrays her as self-serving and money-grubbing, while excoriating anyone who does not accept that the Warren Commission did a stellar job.

> The impact of John Kennedy's death has been overshadowed now by the ghoulish industry that grew out of it. Over forty books have been published attacking the Warren Report, or introducing new theories. Some of these books have been described as "scholarly," which means they contain footnotes . . . others are in the conspiracy game for financial gain, notoriety, excitement, or all of these.[55]

Because of Jaworski's association with the effort to prove that there was no conspiracy in JFK's death, his emergence as part of the group that drove Nixon from office cannot be automatically dismissed as unrelated. Nor can the background as to how he ended up as the Watergate prosecutor.

Jaworski, it turns out, was recommended by national security aide Alexander Haig. General Haig was a career military man and deeply enmeshed in the complicated intrigues and power struggles surrounding presidents Nixon and Ford. A White House survivor, Haig was first a top aide to Henry Kissinger, then became chief of staff after Haldeman resigned; later the military man helped persuade Nixon to resign, and retained power throughout Nixon's fall, inserting himself into the process of determining which of the ex-president's tapes became public. As we now know, this was a crucial function, as certain tapes could be presented in a way that suggested Nixon's guilt, while others would suggest the opposite.[56]

Haig's rapid career rise, from the lowest third of his class at West Point to positions in a succession of Democratic and Republican administrations starting with JFK's, benefited in part from sponsorship by Joseph Califano Jr., a powerful Washington attorney who served in both the Kennedy and Johnson administrations and was considered a close ally of LBJ's.[57] *Washington Post* chair and publisher Katharine Graham initially brought Califano and his law partner Edward Bennett Williams together and the two attorneys spoke of lunching frequently on Saturdays with managing editor Ben Bradlee or "other pals from the *Post*."[58] Complicating matters and illuminating these tangled alliances, Califano served as counsel for both the *Post* and the Democratic National Committee—the very entity purportedly victimized by the president's men. As secretary of the Army under LBJ, Califano had been responsible for looking after veterans of the Bay of Pigs invasion, along with two of his aides: Haig and Alexander Butterfield.

As noted earlier, Haig may have also had a past relationship with Bob Woodward when Woodward was in Naval Intelligence, prior to the latter becoming the reporter who broke the Watergate story. This raises the question of whether the "high White House official" who recommended Woodward to former Naval Intelligence officer Ben Bradlee and/or former Navy secretary Ignatius at the *Post* was not Haig himself. That Haig, who was working in the Pentagon's Operations office in 1963, also had something to do with Jaworski's becoming the Watergate prosecutor, poses intriguing questions—as does almost everything about this remarkable circle of friends.

Jaworski was also, by Poppy Bush's own standards, "a close friend" to the Bushes. He certainly met with George H. W. Bush's approval. In his book *All the Best*, Poppy praises Jaworski as "determined to do a thorough job" and labels him "a respected Houston lawyer and a longtime friend of ours."[59]

The thorough job? Ordering Nixon to turn over a carefully considered group of sixty-four additional tapes—including the smoking gun tape that would implicate Nixon in a cover-up.[60] Two years later, during the Senate confirmation hearings on Poppy's appointment as director of the CIA, Jaworski would go out of his way to give Bush a clean bill of health on Townhouse. Poppy, citing Jaworski's good seal of approval, paraphrased his friend: "clean, clean, clean." Poppy later successfully courted Democrat Jaworski for an endorsement of the Reagan-Bush ticket in 1980.[61]

Jaworski was one of those mentioned briefly by the *Washington Post* in its lengthy 1967 series on CIA-connected foundations. As a trustee and attorney for one of those foundations, he had declined to answer the *Post*'s questions.[62] This factor seemingly went unnoticed when he became Watergate prosecutor. It does not appear in any of the major accounts of that episode.

Also, one thing was clear about Jaworski's Watergate inquiry: he was not interested in pursuing Poppy Bush. "We sat down with Jaworski's staff and went over name after name after name," recalled Jack Gleason. "They were mainly after [Nixon's close friend] Bebe Rebozo. I spent two days at a hundred dollars an hour with my lawyer listening to 'have you ever heard of Jose Martinez' and name after name. At one point we went over the list of the recipients of the six thousand dollars. And I said, . . . the only one I remember clearly is George Bush. And they just brushed right past it . . . It was a name they didn't want to hear. I remember it so clearly because it was such a colossal screw-up."

Assistant special prosecutor Charles Ruff sent Jaworski a memo concerning Poppy Bush. "George Bush received a total of approximately $112,000 from the Townhouse Operation," Ruff wrote. "Bush also received, probably through his campaign manager, $6,000 in cash." Then, he concluded, "Bush is neither a target of our investigation nor a potential witness."[63]

Poppy had the perfect cover. If he was one of the recipients, whether as beneficiary or victim of a setup, how could he be one of the authors of the scheme itself? And if that failed, he also had a perfect friend: Leon Jaworski.[64]

Getting the Tapes

What in the end brought Nixon down was the release of his tapes, in particular, one portion: the "smoking gun" conversation. Whittling down the materials of Watergate to the few select pieces that could be orchestrated to suggest Nixon's culpability was the key.

It would be the responsibility of Poppy's good friend Jaworski to wrest the incriminating tapes from Nixon. Poppy's own diary, noted in *All the Best*, is interesting on Jaworski's appointment and role:

> Nixon had appointed Leon Jaworski—a respected Houston lawyer and longtime friend of ours—to replace Archibald Cox as the special prosecutor. Determined to do a thorough job, Jaworski . . . subpoenae[d] an additional 65 [sic—correct number is 64] tapes and documents . . . Many more shocking revelations were on the tapes, but the most damning—the "smoking gun" tape—were a conversation from June 23, 1972 where Nixon could be heard telling Haldeman to *block the FBI's investigation of the Watergate break-in*, which had occurred just six days earlier. This was proof the President had been involved, at least in the cover-up. [emphasis added]

As noted earlier, Bush, who within eighteen months would become director of the CIA, never mentioned the CIA's involvement in the Watergate break-in. By committing this sin of omission, Bush was leaving out some important context and smudging a trail of clues that might otherwise have led back to himself.

The Loyalty Trail

As noted multiple times in previous chapters, Poppy Bush appears to have labored creatively to create benign explanations for his proximity to controversial operations.

The easiest way to do that with regard to Watergate would be to establish an auxiliary role for him or his close allies in the original plot ascribed to Nixon. That is, were an investigation to look into Watergate, it would find Nixon involved with serious wrongdoing, and find that person ever so slightly tied to that wrongdoing, but in an ultimately harmless way that would have no adverse long-term consequences. That way, he could have his cake and eat it too.

Poppy had achieved that effect when the Townhouse Operation, run by his allies, had made sure that he was one of the recipients of its cash— though guilty of no obvious wrongdoing. The same would need to be true of Watergate.

It is in this light that we now consider the fact that some funds involved in Watergate would be traced back to Texas members of Poppy's team.

In his diary entries, Bush shows no sign of finding it interesting that some of the Watergate monies traced back to close friends of his. Nixon and Haldeman, however, took note. So did acting FBI director L. Patrick Gray. Wrote Gray in his memoirs:

> We had made progress tracing the four Mexican checks to the Texas Finance Committee to Re-Elect the President. Its chairman, the Houston oilman Robert Allen, sent us back to Maurice Stans [treasurer of CREEP] . . . who acknowledged that Manuel Ogarrio may have gotten the funds from a Texas campaign contributor but declined to elaborate without talking to his lawyer . . . On August 24, another Houston oilman, Roy Winchester of Pennzoil, told agents that *in April* a Mexican he believed to be Manuel Ogarrio came to his office and gave him four checks valued at "over $80,000," which Winchester then hand-delivered to [CREEP's] Hugh Sloan in Washington.[65] [emphasis added]

The FBI, in short, was following a trail that led directly to associates of George H. W. Bush. Pennzoil was the oil company of William C. Liedtke Jr. and his brother Hugh, Poppy's former partners in Zapata Petroleum. Winchester had flown the eighty thousand dollars by private Pennzoil jet to Washington in order to get it into Sloan's hands before a new federal election law went into effect in April 1972 that required disclosure of the names of the campaign donors and the recipients of such funds. The ultimate effect of this information was that some people concluded that Poppy was extraloyal to Nixon. And despite the sinister elements, particularly the foreign money, Jaworski found no wrongdoing on Bush's part.

The FBI's inquiries into the Texas money chain went nowhere, thanks to the CIA's interference. Ditto an investigation by Texas congressman Wright

Patman, an old-time populist who was chair of the House Banking Committee. Like FBI director Gray, Patman had been able to trace the money found in the pockets of burglar Bernard Barker back to the Texas chairman of the Committee to Re-elect the President, William Liedtke. But before Patman could issue some twenty-three subpoenas for CREEP officials, his fellow committee members voted 20–15 on October 3, 1972, to stop the investigation.[66]

What was interesting about the Texas connection was that it essentially put everyone in bed together, just as the break-in put Nixon in bed with the CIA. Even though Nixon was secretly feuding with the CIA, in the end it would appear to anyone investigating that everyone was on one team. But of course the Texans would not be found to have done anything wrong.

In fact, nobody did much of anything to pursue that lead. Not the Senate Watergate Committee, not the Watergate special prosecutor's office, and not the intrepid *Washington Post* reporters Woodward and Bernstein, who famously resolved to "follow the money" at the advice of Woodward's mysterious source, Deep Throat. All would claim that they were more interested in the dollar trail than the Watergate burglary itself, but when they got even remotely close to the source of the funds—the Texas money—they all stopped.

For Bush, this was, if anything, proof to Nixon of his loyalty. His group had raised money for CREEP and for the burglars, had sent a jet to bring the money. It was like Bush's Parrott phone call: *I was on the right side, so how could I be a traitor?*

Poppy's Foundation

Perhaps the greatest contribution of the *Washington Post*'s Richard Harwood, whose reporting drew from investigations by House Banking chairman Wright Patman, was his citation of dozens of prominent figures and entities that served as conduits for CIA funds. Although Harwood did not explore these connections in depth, it is striking to discover how many of the CIA-connected figures were Texans. And not just Texans, but Texans with important ties either to Poppy Bush or to November 22, 1963, or both.[67] Among those listed was the family foundation of the head of Dallas's Republic National Bank, whose building was the headquarters of the Dallas oil-intelligence elite, including Dresser Industries and—for years—of

George de Mohrenschildt. Another entity identified by the *Post* as connected to the CIA was the Houston-based San Jacinto Fund, which was incorporated by oilman John W. Mecom Sr., one of George de Mohrenschildt's backers. And a third was the family foundation of Peter J. O'Donnell Jr., who had been the chairman of the Republican Party in Texas at the time of the Kennedy assassination.

O'Donnell was responsible for the candidacies of both Poppy Bush and Army Intelligence man Jack Crichton for statewide office in the fall of 1963. It was O'Donnell, in other words, who provided both men with the cover they needed to move about Texas and meet with all sorts of people in the critical period before and after November 22. The significance of O'Donnell's presence on this list of the CIA-connected, or that of the others mentioned here, was not necessarily apparent at the time, and was not raised in the *Post* or elsewhere.

On Oil Connections

There is one other intriguing aspect to the Texas connection.

It turns out that in March 1974, as the effort to oust Nixon continued to mount, Congress and the Nixon administration were making things very uncomfortable for the Bush crowd.

There were news reports that federal officials and members of Congress were looking into possible antitrust violations by people who sat simultaneously on multiple oil company boards. In a December 1973 letter responding to members of Congress, an assistant attorney general had confirmed that the Nixon Justice Department was looking at these so-called interlocking directorates.

Most striking about the long list of violators is this: a significant majority of them had been friends of, fund-raisers for, or major donors to Poppy Bush. Many had also been employers or sponsors of George de Mohrenschildt. The list included the son of oil depletion king Clint Murchison Sr.; Admiral Arleigh Burke Jr., who had allied himself with Allen Dulles in post–Bay of Pigs inquiries into the disaster and criticized Kennedy's handling of the invasion; George Brown of Brown and Root, backer of LBJ and Poppy and employer of de Mohrenschildt; Dean McGee, former business partner of the late oil depletion backer Senator Robert Kerr; Toddie Lee Wynne, whose family provided lodging to Marina Oswald after Kennedy's assassination; military intelligence man Jack Crichton; and Neil Mallon, Poppy's well-connected "uncle."

Who had been investigating these men? Nixon's Justice Department. It was almost a perfect echo of what was going on in JFK's final year in office—and in life. Jack Kennedy had been fighting with the same group of independent oilmen over the oil depletion allowance, and Bobby Kennedy's Justice Department had sent grudging FBI agents into oil company offices to examine their books. Nixon and his old nemesis JFK had both angered the same people, and both had been removed from the presidency.

The Extent of the Infiltration

Nixon was "paranoid" about the CIA. He imagined that agency operatives were everywhere, working to undermine him. Was he crazy, or was he right?

So far, we have seen many people whose actions undermined Nixon, and found in each case what appear to be CIA connections: Dean, Dean's lawyers, Hunt, Butterfield (who exposed the White House taping system), Jaworski, McCord, Barker, Martinez, Sturgis.

And then there is Jeb Magruder, who played a crucial role in accusing his boss John Mitchell, Nixon's campaign manager, and Nixon himself of being behind the Watergate activities. Magruder was a crucial figure in the downfall of Nixon because he had been the number-two man to John Mitchell, and Mitchell became the highest-ranking member of Nixon's team—indeed, of any administration—to go to jail. Nailing Mitchell was crucial to · nailing Nixon. Magruder would offer detailed, though often demonstrably false, testimony implicating Mitchell, asserting that not only did Mitchell know about the DNC break-ins, but that he was in fact primarily responsible for orchestrating the cover-up.

Back in college, Magruder's adviser had been William Sloane Coffin, the liberal theologian. Coffin is most remembered for his opposition to the Vietnam War. Yet his background included membership in Skull and Bones and service in the Central Intelligence Agency that he himself acknowledged. He also had been chaplain at Andover and was a lifelong friend of Poppy Bush. Indeed, Poppy had brought Coffin into Skull and Bones. "There's no specific creed that they are supposed to go out and spread," Alexandra Robbins, author of a book on Skull and Bones, told the *Washington Post*. "They do have this agenda to further and bolster their superiority complex . . . and to get its members into positions of power, and to have those members hire other members into similar positions of power." Coffin's subsequent liberal credentials notwithstanding, during the period in which he had an influence on Magruder, he was still a creature of that world. Years later, when Magruder became a key witness against Nixon's aides in the Watergate trials, his lawyer was James Bierbower, who had served as vice president of Southern Air Transport, one of the CIA's largest air proprietaries.[68]

Denial

The reader may be wondering why almost everything in this chapter—in particular its theme that Nixon appears to have been ousted in a nonviolent coup—is not common knowledge.

To understand why, it is necessary to contemplate the system through which information is disseminated to the public, and the mind-set with which it is received. The common narrative on the most complex, disturbing events is usually generated by insiders—so-called investigative commissions made up of figures acceptable to the establishment, and by a handful of designated authorities deemed suitably presentable as well. For the rest of us, it is almost always easier on the conscience to accept the most benign interpretation. If everything is tied up neatly, then we do not have to do anything. The key to it all is the gatekeepers.

I got an insight into all this when I telephoned Stanley Kutler, an academic who has authored several books related to Nixon and Watergate, and whose name comes up most often on Internet searches under the term "Watergate scholar." I had hoped to find some "expert" to review my manuscript and poke holes where holes needed to be poked. I later learned that Kutler had testified for John Dean in a legal proceeding against the authors of *Silent Coup*, and in another against Gordon Liddy, who had alleged that Dean was the guiding hand behind the Watergate burglary.

When I called Kutler, he asked, "Have you spoken to John?" When I asked what John he meant, he said, "John Dean. He's a very close personal friend." When I mentioned Dean's aggressiveness toward writers, he replied, "I have enough sense never to challenge him in a court of law. Of course he's litigious, when you have all that crap coming down on you."

(In the end, Dean dropped his *Silent Coup* suit; coauthor Len Colodny, who declined to settle with the former White House counsel, received $410,000 from his own insurance company to allow Dean to dismiss the lawsuit—and a pledge from Dean not to sue in the future. And a federal judge dismissed Dean's suit against Liddy.)

Dean doesn't seem to have suffered inordinately for his role in Watergate. His one-to-four-year jail sentence became, in his own words, just four months, part of it in a government "safe house." He made millions off book deals and moved to the West Coast, where he became an affluent Beverly Hills investment banker. Asked about his business success, Dean has been markedly secretive, declining to name his partners or clients. "I just quietly want to do my own thing, without flash or splash . . . We have no advertising, no marketing, and there's no shortage of business," Dean said.[69]

In the years since Watergate, Dean has assiduously offered himself as available to help others understand the complicated affair, thereby narrating his own saga. In this, he again has positioned himself, with great effect, at the control point for information. These "assists" have ranged from helping an investigative reporting class at the University of Illinois whose project was to try to discover Deep Throat's identity to aiding documentary makers.[70]

Jim Hougan, author of *Secret Agenda*, which posits a CIA role in Watergate, was hired by *Time* magazine to review *Silent Coup* at the time of its release in 1991. Hougan says that after receiving the assignment, he got a call from Hays Gorey, the onetime *Time* correspondent who had lionized Dean in 1973 and later coauthored Maureen Dean's memoirs. Gorey, by 1991 a *Time* editor, wanted to be assured that Hougan planned to pan *Silent Coup*. According to Hougan, when he told Gorey that he found the book, which deeply implicated Dean in the origins of Watergate, to be thoroughly researched and well documented, Gorey pulled the assignment. And in an interesting twist, it turns out that Maureen Dean, before meeting John during his White House residency, had been a Dallas-based flight attendant. She had been married to George Owen, who worked for Clint Murchison Jr.—a central figure in the oil depletion–George de Mohrenschildt circle. At minimum, it certainly is a small world.

Meanwhile, oblivious to the most basic questions about Woodward, everyone continued the parlor game of guessing the "true identity" of Deep Throat. Most folks missed the statement of Woodward and Bernstein's former literary agent David Obst to the *New York Times* that Deep Throat, as such, was a fiction, concocted for purposes of making *All the President's Men* a snappier read. "Mark Felt was an invaluable source . . . but he was not Deep Throat—there

Prescott S. Bush (fourth from left) at his desk at Brown Brothers Harriman, with his partners in 1945. The firm, one of Wall Street's oldest, was tied to the intelligence establishment. *Herbert Gehr/Time Life Pictures/Getty Images*

George H. W. Bush (left of clock) with his Skull and Bones group at Yale University, New Haven, Connecticut, circa 1947. *George Bush Presidential Library and Museum*

Senator Prescott S. Bush and President John F. Kennedy accepting honorary degrees from Yale president A. Whitney Griswold in 1962. Prescott Bush would later say he "never forgave" John and Robert Kennedy for their handling of the Bay of Pigs invasion. *Bob Gomel/Time Life Pictures/Getty Images*

George H. W. "Poppy" Bush with his wife, Barbara; his parents, Dorothy and Prescott Bush; and son George W., in Odessa, Texas, March 7, 1949. Poppy had recently joined a family-connected company, Dresser Industries, which worked closely with the intelligence apparatus. *George Bush Presidential Library and Museum*

George W. Bush stands in front of his father's Zapata Offshore Company in Houston, Texas, 1956. Though a small company, it nevertheless would develop far-flung operations, including in sensitive spots, such as off Cuba. *George Bush Presidential Library and Museum*

Allen Dulles (left), the director of the Central Intelligence Agency, came to Senator Lyndon Johnson's Texas ranch on July 28, 1960, to give the vice presidential nominee a top-secret national security briefing. *AP Photo/Ted Powers*

Front page of the *Times of Viet Nam*, September 2, 1963, alleging a scheme by the U.S. Central Intelligence Agency to overthrow the government of President Diem of South Vietnam. The CIA was implicated in the violent overthrow of several heads of state in the cold war era. *AP Photo/Horst Faas*

CLUB ACTIVITIES

AMERICAN ASSOCIATION OF OILWELL DRILLING CONTRAC-TORS, 6:30 p.m. Thursday, Sheraton-Dallas Hotel: George Bush, president, Zapata Off-Shore Co.

The *Dallas Morning News*, Wednesday, November 20, 1963, announces George H. W. Bush as the speaker for a meeting of the American Association of Oilwell Drilling Contractors on Thursday, November 21—the night before the assassination of JFK.

George de Mohrenschildt, friend of Lee Harvey Oswald and George H. W. Bush, in a 1964 photo. De Mohrenschildt and Poppy Bush shared an extensive web of connections, including ties to the CIA.
Bettmann/Corbis

On November 22, 1963, the open limousine of President John F. Kennedy and First Lady Jacqueline Kennedy passes a public bus advertising the bottlers' convention, which brought eight thousand outsiders to Dallas—including Richard Nixon. Military intelligence figures linked to Poppy Bush's circle were in the pilot car of the motorcade. *AP Photo*

At right, George H. W. Bush campaigns for U.S. Senate in Texas, circa 1963/1964. He announced his candidacy in September 1963. *George Bush Presidential Library and Museum*

16 A 𝔗𝔥𝔢 𝔅𝔞𝔩𝔩𝔞𝔰 𝔐𝔬𝔯𝔫𝔦𝔫𝔤 𝔑𝔢𝔴𝔰
Tuesday, December 5, 1967 ★★★★

ColonelGiven High Award On Retiring

Col. Jack A. Crichton, commanding officer of the 488th Military Intelligence Detachment, was awarded the Legion of Merit Monday night on his retirement from the Army Reserve after 30 years of service.

The medal was presented in a ceremony in the Vaughn Building by Col. Robert D. Offer, commander of the VIII U.S. Army Corps at Austin.

An oil man and petroleum consultant, Col. Crichton organized his Reserve unit in 1956 and has been its only commander. The award cited him for "exceptionally outstanding service" as commander and for the preparation of a series of military intelligence studies.

Col. Crichton was commissioned a Reserve officer after graduation from Texas A&M University and served during World War II as commandant of cadets at Maxwell Field and later as an air intelligence officer in Europe.

At left and below, the *Dallas Morning News*, December 5, 1967. Colonel Jack A. Crichton, oilman and petroleum consultant, and political ally of Poppy Bush with intriguing ties to figures associated with the events of November 22, 1963, retires from the military intelligence unit he founded and headed.

—Dallas News Staff Photo.
Offer, left, presents award to Crichton.

George H. W. Bush pins a lieutenant's bar on his son, after George W. Bush is made an officer in the Texas Air National Guard. Questions about the senior Bush's role in securing the coveted Guard slot for W. during the Vietnam War would dog the son's political career. *AP Photo*

STC Dinner Dance.

It's top photo (from left) Ken Wiley, vice president and director of Marketing; and Mrs. Wiley and Danger Field project manager Fred Traphagen and Mrs. Traphagen and (right) T. and O. Division General manager Bob Lundberg and Mrs. Lundberg at the Service Technology Corp. Dance. Next (from left) it's Gerry Stewart, Dick Stewart, Ruth Armour, Jim Armour, Cassie Hager and project manager Rose Hager. Next photo it's (from left) the Chuck Biggs, Howie Livingstons, Carolyn Detmore, Pres Lockridge and Elwood Johnson. Bottom left is Inge Honneus, senior draftsman for LTV. And right is Carolyn Detmore, secretary to MSC Public Affairs Officer Brian Duff, who sings a few impromptu numbers for the group. — NEWS CITIZEN PHOTOS.

Inge Honneus at a Houston-area dinner dance, featured in a local paper's "Spotlight on Spaceland" column, December 1969. She would become, very briefly, the object of Lieutenant George W. Bush's intense affection.

Vice President Richard Nixon and Senator Prescott Bush enjoying their panama hats, May 6, 1953. The Nixon-Bush relationship is not well understood. Prescott was instrumental in Nixon's rise, perhaps as early as the Californian's first congressional run in 1946. *Bettmann/Corbis*

George H. W. Bush sworn in as United States ambassador to the United Nations by Associate Justice of the Supreme Court Potter Stewart, a fellow Skull and Bonesman, while Bush's wife, Barbara, and his patron, President Richard Nixon, look on, February 26, 1971. *Ron Sachs/CNP/Corbis*

Washington Post reporter Bob Woodward, left, talks with actor Robert Redford following the premiere of *All the President's Men* at the John F. Kennedy Center in Washington, D.C., April 5, 1976. Redford played the part of Woodward in the film. *AP Photo*

Former White House counsel John W. Dean III joins former CIA officer and Watergate conspirator E. Howard Hunt Jr. to field questions from students and faculty as part of a presentation titled "Watergate: Ten Years Later," at Lafayette College in Easton, PA, February 24, 1982. *AP Photo*

George H. W. "Poppy" Bush, director of the Central Intelligence Agency, at the agency's Langley, Virginia, headquarters in 1976. Poppy was named to this important post at a highly sensitive time for the agency, despite claims that he had no relevant background for the job. *Dennis Brack/Black Star*

Vice President George Bush campaigns in Fairfield, Connecticut, with Senator Lowell Weicker, November 4, 1988. The two were ostensibly on opposite sides during the Watergate crisis. *George Bush Presidential Library and Museum*

The Bush family's adviser on religion, evangelical speaker Doug Wead, then special assistant to the president, listens to his boss, George H. W. Bush, at a White House briefing in 1990. Wead helped the Bushes craft a strategy for winning over evangelical Christians. *George Bush Presidential Library and Museum*

GOP presidential front-runner, Texas governor George W. Bush, speaks in front of a painting of Jesus Christ during a campaign stop at a Christian-based community home in Colfax, Iowa, January 21, 2000. W.'s status as a born-again Christian became a key part of his political identity. *AP Photo/Eric Draper*

President George H. W. Bush and King Fahd share a laugh during meetings at the Royal Palace, Jidda, Saudi Arabia, November 21, 1990. No U.S. presidents have been closer to the Saudi royal family than the Bushes. *George Bush Presidential Library and Museum*

James R. Bath, a friend of W.'s in the National Guard, was suspended from flying at the same time as Bush. Bath later became a Houston-based representative for Saudi businessmen closely identified with the royal family. *Dan Ford Connolly/Time Life Pictures/Getty Images*

Above, President Bush and British prime minister Tony Blair following a press conference at Camp David, February 23, 2001. By the time of their first meeting, the two leaders were already linked through a mutual friend. Cooperation on the Iraq invasion came more naturally because of their rapport.
AP Photo/Rick Bowmer

President Bush emerged from the cockpit of a jet on the carrier USS *Abraham Lincoln*, May 1, 2003, where he prematurely declared major combat in Iraq concluded. He also claimed to have helped pilot the plane, though evidence suggests he never flew again after leaving his Air National Guard unit under murky circumstances in 1972, two years before his flying obligation was up.
AP Photo/Pablo Martinez Monsivais

Bush congratulates his former self-described "enforcer," Joe Allbaugh, on his appointment as director of the Federal Emergency Management Agency, March 5, 2001. Allbaugh would bring in Michael Brown as his top aide, and Brown would head the agency during the Hurricane Katrina catastrophe. *Luke Frazza/AFP/Getty Images*

Brown briefs Bush and Homeland Security secretary Michael Chertoff upon their September 2, 2005, arrival in Mobile, Alabama, before they tour the devastation wrought by Katrina. *Jim Watson/AFP/Getty Images*

Poppy and W., presidents "41" and "43," fishing from Lord's Point in Kennebunkport, Maine, June 29, 2007. Despite widely publicized differences, father and son remained close. *Jim Watson/AFP/Getty Images*

was no Deep Throat."[71] Even the book was the idea of Robert Redford, who had initially pitched a movie deal, and thought publishing a book first would make sense.

Questions about the whole Deep Throat exercise can be found buried in many articles on the subject. For example, in the above-mentioned *Times* article, titled "Mystery Solved: The Sleuths," about the Mark Felt revelations, Anne E. Kornblut begins, "With the most tantalizing mystery in recent political history solved," but seven paragraphs below she also notes, "Some cases of mistaken identity appear to be the result of false clues planted by Mr. Woodward and Mr. Bernstein in their book, 'All the President's Men,' as they tried to protect Mr. Felt."[72]

None less than Robert McCandless, Dean's cocounsel and former brother-in-law, would tell an Oklahoma newspaper reporter in a little-noted interview in 1992, on the twentieth anniversary of Watergate, that he had been one of Woodward's sources.

> "I was at least one-third of Deep Throat," Robert McCandless, a Hobart native, told The Daily Oklahoman's Washington bureau in a copyright story in today's editions . . . McCandless, 54, said he met with Woodward and Bernstein "at least four dozen times" at the George Washington University Faculty and Alumni Club . . . He said his worry then was that disclosure of his giving information about his client might lead to his disbarment.[73]

There you have a man with apparent intelligence connections admitting to having fed a story to another man with apparent intelligence connections— yet almost no one knows this.

Indeed, the vast majority of Americans never learned either the key facts about Woodward or of these statements from insiders about the fictitious or composite nature of Deep Throat. Thus, when *Vanity Fair* was approached in 2005 with the claim that former FBI official W. Mark Felt Sr. was the real Deep Throat, it is understandable that the magazine thought it had the scoop of a lifetime. The Felt story generated tremendous publicity and is now the conventional wisdom. Given the above information that there was in fact no single source known as Deep Throat, one has to ask about the motives of those who came forward to offer up Felt, a man who had previously insisted he was not Deep Throat, and who by 2005 was seriously debilitated by old age and could not even speak for himself.

The backstory is that Woodward approached Felt in 1999, showing up at Felt's California house and taking the eighty-six-year-old to a parking lot eight blocks away, where a chauffeured limousine was waiting. Some years later, with Felt incapacitated, a lawyer surfaced to write the *Vanity Fair* article. The lawyer, by the way, mentions in passing that his own father was an intelligence officer.

More recently, the book *In Nixon's Web*, the posthumous memoir of former acting FBI director L. Patrick Gray III, completed by his journalist son, Ed Gray, used Woodward's own archival papers to demonstrate irrefutably that Woodward used the term "Deep Throat" to refer to at least three of his secret sources. At a minimum, that means that Deep Throat was not, as Woodward has maintained, Mark Felt alone.[74]

To be sure, the stakes must have always been high. Not just to get Nixon out, but also, decades later, to preserve the image of Nixon as a monster. In an interview with Gerald S. Strober and Deborah Hart Strober for their book, *Nixon: An Oral History of His Presidency*, Dean says:

> Someone once said to me, "What is Richard Nixon's presidency without Watergate?" This same person—if someone had asked him the question—would have answered it by saying, "Nixon's presidency without Watergate is Hitler's Reich without the Holocaust. How do you separate them?"[75]

As for Bob Woodward, he told the Strobers:

> I disagree very strongly that [Nixon] has been rehabilitated. It's like the three-headed monkey in the circus; he's a bit of a freak. People are interested in him in the same way they are interested in Madonna, or other celebrities, because he does have stamina and endurance, and he has fought a rear-guard action against history to try to blot out what happened and encourage people to forget. It's sad, but it's also endearing, that somebody so old would keep trying to "out, damned spot!" The record is so voluminous on Watergate; there is nothing like it ... It's the most investigated event of all time, perhaps even more so than the Kennedy assassination."[76]

As for the universally reviled Haldeman, whose credibility rating has steadily climbed with corresponding revelations over the years, in 1992 he would insist that the conventional account of Watergate, that Nixon and his top aides had been trying to cover up their illegal activities, was way off base:

> We never set out to plan a planned, conscious cover-up operation. We reacted to Watergate just as we had to other [news-making events]: the Pentagon papers, ITT and the Laos Cambodia operations. We were highly sensitive to any negative PR, and our natural reaction was to contain or minimize any potential political damage.[77]

Haldeman and Ehrlichman would both claim that Nixon never explained his obsession with the Kennedy assassination and the Bay of Pigs. And Nixon wasn't talking about it at all. He refused all interviews on the topic and took whatever he knew to his grave.

Nixon, of course, was no innocent. He played rough with his critics, and he liked intrigue. But the evidence indicates that, despite his documented penchant for dirty deeds, he wasn't behind Watergate and the Watergate-related dirty deeds that ultimately brought him down.

As the former GOP official Ed DeBolt told me: "I think that [Weicker] wanted to hear that Nixon was a bad guy . . . I always say to people, especially if they are liberals, do you like having the Clean Water Act? Do you like having the EPA? Do you like having the government clean up the air?

"He was not controllable," DeBolt said of Nixon. "You wouldn't want to depend on Nixon if you were doing all kinds of clandestine crazy stuff . . . He had his own mind, and he was insecure. You want someone who is good and stable and solid, and who is going to carry out your bidding and do your thing for you . . . He was just a very strong-willed person who had his back up . . . That is not the kind of person, I wouldn't think, that the intelligence people would want to have to deal with."

DeBolt, who left Washington some years ago, said it was only when he got away that he gained some perspective. "There's nothing real, and there's nothing pleasant about the way people live there . . . The administrator of the RNC? I heard that he was CIA, he was running the business part of the RNC." (According to Senate testimony, that man was the person who initially hired former CIA man James McCord, who became a key player in the Watergate burglary.)[78]

"When you get away from the city . . . you realize, wow, the tentacles of the CIA really, really are everywhere."

IN THE END, Nixon acted toward Poppy as he always had—with a kind of restraint. Through all Nixon's tribulations, through all his rants and firings, he had never said a single negative word in public or on tape about Poppy Bush. He had managed to avoid putting Poppy into certain powerful positions—always apologetic about it—but he had always found a consolation prize.

And in 1974, after fighting on and on and on, when Nixon finally agreed to go, it would be after Poppy gave the word. Poppy himself has acknowledged (in his quiet and "unboastful" way) that the day before Nixon resigned, he wrote him and suggested that it was time to go—a view that Poppy said was shared "by most Republican leaders across the country."[79]

When Bush tried to arrange a visit with Nixon the day after the gloomy cabinet meeting and personally convince him to resign, Nixon refused to see him. "The President," Haig explained to an astonished and "somewhat offended" Poppy, "simply cannot bring himself to talk to people outside of a tiny, tiny circle and this has brought him to his knees."[80]

In the midst of this upheaval, Poppy could barely contain his excitement writing in his diary as if he was in the final stages of his own covert operation. "Suspense mounting again. Deep down inside I think maybe it should work this time. I have that inner feeling that it *will finally abort.*" [emphasis added]

He also noted that Nixon's successor, Gerald Ford, was considering him for vice president. *"Another defeat in this line* is going to be rough but then again, it is awful egotistical to think I should be selected." [emphasis added]

Out of Sight, Out of Mind

Less than two weeks after Richard Nixon left Washington in disgrace, and Gerald R. Ford took the oath of office, *Newsweek* reported that the vice presidential prospects of George H. W. Bush—a "youthful, middleground . . . appealing" figure—had suddenly taken a nose dive.

The Bush item appeared within a larger article and few people noticed it. Unnamed White House sources cited questions over Bush's apparent failure to report forty thousand of one hundred thousand dollars in campaign contributions he had received from the secret Townhouse Operation.[81]

Whether the real story was his failure to report the funds—or a more general pressing need to move Poppy far off-screen for a while—within a week Bush was "offered" a job by President Ford at the other end of the world.

And not a bad job. Poppy was to be the United States' envoy to the People's Republic of China, a significant posting in the aftermath of Nixon's diplomatic breakthrough with the Communist country.

Once again, Bush seemed an improbable choice. The awkwardness was apparent when, shortly before he departed for Beijing in October 1974, Poppy was granted an audience with Ford. The meeting lasted under ten minutes and unfolded as follows:

> FORD: You will be leaving soon.
> BUSH: The day after tomorrow. *Don't ask me about China!* . . . I know you're busy. I just wanted to say goodbye.
> FORD: *We couldn't have found anyone more qualified.*
> BUSH: *If there is anything I can do to help you politically as '76 approaches,* just let me know. [emphasis added]
> FORD: Thanks. I may try to visit you there by then.
> BUSH: That would be great! Many thanks for the time.[82]

Bush's jocular admonition not to ask him about China brings to mind a similar, earlier incident, in which a friend had asked what could possibly qualify Poppy to be U.N. ambassador. At that time, Bush had replied, "Ask me in ten days." This time around, Ford was clearly in on the joke.[83]

But shipping Poppy seven thousand miles away made a different kind of sense. With this move, Ford had effectively put Bush outside both domestic politics and the reach of congressional investigators. So important did this piece of business seem to be that Ford took care of it even before he got around to his most famous act: pardoning Nixon.

The Nixon pardon could seem as strange in its own way as sending Bush to Beijing. Nixon had not even been charged with a crime, so he was in essence being given a "premature" pardon. Although this act insulated Nixon against later prosecution, it also branded him forever with the mark of Watergate and its felonious cover-up. As for Ford, while he cast himself as a healer whose only motive was to bring peace to a badly fractured country, the pardon infuriated anyone who wanted to see the full story brought out in open court; the backlash ended up damaging Ford's political future. That he was willing to risk this outcome may say something about the pressures brought to bear to curtail further inquiry into the origins of Watergate. In effect, Ford was sealing away "Exhibit A" of the Watergate mess—before investigators could dig deeper and find out who really was behind it and why.

In explaining away Bush's China appointment, the media reported that he was getting a consolation prize after losing out to New York governor Nelson Rockefeller as Ford's vice presidential pick. According to that version, Poppy had his choice of London or Paris, and he surprised Ford by countering with a third option: Beijing.

An admission by Bush's close friend Robert Mosbacher probably came closer to the truth—namely, that Bush "wanted to get as far away from the stench [of Watergate] as possible."[84] Of course, historians generally attributed that to Bush's desire to keep his own seemingly clear political future unsullied rather than any sort of admission.

Certainly, Poppy urgently needed to get away from the scene of the crime. Throughout his life thus far, and on into the future, Poppy would evince a real talent for edging to the periphery of the crowd, watching like any other bystander while subtly guiding the main action—before slipping away entirely to deny that he had been there at all. In the case of Watergate, his getaway path was clear. A brief exile to China would keep him out of the line of fire, cleanse him of the stench, and burnish his credentials too.

More important, the London and Paris postings would have required Senate confirmation, which could have opened up the very questions he wanted to escape. But the United States did not have full diplomatic relations with Beijing, so that post required no confirmation process (as Bush himself noted in his memoirs).[85]

As for his lack of experience and knowledge, that hardly mattered, as things turned out. The job was largely pro forma, because, as Ford noted to Bush, Henry Kissinger was determined to handle the sensitive Sino-American relationship himself. Poppy Bush's published recollections of his time in China are dominated by leisurely bike rides and barbecues.

The Beijing posting was a fortuitous breather for Poppy, but soon he was ready for the main act. He was finally ready to come in from the cold.

CHAPTER 12

In from the Cold

SHORTLY BEFORE CHRISTMAS 1974, the *New York Times* published an article by Seymour Hersh that chronicled years of CIA covert operations worldwide, known among historians and CIA officials as the "family jewels." These operations ranged from assassination attempts against foreign leaders to CIA-funded drug experiments on unwitting American citizens. Hersh's reporting led to the revelations that the CIA, under director Richard Helms, used physical surveillance and wiretapping against several journalists, notably the investigative columnist Jack Anderson, as well as Victor Marchetti, a former CIA officer turned agency critic.

The CIA's new director, William Colby, had taken office just four months earlier, but he knew all about these embarrassments. On December 31, 1974, Colby briefed the Justice Department on the extent of the transgressions, which had begun in 1953, under then-director Allen Dulles. There was a twenty-year program of reading mail sent back and forth between the United States and both the Soviet Union and China *at American locations*—this despite an explicit prohibition on such domestic activities by the CIA. There were plots to assassinate foreign leaders such as Castro and LSD tests on humans. Several days after Colby brought his information to the Ford administration, Secretary of State Henry Kissinger sent a memo to the president that asserted Hersh's article was "just the tip of the iceberg." "When the FBI has a hunting license into the CIA," Kissinger added, "this could end up worse for the country than Watergate."[1]

IN THIS MILIEU in which Americans learned about the extent of the CIA's involvement in unsavory activities at home and abroad, it was only natural that the public would demand answers to the unresolved questions surrounding the assassination of John E. Kennedy. This subject was not unfamiliar to the now president, Gerald R. Ford. He had been a member of the Warren Commission and had slightly altered text in the commission's report in a manner that supported the "lone gunman" scenario.[2]

Ford appointed a presidential commission to study the indelicate ways of America's spy sector. Commonly known as the Rockefeller Commission, it issued a single report in 1975, which touched on certain CIA abuses such as the mail opening and surveillance of domestic dissident groups. It also conducted a narrow study of issues relating to the Kennedy assassination: the backward head snap evident in the Zapruder film and the possible presence of CIA (and later Watergate) operatives E. Howard Hunt and Frank Sturgis in Dallas at the time of the assassination.

The Rockefeller Report is seen by many historians as a whitewash—an attempt to preclude a more thorough investigation.[3] Even so, there has been little consideration of what it meant that Nelson Rockefeller was chairing such an inquiry to begin with. Rockefeller was himself a devotee of the black arts. As his own former longtime aide William G. Ronan told me in an interview, "Nelson was very active in covert operations. As a matter of fact, he was very supportive, even before we got into World War II."[4] First as coordinator of Inter-American Affairs under President Roosevelt, and then as assistant secretary of state during the war, Nelson had shared oversight of intelligence operations in the western hemisphere with J. Edgar Hoover's FBI. Early in the Eisenhower administration,[5] Rockefeller had been Ike's special assistant on psychological warfare and cold war strategy. He also chaired the National Security Council's special group that oversaw all CIA covert activities. These included some of the agency's supersecret family jewels that CIA director Colby later revealed to Senate investigators.[6]

Given this, and the intelligence background of several other Rockefeller Commission members, one can hardly be surprised at the final verdict. The commission concluded simply that there was "no credible evidence" of CIA involvement in the Kennedy assassination.

Before the commission could issue its report, however, an eight-hundred-pound gorilla appeared on the scene. That was the Church Committee, set up in January 1975 by the Democratic-controlled U.S. Senate. The Rockefeller Commission was in part an attempt to preempt a serious congressional probe of intelligence, but in that it utterly failed.[7] In 1975 and 1976, the Church Committee would publish fourteen reports, which covered the formation of U.S. intelligence agencies, their operations, and their alleged abuses, together with recommendations for reform.[8] Some of these—such as a law requiring warrants for domestic wiretapping—were actually instituted.[9]

The Church Committee documented a mind-boggling array of domestic "dirty tricks." The CIA and FBI would send anonymous letters designed to induce employers to fire politically suspect workers, for example. Similar letters went to spouses in an effort to destroy marriages. The committee also documented criminal break-ins and disinformation campaigns aimed at provoking violent attacks against selected individuals, including Martin Luther King Jr.. The FBI also mailed King a tape recording taken from microphones hidden in his hotel rooms—accompanied by a note warning that the recording, with its evidence of marital indiscretions, would be released to the public unless King committed suicide.

Under pressure from the Church Committee, President Ford issued an executive order banning U.S.-sanctioned assassinations of foreign leaders. In a brief reference to the murder of President John F. Kennedy, the order hinted at a possible scenario that the official investigations had denied. It barred foreign assassinations that "involved the murder of a political leader for political purposes accomplished through a surprise attack," and actually mentioned Kennedy's murder as one that could fit this rubric.[10]

The House of Representatives ran its own investigation, through what came to be known as the Pike Committee. A thorough audit of the foreign-intelligence budget led the committee to conclude that expenditures on overseas spying were three or four times larger than Congress had been told. Meanwhile, in quick succession, former CIA officers began publishing tell-all books about a chilling array of covert schemes. Philip Agee's *Inside the Company: CIA Diary* is probably the best-known of these memoirs. Until then, only books written by outsiders (such as journalists) had been so critical of the agency's activities.[11]

In March 1975, more than eleven years after Henry Luce had purchased the Zapruder film and removed it from circulation, the film was finally shown to a national audience in its entirety. These images spawned a new round of questions regarding the Warren Commission's findings. That September, one of Church's subcommittees was given a staff of nine to investigate the intelligence agencies with respect to the JFK assassination. The subcommittee interviewed over fifty witnesses and gained access to five thousand pages of intelligence agency material.[12] The probe left many lingering questions, but it ran out of steam due to lack of witness cooperation.

Home at Last

On November 1, 1975, while U.S. envoy George H. W. Bush was with his wife, Barbara, riding bicycles through Beijing, he was approached by a breathless messenger with a telegram. It was from Henry Kissinger, and it informed Bush that the president was about to appoint him director of the Central Intelligence Agency.[13]

The current director, William Colby, had been too candid and forthcoming. Without consulting Nixon or Ford, he had released to the Justice Department the 693-page "Family Jewels" document, and confirmed details after it was leaked to *New York Times* reporter Seymour Hersh.[14] Colby was not the one to hold the fort during the coming onslaught; and his ouster was part of what came to be called the "Halloween Massacre," in which the White House rid the administration of elements it deemed undesirable. The orchestrators were Donald Rumsfeld, Ford's young chief of staff, and his deputy, Dick Cheney.

After the putsch, Rumsfeld would become defense secretary and Cheney would take Rumsfeld's post. The new national security adviser, taking Kissinger's place, was Air Force Lieutenant General Brent Scowcroft. Finally, the moderate Vice President Rockefeller was removed from the ticket for the upcoming 1976 reelection campaign.

And whose idea was this dramatic reshuffling? "I did it totally on my own," the relatively moderate Ford assured the press. "It was my decision. I fitted the pieces together and they fitted excellently."[15] This was hardly convincing, since the net effect was to re-empower elements of the security-intelligence elite that had been shunted aside by Nixon and was seriously threatened by the post-Watergate cascade of disclosures.

Ushered into control in one fell swoop was a group that would periodically surface in top positions in Republican administrations over the next three-plus decades. Under President George H.W. Bush, Cheney became defense secretary, with Scowcroft again serving as national security adviser. Under George W. Bush, Cheney returned to power, this time as vice president, and with Rumsfeld, now defense secretary, engineered the disastrous invasion of Iraq.

The appointment that on the surface made the least sense was the decision to place Poppy Bush at the head of the CIA. Why install a purported intelligence virgin—and, moreover, a fellow widely regarded as a lightweight—in this highly sensitive post, and in this period of intense pressure on the agency? The newspapers at the time seemed bewildered, though unwilling to say so explicitly. In an unsigned profile headlined "A Breezy Head of the C.I.A.," the *New York Times* struggled to find some achievements. "As a chief American representative in China, George Bush has succeeded, at least in a limited degree, in erasing the image that many persons in Peking had of America as an elitist country. Instead of formal dinners and receptions, the Bushes entertain by serving soft drinks and popcorn while showing old movies."[16] Another *Times* article noted that on a visit to China, Kissinger "did not set aside any time for consultations with Mr. Bush before plunging into dealings with Chinese leaders."[17]

Yet, just as his brief and undistinguished congressional service had supposedly qualified him for the United Nations, and his unexceptional United Nations service somehow qualified him for the China post, George H. W. Bush's brief experience in China was now invoked as somehow qualifying him to run the CIA. The central assumption in all this was that Poppy did not have an intelligence background. To some, this was seen as a liability, to others an asset. But no one considered the possibility that his supposed lack of experience in spycraft was, in fact, part of that craft, and his long-running cover story.

Indeed, it was unlikely that with all the Sturm und Drang over intelligence, the kind of person that George H. W. Bush appeared to be in public could possibly be the choice of insiders and hard-liners. There had to be more to it. Looking back at old clippings from that period, one can see the tide of inquiry just barely lapping at the story.

Several articles mentioned that Bush had been on the receiving end of largess from the Townhouse fund (covered in chapters 10 and 11), but they failed to inquire into his deeper connections. And there was absolutely no discussion of how Poppy Bush had devoted a substantial chunk of his adult life to intelligence-connected activity. Even the barest hint of this would not emerge until many years later, with Joseph McBride's little-noticed *Nation* article mentioning "George Bush of the CIA."

The Townhouse problem was mitigated by Poppy's old friend Leon Jaworski during the Senate's confirmation hearings. Speaking at a convention of former FBI special agents in Houston, Jaworski gave Bush a clean bill of health on the Townhouse matter: "This was investigated by me when I served as Watergate special prosecutor. I found no involvement of George Bush and gave him full clearance. I hope that in the interest of fairness, the matter will not be bandied about unless something new has appeared on the horizon."[18]

Later, in 1980, when Poppy was campaigning for the presidency and he was asked about the Townhouse fund, he always answered that Leon Jaworski had cleared him: "The answer came back, clean, clean, clean."[19] Not mentioned, perhaps because it was not widely known, was the close relationship between Bush and Jaworski, or Jaworski's own CIA ties—as noted in chapter 11. This mutual admiration resurfaced at Jaworski's funeral, where Bush, Richard Nixon's supposedly loyal retainer, served as an honorary pallbearer for the man who played a key role in driving Nixon from office.

Despite having dodged all the possible bullets related to his questionable personal connections, Poppy nevertheless had a difficult time with the Senate confirmation process. Because of his partisan background and his aspirations to higher office, he was a somewhat controversial choice for a post that required at least the appearance of political neutrality. Senator Frank Church expressed his concern that a political figure would lead what was intended to be the "least political and most sensitive agency in Washington."[20]

Moreover, Bush was being mentioned as a possible running mate for Ford in 1976. "It is wrong for [Bush] to want both positions, even in a Bicentennial year," said Church, only half joking.[21] In response to such criticism, Ford drafted a letter announcing that Bush would not seek the vice presidency. "[Bush] urged that I make this decision," Ford's letter asserted. "This says something about the man and about his desire to do this job for the nation."[22] Bush himself laid it on even thicker. "Old-fashioned as it may seem to some, it is my duty to serve my country," Bush told the Senate Armed Services Committee.[23] The Senate eventually approved Bush by a vote of 64 to 27.

Immediately, Poppy was recognized by elite leaders of other intelligence services as to the manner born. As Count Alexandre de Marenches, head of French intelligence, writes in his memoirs:

> Mr. Bush was introduced to me by the French ambassador to the United Nations in a handwritten note. "He is a real gentleman," the ambassador wrote to me, "born of an old New England family who has had a respect from birth for the kinds of fundamental moral values that we both share."

Shortly after this note arrived, George Bush turned up in Paris. It was March 1976. From the first moment, we got along famously. Our first meeting took place in my office at our headquarters, over a wonderful lunch prepared by our French Navy chef. I still remember the soufflé. Bush was accompanied by his principal aide, General Vernon Walters, who was and remains one of the most extraordinary diplomats and intelligence analysts in the West. Alas, their hands were very much tied by the corrosive and systemic failings of the American intelligence system.

When he returned to Washington, I quickly received a charming, handwritten note:

> Dear Friend:
>   . . . the luncheon was spectacular, but the conversation and getting your impressive views on the troubled world surpassed even that delectable soufflé. An added dividend was Barbara's great feeling of warmth for your charming wife . . .
>   sincerely, George B.[24]

As CIA DIRECTOR, Poppy was a busy man. On the one hand, he needed to repeatedly trot over to Capitol Hill to mollify members of Congress. On the other hand, he needed to help craft the CIA's response to the Church Committee, which was on the warpath over the agency's wrongdoing and excesses. One solution to the scrutiny was simply to scrub the files, and there was precedent for this. Before then-director Helms left the CIA, he had ordered the destruction of files on mind-control experiments and hundreds of hours of secretly recorded tapes of his own conversations.[25]

Senator Frank Church, at least, seemed to have an inkling that something was afoot. "There is no question in my mind," he said, "but that concealment is the new order of the day."[26]

Upon Bush's nomination, former president Nixon, clearly unwitting to Poppy's recent role in his demise, had offered him one bit of advice: "You will be tempted greatly to 'give away the store' in assuring the members of the Senate Committee that everything the CIA does in the future will be an open book," he wrote. "I think you will be far better off to stand up and strongly defend the CIA and the need to maintain, particularly, its covert activities."[27] Bush's handwritten response to these unintentionally ironic remarks suggested that the toppled leader had little to fear. "I couldn't agree more," Bush wrote. "We must not see the Agency compromised further by reckless disclosure."[28]

FOR SOMEONE WHO supposedly knew nothing about intelligence, Poppy made quite an impression on other professionals in the field. As Count de Marenches noted, "The Americans, in my opinion, are the least prepared of all. Few of the heads of American intelligence with whom I came in close contact . . . ever fully understood . . . [the] most basic axioms of war or espionage or geopolitics in the age of South-North conflict. Perhaps the one who came closest was George Bush."[29]

Something truly epochal was going on—but it entirely evaded the ken of the media and public. After sequestering Poppy in China during the bloody aftermath of Nixon's resignation, Ford brought him back to be the chief spy. And then he handed Bush an unprecedented mandate.

Shortly after Poppy took over the CIA—on February 17, 1976—Ford announced a major reorganization that increased both the agency's authority to conduct controversial operations and its director's authority over the larger intelligence community, including agencies that were part of the Defense Department. The *New York Times* reported that Bush now had more power than any other director of Central Intelligence since the creation of the CIA.[30]

Bush wielded this heightened power on behalf of the military-industrial complex that President Eisenhower had so famously warned against in his valedictory speech. Politicizing the process of intelligence analysis, he imposed a systematic bias that supported a new harder line toward the communist bloc. This was a direct reversal of the Nixon-Kissinger policy of détente.

Under the guidance of Rumsfeld, Cheney, a young Paul Wolfowitz, and others who had ascended in the Halloween Massacre, Poppy began finding ways to get around the analysts who did not sufficiently hype the Soviet threat. To that end he created a second analytical team, which produced alarming estimates of Soviet military capabilities. The concept was known as Team A/Team B.

In this way, Poppy was the father of the analytical gamesmanship his son would use to justify war with Iraq nearly three decades later—under the guidance of the same Rumsfeld, Cheney, and Wolfowitz. That makes it particularly ironic that during W.'s presidency, Poppy was widely characterized as the cautious one who was privately troubled by his son's bumptious foreign policy.

In 2003, as it became apparent that the Iraqi weapons of mass destruction, cited as cause for war, did not in fact exist, *Newsweek* observed that "intelligence failure" was a Bush family legacy:

> During the early 1970s, hard-line conservatives pilloried the CIA for being soft on the Soviets. As a result, CIA Director George Bush agreed to allow a team of neocon outside "experts" to look at the intelligence and come to their own conclusions. Team B— which included future President George W.'s Iraq War strategist Paul Wolfowitz—produced a scathing report, claiming that the Soviet threat had been badly underestimated . . . Iraq is part of a pattern. In each of these cases, arguments about the threat posed by a country rest in large part on the character of the regime. The Team B report explains that the CIA's analysis was flawed because it was based on too much "hard data"—meaning facts.[31]

BESIDES THE SCRUBBING operation and the cooking of intelligence to order, Poppy oversaw some intriguing new projects. He enlisted the Saudis to provide financing for agency covert operations that Congress had barred or refused to fund. In effect, Bush privatized U.S. covert operations. This program, which will be detailed in chapters 13 and 14, offered tangible benefits to the Saudis, permitted the continuation of questionable CIA activities, and as we shall see, also enriched Poppy's circle back in Texas.

Farming out CIA operations was risky business, however. In September 1976, Washington was rocked, literally, by a car bombing on D.C.'s Embassy Row that killed Orlando Letelier, the former ambassador of Chilean president Salvador Allende and a critic of Augusto Pinochet's military regime. Letelier's American colleague Ronni Moffitt, also died. Bush insisted that the U.S. government had no knowledge of, nor hand in, this act of terrorism.

But subsequent Chilean investigations and trials showed that the assassination had been carried out by former CIA contract employee Michael Townley, a U.S. expatriate who had gone to work for Pinochet's intelligence chief.

The strangest part was that Townley, who had been on the State Department watch list as a potential terrorist, had nevertheless managed to freely

enter the United States before the assassination. It was an eerie foreshad-
owing of what would happen in the years leading up to September 11, 2001,
when at least one of the hijackers would enter the United States despite being on a CIA watch list. Townley was convicted in the United States in 1978
while the Democrat Jimmy Carter was in the White House; his Chilean
handlers were convicted in 1993, after democracy had returned to that
country. The former Chilean secret police chief admitted that his orders had
come from Pinochet.[32] But the crime was committed on Poppy's turf, and
on Poppy's watch—by one of the agency's former hirelings.

Plenty to Digest

The biggest and most controversial assassination was also back in the
spotlight—and again, there were CIA strands in the picture. Thanks to a
flurry of investigations as George Bush took over at CIA, eyes were turning
back to the unsolved JFK murder. And to Dallas.

Although Poppy couldn't remember where he had been on November
22, 1963, and couldn't be bothered to recall his old friend George de
Mohrenschildt's precise role in the matter or in the life of Lee Harvey Oswald, as CIA director he began paying keen attention to the resurgent assassination investigations.

Director Bush composed a rather strange internal memo asking for a copy
of a report concerning a visit by Jack Ruby (killer of Lee Harvey Oswald—
Kennedy's alleged assassin) to the reputed Mafia leader Santo Trafficante Jr.;
two years after Bush left the CIA directorship, Trafficante would admit to a
House panel that he participated in a CIA-directed 1960 operation to assassinate Castro. Trafficante was also believed by some to have had a role in the
Kennedy assassination. (Another mob figure of interest to Kennedy assassination investigators, Sam Giancana, was killed in 1975 by an unknown gunman shortly before he was scheduled to testify about the plots against Castro.)

In his testimony to the House Select Committee on Assassinations, Trafficante would say that he had been recruited for the Castro project by fellow
mobster John Rosselli, who had testified in 1975 before the Church Committee about efforts to kill Castro. In April 1976, while Poppy was CIA director, Rosselli was again called before the Church Committee, this time to
testify about a conspiracy to kill President Kennedy. Three months later, the
committee decided to recall Rosselli for additional testimony. But by the time

he was called, he had already been missing for several days. His decomposing body was later found inside a fifty-five-gallon steel fuel drum floating in Dumfounding Bay near Miami. He had been strangled and shot, and his legs had been sawed off.

Against this backdrop of new interest in assassinations in general and particularly in possible links between the efforts to rub out Castro and the killing of JFK, George de Mohrenschildt resurfaced.

In January 1976, he wrote to Willem Oltmans, a freelance Dutch television reporter whom he had met eight years earlier. Oltmans's reason for maintaining contact with de Mohrenschildt has been a subject of some speculation, including among his Dutch media colleagues. His profile at times appears less that of the typical left-leaning Dutch journalist and more suggestive of a U.S. intelligence agent. Former colleagues of Oltmans, who is deceased, described him to me as a complex and mysterious figure. As will become clear, Oltmans was a cipher to one and all, sometimes seeming to be determined to expose the truth, and sometimes to do the opposite. Perhaps he was something of a free agent, pursuing a particular course yet unhappy about it. But one thing is certain: just as de Mohrenschildt helped steer Oswald, to a lesser extent Oltmans did the same for de Mohrenschildt.

Oltmans was the son of an affluent family with a history in colonial Indonesia. A Dutch citizen, he had graduated in the same Yale University class as William F. Buckley, and was a strident anti-Communist. Though he had no apparent connections to Dallas, Oltmans was drawn into conservative circles in that city shortly after Allen Dulles's forced resignation and about the time that the CIA's Dallas officer J. Walton Moore began talking to George de Mohrenschildt about Lee Harvey Oswald. Oltmans's reason for visiting at that time was an invitation to give occasional lectures to women's groups. Those female auxiliaries played important support roles in Dallas's highly politicized and archconservative elite, as did the White Russian community, the independent oilmen, and the military contractors and intelligence officers.

Oltmans's name appears on a schedule of upcoming speakers at the Dallas Woman's Club published in the *Dallas Morning News* in October 1961. The leadoff speaker for that season: Edward Tomlinson, "roving Latin American editor" for *Reader's Digest*.

Oltmans's next invitation to speak to the Dallas ladies appears to have been in January 1964, shortly after Kennedy's assassination. At that time, Oltmans met Lee Harvey Oswald's mother on a plane (a coincidence, he said). She mentioned to him her suspicions about the fact that the Dallas police had interrogated her at length about her son but failed to record the important biographical details she provided them. She told Oltmans that she suspected a conspiracy at work.

From that moment forward, in his telling, Oltmans was hooked on the JFK mystery. He interviewed George and Jeanne de Mohrenschildt in 1968 and '69 and remained in touch with them in the years that followed. George de Mohrenschildt got so comfortable with Oltmans that in early 1976 de Mohrenschildt sent him a few pages of a manuscript about his life, with an emphasis on his interactions with Oswald. Oltmans edited the incomplete and stiffly written pages and sent them back to de Mohrenschildt.

Meanwhile, others outside Washington were also becoming interested in reexamining the JFK assassination. One was the world's largest-circulation publication, *Reader's Digest*. With its wholesome portrayal of America, it was almost standard issue in every doctor's waiting room. Less well known are its longtime ties to government, in particular the close historic relationship of the magazine's top brass with J. Edgar Hoover and the CIA. One of the most powerful figures on the board that ran *Reader's Digest* was Nelson Rockefeller's brother, Laurance.[33]

Here's how the magazine explained its interest in the assassination— one that would culminate in its reporter's meeting George de Mohren- schildt in 1977 on the day he died:

> For years *Digest* Managing Editor Fulton Oursler, Jr., had been fas- cinated by the cascade of conflicting reports surrounding the findings of the Warren Commission. In early 1975, as fresh infor- mation began to seep out of the Senate's Select Committee to Study Governmental Operations with Respect to Intelligence Activities, and as certain documents began to be available through the Free- dom of Information Act, Oursler's interest sharpened. "How could it be," he asked his colleagues, "that there was a major investigation in 1964, and that 11 years later people are *still* [italics in original] coming up with new information?" Oursler believed that the *Digest* should attempt a definitive examination of the enigmatic assassin.

As the above excerpt shows, Oursler seemed less interested in uncover- ing new information than in investigating why new information continued to emerge. An extreme conservative and a reliable editorial customer for

Hoover's propaganda wares, Oursler apparently felt that the solution for the *Reader's Digest* editors was to reassure the American mainstream of Oswald's guilt.[34]

The *Digest* editors decided it would be advisable to retain an outsider to write the book, and they turned to Edward Jay Epstein. Epstein had written his master's thesis at Harvard on the Kennedy assassination, as well as a book called *Inquest*, which was a comparatively mild critique of the Warren Commission's investigation.

Epstein's skepticism of the commission's conclusions regarding Oswald made him seem a credible "expert" to later argue the opposite: that Lee Harvey Oswald had indeed shot Kennedy—and moreover, that he had done it as a Soviet agent. This was the version of the assassination tale told by James Jesus Angleton, the CIA's longtime head of security; it became the explanation preferred by hard-line "cold warriors."

That the *Digest* should adopt Angleton's account is not really that surprising, especially when one learns that the magazine's interest was at least to some degree externally stimulated. The magazine editors had been approached by "Jamie" Jamieson, a CIA officer who had purportedly left the agency but now interacted with the media as a "consultant" to it. He arranged interviews with Soviet defectors and ghostwrote articles for them. At this point, Jamieson was ghostwriting a book by Yuri Nosenko, who had defected from the Soviet Union before Kennedy's assassination. Nosenko had originally claimed that Oswald had no ties to Soviet intelligence, but had now reversed himself. Jamieson suggested to the *Digest* editors that they publish a new book about the Kennedy assassination—one in which Nosenko's new claims about Oswald as a Soviet agent would play a central role.

As noted above, in CIA debriefings, Nosenko had originally insisted that the KGB had no ties to Oswald. The defector stuck with that story despite an unusually long and harsh period of interrogation ordered by Angleton. Nosenko had insisted that the Soviets considered Oswald an odd duck and possible CIA double agent during his residency in the Soviet Union; the KGB concluded Oswald had no operational usefulness to the Soviet spy system.

Epstein, however, citing confidential, unnamed sources and classified materials, asserted that Nosenko himself was a double agent who had defected to the United States in order to provide a cover story for Oswald—who, Epstein concluded, was a Soviet agent too. The problem with Epstein's theory, which he revealed later in his own writings, was that his source for most of this was none other than Angleton, the CIA's longtime chief of counterespionage who had been fired by then-director William Colby.[35]

Angleton was considered paranoid by many people in the agency; he saw Russian moles everywhere, and he had been a staunch Dulles loyalist.

Epstein has claimed that he was reluctant to take on the new JFK assassination book project. He did not say why—and did not respond to telephone and e-mail messages from me seeking more information. But once he acquiesced to Oursler's request, he worked quickly. He managed to publish *Legend: The Secret World of Lee Harvey Oswald* in 1978, beating the House Select Committee on Assassinations (HSCA) to the punch, and perhaps partially influencing its conclusions.[36]

With the assistance of two *Reader's Digest* staffers, Epstein was able to contact virtually every witness of interest, thereby getting to them just ahead of House investigators. Among these was Oswald's shipboard roommate from his initial passage to Russia—who coincidentally was from the Bush hometown of Midland, Texas. The roommate, Billy Joe Lord, had just sent a letter to President Jimmy Carter, asserting that there was a conspiracy involving the CIA and FBI. Lord would later complain to the FBI that Epstein's team tried to intimidate him into cooperating. He said the *Digest* researchers even sought to exert pressure by invoking the Bushes, and also Jimmy Allison, Poppy's political lieutenant, who had by then returned to Midland. Allison was the publisher of the local daily, where Lord worked.

For almost a year, Epstein traveled the world with unusual access to top CIA officials. He even stayed as a guest of former-CIA-director-turned-ambassador Richard Helms in Tehran, Iran. He also talked with Angleton at his home in McLean, Virginia, and inspected his famous orchid collection. On April 22, 1976, according to Epstein, he conducted a brief interview with George de Mohrenschildt, but found him less than forthcoming.

Meanwhile, support continued to mount in Congress for a special investigation of assassinations—a list which now included not just John F. Kennedy but also Robert F. Kennedy, Martin Luther King Jr., and Malcolm X. On September 17, 1976, after months of heated debate, the House voted to open a new investigation. The House Select Committee on Assassinations soon had a staff of 170 lawyers, investigators, and researchers.

As the HSCA became a reality, George de Mohrenschildt's urgent plea arrived at CIA headquarters for Director Bush. The missive appears to have been intercepted by a member of Bush's staff, who wrote on a routing slip, "Mr. Bush, do you know this individual?" followed by boxes for "yes" and "no." Bush had marked "yes." Under "Remarks," a staffer wrote: "I was going to forward this to DCI security—but since it's a 'Dear George' letter and from Texas, I thought I should run it through you on the off chance that it is a friend of the Director's."

Bush himself typed an internal memo, which appeared on the director's stationery:

> I do know this man DeMohrenschildt.
>
> I first men [sic] him in the early 40'3 [sic]. He was an uncle to my Andover roommate.
>
> Later he surfaced in Dallas (50's maybe).
>
> He got involved in some controversial dealings in Haiti.
>
> Then he surfaced when Oswald shot to prominence. He knew Oswald before the assassination of Pres. Kennedy.
>
> I don't recall his role in all this.
>
> At one time he had /or spent plenty of money.
>
> I have not heard from him for many years until the attached letter came in.[37]

GB 9-17

Bush's memo appears to be a case study in dissembling and obfuscation: pure spycraft posterior-covering by a consummate intelligence bureaucrat. How could the head of U.S. intelligence "not recall" the role of a friend in the Kennedy assassination, and apparently not even be interested? And if he couldn't remember de Mohrenschildt's role in the assassination, how could he remember that he had gone to Haiti? And why would he even remember such a thing as that de Mohrenschildt had "controversial dealings in Haiti" when he could not recall de Mohrenschildt's certainly more controversial dealings with Oswald? It would have been amusing had the subject not been so literally dead serious.

Poppy was being no more candid in his assertion that he had not heard from de Mohrenschildt "for many years." In fact, the two appear to have maintained sporadic contact. In 1971, as U.N. ambassador, Poppy Bush wrote to the State Department on behalf of de Mohrenschildt, who claimed to be in a dispute with the Haitian government.[38] (A bureaucrat replied to Bush that the matter was essentially a private one and that it would be inappropriate for the State Department to intercede.)

And as recently as 1973, when Bush headed the Republican Party, de Mohrenschildt had sent him an amiable update note, mentioning that he was now teaching at a small private college and urging federal support for such schools.

"And we shall vote for you when you run for President," he had concluded. "Your old friend G. DeMohrenschildt."[39]

From One George to Another

By the fall of 1976, however, when his note was passed through official CIA channels, de Mohrenschildt was no longer upbeat. In fact, as the content reveals, he was terrified:

> Dallas, Sept. 5
> Dear George,
>   You will excuse this hand-written letter. Maybe you will be able to bring a solution to the hopeless situation I find myself in.
>   My wife and I find ourselves surrounded by some vigilantes; our phone bugged; and we are being followed everywhere. Either FBI is involved in this or they do not want to accept my complaints. We are driven to insanity by the situation.
>   I have been behaving like a damn fool ever since my daughter Nadya died from [cystic fibrosis] over three years ago. I tried to write, stupidly and unsuccessfully, about Lee H Oswald and must have angered a lot of people—I do not know. But to punish an elderly man like myself and my highly nervous and sick wife is really too much.
>   Could you do something to remove the net around us? This will be my last request for help and I will not annoy you any more.
>   Good luck in your important job.
>   Thank you so much.
>   Sincerely,
>   G. deMohrenschildt
>   2737 Kings Road, Apt 142
>   Tel 521-1309 (a/c 214) Dallas 75219

This was an interesting letter for a number of reasons. For one thing, what was de Mohrenschildt thinking when he said he "must have angered a lot of people" by trying to write about Oswald? His writing efforts had never been published, nor had any mention of those efforts. The only person who definitely knew about de Mohrenschildt's "writings" was the Dutchman Willem Oltmans. De Mohrenschildt was clearly referring to a limited circle of people who knew about his activities and had something at stake.

To anyone in CIA headquarters who saw the note before it reached the director, it likely appeared desperate and stressed, which explains the comments on the routing slip about passing it along to security.

But to anyone familiar with the saga itself, other things stood out. De Mohrenschildt clearly saw George H. W. Bush as someone he could trust and who had the power to do something about these problems. He appeared to be suggesting that Bush might actually be familiar with the situation and the basis for the harassment.

There's just a hint of the shared shorthand of the sort that intelligence people and others use when communicating something sensitive. It feels as if he is saying to Bush, We both know what is going on here, and please make it stop. There is also a hint amid the ingratiating self-deprecation that there could be adverse publicity consequences should this become public: "to punish an elderly man like myself."

Bush's staff prepared a boilerplate response. And they attached to it this memo to Bush:

> The attached suggested draft to Mr. DeMohrenschildt was written without knowledge of the flavor of your personal relationship with him. The tone may not be appropriate, but the message boils down to the fact that neither CIA nor the FBI appear to have been interested in Mr. DeMohrenschildt for a number of years.

On September 28, 1976, a letter likely reflecting his staff's suggested language went out to de Mohrenschildt at his Dallas address.

> Dear George:
>   Please forgive the delay in my reply to your September 5th letter. It took time to thoroughly explore the matters you raised.
>   Let me say first that I know it must have been difficult for you to seek my help in the situation outlined in your letter. I believe I can appreciate your state of mind in view of your daughter's tragic

death a few years ago and the current poor state of your wife's health. I was extremely sorry to hear of these circumstances.

In your situation, I can well imagine how the attentions you described in your letter affect both you and your wife. However, my staff has been unable to find any indication of interest in your activities on the part of Federal authorities in recent years. The flurry of interest that attended your testimony before the Warren Commission has long since subsided. I can only suspect that you have become "newsworthy" again in view of the renewed interest in the Kennedy assassination and, thus, may be attracting the attention of people in the media.

I hope this letter has been of some comfort to you, George, although I realize I am unable to answer your question completely. Thank you for your good wishes on my new job. As you can imagine, I'm finding it interesting and challenging.

Very truly yours,
George Bush
Director

With his cordial response, Bush could have been strategically establishing a record—a tactic he has been known to employ. This note provides future investigators with alternative explanations for de Mohrenschildt's disquiet: his daughter's death and the attentions of the press, neither of which have anything to do with Poppy personally. And in his backhanded way, Poppy implants a whiff of doubt about de Mohrenschildt's sanity.

For a man who knew what de Mohrenschildt did, the note must have been terrifying.

DESPITE CIA DIRECTOR Bush's assurances that de Mohrenschildt had nothing more to fear than hounding from the media, his life quickly took a turn for the worse. In fact, that turn began almost immediately after de Mohrenschildt's letter arrived on Bush's desk—and before Bush sent his saccharine reply.

Around this time, Willem Oltmans was passing through Dallas from the West Coast and called de Mohrenschildt's apartment. He was surprised when Jeanne de Mohrenschildt answered the phone, as the couple had been divorced for three years and lived separately. Jeanne clearly was not sober. She

told him that her ex-husband was in the hospital, in bad shape. In a subsequent call to George's lawyer, Oltmans learned that de Mohrenschildt was in
a mental hospital receiving electric shock therapy for a persecution complex.[40]

On November 9, 1976, Jeanne de Mohrenschildt had signed papers authorizing that George be committed to a mental institution for three
months. In a notarized affidavit, she claimed that George had made four
suicide attempts in the past, that he suffered from depression, heard voices,
saw visions, and believed that the FBI and the Jewish Mafia were persecut-
ing him—that is, his tormentors were everybody *but* the CIA, though it was
CIA director Bush he had contacted to "remove the net."

George was brought to Parkland Hospital, the same facility where JFK
had been rushed thirteen years earlier. His doctor of record administered
intravenous drugs and a second doctor ordered electroshock therapy.

Two things might shed light on the de Mohrenschildt divorce and Jeanne's
acquiescence in her ex-husband's commitment to a mental hospital. One is
her own familial intelligence connections, as discussed in chapter 5. The second is what appears to have been her own independent history with intelligence work. According to interviews conducted by Michael Kurtz, the dean of
the graduate school at Southeastern Louisiana University and author of several books on the Kennedy assassination, Jeanne had been a friend of—and
apparently at some point a coworker with—Richard Helms, who later would
become the CIA director.[41] She was, according to Kurtz, also acquainted with
James McCord, the ex-CIA man and future Watergate burglar; and David
Atlee Phillips, the head of the CIA's western hemisphere operations, whose
area of responsibility included Cuba and who is believed by many to have
been in Dallas on November 22, 1963.

A year after George de Mohrenschildt's death, Jeanne would tell a journalist a completely different story about what precipitated George's hospi-
talization. She claimed that a doctor had appeared in Dallas for a brief
period and administered injections to him. Following those injections, she
said, George suffered a nervous breakdown, at which point she decided to
have him hospitalized. The doctor, she claimed, vanished into thin air.[42]

Cut Loose

Most people remember George H. W. Bush's tenure as CIA chief, but few recall how short it was. He had been at the helm of the spy agency less than a

year when his boss, President Gerald Ford, was defeated by the Democrat Jimmy Carter. Poppy, who obviously saw some urgency in staying at the agency's helm irrespective of the party in power, actually flew to Plains, Georgia, to urge Carter to keep him on, but the new president was not persuaded.

This was, of course, a source of enormous frustration. Bush felt that he was just starting to reshape the agency. The head of French intelligence at the time agreed: "Even Mr. Bush, during his stay, was unable to change the methods of the CIA. He tried, certainly, and described to me at times the lengths to which he went to move this enormous bureaucracy in a direction that would have created a more effective intelligence apparatus. He had many valuable ideas. But it would have taken years, rather than the time he was given, to put them into effect."[43]

From his exile, Poppy began plotting his comeback—and his operation to rescue his colleagues from the idealistic Carter and his CIA director, Admiral Stansfield Turner. But first, he needed a new command post. Within two months of his departure from Washington, he was hired as a seventy-five-thousand-dollar-a-year (about three hundred thousand in 2009 dollars) consultant to First International Bancshares of Dallas, which was Texas's largest bank holding company. According to an SEC filing, he was to perform "such duties as may be prescribed or assigned by the board of directors." What were those duties? When Poppy was asked that question some years later, he trotted out the same old answer: he could not recall.

In 1988, while Poppy was waging his successful presidential campaign, the *Washington Post* asked the man who hired him, company chairman Robert H. Stewart III, for a description of his job. Stewart declined to answer any questions.

The Cuckoo's Nest

Meanwhile, in February 1977, just after Poppy left the CIA, the Dutch journalist Willem Oltmans was back in Dallas again. He had a conversation with de Mohrenschildt's lawyer, who told him de Mohrenschildt was now out of the mental hospital. Oltmans then met for lunch with de Mohrenschildt and his lawyer.

Oltmans was shocked by the transformation of de Mohrenschildt. "I couldn't believe my eyes," he told the House Select Committee on Assassinations in three hours of closed-session testimony shortly after de Mohrenschildt's death.

"The man had changed drastically . . . he was nervous, trembling. It was a scared, a very, very scared person I saw. I was absolutely shocked, because I knew de Mohrenschildt as a man who wins tennis matches, who is always suntanned, who jogs every morning, who is as healthy as a bull."[44]

At the lunch, according to Oltmans, de Mohrenschildt spoke to him in hushed French, so that their dining companion would not understand. The Russian confessed that he had something troubling to share. Later, sitting in the library of the historically black Bishop College, where de Mohrenschildt now taught French classes, he began to unburden himself. "He said, 'Willem, I have to tell the story as it really was. But don't betray me . . . you are the only journalist I will trust. Don't incriminate me in the Kennedy assassination. I don't want to go to jail. How could we do it in such a way that I don't go to jail?'"

Oltmans said that he then asked de Mohrenschildt, "Well, first tell me, did you do it or didn't you do it?" He said de Mohrenschildt replied: "Yes, I am responsible. I feel responsible for the behavior of Lee Harvey Oswald . . . because I guided him. I instructed him to set it up." At this point, it is certainly possible that George de Mohrenschildt was changing as a person, feeling guilt, perhaps alternating between candor and the instinct to embellish or lie. He could have been saying that his was a somewhat compartmentalized role, never knowing who some of the other players were.

At that point, "He begged me to take him out of the country," Oltmans told the House panel, "'because they are after me.'" With the approval of the head of Dutch national television, Oltmans and de Mohrenschildt flew to Amsterdam. As before, it becomes difficult to ascertain Oltmans's motives in this process, as well as what larger interests he might have been serving.

On the trip, via Houston and New York, de Mohrenschildt purportedly began dropping small pieces of information. He claimed to know Jack Ruby. And he began providing fragments of a scenario in which Texas oilmen in league with intelligence operatives plotted to kill the president.

In Holland, where they arrived February 13, 1977, according to Oltmans, de Mohrenschildt provided names of CIA and FBI people to a Dutch publisher and the head of Dutch national television, with other witnesses present. De Mohrenschildt, awaiting an offer of a deal from the publisher, did not go into greater detail. What happened next may have represented the moment when de Mohrenschildt could read the writing on the wall and knew his ultimate fate.

De Mohrenschildt spent a few days at Oltmans's Amsterdam home, continuing to edit aloud his memoirs of his time with Oswald. Then Oltmans suggested it might do them good to get out of the house. He proposed a day trip to Brussels. When they arrived, Oltmans mentioned that an old friend of his, a Soviet diplomat, would be joining them a bit later for lunch. A few minutes later, they came unexpectedly on the Soviet man. De Mohrenschildt quickly excused himself and said he wished to take a short walk before lunch.

He never came back. Instead, he fled to a friend's house, and after a few days, headed back to the United States. Later, among his effects would be an affidavit he had purportedly prepared, in which he accused Oltmans of betraying him. Perhaps, and this would be strictly conjecture, de Mohrenschildt saw what it meant that he, like Oswald, was being placed in the company of Soviets. He was being made out to be a Soviet agent himself. And once that happened, his ultimate fate was clear.

De Mohrenschildt's affidavit—if he truly wrote it—registered distrust of Oltmans and others, and a fear that people were doing things to him, altering his address book, forging his signature on traveler's checks. He also wrote: "I have a meeting with *Reader's Digest* people on March 15th in New York City . . . The meeting is with Edward Jay Epstein, editorial writer, and the time was agreed upon with the Editor in Chief, Mr. Fulton Oursler, Jr." It was almost as if he knew that he needed to produce a record.

De Mohrenschildt then flew back to New York and later boarded a Greyhound bus for Palm Beach. There, he joined his daughter Alexandra, then thirty-three, who was staying at the beachfront mansion of a relative, Nancy Pierson Clark-Tilton.[45] De Mohrenschildt was installed in the guest room.

A Key to the Mystery

Within days, the Palm Beach County police would be poring over George de Mohrenschildt's blood-spattered corpse. And the FBI would receive a lead about a man named Jim Savage. They did not pursue it very far, but if they had, they would have discovered Savage's connections—right back to the FBI, and to a whole new subterranean level of the story that leads to Poppy Bush.

At de Mohrenschildt's request, Savage, an executive with the Transcontinental Drilling Company in Houston, had been given the keys to the Russian's car with the understanding he would drive it to Palm Beach. The friend of Oltmans's who had delivered the car to Savage told the FBI that Savage had behaved strangely; among other things, he had seemed intent on avoiding a face-to-face meeting. Oltmans's friend was instructed to leave the car in a parking lot and slip the keys under an apartment door.

The entry of W. C. "Jim" Savage into the story at this juncture is significant.

Savage was one of a small cluster of people who had known both de Mohrenschildt and Poppy Bush for many years. In the late 1940s, he and de Mohrenschildt had worked together on an oil field consortium project in Colorado.[46] Then Savage went on to work as an engineer for Kerr-McGee, the oil company of Prescott Bush's friend and fellow senator Robert Kerr.

In 1952, one year before the neophyte Poppy Bush entered the terrestrial oil business and two years before he started his sea-based company, Zapata Offshore, Kerr had been a big help, volunteering Savage to give Poppy a tour of the Kerr-McGee offshore oil rigs and show him the ropes. "I said, 'Sure boss,'" Savage recalled.[47] "I invited [Poppy] out, took a helicopter, flew him around our operations out there (in the Gulf of Mexico), had heliports on all the rigs, wined and dined him." Savage said Bush was "very curious" about the operations and "sort of hooked on to me." But according to Savage, Bush did not mention that he was thinking of forming his own company. When he did take that step, Bush offered top dollar to two Kerr-McGee engineers who left to join Zapata Offshore.[48] Because Poppy Bush knew next to nothing about the oil business, these men ran the operational side of the venture. Yet neither of them merited even a single mention in Bush's autobiography, *Looking Forward*.

The former Kerr-McGee men working for Poppy continued to associate with Savage, and also with de Mohrenschildt, whom they would see at oil-related functions in Houston when de Mohrenschildt traveled there from Dallas. This was in the early 1960s, about the time de Mohrenschildt was squiring Oswald.

De Mohrenschildt was also a close friend of Savage's supervisor at Kerr-McGee, George B. Kitchel, who was a prominent figure in what was then the close-knit offshore drilling industry. Like the others, Kitchel had gotten to know de Mohrenschildt not long after the latter immigrated to the United States. They had met at Humble Oil, where Kitchel managed oil drilling operations for most of the 1930s and 1940s; de Mohrenschildt had worked for the company briefly as a "roughneck" in 1938. Kitchel, whose name appears in de Mohrenschildt's address book, said he knew the Russian "very well," and considered himself a "great admirer."[49]

IN THE EARLY 1960s, George Kitchel was also close with Poppy Bush and played a role in launching Poppy's political career in Houston. Among other things, it was Kitchel who introduced candidate Bush, in a ten- to fifteen-minute peroration, to a gathering of several hundred Houston oilmen.

Years after the JFK assassination, Kitchel would confirm that he had been friends with both Poppy Bush and George de Mohrenschildt.[50] He denied, however, that he had been aware of any friendship between the two—which seems highly unlikely given the tight web of relationships of which they were part. The denial did, however, suggest that Kitchel understood the ramifications.

There turns out to be a reason for Kitchel's improbable denial: his own brother was none other than Graham Kitchel—the FBI agent to whom Poppy Bush called in his Kennedy threat from Tyler, Texas, on November 22, 1963. Thus, the man who helped start Poppy Bush's political career shortly before the Kennedy assassination was at the same time a close friend of Lee Harvey Oswald's handler, while his own brother was the FBI agent who created an alibi paper trail for Poppy Bush.

After the assassination, FBI agents interviewed George Kitchel about his friend de Mohrenschildt. Kitchel told them that the Russian was close with the powerful right-wing oilmen Clint Murchison, H. L. Hunt, Sid Richardson, and John W. Mecom Sr. The FBI report did not mention Poppy Bush, or that Kitchel's brother was an FBI agent, with his own curious walk-on part in the assassination story.

BOTH JIM SAVAGE and George Kitchel were more than casual friends of the de Mohrenschildts. Their activities raise the question of whether they might have been serving as contacts and handlers. In late 1961, when the de Mohrenschildts returned by boat following their "walking tour" through Central America (the one where they happened upon Bay of Pigs invasion preparations), Savage and Kitchel were waiting at quayside. Savage took them to his home in

Houston, where they remained for a few days, before returning to Dallas.[51] In early 1962, when the de Mohrenschildts returned from a short trip to Haiti, arriving by ship, Savage and Kitchel picked them up again and drove them back to Houston and then on to Dallas. That two oil executives had the time and inclination to perform such errands at the least invites interest.

Prior to the Kennedy assassination, Savage was working for Sun Oil, the firm owned by the Pew family of Philadelphia, which was rabidly and outspokenly anti-Kennedy. Sun Oil also employed the far-right Russian émigré Ilya Mamantov, who frequently gave political speeches and was active in the Texas GOP when Poppy and Jack Crichton were its nominees. It was Mamantov who, as noted in chapter 7, would "translate" Marina Oswald's remarks on November 22 in a manner that underlined Oswald's guilt.

Blast from the Past

In March 1977, when George de Mohrenschildt fled Belgium for Florida, the House Select Committee on Assassinations learned of his return and quickly sent its investigator Gaeton Fonzi after him. But *Reader's Digest* was a step ahead.

On March 27, de Mohrenschildt arrived at the famed Breakers Hotel in Palm Beach and spent the day being interviewed by the *Digest*'s Epstein. It was to be the first of four days of interviews, for which Epstein had agreed to pay the Russian a thousand dollars a day. That day, de Mohrenschildt talked about his life and career up until the time he met Oswald. The next morning, they began again, continuing until lunch.

De Mohrenschildt returned to the seafront mansion where he was staying, had a light lunch, and then learned from his daughter that the House investigator Fonzi had stopped by to see him. He apparently took in this information with no visible upset. A little later that afternoon, a maid found George de Mohrenschildt slumped over in his chair, surrounded by a pool of blood. The cause of death: a 20-gauge shotgun blast through his mouth.[52] After an investigation, the authorities proclaimed it suicide.

The weapon had been left by de Mohrenschildt's hostess, Nancy Pierson Clark-Tilton, loaded and leaning against a wall near his guest room. Tilton told police she left the gun out because she had heard noises in the house in recent days.

When police searched the room, they found in de Mohrenschildt's brief-case the two-page personal affidavit that he had prepared on March 11, 1977. That was the day he had learned about Oltmans's plans for them to lunch with the Soviet diplomat and had bolted. In his left front pants pocket, they found a newspaper clipping that Epstein had given him. It was a front-page article from the *Dallas Morning News*, dated Sunday, March 20, 1977, with the headline MENTAL ILLS OF OSWALD CONFIDANT TOLD.

De Mohrenschildt's stay in the mental hospital had remained a secret un-til the Dallas paper persuaded a judge that it was in the public interest for the patient's private medical records, which were part of a court record, to be released. Thus, when de Mohrenschildt died, the Dallas public already had reason to believe him a candidate for suicide. The disclosure of his pur-ported mental state also served to discredit any of his recent claims.

Epstein told police that he had brought the clipping to de Mohrenschildt. Presumably, that action could be seen as an innocent act that unintention-ally led de Mohrenschildt to take his life. That is, if de Mohrenschildt took his own life, and did it entirely unassisted.

One person who challenged the idea that George de Mohrenschildt died by his own hand was his ex-wife. In a May 11, 1978, interview with the *Fort Worth Star-Telegram*, Jeanne de Mohrenschildt said that she did not accept that her husband had committed suicide. She also said that she believed Lee Harvey Oswald was an agent of the United States, possibly of the CIA, and that she was convinced he did not kill Kennedy. As to whoever she believed *did* do it, she said: "They may get me too, but I'm not afraid . . . It's about time somebody looked into this thing."[53]

In fact, a serious investigation would have turned up a surprising lead. In de Mohrenschildt's battered address book was an entry for "Bush, George H. W. (Poppy) 1412 W. Ohio also Zapata Petroleum Midland."

There is no evidence that anyone interviewed the recently departed CIA director.

THE SAME MONTH that de Mohrenschildt died, so did Paul Raigorodsky, his onetime White Russian mentor. On November 22, 1976, while Poppy Bush was still CIA director, author Michael Canfield paid a visit to Raigorodsky. The oilman told the researcher, "I told everything I knew to the Warren Commission. What is your interest in all of this?" When Canfield answered,

"Oh, I'm just curious, that's all." Raigorodsky retorted, "But don't you know that curiosity killed the cat?"[54]

Yet it was Raigorodsky, not Canfield, who was soon dead, on March 16, 1977, less than two weeks before his friend de Mohrenschildt's death, at a time when HSCA investigators were seeking to interview both men about the assassination. Raigorodsky, who suffered from chronic gout, is said to have died of natural causes.

CHAPTER 13

Poppy's Proxy and the Saudis

ONE DAY IN MARCH 1976, SEVERAL months after Poppy Bush was sworn in as CIA director, W.'s old National Guard buddy Jim Bath, who had just launched his own aircraft brokerage, picked up the phone and heard a voice from afar.[1] The caller, according to accounts Bath has provided, was interested in buying an F-27 turboprop, an unexceptional and sluggish medium-range plane that no one else seemed to want. The man said his name was Salem bin Laden.

Bath personally flew the F-27 to Saudi Arabia to make the delivery—an arduous trip since the plane averaged an airspeed of just 240 knots, or about 275 miles per hour.[2] He remained in the city of Jidda for three weeks and became close to bin Laden, who was then the thirty-year-old heir to the Saudi Bin Laden Group. This was a vast construction and engineering empire that built roads, schools, hospitals, and hotels and had played a key role in the modernization of Saudi Arabia.[3]

Bath also grew friendly with another young scion, Khalid bin Mahfouz, then twenty-five, heir to the National Commercial Bank of Saudi Arabia, the biggest bank in the kingdom. The bin Laden and bin Mahfouz families were close with Saudi king Fahd.

Almost immediately, this seemingly random connection turned into a formal business arrangement. On July 8, 1976, Salem bin Laden signed a notarized trust agreement in Harris County, Texas, establishing Bath's role as his business representative in the United States. Mahfouz, too, hired Bath.

Salem bin Laden was the eldest of fifty-four children of Mohammed bin Laden, a one-eyed bricklayer who became a close friend of King Faisal and then the most powerful construction magnate in Saudi Arabia. After Mohammed died in a 1967 air crash, King Faisal sent the head of his own construction company to serve as a kind of trustee for the bin Ladens until Salem was old enough to take the reins.[4] One of Salem's half brothers, Osama, would go on to lead the terrorist network al-Qaeda. While Osama became estranged from the Saudi royals, most of the family, including Salem, would remain very much in the fold.[5]

Certainly, the bin Ladens and bin Mahfouzes were stars in the Saudi firmament. Thus the question: How did it happen that Jim Bath, close friend and National Guard minder to George W. Bush and acquaintance of Poppy Bush, suddenly became a business partner of these two powerful Saudi families just *weeks* after Poppy took over at the CIA? Is it likely that this was mere coincidence? Bath clearly preferred that explanation. When the author Craig Unger obtained a rare interview with Bath several years ago and asked him how he came to be in business with these powerful Saudis, Bath offered the story of the unexpected phone call, although he claimed not to recall what year it had taken place.

Thus, Unger wrote in his book *House of Bush, House of Saud*, that Bath said the call came "sometime around 1974." This claim appears to have been off by two years, considering that he had not even launched his airplane brokerage until 1976—just after his friend Poppy Bush became the head of American intelligence. One wonders if that misstatement could have been an accident. More likely, neither Bath nor Bush would have wanted anyone to note the synchronicity of these events.

If people had looked more deeply into Bath's activities, they would have discovered what appeared to be a covert private foreign policy benefiting the wealthy and implemented by Poppy Bush and his associates—with Jim Bath acting as a key intermediary to the Saudi royal house.

Indeed, the year 1976, when Jim Bath went into business with the two young Saudis, was a strategic turning point. Poppy Bush was a central participant in an effort to secretly engineer a deepening of the relationship between America and the kingdom. One purpose was to ensure a stable supply of oil for America. Another was to create a vehicle for evading congressional restrictions on covert operations by enlisting the Saudis as outside funders, surrogates, and cutouts—trusted confidential intermediaries. The result was a secret intelligence partnership that would come to rival that between the United States and Israel.

The story of this secret partnership is directly connected to the story of how the Saudi royal family became the benefactors of the Bush family. It also raises questions—not answered here—that warrant further investigation. These include the urgency with which the George W. Bush administration moved to transport members of the extended bin Laden family from the United States back to Saudi Arabia in the early hours after the September 11 attacks—even in contravention of the no-fly rules in effect at the time.[6] These and other questions, explored in books, articles, and even in Michael Moore's controversial award-winning film *Fahrenheit 9/11*, provide an intriguing perspective for contemplating the material that follows.

A Bath or a Sheep-Dipping?

Ostensibly, Jim Bath came to the attention of the Bush family in 1969, when W. reported for duty at Ellington Air Force Base, to a unit in which Bath was already serving. The two promptly became buddies. This was a little surprising, really, given that George W. Bush has tended to socialize almost exclusively with people of his own social and economic class. James Reynolds Bath did not go to Yale. He was not an oil heir or from a Wall Street blueblood clan. He was older than W., had grown up in a small town in modest circumstances, and had already served an impressive stint in the Air Force before moving to Houston and joining the Air National Guard. He was not the typical Champagne Unit prince.

As a youth, Bath had developed two interests that he would maintain through much of his adult life: media and flying. Upon graduation from Louisiana State University with a degree in publishing management, Bath joined the Air Force, where he served as a fighter pilot for five years. While there he did publicity work, partly as a top aide to a powerful military officer. Later, while living in Texas, Bath would own and fly a V/STOL plane, typically used by the CIA in Vietnam for short-field takeoffs and landing on rugged mountain airstrips.[7]

Because of Bath's skills and background, he would have been a prime candidate for what is called "sheep-dipping." In this process, the Air Force typically loans a pilot to the CIA, and the pilot ostensibly becomes a civilian, but all his military records are transferred over to a clandestine department within the Air Force. The pilot gets routine promotions and retirement credit points, just as if he were on active duty, except that this part of his record is missing from files released under the Freedom of Information Act. If there are "missing" periods within a span of military service, when no active duty is documented, that is a sign that a flier was sheep-dipped.

(In fact, when I asked the military for Bath's records, I got an extraordinary runaround, with two different records centers insisting that the other ought to have the file. The George W. Bush administration never did provide me with his records.)

Oftentimes, a dipped sheep's own family and friends are kept in the dark and told simply that the individual has resigned from the Air Force to become a civilian.[8]

In 1965, Bath received an honorable discharge, and at the age of twenty-nine, he moved to Houston, where he joined the Texas Air National Guard as a part-time member of the 147th Fighter Wing at Ellington Air Force Base.

Jim Bath was a unit star, and a versatile one. "Bath could fly upside down on your wing," recalls Dr. Richard Mayo, another member of the unit.[9] "He was a supremely talented guy. He was charming, smart, trained in journalism and PR, and a fabulous pilot." All that made him a valued asset for Colonel Walter B. "Buck" Staudt, the unit's highly political and ambitious commandant. It also gave Bath enviable connections to powerful men who were looking not just to keep their sons out of Vietnam, but to put the best possible spin on the situation as well. People like Lloyd Bentsen, John Connally, and soon Poppy Bush were well aware of Bath's usefulness, and so were indebted to him.

Bath's decision to join the Texas Air National Guard would have been purely voluntary, since he had already fulfilled his military service obligation. As a "weekend warrior," working in aircraft sales for a Dallas-based company (Brown Aero), Bath was hired in 1968 as Houston vice president for Atlantic Aviation. That firm, a holding of the fabulously wealthy Du Pont family of Delaware, has been identified as associated with the CIA.[10] Among other things, Bath would be given the exclusive contract to sell the corporate jet manufactured by Israeli Aircraft Industries in the United States.

During these years, Bath appeared regularly as a speaker before the Houston Chamber of Commerce, the Kiwanis, and other business and social groups. In 1966, Bath and Poppy Bush were both on the lecture circuit, with the congressional candidate and the Guardsman making the rounds of the same set of civic and fraternal associations.

Bill White, Bath's former longtime business partner, said Bath told him that he would still be "cleaning the toilets in the aircraft" instead of running the show for Atlantic had Poppy Bush not intervened. If correct, this would place Bath and Poppy in cooperation at least as early as 1968, the year W. was admitted to Bath's Guard unit.

Suspended Disbelief

When the younger George Bush arrived at Ellington Air Force Base from his Georgia pilot training in late 1969, he and Jim Bath quickly became a dynamic duo. Both were charmers, both liked to wisecrack and push the limits, both enjoyed a good party. But Bath far outshone his younger friend: people considered the Louisianan smart, focused, an engaging speaker, and an amazing pilot.

Bath seemed to have been tasked with both minding W. and turning his mediocre performance and party-boy lifestyle into something more conducive to future prospects. Hence the press release, cited in chapter 8, which sang George W. Bush's praises as a pilot to local newspapers. Bath had impressed Poppy Bush, and the two are said to have become regular dining companions.

But was the relationship between Bath and Poppy strong enough that the elder Bush could prevail upon Bath—as he had so often with others—for a major sacrifice in a greater cause? Would he take a dive for Poppy's trouble-prone namesake? There are indications that this may have happened.

As noted earlier, George W. Bush left the 147th Fighter Wing in May of 1972. He would later claim that he had left his unit and moved temporarily to Alabama because of a keen desire to work on the Senate campaign of his father's friend Winton Blount. But records show that at the time of his departure he was experiencing problems in the cockpit and had stopped flying. It appears that for some reason W. began having trouble handling his F-102's controls and may have been judged a danger to himself and others. Under this scenario, the flying problems necessitated creation of an excuse for leaving the unit, i.e., getting out of town.

Years later, when Bush's cessation of flying became a subject of speculation, Bush's White House staff explained that his departure for Alabama had caused him to miss his annual pilot's physical exam, and that this in turn had caused his routine suspension from flying.

To bolster this, the White House released a document that showed Bush's suspension for failure to take a physical. The document also showed that a second airman from Bush's unit had been suspended around the same time for the same reason. One might have concluded from this that such suspensions were commonplace. One might have concluded—if one did not know the identity of the other airman, whose name the White House had redacted from the form, purportedly to protect his privacy.

But Marty Heldt, an Iowa railroad worker, corn farmer, and amateur researcher, came forward to identify the mystery man, based on an unredacted document copy he had obtained in 2000 through a Freedom of Information request and posted to his Web site.[11] The airman who was suspended along with W.? Major James R. Bath.[12]

Once this information became known, some wondered if it could be a coincidence that the two good friends were suspended at the same time for the same reason. And since W.'s real reason seemed to be that he needed an excuse to justify that he had let down the Guard—and perhaps disappointed his family—Bath would need some reason too.

But unlike W., Bath's Guard service was not compulsory; it was a beloved avocation. If W. had purportedly been suspended for failure to take his physical on account of his being out of state, Bath had no such excuse. Also perhaps significant is that while George W. Bush appears never to have piloted aircraft of any kind again after the suspension, Bath returned to the sky after he left the unit, flying commercial and private planes.

One conclusion, then, was that Bath had agreed to take a dive in order to provide W. with cover. If this is correct, and Poppy did ask Bath to essentially provide cover for W., he would have been taking another page straight out of the spymaster's playbook—something like the two George Bushes in the CIA at the same time, and the Tyler, Texas, alibi.

In fact, both George W. and Jim Bath have played along, with the men portraying their dual suspensions as minor matters, and as commonplace.[13] "It happens all the time, especially in the Guard," Bath told the author Craig Unger. "In a regular squadron it is real easy to get your physical, but in a Guard unit, it is a different kettle of fish because the flight surgeon is also a civilian . . . The base is a ghost town except when the whole unit is there. When you fall out of requirements, it is no big deal, you are simply not able to be on the flying schedule. That is it, full stop."

But in fact, being suspended is apparently not a minor matter, and such a lapse would have been highly unusual for any unit member; for two men to be suspended at the same time for the same reason was extraordinary. When I asked General Belisario J. Flores (Ret.), a former assistant adjutant general of the Texas Air National Guard, he told me that suspensions for missing flight physicals were rare. Moreover, he said, he had never, in all his years with the Texas Air National Guard, heard of two members of the same unit being suspended from flying for failure to take physicals, much less at the same time.[14]

From the point of view of the National Guard, which had invested so much time and money in these men, it defies reason that the punishment for missing a physical exam would be suspension from flying. For such an offense, I was told by a cross-section of military people, a crack flier like Bath would most likely have been ordered to take the exam at a later date.

For someone like Bush, who had not completed his compulsory military service, the consequences could have been more severe; indeed, a Guardsman in this situation without Bush's connections might have found himself ordered to Vietnam, where the war at this time was very much a hot one. (Logic alone suggests that if everyone knew they could abandon their obligations during an unpopular war by simply not taking a medical exam, the drain on the military would be substantial.)

According to General Flores, the ongoing failure to take a required physical would definitely have triggered disciplinary action. In a 2004 interview, Flores told me: "If a person does not fulfill his training requirements, he is counseled by his commander, then meets a board, and then the case is forwarded for further action." He said that a special board would have to be convened, and during this time the person suspended from flying would continue to serve in a nonflying capacity. In any event, a record of the board proceedings should have been created. Yet no such record regarding the disposition of the Bush and Bath cases has ever been released. Nor is it even known to exist.

Was there more to Bush's grounding than simply nerves?

When reporters raised allegations that Bush had been grounded for using drugs, Bath characterized it as a "bogus issue." Bath has declined to publicly explain precisely why he and Bush—whom he calls "Geo," after the name on his Guard uniform—had failed to take their physicals. "I'm telling you that it [drug use] did not happen. It is beyond laughable. I wasn't with him 24/7, but Geo did not use drugs. Geo did not use drugs, and I really know the facts."[15] Actually, as noted in chapter 8, the facts were a little more complicated in W.'s case. And they certainly were in Bath's. His own divorce proceedings involved allegations by his ex-wife of his use of cocaine and its detrimental effects on his business and personal life.

While the grounding came back to inconvenience W. decades later at a key moment in his political career, it seems not to have hurt Jim Bath. To the contrary. Within a few short years, at a turning point for the American intelligence establishment under Poppy Bush, a man with no particular experience in finance or administration became the investment manager for the scions of two of the wealthiest families in Saudi Arabia and the world.

Drilling Deep for Answers

Was Jim Bath connected to American intelligence, in an official or unofficial capacity? Craig Unger's 2002 interview is the only in-depth one that Bath ever gave. I had a couple of brief conversations with Bath, in which he declined to answer any questions on the record. Unger wrote that Bath "equivocated." "There's all sorts of degrees of civilian participation [in the CIA]," Bath said. "It runs the whole spectrum, maybe passing on relevant data to more substantive things. The people who are called on by their government and serve—I don't think you're going to find them talking about it. Were that the case with me, I'm almost certain you wouldn't find me talking about it."[16]

Once the business relationship between Bath and his partner Bill White had turned into a fractious legal battle, a curious White decided to research Bath's hints of a secret agent past, and used the phone book to find a local number for Houston's CIA outpost.

"I hooked up a Radio Shack tape recorder to my office phone and called the number. I gave my name in a familiar, friendly tone of voice like I was one of the boys. I told the man who answered that I was working with the Financial Crimes Enforcement Network and that I was attempting to locate Jim Bath. He was apparently caught off guard and assumed that I was with one of the federal alphabet agencies, as he never asked for credentials. He responded without hesitation, saying in effect: 'Oh, it's been a few years now since we've heard from Bath. Give me a minute and I'll pull his file.' After a short delay he came back on the line and told me that Bath's file had been sent to DC." When White called again to request the file, he was given the runaround.[17]

To understand the roots of this tangled tale, in which the Bushes' friend

Jim Bath turns an unexpected order for an outmoded plane into a relationship with representatives of the most powerful oil empire in world history,
one has to look back seventy years or so, to the foundations of the American
relationship with the House of Saud.

Friends with Benefits

The friendship of the Saudis has long been sought by Westerners. Even before Americans got into the kingdom, the British were there. In the 1930s,
the founder of modern Saudi Arabia, King Abdul Aziz ibn Saud, was advised by British expatriate St. John Philby. A former British intelligence operative who "went native," Philby represented King Saud in negotiations with
foreign suitors eager to explore for oil beneath the shifting sands. The wily
Briton soon realized that the Americans were showing more interest than
were the British, and so—much to Britain's everlasting regret—he helped ne-
gotiate Saudi Arabia's first oil contract with a premier American company,
Standard Oil of California (SoCal), one of the spin-offs of John D. Rockefeller's original Standard Oil Company.

Philby advised the king to give SoCal a sixty-year exclusive contract for
exploration and extraction along the shores of the Persian Gulf. It didn't
hurt the company's standing that it was quietly compensating Philby on the
side. In 1938, SoCal struck oil in commercial quantities. Shipments abroad
commenced the next year.

World War II firmly established oil as the preeminent strategic resource,
and the United States and the Soviet Union as the world's two superpowers.
As one member of an official U.S. delegation visiting Saudi Arabia in 1944
put it, "The oil in this region is the greatest single prize in all history." The
delegation was led by Everette DeGolyer, a central player in the Dallas oil
crowd who was back then a deputy to Secretary of the Interior Harold Ickes
in the Petroleum Administration for War.[18] In February 1945, Abdul Aziz
met with President Franklin D. Roosevelt on board the USS *Quincy* in the
Suez Canal, and the two cemented what would become one of the most consequential agreements in world history: the trade-off of oil for security.[19]
This led to the establishment of a U.S. training mission in Saudi and the
onset of a long-term U.S. military aid program, one that continues to this
day. As part of that assistance, the United States helped create the modern
Saudi army as well as the Saudi Arabian National Guard (SANG), a rival or-

ganization responsible for internal security and protection of the royal family.[20]

The allure of the seemingly unlimited Saudi petroleum deposits (and of the profits the kingdom was beginning to amass) beckoned increasingly as the limits of domestic U.S. oil production became apparent. Moreover, the United States increasingly looked like a good bet as protector of the Saudi royal house, especially after the humiliation of the British and French in the 1956 Suez Canal crisis. The Eisenhower Doctrine of 1957 led to a deepening of America's commitment to the Saudis.

The rise of the nationalist Gamal Abdel Nasser and his dalliance with the Soviets, coupled with fears of rebellion in Saudi Arabia, led to U.S. military support of Saudi Arabia in the Yemeni Civil War (1962–70). President Kennedy was the first to order U.S. troops into the kingdom, during the Yemeni crisis.

But the outright defense of Gulf states by the U.S. military would soon end. In response to growing public distaste for American military entanglements in the developing world, the Nixon Doctrine (1969) declared that the United States would no longer bear the main responsibility for the defense of Gulf states. Rather than sending troops to protect developing countries, the Nixon administration sent billions of dollars' worth of equipment. This led to even greater U.S. military investment in Saudi Arabia. During this time, the U.S. Army Corps of Engineers was charged with constructing a new headquarters for SANG.

As the Saudis became cognizant of the full extent of their natural riches, they took steps to gradually get control of them, and especially the revenue they produced. The vehicle for this was Aramco, which was SoCal's postwar consortium that included Texaco, Standard Oil of New Jersey, Standard Oil of New York, and later, as a nationalized Saudi-controlled concern, Saudi Aramco, the world's richest oil company. The turning point came during the 1973 Arab-Israeli War, in which the Nixon administration tilted decisively in support of Israel, after which Saudi Arabia nationalized its oil deposits. In response the United States turned to new ways of maintaining the relationship, and in the process retain access to Saudi oil supplies on favorable terms. Mostly, this meant a kind of mutually beneficial shotgun marriage between the two highly dissimilar cultures, which brought more military dependence and increased financial and personal ties.

Saudi Arabia would become—and remains today—the leading recipient of U.S. arms and military services, far exceeding Israel and all other U.S.

allies. Much of this assistance goes to SANG rather than the army, and therefore is intended specifically to protect and sustain the Saudi royal family.[21]

This military assistance extended to pilot training. Previously, the United States had concentrated on training its own aircrews for operations over Saudi Arabia. Now it was equipping and training the Saudi Royal Air Force to operate Saudi aircraft—planes that had been purchased from the United States.[22] This was an approach that President Richard Nixon also favored: take care of the despotic rulers who sat upon these thrones of petroleum, equip and train their military, and direct juicy contracts to U.S. defense contractors at the same time. The Pentagon convinced the Saudis to buy Lockheed's new F-104 Starfighter, the first service combat aircraft designed to fly at twice the speed of sound.

The United States hosted Saudi princes and other Saudi scions in American universities, fostering deeper personal ties as well as inculcating American-style values and perspectives on such topics as economics and investing. The princes, exposed to American planes, fell in love with the toys—and then with others, including American ranches, mansions, and the like.

One aspect of this deepening bond was the increasing frequency with which Saudi princes came to United States for education and military training. The latter was a crucial aspect of the effort to protect the royal family from kingdom intrigues and plots and to reinforce Saudi dependence on the U.S. military. For example, in 1970, Prince Bandar bin Sultan bin Abdul Aziz, a grandson of the late king Abdul Aziz, was at Perrin Air Force Base near Sherman, Texas, in the Dallas area, being trained as a fighter pilot on the F-102.[23]

Access to the world's most expensive toys—American high-performance aircraft, and even spacecraft—was a significant attraction to the Saudi princes. Bandar's father, the longtime Saudi defense secretary Prince Sultan, was training in Houston at NASA and became the first foreign national to fly on the American Space Shuttle in 1985.[24]

Bandar became the Saudi ambassador to the United States in 1983 while Poppy Bush was vice president and remained in the post for twenty-two years. Bandar would grow so close to the Bush family that W. nicknamed him "Bandar Bush."[25]

In 1973, the evolution of the U.S.-Saudi relationship quickened. Paradoxically, this heightened cooperation emerged from discord. U.S. support for

the Israeli victory in the Yom Kippur War prompted the Arab nations to embargo oil and gas deliveries to the United States. Politicians felt the wrath of
voters fed up with long lines at the gas pump and considerably higher
prices.[26] Saudi revenues increased dramatically, as the selling price of Saudi
crude nearly quadrupled between 1970 and 1974.[27]

To forestall any more such upheavals in the supply pipeline, the United
States quickly struck a secret deal. Thanks to a covert agreement between
the Saudi Arabian Monetary Agency (SAMA) and the U.S. Treasury, Saudi
petrodollars would pour back into the United States in the form of investment in American businesses and prime real estate. In effect, the Saudis
were using the gas being pumped into American tanks to buy America out
from under the Americans. It was, to quote Saudi prince Fahd, "a new and
glorious chapter in relations between Saudi Arabia and the United States."

The United States would continue to serve as protector of the Saudi royal
family—assuring its continued survival against domestic and foreign enemies—despite its authoritarian and anti-democratic foundations.[28] U.S. companies, particularly Texas-based ones such as Bechtel and Brown and Root
(later bought by Halliburton), would make vast fortunes by helping Saudi Arabia develop its infrastructure. This further benefited the royal family and (it
was assumed) secured goodwill with the Saudi people. In return, the Saudis
would agree to provide a stable oil supply and to invest a substantial percentage of their petroprofits in the United States. As noted by John Perkins, a former economic consultant who says he worked secretly for the National
Security Agency, "What had initially appeared to be so negative [about the oil
embargo] would end up offering many gifts to the engineering and construction businesses and would help pave the road to global empire."[29]

Which brings us back to Poppy Bush and his special position at the
nexus of oil and intelligence. The United States agreed—secretly, of
course—to help develop the Saudi military and intelligence service, and to
work closely with the latter. The United States also agreed to pass along intelligence gathered by the Israelis throughout the Arab world on radical Islamic elements.

As a result of the deal, not only did Saudi funding for unauthorized
American covert operations increase, but Saudi money also flowed to American friends of the royal family. Law firms and others who secured the
Saudis as clients significantly increased their role in raising and bundling
political contributions while handling Saudi business.

There was also a calculated decision to use the Saudis as surrogates in the cold war. The United States actually encouraged Saudi efforts to spread the extremist Wahhabi form of Islam as a way of stirring up large Muslim communities in Soviet-controlled countries. (It didn't hurt that Muslim Soviet Asia contained what were believed to be the world's largest undeveloped reserves of oil.) The Democrats played a role in all this, too. Jimmy Carter's national security adviser, Zbigniew Brzezinski, has proudly asserted that the unleashing of radical Islam played a crucial role in destabilizing the USSR and ending Communism as a dominant world force.

In retrospect, it was not among the more farsighted policies in American history. It elevated a radicalized element of Islam with military training over what had been largely a moderate and insular Muslim population, and it prepared the militants to play a significant role around the world as well-trained and well-financed terrorists.

In the two years leading up to the oil embargo, Poppy Bush had been United States ambassador to the United Nations. In this capacity, he had worked for the foreign policy czar Henry Kissinger. By the time of the oil embargo, Poppy was the chairman of the Republican National Committee, which of course was concerned with the political consequences of the embargo—in particular, the public anger over the long gas lines. On top of all this was his close relationship with Texas petroleum refiners, who not only were among the GOP's top funders but also were staring at dwindling domestic reserves. The Texas oilmen were eager for both the crude and the petrodollars the former Bedouins had in abundance.[30]

The point man for weaving together the complex economic relationship with the Saudis was a little-known fellow by the name of Gerald Parsky. His grasp of U.S. tax laws enabled him to advise Arab countries how to benefit from IRS tax exemptions for foreign investment in real estate. Parsky's enthusiasm and expertise landed him a slot as assistant to Treasury Secretary William Simon, who was often referred to as Nixon's "energy czar." Between 1974 and 1977, Assistant Secretary Parsky visited many oil-rich Gulf states—Saudi Arabia, Kuwait, the United Arab Emirates, and Qatar—and worked every angle to ensure that petrodollars would flow back to the United States. He soon became known as the "whiz kid" in the Treasury for his mastery of details related to the Arab countries—revenues, development plans, investment strategies, and the rest.[31] Parsky also developed a close relationship with the Bushes, and would later serve as one of W.'s top California fund-raisers.

The Men to Know

Meanwhile, other alliances were being forged that would play a significant role in the rising fortunes of the Bush dynasty. Bill White, Jim Bath's onetime business partner, first met Ken Lay in the early 1980s when Lay was being trained to succeed Robert Herring as CEO of Houston Natural Gas Company. That company would become the energy trading giant Enron, whose spectacular collapse amid widespread fraud under Lay's leadership would make headlines in 2001. In the early eighties Herring was dying of cancer. His socialite wife, Joanne, a hostess of Saudis and honorary ambassador to Pakistan at the time, is credited with bringing James Baker, Prince Bandar, and Congressman Charlie Wilson together to arm the mujahideen to fight the Soviets in Afghanistan. In the film *Charlie Wilson's War*, Joanne Herring is played by Julia Roberts.

It is a little-known fact that Ken Lay played a central role in the new relationship between the United States and Saudi Arabia that developed in the 1970s.[32] Lay did so as one of Gerald Parsky's young colleagues in the Nixon White House energy operation. Lay had gone directly from college to senior economist and speechwriter for the chief executive of Humble Oil in Houston, the Texas subsidiary of the Rockefellers' Standard Oil of New Jersey, which later became Exxon. His professor Pinkney Walker had been named by Nixon as vice chairman of the Federal Power Commission, the precursor to the Federal Energy Regulatory Commission, and he brought Lay with him as his aide.[33] After less than two years, Lay was put in charge of coordinating government energy policies, as deputy undersecretary of interior (the Department of Energy did not yet exist).[34]

It happened that Lay was in charge of energy policies just when the oil embargo hit in 1973. In the Nixon administration, as would be true later with the Bush-Cheney administration, the person in charge of energy policy was in effect the point man to the industries he was expected to regulate. This of course was the energy industry so closely tied to Poppy Bush, who became the chairman of the Republican Party in 1973. Resolving the supply instability issue highlighted by the embargo was not just good policy. It was good politics.

Though the crisis created hardships for most Americans, it meant enormous opportunity for some: Lay left Washington in 1974 and eventually signed on with Houston Natural Gas (later called Enron). Citing the embargo, he began pushing for complete deregulation of the industry. By 1974,

Aramco could see the power shift and moved its headquarters from New York to Houston.

Another person who would figure prominently in Bush-circle dealings with the kingdom, and who will resurface in subsequent chapters, was a young Saudi named Ghaith Pharaon. A soft-featured man with the requisite Vandyke beard, private jet, and French château favored by the Saudi elite—and like George W. Bush a graduate of Harvard Business School—he was the son of a political adviser to the Saudi royal family. In 1975, Pharaon became the first Saudi to purchase a controlling interest in a domestic American bank—Detroit's ailing Bank of the Commonwealth, the biggest in Michigan, with assets of one billion dollars. The firm's real value, though, was as a foot in the door of the American banking system and a potential stepping-stone for further acquisitions.

Pharaon soon turned his attention to Texas and established Houston as his base of operations.[35] He created a holding company called Arabian Services Corporation, quickly took control of a number of American firms, and eventually built a global corporate empire. His approach to business would be characterized by *Time* as a "tendency to leave many major decisions to others, combined with a rather offhand manner when discussing business and money." One of his domestic companies, a Dallas-based contractor, would plead guilty to bribing foreign officials in the Caribbean.[36]

By 1976, Gerald Parsky was assistant secretary of the Treasury, the undisputed go-to man for the Saudis on oil and money. And by then Poppy Bush had been brought back from China and installed as CIA director. One reason, already mentioned, was to put a benign face on the controversial agency at a time when it was receiving harsh public criticism. But there was another reason. Poppy's secret past with the agency and his powerful connections at the epicenter of the oil-money culture in Texas would help him to implement the growing secret relationship with the Saudis. In this, Poppy worked closely with his counterpart at the Saudi General Intelligence Division (GID), Kamal Adham, who was also head of the separate agency charged with protecting the Saudi royal family. Adham had a third important connection, his longtime friendship and business partnership with bin Mahfouz—the man who hired Jim Bath.

In a now familiar pattern, years later, when Kamal Adham would be caught up in an explosive banking scandal, Poppy Bush would, improbably, deny even knowing him. It was implausible that the U.S. spy chief would not know his Saudi counterpart during that era, but that did not stop Poppy, who said, "I don't know anything about this man except I've read bad stuff about him."[37] Indeed, when Adham was told that the White House press office had reconfirmed Bush's disavowal, the Saudi expressed disbelief and even amazement, remarking, "It is not possible for the president to say that."

For his end of the bargain, Poppy had quickly begun to put all manner of heightened protective measures in place on behalf of the Saudi leadership. The danger to the top Saudis was real. A mullah had issued an edict proclaiming the Saudi royal family corrupt. And in March 1975, at a conference, one of King Faisal's nephews pulled a gun out of his *shumagh* (the traditional Saudi headdress) and shot the king dead. As rumors circulated that Faisal had been assassinated in a foreign plot, the CIA and Saudi security authorities launched an investigation. Meanwhile, the royal family moved swiftly to name his successor: Crown Prince Khalid would become king, and Fahd, known for his pro-Western views, would be his crown prince.

Three days after Faisal's death, his successor, King Khalid, told the Beirut *Daily Star* that the killing had been "an isolated act by a deranged person without any foreign scheming."[38] The assassin was swiftly beheaded in public eighty-five days after Faisal's death,[39] and life went on in Saudi Arabia. But at the highest levels, the leadership knew that it could not trust many of their own relatives. Poppy is believed to have dispatched his former number-two man in the CIA, Vernon Walters, to work full time with the Saudi government to improve security.[40]

Trading on the Saudis' fear, Poppy was in a position to ask for almost anything. And apparently he did. As we shall see, for many ensuing years almost everything that he, his friends, and his family members—including George W. Bush—were involved with was subsidized, mostly secretly, by the Saudis. The Saudis began to play a role comparable to that played earlier by the shah of Iran and the Philippine dictator Ferdinand Marcos as secret benefactors of Richard Nixon. In all, the relationship would result in more than $1.4 billion in investments and contracts passing from the wealthiest family in the world (and its surrogates) to the Bush apparatus over the course of two decades.[41]

The House of Bath

"Bush was responsible for Bath's relationship with the Arabs from the onset," said Charles W. "Bill" White. Much of the Bath-Saudi story would not be known were it not for White, a former Navy pilot and Annapolis graduate who was recruited from the Harvard Business School in 1978 by Lan Bentsen, Bath's real estate partner, to provide what Bentsen described as "pedigree" for Bath.

Bentsen was himself a graduate of the Harvard Business School and the son of Texas's Democratic senator Lloyd Bentsen, who had defeated Poppy Bush in the Texas Senate race in 1970. White told the Canadian Broadcasting Corporation,

> When [Lan] found that I was a Navy fighter pilot, he said that there was an Air Force fighter pilot in Houston that I should meet—a pilot who the Bentsen family and the Bush families were already in business with. And he said that this fellow James R. Bath needed someone to run a series of real estate companies that would be grubstaked by not only the political families, but also by some foreign nationals—the Saudis. And so I came down for an interview and met Jim Bath.[42]

Bath interviewed White in his Rayalle Minerva V/STOL aircraft, which he kept at Houston's Hobby field. During the interview, Bath actually landed this plane on a farmer's field to relieve himself off the wing—a display of bravado presumably intended to impress White.

Though both were bright, personable, and former fliers, White and Bath couldn't have been more different: White was an earnest, spit-and-polish man with a talent for balance sheets and an obsession with playing by the rules. Bath was a folksy and crafty wheeler-dealer with a passion for secrets and bold schemes.

Nevertheless, Bath took quickly to White, dubbing him "CW." And in his relationship to White, Bath began showing why he and George W. had been kindred spirits. Not only did Bath, like W., enjoy joking and assigning nicknames, but, as he moved away from his role as W.'s minder, he also revealed the extent to which he too could be something of a wild man.

"Bath was very forthright with me when we went into business together in 1978. He said: 'Bill, I come from a poor background, I have no money of my own and this relationship with the Bushes and the Saudis is of paramount importance to me because I derive all of my capital and all of my business contacts from that relationship.' "[43] White says Bath told him that he was personally recruited by George H. W. Bush when the senior Bush was CIA director in 1976. In all likelihood, though, he was actually recruited much earlier.

"He explained that the Saudis had basically entered into a quid pro quo relationship with Bush and that Bush when he was CIA director worked with the head of Saudi Intelligence, and the CIA trained the Palace Guard to protect the Saudi royal family, who was concerned about a fundamentalist revolution."[44]

"My understanding of it is that Bath represented the Bush interests and bin Laden/bin Mahfouz interchangeably represented the Saudi royal family interests," said White. "People who have tried to vilify the bin Laden family or the bin Mahfouz family fail to realize that the Saudis have a very patriarchal society and that, according to Bath, neither of those families sneeze without the Saudi royals' blessing. I mean everything they do is at the [behest of] the Saudi royal family. As a matter of fact, bin Mahfouz's bank, NCB, is the only bank that was not nationalized in Saudi Arabia. All the rest of the banks were nationalized in 1974 except National Commercial Bank (NCB), which is privately owned by bin Mahfouz. That's where the Saudi royals keep all their personal money."[45]

The two Saudis entered into a business relationship with Bath. They would provide the money, and he would be the front man and manager of the enterprises.

Salem bin Laden and Khalid bin Mahfouz arrived in Houston shortly after Jim Bath flew that clunky plane out to Riyadh. In sharp contrast to his notorious brother, Bin Laden was a gregarious, Westernized, English-speaking, cocktail-loving international playboy. He traveled with an entourage and threw parties with prominent Houston businessmen and attorneys in attendance; Salem entertained the crowd by playing the piano and singing. Bin Mahfouz, tall and thin, was more enigmatic and reserved—the scion of a Saudi banking empire with hopes of expanding its franchise into the United States. One helpful asset was his $3.5 million French château-style house in the posh River Oaks section of Houston, which would become known as Houston's Versailles. Huge crowds would gather at what the irreverent Bath referred to as "the Big House."

It would soon be apparent that some, if not most, of this Texas-Saudi connection had to do with the growing off-the-books covert intelligence operations in which Poppy was deeply immersed. Between them, the wealthy Saudis and Americans controlled what amounted to an empire. And that empire needed planes, income, and intelligence.

On his arrival in the United States, Salem bin Laden had immediately set about purchasing planes and equipment for his family's giant construction firm. He also bought houses in Central Texas's Hill Country and outside Orlando, Florida. He launched an aircraft services company in San Antonio, Bin Laden Aviation, ostensibly to manage his small fleet of airplanes.[46]

Bath's principal business was JB&A, Jim Bath and Associates, his aircraft brokerage company.[47] It was staffed almost exclusively by former military pilots who held top-secret security clearances. From the same offices, he also ran an entity called Binladen-Houston, which procured heavy construction equipment for shipment overseas. Bath received a 5 percent personal interest (in lieu of a paycheck) in every purchase that he made using bin Laden money.[48]

The growing holdings of Saudis, such as Khalid bin Mahfouz and Salem bin Laden were almost always hidden in trusts, which were set up by some of Houston's biggest law firms. Baker Botts and Vinson & Elkins both represented the Saudis.[49] The names of the Saudis almost never appeared, but rather those of nominees, front men, or lawyers functioning as trustees.

"He spent probably ninety-five percent of his time, I'd call it handholding the Arabs," said White. "He bought a bank for them. He bought an airport for them. He started an airline for them among other ventures in Houston, and was the nominee or the front man for their ownership of these various entities. He would spend most of his time dealing with their interests while I concentrated on running our real estate development company."[50]

It is important to note that White's bona fides and credibility as a source have been verified by numerous journalists and government investigators who have consulted him, and he has been cited over a period of nearly twenty years by news organizations ranging from the *Wall Street Journal* to *Time* to the Canadian Broadcasting Corporation.

Certainly no one was in a better position than White to observe the origin and growth of the Saudi-Texas connection.

CHAPTER 14

Poppy's Web

S O LONG AS POPPY HEADED THE CIA, working to build an extended off-the-books intelligence network, the center of action was at agency head-quarters in Langley, Virginia. But with Poppy's ouster from the CIA directorship in early 1977, the hub shifted with him to Houston. Officially, Poppy was returning to the traditional family business: banking. Wealth in America had been steadily shifting westward since Prescott Bush turned in his Yale baseball cleats for a banker's wing tips, so it was fitting that the son should become a *Texas* banker.

And what a great time to get back into the business. A 1970 law had made it possible for banks to expand rapidly into giant holding companies. One such entity was the Dallas-based First International Bancshares (FIB). At FIB's Houston location, Poppy set up his government-in-exile. During his time with the company. Bush would serve as chairman of the Houston subsidiary's executive committee and join the boards of the Dallas-based parent and a subsidiary of First International in London.

First International had no trouble getting the needed approvals from the Federal Reserve for its steady diet of acquisitions. While it brought fifty banks under its umbrella, FIB was turned down only once.

In some ways, First International was a kind of twin to Republic National Bank in the Dallas oil-intelligence world. In the 1950s, when Poppy's "uncle" Neil Mallon was assembling his off-the-books covert operations via Dresser Industries and the Dallas Council on World Affairs, First International had sent high executives to the council's first planning meeting. (Its competitor, Republic, had done so as well.) First International's association with the Bush family went back many years. In the summer of 1967, young George W. Bush worked as a clerk-bookkeeper at its Houston affiliate, earning $250 for the stint.[1]

First International was not your friendly neighborhood bank. Rather, it was a Texas powerhouse whose principals reached well beyond banking into the netherworld of intelligence and intrigue. The holding company chairman, Robert H. Stewart III, came from a family with long-standing personal ties to J. Edgar Hoover. FIB was intimately associated with the powerful Bass, Hunt, and Murchison families. Its largest shareholder was Joe Allbritton, whose D.C.-based Riggs Bank held the accounts for several embassies, including Saudi Arabia.[2]

Most important, First International itself did a lot of business with Saudi Arabia. George H. W. Bush has said he cannot remember what he did for the bank, but Bill White claims Poppy was a Mercantile Division consultant paid to bring in Arab deposits. According to White, the bank played an important role in handling massive transfers of Saudi funds. It even provided a revolving line of credit for Salem bin Laden. The president and CEO of FIB's London merchant bank, on whose board Poppy Bush sat, was a former FBI agent and employee of Magnolia Oil, the company that provided employment to several figures who associated with Lee Harvey Oswald. It is believed that much of the Saudi business flowed through the London affiliate.

After Bush came on board in 1977, FIB began a massive expansion. First International (known as "Interfirst" by 1980) would merge with its rival Republic to form First RepublicBank, which became the biggest commercial bank in Texas. Fourteen months later, the giant holding company failed, resulting in a $3.5 billion federal bailout.

The demise of First RepublicBank was part of a broad-based failure of financial institutions that—encouraged by the Reagan, Poppy Bush, and Clinton administrations—had combined voracious acquisitions of smaller banks with a spree of speculation and usury that in particular devastated the Texas economy and sent commercial banks into bankruptcy.

A major cause behind the bank failures was the erosion of consumer protections that Franklin Roosevelt had put in place in the aftermath of the Wall Street crash of 1929. The effort to weaken FDR's protective mechanism began under President Nixon, continued under Ford and Carter, and was characterized as a positive development called "deregulation." It greatly accelerated under the Reagan-Bush administrations, finally imploding under

W. in the form of a collapsing housing market and fortunes lost in arcane financial instruments called "derivatives."

The collapse of FDR's safety net may have looked like a disaster to economists and to the ordinary taxpayers footing the bill for these risky ventures, but it also represented the fulfillment of a dream expressed by Prescott Bush and his confreres: to see Roosevelt's hated New Deal brand of "socialism" undone. That it was undone, in steps, by Prescott's son Poppy and grandson W. is hardly coincidental.

Banking institutions of all sizes have played crucial roles, wittingly and unwittingly, in the repatriation and investment of petrodollars in the West, and in the movement of monies to finance intelligence operations and undeclared wars. But all of this was nothing compared to the role played by an enterprise called BCCI. The involvement of the Bushes and their friends in this international scheme is not easy to tease out of the welter of sub rosa actions and relationships, but it is there nonetheless.

The Outlaw Bank and Its Spooky Customers

The sprawling global banking empire called Bank of Credit and Commerce International (BCCI), which emerged in the 1970s and was shuttered in 1991, is largely forgotten today. But not long ago it was occupying headlines as the world's biggest-ever financial fraud. BCCI, though it called itself a bank, was really much more. It was a vast entity connected to the Pakistani military regime and key Gulf states, with banks and branches in seventy-three countries, including at least fifty developing ones. Although its founder, Agha Hasan Abedi, along with his top brass, emphasized their Muslim religiosity, the institution would apparently do anything for anyone willing to pay for services that needed to be kept quiet. These ranged from helping Pakistan obtain a nuclear bomb to financing secret arms deals on behalf of the West, while simultaneously serving as a money-distribution network for West-hating terrorist organizations.

At its peak BCCI wielded immense political and financial power in world capitals. It was a de facto international crime syndicate, a one-stop banking center for everyone from dictators to drug lords to intelligence services. BCCI engaged in blackmail and provided underage girls to major clients. The reality was like a scene out of a James Bond movie, replete with every imaginable form of villainy and the obligatory bikini beauties. BCCI provided "banking

: DRIFTWOOD PUBLIC LIBRARY
801 SW HWY. 101
LINCOLN CITY, OREGON 97367

services," broadly defined, to the likes of Saddam Hussein, terrorist master-mind Abu Nidal, Panamanian dictator Manuel Noriega, and even the elusive heroin kingpin of Asia's Golden Triangle, Khun Sa.

Completely amoral, it seemed to be connected to people in power throughout the world. It was the ultimate expression of the dark side of strategies purportedly designed to help people and produce peace and security. The funding for BCCI had, since its inception, come from ordinary people in developing countries, particularly in the form of remissions from guest workers, such as Pakistanis and Filipinos working in Persian Gulf countries. When it collapsed, literally millions of BCCI patrons, scattered throughout the developing world, suffered, and many lost their life savings.

Starting in 1988, during Poppy Bush's last year as vice president and continuing through his presidency, a handful of investigators and prosecutors—notably Manhattan District Attorney Robert Morgenthau and Senator John Kerry—got on the trail of this syndicate. Although they met mysterious resistance from the highest levels of the Reagan-Bush and then Poppy Bush administrations, by 1991 they managed to persuade British banking authorities to spearhead a global raid that brought the bank's activities to a halt. The Manhattan District Attorney's Office told the Bank of England, directly and indirectly, that it would be seeking to indict the London-based BCCI for operating as a Ponzi scheme. The Bank of England recognized that a New York indictment would precipitate a run on the bank, with an unfair distribution of bank assets to the first people who could withdraw their funds and nothing for the rest. To prevent that, the Bank of England, working with authorities in other countries, closed BCCI worldwide.

But the complicity of high officials in the United States and elsewhere, in at least some aspects of BCCI's operations, was never fully exposed, as inquiry after inquiry hit walls where supposed "national security" interests were involved. BCCI had aided the CIA, British MI-6, the Israeli Mossad, Saudi and Iranian intelligence together with the North Koreans, the Chinese, and above all the Pakistani military, and all parties were afraid that their own secrets would be compromised.

Robert Mueller, chief of the Justice Department's criminal division under Poppy (and later FBI director under W.), failed to establish any high-level governmental culpability—though BCCI could never have functioned without protection at the highest levels.

Had Mueller looked at what his own investigators had found, he might have discovered the identity of one such enabler: William Casey, who was

DRIFTWOOD PUBLIC LIBRARY
801 SW HWY. 101
LINCOLN CITY, OREGON 97367

CIA director during the Reagan-Bush administration. According to reporters Jonathan Beaty and S. C. Gwynne, Casey had met regularly with Abedi, the founder and de facto head of BCCI.[3] Casey allegedly struck a deal in which BCCI would serve as a major conduit for covert operations—that is, a way to wash the hundreds of millions in funds that were not authorized by Congress or the American people for use in Afghanistan, Central America, and elsewhere. The Senate Committee investigating CIA-BCCI ties also found evidence of meetings between Casey and Abedi.[4]

One of the figures implicated in BCCI's activities in the United States was its largest shareholder, none other than Jim Bath's partner Khalid bin Mahfouz. Mahfouz ended up paying $225 million to settle fraud allegations in 1993 as part of a deal in which New York state dropped criminal charges. Mahfouz's own Saudi bank, National Commercial Bank, was barred from operating in the United States.

Nothing, however, was ever made of the Bush connection to all this. Mahfouz's ties to Jim Bath were not raised, and therefore, neither was Bath's connection to the Bush family. It is worth noting that the Treasury Department official responsible for scrutinizing BCCI's affairs in the Reagan-Bush administration was assistant secretary for enforcement John M. Walker Jr.—who happened to be Poppy's cousin.

A Veiled Attempt at Banking

Even before John Walker got the job of overseeing such institutions as BCCI, others close to Bush were already on the other side of the covert banking customer-service counter. At the very time Poppy was at First International Bank, across town in Houston a number of his friends were starting up the Main Bank, with a paltry seventy million dollars in assets.

Main was to BCCI what a tiny hatchling is to a giant condor. But it achieved one thing that BCCI failed to do: publicly creating a joint banking venture between Saudis and Texans. The name conjured up images of Main Street, USA, though it would more accurately have been named after one of the wide, palm-lined boulevards of Riyadh.

In fact, the innocent name cloaked a darker reality. Main Bank brought together the Saudi geopolitical agenda, funding for U.S. covert operations, and related money-laundering, as well as the chance to make a buck. Among Main's principal investors were Bush's friend Jim Bath, his Saudi billionaire business partner Khalid bin Mahfouz, and Mahfouz's fellow Saudi billionaire, Ghaith Pharaon.

A fourth member of the Main Bank team was John Connally, the former Texas governor and former secretary of the Treasury under Nixon.[5] Connally was by then a partner in the Houston oil industry law firm of Vinson & Elkins, and probably the top Texas lawyer handling Arab money. Poppy Bush had worked with Connally over the years, but they had always been political rivals. Now both men were gearing up to seek the Republican nomination for president—and here Connally was enmeshed in Bush's convoluted milieu.

What most distinguished the tiny Main Bank was the highly unusual amount of *cash* the bank disbursed—more than ten million dollars a month in hundred-dollar bills.[6] The authorities often consider such untraceable money flows to be signs of criminal activity, particularly money laundering, and often connected with drugs. Cash, however, is also the principal tool of covert operations. In the case of Main Bank, whatever the intent, the practice brought no substantial scrutiny.

Lancing Carter

Such operations were, of course, small potatoes compared to the real action: controlling the White House. Even before Poppy Bush reached the pinnacle of the intelligence establishment, he and his associates knew that given the cries for reform in America following Watergate, there was a strong chance that Gerald Ford, who had succeeded Nixon, would not be reelected. As the 1976 election approached, there was a great likelihood a Democrat would prevail. If you had to hedge your bets, you'd look for a Democratic nominee who would be as cooperative as possible. Thus, key power brokers embraced Jimmy Carter, who then was governor of Georgia.

Powerful forces were moving in, influencing Carter's presidency from day one.

The peanut farmer lacked experience with foreign affairs. This put him somewhat at the mercy of the better-connected; and the Trilateral Commission, a private international policy group started in 1973 by David Rockefeller, stepped into the void. Carter turned his national security portfolio over to the commission's executive director, Zbigniew Brzezinski. Without Carter's knowledge, moreover, Bert Lance, the adviser he trusted most—

and the one he prayed with every morning—would be compromised by powerful forces.

Lance was a small-town Georgia banker who had practically bankrolled both the Carter family peanut warehouse and Carter's successful run for governor of Georgia. Lance had pressing financial needs, which proved his—and to some extent Carter's—undoing. In early 1975, as Carter and Lance were planning the presidential campaign, Lance was approached by one of the biggest bank-holding companies in Washington, Financial General Bankshares (FGB). Although federal law barred American banks from engaging in interstate banking in those days, FGB had a special exemption. It owned banks in a number of states; and as the only such company it was potentially quite valuable. It was controlled by General George Olmsted (Ret.), a former OSS chief in China, an old intelligence hand with longstanding ties to the late Allen Dulles. FGB's true essence was under wraps, but it sent out a message of its quiet power to the discerning by locating its headquarters at 1701 Pennsylvania Avenue, diagonally across from the White House.

FGB's stable included the National Bank of Georgia, and that entity offered Bert Lance the job of president. Lance readily agreed, and took a large stock position in the firm. He was now in deep.[7] Before long, Jimmy Carter would be too.

PRESIDENT JIMMY CARTER was a sharp fellow, and no pushover. He had been elected with a mandate and an ambition to open up the government. He would not stand in the way of the ongoing congressional inquiries into abuses of power by federal agencies, in particular, the CIA. In fact, one of Carter's first steps was to try to reform the intelligence agency. Ignoring Poppy Bush's entreaties to leave him at the helm in Langley, Carter brought in Admiral Stansfield Turner, whom he had known since their days at the Naval Academy, where Turner had been first in his class. But despite a successful career in the Navy, Turner was a fish out of water—actually as unfamiliar with the inner workings of the agency as George H. W. Bush pretended to be. The silver-haired patrician was unprepared for the ruthless internal politics of the CIA, which was more an assemblage of compartmentalized fiefdoms than a top-down military organization.

Nevertheless, Carter and Turner were determined to regain White House control over the CIA. One of Turner's first steps was to force out hundreds of officers from the Operations ("Dirty Tricks") Division—the perceived "rogue element"—along with their paid outside agents. Since the CIA's clandestine services already had been purged by previous directors Schlesinger and Colby, Turner was stepping onto an angry anthill.

To the intelligence brotherhood, Admiral Turner was a dangerously naïve man. Turner's foreign counterparts, who had liked Poppy Bush because he "got it," shared the domestic view. Recalls Count Alexandre de Marenches, the former head of French intelligence, in his memoirs:

> Admiral Stansfield Turner . . . had perhaps the most corrosive in-
> fluence . . . he never ceased to amaze me . . . "Call me Stan," he
> opened our conversation. I cringed. "In today's world, do you think
> communism is still something to be feared?" . . . I giggled. But he
> was serious. Deadly serious. As far as I was concerned, our con-
> versation had begun and ended there. "Jesus, this is the man," I
> thought, "who serves on the national Security Council and who
> helps to form the opinion on world affairs of the president of the
> United States . . . If the head of the CIA began by questioning the
> power and tenacity of his country's principal enemy . . . there was
> little hope for the integrity of the agency . . . It was not surprising
> that the Carter administration all but succeeded in destroying
> America's human intelligence capability.[8]

Turner's reforms created bitter internal resistance and fostered the establishment of a kind of CIA regime in exile. In 1977, former CIA counterintelligence czar James Angleton and some former colleagues started an organization, the Security and Intelligence Fund (SIF), ostensibly to defend U.S. security and intelligence organizations. The new organization also raised money for the defense of two FBI officers then under indictment. Within six months it was reported to have more than seventeen thousand members. Meanwhile, inside the agency, Hank Knoche, whom Turner retained as his number-two man and de facto chief of operations, was patently disloyal to his boss and frequently communicated directly with the National Security Council without even consulting him. Of all these disgruntled ex-CIA officers who had been turned out from their home, none was more disgruntled than the immediate past CIA director, George H. W. Bush.

Obviously, Jimmy Carter and Stansfield Turner and their reformist ideas represented a major threat to the status quo, and there were many people, both within the Beltway and outside it, who wanted to see them reined in. It was in this time frame that the Senate Governmental Affairs Committee began poking into the financial affairs of Bert Lance, whom Carter had appointed director of the Office of Management and Budget (OMB). *New York Times* columnist William Safire, a former Nixon speechwriter, had raised the question of whether a $3.4 million loan that Lance received from yet another murky bank after being picked for the OMB job was a "sweetheart" deal. Safire accused the chairman of the First National Bank of Chicago, A. Robert Abboud,[9] who was prominent in Chicago Democratic politics, of trying to "to gain life-and-death financial control over the man closest to the President."[10]

At issue were loans Lance had used to comply with terms of his stock purchase in the National Bank of Georgia. It was a highly technical matter. As James Ring Adams and Douglas Frantz of the *Los Angeles Times* wrote in their book *A Full-Service Bank: How BCCI Stole Billions Around the World.* "This was not a terrible offense and no criminal violation [was] involved. But Bert Lance was budget director of the Carter administration and the Senate investigation did not die after just a few headlines."[11]

Shortly after Labor Day 1977, Lance resigned as director of the Office of Management and Budget. He was out of work and nearly broke—and susceptible to being compromised further. It was at this time that he was introduced to Agha Hassan Abedi, the Pakistani who headed BCCI. Abedi ostensibly wanted to use Bert Lance as a front man for acquiring a banking operation in the United States, something foreigners then could generally not do under U.S. law.[12]

In November 1977, just three months after the group of which he was part purchased Main Bank of Houston, the charming, gift-bearing Ghaith Pharaon, now a business partner of Jim Bath, came into the harried life of Bert Lance. The matchmaker was none other than Agha Hassan Abedi. In what was to transpire, Pharaon's true function became apparent: he was essentially a front for BCCI.

Abedi explained to Lance that Pharaon was interested in buying Lance's bank stock—which Pharaon, unlike Abedi, could do because he had already been approved by American regulators and had already acquired substantial interests in domestic banking. Lance, who was deeply in debt, agreed enthusiastically, and Pharaon bought out his shares in the National Bank of Georgia at a 25 percent premium over market value.[13] Soon, Pharaon was practically moving into the Peachtree State. He bought Henry Ford II's eighteen-hundred-acre plantation outside Savannah, threw big parties for the state's elite, and generally established himself as a formidable local figure.

That Pharaon was essentially a middleman in those days would be corroborated years later, in a U.S. government investigative memo from the summer of 1988, as the problems with BCCI were becoming increasingly evident. The memo cited a source from inside the bank:

> Source said everything that Pharaon had came from BCCI. In effect Pharaon was an invention of BCCI . . . After Pharaon had returned from college, he in fact was "recruited" by [the bank] and for years had been used to "front" for BCCI . . . Whenever the BCCI group wanted to buy anything that they perceived was difficult for them to acquire directly, Pharaon would be used. This included, according to the source, the National Bank of Georgia.[14]

AROUND THE SAME time in 1977 that BCCI bought out Bert Lance's bank shares, he was approached separately by a purportedly disgruntled shareholder faction of the giant Washington-based Financial General Bankshares (FGB), whose intelligence connections were discussed earlier. These shareholders told him they were looking for a bank to acquire their FGB stock. In retrospect, this all seems a little too neat. Lance was now essentially the possibly unwitting midwife for both the entry of the criminal bank BCCI into the United States and its assumption of the CIA-connected banking activities previously handled by FGB. If anyone were to investigate BCCI's activities in this period, Lance's involvement would be prominent, and any scrutiny of Lance's role could not help but point a finger at his close friend and former business associate Jimmy Carter.

Meanwhile, Carter soon became pals with Abedi. In the 1980s, the now ex-president and the banker would spend holidays together in Switzerland and make missionary appearances in Bangladesh, China, and Pakistan, among other countries. (Coincidentally or not, BCCI had development interests in each country.) Abedi even donated five hundred thousand dollars to help create the Carter Center at Emory University.[15]

As if the scandal over Lance's banking dealings weren't enough of an embarrassment for Jimmy Carter—seriously tarnishing his image of rectitude—intermediaries connected with American and Israeli intelligence managed to woo Carter's brother Billy into a lucrative arms deal with the reviled Libyan dictator Mu'ammar al-Gadhafi. For obvious reasons, this looked very bad. The president was further embarrassed when it was revealed that Zbigniew Brzezinski, Carter's national security adviser, was providing Billy with classified information.[16]

That the Bush name disappears for so long from our narrative is less a symptom of the family's lack of involvement than a testament to its legendary caution. For Poppy Bush was connected to almost everything cited above. He was deeply involved with the outsourcing of unauthorized covert operations and illegal wars. He had created Bath's setup and the relationship with the Saudis. It's not too hard to imagine that, having been exiled by Jimmy Carter, he had mobilized the forces under his control to pay the president back.

Shah? Shush!

Iran was another crucial piece of the geo-petroleum mosaic. And where oil was, George H. W. Bush and his coalition were often not far behind.

In 1979, after years of oppressive rule, the U.S.-backed shah was overthrown, he was given sanctuary in the United States, and angry crowds in Tehran seized the U.S. embassy. The resulting hostage crisis dominated world headlines and began inflicting what would be a mortal wound on Carter's presidency. It was about this time that a young dark-haired visitor arrived at Bath's offices.

Bill White would never forget the encounter. "The Secret Service comes in with an Iranian guy who is ostensibly an aircraft salesman, and Jim introduces me and he says, 'Bill, I'd like to introduce you to His Royal Highness Reza Pahlavi, the shah's son.'"[17]

Like the Saudi princes, the young man had come to the United States to train as a jet fighter pilot, and spent the previous year at Reese Air Force Base in Lubbock, Texas. But in 1979, with his father overthrown, the shah's son needed to lay low. The Ayatollah Khomeini had just put out a contract on the shah's family, and by December, a nephew of the shah would be assassinated in Paris. So Reza was hiding out at Jim Bath's place, pretending to be an aircraft salesman.

His father, Shah Reza Pahlavi, had been installed by two coups—one British (1947), the other American (1953)—and was incompetent, fabulously corrupt, and gratuitously brutal. The shah's first national police force, the Gendarmerie, was trained by U.S. World War II veteran General Norman Schwarzkopf (whose namesake son led Poppy Bush's "Desert Storm" war on Iraq's Saddam Hussein in 1991). After the 1953 CIA-sponsored coup that toppled a popularly elected prime minister and restored the shah to dictatorial power, it was clear that Reza Pahlavi needed protection against his own people. So the CIA, under Allen Dulles and deputy director Richard Helms, helped train a new Iranian secret police force, the dreaded SAVAK. (This was the template later used by CIA director Bush for formulating his secret pact with the Saudis.) After Helms was removed from the CIA directorship by Nixon in the wake of Watergate, he was shipped off to Iran as U.S. ambassador. This was perhaps not as much of a demotion in the eyes of his colleagues as one might think, considering the looming importance of Iran and its oil reserves.

In October 1979, Brzezinski would, on the urging of the Rockefellers, persuade Carter—despite his grave doubts—to admit the fleeing shah for medical treatment. This enraged the Iranian populace, which in turn prompted the takeover of the U.S. embassy in Tehran and the seizure of fifty-two American hostages there. The resulting tensions between the two countries persist to the present day—and continue to stoke the political success of extremist elements in Iran and to heighten the risks of a military showdown.

Less well known is that David and Nelson Rockefeller used the takeover as a pretext to prevent the Iranian revolutionaries from withdrawing petrodollars from the Chase Manhattan Bank in London, where the shah kept most of his assets. According to several thoughtful accounts, the shah's looted billions were crucial to Chase's then-shaky finances. Their withdrawal could have precipitated an international financial crisis.[18] The hostage crisis then provided a justification for the Carter administration, under pressure from Rockefeller interests, to seize *all* of Iran's assets.

The presence of the shah's son in the Houston offices of Jim Bath might have surprised Bill White. But it made sense for the Poppy Bush operation to serve as guardian of the shah's most prized possession: the heir to the Peacock Throne. The shah had already been an important—if secret—benefactor of Richard Nixon and the GOP. And Poppy knew that if he was good to the shah, the shah could still be good to him—as would become clear with a series of investments that would shortly flow into businesses connected with Poppy's son George W.

Poppy for President

The intelligence apparatus has long meddled in elections abroad. But it took its first known step toward compromising a domestic election when Poppy Bush decided to launch his own bid to become the Republican nominee against Carter.

With James Baker as campaign manager and a young Karl Rove in a supporting role, Poppy began assembling a campaign organization full of former intelligence officials. Their enthusiasm could hardly be explained by his single year at the helm of the CIA. Part of it, certainly, was Stansfield Turner's decision to fire so many covert operations officers. A group of them formed Spooks for Bush; the former deputy director of the Defense Intelligence Agency was on Bush's national steering committee; the CIA director of security actually resigned his position at Langley to work for the campaign full-time; the former CIA Bangkok station chief also came aboard.[19] At CIA headquarters, nervy employees even affixed Bush stickers to their cubicles. Nothing remotely like it had ever happened in the history of the agency, though surprisingly little was made of it in the press.

Clearly, though CIA operatives worked hard to influence election outcomes—abroad, at least—they were not so effective this time around. Ronald Reagan surged past Poppy and claimed the GOP nomination. Soon, however, Reagan was persuaded—thanks in part to some negotiations by James Baker that were supposedly conducted without Poppy's consent—to make Poppy his running mate. And Poppy brought with him the tricks and mind-set of spycraft.

The greatest fear that Bush and his fellow Republicans had was that the Carter White House would resolve the Iranian hostage crisis in the final weeks of the 1980 campaign and throw the election back to the Democratic incumbent. Within the Reagan-Bush campaign, this threat was termed the "October Surprise."

Gary Sick, Carter's National Security Council expert on the Middle East, contends in his book *October Surprise* that William Casey, then manager for the Reagan-Bush campaign, worked out a clandestine deal with the Iranians during the summer and fall of 1980. This involved a quid pro quo: if the fifty-two American hostages were held until after the election, the Republicans vowed to deliver desperately needed arms and spare parts to Iran. The 1980 election involved, in Sick's words, a "political coup" that handed the Reagan-Bush ticket the White House.[20]

Robert Parry, who covered the Iran-contra story for *Newsweek* and the Associated Press, reported:

> According to handwritten notes of Reagan's foreign policy adviser Richard Allen, Bush called on Oct. 27, 1980, after getting an unsettling message from former Texas Gov. John Connally, the ex-Democrat who had switched to the Republican Party during the Nixon administration. Connally said his oil contacts in the Middle East were buzzing with rumors that Carter had achieved the long-elusive breakthrough on the hostages.
>
> Bush ordered Allen to find out what he could about Connally's tip. "Geo Bush," Allen's notes began, "JBC [Connally]—already made deal. Israelis delivered last wk spare pts. via Amsterdam. Hostages out this wk. Moderate Arabs upset. French have given spares to Iraq and know of JC [Carter] deal w/Iran. JBC [Connally] unsure what we should do. RVA [Allen] to act if true or not."[21]

In a still "secret" 1992 deposition to the House October Surprise Task Force, Allen explained the cryptic notes as meaning Connally had heard that Carter had ransomed the hostages' freedom with an Israeli shipment of military spare parts to Iran. Allen said Bush instructed him, Allen, to get details from Connally. Allen was then to pass on any new details to two of Bush's aides.

According to the notes, Bush ordered Allen to relay the information to "Ted Shacklee [sic] via Jennifer." Allen said the Jennifer was Jennifer Fitzgerald, Bush's longtime assistant, including during his year at the CIA. Allen testified that "Shacklee" was Theodore Shackley, the legendary CIA covert operations specialist.

Whatever one makes of the allegations and purported evidence that the Reagan-Bush forces were able to intervene to block Carter's October Surprise, the fact is that the hostages were not released before the election. Instead, they were released the day Reagan and Bush were inaugurated. The scenarios suggest that the Reagan-Bush campaign relied heavily on Bush and William Casey's off-the-books operations and contacts to deal successfully with the Iranians.

If this October *Anti*-Surprise actually took place, it would have been an act of treachery, and even treason.

CIA off the Books

Once in the White House, Poppy quickly asserted his desire to oversee national security issues. His Texas operation—and in particular the arrangements with the Iranians—became useful in a new and perhaps unexpected way. They provided a vehicle for funding unauthorized wars in Central America, especially the American-created contra rebel army fighting against the leftist Sandinista regime in Nicaragua. These wars were costly, and they required funding from a variety of sources; it took a vast array of airlines, weapons suppliers, and operational entities to run such an operation, keep it shielded from Congress, and provide the president and his aides their all-important "deniability" in case the press came snooping.

That's where Jim Bath's Saudi-Texan operation proved especially useful. Bath's partner Bill White recalled Bath saying that he "had been tapped by George Senior to set up a quasi-private aircraft firm that would basically engage in CIA-sponsored activities funded by the Saudi royal family."[22] As a military pilot who had top-secret clearance and had been vetted by the FBI, Bath was a perfect candidate to organize and run covert aviation operations.

Since the Federal Aviation Administration will certify only planes owned by Americans, Bath acted as the front man for Saudi aviation purchases. In 1977, ostensibly on behalf of Salem bin Laden, Bath bought the Houston Gulf Airport, a small, private facility in League City, Texas, twenty-five miles east of Houston. Bath also bought aircraft for bin Laden.[23] Upon purchase, Bath immediately renovated the airport and extended and reinforced the runway to accommodate what he referred to as "heavy iron"—large corporate jets and even light commercial aircraft. Bath bragged that Houston Gulf—unlike the city's other airports—had no U.S. Customs presence. This absence of oversight could prove handy in many an instance. Another property Bath bought as front man for the Saudis was the Express Auto Park garage at Houston's Hobby Airport, which fetched a price of $8.4 million.

By the time Poppy Bush became vice president in 1980, this Bath-fronted, Saudi-funded cover for American intelligence was involved in a broad range of covert activities. These ranged from supplying BCCI with airplanes to playing an integral role in what came to be known as Iran-contra. Bath set up Skyway Aircraft Leasing Ltd. in the Cayman Islands and became the sole director. A deposition of Bath in a subsequent lawsuit would reveal that the real owner was his Saudi friend Salem bin Laden. In essence, Bath was the vehicle through which Osama bin Laden's brother owned a CIA-connected airline.

Via Skyway, Bath brokered about $150 million worth of private aircraft deals to major BCCI stockholders. The firm that handled the incorporation of his companies in the Caymans was the same one that set up a money-collecting front company for White House aide Lieutenant Colonel Oliver North in the Iran-contra affair. Tentacles ran in and out of North's private network for funding the contras. Some of the money came from wealthy widows such as Ellen Garwood, a good Texas friend of Poppy Bush's.

On March 7, 1987, the *Washington Post* published what may have been the only public account of these transactions, noting the "circuitous route" the money followed through a curious company known as I.C. Inc., which also was incorporated in the Caymans.[24] The reporter could not determine who was behind I.C. Inc., nor why this entity was needed to transfer the money. Privately, insiders came to believe that I.C. was a kind of inside joke, and actually stood for "Iran-contra."

Arm's Length

Not only were Poppy and Bath deeply immersed in these operations—but the next-generation George Bush was himself privy, according to former White House adviser Doug Wead. The telling incident came during the early days of the Iran-contra operation, at a Christmas party thrown by Vice President George H. W. Bush at his official D.C. residence, known as the Admiralty. Wead was standing on the stairs with W. As the guests arrived, Poppy rushed to W.'s side and pointed out a young fellow in military garb. Wead said he heard Poppy whisper into W.'s ear, "That's the guy I was telling you about right now walking in the door." Was that fellow Oliver North, who would later be revealed as the point man for the secret and unauthorized war in Nicaragua? Wead believes so.

Poppy, as was his custom, would claim to know nothing about Iran-contra, contending famously that he was "out of the loop." But when North's diaries were released, they showed an August 6, 1986, meeting between North and Vice President Bush—at the height of North's activities coordinating the illegal effort.[25]

It was often the people they claimed not to have known, the ones they felt they had to whisper about, who really mattered. Jim Bath was one of these people. Beginning when he and George W. were suspended from flying in 1972, Bath's relationship with the Bush family, which had been common knowledge, became akin to classified information. For years thereafter, W. sought to create distance from his friend while Poppy Bush denied knowing him at all.

Bill White witnessed this public distancing when he accompanied Bath to a luncheon in 1982 at Houston's Ramada Club, where Poppy Bush was scheduled to speak. According to White, he and Bath were seated on a sofa facing the elevators when the doors opened and the vice president emerged with his Secret Service entourage. "He just looked at us and said, 'Jim'—and kind of winked at him and nodded—and then went off. It was kind of a knowing look, as they were obviously very guarded about any public display of familiarity," White said.[26]

That year, Bath donated five hundred dollars to the campaign of Poppy Bush's brother Prescott Jr., who was running for a U.S. Senate seat in Connecticut against Lowell Weicker.[27] In 1991, Bath acknowledged to *Time* that he was friends with George W. Bush as a result of their time together in the Texas Air National Guard but described himself as only "slightly" acquainted with Poppy Bush.

Railroaded

Whoever may be said to have benefited from the Saudi Houston operation, Bill White is not one of them. At first, things went well enough. For fourteen years, he was partner to Jim Bath in what appeared to be a thriving assemblage of enterprises. He was Mr. Inside to Bath's Mr. Outside, the one who managed the details while Bath hustled business with his connections and charm. White did well. According to White's recollections, by 1985 he was "hobnobbing with the rich and famous in Houston," enjoying "lunches at the River Oaks Country Club and the exclusive Ramada club, Lear jet junkets to Nashville, Las Vegas shows with Siegfried & Roy." Parties "at the Saudi Big House" and in the "high-rise digs . . . at the Olympic Tower in Manhattan were the order of the day."

Today the roof of White's own house is collapsing; his finances did so long ago. He has been through multiple bankruptcies, been sued untold times, besieged by threats, accidents, and other misfortunes. He even was accused by a man with alleged organized crime ties of not delivering an expensive model train White had sold him. All of this, White contends, is related to his refusal to cover for Bath when, he claims, his partner misappropriated loan funds intended for the Saudi-funded ventures for his personal use. After Bath and InterFirst Bank cut off funding to the Bath-White real estate development companies and partnerships, two main lawsuits mushroomed into dozens, as disgruntled employees, company creditors, and even the IRS joined the onslaught against White, focusing on his liability rather than Bath's.

Bath instigated four criminal charges against White, who was accused of assaulting a twelve-year-old boy, beating up a pregnant woman, setting fire to one of the Bath-White apartment complexes, and forcing a company employee to file a false insurance claim to recover for the fire damage.

InterFirst—which once employed Poppy, and which funded Bath's business—hit White with twenty-eight lawsuits in all. White got top Houston attorneys to take his case on a contingency basis, and they filed counterclaims against Bath, though they were careful to remove most references to threats, the Saudis, and Bush.

Due to the litigation, White, a full Navy commander, lost his chance to qualify for retirement benefits,[28] and most recently, there have been attempts to seize his mother-in-law's house. At one point, White told a Texas court that Bath and the Justice Department had "blackballed" him professionally and financially because he refused to keep quiet about his knowledge of a conspiracy to launder Middle Eastern money into the bank accounts of American businesses and politicians. That got action, and Bath and the bank abruptly shifted gears, offering him a package worth millions of dollars if he withdrew his own legal efforts and stopped speaking publicly about the dispute, but White refused.

"The settlement proposal was nothing but a 'hush money' agreement," White told the Canadian Broadcasting Corporation in an interview. "It said basically that we could never have this conversation and that I could never disclose the Bush-Saudi relationship. I felt that to take that money and to sign that agreement would have been to basically spit on the graves of all of my friends who died in Vietnam and were fighting to fulfill the oath we took to protect the Constitution. So I've paid a heavy price, but I really feel like some of us have a destiny. I certainly didn't choose this destiny, but it was thrust upon me and I'm trying to do my best to get the truth out. And again there's really no ill will toward Jim Bath or George Bush. It's just a matter of getting the truth out on the table and letting the consequences be what they may. But I think the truth's important."[29]

In June 1992, the *Houston Chronicle* reported that the federal authorities were investigating whether Bath had failed to register as a foreign agent and therefore was illegally representing Saudi interests in the United States. More important, it suggested that the Saudis were seeking to buy influence at the top:

> Federal authorities are investigating the activities of a Houston businessman—a past investor in companies controlled by a son of President Bush—who has been accused of illegally representing Saudi interests in the United States. The Financial Crimes Enforcement Network—known as FinCEN—and the FBI are reviewing accusations that entrepreneur James R. Bath guided money to Houston from Saudi investors who wanted to influence U.S. policy under the Reagan and Bush administrations, sources close to the investigations say. FinCEN, a division of the U.S. Department of Treasury, investigates money laundering. Special agents and analysts from various law enforcement agencies, including the Internal Revenue Service and the U.S. Customs Service, are assigned to work with the FinCEN staff.[30]

The unnamed "son of President Bush" was George W. Bush.

For federal employees to investigate such a thing at a time when the investigators' ultimate boss was Poppy Bush is in itself remarkable; that the investigation was occurring while Poppy Bush stood for reelection in a difficult campaign is also remarkable. Perhaps it is not surprising that nothing came of the investigation. As for the coverage, the *Houston Chronicle*, Bush's hometown paper, relegated the potentially explosive story to page 21, and it received no national attention. Earlier, with Poppy Bush in the White House as VP, Bath had come under scrutiny by the same paper. In 1985 he had obtained a unique federal contract to service transiting military aircraft at Houston's Ellington Field. According to the *Chronicle*'s competitor, the *Houston Post*, the U.S. government spent millions of dollars more than necessary by fueling military aircraft, including Air Force One, at Bath's facility, Southwest Airport Services, at Ellington Field, rather than using a government fuel station at the same airfield. Bath was said to be charging a markup of as much as 60 percent on fuel, but even after the newspaper's report, no investigations were launched. Bath would go on to refuel Air Force One for Poppy whenever it came to Houston, at a drastically inflated rate.

A Saudi connection to Bath's refueling facility emerged as a result of a lawsuit filed by Bath's former wife, Sandra, in the early 1990s. According to documents revealed in the suit, the Saudi bank controlled by bin Mahfouz claimed ownership of 90 percent of the shares in Southwest Airport Services, as compensation for a default by Jim Bath on a loan granted him for his airport parking company, which went bankrupt in 1989. However, Sandra Bath alleged that the bank was merely trying to seize control of the lucrative Southwest Airport Services as a favor to her ex-husband.[31]

Under President George W. Bush, Air Force One continued to use the facility.[32]

CHAPTER 15

The Handoff

I don't understand how poor people think.
—GEORGE W. BUSH, CONFIDING IN
REVEREND JIM WALLIS

A S GEORGE W. BUSH MOVED FROM college through adulthood, his activities fulfilled a kind of Bush family pattern of fuzzy implausibility. Things were not quite what they appeared at first to be.

A series of improbable choices and opportunities presented themselves—extraordinary ones even by the standards of his privileged life. Thus it was that in 1973, Bush, having inexplicably managed to opt out of the final two years of his military service obligation, instead began playing basketball with and giving pep talks to inner-city youth at Houston's Professionals United for Leadership League (PULL). As noted in chapter 8, this appeared to be some kind of compulsory (albeit rather pleasant) "community service" gig.

Then he entered Harvard Business School. That W. would again essentially pull rank on what must certainly have been hundreds of better-qualified and considerably more motivated applicants should really be no surprise to students of the system. From Harvard's understandable perspective, even if W.'s association with the school was not likely to confer any additional distinction upon the school itself, it did not hurt to have the son of the incoming chairman of the ruling Republican Party on the premises.

Yet even this opportunity for conventional success did not play out in a conventional manner. At the end of his first year in Cambridge, Massachusetts, while his classmates were taking summer internships with Wall Street firms and major corporations, George W. Bush was braving the wilds of the North. This could have been publicly spun in the same way as Poppy's decision to head off to the oil patch: as an appealing act of individuality, initiative, and grit. But this intriguing if short sojourn was left out of the bland résumé of W.'s past that was offered up for public consumption as he sought political office.

It turns out there was a reason for this reticence.

That summer of 1974, Bush flew to Fairbanks, Alaska, where he began working for Alaska International Industries, a company with airline and construction operations on the ground floor of the eight-hundred-mile trans-Alaska pipeline boom. It was a potlatch for all concerned: pipeline workers drove off with trucks from work sites and flew home to the Lower 48 with duffel bags full of stolen tools, with few adverse consequences. There was money for all.

How and why did W. get the job? As with virtually every other position in his life, someone—whose identity is not always clear—provided a boost. "He was actually a political hire," explained Neil Bergt, owner of the privately held Alaska International, in a 2008 interview.[1] Bergt said that someone from a Houston construction company with which he did business had called him and "asked us if we could put George Bush's kid to work for the summer, give him a summer job."

Nothing unusual about that, and, according to Bergt, W. did real work and was pretty good at it. "The bank was always bugging me for a business plan, and gee, I didn't have a business plan in those days," said Bergt. "I asked him if he could write a business plan. He said yeah . . . He knew enough about writing a business plan to ask the right questions and put it together . . . in a business plan format, and produced a nice-looking document . . . I enjoyed reading it, frankly."

Why Bush wanted to work at this particular company, or why someone thought he ought to, is a question with no clear answer at this date. A woman who met W. at a wedding in 1976 recalls asking him about Alaska. He replied, "Juneau's O.K. if you like mildew growing between your toes."[2]

One could argue that Alaska wasn't a bad place to be for someone looking to get into the oil business. Yet even Bergt can't help speculating about why W. was there. "I've often wondered what he did to piss somebody off and get sent to Alaska over the summer," he said. "Why he'd be working for a chickenshit company up in Alaska . . . The only thing that's ever crossed my mind is whether he was up here this summer he was supposed to be in the National Guard someplace."

In fact, Bergt's hunch might not be far off the mark. In the summer of

1974, W. should have been completing his six-year Air National Guard service obligation. What better place to remain off the radar than some mildewed Alaskan backwater? This could also explain why W. has omitted this work experience from his slim pre-politics résumé. Otherwise, why hide a job your boss thought you were good at?

Well, maybe because of the company's spookier aspects. In our conversation, Bergt described his company's activities in those days. These included refueling stops in Baghdad and business transacted with the Ugandan dictator Idi Amin and other leaders of what he described as "these weird countries."

"We were all over the world," Bergt said. "And we did all kinds of weird stuff." He described doing off-the-books work not authorized by the Democratic president. "We did some spying for the CIA after Jimmy Carter went in, gutted the CIA, and almost ruined them. They came to people like me because they didn't have any money, and by law they couldn't be in some countries—Libya, for one. We were still flying into Tripoli, and they asked us if we would count the number of MIGs on the runway, stuff like that.

"We did some work for the CIA in Guatemala . . . [when] Reagan was president," said Bergt. "The CIA had a captive airline, Southern Air Transport, and the only time we would ever get any call from them was when there was some kind of overspill . . . I think we may have gotten involved with Ollie North's funding of that [illegal Iran-contra] operation when Congress had refused . . . and then Ollie went to Iran . . . We hauled boots and pants." Bergt said he would have absolutely flown weapons if asked. "When my government calls . . . The politics of it, that's irrelevant to me."

"They would never admit they were CIA," Bergt said of one outfit that contracted with his firm. "They were a company out of New York. I remember one time they got an address. We hired somebody to go check it out, and it was an empty lot.

"The CIA wanted to do business . . . and they wanted to debrief some crew members and it was always in the southeast corner of Hyde Park, on the bench, in a trench coat, and the London *Times* under my arm. . . . It was like out of a bad movie."

Whatever he was doing that summer of 1974, W. kept the details to himself. Even later, when he was desperate for professional credentials, he did not speak of this job, just as he rarely mentioned his earlier international travels for Bob Gow's company, Stratford. As a result, none of the three principal biographies that were published during the 2000 campaign made any mention of his Alaskan sojourn. Reporters who traveled on his campaign plane could not recall his ever talking about it.

Bush's interlude in the forty-ninth state did attract fleeting public notice during his first presidential campaign, when Alaska Republicans produced a leaflet for local distribution that referred to him as a "former Alaska resident." Playing to local audiences with even the most meager connection is a common political tactic. But given their many secrets, that is a tricky game for a Bush to play.

Probably prompted by the leaflet, a short account of W.'s time in Alaska appeared in the state capital newspaper, the *Juneau Empire*, in September 2000. The *New York Times* followed up with a lengthier piece, based on original reporting and written with a tone of polite suspicion. But that article did not appear until October, just a few weeks before the election, and the story gained no traction.[3] (Bergt said that when word reached Poppy that a reporter was checking out an unfounded rumor that Alaska International had given W. the job in return for a favor with federal aviation authorities, the elder Bush, believing Bergt to have been the source, angrily rang him up. "George Senior was pissed off," Bergt recalled. "He lit into me: 'What the hell is going on?' I had to calm him down . . . Man, he could chew at you.")

Asked during the 2000 campaign about Alaska International and its business dealings with the Central Intelligence Agency and the shah of Iran, Dan Bartlett, a Bush spokesperson, said W. was unaware of those clients. "The only thing he knew the company was doing was flying freight in C-130s to the north Alaskan slope," Bartlett said. "That is the extent of his knowledge."

Bartlett speculated that Bush hadn't spoken of the job before because it had occurred so long ago and was so uneventful that it didn't seem worth mentioning. Yet Bush chose to cite a number of other jobs that were equally short and decidedly more banal—from delivering mail at a Houston law firm to working for a stockbroker to selling sporting goods. It was only the Alaska position and the Stratford foreign travel about which he kept strictly mum.

In any case, given Poppy's expressed concerns about his eldest son, it is likely that Bush Sr. had a role in arranging W.'s Alaska job. Yet, in typical fashion, the senior Bush left no fingerprints. It would not be wise for him to reveal connections with the Central Intelligence Agency, even indirect ones, in the summer of 1974, since he would not become publicly associated with the agency, as director, for another year and a half.

Starting at the Bottom . . . of the Top

Soon enough, it was Graduation Day, 1975. America's top companies made a beeline for the Harvard Business School. They were looking for talent—but they did not see it in W.

"Did you know that George W. Bush is the only Harvard Business School graduate that I know of who ever left there without a goddamned job?" asked Bill White, former business partner of W.'s friend Jim Bath and himself a Harvard Business School graduate. "He had fifty-three job interviews with Fortune 500 companies, McKinsey and Company, Booz Allen, everybody wants Harvard people. But Bush came back to [Texas] with no job!"[4]

Well, perhaps. But opportunity knocked just as it had for his father—in Midland, the land of his early youth. Emulating his father, as he would do time and again, he became what is known in West Texas parlance as a landman—convincing landowners to turn over the rights to potential drilling sites on their property, as Poppy himself had briefly done in the early 1950s. Fittingly, this involved a kind of rudimentary intelligence work: finding out who had a good handle on where oil deposits might be.

Thus W. joined dozens of other hopeful souls at the county courthouse, sifting through records to see who owned certain pieces of property on which others might wish to drill, and then persuading the landowners to part with their mineral rights. This was a tricky business, and one that required just a bit of a respectable front, at least a business card with a decent local address. For this, friends of his father's with offices in a downtown petroleum building turned over to W., rent-free, their water cooler room, where he used old soda crates for chairs. Beyond that, he didn't do much to knock out the West Texas locals. He dressed like a rumpled preppy, in wrinkled shirts and loafers with their tassels falling off. Friends of his father's got him into the Petroleum Club and the Country Club, and he worked the system. He initially called his modest venture Bush Oil. But he soon displayed a flash of his irreverent humor and incorporated under the just slightly disguised title of Arbusto—Spanish for "Bush."

An Early Political Ambition

There is some reason to think that W.'s sojourn in Midland was at least partly a political ploy. For one thing, before making his move he flew out to the dusty West Texas city for a chat with Poppy's longtime political aide Jimmy Allison. At that time Allison was the publisher of the local newspaper. He knew W.'s strengths—and weaknesses—better than most, having been assigned to keep an eye on him in Montgomery, Alabama, just a few years before, when W. had abruptly bailed out of his flying obligations. Some of W.'s closest friends also moved back to or settled in Midland around the same time: Joey O'Neill, Charlie Younger, and Don Evans, who would form a kind of inner circle for Bush and remain staunch loyalists throughout his life. Indeed, all would tell stories to inquiring reporters that helped shape the Bush narrative the public came to know.[5]

W. had just enough time to scrape together the cash to take a small position in one drilling deal when, in July 1977, the area congressman, Democrat George Mahon, announced he was retiring. This was exciting news, and perhaps not unexpected; the man had held the seat for four decades. It represented a singular opportunity in Poppy Bush's ongoing project of converting Texas to the GOP column. The longest-serving Democrat in the state's congressional delegation was giving up his seat in an extremely conservative area—and one where Poppy's son just happened to be hanging out his shingle.

For the many Americans who became aware in the 1990s that there was "another George Bush" with political ambitions, it might be surprising to learn that W. considered himself prepared for public office as early as 1971.[6] Back then, just three years out of university, W. had flirted with running for the Texas legislature, but was discouraged by his father, who thought he first needed to establish himself. Given Poppy's own rapid political rise, it might seem strange that he would be the one dispensing such advice. But even in his younger days, the father seemed more mature and accomplished than his unseasoned and impatient son.

W.'s 1978 congressional campaign, unfolding as Poppy was in the planning stages of his 1980 presidential campaign, could be seen as a kind of test run of the money machine for the larger cause. Indeed, it's likely that the donors understood what they were investing in. W.'s campaign raised $450,000—at that time an astronomical amount. Thus, twenty-two years before his presidential candidacy, at a time when his own father was preparing for a losing presidential race, the people who mattered were already betting smart money on George W. Bush's long-term prospects, or at least responding to the entreaties of his famously persistent father.

Asked later about his fund-raising success, W. explained that he had relied on his parents' Christmas card list. For context, one must consider that this document combined the cachet of an all-American social register and the heft of a big-city phone book. W.'s 1978 donor list, which goes on for pages, is a who's who from Midland, Houston, and Dallas—and includes entries substantiating the Bush family's long-standing ties to national elites. Contributors included William Ford of the Ford Motor Company; Robert Taft (whose ancestor was a founder of Skull and Bones); Frank Shakespeare, the longtime CBS president who headed the government's propaganda entity Radio Liberty; and a massive outpouring from every corner of the oil and energy industry. W.'s future defense secretary Donald Rumsfeld also contributed.

Bath also helped Bush by introducing him to big-money people in Houston. This included members of the Houston Chamber of Commerce, where Bath was a major player.

One day in 1978, Bath picked up his business partner Bill White en route to a Chamber of Commerce luncheon.[7] "As we were driving downtown, he said, 'Bill, I can't wait for you to meet the guest speaker . . . the two of you are cut from the same cloth. You're both fighter pilots. You're both Harvard Business School graduates. You're going to love this guy.' "[8]

White recalls that day, on which he first met George W. Bush, several months after White had moved to Texas:

> I'll never forget as long as I live, it was the first time I saw somebody dress in a suit wearing high-heeled cowboy boots. And it just struck me as a guy who was desperately trying to be six foot tall, irrespective of his natural height. Somehow he equated importance with height, which I thought was ludicrous because most of the fighter pilots that I flew with were shorter in stature, but were guys who were seven feet tall in my mind's eye because they had integrity, confidence and they didn't care about the superficial.
>
> My observation was that he was not comfortable around people who were "looking down" on him. I think that if you check the Presidential cabinet appointments and study photos of W. with his staff that you'll see what I mean. The company surrounding the President

in 99% of the photo ops that I see are carefully staged to make W.
look like "the big man."[9]

White recalled that Bath was animated on the way back from the luncheon and kept pressing his partner to say what he thought of Bath's friend.
There was a long silence. Bath could see that White was not impressed. Finally White spoke up. "Jim, I've known a lot of fighter pilots and this guy
didn't have any of the fighter pilot's attributes . . . that I admire and respect."

Bath was annoyed, according to White, who recalled Bath saying, " 'God-
dammit, that guy is going to be President of the United States one day. He's
going to be President of the United States.' "

The reason Bath could imagine such a thing in those early days was that
he had personally experienced the power of the Bush family connections.
Bath was already trustee for Salem bin Laden, and a millionaire. And he had
seen the skill with which the Bush family repeatedly made W.'s problems—
girlfriends, military service, and other matters—simply go away.

Yet Bath's prescient assertion that W. would one day be president seemed
astonishing, so White merely bit his tongue. But at the time, he mused
upon how bizarre it was: "And I just thought, no way in hell . . . Famous last
words."

And He Shall Have a Wife

Back in Midland, there was other matchmaking going on.

By their own accounts, George and Laura Bush first met at a Midland
barbecue in the summer of 1977. According to the official story, W.'s good
friend Joe O'Neill and his wife, Jan Donnelly O'Neill, a close friend and former roommate of Laura's, thought W. was a bit lonely and in need of a good
woman. And they thought they had the perfect one: Laura Welch, who had
grown up in Midland and then gone away to college and become a librarian.
The whole purpose of the barbecue, we are told, was to introduce the George
and Laura.

That made sense. Even today, but especially in those days, and especially
in a place like West Texas, there was something fishy about a candidate who
did not have a wife. Though most in his circle were already married, it
seemed to his friends as if finding a mate was the furthest thing from W.'s
mind when he announced his candidacy in July 1977. But when he met

Laura at the O'Neills' just two weeks later, he quickly reversed himself. They would wed in three months' time.

In a family where many things don't add up, the claim that George and Laura hadn't met before was certainly one of them. Laura and W. had both spent childhood years in Midland, if only minimally overlapping. Even if they did not meet then, or did not notice each other, by 1970, Laura and W. were both living in the same wild-and-crazy Houston apartment complex known for its eligible bachelors on the make and women looking to get made. Moreover, Laura's Houston roommate was Jan Donnelly, who was dating Joe O'Neill, already one of W.'s pals from Midland.[10] It's hard to believe that when Joe O'Neill came to visit his girlfriend at Chateaux Dijon, his old friend W. and his girlfriend's roommate Laura never encountered each other.

But a connection to those Chateaux days would not have fit the need in 1978 to clean up W.'s party-boy past—and indeed present.

At the barbecue, according to Bush biographer Bill Minutaglio, "Bush talked nonstop, and Laura Welch seemed to listen to every word."[11] In any case, the result was that W. the bachelor candidate instantly became a "family man"—and Laura a highly visible part of the campaign team. Laura would become W.'s best asset, even years later when his own popularity plunged.

Back to Business

Bush lost the 1978 election but collected a respectable 47 percent of the vote. The victor was the Democratic conservative Kent Hance, a thirty-five-year-old good old boy and state senator. The Bushes were reported to be utterly disconsolate about the loss.

But there were some lessons to take away from this. W. had been tarred as a carpetbagger, and leaflets warned that his father was a member of the ominous-sounding Trilateral Commission. Also, some things that bordered on dirty tricks were used *against* Bush. A Texas Tech student organized a "Bush bash" to recruit new voters, promising free beer to all attendees. Though the event was essentially harmless, a Hance surrogate drafted a public letter condemning Bush's campaign, and sent four thousand copies to the Church of Christ in Lubbock. "Maybe it's a cool thing to do at Harvard or Yale," Hance told local newspapers.[12] Hance also accused W. of trying to buy the election with out-of-state money.[13] That was the last time W. would allow an opponent to define him.

The lost election also served as the first indication of what the extended Bush operation could, and would, do on W.'s behalf. Younger brother Neil had moved temporarily to the district to help manage the operation. Other clan members were constantly in and out. Poppy's involvement as always was quiet and arm's length. But most significant was that one of Poppy's lieutenants, a young man named Karl Rove, was frequently on the phone offering advice to W.

That 1978 campaign was also an indication of the remarkable willingness of people who knew the Bushes to step up and put their own (or someone else's) money on the table. And it hardly mattered whether it was nominally for a political campaign or a business venture. That became evident after the election, when W. turned back to business and began aggressively working the same circles that had backed his campaign.

Monopoly Money

In 1982, Ronald Reagan instituted a huge tax cut. This boon to the wealthy had an unintended though inevitable by-product: it eliminated the attractiveness of oil and gas investments as tax shelters, and the oil business began to experience a drastic slide in prices and an exodus of capital.

Arbusto was hitting one dry hole after another, and running out of ready sources of cash. In the same year, Arbusto was renamed Bush Exploration. Perhaps this was an acknowledgment that a less subtle approach to the game was now required, a slight reminder that the supplicant was the son of the man a heartbeat away from the presidency.

Soon people were again salivating at the prospect of betting a fortune on businessman George W. Bush. One such investor was Philip Uzielli, an associate and sometime trustee of the New York–based Toqueville Asset Management, who flew into Midland with a check for a million dollars. When Robert K. Whitt, the attorney handling the paperwork, began reciting boilerplate about the inherent risks of such a deal, Uzielli brushed it off. "Not my money," he said.[14] Uzielli had never met W., but he did know James Baker, Uzielli's best friend at Princeton. Uzielli later explained that he had been asked to invest the money by George L. Ohrstrom Jr., a friend of Poppy Bush's from Greenwich Country Day School. When I questioned the late Ohrstrom's son, Wright, about this, he volunteered that his father was very secretive and that he heard rumors about his being in the intelligence services.[15]

For his million dollars, Uzielli received a 10 percent stake in Bush's venture. But given that the company's entire valuation at the time was under four hundred thousand dollars, Uzielli had paid about twenty-five times more than book value.[16]

Uzielli's cash infusion came in January 1982, about the time of another large and equally carefree cash injection—this one never previously reported. It came from a small Houston-based independent oil company called Moran Exploration, which had done some business with Dresser Industries, the company that had long been run by W.'s "favorite uncle" Neil Mallon, with Prescott Bush a longtime board member. At Moran's Midland, Texas, office, the geologist James Lee Brown got an odd request from the company's then-headquarters in Houston: put about $1.4 million into some wells Bush's company was hoping to drill, despite geological data showing they would be a bust. When he and a colleague objected, the word came back from the main office: just do it.

"I didn't even know George W. Bush, the son, existed, until he came in," Brown explained to me in a 2006 interview at his home in Midland. At the time of the early-eighties meeting, Brown knew about Poppy, of course, because he was vice president. But the son had never registered significantly on his radar up to that time, notwithstanding his losing 1978 congressional bid.

As for the investment W. was now touting, Brown said, "Dick Kramer Sr., my immediate boss, he and I didn't think it was a good deal, so we recommended they not do it. [Later] he popped his head in my door, told me it didn't matter what we thought—we're doing it anyway."

Brown, who was well paid at Moran, shrugged and went to work. If he was unenthusiastic about the prospects, meeting Bush did nothing to persuade him otherwise. "At the two or three meetings I sat in with him . . . he was usually the guy in the corner sound asleep," said Brown. "Trying to work over a hangover."

"Years later, I thought, 'Mr. Moran must have pissed away that million bucks because he's trying to grease the skids for something,'" Brown added.[17]

In 2006, I met with Dick Moran, head of the company, at his office in Wichita Falls, Texas. Moran was by then an octogenarian who still reported to work every day. He recalled making donations to various Bush campaigns but couldn't remember his company putting more than a million dollars into Bush's company. However, he didn't register surprise when I raised the issue.

The next time W. crossed James Lee Brown's radar was when he was running for governor. "I was hearing a completely different story than the story that I knew about him," he said. "All of a sudden he was this big-time oil man, doing quite well. He was a mover and shaker in the Midland oil business. And of course Midland was in love with him."

Saudis in Early

Another investor was W.'s old Guard buddy Jim Bath. Or at least he appeared to be. His deal with the Saudis and his own circumstances suggest that he may have been simply a middleman for the fifty thousand dollars he plunked down for stakes in two oil exploration partnerships that George W. had put together. "I know that it was Saudi money because Bath had no money of his own," said Bath's former partner Bill White. "We were in business together. I saw his personal financial statements. I knew the amount of cash he had available at any given time. And he also confided in me that the money invested both in our real estate business and in Dubya's energy business was Saudi money . . . One hundred percent of it was Saudi money."[18]

Given Bath's customary deal with the Saudis—a 5 percent management fee for any Saudi dollars he invested—this fifty thousand dollars from Bath raises the possibility of a corresponding one million dollars of Saudi money invested directly in W.'s drilling ventures. It's not possible to know for sure. But recall the million from Uzielli, who admitted the money was not his.

Remarkably, when *Time* reporters asked W. about his post-Guard relationship with Bath—for an article on Bush Sr.—he denied having one. The reporters were visiting Bill White in Houston at the time. When White told them that he had retained old financial statements showing that Bath had invested in Bush's firm, the reporters called Bush and asked him about it. In their subsequent article, they noted:

> The President's son has denied that he ever had business dealings with Bath, but early 1980s tax records reviewed by TIME show that Bath invested $50,000 in Bush's energy ventures and remained a stockholder until Bush sold his company to Harken in 1986.[19]

In the light of this information, those widely published pictures of Bushes shaking hands with Saudi royals come into clearer focus. That some of the money invested in W.'s first business ventures may have come from the bin Laden family shows how prudent the Bushes were to stonewall inquiries into anything Bath-related. As noted in chapter 14, Bath confirmed in a legal proceeding his compensation arrangement with the Saudis—in which his small piece of the action was his compensation for arranging a larger Saudi piece. From that, and from Bath's own limited resources, it appears that Bath's involvement in any Bush enterprises may have translated into secret Saudi involvement as well.

A Broad Spectrum

When, despite this outside funding, W.'s company continued to slide into the red, yet more investors stepped in. The next chunk of capital came from Spectrum 7 Energy, an oil fund with Midland operations run by two Cincinnati money managers, William O. DeWitt Jr. and Mercer Reynolds III. Spectrum was just one of their ventures, started in better times, largely for tax shelter purposes. In September 1984, as Bush Exploration neared financial collapse, Spectrum 7 merged with it. George W. became chairman and CEO of the parent company, still called Spectrum 7, for which he was paid $75,000 a year.[20] He also was given 1.1 million shares of Spectrum stock, worth about $150,000 in 2008 dollars.

The official version put forth during W.'s first presidential campaign is that in late 1983, DeWitt was too busy with other affairs and wanted someone to take over his oil enterprise. "He asked me to find someone in Midland who would be able to run the business down in Texas," said Paul Rea, a DeWitt relative who had been in oil in Midland for years. Rea was an old friend of oil attorney Martin Allday, a longtime friend of Poppy Bush's. The DeWitt family had owned the Cincinnati Reds baseball team and were major figures in Cincinnati.[21]

According to the official account, Rea arranged a meeting with W., and DeWitt quickly decided that Bush was the ideal candidate. Since that explanation is so unlikely on its face, given W.'s track record as a businessman, other factors must be considered.

What those might be is suggested by DeWitt and Reynolds's subsequent activities. These were of a complexion with which the reader is now familiar.

In 1986, two years after the duo rescued W., DeWitt and Reynolds were on the ground floor of a new player in the lucrative and often tax-free offshore reinsurance business, a way for insurance companies to protect themselves against unnecessary risk.[22]

The firm, Midwest Employers Casualty Company (MECC), had an all-star cast, with names that figured in other Bush-related enterprises flavored with a hint of intelligence activity.[23] The largest shareholders included Stephens Inc., the Little Rock–based investment bank whose owner had been involved in bringing Jimmy Carter's aide Bert Lance into the fold of the criminal bank BCCI. There was also Schroder Venture Trust of New York, an affiliate of a London-based bank on whose board Allen Dulles once sat.

W.'s oil enterprises do not seem to have made his partners any money. Still, Reynolds in particular has collected large amounts for his political campaigns. He served as chief fund-raiser of W.'s presidential race in the crucial state of Ohio in 2000 and 2004. People in Reynolds's zip code in the exclusive Indian Hills section of Cincinnati gave more to Bush's reelection effort than did those in any other zip code except Manhattan's Upper East Side. Ohio, of course, was the key to Bush's close reelection victory over John Kerry.

There is a neat conclusion to this pas de deux: President George W. Bush named Reynolds as his ambassador to the banking havens Switzerland and Liechtenstein. As for William DeWitt, Bush appointed him to his Foreign Intelligence Advisory Board. Unless multimillionaire baseball team owners have special gifts for intelligence beyond scouting prospects and stealing signals, there could be something else going on.

W.'s Lucky Chance

During the 1980s, George W. Bush kept busy with other undertakings, most of them scrutinized little if at all in the years before he was elected president. In 1984, while his father was vice president, Bush was invited onto the board of a company called Lucky Chance Mining—whose name somehow evoked W.'s charmed life but which itself suffered a different fate. Lucky Chance was a penny stock—the category of investments in which individual shares usually can be bought for fractions of a dollar.

The main thing one concludes from a close look at Lucky Chance is that it

- was far more complicated than your average investment.
- involved figures connected with intelligence and with foreign money associated with regimes closely tied to the U.S. government.
- was not a venture of which W. was inordinately proud.

Lucky Chance was a small Arizona-based company that had cobbled together inactive gold and silver mines before Houston stock promoter David Klausmeyer took it over in the early '80s. Klausmeyer was an old friend of Bob Gow's. Gow had been both Poppy Bush's lieutenant at Zapata Offshore and the employer of George W., in 1971 at Gow's agricultural company, Stratford of Texas. Klausmeyer himself had worked as an in-house consultant at Stratford when George W. was there and also recalled meeting the elder Bush on numerous occasions. W. apparently asked him for career advice.

In a 2006 interview at his Houston home, Klausmeyer reconstructed for me his memories of those days. He recalled that he was looking for penny stocks from which he might be able to make some money. He was not particularly choosy; indeed he assigned his teenage son to scrutinize the so-called pink sheets that list these small-time companies. His son liked the name of the company, and that was that, he said.

The funding was arranged through Marion Gilliam, a pedigreed New York investment banker. In a telephone interview, Gilliam told me he vaguely recalled being approached by Klausmeyer to get involved with Lucky Chance. "It may very well have been that he once came on a totally unrelated matter, he mentioned that he had a client or a person interested in gold mining, and asked, did we have any people interested in investing in mining?"[24] Gilliam worked in New York at Schroder Bank and Trust, a firm represented decades earlier by Allen Dulles that repeatedly shows up in connection with Bush-related ventures.[25]

Money came in from Iranians and Saudis who claimed ties to their royal houses.[26] Houston-based Gamal Gamal, an Egyptian native, told Klausmeyer that he had connections with the Saudi royal family. "His connections must have checked out because I remember attending a function in L.A. with [TV personality] Art Linkletter and Marion Gilliam when we were introduced to a 'Saudi princess,'" recalled Klausmeyer. "Marion took me aside and laughed about her because he knew right away she was phony—as Marion knew all the royal family, who were clients of Schroder Bank."[27]

Despite its high-powered investors, Lucky Chance declared bankruptcy in 1982. Later, a company in which Gilliam owned stock received two hundred thousand dollars and five million Lucky shares for reorganizing the mining outfit.[28]

W.'s entry onto Lucky Chance's board came in 1984 via Walter "Del" Marting Jr., an undergraduate roommate at Yale and classmate at Harvard Business School.[29] When Marting was asked to assume the presidency of Lucky Chance, he agreed—but only on the condition that George W. Bush be brought onto the board, according to Klausmeyer. It was a kind of quid pro quo, as Marting sat on the board of W.'s oil company, Bush Exploration. Thus, both Marting and Bush got salaries from their respective companies, and blocks of stock in their friends' company. (Klausmeyer believes that Bush got about fifty thousand shares per meeting.)

Bush served several years on the Lucky Chance board. He attended board meetings in various locales and visited the mines—until things got hot. For one thing, the other board members believed that Marting was investing funds in things they had not authorized. For another, the press had come calling.

A *Forbes* magazine reporter wasn't really focusing on Lucky Chance, nor on Bush's role, when he stumbled into the scene. The reporter, Stuart Flack, was looking into offshore shell corporations, in particular ones arranged by Gilliam and Klausmeyer.[30] The whole matter of using offshore entities to avoid U.S. taxes had come up before, at Dresser and Zapata. Now, it could be a big problem because attention was focusing on Lucky Chance itself. "Both Dave [Klausmeyer] and Gilliam had accounts in Bermuda," said Ernest Lambert, a former board member. "They could sell their stock through Bermuda—through, I think, Schroder's. They would sell it through their account in Bermuda, and brought back the cash in suitcases."[31]

Lambert, described by several former Lucky Chance figures as a rare person of rectitude in the enterprise, said the Bermuda bank was used by some to sell their Lucky stock after the restructuring, when it was as high as fifty cents a share. That's compared with less than a penny during many periods; and in fact the stock later plummeted. Lambert sold his own shares, legally, for just a nickel apiece. Because he had been able to acquire the stock for even less, Lambert was still able to make a $180,000 profit on the sale.

It was Klausmeyer who warned W. that a reporter was sniffing around. "I told George that *Forbes* magazine is doing this article," Klausmeyer recalled when I visited him at his Houston home in 2006. "I said, 'I think since your name was mentioned, if your father wants to be president, you proba-bly should resign.' And he said, 'You're right. I resign right now.'"

Klausmeyer recalled the scene vividly: "[Marting] was practically on his knees saying, 'Please, George, don't leave me alone here. Please don't re-sign.' And Bush says, 'No, Klausmeyer is right. You don't know the press. They get a hold of something like this and they'll blow it up all out of pro-portion. I'm out of here.' He didn't call anybody. He didn't think about it more than [that]—as soon as the words were out of my mouth."

When I called Marting to ask him about this, he asked that I call him back later, but never responded to my messages.

CHAPTER 16

The Quacking Duck

My pet belief, and I think it's grounded in some good research and reality, is that George W. Bush would not be president of the United States today if not for that starting point of this controversial Harken sale.

—BILL MINUTAGLIO, TEXAS JOURNALIST
AND AUTHOR OF THE BUSH BIOGRAPHY
*FIRST SON: GEORGE W. BUSH AND
THE BUSH FAMILY DYNASTY,* APPEARING
ON ABC'S *NIGHTLINE*

I F IT WALKS LIKE A DUCK AND TALKS like a duck, the saying goes, then maybe it really is a duck. Over at Harken Energy—George W. Bush's next corporate home—the ducks were quacking plenty loud. Bush-connected enterprises were just not the kinds of businesses with which the rest of us are familiar. There always seemed to be something more going on: that overlay of peculiar money-moving, a general lack of profitability, the participation of foreign interests, and a hint of black intelligence operations.

In September 1986, as oil prices continued to collapse and W.'s previous financial savior, the Cincinnati-based Spectrum 7 Energy, was itself failing, along came the Dallas-based Harken, a comparatively little-known independent oil and gas company, riding to the rescue. Harken snapped up Spectrum, put W. on its board, and gave him a handsome compensation package.[1] In return, W. was allowed to go about his business—which at the time meant playing a crucial role in his father's presidential campaign. But the Harken assist didn't just benefit Poppy's political fortunes. Profits from W.'s subsequent sale of his Harken stock would jack up his own political career. The Harken deal ultimately made it possible for him to become part owner and highly visible "managing director" of the popular Texas Rangers baseball team—a position that would enhance his modest résumé as a candidate for governor a few years later. Thus, the largesse of the figures behind Harken played a key role in George W. Bush's quick march to the presidency.

Virtually everyone who has looked at Harken over the years agrees that it is some strange kind of corporate beast, like a newly discovered species of manatee. The company's books have never made any sense to outsiders— which might have had something to do with the fact that the only people who seemed to make any money were the insiders. In 1991 *Time* proclaimed Harken "one of the most mysterious and eccentric outfits ever to drill for oil."[2]

The Harken story reads at times like the stuff of an airport bookstore thriller. One finds figures associated with BCCI, gold caches, and an alphabet soup of secret societies appearing at critical junctures to bail out Harken, traveling to the White House to meet with President George H. W. Bush, then flying off to make deals with the likes of Saddam Hussein or the Chinese in the wake of the Tiananmen Massacre. In Harken we find the future president of the United States deeply involved in an enterprise whose every aspect raises questions about control of power in our country, because it draws our attention to complex and little-understood international alliances that bring America's leaders, past and future, together with individuals and forces of dubious integrity and ambitions that appear far removed from the public interest. Harken also pulls the curtain back further on subjects we examined in past chapters—collusions and interferences in a broad range of institutions, from precious metals to the awarding of drilling contracts—and raises questions about a host of institutions, including even top universities. It shows us how very little we understand about power at the highest levels—and indicates how much more work needs to be done.

One thing, though, is clear: The story of Harken fits in perfectly with our evolving exploration of the Bush family's role in a globally reaching, fundamentally amoral, financial-intelligence-resource apparatus that has never before been properly documented.

AT ONE TIME, Harken Energy was not such an odd duck. For the first decade of its existence, Harken was a fairly conventional, and mostly profitable, oil exploration firm.[3] But in 1983, things began to change. Having been in business for nearly a decade, and now suffering from the collapse of oil prices, founder Phil Kendrick traveled to Asia to consider potential buyers for his Australian subsidiary. One Singapore-based broker happened to bring up a name. "He told me about a guy named Quasha—said he was the man behind Marcos," Kendrick recalled. "He said he was the one who put him in power." That may have been something of an exaggeration, but William Quasha was a man to know in the Philippines. An American citizen who had served there during World War II and stayed on to become a powerful lawyer in that country, he was head of the local expatriate group Republicans Abroad, and so well connected that he even played host to a Democrat, President Bill Clinton, when he came through the isles.

William Quasha's ace in the hole was his relationship with the long-ruling president and strongman Ferdinand Marcos. And Marcos, accused of stealing billions of dollars from the public treasury of the poor country during his twenty-year reign, needed friends with connections abroad.[4] Recalled Kendrick: "The word was, Marcos was trying to get money out of [the] Philippines—he had a lot of money—and place it in legitimate businesses."

In a curious coincidence, not long after Kendrick first heard the Quasha name, one of Harken's investment bankers in New York mentioned a client looking to take a major position in an oil company, a New York lawyer named Quasha. He turned out to be William Quasha's son, Alan.

Phil Kendrick and Alan Quasha quickly struck a deal. "He wanted control of the board, so we sold our stock to him, and that gave him control," Kendrick explained to me in what began as a phone conversation and ended up weeks later as a dinner at his country club in Abilene, Texas. With Quasha's arrival, Kendrick stayed on as a consultant and as president of the Australian subsidiary, for which he had high hopes. Quasha assured him, Kendrick said, that he was going to make Kendrick's stock options valuable.

According to Kendrick, he did exactly the opposite. "I finally figured out what his game plan was," Kendrick said. Kendrick alleges that this initially consisted of a press release that portrayed the company as a giant mess that needed to be fixed. "The stock just crashed; it went down to nothing—below a dollar." Then, the new management announced a rights offering, which allowed people like Quasha to buy still more stock, at a heavily discounted price.

This, of course, destroyed Phil Kendrick's stock options while giving the newcomers even more control. Then the company instituted a one-for-ten reverse split, which brought the stock price up to a no-longer-embarrassing level.[5] Meanwhile, management sold off the Australian subsidiary that Kendrick had been told he could run, and, according to Kendrick, pushed him out. (Kendrick, it should be noted, is a lifelong Republican who voted for George W. Bush in both 2000 and 2004.)

The funding for all this was baffling. When Quasha bought Kendrick's stock, the money came through an entity in Bermuda, a trust in the name of Quasha's mother, with major blocks of shares taken by other members of the Quasha family.[6] According to company filings, his father, William Quasha, bought 21 percent of Harken's stock.

Why did the Quasha family find this particular company so interesting? Kendrick couldn't stop thinking about what he had heard about the Quashas and Marcos—and couldn't help wondering whether the money going into Harken wasn't really Marcos's money—or, put another way, the money of the people of the Philippines. I had hoped to get some insight, at least a limited one, from Alan Quasha, but he has repeatedly ignored requests for an interview.

School for Scandal

With Kendrick out of the way, Harken began metamorphosing in strange and wondrous ways. As mysterious as the workings of the company was its allure for powerful figures and institutions—almost all of whom piled into the company after George W. Bush came on board in 1986.

One of the oddest investors in Harken was the billionaire speculator, investor, and philanthropist George Soros, who first became involved shortly after Alan Quasha took over the company by swapping oil company stocks for Harken shares; Soros was a major shareholder in the first years following Quasha's takeover, at one point holding one third of the stock.[7] That George Soros held a big stake and served as a board member at the time George W. Bush was welcomed into the company that would make his fortune is rife with irony. Soros, a refugee from Communist Hungary, would found a variety of progressive philanthropies in the United States and abroad, whose causes included promoting democratic institutions, campaign finance, and drug policy reform. Eighteen years after George W. Bush joined him in Harken, Soros would become the leading financier of efforts to deny W. a second term as president.[8] More consistent with

Harken's geopolitical texture is Soros's longtime backing of Central and Eastern European democracy movements during the Soviet era. Though Soros exited Harken years ago, he continues to play tennis with Alan Quasha.

By far the biggest—and ultimately the most improbable—of Harken shareholders was Harvard University.[9] Harvard, currently the second wealthiest private institution in America after the Bill and Melinda Gates Foundation, entered the picture in October 1986, right on the heels of George W. Bush.[10] Through its investing arm, Harvard Management Company, it agreed to buy 1.35 million shares of Harken for two million dollars and invest another twenty million dollars in Harken projects—eventually pumping fifty million dollars into the company and owning 30 percent of its stock.[11] Harken, in fact, was one of the largest investments the university ever made. "It was not typical," one former member of Harvard Management Company's board of directors told the school's newspaper.[12]

Harvard's initial purchase of Harken shares worked like a booster rocket. The next month, Harken began trading on the NASDAQ exchange. The month after, the firm scooped up E-Z Serve Inc., a chain of nine hundred rural convenience stores and gas stations, in its largest acquisition to date.

In this period, George W. Bush acquired options for eighty thousand additional shares of the company's stock. And no wonder. The company was about to turn from an ant into an anteater—and a particularly voracious one at that. In 1986, it had a total revenue of four million dollars. In 1989, thanks to a flurry of acquisitions and infinitely complicated transactions, revenue would exceed *a billion dollars*. Yet few outside investors made any money. Which might have raised more than a few eyebrows about where all that cash was coming from and going to.

Equally mysterious is how and why the financial whizzes at Harvard chose to bankroll the apparent clunker. In 2002, when the *Boston Globe* asked for an interview on the subject of Harvard and Harken, Michael Eisenson, managing director and CEO of the Harvard Management Company, who sat on the Harken board with George W. Bush, declined.[13] The university's motto—*Veritas*—apparently does not apply to its financial dealings.

The truth about Harvard's involvement begins to open a window on something that does not appear in the university's brochures, nor in the *U.S. News & World Report* rankings of America's top colleges.

Sly and the Family Stone

In 2002, the *Boston Globe*, seeking to understand the local school's involvement with Harken, spoke with Robert G. Stone Jr., the longtime chairman of the seven-member Harvard Corporation, the university's highest governing board. Stone sought to distance himself from the matter.

> "I never recommended Harken. I didn't know anything about them," Stone said in a telephone interview from his New York City office in what appears to be his first interview about the matter. "I don't tell them what to invest in." He said that at the time of Harvard's investment, he knew then-Vice President George H.W. Bush "very, very slightly."
>
> "I was at Harvard the same year he was at Yale. I met him a few times, and that was that," Stone said. "I had nothing to do with his administration."[14]

As for Bush's son, a graduate of Harvard Business School, Stone said, "I don't know the current president at all."[15]

It was an artful answer, and also disingenuous. Records show that in 1979, Stone, a resident of the Bush hometown of Greenwich, Connecticut, was—along with his brother David—an early donor to Poppy Bush's Republican primary race against Ronald Reagan. In 1982 Robert and David Stone again supported a Bush campaign: this time Poppy's brother Prescott Bush Jr.'s unsuccessful and quixotic 1982 U.S. Senate campaign in Connecticut against Lowell Weicker.[16]

Despite Stone's efforts to distance himself from the Bushes and from Harvard's entry into Harken, Stone himself turns out to have both oil and CIA connections—or, perhaps it can be said, CIA-oil connections. Most intriguingly, Stone turns out to have been in business with the "former" CIA officer Thomas J. Devine. That's the same Thomas J. Devine who purportedly retired from the agency in order to help Poppy Bush start up Zapata Offshore.

In 1950, the same year that Dresser Industries relocated to Dallas and the whole Dallas intelligence complex was coming together, Stone started Stonetex Oil Corporation, a Dallas-based oil company. Some years later, Devine became Stonetex's treasurer. (When I asked Devine about his association with the Stone family, he explained that the same ground rules applied as with the Bushes before he could speak to me: "That makes two families I need to get clearance from." He apparently never did get that clearance.)

Part of the mystery of the Bush connection turns out to once again revolve around old relationships. Stone came from a powerful old Boston family and married the daughter of a Rockefeller. His in-laws, it turns out, were close personal friends of Prescott Bush and his wife, Dorothy, George W. Bush's grandparents. And his father-in-law, Godfrey Rockefeller, had his own CIA ties.[17]

But there was much more to Robert Stone and to Harvard's decision to invest in Harken Energy. For one thing, Stone played a significant role in Harvard University's decision to move into private equity investing—which made it possible to get deeply involved in a company like Harken. For another, Stone's own business activities suggest that Stonetex and Harken were not anomalies, but rather that he was cobbling together some kind of empire with strategic objectives beyond profits at their heart.

Stone was a board member and sometime chairman of a whole range of companies involved with international shipping, the use of inland barges to move oil, and oil exploration. At one point he controlled one of the world's largest cargo fleets. And he was intimately associated with a small circle of highly politicized oilmen whose names have appeared in previous chapters. He served as chairman of the board of the Houston-based Kirby Corporation, a shipping and oil concern substantially controlled by the family of the oil depletion allowance king, Clint Murchison.

Stone kept building the requisite connections and power base contacts in East Coast establishment circles. He served as commodore of the exclusive New York Yacht Club—the ultimate gathering place of the upper class. He was an apt bridge between the worlds of Wall Street and oil, and the type of "master of the universe" who would have been useful in the management and financing of covert intelligence entities. As an obituary in the *Boston Globe* put it: "Robert G. Stone Jr., who served a record 27 years on Harvard University's governing board, had unparalleled gusto and talent for fundraising, eagerly jetting off to woo potential donors wherever they could be found."[18]

In a 1985 interview with the *Harvard Crimson*, a decade after Stone had joined the university's board, fellow board member Hugh D. Calkins called Stone "the world's finest fundraiser," noting that Stone "would hear about an Arabian sheik who had some remote connection to Harvard, and he would hop on the next plane there." At the same time that Harvard was propping up Harken Energy, Stone was also executive committee chairman of Combustion Engineering, a large company that was deeply involved in Saudi Arabia.

And there was more, as intimated by Michael Eisenson, the president of the Harvard Management Company. Eisenson, somewhat cryptically, told the *Boston Globe*, "There were not too many degrees of separation between Stone and Quasha."[19] The *Globe*'s reporters, pressed as daily newspaper reporters generally are, do not seem to have followed that intriguing revelation any further. But it is now possible to report the story of the relationship between the two men.

A Golden Opportunity

The importance of controlling natural resources is not something most of us discuss on a regular basis. But it is a principal motivation—and often *the* principal motivation—behind foreign policy decisions, wars, and coups.

As a young man, Robert Stone's marriage into the Rockefeller clan would result in his joining the board of Freeport Mining, a huge Rockefeller-dominated company with gold, silver, copper, and other mineral-extraction operations throughout the world, including major mines in Indonesia and the Philippines. The partners of Freeport Mining were a powerful bunch with an appreciation for the strategic value of minerals. Among the board members over the years was Prescott Bush's business partner Robert A. Lovett, who served in various administrations as undersecretary of state, assistant secretary of war, and secretary of defense, and is widely regarded as one of the architects of America's cold war strategy.[20]

Freeport's largest mine was and is in Indonesia—and Freeport is closely identified with the CIA-backed coup that brought the dictator Suharto to power in 1965. Efforts to topple his predecessor, the nationalist Sukarno, were the province of Alfred C. Ulmer, the Allen Dulles confidant who, as noted in chapter 4, visited Poppy Bush in Texas the week of the JFK assassination. Other Freeport board members have included Henry Kissinger and Admiral Arleigh Burke, chief of naval operations under Ike and JFK. Burke was an ardent advocate in National Security Council meetings for the assassination not just of Fidel Castro but also of others in the Cuban leadership as a "package deal."[21] JFK, just prior to his death, was taking policy stances on Indonesia inimical to the interests of Freeport.

It is in this context—the control and extraction of precious resources—that we meet Robert G. Stone Jr. and William H. Quasha (Alan's father), as young men doing their World War II service in the Philippine Islands.

The Philippines had been a gem in the American colonial empire since it, like Cuba, became an American possession after the Spanish-American War in 1898. The Philippines, even more than Cuba, was rich in resources, including gold, copper, sugar, and other strategic commodities.

And more than a few big names did their apprenticeship in the fertile islands. Before he became president of the United States, Bush family associate and Bonesman William Howard Taft was the civilian governor there. So was Henry L. Stimson, the Bonesman who would serve in five presidential administrations—and would address Poppy's Andover graduating class.[22] The family of future American general Douglas MacArthur was part of this same American cadre "managing" the Philippines. Douglas MacArthur's father, Lieutenant General Arthur MacArthur Jr., was the military governor.

Two other Americans spent time in the Philippines—both in the company of General Douglas MacArthur: Robert G. Stone Jr. and William Quasha.

From a young age, even before marrying into the Rockefeller family, Stone was trusted at the highest levels. In World War II, he did intelligence work related to ports and oil in Iran for the acclaimed marine engineer Benjamin Casey Allin III.[23] After working with Allin, Stone was then sent to the Pacific to serve General Douglas MacArthur, where, among other things, he took personal charge of the security of MacArthur's yacht and oversaw the sensitive landing preparations for MacArthur's retaking of the Philippines.

William Quasha, hailing from New York, obtained his law degree from St. John's University, graduating a year ahead of William Casey, the future CIA director. During the war, Quasha was also sent to the Philippines, where he worked in General MacArthur's legal department.

Allin, Stone, and Quasha all attained high status within the secrecy-prizing Freemasonry, with Allin and Stone becoming thirty-second-degree Masons and Quasha eventually attaining the coveted rank of Grand Master. One does not need to put too fine a point on this to recognize that such bonds of loyalty and discretion, seen elsewhere in Skull and Bones, do wonders for preserving secrecy over long periods of time, and are therefore enormously useful for maintaining discipline within vast covert operations networks.

Manila Poppy

Poppy Bush himself doesn't talk much about the Philippines, but he too did service there. Among other things, he participated in numerous bombing runs over the islands when they were in Japanese hands—including Manila Harbor as part of MacArthur's effort to retake the territory.[24]

And of course there was his intelligence work. As noted in chapter 2, on his way to the Pacific, Poppy stopped off at Pearl Harbor for some face time with officers assigned to the Joint Intelligence Center for the Pacific Ocean Areas (JICPOA). The early incarnation of JICPOA was headed by Admiral Roscoe Hillenkoeter, who would after the war become the director of the CIA. JICPOA remains little known and little discussed, but it was a crucial development in wartime intelligence, and played a key role in Admiral Chester Nimitz's successful island-hopping campaign, of which Bush was a part.

Franklin Roosevelt created the Office of Strategic Services (OSS) in July 1942 to replace a previous intelligence system that was deemed ineffective. General MacArthur, however, barred the OSS from operating in the Philippines, so that battleground was pretty much his own show.

Thus Bush became part of a joint intelligence effort coordinated with MacArthur's command. The association with the Bush circle would date back to the days when Douglas MacArthur was a young man and his mother contacted E. H. Harriman, father of Prescott's future business partners, to ask the railroad tycoon to give her son a job.[25] Years later, when Poppy Bush became U.N. ambassador, he took an apartment next to Mrs. Douglas MacArthur, and in 1978 the widow contributed to George W.'s Midland, Texas congressional campaign.[26]

Gold Busters!

Being in the Philippines at the close of World War II was a golden opportunity—literally as well as figuratively. The Philippines were chock-full of gold. There was gold in the mines, and rumor had it, there was gold being hoarded.

Even before Douglas MacArthur commanded U.S. troops in the country, he had major holdings in the largest Philippine gold mine. MacArthur's staff officer, Major General Courtney Whitney, had been an executive of several gold mining companies before the war.[27]

Besides the indigenous gold, a great fortune in gold booty was rumored to be buried in the Philippines, seized by the Japanese as they plundered one East Asian country after another. Marcos's widow, the famously extravagant Imelda, has claimed that her husband and his buddies got hold of this so-called Yamashita treasure. Several journalists, who have spent combined decades on the Philippines gold story, assert that the cache was actually seized by American forces under MacArthur and that its very existence is a sensitive secret. One reason is that knowledge of this gold could cause world gold prices to plunge and wreak havoc with currency markets. Estimates of the cache vary from forty-five billion dollars to hundreds of billions.

This may help to explain why so many of the companies mentioned in this book seem able to function in apparent defiance of economic logic. Entities such as Zapata Offshore, Stratford, Arbusto, and Harken appear to persist without profits for great stretches. To the trained eye, they look like classic money-laundering ventures, raising the question of where all that money originates. And that leads in turn to another explanation proffered about the Philippine gold: that it has been used—and perhaps is still being used—to fund unauthorized covert operations. This would not preclude a variety of funding sources, ranging from oil concessions to profits generated by the "legitimate" side of airlines and other enterprises. But it is hard to top gold as a negotiable mineral.

Rumors about MacArthur's involvement with gold were so widespread that the general himself called a press conference to dispel such notions. In his statement, he sought to downplay his own gold investments, and did not mention the Japanese gold at all.

At the end of the war, MacArthur appointed William Quasha as alien property administrator.[28] "Alien property" would have included anything of value captured from the Japanese. If in fact the Japanese possessed gold, this would have been by far the top priority.

Authors Sterling Seagrave and Peggy Seagrave contend that former CIA deputy director Ray Cline told them that the United States did locate the Japanese gold and used it to fund anti-Communist operations the world over.[29] Investigators in the Philippines have said that the gold was stashed in bank vaults in forty-two countries. Some of the money is believed to have been used in Japan, to quickly reestablish the ruling clique, and a pro-U.S.

ruling party, the Liberal Democratic Party; MacArthur oversaw the postwar occupation of Japan. The administrator of the so-called M-2 slush fund that secretly channeled these monies to Tokyo was none other than Poppy Bush friend and CIA officer Alfred C. Ulmer.

The Seagraves cast the Pacific gold operation as an offshoot of a secret program that began in Europe after the war. The key figures will be familiar to readers of this book:

> The idea for a global political action fund based on war loot actually originated during the Roosevelt administration, with Secretary of War Henry L. Stimson. During the war, Stimson had a brain trust thinking hard about Axis plunder and how it should be handled after the war. As the tide turned against the Axis, it was only a matter of time before treasure began to be recovered. Much of this war prize was in the form of gold looted by the Nazis from conquered countries and civilian victims ... Stimson's special assistants on this topic were his deputies John J. McCloy and Robert Lovett, and consultant Robert B. Anderson ... (This was confirmed, in documents we obtained, by a number of high-level sources, including a CIA officer based in Manila, and former CIA Deputy Director Ray Cline ...) [The next target was Japanese gold.] After briefing President Truman and others in Washington including McCloy, Lovett and Stimson, [intelligence officer] Captain [Edward] Lansdale returned to Tokyo in November 1945 with Robert B. Anderson. General MacArthur then accompanied Anderson and Lansdale on a covert flight to Manila where they set out for a tour of the vaults [that] already had [been] opened.[30]

Probably the key figure in all this was Edward Lansdale, who, according to the Seagraves, was the point man for the gold operation. Lansdale was almost larger than life, a figure deeply involved with high-stakes covert operations for many presidents. He was said to be an inspiration for the popular novel *The Ugly American. New York Times* Pulitzer Prize–winner Tim Weiner writes of Lansdale: "His specialty was counterinsurgency, and his trademark was winning third-world hearts and minds with American ingenuity, greenback dollars, and snake oil."[31]

This much is clear: Lansdale helped direct counterinsurgency operations in the Philippines in the 1950s. He was prominent in counterinsurgency meetings in the Kennedy White House, in which Averell Harriman, Prescott Bush's friend and business partner, was an ardent advocate of such activities.[32] Lansdale was also the titular head of Operation Mongoose, the part-CIA, part-Pentagon project to assassinate Cuban leaders, as well as a top figure in counterinsurgency operations in Vietnam.[33] If indeed Lansdale was involved with gold operations in the Philippines, then the gold operations were of paramount importance in the larger cold war battle.

IN THE POSTWAR period, and especially the 1950s and '60s, the United States was desperate for allies in East Asia. The deal, at least as U.S. officials saw it, was that Marcos would hold the fort against Communist incursions in the region as well as allow the continued operation of giant U.S. military bases, notably Clark Air Force Base and Subic Bay Naval Station, that would serve specific cold war strategic objectives.

In return, he would receive protection from the U.S. embassy and intelligence operations emanating from it, as well as from prominent local Americans acting as surrogates.

As part of the deal, Marcos would play a role in the international money machine through which vast undocumented sums sloshed, ostensibly to pay for covert operations. Implicit in this was a wink when he looted his own country—and maybe even an assist.[34] Whether the wealth he amassed included the Yamashita gold is uncertain. After his death, his wife, Imelda, would claim that Marcos had indeed found some of the stash—which at least was justification for the couple's ability to amass such a fortune.[35] But even without the Japanese treasure, the Philippines certainly had a domestic supply—which had been mined steadily, including during the war years, when the Japanese occupiers oversaw continued production.[36]

In 1978, Marcos issued a decree mandating that all gold mined in the islands had to be sold directly to the government. As the Seagraves note: "This made it possible for him to sell some of his own gold to the Central Bank through a variety of intermediaries, and the bank could then send the gold to financial centers without attracting attention." In effect, Marcos seems to have turned the Philippine government into a laundry for his own stash. From there, according to this analysis, the gold, its origins obscured, made its way into bank vaults abroad and into international markets.[37]

Poppy Bush and Ferdinand Marcos cultivated a relationship of mutual appreciation. "We love your adherence to democratic principles," Poppy gushed during a visit to Manila in 1981.[38] Marcos knew how to play the anti-Communist card, and like nearly all U.S. leaders, Poppy avidly helped prop up the dictator. A number of Poppy's lieutenants, including Lee Atwater, Paul Manafort, and the notorious "dirty trickster" Roger Stone (no relation to Robert G. Stone Jr.) did political consulting for Marcos.[39] Ed Rollins, the manager of the Reagan-Bush 1984 reelection campaign, admitted that a top Filipino politician illegally delivered ten million dollars in cash from Marcos to Reagan's 1984 campaign, though he declined to name him.[40]

Poppy also is known to have personally urged Ferdinand Marcos to invest money in the United States.[41] Imelda has claimed that Poppy urged her husband to put "his" funds into something that Imelda knew only as the Communist Takeover Fund. That suggests that gold in the Philippines has long been seen as a funding vehicle for off-the-books intelligence, covert operations, weapons trafficking, and even coups—plus protection money that Marcos felt he had to pay.[42]

To be sure, there *was* something of a Communist threat to the Marcos regime, albeit an exaggerated threat, and one Marcos himself used to good advantage. But the real threat to the dictator was a *democratic* takeover. By 1983 he was on rocky ground. His health was failing, and his regime's corruption was increasingly apparent—and embarrassing for his allies, including the United States, which soon began distancing itself. When Benigno Aquino, Marcos's political rival, returned in August 1983 from a self-imposed three-year exile in the United States, he was gunned down on the tarmac of the Manila airport. In 1986 Aquino's widow, Corazon, challenged Marcos in an election; when Marcos-regime officials announced that Corazon had lost what was likely a rigged count, a military rebellion finally forced the Marcoses to flee the country.

Amid the upheaval, William Quasha issued a statement of support for Marcos. The disputed election, he declared, was "the least dishonest and least bloody" since the Philippines gained independence from the United States.[43]

On the Home Front

If all this gold was going somewhere, we have to ask: Was some of it going into Harken Energy, where George W. Bush was deeply involved? Certainly, Alan Quasha had a relationship with his father that somewhat paralleled that of W. and Poppy's.

Having remained in the Philippines after the war, William Quasha eventually attained the rarefied status as the only American licensed to practice law there. He also picked up some intriguing clients, including the CIA-tied Nugan Hand Bank.[44]

Quasha and some American expat friends living in Manila also established a trail of disbursements outside the Philippines in the carefree manner of people who seemed to be spending someone else's money. The peculiar approach that this group brought to investing was described, almost in passing, in a Portland *Oregonian* profile of a local developer who received funding from them. In 1972, according to the article, Homer Williams was fretting about his lack of funding for a desirable real estate purchase when out of the blue he received a call from halfway across the world. Soon, Bill Quasha himself was flying in, making an offer for the property on the back of an envelope. A few weeks later, as the option was about to expire, Quasha's lawyer called Williams and flatly reported: "We just had $600,000 wired into your trust account."[45]

After three years of facing various legal hurdles relating to the property, Quasha dispatched his partner Lou Sheff to Portland. What struck Williams—and apparently the *Oregonian* reporter—was the man's slightly indelicate approach, perhaps the result of a few too many years living under Marcos.

> "Homer," Sheff asked, "who do we have to pay off?"
>
> "Lou, this is Portland," Williams replied. "You don't pay anyone off. It's not the way it works here."
>
> Two years later, Sheff passed through Portland again. He had a different question.
>
> "Homer," he asked. "Who do we kill?"[46]

This is not, one hopes, normal investment behavior.

Quasha senior himself was a far smoother operative. He was well-off and well connected with capital sources. In the final days of the Marcos reign, after nearly all the expatriates had abandoned him, Quasha continued to stick by his man, leading the American Chamber of Commerce to condemn his "partisan approach."

He also may have been a Marcos money man, just as Phil Kendrick had heard. Philippine investigators seeking to track the billions Marcos had embezzled from the Philippine treasury or obtained as bribes found that most of the money had been moved overseas through intermediaries. In 1986, the *New York Times* reported that Marcos-connected transactions involving tens of millions of dollars went through U.S. institutions such as the Rockefellers' Chase Manhattan Bank.[47] During a federal racketeering trial against Imelda Marcos in New York in 1990, the *New York Times* reported that Imelda's lawyer Gerald Spence said, "President Bush had urged Mr. Marcos to invest in United States real estate."[48]

During the years William Quasha was living in Manila and conducting his law practice, his son Alan attended Harvard Law School and Harvard Business School—even studying in years that overlapped W.'s time there. Then Alan Quasha set up a law practice specializing in the alchemy of corporate restructuring. News reports have characterized his approach to acquiring companies on the cheap as bottom-feeding,[49] and noted that the provenance of the funding was not always clear. Additionally, at the time of the Harken purchase, Poppy Bush, a former CIA director, was vice president, with the portfolio for managing covert operations—an empire that was undergirded by laundered intelligence funds.

When Alan Quasha took control of Harken in 1983, he was essentially an unknown and a small-timer. Several years later, he appeared to be on top of the world. Did gold and/or Marcos's billions have anything to do with this? What about Harvard's role? It is possibly a coincidence that Robert G. Stone of the Harvard Corporation also served on the board of the Gold Fund of the investment giant Scudder Investments. The Gold Fund was established in 1988, shortly after Stone brought Harvard's money into Harken. Four years later, Harken chairman Alan Quasha joined the board of American Express's AXP Precious Metals Fund.[50]

By 1994, the once little-known New York lawyer had advanced so far up the ladder that he became a governor of the American Stock Exchange. And in May 2002, he joined the board of American Express Funds, the mutual fund arm of Amex. And fittingly, Quasha joined the board of Harvard University's foreign affairs center.

An Alpine Rescue

By joining the Harken board of directors in late 1986, George W. Bush was entering this dense financial web. The next year he took time out from his father's presidential campaign to travel to Little Rock, Arkansas, where he met with Jackson Stephens, head of Stephens Inc., the largest private investment bank outside Wall Street. Stephens, as noted earlier, had a proclivity for befriending presidents and would-be presidents of both parties. He had previously established financial ties to Jimmy Carter—and would later do so with his fellow Arkansas native Bill Clinton, for whom he was a particularly crucial savior. The Stephens family rode to Clinton's rescue both during his 1990 reelection bid for governor of Arkansas and in March 1992, when his presidential campaign was broke. Noted the investigative magazine *Mother Jones*: "It may not be too much to say that their Worthen Bank's emergency $3.5 million line of credit saved the [Clinton] presidential campaign from extinction."[51]

Following W.'s visit in 1987, Stephens brought in the Union Bank of Switzerland (UBS), the largest financial institution in that secretive Alpine enclave. According to Harken filings, the London branch of that Swiss bank underwrote Harken's twenty-five-million-dollar stock offering. The bulk of the UBS shares, in turn, went to a Saudi operating through a Caribbean shell company.[52]

In the final analysis, George W. Bush, Stephens, and even UBS appear to have been midwives to create an arm's-distance between Harken and its U.S. intelligence connections and some ultimate funders: the Saudis.

The Marcos clique and the Saudis were not the only international elites connected with the Harken-Quasha group while George W. Bush was involved. The South African white apartheid regime was also a bulwark in America's global anti-Soviet strategy, and like the Marcos government, looked to the Reagan-Bush and then Poppy Bush administrations for protection from the growing demands of home-grown insurgents—in this case, black anti-apartheid activists. Through its gold trading activities on behalf of South Africa, the Union Bank of Switzerland was influential in preserving the African apartheid system for many years.

In 1983, as Alan Quasha was taking over Harken, UBS chairman Nikolaus Senn publicly expressed doubts about democracy in South Africa, reflecting a general sentiment among Swiss bankers that the black majority was not capable of self-governance.[53] At the time, UBS was providing banking services for funds from South Africa, the Philippines, and Saudi Arabia. When a Swiss referendum proposed in 1984 to lift the veil on bank secrecy, threatening to reveal the criminal origins of so much money sloshing through that pristine country, Senn was quoted as warning that it could lead to the withdrawal of so many funds as to cause the collapse of the Swiss economy.[54]

In an unapologetic 1988 acknowledgment of the mutual obligations incurred, P. W. Botha, the president of the South African apartheid regime, personally bestowed a medal of honor on a UBS official for services rendered to the regime.[55]

Around this time, with Poppy Bush running for president and George W. Bush sitting on the board at Harken, the company received an infusion from the billionaire Rupert clan of South Africa, which had important holdings in diamonds, gold, liquor, and cigarettes and close ties to the apartheid regime. The Ruperts also invested with Quasha in an American petroleum refiner, Frontier Oil, and became involved in the takeover of the Swiss company Richemont—whose top-drawer luxury brands included Cartier, Montblanc, and Dunhill—and put both Alan Quasha and Senn on the board.[56]

FOR PART OF George W.'s term on the Harken board (during which time he also received a consultant's fee from the company), he was living in D.C. and working full-time on his father's presidential campaign, where he was both one of his father's top advisers and his "enforcer" on the campaign staff. Poppy would certainly have known about his son's principal business activities at the time. And yet, as far as can be ascertained, neither of the George Bushes has been pressed to explain the geopolitical ramifications of Harken—or even to address the transparent illogic of it as a business enterprise.

Bahrain, in Vain

What W. got out of it—and why he was put into it—gradually became clearer. In December 1988, after Poppy Bush won the election, Harken's board gave W. an option to buy twenty-five thousand shares of stock. W. exercised the option immediately with the help of a low-interest loan from the company. This was the same type of loan that W.'s own White House would later criticize in regard to Enron and other malfeasance-driven corporate collapses.

The following June, Harken extended W.'s consulting agreement, citing the "positive image" the younger Bush helped create for the company. Who

perceived that "positive image" was not clear. It certainly was not the investing public. That year, the company's problems grew grave. Its petroleum
commodities trading subsidiary suffered seventeen million dollars in
losses.

In January 1990, Harken, which had never drilled overseas or in offshore
waters, came out of nowhere and beat the oil giant Amoco for the rights to
drill in the offshore waters of the Persian Gulf island nation Bahrain.[57]

Asked how Harken got the deal, Quasha, who back then apparently took
press calls, replied, "It was not some sort of fix." But he did not offer a persuasive explanation of what exactly it was instead. Eventually, Harken claimed
that Bahrain picked the company *because* of its inexperience, arguing inven-
tively that the emirate wanted a small outfit that could give the project all of its
attention.[58]

The actual drilling work was assigned to major political backers of the
Bushes. Harken Energy, of course, lacked not only the experience but also
the capital to finance the Bahrain exploration. So it chose, from dozens of
suitors, a Fort Worth company owned by the politically wired billionaire
Bass family, major GOP donors and friends of the Bushes—who will soon
show up in connection with other George W. Bush financial matters, including the Texas Rangers baseball team and a film financing company
called Silver Screen.

Lurking in the background of Harken's activities was the shadow of the
Saudi royal family and of BCCI, the intelligence-connected global banking
laundry. Indeed, three key figures associated with the drilling deal—the
Houston oil consultant who put Bahrain together with Harken, the U.S.
ambassador to Bahrain, and Bahrain's prime minister—all had connections
to BCCI.[59]

Timing Is Everything

Harken may have been an unlikely candidate to look for oil off Bahrain—
none was found anyway, but W. did nicely regardless. The announcement of
the Bahrain deal sent Harken stock soaring. In April, Bush signed a "lockup"
letter requested by underwriters of a planned public stock sale, pledging not
to sell his shares for six months after a proposed public offering. Nevertheless, two months later, he cashed out his Harken shares for nearly
$850,000.

This transaction, which enabled him to cover a loan he earlier used to join a group in purchasing the Texas Rangers baseball team, was another example of Harvard appearing to take steps to benefit the president's son.[60] The broker who handled the deal has steadfastly refused to identify the institution that bought Bush's stock. But a former Harvard Management Company accountant, Steve Rose, told me that he found an SEC filing on which the broker had written on a trade ticket "Michael Eisenson," the name of Harvard Management Company's president—and also a Harken board member.

Further, Rose found an inexplicable gap of 212,750 shares in Harvard's total Harken holdings, or almost exactly the 212,140 shares sold by Bush. "That is evidence that Harvard bought Bush's stock," he said.[61] So there was Harvard, having already come into Harken at a crucial moment to save the company in 1986, secretly coming to the rescue of George W. Bush personally, and helping him make a bundle. If Harvard did that, it would seem to be a rather bold use of university funds for some kind of private game well outside the purview of Harvard's trustees and money managers—and certainly an egregious conflict of interest in the truest sense of the term.

A week after Bush sold his stock (and the day a largely favorable *Forbes* magazine profile of the company appeared), Harken announced a second-quarter loss of $23.2 million. The stock plunged 20 percent. In 2002, it came out that Bush and other insiders had received internal warnings of impending financial collapse just sixteen days before Bush sold his own shares.[62] The company's problems, according to an internal memo, were mostly caused by losses from impenetrable Enron-type transactions that may or may not have signified true losses.[63] They came also from Harken's repurchase of the shares held by George Soros, who himself came out with a handsome profit.

Six weeks after Bush sold his shares, the plans to begin exploratory drilling off Bahrain got a jolt. On August 2, Iraq invaded Kuwait over disputed oil lands. Saddam Hussein had received what he interpreted—or at least said he interpreted—as assurances from the U.S. ambassador that the United States would not object. Eight days later, Harken board member Talat Othman, who had been part of a three-man delegation along with Quasha sent from Harken for the Bahrain signing ceremony, joined a small group of Arab Americans in a private meeting with President George H. W. Bush and his top aides.

Another person attending the meeting was A. Robert Abboud, head of

First City Bancorp of Texas, one of Harken's principal banks. Days after that White House meeting with Poppy Bush, the other Harken creditor, Bank of Boston, demanded Harken's immediate repayment of its loan because of a technical default—and Abboud stepped into the breach by agreeing to assume the Boston bank's loan. If Abboud had not shown up when he did, Harken might have collapsed, and certainly its stock would have plummeted further. A Poppy Bush supporter with three degrees from Harvard, Abboud claimed he was moved to play white knight based on Harvard's involvement, not Bush's. Certainly, the continued Harken rescue operations, even as W.'s own ties to the firm were being severed, suggest the overall importance of the largely unprofitable venture to some larger purpose.

As for George W. Bush, he was never seriously held to account for any of these dealings. Along the way, W. not only accepted remuneration from dubious characters for work he scarcely performed, but he also committed repeated acts of gross negligence. He had seemingly ignored *two* warnings from Harken's attorneys: about insider trading and about filing forms relating to insider trades in a timely fashion. Eight months would pass before W. filed the required forms. Bush claimed at the time that the SEC had lost his original filing; White House spokesman Ari Fleischer said the delayed filing had been caused by Harken's lawyers; and at a press conference, Bush himself said he hadn't "figured it out completely."[64]

An inquiry by the SEC under the Poppy Bush administration raised questions about the circumstances of the trade. But somehow no investigators ever spoke with W.; they concluded that he and other company officials were probably unaware of the extent of the losses. Thus, the president's son faced no consequences for his actions, and the peculiar activities of Harken and its affiliates drew no serious governmental scrutiny. By October 1993, with Bill Clinton in the White House, an SEC memo declared the investigation terminated with regard to Bush's conduct. It noted, however, that this did not mean that he had been exonerated or that future action was ruled out. Needless to say, there has been no further action.

A month after that SEC memo, Bush resigned as a Harken board member and consultant. He was now a baseball team owner and running for governor of Texas. Asked in 1994 about the Bahrain deal, candidate George W. Bush dismissed speculation about it as "all a giant conspiracy theory."[65]

But Alan Quasha and Harken are still around. And Quasha is still interested in relationships with presidents and would-be presidents of both parties. In the period leading up to the 2008 elections, Quasha and his business partner Hassan Nemazee hired Terry McAuliffe, the former chairman of the Democratic Party, to work for them. From there, McAuliffe went on to be Hillary Clinton's campaign chairman in 2008, with Nemazee serving as a major campaign adviser.[66]

Like Quasha, UBS retains its own strong interest in people on the path to the White House irrespective of party affiliation: UBS America raised more than one million dollars for Barack Obama's presidential bid. After a sit-down chat with Obama, the firm's CEO pronounced himself delighted with the candidate, whom he called "unbelievably smart and refreshing and thoughtful."[67]

CHAPTER 17

Playing Hardball

W. WAS NOT QUITE THE BASEBALL player his father and grandfather had been—but he was the master of a certain kind of pitch.[1] In the days leading up to the 1988 election, W. was on the phone constantly making sales calls, though not for his father's candidacy. As Bush family adviser Doug Wead recalled: "It was interesting to sit and listen to him pick up the phone again and again and say: 'Well, we're gonna buy a baseball team. Want to buy a baseball team?'"

Maybe George W. Bush felt that his father's election was in the bag. Or maybe he was in a hurry because he thought it was less unseemly for the son of a vice president seeking the presidency to be soliciting funds for personal reasons than for the son of a sitting president to be doing so. Whatever his reason, at that particular moment, baseball was on his mind.

W. has genuine affection for "America's pastime," but his decision to acquire the Texas Rangers baseball team was not just about fun. He was creating a legend that would set him on the path to the presidency. How could a man with so few accomplishments be made into an impressive public figure? How could a fellow who had few prospects of honestly earning a fortune be set up in the sort of lifestyle he and his friends expected?

Such questions were certainly on the mind of his informal political adviser Karl Rove. Although the Bush forces would claim that W. had not seriously thought about running for higher office until well into the 1990s, as far back as Poppy's inauguration Rove had been letting reporters know that there was another Bush waiting in the wings.[2] In fact, W.'s name was floated as a possibility for the 1990 Texas governor's race, but W.'s mother publicly opposed his bid because of concerns that a loss would be seen as a referendum on Bush Sr.'s presidency.[3]

Even back then, Rove was envisioning a path for him and his friend straight to the White House. The Texas governorship would give W. a base, and a bucketload of electoral votes to start with. So in the final days before his father's victory over Democrat Michael Dukakis, George W. Bush was looking toward his own future—first, a brief baseball "baptism" as a public figure, then political office. "Mostly he was talking about his plan with the Rangers and governor, back then," recalled Wead. "It was Rangers and governor, Rangers, governor, *Rangerrrrs* . . ."[4]

ANYONE SEEKING A path to the big leagues could do worse than owning a ball team. George W. Bush and his cadre well understood that a winning sports play, like a steady spot in a forward church pew or an art museum with one's name on it, accorded instant points—and went a long way toward ameliorating deficiencies (particularly moral ones) on other fronts.

The Bushes and their friends had ownership stakes in a lot of teams—the Reds, the Mets, the Tigers, and other favorites. It all started with W.'s great-grandfather George Herbert "Bert" Walker, who was a force behind professional golf's Walker Cup and, in fact, the introduction of golf itself into America. He was also a prominent booster of the New York Yacht Club, professional tennis, and premier horse racing. This family legacy culminated in George W. Bush's successful effort at capturing a new constituency known as the NASCAR voter. Of course, being associated with sports offers obvious benefits in terms of pleasure and ego, but there is little question that the Bush group was adept at leveraging yet one more beloved American institution.

As would be demonstrated by the Supreme Court that would decide the 2000 election in W.'s favor, getting a "fair break" for oneself begins with knowing the referee. Peter Ueberroth, the baseball commissioner at the time W.'s group acquired the Arlington, Texas–based Rangers, was known to be looking for opportunities in politics as he left baseball in 1989, the year Poppy took office. One source close to the negotiations told the *New York Times* that after W. had failed to persuade the wealthy Texan Richard Rainwater to join the investment group, Ueberroth himself had approached Rainwater and suggested that he team up with Bush, at least partly "out of respect for his father."[5] As commissioner, Ueberroth was succeeded by Bart Giamatti, an Andover alum who became president of Yale; he was succeeded by

Fay Vincent, another old friend of the Bushes who had roughnecked in the oil business in Midland, and even lived at the Bush house briefly when W. was growing up.

W. was relentlessly optimistic about his plans to get into baseball. "He'd get off the phone after somebody said no, and there was not even the slightest disappointment or discouragement," recalled Doug Wead. "You couldn't even see a whiff of self-doubt. I thought, man, he'd be a great salesman, he doesn't even have any [sense of] rejection."

Not that there was too much rejection. Smart men—and it was virtually only men who invested—knew that this was a good moment to be in business with George W. Bush, the president's son.

Family and friends understood the plan: turn a nobody with a famous name into a "somebody," and, while you're at it, use the famous name, insider connections, and the implied glamour of the project to make a bundle.

According to Comer Cottrell, a black Republican hair products entrepreneur who put up half a million dollars to become a limited partner, "George brought a lot to the table just by being the president's son and running for governor . . . Everybody wanted to know him."[6]

Bush paid six hundred thousand dollars in borrowed money for a 2 percent stake in the Rangers. However, he secured the generous proviso that his share would jump to 11 percent once the partners had gotten their investment out. Thus, the entire deal seems designed to benefit Bush.

Inside Baseball

For about eighty-six million dollars, Bush and seventy investors bought the team.[7] Among the investors were William O. DeWitt Jr. and Mercer Reynolds III, the fellows who had bailed out W.'s Arbusto Energy. This new deal was certainly a natural for DeWitt, who grew up around baseball and whose father served as general manager of the Detroit Tigers and later owned the Cincinnati Reds. Other Rangers investors included the much-investigated Nixon administration "Jew-counter" Fred Malek, who managed Poppy Bush's 1992 presidential campaign. Malek, who by 2008 was making a bid for the Chicago Cubs, has long been a kind of Bush family handyman. It was he who arranged a job for W. on the board of CaterAir, a subsidiary of the secretive global holding company the Carlyle Group.[8]

Typically, sports team ownership is a badge of pride. Yet, as with so many other ventures involving George W. Bush, many of the people who invested in the Rangers with him preferred to remain below the radar. "The city went berserk when I got a list of owners," said attorney Glenn Sodd, who represented plaintiffs suing the city of Arlington and the team owners over private land seizures to make way for the new stadium that would exponentially increase the value of the franchise. "They got the court order to prevent names from coming out. The team was desperate to keep it secret . . . The list didn't tell you a whole lot, because there were some partnerships [hiding] who the actual people were. For all you and I know, there were Saudis."[9]

There certainly were Saudi connections, including the attorney representing Bush as he pursued the Rangers. James R. Doty was a partner with Baker Botts, which represented major Saudi interests, as well as many American companies doing business with the kingdom. Doty had also represented W.'s old friend and Saudi financial agent Jim Bath when Bath sued his business partner Bill White, a saga described in chapter 14. Shortly after handling Bush's Rangers deal, Doty was named general counsel to the SEC under Poppy Bush's administration, and though he recused himself, he was there when the agency investigated the possibility of insider trading on W.'s Harken stock sale—and closed the file with no action.[10]

Roland Places His Betts

If Harvard deserves much of the credit for the boost Harken Energy provided George W. Bush on his path to the White House, then Yale deserves some credit for the boost that the Texas Rangers provided. With Yale, however, it was not the school's money so much as the clubby milieu the school created for private arrangements.

The largest investor in the Rangers deal was Bush's Yale friend Roland Betts, who put in a hefty $3.6 million. "I'm George's biggest fan," Betts once told the *New York Times*. Betts, who served as rush chairman of Delta Kappa Epsilon at Yale while Bush was the fraternity's president, would subsequently play a unique role over the years in persuading the media that W. was really quite a moderate fellow. As the *Times* wrote in 2005:

When people ask Roland Betts how a New York Democrat can be such a good friend of President Bush, he whips out a ready answer. "Which would you prefer: my being close to him, or some right-wing zealot being close to him?" Mr. Betts said in a recent interview. "Who do you want to have his ear? So it's not a bad thing. Maybe I give him a little balance. . . . I don't think he's as conservative a person as the media generally characterizes him as," Mr. Betts said.[11]

The media loved Betts: not only was he a Democrat friend of Bush's, but he had also worked for a while in an inner-city school, and he had a black wife. Moreover, Betts was founder and chairman of Chelsea Piers, a popular sports complex on Manhattan's West Side. After Yale, and after a spell as a teacher and assistant principal during the Vietnam War, Betts moved on to Columbia Law School and then became an entertainment lawyer with the white-shoe Manhattan firm of Paul, Weiss, Rifkind, Wharton & Garrison.

Even better, Betts started his own limited partnership, which cut a deal with the company that is practically synonymous with Hollywood entertainment culture—the Walt Disney Company—and put George W. Bush on the board. Betts's Silver Screen Management financed nearly every Disney movie made between 1985 and 1991, including *Pretty Woman, Beauty and the Beast,* and *The Little Mermaid.* The company also backed *The Hitcher,* with Rutger Hauer as a psycho-killer hitchhiker, which was derided for its "gizzard-slitting depravity."

Asked why he brought W. into the film-financing business (Bush remained on the board from 1983 to 1992), Betts told the *Times* it was to benefit from his friend's common sense. If anyone had common sense, it was Betts himself. Silver Screen got its start-up funding courtesy of the investment house E. F. Hutton. In that period, E. F. Hutton was being run by W.'s uncle Scott Pierce. Before coming to E. F. Hutton, Pierce had worked for the "other" Bush-Walker clan investment firm, G. H. Walker and Company. And the man who preceded Pierce at Hutton and brought him into the company, George Ball, was both a funder of W.'s Arbusto oil venture, and, as noted in chapter 15, presided over Hutton in a period when it engaged in a major check-kiting scheme; the firm later pleaded guilty to two thousand counts of mail and wire fraud.

The Betts family, meanwhile, turns out to mirror the Bushes in many respects: Yale legacy, employment in the Walker brokerage, roots in the spy world.[12]

The most visible Rangers investors, including Betts, were thought of not just in terms of the financial resources they could provide, but also of demographics. "The first time I met George, he came up to my office and wanted to meet me and told me that he was wanting to have a true American diverse team partnership," recalled Cottrell, one of Bush's co-investors. "He says, I would be his black partner, Afro-American. Then he had some Jewish people, and he had some European Americans from Yale. Half the guys were from Yale."[13]

Besides Betts, another strong Yale connection was the Bass family of Fort Worth, famously right-wing heirs to the vast Richardson-Bass oil fortune. The man who is generally characterized as putting the baseball financing deal together, the brilliant Texas investment manager Richard Rainwater, had been the investment manager for the Basses. Rainwater was a Wall Street legend for transforming a Bass inheritance of about fifty million dollars in 1970 to more than four billion dollars by the time he went out on his own in 1986. At the time Rainwater partnered with W., the Basses were involved with W. through Harken's Bahrain drilling deal.

Bush, Betts, and Ed Bass had all been at Yale at the same time, and Bass Brothers Enterprises—Lee, Ed, Sid, and Robert Bass—would be the fifth-largest donor to W.'s Texas gubernatorial and 2000 presidential campaigns, and ninth among his 2004 presidential campaign donors.

Betts's good fortune with regard to Silver Screen—and W.'s as well—may have come courtesy of the Bass family, who were Disney's largest stockholder, having saved Disney from a hostile takeover and selected Michael D. Eisner to run the studio.[14]

The Basses shared the ideological and cultural interests of the Bush clan and their secret society confreres. In 1991, Ed Bass's brother Lee donated twenty million dollars to Yale, his alma mater, and specified that the money—one of the largest donations ever made to the school—was to be used for revitalizing the Western civilization program. In fact, Bass hoped to limit the growing emphasis on multiculturalism; he was worried that the study of Toni Morrison and Malcolm X was pushing out the "classics." A controversy ensued, and Yale returned Lee Bass's money. To some, the problem with the Bass's gambit was not their ideology, but rather their apparent belief that money, rather than vigorous open debate, should be the deciding factor in a matter of broad public concern. As if to confirm this, when Lee Bass's effort backfired, Lee's father, Perry (Yale '37), offered five hundred million dollars to the school to formally declare that his son had done nothing wrong; Yale president Richard C. Levin refused that deal.

Nevertheless, by the time George W. Bush had become president, Ed Bass was one of Yale's nineteen trustees, along with Roland Betts.[15] Capping it off, in 2005, the Yale Athletic Department presented Betts with a George H. W. Bush Lifetime of Leadership Award.

Probably the most interesting thing of all is that the top men at America's top two universities would have a hand in enriching George W. Bush. W.'s apparent secret friend on the Harken transaction, Robert G. Stone, was the most powerful board member at Harvard, while Betts, the largest single investor in W.'s next enterprise, the Rangers, would become Stone's equivalent as senior fellow of the Yale Corporation.

W.'s Domain

Financially, the Rangers deal was basically about real estate. By getting the city to build them a new stadium, Bush and his partners increased the team's book value from $83 million to $138 million. This required convincing the city's taxpayers that they would lose the team if they did not pay up for the stadium. To raise the $191 million it would cost to build the Ballpark at Arlington, residents were asked to add a half cent to what was already one of the nation's highest sales tax rates.

According to attorney Glenn Sodd, W.'s group helped egg along Arlington by leaking a story that Dallas was competing for the team and had offered to build them a stadium. "We found out that this was untrue," said Sodd. In any case, Arlington mayor Richard Greene used the supposed threat to rush a deal through.

Bush put aside his much-touted antitax, free-market principles just long enough to get the city of Arlington to increase taxes on ordinary people there in order to build a stadium for—and then give both the stadium and the land underneath it to—Bush and his partners.

This subsidized land and stadium windfall was engineered at a time when Poppy was president and the savings and loan industry was in a free fall, with real estate being dumped for a pittance. To get the land, the new owners went to governmental agency liquidators and banks handling land liquidations and snapped up property. "Essentially, Bush's daddy sold him property for pennies on the dollar," said Sodd. What they couldn't get on the market, they grabbed with government assistance.

Bush and his partners wanted over two hundred acres of land to develop an entertainment complex around the seventeen-acre stadium. So they used the state's power of eminent domain to force out landowners without the inconvenience of free market negotiation. As *New York Times* reporter David Cay Johnston discovered, the Texas Republican Party had already expressed official disapproval of such activity, having stipulated: "Public money (including taxes or bond guarantees) or public powers (such as eminent domain) should not be used to fund or implement so-called private enterprise projects."[16]

W. would later campaign for governor as a defender of property rights. Speaking to the Texas Association of Business, he said: "I understand full well the value of private property and its importance not only in our state but in capitalism in general. And I will do everything I can to defend the power of private property and private property rights when I am the governor of this state."[17]

So the Rangers deal was essentially predicated on public funding through a tax increase and the seizure of private land through eminent domain. One attorney called it "welfare for billionaires."[18] To make money, the owners needed a new stadium, and they needed someone else to pay for it.

To engineer the crucial land deal, the Bush team found an inside man and an inside-inside man. The inside man was Tom Schieffer, brother of CBS News correspondent Bob Schieffer. A former Texas state representative once dubbed one of the "ten worst legislators" in Texas by *Texas Monthly*, Schieffer had already been involved with a competing group seeking to buy the team, but was persuaded to transfer his allegiance, as well as to bring in a $1.4 million investment.[19] As president, W. would appoint Schieffer ambassador to Australia and then to Japan.

Along with Bush's lawyer in the Rangers deal, James Doty, the Baker Botts lawyer working for the Saudis, the person who recruited Tom Schieffer also represented both the American oil industry and the Saudis. James C. Langdon Jr. was a Washington attorney who ran the energy practice for the prominent Dallas firm of Akin, Gump.[20] Langdon would give $3,500 to Bush during his gubernatorial campaign and become a principal fundraiser in 2000; he and his wife would be overnight guests at Camp David, and Langdon would be named to President George W. Bush's Foreign Intelligence Advisory Board. *Again that board.* It is not a certainty that Saudi money was involved, but as in past deals, the smoke suggested a fire of some kind.

The inside inside man was the mayor of Arlington, car dealer Richard Greene. Greene played a key role in the city's decision to heavily subsidize Bush and his group. At the time he began working to secure a home on favorable terms for Bush's Rangers, he was in trouble with federal banking regulators working for W.'s dad.

In 1990, at the same time he was talking with the Rangers about a new stadium, Greene was negotiating with the Federal Deposit Insurance Corporation (FDIC) to settle a large lawsuit it had filed against him. He had headed the Arlington branch of Sunbelt Savings Association, which the local *Fort Worth Star-Telegram* described as "one of the most notorious failures of the S&L scandal." Sunbelt lost an estimated $2 billion, and the feds (and the nation's taxpayers) had to chip in about $297 million to clean it up. Greene and the FDIC reached an agreement on the pending suit just as he was signing the Rangers deal.

The Arlington mayor paid just $40,000 to settle the case—and walked away. "George had no knowledge of my problems; there is no connection," he assured the *New York Times* in September 2000.[21] All of the bank's key figures were charged except for him. Not only was Greene not criminally indicted, but he also escaped with minimal monetary pain. Ten days before Arlington's 1991 public referendum on a special sales tax hike to help finance the stadium, Greene, now charged in losses of $500 million, settled all of his civil litigation for a modest $165,000.[22]

Greene Becomes Green

Greene's tenure was identified principally with pro-growth and business-friendly policies. Yet after George W. Bush became president, he appointed Greene to be a regional administrator for the Environmental Protection Agency, where he oversaw federal environmental programs throughout Arkansas, Louisiana, New Mexico, Oklahoma, and Texas. These states have some of the nation's most severe pollution problems, most of which are connected to petroleum, and thus of central interest to the Bush political clan— which has typically fought emissions controls.

The announcement of Greene's EPA appointment, which required no Senate approval, cited no environmental accomplishments or related experience for Greene.[23] It did note that his wife was founder and current director of the River Legacy Foundation, which created trails and a nature center along undeveloped portions by the Trinity River. But it failed to add that she had been named to that post by the city government that her husband ran. In 1997, then-governor George W. Bush appointed Mrs. Greene to the Trinity River Authority board of directors. It all raised the question: Why was a car dealer in charge of environmental protection efforts in a part of the country befouled by some of the most noxious emissions found anywhere?

Greene's EPA appointment was a nice farewell gift from his friends in the White House. He will get a pension equivalent to 100 percent of the highest pay he received at the EPA—this for a man who helped bankrupt two S&L's at massive cost to the public, and who walked away with just a forty-thousand-dollar fine.

Owning Up to It

It didn't take special political acumen to see that association with the Rangers would be helpful for anyone with political aspirations. For one thing, it appealed to state pride. After all, this wasn't the Arlington Rangers, or even the Dallas–Fort Worth Rangers; it was the *Texas* Rangers. Not only that, the team was named after an institution dear to the hearts and minds of all Texans. Since its founding in 1823, the original Texas Rangers, heroic upholders of law and order, have attained a near-mythic aura based on exploits that range from routing Comanches and Mexican soldiers to chasing down outlaws such as John Wesley Hardin.

Years later, W. would refer to his Ranger years as simply "a win-win for everyone involved."[24] But the business dealings that extracted $135 million from taxpayers should have made Bush a juicy media target in the 2000 presidential election. *New York Times* reporter Nicholas Kristof ferreted out the truth behind W.'s baseball bonanza in a front-page article in September 2000.[25] Unfortunately, it took the *Times* six paragraphs to even hint that the report was more than a puff piece about a successful Texas businessman.

Arlington attorney Jim Runzheimer was surprised that rival campaigns dismissed the reporting. "I thought at that point for sure the Gore campaign would have picked up on Nick Kristof's article," Runzheimer said. "I mean, they don't know who some local yokel is, who might be saying certain negative things about Bush. But hey, if Nick Kristof . . . obviously he's got some stature. He's a Pulitzer Prize–winner, if nothing else. But they didn't follow up." Even if Gore had trouble untangling the thorny financial web of Harken Energy, the story of Bush and Arlington provided ripe material for debunking his supposedly antitax opponent. "The ballpark would have been an easy issue. Kerry didn't do anything with it either . . . Bush would have been on defense if he would have had to explain, but not once did that come up in either campaign."[26]

At the very least, voters would have realized that they were dealing with, per David Cay Johnston, "arguably the greatest salesman of our time," who would end up "having sold not just friends but political opponents on a war costing more than a trillion dollars and thousands of lives with the kind of pay-no-attention-to-that-pool-of-oil-under-the-engine polish that used car salesmen only dream about."[27]

W.'s public sales jobs thus began with his successful effort to sell the citizens of Arlington on a tax increase—one that ran counter to his stated antitax principles, but also one where the beneficiary would be himself.

A Good Job—If You Can Get It

All W.'s Texas Rangers position really required was for him to show up at baseball games—which, of course, he was eager to do because of the public exposure it gave him. For this he received a salary of $200,000, about $350,000 in today's dollars—his largest compensation ever—for what was at most a part-time job.

Besides the constant association of his candidate with this beloved team in this beloved sport, Karl Rove loved to promote the public impression that Bush played an important role in the administration of the team. Given his conspicuous lack of experience in running ventures of any size or success, Bush needed to be seen as substantially engaged with the team's operations in order to ask the people of Texas to elect him governor. Rove would insist that newspapers refer to Bush as the "Rangers owner," though W. was just one of many owners, and certainly not the principal or most active one.[28] He also was not at all engaged in daily operations. As Glenn Sodd, the opposing attorney on the Rangers' land seizures recalled: "Bush never showed up at any of the key meetings about the [stadium deal]. If Bush spent two hours a week working on the baseball team, I'd be surprised."

While he was ostensibly toiling for the Rangers, Bush traveled widely on the company budget and delivered hundreds of speeches. He was building a following throughout Texas—as Bush explained in an exchange of notes with David Rosen, an oil geologist and acquaintance from Midland. Rosen had seen W.'s face on the cover of *Newsweek*, and an accompanying article in which he said he might run for governor. "I dropped him a letter suggesting that he would be much better suited for the House of Representatives, inasmuch as it's a gentleman's club, a lot of Yale graduates there," recalled Rosen. "Not a rough job. But I think he dropped back this note that he was more interested in what he could do for Texas."[29]

To be precise, the note read:

> Dear David, thanks for the letter and thoughts. I will not run for the House. It is a young man's seat and you and I are not young. I don't have any specific plans except to run the Rangers and work hard for candidates and the party—100 plus speeches in 1990.

W. commented on how the Republican gubernatorial nominee Clayton Williams had virtually handed the nomination to Democrat Ann Richards through his intemperate remarks,[30] then added:

> Let's hope she does well. If not there will be some folks after her . . . Sincerely, George.

Having egregiously gamed the system for years without being called to account, W. saw little reason to settle for so meager a prize as a congressional seat.

CHAPTER 18

Meet the Help

*Tell me what company you keep, and I'll tell
you what you are.*
—Miguel de Cervantes

The moral atmosphere of the George W. Bush presidency—and a growing list of revelations concerning improprieties, politicizing of agencies, and self-dealing—should not have come as a surprise. Warning signs abounded in W.'s gubernatorial campaign, his term and a half as governor, and his presidential campaign. There were the issues he championed, his management of the press, and his intimidation of everyone who got in his way. Most telling of all: the kind of people with whom he chose to surround himself. Taken together, these factors strongly suggested what a W. presidency would be like.

Yet the signs were mainly overlooked, especially by the people in the best position to shed light on them—reporters. With some conspicuous exceptions, the media was positively gleeful about nailing Bush's 2000 opponent, Al Gore, for alleged boasts and exaggerations (e.g., "I invented the Internet") that were in reality either misquotes or taken out of context. But when it came to Bush, the "liberal" media was strangely silent. It took a conservative pundit, Tucker Carlson, to question the resolve of his media peers. After one Bush-Gore debate, Carlson put it this way on CNN:

> There is this sense in which Bush is benefiting from something, and I'm not sure what it is. Maybe it's the low expectations of the people covering him. You know, he didn't drool or pass out onstage or anything, so he's getting credit for that. But there is this kind of interesting reluctance on the part of the press to pass judgment

on it. I think a lot of people—they don't, necessarily, break down along ideological lines—believe that, you know, maybe Bush didn't do as good a job as he might have. And yet, the coverage does not reflect that at all. It's interesting.[1]

In many respects, the media was so eager to "discern" W.'s character—and to bend over backward to be "fair"—that reporters often ended up being suckers for spin. And whenever they tried to just tell it like it seemed to be, their editors had to worry about complaints from the Bush campaign and elements of their audience decrying perceived bias.

Certainly, W. did have an aw-shucks charm that was especially effective on Eastern reporters who didn't want to appear prissy. But even more, he had better handlers. As Gore adviser Tony Coelho put it, "Karl Rove and Karen Hughes outmaneuvered and out-strategized us. We weren't in the same league."[2]

Karl the Killer

The personnel protecting and propelling George W. Bush as he rose toward the governorship and then the presidency resembled less a team of policy advisers than an offensive blocking squad—or perhaps a gaggle of underworld capos. None better played the role than Karl Rove.

Few people realize that Rove, perhaps the most important figure in W.'s political rise, got his start as a handpicked apprentice to Poppy Bush.

A self-described nerd who spent his teenage years in Salt Lake City, Utah, carried a briefcase to school, and wore a pocket protector, Rove was a devoted high school Republican and avid debater with a remarkable mind for facts and figures. Rove attended four colleges but never graduated. Yet it was Rove's role in College Republican circles that brought him to Washington, and in 1973, into the offices of Poppy Bush. At that time, Poppy was the chairman of the Republican National Committee (RNC), and Karl Rove was an ambitious twenty-two-year-old who had just quit his position as executive director of the College Republican National Committee in order to spend five months campaigning for the position of chairman. He had been accused of engaging in dirty tricks and of teaching his methods to others. Worse, a rival candidate had leaked to the

Washington Post a tape of Rove and a peer comparing notes on prior electoral espionage. In the middle of the Watergate scandal, a *Post* story titled "GOP Probes Official as Teacher of 'Tricks'" couldn't have pleased party elders.

Poppy "investigated" Rove, and even went so far as to have an FBI agent sent out to question him.[3] On what authority the chairman of the Republican Party could get the FBI at his disposal, and what such access might have meant, especially coming at the height of Watergate, is not clear. In any case, with that bit of business concluded, Poppy did what his friend, Watergate prosecutor Leon Jaworski, would later do for Poppy with regard to the Townhouse affair. He declared young Rove clear of all charges—then hired him as a special assistant.

Not only did he clear him and hire him, but he went right after Rove's critics. After the surrogate of one College Republican, Robert Edgeworth, spoke to the *Post* about the dirty tricks, Edgeworth asked Bush to explain the basis for his decision favoring Rove. "Bush sent me back the angriest letter I have ever received in my life," Edgeworth said. "I had leaked to the *Washington Post*, and now I was out of the Party forever."[4]

The irony of this lecture on disloyalty cannot be overstated, since this was the same Poppy Bush who appears to have been so diligently undermining his own president and boss at precisely this moment.

ROVE IMMEDIATELY REPAID Poppy's kindness by introducing him to the man who would help him become president.

The new College Republican National Committee executive director, Lee Atwater, would become a top Bush operative and later Poppy's RNC chairman. Atwater's crowning achievement would be the political destruction of Michael Dukakis, Poppy's Democratic opponent in the 1988 presidential election, who had started the race well in the lead.[5]

When Poppy returned from his year in China to serve as CIA director in Langley, Virginia, Rove was nearby, working for the Virginia Republican Party. When Jimmy Carter ousted Poppy from his directorship and Poppy headed back to Texas to plot his presidential campaign, Karl Rove headed back there with him. Working from their Houston base in the First International Bank building, Rove helped James Baker run Poppy's political action committee, the Fund for Limited Government, then hung out his shingle in Austin as a specialist in "direct mail"—the use of demographic and other information to send targeted letters for business and political purposes.

The Texas Hustle

There was direct mail, and then there was indirect mail. Former *Newsweek* senior editor John Taliaferro and his business partner found out about the latter form of communication when they were late in paying Rove's bills for work he did on behalf of their Austin-based magazine *Third Coast*. Rove had been calling repeatedly demanding payment. Suddenly, the magazine's post office box began filling up with blank subscription cards. "These, we came to realize, were [the result of] Karl Rove, madly pulling these cards out of magazines and stuffing them in the mailbox, knowing we would be required to pay twenty-five cents each or whatever," recalled Taliaferro.[6] "It was a huge annoyance, and a prank that made sure we got the message that Karl Rove didn't like being messed with. It was petty—rat fucking. But you could just see that instinct magnified twenty years later."[7]

In 1986, on the eve of a gubernatorial debate between Rove's candidate, former governor Bill Clements, and Democratic incumbent Mark White, and with Clements's opponent closing the gap in the polls, Rove called a press conference to announce the discovery of a bugging device behind a picture frame near his desk. "Obviously, I do not know who did this," Rove said, "but there is no doubt in my mind that the only ones who could have benefited from this detailed, sensitive information, would have been the political opposition."[8]

The story easily trumped news coverage of a debate on public policy and left White flustered. According to his speechwriter, "Mark White was told all about this minutes before going on, and it just really rattled him. And he didn't give a very good performance. It was really from that moment on that things started going not so well for Mark White."[9] Indeed, White's poll numbers dropped precipitously, and he lost.

Meanwhile the FBI concluded that the bug's tiny battery would have needed to be changed every few hours, and thus didn't look like the work of Democratic operatives. Nevertheless, it was a brilliant tactical move. "I will go to my grave convinced [Rove] planted the bug," said former Texas Republican Party political director and campaign consultant Royal Masset. "He's one of these art-of-war guys. To him, winning is everything. With Karl it's all a game; it's all a pure zero-sum game: we win, you lose—always."[10]

Rove's growing repertoire of tricks was tradecraft of the type that Poppy Bush's CIA associates would have admired. It was what they themselves routinely did around the world, ostensibly in the service of the nation. And Rove was hardly alone: former House Speaker Newt Gingrich, whose Republican revolution of 1994 bedeviled Bill Clinton's presidency, quietly brought a military psy-ops specialist onto his staff.[11]

Like Poppy, Rove would develop informal relationships with FBI and other law enforcement personnel.[12] Rove was not just ambitious and often brilliant. He was, in fact, the most effective of a long line of covert operatives recruited as young men into a pervasive extralegal apparatus. Perhaps more than any other person, Rove represented the sub rosa convergence of politics with intelligence and espionage—truly the embodiment of the Bush political psyche.

Rove at First Sight

When Rove first met George W. Bush, in 1973 at RNC headquarters in Washington, the circumstances couldn't have been more humdrum. As the story goes, W. was visiting from Harvard Business School, and Poppy assigned Rove the mundane task of delivering his car keys to the eldest son. But Rove, his eye ever on the main chance, was impressed: One look at W., handsome and brimming with charisma, in his cowboy boots and flight jacket, struck a chord in the pudgy, bespectacled Rove. "Bush is the kind of candidate and officeholder political hacks like me wait a lifetime to be associated with,"[13] Rove would muse years later.

They stayed in touch over the years, as W. served as an adviser to and sometimes surrogate speaker for his father. In 1978, as W. sought the congressional seat from Midland, Rove was already providing guidance. By the late eighties, he was actively touting W.'s political prospects. And by 1994, he was orchestrating the manufacture of a legend.

So dedicated was Rove to George W. Bush that not only would he labor assiduously to muddy W.'s opponents, from Ann Richards to Al Gore to John Kerry; often he took it upon himself to clean George W. Bush up—sometimes literally. On one occasion, shortly after W. filed to run for governor, when Rove brought his client around for a meeting with Texas Republican Party officials, it soon became apparent to everyone present—apparently excepting W.—that the aspiring candidate had stepped in some dog poop. Eventually,

Rove got Bush to the men's room for some corrective action, which was when political director Royal Masset walked in.

"Karl's there on his hands and knees wiping off the dogshit," Masset recalled with a chuckle.

The Rainbo Coalition

In one sense, George W. Bush has led a charmed political life. With a little help from his friends, he has consistently managed to avoid critical scrutiny of dubious public and private behavior. One incident that might have derailed his political rise came while Karl Rove was working as an independent political consultant and W. was using the Rangers to build his political legitimacy.

In 1991, Bush was invited to buy a house in an exclusive fishing resort—a twelve-hundred-acre lakeside reserve near Athens, about ninety miles from Dallas, called Rainbo Club Inc. Among the members was Harvey "Bum" Bright, a Dallas oil, real estate, banking, and trucking magnate, who owned more than 120 companies, including, for a number of years, the Dallas Cowboys.

Bright was a member of a group of powerful right-wing businessmen and a friend to Poppy Bush, who had helped pay for a vitriolic, black-bordered anti-Kennedy ad that ran in the *Dallas Morning News* on the day JFK was assassinated.

Through an artful arrangement, the Rainbo Club members managed to have their private retreat declared a recreation sanctuary, thereby reducing their property taxes, while keeping the land effectively closed to the public. This neat little dodge, while hardly on the scale of the Arlington stadium deal, epitomizes the double standard that the rich and powerful apply to maintain, and extend, their privileges.

Press exposure of this arrangement could have been embarrassing to George W. Bush when he ran for president in 2000. But by that time, W. had sold his stake in the Rainbo Club, and the press showed little inclination to pursue this "old" news.

The Rainbo connection proved useful to W. in another context. In 1994, ten days after gubernatorial candidate Bush laid out a nine-point plan "to prevent frivolous and junk lawsuits," a former caretaker at the club sued W. and his fellow members over his firing, which he said was on account of "spite and ill will." W. was concerned enough about adverse publicity to hire Dallas attorney Harriet Miers to represent him. Nothing came of the suit, but Miers soon joined the Bush team to fix other messes, and eventually became his White House counsel. According to a White House speechwriter, Miers once called Bush the most brilliant man she had ever met.[14] W. rewarded her loyalty in 2005 by nominating her for a seat on the Supreme Court. She had to withdraw from consideration in the face of a firestorm of criticism from both sides of the aisle, mainly regarding her lack of qualifications.

When W. assembled his 1994 gubernatorial campaign committee, his chairman was Jim Francis, who had spent most of his adult life as chief political operative for Bum Bright. In that capacity, Francis had played a kind of kingmaker role for a number of Texas politicians: Governor Bill Clements (on whose behalf he hired Karl Rove in 1979), and Senators Kay Bailey Hutchison and Phil Gramm. In the 2000 presidential race, Francis would run W.'s big-money fund-raising effort called the "Pioneers."

For his campaign manager, W. turned to Brian Berry, the man who had just managed Hutchison's successful 1993 special-election campaign. Though he would run W.'s 1994 primary campaign until March of that year, Berry was never admitted to the true inner circle. "There was a compartmentalization," he told me. "You literally had a senior level team—Francis, Karl, etc.—and I was left to be the mechanic." As for W.'s liabilities, Berry said, "That kind of stuff was rarely discussed, if ever."[15] Francis, a, bullish guy who had been Hutchison's campaign chairman and didn't seem to trust Berry, soon replaced him with Joe Allbaugh.

Allbaugh's name to this day is largely unknown, but he is an essential character in the George W. saga. They first met in 1984, when Allbaugh was serving as deputy regional coordinator for the Ronald Reagan–Poppy Bush reelection campaign, responsible for eleven western states. Allbaugh became in steady succession Bush's gubernatorial campaign manager, gubernatorial chief of staff, presidential campaign manager, on-the-ground leader of the Bush team during the Florida recount battle of 2000, and finally, the head of the Federal Emergency Management Agency (FEMA)—which would become infamous following Hurricane Katrina under Michael Brown, a friend whom Allbaugh brought to Washington and installed as his successor.

When Allbaugh entered W.'s inner circle, he was little more than an

Oklahoma apparatchik with a spotty record. He'd started in college as a driver for Senator Henry Bellmon (Republican of Oklahoma and longtime friend of George H. W. Bush), then climbed his way up the political ladder. He worked in government, politics, and business while pursuing deals of questionable ethical probity. In 1987, as a top aide to then-governor Bellmon, he worked closely with state highway officials. But he also took a thirty-thousand-dollar bank loan guaranteed by a large road contractor who was engaged in a steady stream of disputes with the state over shoddy work practices.

Allbaugh's ability to hop back and forth between the letting and the getting of contracts was clear to all—including Allbaugh himself. When a reporter from the *Daily Oklahoman* observed to Allbaugh that he had gone from serving as Bellmon's Oklahoma Turnpike Authority liaison to working for a bond underwriter that was hoping to do business with the authority, Allbaugh replied, "Golly, what a coincidence."

On the side, Allbaugh started an oil-and-gas partnership called Great American Resources. The secretary and treasurer of that firm was Allbaugh's then-wife Gypsy Hogan, a former journalist who grew increasingly upset about the fact that she had no idea what the business was about. She also wasn't comfortable with large amounts of unexplained cash flowing in—and with Allbaugh's request that she sign a series of blank checks. When she began to demand answers, she said, Allbaugh got angry and warned her to mind her own business. Hogan, whom I interviewed at the University of Central Oklahoma, where she is publications editor, also remembered that, shortly before she asked him for a divorce, Allbaugh claimed to be in the CIA.[16] Maybe he was. But there is no doubt that Allbaugh was a loyal soldier in the Bush machine, whose devotion was amply rewarded.

In 1988, Allbaugh left government and took a job with the Little Rock investment banker Jackson Stephens.[17] Stephens had repeatedly shown up in intelligence-tinged, Bush-related operations, including Harken Energy and BCCI; at the time he employed Allbaugh, the banker was one of Poppy Bush's key fund-raisers. That Poppy Bush was keeping an eye out for Joe Allbaugh was suggested again in 1992 when the president appointed him to an obscure regional entity called the Arkansas-Oklahoma Arkansas River Compact Commission. That entity's jurisdiction included the movements of oil barges.

One manager from the Stephens bank told me that Allbaugh produced little for the firm. But by the time he arrived in Texas in 1994 to run W.'s gubernatorial campaign, he had settled into his ultimate persona: the enforcer. In newspaper articles, Allbaugh explained his role in the Bush gubernatorial campaign was making sure the trains ran on time, and mediating the strong personalities of Karl Rove and communications director Karen Hughes. If Rove was Bush's brain and Hughes was Bush's mouth, Big Joe Allbaugh, at six foot four and 275 pounds, was Bush's muscle.

"It was clear he wanted to use his size to project a strong or menacing sense of himself," said Wayne Slater, senior political writer for the *Dallas Morning News.*[18] Indeed, Allbaugh's propensity to turn bright red when enraged led Bush to give Allbaugh the nickname "Pinky." But if anyone other than W. dared to call him by that name, Allbaugh would whirl around and growl, "I will pinch your head off," and make pinching motions with his fingers.

W. prized loyalty above all, and Allbaugh's was unquestioned, even fanatical. "There isn't anything more important than protecting him and the first lady," Allbaugh once told the *Washington Post* from the governor's office. "I'm the heavy, in the literal sense of the word."

BUSH'S RUN FOR Texas governor in 1994 was the first big test for his crew of handlers and enablers. The methods they used foreshadowed those employed in W.'s two presidential campaigns. His opponent, Democratic governor Ann Richards, was characterized as an effete Austin liberal. Beyond this, there were rumors of uncertain provenance that Richards was a lesbian. No one could doubt that the Bushes had a grievance with her. At the 1988 Democratic convention, she ridiculed the malapropism-plagued Poppy for having been "born with a silver foot in his mouth."

For W. himself, the main task was to shed the vestiges of the Eastern Establishment that still clung to him. To achieve this, he talked fondly of his days at the public San Jacinto Junior High, neglecting to mention that he had transferred to the exclusive private Kinkaid School, and from there to that most un-Texan institution, Andover.

The issues, such as they were, involved popular fare such as improving education and getting tough on crime. Perhaps most important, W. benefited from good timing—as one of many Republicans swept into office nationally on the wave of the Newt Gingrich revolution. Bush beat Richards with 53 percent of the vote to her 46.

Tough on (Some) Crime

From the moment Bush was inaugurated, everything he did seemed calculated to boost him to an even higher stage. His upward trajectory benefited from the unique structure of Texas government. By design, Texas's governor has limited say in state affairs; curiously, the lieutenant governor wields more influence. This dispersal of power among elected officials, called a *plural executive*, enabled W. to selectively associate himself with issues that would boost his appeal, while distancing himself from unpleasant ones. Such a system was tailor-made for a neophyte politician with national ambitions.

The issues W. and Rove chose were rather predictable: W. would be for children and against criminals. Bush received requests from the highest levels that he commute the death sentence of the killer Karla Faye Tucker, who had expressed remorse and, like W. himself, found religion. But for Tucker, there would be no second chance, and she became the first woman executed in Texas since the Civil War. Journalist Tucker Carlson later claimed that during an interview for a print article, the governor had been particularly callous toward the late convict, even mocking her stated fear of death.

Bush also withheld compassion from first-time drug offenders. His approach was in stark contrast to that of his predecessor, Ann Richards, under whom first-timers received automatic probation with counseling. In W.'s campaign against her, he disparaged this approach as "Penal Code Lite." Once in office, he signed a law ensuring that first-time offenders and those caught with under a gram would face six months to two years of jail time.

Many of those apprehended under this system have been people of color to whom the state provided only the most minimal legal representation. In Texas, being stopped by police on suspicion of using drugs often leads inexorably to prosecution and incarceration. Bush parroted the conventional tough-guy line: "Incarceration is rehabilitation."

The release rate for parole for first-time, nonviolent offenders dropped from nearly 80 percent of eligible inmates under Richards's predecessor, Bill Clements (high largely because of prison overcrowding) to about 20 percent under Bush. "Below 30 percent is a crime," Bill Habern, cochair of the parole and prison committee of the Texas Criminal Defense Lawyers' Association, told *Salon*. "This 'compassionate conservative' line is horseshit. It may be conservative but it sure ain't compassionate."[19] It also didn't make a lot of sense, considering the nature of their crimes and their pasts, to treat such offenders so harshly—at least not from a practical or fiscal standpoint. But it did make sense politically.

This judgmental tendency did not extend to his own circle. Putting aside W.'s own apparently murky record with drugs, he had friends who partied with impunity. James Bath's extensive use of cocaine emerged in a divorce proceeding. So did that of W.'s friend Jerry Chiles, a major party-giver at Chateaux Dijon, whose father, Eddie Chiles, would sell his Texas Rangers baseball team to W.'s investor group.

In a well-publicized divorce case, Chiles's wife accused him of abusive behavior and claimed that her addled spouse had snorted cocaine with a prostitute on the marital bed. A Houston jury awarded her five hundred thousand dollars for emotional distress, in a verdict that *National Law Journal* said, "blazes new legal compensatory ground for divorcing couples."[20] None of this estranged W. from Chiles, who remained a major donor and supporter throughout Bush's political career.

While crime was a hot issue at the polls, W. also needed something that would bring in money from the deepest pockets. Tort reform filled that bill. Tort law serves two purposes: to compensate victims for the negligence of others and to deter such negligence—including, for example, the manufacture of shoddy and unsafe products. Reforming the law sounded reasonable enough—stop greedy lawyers from shaking down the system and driving up insurance rates. But many claims turn out to be valid. Indisputably, manufacturers sometimes do make shoddy products and employers do not always consider the well-being of their workforce or the public. In fact, tough financial penalties are broadly considered the single most effective form of corporate rehabilitation. With the political system heavily influenced by corporations, the courts are often the only resort for ordinary people. Which is why, of course, corporations seek to restrict the courts' power, and thus end the one form of accountability to which they are still subject.

W. chose to champion the cause of a corporate front group called Texans for Lawsuit Reform (TLR), and as governor greatly curtailed the rights of the injured. For would-be plaintiffs, the legal system became a bureaucratic morass. Thanks to "tort reform," reported *Texas Monthly*, "if you go to an emergency room [in Texas] with a heart attack and the ER doctor misreads your EKG, you must prove, in order to prevail in a lawsuit, that he was both 'wantonly and willfully negligent.' "[21]

By the time he left for Washington, W. had played a key role in eliminating deterrence. Thus, his legacy was to be spectacularly tough on individuals, even single mothers with a first-time narcotics-possession offense, while going easy on enormously wealthy and powerful interests whose practices—like dumping toxic waste—were an integral part of how they did business. Karl Rove, meanwhile, built a big part of his political consulting practice around weakening consumer protections. In Alabama, he helped engineer a takeover of the state's judicial system by Republican judges sympathetic to the corporate take on tort reform.[22]

Business showed its appreciation. Houston-based home builder Bob Perry, a major bankroller of tort reform efforts in Texas, remained so loyal to W. that when John Kerry ran against Bush in 2004, Perry donated millions of dollars to the so-called Swift Boat Veterans for Truth in their fact-challenged attack on Kerry's military record.

Sophisticated Hicks

One of the investments Bush had not shed until well into his gubernatorial years was his stake in the Rangers. It was a wise move, financially speaking. Bush's personal stock rose with the value of the team, and when he and his group sold out in 1998 for $250 million, Bush took out $15 million—not bad for an initial $600,000 investment, which was borrowed money to begin with.

The buyer was a financier named Tom Hicks, a man who embodied the values that would come to the fore when W. captured the White House. Hicks made his fortune using other people's money, through leverage, political connections, and hardball. In 1977, he left his job as president of First Dallas Capital Corporation, an affiliate of First International Bancshares—the company where Poppy Bush first worked after leaving the CIA directorship—to begin a career in leveraged buyouts.

Hicks would eventually become a billionaire. Besides the Texas Rangers, he would come to control the National Hockey League's Dallas Stars as well as the Mesquite Championship Rodeo. He also bought 50 percent of the Liverpool Football Club, an English soccer team. Hicks's most controversial play came in the early nineties, when he became enraged after the University of Texas refused to invest part of its endowment in a dental company he owned. Not one to take defeat lightly, Hicks launched a concerted effort to secure control of university investments.

There was nothing subtle about Hicks's attempts to buy influence. He and his brother Steven gave a total of $146,000 to W.'s 1994 and 1998 gubernatorial campaigns. At the same time he was lobbying heavily for the creation of the University of Texas Investment Management Company (UTIMCO)—the first external investment corporation ever formed by a public university system. In his first year in office, W. approved legislation creating UTIMCO; then he appointed Hicks as its first chair.

Acting in secrecy, UTIMCO handed out public funds to friends and cronies. About $252 million went to projects run by associates of Hicks and other large Republican donors. Among the investments: the Carlyle group (heavily into military contracting, with the involvement of Poppy Bush and James Baker and the bin Laden family); Maverick Capital Fund, a project of the Wyly brothers, who would in 2004 donate thousands of dollars to the Swift Boat Veterans' attack on the military record of W.'s opponent John Kerry; and Bass Brothers Enterprises (investors in Harken Energy).

After the *Houston Chronicle* exposed these insider dealings in a 1999 article, Tom Hicks, while denying any improprieties, resigned from the board.[23]

When he bought the Texas Rangers, in which Bush retained his stake after becoming governor, Hicks helped make his influential friend a multimillionaire. Hicks's investment company would also be the fourth-largest overall donor to W.'s political career.

More controversially, Hicks aided W. through his control of Clear Channel Communications, the largest chain of radio stations in the United States. In 2003, affiliate stations sponsored and organized pro–Iraq War demonstrations, a clear show of support for W.'s most ambitious policy initiative.[24] A year later, Clear Channel, which also handles outdoor advertising, blocked an antiwar group's attempt to rent a Times Square billboard for a feisty message, complete with a red, white, and blue bomb, criticizing the war.[25]

The Seduction

Whether W. really needed this help is open to question. His cultivation of the news media was one of the great political seductions of the twentieth century. Perhaps never before had someone so flawed been treated so well.

In memos written in the 1980s to both George Bushes, presidential aide

Doug Wead sought to convince Bush father and son that they needed to woo journalists and writers. Wead made a historical analogy. "I used the illustration . . . that Napoléon is seen in history as this great conqueror. He is quoted. It's like he's a winner or something. And Louisa of Prussia—nobody knows who she is, and she beat him socially and militarily and diplomatically and economically. But he's a star because he cultivated the arts and had favored artists and he had favored writers, and so [while] she ends up on a trash heap . . . he's romanticized and celebrated and glorified."[26]

Karen Hughes understood this. A former television reporter turned Republican Party official, she became Bush's communications director. Royal Masset, who worked for Hughes at the Texas Republican Party, gives her an enormous amount of credit for W.'s political success. "I didn't like working with her, but she was the best," said Masset. "She was absolutely relentless." Masset believes that Hughes played a crucial role in winning media approval for Bush as governor by her constant attention to reporters' needs, and her rapid response when anything controversial emerged. It was her style to strategically and selectively admit error before a scandal could grow—and be out like lightning with a response. "You guys have the power," Masset told me. "She understood that better than a lot of us."

Borrowing a Persona

Karl Rove loved legends. He understood their power to distract the media—and therefore the public—and to frame the entire political debate. And so he began constructing the legend of George W. Bush, reluctant candidate and compassionate conservative.

Rove began his research in 1998 as part of a professed effort to secure his long-delayed bachelor's degree through so-called conference courses at the University of Texas, Austin. (Rove never did get that degree.) At a time when the Internet was still in its infancy, everything was done by phone and mail. Working with Professor Lewis L. Gould, Rove sought to identify a former president who could serve as a model for George W. He focused initially on Teddy Roosevelt, but Gould recommended William McKinley as a better choice. Rove quickly took to McKinley: though a Republican, he was a compassionate one, breaking with Gilded Age values to appeal to working-class immigrants.[27]

Even better, there was a Karl Rove in the story: Mark Hanna, the first political operative publicly identified as having created a president. Getting himself cast as the new Mark Hanna would serve him well professionally. It also would further the notion that W. was a reluctant politician, and shift blame for anything that went wrong to his Mark Hanna–like Svengali. Best of all was the way that it set Bush up as a compassionate conservative, covering up the fundamental pathology of W.'s character, including a deep-grained incomprehension of the problems of the less fortunate.

By the summer of 1999, Rove had hit on his formulation. He called Gould to let him know that he was drawing a parallel between Bush and McKinley for reporters, and that the professor might expect some calls from the media.

"McKinley fit into the compassionate conservatism they were pitching at that time," Gould told me in a 2006 interview. The professor himself did not buy the comparison, but that did not matter. He did not think it appropriate to be offering his own opinion, so on background he simply answered reporters' questions about McKinley.

In retrospect, Gould realizes just how inapt the comparison was. "The differences between McKinley and Bush have become so palpable—McKinley was a very kind man, in a genuine kind of way," said Gould. "He was able to work with Democrats. One of his sayings was, Never keep books in politics, don't hold grudges. He would say, 'I will always love you no matter what you do.' "[28]

Gould thinks the press was easily bamboozled. "In your business, people love historical parallels, but they don't [feel they] have to check them . . . Some reporters' sense of history ended when their college [years] did."

The better parallel, but only in a limited and superficial sense, was with Reagan. As the first actor in presidential politics, the Californian had quickly mastered every aspect of the public stage—the uniforms, the gestures, the stirring words and music. Reagan was photographed chopping wood and riding horses, and the media lapped it up.

Then there was Poppy. Image-wise, he had gotten it all wrong: preppy, goofy, bad speaker, no "vision thing," stood for nothing, inspired nobody. A disaster in every way. Pretending to enjoy pork rinds.

Clinton was much better. Forget the Oxford stint; here was a colorful, exuberant everyman: jogging, living large, tooting the saxophone. Not quite Reagan, but a good act nonetheless. Bush and Rove and their team watched and discussed. When they moved into action, they took nothing for granted. If there were an Academy Award for Best Pre-Presidential Set Design, they would have won hands-down. The secretive Rainbo Club membership disappeared, and in its place came a more acceptable "ranch." The ranch was as improbable as the rest. Purchased in 1999, it played a crucial role as a campaign prop, making the Andover-bred W. into a cowboy. By 2004 the notion seemed ludicrous enough that an ad for the anti-Bush group America Coming Together cast comedian Will Ferrell as a convincingly bumbling W. who fears horses and pretends to mend his fence with tools he hardly knows how to hold. But in the early days the imagery held sway.

The real W., a man with no interest in foreign affairs, was suddenly receiving foreign leaders and dignitaries, in a carefully manipulated limelight. A governor whose state had the dirtiest air in America was now talking about protecting the environment. And a contentious, bullheaded fellow was cast as a thoughtful moderate, a "uniter not a divider."

The Texas Education Miracle

During the 2000 campaign, Bush made clear that he wanted to be the "education president." His staff would tout to reporters his success in improving educational results, which they dubbed the "Texas Miracle." It was a catchy phrase, but truth in advertising would have required Bush admit the only "miracle" was the fact that anyone believed it.

A report by the nonprofit RAND Corporation debunked the "miracle" story just two weeks before the election. Though Texas students had made gains on statewide tests—the result of classroom coaching, RAND said—they did not score better on national standardized tests. "The very foundation of the Bush campaign just crumbled," Gore's deputy campaign manager said at the time, in a bout of wishful thinking.[29] The truth about Bush and the schools received a mere fraction of the media coverage given to the myth.

Credit for W.'s supposed success was initially given to Houston school superintendent Rod Paige, whose popularity reached across party lines. Dropout rates in Houston had dwindled, and test scores had soared. Once W. was elected president, he named Paige as his education secretary, and used Houston as the model for "No Child Left Behind." Despite the fact that polls consistently show education as a primary voter concern, few have heard of Rod Paige—and few realize what actually happened in the Texas schools.

It turns out that Paige's district was cooking the books. According to a 60 Minutes II investigation, one high school "reported zero dropouts, but dozens of the students did just that. School officials hid that fact by classifying, or coding, them as leaving for acceptable reasons: transferring to another school, or returning to their native country."[30] Though Houston's school district reported a dropout rate of 1.5 percent, experts estimated the true rate as being between 25 and 50 percent. The lower rate was cited by W. on the campaign trail as evidence of his educational prowess.

Upon leaving the administration, Paige joined the board of News Corp, the parent of the Fox News Channel, and cofounded a firm that offers consulting on education reform, ostensibly attempting to spread Texas-style "miracles" across the country.

Compassionate Conservative

The same kind of "creative fiction" approach to political campaigning could be seen in the way the Bush team deployed faces of color to imply a kind of egalitarianism and embracing social concern—a concern that seemed to vanish the moment he gained the White House.

While W. followed the conservative playbook in preaching against affirmative action for minorities "on principle," he practiced the most morally repugnant form of it: the advancement of easily manipulated second-raters to serve his own purposes.

The notion seems to have originated with W.'s elders. Prescott Bush, who, as noted in chapter 10, did not like Italians in Greenwich getting into Andover, had served as Connecticut chairman of the United Negro College Fund. Early in his political career, Poppy had gone after black votes, hoping to win just enough to eke out a victory. Recalled Poppy's friend and employee Bob Gow: "Most of the blacks in Texas at that time were Democrats, but George had one prominent black man who was staunchly for him. This man ran a tire distribution company . . . [that] was failing and George asked me to go and meet with this man . . . with the objective of helping them make the company prosper, if possible, but if not, at least stay solvent through the election."[31]

Poppy nevertheless did badly among blacks in 1964, and resolved to reposition himself from a "Goldwater Republican" to a moderate for his 1970 Senate race. He got in contact with Ernie Ladd, who had recently moved to Houston to join the Oilers, and the two became friends. In a published account, Ladd claims that he met Poppy Bush because Bush "wanted to know who the most popular black person was in the city of Houston and someone told them Ernie Ladd was getting a lot of newspaper coverage."[32]

Besides appearing in a video presented at the 2000 Republican National Convention, Ladd, a professional wrestler and minister after retiring from football, helped organize W.'s inauguration.

A close friend of Ladd's, Ernest L. Johnson, the head of the Louisiana NAACP, provided Bush with another kind of cover during the 2000 campaign. This took place when W. attended a lunch honoring Governor Mike Foster, a Bush supporter with ties to former KKK grand wizard David Duke. Johnson actually joined Bush at the lunch and waded through a crowd of African American protesters. That same year, Johnson received a state contract for affirmative-action programs. Johnson also endorsed a chemical plant that was vigorously resisted by environmental and citizen groups outraged by Louisiana's role as a kind of toxic dumping ground, especially in areas whose large poor black populations were historically bedeviled by high cancer rates.

Johnson, who claims to have known W. since the early 1980s, described him as "a person we could sit down with and talk to about issues."[33] (Although W. may have been willing to sit down with his friend Johnson, he was considerably more leery of the NAACP itself. He declined five straight annual invitations to address the NAACP's national convention, before relenting in 2006 in the wake of his government's botched response to Hurricane Katrina, many of whose victims were African Americans.)

In 2001, President George W. Bush appointed Johnson as alternate representative to the General Assembly of the United Nations. Oddly, this fact does not seem to have been publicized in Johnson's home state. When I mentioned it to several prominent community figures in Louisiana who know Johnson well, they laughed out loud in disbelief.

Bush's most illustrious and accomplished black appointee was Colin Powell. During the tumult in Florida after the 2000 election, the campaign promoted the idea that Powell was Bush's "near-certain choice" for secretary of state,[34] a move that seemed intended to silence the accusation that thousands of Florida blacks had been disenfranchised. But after W. took office, Powell was largely ignored and disrespected by administration insiders. Eventually, he was put in the untenable position of trumpeting false evidence on behalf of a war in Iraq he dreaded.

Meanwhile, Education Secretary Rod Paige strove assiduously to fit in, right down to his black cowboy boots. Yet, Bush basically ignored him. The *New Republic* noted, "In any Administration, The blatant marginalization of the only African American domestic Cabinet secretary would be noteworthy. In an Administration that loudly trumpets its commitment to Cabinet government and racial diversity, it's stunning."[35]

W.'s high-profile African American hires besides Powell and Condoleezza Rice also included housing secretary Alphonso Jackson, whose inattentive and misdirected policies may have contributed to the collapse of the home mortgage market—a disaster that hit African Americans especially hard. A front-page *Washington Post* article written the week Jackson left office characterized the secretary as a spendthrift who had a private chef and commissioned expensive personal portraits at taxpayers' expense. His office also spent seven million dollars on a new auditorium and cafeteria at Housing and Urban Development headquarters. "How can you spend that much money on building a shrine to yourself?"[36] asked the vice president of the fiscally conservative National Taxpayers Union. Meanwhile, said the *Post*, Jackson repeatedly ignored warnings from his colleagues that his policies on mortgage loans were putting poor families at risk.[37] Perhaps the most striking fact about Jackson—generally ignored by the media—was that Bush's housing chief had rather quietly exited the administration right in the middle of the housing crisis. That few noticed was in itself telling.

W.'s domestic policy adviser was Claude Allen, a black Republican who had served as campaign spokesman for Senator Jesse Helms, the man the *Washington Post*'s David Broder once referred to as "the last prominent unabashed white racist politician in this country."[38] W. appointed Allen after his nomination for a federal judgeship stalled in the Senate. In 2006, Allen resigned from his White House position ostensibly to spend more time with the family. But it soon came out that he had perpetrated a refund scam to swindle five thousand dollars out of Target and Hecht's department stores. On at least twenty-five occasions Allen attempted to collect refund money on items he hadn't purchased.[39] At the time, he was the highest-ranking African American on the White House staff.

The irony was that W., an opponent of affirmative action designed to help minorities get a leg up, was using his own distorted form of it to reward loyal hangers-on, and to help perpetuate a self-serving myth of compassionate, diversity-friendly conservatism.

CHAPTER 19

The Conversion

*I say unto you, that likewise joy shall be in
heaven over one sinner that repenteth, more
than over ninety and nine just persons, which
need no repentance.*

—LUKE 15:7

GEORGE W. BUSH AND HIS HANDLERS knew that his behavior before becoming governor—his partying, his womanizing, and in particular his military service problems—posed a serious threat to his presidential ambitions. Their solution was to wipe the slate clean—through a religious transformation.

The wholesale remaking of the man would require a credible conversion experience and a presentable spiritual guide. For the latter, they settled on the popular and respectable Billy Graham. He had proven a trustworthy friend to the powerful, and he happened to have visited the Bushes at a crucial time for W. and the Bush family.

In 1985 Poppy invited Reverend Graham to join the Bushes at their summer retreat in Kennebunkport. Though the Bush family was Episcopal and Graham Southern Baptist, Graham had for years been widely recognized as the religious leader in residence for the White House. Just associating publicly with him bestowed a certain moral legitimacy in the eyes of untold voters.

The Graham invite was likely part of an effort to build support for Poppy among self-identified Christian voters. But it included a bonus, because W. got his own path to validation too. According to a story that would later be repeated widely in the media, Graham preached at the tiny church favored by the Bushes. Afterward he engaged the Bush clan in private discussions of faith, including a chat beside the fireplace. W. would claim later that this

chat, along with a walk on the beach, left him a changed man. He wrote in
A Charge to Keep:

> Over the course of that weekend, Reverend Graham planted a
> mustard seed in my soul, a seed that grew over the next year. He
> led me to the path, and I began walking. It was the beginning of a
> change in my life. I had always been a "religious" person, had reg-
> ularly attended church, even taught Sunday School and served as
> an altar boy. But that weekend my faith took on a new meaning. It
> was the beginning of a new walk where I would commit my heart
> to Jesus Christ . . .
>
> When I returned to Midland, I began reading the Bible regu-
> larly. Don Evans talked me into joining him and another friend,
> Don Jones, at a men's community Bible study.[1]

RELIGIOUS AFFILIATION HAS long offered the ambitious more than just
spiritual comfort. It presents opportunities for social and business network-
ing, and for some a convenient counterweight to questionable behavior.
John D. Rockefeller's longtime involvement in the Baptist Church, along
with his philanthropic activities, went a long way toward redeeming in
some minds his ruthless business practices. Allen Dulles, the CIA's master
of assassinations and coups, served on the national board of the Presbyte-
rian Church. Even Poppy Bush would become a board member of the Episcopal Church Foundation.

Among the moneyed and well-established, it once was typical that one
son become an attorney and another a clergyman—occupations preferred
over commerce, which was generally frowned upon. When the first wife of
Poppy's great-grandfather James Smith Bush died in childbirth, James entered divinity school. Originally trained as a lawyer at Yale, he ended up
serving as minister to some of America's most powerful congregations,
from bastions of great wealth on the East Coast to San Francisco's exclusive
Nob Hill at the height of the California gold rush.

Of course, George W. Bush is not the first politician to tout his religious
devotion. Certainly he will not be the last. The conversion narrative is a staple, and one that reporters are loath to question. It was especially appealing
in 2000, given Bill Clinton's sexual misconduct and the consequent large
role of "character" in the election.

As he noted in *Charge to Keep*, Bush had served communion during his Houston youth and taught Sunday school when he moved back to Midland in 1975.[2] But the Bush family had long treated such activities as civic and political obligations. Inge Honneus, the woman Bush pursued when he was in the National Guard, recalled how W. felt free to discuss all manner of topics with her since she was so far out of his normal circle. "We talked about religion," she said, and "he thought it was a joke. And when he started going and running for president, and trying to get the religious votes, I'm thinking, 'What a hypocrite.' I don't know if he all of a sudden turned religious. But the core of him was not a very nice man." Nice man or not, one thing is certain: with his entry into Bible study, Bush was reinventing himself.

It was a politically savvy idea, but, in truth, it was not his own. It appears that it was neither W.'s Midland friends nor the Reverend Billy Graham who helped him see the light. It was Doug Wead, marketing man.

The Religion Coach

Before W. sought to establish his credentials with the religious right—during his father's vice presidency—Wead had written the Bushes a memo stressing the potential political benefits of preaching to that particular choir.

Wead, a handsome, amiable former minister of the Assemblies of God, had built a career as a motivational speaker. He was a master networker who had moved up the ranks at Amway, the multilevel marketing company run by the fundamentalist DeVos family, big players in the Republican Party. And he had used his charm and his unusual position as a bridge between the moneymaking world and the evangelicals to meet and build relationships with a range of powerful people. He got to know Jimmy Carter. In 1980 he wrote a quickie book, *Reagan in Pursuit of the Presidency*, timed for release just before the Republican convention. He studied the potential of the evangelical vote, and was soon a hybrid marketer-author-speaker-historian-religious-political-consultant.

Wead's entry into the Bush circle had nothing to do with religious politics. He came in as a ghostwriter. It was in this role that Wead was recommended to Senator Lowell Weicker in 1981 to help with the senator's memoir—the revelations of which, Weicker believed, would finish off Vice

President Poppy Bush. But as Weicker narrated his interactions with Poppy over the burning of the Townhouse documents, Wead began to imagine that Weicker was misreading his rival. And so, paradoxically, the more Weicker vented, the more Wead felt a growing sense of affection, from a distance, for Poppy Bush. (On a practical level, it also was certainly more useful to be friends with a vice president who might become president than with a maverick senator who most certainly would not.)

The ghostwriter contacted deputy assistant White House chief of staff Joe Canzeri, whom he knew. Almost immediately, Wead found himself ushered into a meeting in Poppy's vice presidential offices at the Old Executive Office Building with Pete Teeley, the vice president's press secretary. Teeley had been recruited onto Poppy's 1980 campaign by none other than W., and the two men remained close.[3]

"I tell him what Weicker has, the goods he has," Wead recalled in one of numerous conversations I had with him over several years. "And Teeley says: 'Maybe Weicker is right. Maybe George Bush shouldn't be president of the United States.'" Wead realized that Teeley was egging him on. Moreover, Wead recalled, "I had the distinct impression later—after I got to know all these characters—that Herbert Walker [Bush] was sitting in the next room," listening to the conversation through an open door.

Teeley soon introduced Wead to Poppy's aide Ron Kaufman, with whom he began having long discussions about the importance of the evangelical vote.

Some time later, Wead was speaking at a conference in Miami when he got an emergency phone call from Teeley, who informed the surprised Wead that he was staying at the hotel next door. "Now, I've always assumed, and always thought, it was a coincidence," said Wead. "We ended up meeting together for lunch several times that week. I literally just walked down the beach and met with him." Teeley claimed to have taken a leave of absence to write a book about the Colombian cocaine kingpin Carlos Lehder. "[The Vice President's office] had all this CIA information on him, and they couldn't go public with it and they couldn't get him legally, and they were trying to put him out of business. They had finally decided a book was the best way," Wead said.

In fact, on January 28, 1982, around the time Teeley reached out to Wead, President Reagan had created the high-profile South Florida Task Force, under Poppy's leadership, ostensibly to control narcotics flowing into the United States. Poppy's "war on drugs" as vice president and later president would become one of his signature issues.

Teeley told Wead that since he himself lacked experience writing books, he was hoping that Wead might offer guidance. Whatever the true reason for Teeley to be in Florida and seek out Wead, it did not benefit the purported Lehder book. Said Wead: "Come to think of it . . . I don't think he ever wrote the book."

In fact, Wead is correct. Teeley never wrote the book—if there ever was a book to write. But Teeley did use this tropical interlude to develop a closer relationship with Wead, and to examine him up close. In retrospect, Wead wondered whether Teeley's confiding in him on this "confidential topic" was some kind of test.[4]

Wead soon was being ushered into the presence of Poppy himself. The ostensible reason was an opportunity for Wead to interview the VP for a cover story in an obscure publication Wead put out called *On Magazine—Positive News of People and Events*. This first meeting with Poppy, Wead recalled, took place in early 1982—not long after his lunch with Pete Teeley in Florida, and while Wead was still working with Senator Weicker. Soon Wead was a regular in Bush circles.

Doug Wead's relationship with Poppy Bush grew stronger in June 1984, when Wead sat next to Barbara Bush, and Poppy sat next to Wead's wife, at a Washington charity dinner honoring Poppy for the "humanitarian" work he had done in Central America. (The Reagan administration's secret arming of the Nicaraguan rebels, and Bush's role in the so-called Iran-contra scandal, were not yet publicly known.)

In February 1985, the new friends got down to business. "One day I'm sitting in the office with Pete Teeley, and we're talking about how to get some water-treatment systems for the vice president to take to Africa," Wead recalled. "The vice president was there, and he said, 'Oh God, I've got to go speak to the National Religious Broadcasters. I'd like to stay here and shoot the'—whatever he said it was—'with you guys, but I've got to go speak to the National Religious Broadcasters.' And Pete Teeley said, 'Well, Mr. Vice President, Doug here is a born-again Christian.' And he was bowled over. He couldn't believe it. It was like he was stunned. He said, 'You've got to be kidding.' I said, 'No, I am. Sorry.' He said, 'I can't believe that. You're a born-again Christian?' I said, yeah . . . I think he didn't know anybody in his circle that was born-again. He had never met one." Poppy was almost certainly being disingenuous and making Wead feel special. After all, there were many evangelicals around Reagan, and the GOP in general.

Wead then explained to Poppy that the wife of Poppy's close friend James Baker was a Catholic Pentecostal, which is not unlike an evangelical, and again, though it is hard to see how the vice president could not have already known about Mrs. Baker, he expressed amazement. And then he asked Wead what he was doing right that minute, whether he would come with him to the National Religious Broadcasters speech.

"So we're sitting in the car, in the motorcade . . . and he said, can you look at my speech. And I said sure. So I start to read his speech, and it's just awful—for evangelicals it's just terrible. He's quoting Thomas Dewey. And I said . . . you know, you don't want to quote him." Wead felt it showed Poppy's tin ear that he imagined evangelicals would want to hear sayings from Dewey, the mustachioed New York Episcopalian.

Certainly, it was a challenge for someone perceived as a preppy moderate to play well to that crowd. But Poppy could hardly have been unaware of the growing influence of the religious right on American politics. Indeed, even the pro-choice, socially liberal Jimmy Carter had very effectively garnered fundamentalist support in 1976 as the first self-described born-again Christian president. And of course Poppy would have known how effectively Ronald Reagan had wooed the same constituency.

When Reagan stood in front of a crowd of fifteen thousand evangelicals in Dallas in August 1980, his message had been framed in the most reassuring terms: "All the complex and horrendous questions confronting us at home and worldwide have their answer in that single book."[5] He eagerly tore into the ACLU, the NEA, and the USSR. Evolution, he assured his audience, "is a scientific theory only."[6]

Poppy did not have Reagan's oratorical gifts—nor his actor's relish for a good role. Instinctively, he was uncomfortable with pandering to the masses, and uncomfortable too with ascribing deep personal values to himself. For that matter he didn't like to reveal much of anything about himself, which was partly patrician reserve and partly, perhaps, an instinct reinforced by his covert endeavors over the years.

Wead knew none of this at the time. "So afterwards I tell Pete, I said, boy, if he's going to be president of the United States, he's got to have a little better working knowledge of who these people are because it's going to come off, either it's going to be terribly offensive that he doesn't know about them and doesn't care or that he's missed one of the greatest religious revivals of his generation and he's totally unaware of it. Either it's ignorance or it's going to be perceived as bias."

The next thing he knew, Wead was meeting, this time formally, with Ron Kaufman, now Poppy's national campaign director; their conversation late into the night led to a full week of intense dialogue, and then Kaufman asked Wead to write Poppy Bush a memo on the religious right.

Wead wrote up everything he could think of about the evangelical movement—who they were, how they thought and why they thought that way, and how to cater to them. It took him six months, and it amounted to something like 120 pages. But Kaufman said that wouldn't do. "He said . . . [Poppy] only reads one-page memos." Wead got it down to 44 pages, and despite Kaufman's doubts, Teeley walked it over on a Sunday to Bush at the Admiralty (the vice president's residence) and handed what became known as the Red Memo to the people at the gate. Shortly thereafter, Poppy sent Wead a note, telling him how helpful it was, that he had read and reread it, and that they needed to talk.

"That was the beginning," said Wead. There would be much more—in total, according to Wead, thousands of pages anatomizing the evangelicals of the religious right and how to win their support. Wead provided me with copies of some of those memos.

Teeley, Poppy's former press secretary, recalled Wead's influence. "I was a little bit dismissive of the numbers of evangelicals and what they could do and one thing or another," Teeley told me. "So Wead wrote this memo; it was forty pages. It was brilliant. It was one of the best documents that I have ever read in terms of a grassroots operation in politics. And that was basically his—basically Doug was saying, look, here's the plan, and you should carry this out, and if you do, you're going to get a lot of support from newborn Christians and one thing or another. Now the question that I had was, was that ever carried out? I don't know if it was or not, because George Jr. and Doug Wead were fairly close at that time." The fact that Teeley didn't know more about what happened was typical of the compartmentalization that Poppy so rigorously enforced.

Wead recalled: "So then I started writing these memos and [Poppy] would write back and say, 'What does this mean? And why does a Baptist do this? And does a Nazarene have, like, an emotional experience when they have sanctification? And does a Nazarene grow up a Nazarene? Do they have to have a separate experience then, separate from their born-again experience?' Minutiae. So I realized, very quickly I realized, you know this is more than intellectual curiosity; this is, he is on his way to the White House and he's also refining what he believes and what he doesn't believe himself. This is a journey too, because it wasn't a sufficient reason just for political purposes."

Though Wead met Poppy Bush in 1982 and got him thinking about the need to understand and embrace religion in 1985, Wead would not actually meet the eldest son until March 1987. But it turns out that W. knew about Wead and his advice long before that.

"I knew the memos that I was sending to his dad were being vetted, and I assumed that they were being vetted by Billy Graham, because of the things his dad would say about Billy Graham," Wead said. "Well, that was pretty naïve of me to think that."

Wead realized that Poppy had to be talking with someone about the advice he was being given. "He's making decisions based on what I'm writing him. Like he started developing his born-again thing, Senior, based on—I gave him several choices and he picked one of them. He's making big decisions based on this paperwork back and forth, and that was making Atwater real nervous. So I assumed it was Billy Graham.

"It wasn't: *It was* W. I hadn't met W. yet, but he knew me because he was getting all these memos, and he was basically saying, 'Dad, this is right. This is what people in Midland think. My born-again friends say this. He's right.'

"When I finally met W., [he said] 'I've read all of your stuff—it's great stuff.' He said, 'We're going to get this thing going.' "

Family Powwow at Camp David

As noted, when W. told the story of his own transformation, he credited Billy Graham's summer 1985 visit to Kennebunkport. But an equally relevant event took place three months earlier. In the spring, the Bush family had gathered at Camp David with its closest advisers to mull strategy for Poppy's upcoming 1988 presidential race. (Only a few months earlier, the Reagan-Bush ticket had been reelected to the White House, and in Poppy's world, all eyes were already on the *big* prize.)

One factor that constituted both an asset and a liability was W. himself.

He was the family's enforcer, expected to play a prominent role in maintaining focus and discipline among staff—and to "handle" the media. W. had a talent for such things, but he also brought with him a lot of baggage that was certain to become fodder for the press, as well as for the religious right, the influence of which was cresting.

At the Camp David gathering, George W. and Jeb took the lead in questioning the loyalty of the hired hands. A particular concern was Lee Atwater, whose GOP consulting firm partners were at the same time doing work for Jack Kemp, a rival to Poppy. According to some accounts, Atwater tried to reassure W., and even suggested the VP's son move to Washington and keep an eye on him.[7] Though it would be more than two years before W. physically moved to Washington, he would be very much involved with his father's 1988 campaign from the outset, and would eventually be called on to serve as liaison to the evangelical community. The mere fact that W., of all people, was in charge of wooing this crucial group is striking. Without his own convincing redemption tale, he would never have been acceptable in that position.

Members of the media might start digging into the backgrounds of the Bush offspring. If they did, they would likely learn that W. had never accomplished anything of note, save for learning to fly a jet in the National Guard (and then cutting out prematurely), and that his businesses were family-and-friend-funded failures whose trail led to covert operations. They might also find that much of his social behavior since college had been an embarrassment. After all, he would soon turn forty.

W. Sees the Light

W. had reason to believe that his efforts to redefine himself would not receive heavy scrutiny in Texas. "Attacks on moral character are the province of the GOP," said Mike Lavigne, a former Texas Democratic Party official. And being reborn was double insurance. "People figure what you did for forty years of your life doesn't matter if you're reborn. And Texas culture is very accepting of born-agains."

W. saw how people turned to religion when everything seemed lost. He had seen it right there in Midland. At the same time, W. himself was looking for ways to cope with his worsening situation at home—where, according to some Midlanders, his relationship with Laura had become badly strained.

And, with his father preparing to run for the White House, the whole family would have to bear up well under media scrutiny.

The beauty of the religious right as a political bloc was that it provided a large pool of voters that often acted in unison, based on a narrow set of issues that had relatively little to do with actual governance and did not inconvenience the corporate interests that finance the Republican Party. By and large, the things that mattered most to these voters mattered least in the Oval Office. Despite the Bush family's traditional aversion to its culture, Rove and the other strategists knew that they had to have that bloc.

In March 1987, after years of reading and vetting Wead's memos, W. finally met the influential evangelical. He quickly developed a close relationship with the man he came to call "Weadie." Wead would later use his experience with W. and other members of the Bush family as a basis for his accounts of presidential family dynamics, including 2004's *All the President's Children*.[8]

One day, the two were sitting in W.'s office on Fourteenth Street in Washington, discussing strategies for approaching various evangelicals. "We're going through a list of the names of these religious leaders," Wead told me in a 2006 interview, "and . . . [W.]'s not into details at all . . . His eyes glaze over in thirty seconds; you got to be right to the point, quick. We're going over these leaders and how his dad can win them over one by one, discussing different strategies. And he looks down the list and bing! He sees this guy's name, the guy with the cross. He says, tell me about *him*, tell me about *this* guy." The guy was Arthur Blessitt.

At the time, Blessitt was perhaps best known for earning a mention in *The Guinness Book of Records* by dragging a ninety-six-pound cross on wheels across six continents. (It is apparently the "world's longest walk.") Author Jacob Weisberg notes that a decade earlier, Blessitt "declared he was running for president, though it wasn't clear which party, if any, he belonged to."[9] In August 2008, the ambitious evangelist fulfilled a lifelong dream by launching the first-ever cross into outer space.

Recalled Wead: "I said basically, well, he's very beloved, an honest person, innocent person. The rap, which may be very unfair, is that before his conversion he was very much into drugs; he is like a born-again Cheech and Chong sort of thing. He's got a great sense of humor and [is] a loveable guy, seen [as] a little bit of an oddball to some, but certainly seen as someone who has integrity and [is] without guile and . . . And [W.] said, 'Yeah, yeah, uh-huh.' "

W.'s Ears Prick Up

In fact, W. was playing dumb with Wead, because he already knew all about the fortuitously named Blessitt. He had met him in April 1984 when the itinerant minister had come to Midland on a crusade. It was a particularly bad moment for the oil-dominated town. The bottom had fallen out of the oil business—including W.'s small piece of it—and former playboys found themselves facing hard times; some suffered the humiliation of having their luxury cars repossessed. In their extremity, some turned to religion. An oil industry Bible study group had been formed that year, and W.'s friend, the banker Don Jones, who had put W. on his bank board, was a member. But Bush himself had not felt the need to join at that time. Raised Episcopal, he had begun attending a Methodist church when he married Laura, but it had been the normal Sunday-morning brand of religiosity.

W. has never spoken about his encounter with Blessitt, but the story emerged on the preacher's Web site in October 2001.[10] According to Blessitt, an intermediary contacted him during his 1984 crusade stop in Midland to say that the vice president's son had heard him on the radio and wished to meet with him discreetly. Blessitt invited Bush to meet with him, led him in a sinner's prayer and praise, and then said, more or less: that's it, your sins are forgiven, you're a new creature, you're born-again.

By 1987, when W. saw Blessitt on Wead's list of evangelical leaders, he was being a bit disingenuous in asking Wead to tell him about the man—or why he was so interested. Paying it no further heed, Wead continued reading names. "But later, when I heard the story that [Blessitt] said Bush [became born-again through him] . . . I believed him."

However, Wead had warned the Bushes that they had to be careful how they couched their conversion story. It couldn't be seen as something too radical or too tacky. Preachers who performed stunts with giant crosses would not do. Billy Graham, "spiritual counselor to presidents," would do perfectly. "My point to him was that evangelicals are not popular in the media and therefore you take a risk by identifying with any of them, and Graham may be the only one that you can," said Wead. "So G. W. was aware of that before he told me the story that he had a walk with Graham." Thus, W. was just repeating back to Wead what Wead had advised the Bushes, but with a twist.

"Something in that exchange [about Blessitt] told me that Bush decided Billy Graham's got to be the guy. It can't be this guy. It's got to be Billy Graham."

The Corporate Confessor: Billy Graham to the Rescue

Billy Graham was a congenial political confessor.[11] He was forgiving of the misdoings of his powerful friends—such as Nixon and former Texas governor John Connally. In 1975, when Connally went on trial, accused of taking ten thousand dollars to influence a milk-price decision, one of his character witnesses was Billy Graham. Connally was acquitted.

Graham was also a friend to the Bushes, one who met their test of loyalty. He reportedly had even been among those urging Nixon to make Poppy his running mate back in 1968. In the final Sunday before the 2000 election, Graham would travel to Florida and very publicly embrace his supposed disciple. Speaking on W.'s behalf, Graham said, "I don't endorse candidates, but I've come as close to it now as any time in my life. I believe in the integrity of this man."[12]

Of course Billy Graham was often around political families, and of course he talked about his work. And of course they probably took that walk on the beach to which W. would refer. The misdirection came in the way the conversion story was worded. Reporters leaped to the assumption that Bush and Graham had had a private walk and a heart-to-heart, but the words in *Charge to Keep* don't really say that. "We walked and talked at Walker's Point," Bush says, which is what everyone did while staying there. After W. began recounting the story publicly, Billy Graham admitted to one journalist that he didn't remember the encounter.

In 2006, Graham told two *Time* reporters who tried to jog his memory: "I don't remember what we talked about. There's not much of a beach there. Mostly rocks. Some people have written—or maybe he has said, I don't know—that it had an effect, our walk on the beach. I don't remember. I do remember a walk on the beach."[13]

Rocky Mountain Not High

Even after a conversion experience, it is hard to argue that you have changed your ways unless you actually . . . change your ways. And the iconic moment for that, a staple of virtually every profile written during Bush's first presidential campaign, was the night he swore off drinking.

One of the rules of propaganda is that a transformative event must be dramatically staged. And so W.'s forswearing booze takes place the day after

DRIFTWOOD PUBLIC LIBRARY
801 SW HWY. 101
LINCOLN CITY, OREGON 97367

his fortieth birthday—July 7, 1986—and with the majestic Rocky Mountains as the backdrop. For the occasion, Bush had assembled a small group of close friends at the Broadmoor Hotel, a renowned resort in Colorado Springs.

As Bush tells it, he had had a few too many drinks at his birthday dinner the night before, and had awoken the next morning feeling awful. On the spot he decided never to drink again. Like all the significant changes in Bush's life, this one was described without inner texture or process. He simply flipped a switch. "People later asked whether something special happened, some incident, some argument or accident that turned the tide, but no, I just drank too much and woke up with a hangover. I got out of bed and went for my usual run . . . I felt worse than usual, and about halfway through, I decided that I would drink no more."

It was not that his drinking had taken so much of a toll. Rather it was an act of prudent foresight. "I realized that alcohol was beginning to crowd out my energies and could crowd, eventually, my affections for other people . . . When you're drinking, it can be an incredibly selfish act," Bush said. "Well, I don't think I had [an addiction]. You know, it's hard for me to say. I've had friends who were, you know, very addicted . . . and they required hitting bottom [to start] going to AA. I don't think that was my case."[14]

Actually it is quite believable that Bush could abruptly end a longtime habit in this way. He has a steely resolve and a self-assurance that in some contexts can be a plus. He has talked about "not getting into a debate with myself."

In his professional as well as personal life, W. often made snap decisions and stuck to them, no matter what. "It took my breath away," recalled Wead. "When he first came in, we had a long list of things that needed to be done. He just went down the list, yes, yes, no, no, yes—things that for months we couldn't get any action on. I said, 'Why yes to number three? I mean, I'm glad you said that, but why yes to three?' Well, he'd give his answers that just blew me away. I never met anybody that decisive in my life.

"I once met a guy named Nicholson . . . He was working for Gerald Ford, and he went on to corporate work, and he was like that. You'd be having a conversation like this, and he'd say, wait, that's a good idea. And he'd get the phone, and he'd call somebody and say, sell this, do this, do that, build that. And then he'd say, OK, go on. And he was amazing, a businessman, a multimillionaire. But other than him, I've never met anybody else like that—and Bush Jr. was far more decisive than Nicholson. I just couldn't believe it."

DRIFTWOOD PUBLIC LIBRARY
801 SW HWY. 101
LINCOLN CITY, OREGON 97367

Alcohol served well as a representative sin—a part that avoided the need to talk about the whole. It is a far more acceptable sin than, say, buying, selling, or using illegal drugs, or committing spousal abuse. And millions of Americans would relate to him. A weakness overcome could end up actually attracting voters. A negative would become a positive.

W. had been dipped into the cleansing waters, and he was triply absolved: 1) No one could criticize him for anything he had done before he had found the Lord and abandoned the bottle; 2) fundamentalist Christians would embrace him in large numbers; and 3) by emphasizing his "wild youth" he would create a striking contrast to stuffed shirts like his father, Al Gore, and John Kerry. To pollster after pollster, voters would admit that they liked George W. Bush largely because of what a regular guy he was. And he certainly was—even when in his post-born-again life, he didn't take his conversion experience too seriously. When a Midland Bible teacher asked W.'s prayer group to define a prophet, the irreverent Harvard Business School grad piped up with this quip: "That is when revenues exceed expenditures. No one's seen one out here in years."[15]

Spy vs. Spy

If there were ever any doubts about just how crucial the religious right vote was to political success, they evaporated the moment the televangelist Pat Robertson entered the 1988 GOP race against Poppy. Then things moved beyond simple outreach.

"I ran spies in our opponents' political camps," Wead said. "We recruited precinct delegates that ran for office for Pat Robertson in Michigan. We helped them win, get elected, go to the state, and totally infiltrate Robertson's campaign. I ran them essentially for [Lee] Atwater, but W. knew about them."[16] Wead said that front-page headlines in Detroit were declaring "Robertson Delegates Switch to Bush," but of course these delegate spies were supporting Bush from the get-go. The spy argot here is suggestive. In the Bush milieu, an intelligence mentality spills over not just into politics generally, but even into dealings with the church-based right. Domestic political constituencies have replaced the citizens of Communist countries as a key target of American elites. They seek to win the hearts and minds of devout Christians through quasi-intelligence techniques.

Wead was struck by W.'s own mastery of the dark arts. "I've had long discussions with W. about planting stories deep so that journalists who find them have a great sense of authorship and so that they have great authenticity," Wead said. "Like doing a good deed and planting it real, real deep, knowing it will be found." It was subtle, and therefore it was effective, a classic strategy of misdirection that is one of the oldest weapons in the arsenal of the covert operative. "We talked about the importance of things that the press would have to find, that you leave a little nugget there, and you got to bury it deep enough that as [for example, *Washington Post* reporter] Lois Romano goes for it and finds it, she would never ever guess that it was planted. She would die for her story—pride of authorship. She'd fight her editors all the way. We talked about that."

Once, Wead recalled with amusement, they were talking about *Mad* magazine, and which features were their favorites. W. volunteered that he particularly loved the intrigues of *Spy vs. Spy*. "He was talking about the subtlety of politics and how what meets the eye is so different from the political [reality]," Wead told me. "I'm still amazed how naïve so many journalists are who have covered politics all their life."

In former White House press secretary Scott McClellan's 2008 tell-all, *What Happened*, he recounts being invited to W.'s hotel suite during the 2004 campaign while the president is on the phone with a supporter. "The media won't let go of these ridiculous cocaine rumors," W. says into the phone as he motions for McClellan to sit and relax. "You know, the truth is I honestly don't remember whether I tried it or not. We had some pretty wild parties back in the day," the president continues.

In his book, McClellan recalls his own bewilderment. "How can that be? How can someone simply not remember whether or not they used an illegal substance like cocaine?" Though McClellan remembers that the phone call was arranged, and that W. "brought up the [cocaine] issue," he doesn't seem to realize that the president is indirectly relaying a message to the man who serves as his mouthpiece. If W. could only convince his press secretary, through an offhand moment of candor, that he didn't remember using cocaine, then McClellan might repeat the statement to the press with all the conviction of someone telling the truth as he saw it.[17]

In politics, the essence of deceit is deniability: getting something done in such a way that you can plausibly claim that you had nothing to do with it. Not surprisingly, the first son of a longtime CIA operative was obsessed with deniability for both himself and his father. "What they did in '85, '86, '87, '88, '89, is they didn't have me write the memo to him," said Wead.

"They had me write the memo to Atwater or to Fuller or to Kaufman, so I've got a ton of memos that I can show you that are written to Kaufman, but they were for [both Georges] Bush."

W. went to great lengths to remind "Weadie" of his value to the operation. "He would say to me, 'Did you get reimbursed for that airline ticket?' And I'd say, no, but it's no problem. He'd yell to Gina or whatever her name was, 'Get in here.' And she'd come in, and he'd say, 'Why haven't you reimbursed him?'

" 'Well, we were going to do it.'

" 'Pay him now, *now!*'

" 'Well, I've got to—'

" 'Now!'

" 'OK.' "

The Safe with Two Keys

Given all they had to hide, it makes sense that the obsession with secrecy by George Bush, father and son, would be all-consuming.

Wead recalls that sometimes during the 1980s he would be talking on the phone with Poppy Bush and Poppy would say that he wanted to ring off and call Wead back on the "secure phone"—though what they were discussing was inherently political and in no way dealt with national security.

W. was sometimes more careless than his father, but he was always vigorous about cleaning up after the fact. This appears to have been the case in a previously undisclosed arrangement he made with Wead to safeguard tapes of conversations between the two aboard campaign planes in the 2000 election period.

During the 1980s, Wead had routinely taped some conversations with Poppy with the elder Bush's permission. He had also instinctively taped his discussions with W. more than a decade later, for reasons Wead says were benign—a capturing of history, and a means of retaining a record of W.'s sentiments and instructions. But he had neglected to tell W. Those tapes would provoke a brief scandal some years later.

In 2005, the *New York Times* persuaded Wead, a self-styled presidential historian, to play snippets of those tapes, and the result was a front-page story—and a huge row with the White House. The excerpts Wead had chosen to play were largely benign, and featured W. discussing faith, politics, and the weaknesses of rival candidates—without making too many major gaffes. Yet the White House reacted with anger. In an unusual step, Laura Bush was sent out to chastise Wead and nip the story in the bud. With the resulting media hullabaloo, Wead was faced with a difficult decision. He told CNN's Anderson Cooper that he'd had lucrative offers to sell the tapes: "Tonight, my agent called me and said, 'Well, do you want to retire a multimillionaire?'" But ultimately, Wead decided to hand the tapes back to the White House. "History can wait," he said.[18]

What was not reported at the time was what else was on the tapes—or what became of them. I asked Wead, and he told me. "It's a president speaking. He's talking and he's strategizing and he's talking about rumors about his sex life, why they're not true and details about his life and reporters and how he reacts to them and he's putting me on assignment to go and put out some of these stories."

Understandably, the White House did not want Wead sharing any more of their content than he already had, and he quickly heard from W.'s personal attorney, Jim Sharp. "He'd come out here, and we'd meet and talk and I gave him the tapes, and Bush listened to them . . ."

Wead and Bush signed an agreement that they would jointly own the tapes. The White House people proposed that Wead turn over the tapes, and that they be stored in a box to which he would have a key. But Wead's son, an attorney, proposed instead that the parties get a safe that required two keys to open: "He said, 'No, no, no, get a safe that has two keys, one for the president and one for you.' And Sharp said, 'We can't do that, there is no such thing.' And he insisted, 'The president wants this resolved right away.' And I go back to my son, and he says 'There is *too* such thing.'"

And indeed there was. "We found that safe. My wife and I went to downtown Washington with the tapes, and we deposited them in a satchel. We locked the satchel, put it in the safe, and locked the keys. [Sharp] took it to the president, and I locked my key and I took that for me. And rolled it down the street to a bank."

CHAPTER 20

The Skeleton in W.'s Closet

EVEN BEFORE GEORGE W. BUSH ATTAINED his first public office, his handlers were aware of a skeleton rattling noisily in his closet. It was one that undercut the legend of principle and duty—the story of a man's man and patriot. It would have to be disposed of.

At a televised debate in 1994 between incumbent Texas governor Ann Richards and challenger George W., Austin television reporter Jim Moore asked Bush to explain how he had gotten so quickly and easily into National Guard pilot training as an alternative to serving in Vietnam. Candidate Bush simply asserted that favoritism had played no role and that he had honorably served. End of discussion. There were no follow-up questions. But the moment the debate was over, Bush's communications director, Karen Hughes, came at the journalist.

"Karen just makes a beeline for me and gets in my face and tries to separate me from the crowd," Moore said. "Then she starts a rant. 'What kind of question is that? Why did you ask that question? Who do you think you are? That's just not relevant to being governor of Texas. He's not trying to run the federal government. He's going to run the state of Texas. What does his service in the National Guard have to do with anything? He doesn't have an army to run here in Texas. Why would you ask such a question, Jim?'" (Some years later, when Bush actually *was* running an army, each time a reporter asked the same question, he or she was told that it had been "asked and answered" long ago.) In response to Hughes, Moore said, "It's about character, Karen. It's about his generation and mine coming of age, and how we dealt with what we all viewed as a bad war."[1]

As the reporter was turning to go file his story, Bush's chief strategist, Karl Rove, came at him next. " 'What was that question, Moore?' And I said, 'Well, you know what it was, Karl.' I said it's a fair question. And he said, 'It wasn't fair. It doesn't have anything to do with anything.' And his rant was less energized than Karen's, but it was the same thing—trying to say, 'You're stupid. You're a yokel local and you're stupid and you don't know what you're doing.' "[2]

Bush's handlers thought they could get reporters off a story by intimidating them. Often they turned out to be right.

IT SOMETIMES SEEMS that the entire story of George W. Bush's life has been rewritten by hired hands. As each exaggeration, distortion, or factual error is uncovered, Bush has ducked and bobbed; only rarely has he been forced to concede anything.

Just one of hundreds of such examples: During his unsuccessful Midland congressional bid in 1978, W.'s campaign literature described his wartime service as "Air Force"—a claim also made for him in Poppy's autobiography. Presumably both men knew the difference between the National Guard and the Air Force. Nevertheless, that claim remained in W.'s official biography until the 2000 presidential campaign, at which point the correction was quietly made.[3]

On no subject were Bush and his team more intransigent than on the particulars of his military service. One cosmetic concern was that the favoritism shown young Bush in his National Guard assignment did not fit the legend Karl Rove was developing for him. This was the tough, no bullshit, "mano a mano" kind of guy, the cocky kid who challenged his famous father to a fight, the self-made oilman in flight jacket and cowboy boots, the straight-talking "ranch hand" with the John Wayne swagger ("in Texas, we call that walking"). Even the name of his campaign plane (*Accountability One*) was crafted to the image. He could not be seen as someone who used family connections to get a cushy home-front assignment while thousands of his peers went off to die in Vietnam.

After Bush's election as governor in 1994, his political team worked to inoculate their man against further inquiries into his Guard service. Dan Bartlett, an eager staff aide then in his twenties, and with no military service of his own, was named as liaison between the governor and the National Guard. And Bush replaced Texas's adjutant general Sam Turk, the administrative head of the Guard, who had been appointed by Governor Richards, with General Daniel James.

Cleaning up the Texas Guard records became a lot easier once W. was the titular commander in chief of the state's National Guard units. The effort got under way just months after Bush's inauguration. On May 16, 1995, Joe Allbaugh, by then Bush's chief of staff, met with Guard officials and asked to see Bush's personnel records. Three days later, they were sent over to the governor's office from the office of the outgoing adjutant general. "I am enclosing copies of the Texas Air National Guard personnel records for Mr. Daniel O. Shelley and Governor George W. Bush," wrote Turk. It is not clear why Shelley's records were also requested, except that he was about to be named Bush's legislative director. In any case, asking for two records rather than one likely was a form of cover—comparable to what happened in 1972 when George W. Bush failed to take his mandatory National Guard physical and was joined in this violation by his friend Jim Bath. In each instance, the special treatment accorded W. was made to seem more "routine" by the fact that at least one other person was included.

That the people around the governor were concerned was evident when Dan Bartlett traveled to Denver to personally review the microfiche copy of Bush's records on file at the Air Reserve Personnel Center.[4] Although Bartlett had little or no knowledge of the military, he would turn out to be a good man for the job. As was true of most Bush appointees, his primary qualification was loyalty. Bartlett had gone to work for Karl Rove's political consulting business in 1992, right out of college, and so by the 2000 presidential campaign, his entire adult life had been in service to Rove and Bush.

In 1996, the new adjutant general, Daniel James, hired Lieutenant Colonel Bill Burkett, a former Guardsman and tough cattle rancher who doubled as a private management consultant, to lead a task force assessing the state of the organization. Even the top brass believed it had become lax and inefficient; Burkett's mission was to create a strategic plan to bring the Guard back into fighting trim. Burkett returned several months later with a devastating report, documenting how outmoded, inefficient, unprepared, and even corrupt the service was. The report suggested sweeping reforms.

What Burkett and his team discovered went way beyond unjustified promotions of politically connected officers, as bad as those were. (One officer whose promotion was judged improper nevertheless went on to head a unit that was sent to Iraq in 2004.) They also uncovered that the Texas

Guard rolls were full of "ghost soldiers," military personnel kept on the books after they had left the unit to justify the continued flow of money allocated for their pay. Equally important, the ghost numbers made units appear to be at authorized troop levels when reviewed by state and federal authorities.[5]

Burkett and his team believed their findings were so important and so sensitive that they had to take them straight to the top. Not knowing who was responsible for the fraud, "we decided we had to go to the boss," Burkett recalled. But James, the man governor Bush had handpicked to run the Guard, seemed far more upset about the breach of military procedure in reporting the news of corruption and malfeasance than in the news itself. According to Burkett, James responded: "Now guys, I want to know what I'm supposed to tell the chief of staff, Colonel Goodwin, when he wants to have your heads 'cause you violated the chain of command and came in here over his head."[6]

When Burkett asked for—and received—a promise of funding from the Clinton-Gore administration to begin repairing holes in the Guard, Governor Bush angrily declined the help. According to Burkett, Bush's chief of staff, Joe Allbaugh, informed General James that henceforth his primary function was to ensure that Bill Burkett be kept as far as possible from the media.

Meanwhile, according to Burkett, there was discussion of Bush's impending presidential bid and how it would become a priority for state officials. One day in 1997, Burkett said, he was in the vicinity of General James's office when a call came in. James took it on the speakerphone. It was Joe Allbaugh, with Bush's Guard liaison Dan Bartlett on the line. According to Burkett, Allbaugh told James that Karen Hughes and Bartlett would be coming out to Camp Mabry, which was on the outskirts of Austin, to comb through the records in preparation for a book on Bush, and he instructed the general to have the records prescreened. According to Burkett, Allbaugh said, "Just get rid of the embarrassments."

About ten days after Allbaugh's call, Burkett claims, he came upon Guard officials going through Bush's records and observed a trash can nearby that included between twenty and forty pages of Bush's military documents. Burkett had a few moments to see what they contained. Another Guard officer and friend of Burkett's, George Conn, would later corroborate much of this story, but then withdraw confirmation while steadfastly maintaining that Burkett was an honorable and truthful man. Clearly, Conn was in a difficult position, working for the military on a civilian contract, while his wife served as head of the secretarial pool for a large law firm that was a leading bundler of campaign contributions to the Bush campaigns.

"I was there. I know what I saw in the trash. I know what actions I saw taking place," Burkett told me during one of several lengthy conversations.[7] One of the documents that has been missing from the released files, Burkett claims, is a "counseling statement" from a senior officer to Bush, explaining why he was grounded and the changes to his assignment, slot, and pay rate. Burkett told me he glimpsed Bush's counseling statement at the top of the discard stack, but did not have time to read it through. "In a perfect world, I guess I should have just stepped up and grabbed the files and made a federal case of it all right there," he said. "Looking back, I probably would have. It would have been simpler to have confronted the whole mess right then and there."[8]

Burkett, whose claims would surface publicly on a Web site for a Texas veterans' group in 2000 and were subsequently detailed in Jim Moore's 2004 book, *Bush's War for Reelection*, first made his allegations within Guard circles in 1997. The next year he laid them out in letters to state legislators and in eight missives to Bush himself, addressing broad problems with the Guard, as well as in sworn public testimony. "Dan Bartlett knew about it," Burkett said. "I called Dan in May or June 1998. I told him it's gotten to the point where you need a new [National Guard] adjutant general."

Burkett was pulled away to other projects, and then in 1998 abruptly and unexpectedly dispatched on federal orders to Panama. On his trip home, he fell seriously ill. It was when he had trouble receiving proper medical care under his benefits package that he tried to use his knowledge of the destruction of Bush's military record as leverage. Even efforts by Texas congressman Charles Stenholm and the surgeon general to arrange hospital care for Burkett were rebuffed by Guard headquarters.[9] Two close friends of Burkett's within the Guard who tried to get him help for emergency medical bills—George Conn and Harvey Gough—would themselves be fired from the Guard.[10]

To this day, it remains unclear whether the treatment of Burkett was retribution for embarrassing the Guard with claims of corruption and of the destruction of documents concerning George W. Bush's service. The undeniable fact is that essential paperwork one would expect to find in W.'s file somehow was missing. This included records of how the military handled Bush's transfer to Alabama, documentation of additional service after May

1972 or an explanation of why no such evidence existed, and a report from the panel that typically convened when a pilot stopped flying prematurely. However it happened, it certainly would appear that someone purged parts of the governor's National Guard file.

Circa 1997, the same year as the trash-can incident, microfilm containing military pay records for hundreds of Guardsmen, including Bush, was irreversibly damaged at a national records center. When the government finally acknowledged the incident seven years later, it was described as an accident during a routine "restoration" effort.

Until May 23, 2000, the efforts of Bush's team to keep their man's military record from public view seemed to be succeeding. Then, with Bush closing in on the GOP presidential nomination, the *Boston Globe* ran a story headlined I-YEAR GAP IN BUSH'S GUARD DUTY: NO RECORD OF AIRMAN AT DRILLS IN 1972–73. Reporter Walter Robinson had obtained and reviewed 160 pages of military documents. It was Robinson who first interviewed Bush's former commanders, only to discover that none could recall Bush performing service during that period.

The *Globe*'s revelations gave rise to a veritable cottage industry of bloggers, with citizen journalists launching their own inquiries, complete with their own Freedom of Information requests.[11] Together they provided sophisticated, rigorous analysis of the fine points of military procedure and record keeping.

The Bush camp swung into damage-control mode. Bartlett called in the retired Guard personnel director, General Albert Lloyd, and asked him to review W.'s record to look for any proof of his service. Armed with a request letter from Bush for access to his files, and, as he confirmed to me, left alone in the records room at Camp Mabry, Lloyd found a torn piece of paper with Bush's social security number and a series of numbers.[12] Though no one explained why the paper had come to be torn, or established the authenticity or validity of the document, it would be turned over to news organizations and the visible partial-date information extrapolated upon as evidence of service.

BUSH CARRIED INTO the White House with him an official biography that by now reflected an already thoroughly discredited scenario: "George W. Bush was commissioned as second lieutenant and spent two years on active duty, flying F-102 fighter interceptors. For almost four years after that, he was on a part-time status, flying occasional missions to help the Air National Guard keep two of its F-102s on round-the-clock service." Yet, in actuality, after he went on part-time status, Bush did not fly for four more years, but rather just one year and nine months.

Since that time, the White House has, without acknowledging or explaining the changes, repeatedly revised the script. Ultimately, the latter period of Bush's Guard service would be presented this way: after April 1972 the high-flying and highly visible pilot suddenly becomes a ground-hugging reservist reading manuals in back offices both in Alabama and in Texas, unobserved by his former flight mates, and therefore unnoticed and unremembered. The personable Bush, once nicknamed "the Lip" and "the Bombastic Bushkin," had disappeared into a cubbyhole. In spite of this, when he became governor, his F-102 was symbolically refurbished like new, and a ceremony honoring his service was held, featuring Bush-supplied promotional materials containing the misleading biographical information.

Meanwhile, the original justification for Bush's staff to review his Guard records—that they were seeking information to include in his "autobiography"—proved suspect. When the book, *A Charge to Keep*, finally appeared, all mentions of his Guard duty were couched in the vaguest possible language. "It was exciting the first time I flew and it was exciting the last time . . . I continued flying with my unit for the next several years . . . My fellow pilots were interesting people . . . We were different, but we worked well together . . ."[13]

From the moment journalists started to look into Bush's military records, it was clear that some essential documents were missing.[14] But after initial Freedom of Information requests had elicited the "complete record," other documents—such as laudatory press releases—were mysteriously supplied in response to later rounds of FOIA requests. There was no adequate explanation of where these new documents came from.

Bush Accused: The Lottery Gambit

In 1996, an anonymous letter reached the U.S. attorney in Austin. The letter, whose existence was revealed in a later legal proceeding, was apparently written by someone with knowledge of the situation. The letter referred to former Texas house speaker Ben Barnes, and alleged that in 1968 Barnes knew about or was involved with favoritism in dispensing of coveted Guard slots, including Bush's. According to the letter writer, Governor Bush had been so desperate to suppress information about his admission to the Guard that he had rewarded Barnes with a lucrative contract.[15]

The letter alleges that the situation unfolded in the following way:

The state of Texas had, under Democrat Ann Richards, awarded the lucrative state lottery contract to GTech Corporation, which was represented by Barnes, who had signed a lifetime deal with the company. It gave Barnes a percentage of revenues generated by the lottery; the arrangement, worth millions, made him the highest-paid lobbyist in Texas history.[16]

When Bush came into office, he appointed his attorney Harriet Miers to head the Lottery Commission. Miers, consulting closely with Karl Rove, went right to work scrutinizing the GTech deal and quickly decided the state could do better than continue with the firm appointed by a Democratic predecessor. "The time has come," Miers wrote in a February 18, 1997, memo. "I am convinced the Texas Lottery Commission and the State of Texas will be best served by the re-bid of the Lottery Operator contract as soon as possible."[17]

The commission hired a lottery expert, Larry Littwin, who moved aggressively for rebidding. At that point, according to the anonymous letter writer, Bush's aide Reggie Bashur got Barnes to agree—in return for GTech keeping the lucrative lottery contract—not to talk about Bush's fortuitous admission to the Champagne Unit. Added the letter writer: "Governor Bush knows his election campaign might have had a different result if this story had been confirmed at the time."[18] Littwin was abruptly fired by the commission after he resisted renewing the GTech contract. He then filed a wrongful termination suit. In court pleadings at the time of the lawsuit, Barnes and his attorneys described the notion that the contract renewal was a favor repaid as "fanciful and preposterous."

After being deposed as part of Littwin's lawsuit, Barnes issued a statement saying that "neither Bush's father nor any other member of the Bush family" asked Barnes for help getting W. into the Guard. Instead, Barnes indicated in his written statement that he had been contacted by a third party, Houston businessman Sidney Adger, a wealthy friend of George H. W. Bush's, who, Barnes claimed, had asked him to recommend the younger Bush "for a pilot position at the Air National Guard." Barnes said he did just that.

In September 1999, at the time Littwin's lawsuit was being adjudicated, the *Dallas Morning News* published the more benign Adger narrative. "Former Texas House Speaker Ben Barnes has told friends that in the late 1960s, a well-known Houston oilman asked him to help George W. Bush get a spot in the Texas Air National Guard," the newspaper story reported.

"Two of those friends, who spoke on the condition of anonymity, said in recent interviews that Mr. Barnes identified the oilman as Sidney A. Adger, a longtime Bush family acquaintance who died in 1996."

And there was a requisite nondenial denial. "'All I know is anybody named George Bush did not ask [Barnes] for help,' said the governor and GOP presidential front-runner while campaigning in New Hampshire."

It was a wonderful nonstory—a dead man had supposedly called someone to request assistance in gaining W. admission to a unit filled with children of privilege who had gotten into it through connections. In another break for W., though copies of the accusatory anonymous letter were leaked to a few Texas reporters, they were never published.

As part of the cleanup operation on Bush's Guard years, Don Evans, who ran Governor Bush's 1998 reelection effort and chaired his presidential campaign, was dispatched for a chat with Barnes. The purpose was to dispel a rumor that the senior Bush had solicited Barnes's help during an encounter in a private box at the Bluebonnet Bowl football game in December 1967.[19] Evans returned with word that Barnes had no memory of the elder Bush asking for any such consideration. W. wrote Barnes personally to express his thanks and also to add another denial to the paper trail. "Dear Ben," Bush wrote, "Don Evans reported your conversation. Thank you for your candor and for killing the rumor about you and dad ever discussing my status. Like you, he never remembered any conversation. I appreciate your help."

Why did Bush choose Don Evans for this sensitive mission? The most likely explanation seems to be a prior connection between Evans and Barnes, one that was carefully guarded for many years.

The delicacy of Evans's position became apparent when Fox News' Brit Hume was interviewing him at the 2000 convention.

Only an extremely observant viewer might have noticed how evasive Evans was on a particular point: the exact year he had first come to know George W. Bush. Here's a transcript excerpt from Fox:

> HUME: And awaiting Texas' turn to finally cast its votes, we are joined by Governor George W. Bush's very good friend and campaign chairman, *Don Evans, a fellow Texan. Known him for what 30, 31 years?*
>
> EVANS: About 30 years . . . He's a guy that I knew early on. *And we met in 1975 really is when we became great friends.* [italics added]

Evans starts to say that he met Bush in 1975, then realizes that he can't say that because it is not true. Midsentence, he makes a subtle shift: 1975 is when the two really became great friends. It is not when they first met. The distinction might seem trivial. But consider the backstory.

It turns out that Evans, the man most responsible for raising the massive sums that made W. president, had firsthand knowledge of W.'s National Guard saga. Back in 1968, Evans was attending the University of Texas at Austin and dating the woman who would become his wife, Susie Marinis. A childhood friend and neighbor of George W. Bush's, Marinis would stay with the Bush family when visiting Houston from Midland. But most significant of all is this: Susie Marinis was Ben Barnes's secretary. Ben Barnes confirmed this to me in 2004. He said that he remembered Don Evans from those early days, and recalled congratulating Evans on his engagement to Marinis, while grousing good-naturedly that Evans was "taking her from him." Thus, Marinis is the reason that Evans and Bush knew each other in the first place—and the glue between Barnes and Bush.

Whatever Evans knew about Bush's activities in 1968, he and Bush quickly became fast friends. The two would move to Midland about the same time, with Evans quickly being placed on the executive track of Tom Brown, Inc., a drilling company run by an old friend of the Bush family. Soon Bush would be running for Congress, with Evans playing a central role. As Bush set up his own oil business, and Evans rose at Tom Brown, Evans would join Bush's company board. And Evans, now president of Tom Brown, would put Bush on his own board.

Meanwhile, Susie Marinis's brother (Don Evans's brother-in-law) Thomas Marinis would go on to become the head of the political action committee at Vinson and Elkins, the powerful Houston law firm that represented Enron and became one of the largest corporate bundlers of funds to George W. Bush's 2000 presidential campaign.[20] Evans himself would become W.'s secretary of commerce soon after the 2000 election.

Ultimately, the most telling detail may be the simple fact that at the time Ben Barnes helped George W. Bush get into the National Guard, his secretary was Bush's childhood friend. With connections like that, who needed a phone call from Sid Adger? In 2004, when Barnes finally "went public" with what he knew on CBS's *60 Minutes II*, that point about Marinis and Evans was never raised.

Spelling W.

Another person who figures in the Bush Guard story is Robert Spellings, who in 1968 was Ben Barnes's chief of staff. According to the anonymous letter sent to the U.S. attorney in 1996, Spellings not only knew about the favoritism shown to W., but in the midnineties was gossiping about it. "Robert Spellings also knows about this and began telling the story which made a lot of people nervous," wrote the informant. "I am told that Spellings was also an aide to Barnes at the time this took place."

The authorship of the letter never was determined. But one of its effects was to give a boost to Spellings's personal fortunes. After leaving government, Spellings had been through a lot of ups and downs, both in his personal life and in his work as a lobbyist. He had gained clout with the 1990 victory of Ann Richards, with whom he had been close. But when Bush beat Richards, Spellings was on the outs—a bad position for a lobbyist. Soon after the letter arrived at the U.S. Attorney's Office, however, Spellings's luck and life changed dramatically.

Spellings was introduced to Margaret LaMontagne, a longtime Karl Rove protégé serving as an adviser to Governor Bush. The two, both previously married, began dating. Spellings's new clients included the Texas Thoroughbred Association, one of whose directors was John Adger, a friend and former Champagne Unit colleague of George W. Bush's, and the son of the man Barnes claimed he had called to get W. preferential treatment in the National Guard.[21]

With W.'s 2000 victory, LaMontagne moved to Washington, where as assistant to the president for domestic policy, she helped create the "No Child Left Behind" program.[22] In 2005 Bush named her secretary of education. In 2001, Spellings and LaMontagne were married—after he proposed to her over the microphone at an Austin dinner held, fittingly, to honor Karl Rove.

Perhaps Rove's involvement in this political love match was no more than that of a friend. But it also served a larger purpose: once Spellings became LaMontagne's boyfriend and then husband, he was effectively removed as a witness to the suppression of Bush's National Guard service story—an obvious political time bomb for Governor Bush.

Spellings is sensitive about inquiries. When he heard that I had been asking questions about him, he called me and demanded to know why. I arranged to see him at the Washington law firm he had joined after marrying LaMontagne, and through which he works as a lobbyist. When I arrived at his offices with a colleague in December 2006, he ushered us into a conference room, spent the first minutes or so in a tirade against the press, and then insisted he would only consent to an interview if he was allowed to videotape me—so that he could "study my body language" later.

Studying body language is a favorite gambit of George W. Bush, as Ron Suskind recounts in *The One Percent Doctrine*.[23] It is not clear whether Spellings picked it up from the president. But videotaping a private meeting with a print journalist in which note taking and audio recording are the norm seemed in this instance an effort to intimidate. When Spellings insisted on this, I left.[24]

MORE THAN ANY other president in history, Bush would embrace the title "commander in chief" and wrap himself in the raiment of military service. This was evident long before 9/11 and the Iraq War, and long before he became unpopular. But this tendency was not apparent during his eight years as Texas governor. Then, he steered clear of the base where his Guard secrets happened to be buried.

Texas governors from Republican Bill Clements to Democrat Ann Richards routinely visited Guard headquarters at Camp Mabry. All except George W. Bush. "In his eight years as governor, he never one time went to Camp Mabry," said one Mabry veteran. "How far was it from the office? A five-minute drive if you are driving in a normal car. If you had an escort, it's a three-minute drive. You could almost hit it with a tank round."

A Flight of Fancy

All this makes doubly interesting a lengthy anecdote Evans shared during Bush's first presidential race.[25] According to Evans, during the summer of 1976, in Midland, W. took Evans up in a Cessna. Evans chortled over Bush's problems with the controls—though Bush's original flight training was in a Cessna. Evans actually had to issue instructions: "Give it some gas!" It was a heart-stopping landing and—according to Texas reporter and author Bill Minutaglio—"the last time [Bush] flew a plane."

Evans told this story to Minutaglio in June 1998, at the precise time that Evans and his team were busy cleaning up the messy spots in Bush's résumé, especially his National Guard service. In their world of deception, calculation and counter-calculation, it is impossible to know with certainty why Evans thought it important to share this seemingly embarrassing story about his friend and candidate with a reporter, or whether it simply slipped out. Nevertheless, while this story presents W. as a bumbler, it also appears to refute the evidence that W. never flew again after walking away from his duty as an Air National Guard pilot in 1972. That's important, because of Janet Linke's story, recounted in chapter 8, about W. being afraid to fly and having trouble handling the controls of his jet—a story that could have been politically damaging if it gained momentum.

And they cannot have it both ways. If the Evans story of W.'s shaky performance in a small, simple civilian plane were true, it would cast doubt upon the carefully choreographed moment in which Bush emerged in pilot's garb from a jet on the aircraft carrier USS *Abraham Lincoln* in 2003 to celebrate "Mission Accomplished" in Iraq. The image—instantly telegraphed around the globe and reinforced by subsequent White House statements about his capacity in the cockpit—created the impression that a heroic Bush had played a role in flying the craft.

A Charge to Keep

During his presidential campaign, W. collaborated with a professional writer on *A Charge to Keep*, a book that was intended to introduce the candidate to the American public. Mickey Herskowitz was a longtime Texas journalist, known both as a sports columnist and as a prolific ghostwriter of biographies. He had worked with a wide range of political, media, and sports figures, including Texas governor John Connally, Yankees slugger Mickey Mantle, Reagan adviser Michael Deaver, and newsman Dan Rather.

The project originally had been his agent's idea. Herskowitz whom I interviewed in October 2004, considered himself a friend of the Bush family, and has been a guest at the family vacation home in Kennebunkport. In the late 1960s, Herskowitz designated President Bush's father, then-congressman George H. W. Bush, to replace him briefly as a guest sports columnist at the *Houston Chronicle*, and the two had remained close since.

In 1999, when Herskowitz called the George W. Bush presidential campaign, to propose a book "by W.," it was supposed to be Karl Rove's decision on whether to green-light the book project. But Rove was busy with other things, and he said that if it was okay with W., it was okay with him. W. said he was amenable as long as he didn't have to do too much. Most of all, he wanted to know how much money was involved. Herskowitz, whom I interviewed in 2004, said that he and Bush quickly arrived at an agreement in which they would split the proceeds.

W. did have one other concern: he worried whether there would be enough content for such a book. He openly fretted to Herskowitz: what had he accomplished that was worth talking about? Bush thought it a better idea for the book to focus on his policy objectives. And what might those be? Herskowitz inquired. Ask Karl, Bush replied.

Finally, though, the two began what would total approximately twenty meetings so Bush could share his thoughts. As a writer, Herskowitz knew that too much canned, self-serving material could be commercially toxic. Even in a book intended to be self-serving, it could destroy the credibility—and hence the marketability—of the product. So he hoped to tease out some unguarded revelations, on the assumption that these would simply humanize his subject. At the beginning, Herskowitz had no idea the extent to which W. was treading on eggshells.

According to Herskowitz, W. was a confusing combination of cautious and candid. Sometimes, he would say something in an offhanded way that would later prove to be explosive. One such bombshell concerned his military service.

Herskowitz says that Bush was reluctant to discuss his time in the Texas Air National Guard—and inconsistent when he did so. Among other things, he provided conflicting explanations of how he came to bypass a waiting list and obtain a coveted Guard slot as a domestic alternative to Vietnam.

When the subject came up, W. sought to quickly deflect the conversation to the summer of 1972—when he moved to Montgomery, Alabama, to work on the Winton Blount senatorial campaign. And what did you do about your remaining military service? Herskowitz asked. "Nothing," Bush replied. "*I was excused.*" [emphasis added]

Of course, W. had not been excused, so this was not true. Even more interesting, however, is that this would constitute Bush's only admission that he had not continued to fulfill his military service obligation. Thus, he was directly contradicting what he had said earlier, and what he and his spokespeople would later claim.

At the time, however, Bush's service record had not become a subject of contention, so his answers seemed only mildly interesting to Herskowitz. Pressing on, the biographer asked W. if he ever flew a plane again after leaving the Texas Air National Guard in 1972. He said Bush told him he never flew any plane—military or civilian—again.

But a story had circulated among the press, in which W. took some of the inner-city children at PULL up in a plane in 1973—and stalled the engine to teach the unruly kids a lesson.[26] If Herskowitz is correct, then the PULL story, combined with Evans's yarn during the 2000 election, look like deliberate attempts to foster the impression that he did indeed fly again. The bit about scaring the children looks like the kind of compelling detail that ensures the wide circulation of a story. This is an apt example of Bush's favored technique, as described in chapter 19, of intentionally burying stories in plain sight for enterprising reporters to find and publicize.

Getting Rid of Mickey

Herskowitz began writing W.'s book in May 1999. Within two months, he says, he had completed and submitted some ten chapters, with a remaining four to six chapters still on his computer. Then he began hearing of concern from within the Bush campaign.

Ostensibly, the matter that troubled the Bush team the most was a trifling one. W. had described his Midland-based oil companies as "floundering," seemingly an innocuous and even understated characterization of his undistinguished business career. But his handlers were steamed. "I got a call from one of the campaign lawyers," Herskowitz recalled. "He was kind of angry, and he said, 'You've got some wrong information.' I didn't bother to say, 'Well, you know where it came from.' [The lawyer] said, 'We do not consider that the governor struggled or floundered in the oil business. We consider him a successful oilman who started up at least two new businesses.' "

It was downhill from there. Before long, Herskowitz was told that he was being pulled off the project, that his work would not be used, and they demanded all his materials back. "The lawyer called me and said, 'Delete it. Shred it. Just do it.' "

A campaign official arrived at his home unexpectedly at seven A.M. on a Monday morning and took his notes and computer files. He had not expected them to come so abruptly, nor so early in the morning, nor to be quite so aggressive in seizing and removing all his documentation of Bush's thoughts. Mickey summed up the end of his book labors this way: "They took it, and [communications director] Karen [Hughes] rewrote it."

After Herskowitz was pulled from the Bush book project, he learned that a scenario was being prepared to explain his departure. "I got a phone call from someone in the Bush campaign, confidentially, saying, 'Watch your back.'"

Reporters covering Bush say that when they asked why Herskowitz was no longer on the project, Hughes intimated that Herskowitz was hitting the bottle—a claim Herskowitz said was unfounded. Later, the campaign put out the word that Herskowitz had been removed for missing a deadline. Hughes subsequently finished the book herself; it received largely negative reviews for its self-serving qualities and lack of spontaneity or introspection. Meanwhile, Poppy took care of Mickey.

In 2002, three years after he had been pulled off the George W. Bush biography, Herskowitz got a message that the senior Bush wanted to see him. At that meeting Poppy asked him to write a book about the current president's grandfather, Prescott Bush. "Former president Bush just handed it to me. We were sitting there one day, and I was visiting him there in his office . . . He said, 'I wish somebody would do a book about my dad.'"

"He said to me, 'I know this has been a disappointing time for you, but it's amazing how many times something good will come out of it.' I passed it on to my agent; he jumped all over it. I asked [Bush Senior], 'Would you support it and would you give me access to the rest of family?' He said yes." The resulting book, *Duty, Honor, Country: The Life and Legacy of Prescott Bush*, was published in 2003. Not surprisingly for an authorized biography, it was a sympathetic portrait.

As for *A Charge to Keep*, Herskowitz keeps thinking about what might have happened if the public had learned how W. really thinks. "He told me that as a leader, you can never admit to a mistake," Herskowitz said. "That was one of the keys to being a leader."

There were other things that W. told Herskowitz about what makes a successful leader. Prominent among them, the future president of the United States confided, was the benefit of starting a war.

CHAPTER 21

Shock and . . . Oil?

It didn't take Herskowitz and Bush long to work through W.'s life story and accomplishments. Soon they were discussing what Bush hoped to achieve as president. While W. seemed somewhat hazy on specifics, on one point he was clear: the many benefits that would accrue if he were to overthrow Saddam Hussein. Herskowitz recalled that Bush and his advisers were sold on the idea that it was difficult for a president to realize his legislative agenda without the high approval numbers that accompany successful—even if modest—wars.

"He was thinking about invading Iraq in 1999," Herskowitz told me in our 2004 interview, leaning in a little to make sure I could hear him properly. "It was on his mind. He said to me: 'One of the keys to being seen as a great leader is to be seen as a commander in chief.' And he said, 'My father had all this political capital built up when he drove the Iraqis out of Kuwait, and he wasted it.' He said, 'If I have a chance to invade . . . if I had that much capital, I'm not going to waste it. I'm going to get everything passed that I want to get passed, and I'm going to have a successful presidency.' "

Herskowitz said that Bush expressed frustration at a lifetime as an underachiever in the shadow of an accomplished father. In aggressive military action, he saw the opportunity to emerge from his father's shadow.

That opportunity, of course, would come in the wake of the September 11 attacks. "Suddenly, he's at ninety-one percent in the polls," Herskowitz said, "and he'd barely crawled out of the bunker." Just four days before, according to a Gallup poll, his approval rating was 51 percent.

Herskowitz said that George W. Bush's beliefs on Iraq were based in part on a notion dating back to the Reagan White House, and ascribed in part to Dick Cheney, who was then a powerful congressman. "Start a small war. Pick a country where there is justification you can jump on, go ahead and invade."

Bush's circle of preelection advisers had a fixation on the political capital that British prime minister Margaret Thatcher had amassed from the Falklands War with Argentina. Said Herskowitz: "They were just absolutely blown away, just enthralled by the scenes of the troops coming back, of the boats, people throwing flowers at [Thatcher] and her getting these standing ovations in Parliament and making these magnificent speeches." It was a masterpiece of "perception management"—a lesson in how to maneuver the media and public into supporting a war, irrespective of the actual merits.

The neocons backing Bush believed that Jimmy Carter's political downfall could be attributed largely to his failure to wage a war. Herskowitz noted that President Reagan and President George H. W. Bush had (in addition to the narrowly focused Gulf War I) successfully waged limited wars against tiny opponents—Grenada and Panama—and gained politically. But there were successful small wars and then there were quagmires, and apparently George H. W. Bush and his son did not see eye to eye on the difference. Poppy, the consummate CIA professional, preferred behind-the-scenes solutions over grand-scale confrontation—indeed, Poppy is remembered largely for that. In 2008, with memory of Poppy's 1989 invasion of Panama long faded, Democratic presidential candidate Barack Obama praised the elder Bush for his seemingly prudent foreign policy.[1]

Not surprisingly, Poppy harbored serious doubts about his son's plan to finish the job with Saddam. Said Herskowitz: "I know [Poppy] would not admit this now, but he was opposed to [the 2003 Iraq invasion]. I asked him if he had talked to W. about [it]. He said, 'No I haven't, and I won't, but Brent [Scowcroft] has.' Brent would not have talked to him without the old man's okaying it." Scowcroft, national security adviser in the elder Bush's administration and chairman of W.'s Foreign Intelligence Advisory Board, penned a highly publicized warning to George W. Bush about the perils of an invasion.

Herskowitz's revelations are not the sole indicator of Bush's preelection thinking on Iraq. In December 1999, some six months after his talks with Herskowitz, Bush surprised veteran political chroniclers, including the *Boston Globe*'s David Nyhan, with his blunt pronouncements about Saddam at a New Hampshire primary event that got little notice. As Nyhan described the event for his readers:

It was a gaffe-free evening for the rookie front-runner, till he was asked about Saddam's weapons stash. "I'd take 'em out," [Bush] grinned cavalierly, "take out the weapons of mass destruction . . . I'm surprised he's still there," said Bush of the despot who remains in power after losing the Gulf War to Bush Jr.'s father . . . It remains to be seen if that offhand declaration of war was just Texas talk, a sort of locker room braggadocio, or whether it was Bush's first big clinker.[2]

The suspicion that W. held unrealistic or naïve views about the consequences of war was further corroborated by a supporter, the evangelist Pat Robertson, who revealed that Bush had assured him the Iraq invasion would yield no casualties.

For George W. Bush, careful and rational calculations were not important. If he could become a heroic commander in chief, he'd have the political capital to go quickly through the Republican wish list: appoint right-thinking Supreme Court nominees; make massive tax cuts to starve the federal government; bury evidence of climate change. It all flowed from that irresistible Thatcherite image. Plus, there would be the oil, and the contracts for an expanded military.[3] It was a fantasy that mesmerized the neocon imagination.

IN THEIR THINK tanks—most notably the Project for a New American Century (PNAC) and the American Enterprise Institute—the neocons had made no secret of their desire to use Iraq as a showcase for a reprojection of American military might. Some spoke of installing a U.S-style democracy in the heart of the Arab Middle East; others of Iraq's huge oil reserves. Lurking just offstage was the inescapable fact that America's vast military economy needed a steady stream of projects and perceived threats—a particularly vexing challenge in a post-Communist world. As *Shock Doctrine* author Naomi Klein astutely noted, the war on terror forms an unbeatable economic proposition: "Not a flash-in-the-pan war that could potentially be won but a new and permanent fixture in the global economic architecture."[4]

The big kahuna, without question, was the seizure of the Middle Eastern country sitting on some of the world's largest untapped oil reserves. One 2000 PNAC study, *Rebuilding America's Defenses*, called for an increased defense budget, Saddam Hussein's removal, and the presence of U.S. troops in the Middle East even after regime change in Iraq. It noted suggestively that these steps would be difficult "absent some catastrophic and catalyzing event—like a new Pearl Harbor."[5]

Vice in Charge

Once W. settled into the White House, foreign policy, and in particular Iraq, was largely Dick Cheney's show. Cheney had spent most of his adult life catering to corporate interests, particularly military contractors. He and his mentor Donald Rumsfeld had seized power by orchestrating Gerald Ford's Halloween Massacre, in which they marginalized the "realists," Henry Kissinger and Nelson Rockefeller, and began destroying détente. Ever since, Cheney had been obsessed with restoring a strong executive branch. He wanted it unencumbered by other branches of government, the public, and even by law itself. Cheney would take all the power W. would give him, and become by far the most powerful vice president in American history.

Cheney and Rumsfeld's role in the Ford White House coincided with Poppy Bush's rising influence—as a result of Richard Nixon's resignation and Ford's subsequent decision to appoint Poppy director of Central Intelligence. After Poppy became president, he named Cheney as secretary of defense, and it was Cheney who presided over Poppy's war with Iraq following the latter's invasion of Kuwait. Cheney remained in the Bush orbit after Bill Clinton's victory in 1992, with his selection to head Halliburton, the company that he would merge in 1998 with Dresser Industries to create the largest oil field services firm in the world.

Halliburton was also deeply involved in defense contracting, through its subsidiary Brown and Root (later Kellogg Brown and Root: KBR), the politically wired Texas engineering firm. Brown and Root had taken a giant leap into military contracting when Lyndon Johnson, its political protégé, became president. It would receive giant contracts from both the Clinton and George W. Bush administrations. The company, with forty thousand employees in Iraq and twenty-eight thousand more in Afghanistan and Kuwait, had a near monopoly on a wide range of services, from construction to food handling to disco nights for the troops. By 2008 Halliburton had been paid more than $24 billion.[6] Halliburton's contract in Iraq has been repeatedly marked by corruption: In 2004 the company had to repay the government for $6.3 million in "improper payments" to its employees.[7] Halliburton also overcharged the government for importing gasoline into Iraq and even for meals supplied to the troops.[8] Most recently, KBR admitted a "systemic problem" with its electrical work at U.S. military bases in Iraq. The company had to conduct its own study after a six-month period in which there were 283 electrical fires, and numerous soldiers were electrocuted.[9]

Dick Cheney was the right partner for President Bush. W. was short on experience, had an attention span that was even shorter, and was a serial delegator. Cheney knew Washington inside and out, was hardworking and focused, and was a practiced courtier who knew how to get his way with a boss. W. had to count heavily on Cheney, especially with so much of W.'s senior staff having come directly from Austin with little Washington experience.

As Texas journalists Lou Dubose and Jake Bernstein note in their book *Vice: Dick Cheney and the Hijacking of the American Presidency*, Cheney was not supposed to generate fireworks. "Cheney had served three presidents, had spent ten years in Congress, and as secretary of defense had coordinated the first Gulf War. He was Bush père's preferred candidate, the Washington insider who would provide adult supervision in the White House. Nothing exciting, just competent and steady. Dick Cheney was the safe, reassuring presence whose experience would ensure that public policy, in particular foreign policy, would not career off track."[10]

The public would soon learn that as Halliburton chief executive, Cheney had grown used to calling the shots. The full extent of Cheney's clout would not become apparent for years, in part because of his extraordinary penchant for secrecy. So much so that six and a half years into the administration, when the *Washington Post* released an excellent series on Cheney's power and influence, it was still something of a shock.

Cheney dominated more than foreign policy. Noted the *Post*:

> In roles that have gone largely undetected, Cheney has served as gatekeeper for Supreme Court nominees, referee of Cabinet turf disputes, arbiter of budget appeals, editor of tax proposals and regulator in chief of water flows in his native West. On some subjects, officials said, he has displayed a strong pragmatic streak. On others he has served as enforcer of ideological principle, come what may.[11]

Practically the first thing Cheney did when he took office was to convene a secretive energy task force whose advisers would meet with officials from the oil and energy industry.[12] It soon became clear that securing additional oil reserves and projecting American power in oil-rich regions was the top priority. A lawsuit, filed by Judicial Watch, a conservative group that opposes abuses of government power, unearthed maps of Iraqi oil fields prepared by the task force, along with lists of the American oil companies interested in each field.

At the time, Iraqi oil was under an embargo and controlled by the United Nations as part of the peace accords imposed after the first Gulf War. Yet the documents, dated March 2001, list "foreign suitors for Iraqi oilfield contracts" long before the administration began justifying an invasion of the country. "These documents show the importance of the Energy Task Force and why its operations should be open to the public," said Judicial Watch president Tom Fitton.[13]

If Cheney's interest in Iraqi oil fields seemed speculative at the time, it was no longer so after the September 11 attacks. The administration would turn quickly to manipulating intelligence in order to achieve what had always been its goal.

From One Bunker to Another

From the time of his inauguration, Bush's approval ratings had been hovering around 55 percent. Then came the 9/11 attacks, and a surge of support. PNAC's 2000 report had been prescient when it anticipated the potential response to a catastrophic and catalyzing event—to the "new Pearl Harbor."

For a time, the world rallied around the United States. Americans generally backed Bush and what seemed his decisive and appropriate response to the attack: an assault on al-Qaeda and the ruling Taliban regime of its host country, Afghanistan. Yet, as time passed, Bush's poll numbers gradually eroded, at least in part due to the failure to capture Osama bin Laden. By the spring of 2002, the White House political team was growing concerned, and others were beginning to speculate as to what an administration devoted to the so-called permanent campaign might do next.

Former Texas GOP political director and political consultant Royal Masset recalls what went through his head. "In the spring, I said, 'Karl is going to push the war button—because that is going to resuscitate George. It will be good for the midterm elections.' The Karl Rove I know would have been pushing the war for all it was worth."[14]

Iraq

Things might have gone differently if it were easier to bring a historical perspective to news reporting. The public would then have grasped the fundamental hypocrisy of the administration's building a case against Saddam. Throughout the Reagan–Poppy Bush years, the White House had been an eager backer of Saddam. The two administrations had provided millions of dollars in aid and had permitted the export of U.S. technology that Iraq used to build a massive arsenal of chemical, biological, and possibly nuclear weapons.[15] George W. Bush would repeatedly express outrage over Saddam's 1988 gassing of the Kurds, neglecting to mention that Donald Rumsfeld, now his defense secretary, had visited and talked business deals with Saddam back in the eighties—and that the Reagan and Poppy Bush administrations continued to support the Iraqi dictator *after* the gassing.[16] The larger goal, however, was a so-called balance of terror that would prevent any country from gaining ascendancy in the strategic Gulf region, and so the United States actually provided materiel and intelligence to both sides in the brutal, nearly decade-long Iraq-Iran war, in which over a million people died.

In a paradoxical twist, when W. sought to justify the invasion of Iraq in 2003, he cited those same weapons—without mentioning that his own father had helped to provide them. He also failed to mention what many proliferation experts correctly believed: that most or all of those weapons had been destroyed as part of Saddam's scale-down after the imposition of the no-fly zones and President Clinton's own threats to invade.

Surprisingly, the United States' secret relationship with Saddam Hussein goes back even further—a remarkable forty years. This information was published by the wire service UPI in April 2003, shortly after the invasion, while U.S. forces were hunting for the reviled Saddam Hussein, but it was generally ignored.[17] The report noted:

> U.S. forces in Baghdad might now be searching high and low for Iraqi dictator Saddam Hussein, but in the past Saddam was seen by U.S. intelligence services as a bulwark of anti-communism and they used him as their instrument for more than 40 years, according to former U.S. intelligence diplomats and intelligence officials . . . While many have thought that Saddam first became involved with U.S. intelligence agencies at the start of the September 1980 Iran-Iraq war, his first contacts with U.S. officials date back to 1959,

when he was part of a CIA-authorized six-man squad tasked with assassinating then Iraqi Prime Minister Gen. Abd al-Karim Qasim.

The article noted that Qasim had overthrown the Iraqi monarchy and participated in a U.S.-backed cold war coalition. But when Qasim decided to withdraw from the alliance and began warming up to the USSR, CIA director Allen Dulles publicly declared that Iraq was "the most dangerous spot in the world."

> According to another former senior State Department official, Saddam, while only in his early 20s, became a part of a U.S. plot to get rid of Qasim . . . In Beirut, the CIA paid for Saddam's apartment and put him through a brief training course . . . Even then Saddam "was known as having no class. He was a thug—a cutthroat."
> . . . During this time Saddam was making frequent visits to the American Embassy . . . In February 1963 Qasim was killed in a Baath Party coup . . . But the agency quickly moved into action. Noting that the Baath Party was hunting down Iraq's communists, the CIA provided the submachine gun–toting Iraqi National Guardsmen with lists of suspected communists who were then jailed, interrogated, and summarily gunned down.

Saddam Hussein is hardly the only dictator whom the United States essentially created, long supported, and then turned on when circumstances changed. Panamanian strongman Manuel Noriega, a longtime CIA asset, was another. Poppy, as Ford's CIA director and then as Reagan's vice president, had fostered a relationship with the notorious drug trafficker during the seventies and eighties, even keeping him on the U.S. payroll at more than a hundred thousand dollars a year.[18] But Noriega did not always do as the Americans wanted. While Noriega sold arms and provided intelligence to the Sandinista government in Nicaragua, he refused to supply weapons to the U.S.-backed contras to help overthrow the Managua government.[19]

According to Larry Birns, director of the Washington-based Council on Hemispheric Affairs, Noriega insisted to him that he had had the best of relations with Bush for years. But Noriega told Birns that at an airport meeting in Panama shortly before the invasion, he had had a spat with Vice President Dan Quayle when he refused to commit Panama to a more confrontational role in fighting against Washington's Central American enemies. Birns, who was in Panama as Noriega's "honorable enemy" guest only hours before the U.S. invasion and was arguably the last American to meet with Noriega before U.S. troops arrived, told me that the Panamanian strongman was bitter because after years of servitude to Washington's various regional crusades, Bush was unceremoniously dumping him.[20]

As former head of French intelligence Count Alexandre de Marenches puts it in his memoirs:

> If it's proved that Noriega was on the US payroll, then it was a shameful mistake . . . Never use shady characters . . . I expressed this philosophy to George Bush . . . Now years later, the worst nightmare has come to haunt the Americans—a protracted and messy jury trial following a lethal and embarrassing military operation in Panama—all designed to get rid of the rat they should never have hired in the first place . . . If you do, after all, hire the rat, and are ultimately forced to get rid of him, then by all means do so quickly and permanently.[21]

Though Jimmy Carter had agreed to return the Canal Zone to Panama by 2000, that did not mean Poppy was willing to give up influence in the tropical republic. At the end of 1989, Poppy ordered an invasion of the country, which resulted in the deaths of hundreds and the imposition of a more compliant government.

Twisting Arms

For W., one benefit of turning attention toward Iraq and touting Saddam as a major threat was to take the world's eye off more than a few potentially embarrassing balls. What, for example, had led to 9/11? What about the U.S. role during the 1970s and '80s in creating a global mujahideen force as surrogates in Afghanistan against the Soviet Union? Or the objective of actually fostering the USSR's Afghan invasion in the first place by baiting the Soviets into what Zbigniew Brzezinski hoped would be quicksand for the Communists? These global gambits, acknowledged in memoirs of key decision makers, including Brzezinski, have seldom been widely discussed or generally understood.[22]

Then there was the politicization of intelligence, which began under

Poppy Bush's CIA directorship with his creation of the "Team B" that sought to refute the agency analysts who had accurately determined that the USSR was already in decline. Some intelligence analysts had also warned— only to be ignored—about the risk of creating an extremist Islamic force armed to the teeth.

And there was the simple fact that fifteen of nineteen hijackers on September 11 were Saudis. What could or should the Saudi government have known about these people? And what about the deep and long personal relationship between the Bushes and the Saudi royal family? All the public ever learned, thanks in good part to the film *Fahrenheit 9/11*, was how W.'s administration showed remarkable diligence in spiriting Saudi royals out of the United States right after 9/11—an operation about which the administration has maintained silence.

And what of the manner in which the 9/11 attack itself was handled— most notably the failure to act on intelligence leads in advance and the competing accounts of the activities of Vice President Cheney in those crucial minutes and hours after the attack? And what of the mystery of Secretary of Defense Rumsfeld's equally peculiar actions, including his odd decision to "assist" at the scene of the Pentagon attack rather than assume command?[23] There were so many questions, and all they did was undermine confidence in the competency and candor of the administration.

Absent a distraction, the media and a few public intellectuals were bound to raise such potentially embarrassing topics. Indeed, some did—but a war always takes center stage.

Help, Britannia

Put aside the compromising connections and troubling pre-9/11 history with Islamic fundamentalism. There was still the simple fact that al-Qaeda was an elusive military target—an amorphous fighting group that could not be pinned down to a single geographical location. By contrast, Iraq was easy to find on a map and Saddam a bona fide villain who could be taken out with telegenic flair.

However, not everyone agreed about the nature of the Iraqi threat, and so the Bush administration faced a huge public relations challenge. In its response, truth—not surprisingly—was the first casualty. Appearing on CNN, Condoleezza Rice warned: "We don't want the smoking gun to be a mushroom cloud."[24] And Colin Powell delivered his dramatic show-and-tell presentation on Saddam's alleged weapons of mass destruction—complete with a vial of "anthrax" as a prop. Though no U.N. action followed, the United States could hardly be seen to act alone.[25] It needed an appearance of broad international support, and that meant allies. The most important, by far, would be the former (post–World War I) ruler of Iraq, Great Britain.

The affection felt by the Bushes and their friends for the British Isles has been remarked on by numerous authors. It is manifested in a variety of ways, from a passion for Scottish tartans to claims of distant blood relationships to the queen. The Bush family moneyman, William Farish, even stables Queen Elizabeth's horses in Kentucky and was dispatched by President George W. Bush as ambassador to the Court of St. James. And the guardians of royalty returned the favor. The publishing director of *Burke's Peerage* enthused that while other presidents had royal connections, "none [are] as royal as George Bush." Aspirants to royalty, the Bushes owed deference to the real thing. "While no American presidential family can actually be royal," writes Kevin Phillips, "the Bushes' triple predilection for royal genealogy, restoration, and an unacknowledged dynasty is an extraordinary coincidence."[26]

As always with the Bush family, there were long-standing relationships that helped smooth cooperation in sensitive areas. One little-understood factor in the role Britain played in the "coalition" that invaded Iraq was the personal relationship between George W. Bush and Tony Blair. Many were surprised that Blair, a Labour Party politician who had gotten on famously with Clinton, quickly developed a similar rapport with Bush. But once again, there was a backstory, this one involving a mutual friend of both Blair and Bush. The story also involved oil.

Going back several generations, the Bush family has been close friends with a powerful Scottish banking family, the Gammells. After World War II, J. A. H. Gammell ran the British military mission to Moscow, while Averell Harriman, Prescott Bush's business partner, was the U.S. ambassador there. Gammell's son, James "Jimmy" G. S. Gammell of Edinburgh, somehow became close with Poppy, and was an early investor in Bush-Overbey, one of Poppy's first intelligence-tinged "business" ventures in Midland, Texas, in the early 1950s. This same Jimmy Gammell would head the investment firm Ivory and Sime, of which one former staffer told a Scottish newspaper: "The joke [around here] was that we were the CIA's station in Scotland."[27]

The Gammells and Bushes remained close, and Poppy seemed to want to further develop this relationship. Poppy visited the Gammells while on "business trips"—accompanied by young George W. Those repeat visits to the Gammell farm in Perthshire, Scotland, would yield a friendship between W. and Jimmy Gammell's son, Bill. In 1959, when W. was thirteen, Poppy sent him to spend the summer with the Gammells. Apparently he made a big impression on Bill, who was just seven at the time.

After a career as a Scottish rugby star, Bill Gammell went into business—eventually gaining the type of success that got him dubbed "the JR Ewing of Scotland" by the London *Observer*.[28] In 1980, the young Gammell, who like W. had spent summers in college on Texas oil rigs, set up Cairn Energy Management to look for North American oil and gas deals for Scottish high rollers. His first deal was as one of W.'s earliest investors, supposedly after W. traveled to Scotland to pitch the idea. For their stake in Arbusto Energy, Gammell and his investors got back just twenty cents on the dollar, but there were no hard feelings—in 1983, W. was back in Scotland for Bill's wedding.

In 2006 I interviewed Mark Vozar, a partner in CVC, a little-known oil exploration company that was created to serve as a subcontractor for W.'s companies. Vozar told me that Bill Gammell and Cairn Energy Management also provided substantial funding for CVC.[29] Vozar said Gammell covered CVC's entire overhead and all salaries and promoted some Bush oil deals abroad. Vozar said Gammell wrote his checks to Bush, who then transferred the money into CVC. There also appeared to be a geopolitical backstory to the investments in W.'s oil ventures, full of names from Zapata, British Petroleum (now BP), and Scottish entities, that suggested more than the normal marketplace at work.[30]

George W. and Bill remained close, and the two talked the day Bush was elected governor of Texas in 1994. The following year, Bill Gammell, whose company vice chairman was a former Labour energy minister, renewed his relationship with British Labour leader and soon-to-be prime minister Tony Blair.

Bill Gammell's ties to Blair date back to prep school in Edinburgh, where the two had been friends and basketball teammates. Gammell arranged the initial meeting between the two world leaders, and Bush's first words to the British prime minister were: "I believe you know my old friend, Bill Gammell."[31]

W. would mention his family's connection to the Gammells in a 2005

Oval Office interview with the *Times* of London. In answer to a question about whether he planned to eat haggis on a forthcoming trip to the U.K., W. talked about "a fellow named James Gammell," his "fabulous family" and their beautiful sheep farm in Glen Isle. He discussed past business deals with Billy Gammell, an "oil and gas guy" who used to visit Midland, Texas, and became "a very successful entrepreneur."[32] The British reporter quickly moved on to a question about golf.

W.'s reference to the Gammells in such an innocuous context is a typical Bush family device. Get the information out so it is no longer news, to ensure the trail stops there. Journalists will continue to construe the "special relationship" between the United States and Great Britain as based on fellowship and history. The CIA and oil connections loom as unseemly mood breakers, and so remain unexamined.

Either Gammell was an extremely visionary businessman or he had great connections—or both. One way or the other, along with Enron and Cheney's Halliburton, Gammell's Cairn was soon making a fortune off oil in India—a country not noted for its prospects in that regard. These Western relationships with India got a boost when George W. Bush succeeded Bill Clinton and replaced the United States' tough stance on the South Asian country's nuclear weapons program with one that was more forbearing.[33]

Meanwhile, an odd political twist: Bill's father, Jimmy, once was a director of the Bank of Scotland. There he mentored Peter Burt, who, as chairman of the Bank of Scotland in 1999, named Reverend Pat Robertson to head a new joint venture in the United States, in which Robertson's followers would form the initial customer base. Is it possible that Burt was doing this deal to reward Robertson for bringing the Christian conservatives, who formed one third of the GOP base, into the fold of the Bush campaign? Of course, as Scotland's national poet Robert Burns noted, "the best-laid schemes o' mice and men" often go awry: the Bank of Scotland deal fell apart over U.K. public outrage concerning Robertson's views, in particular his remark that Scotland was "a dark land" overrun by homosexuals.

Blair's decision to back Bush enthusiastically on Iraq appears to have paid dividends. In 2008, when Iraq's oil ministry began handing out no-bid development contracts to a select group, one of the lucky parties was BP—a company that had as much influence in the Blair government as American oil companies had in the Bush-Cheney White House. Blair surrounded himself with at least a dozen executives from BP. In 1997, for example, he appointed BP chair David Simon to a newly created position, minister of trade and competitiveness in Europe. The prime minister maintained such a close relationship with BP's CEO Lord Browne that newspapers dubbed the giant oil company "Blair Petroleum" (although some wondered if it wouldn't be more fitting to call the British government the British petroleum government).[34]

Another of Blair's closest confidantes and aides, an old friend from his native Edinburgh named Anji Hunter, left her job at 10 Downing Street in November 2001 to become director of communications at BP. Blair said he was "sad" over losing such a close confidante after thirteen years, but Hunter's timing was fortuitous, as discussions were already under way about invading Iraq.[35] According to the *Observer*, Bush raised the issue of removing Saddam with British support over dinner with Blair just nine days after September 11.[36]

Where such old-school ties did not exist, the Bush administration used hardball against allies that would not go along with its wartime objectives. According to a 2008 book by Chilean diplomat Heraldo Muñoz (with a foreword by former U.N. Secretary-General Kofi Annan), the so-called Coalition of the Willing was anything but willing. Muñoz notes that in the march-up to the invasion, the White House virtually declared war on allies who did not fall into line. The administration threatened trade reprisals, spied on them, and demanded that U.N. envoys who resisted U.S. pressure to endorse the war be recalled.[37]

Making the Case

The news media, opposition politicians, and even popular entertainers faced intense pressure, overt and implied, to support the invasion. When political comedian Bill Maher questioned whether terrorists who turned themselves into missiles were really "cowardly" as opposed to those who launch missiles from afar, expressions of outrage came quickly. "People need to watch what they say, watch what they do," said presidential press secretary Ari Fleischer.[38] The controversy over Maher's remarks was widely believed to be a factor in the later cancellation of his show.

Fury followed ABC News anchor Peter Jennings's musing after the September 11 attacks that "the country looks to the president on occasions like this to be reassuring to the nation. Some presidents do it well, some presidents don't." Syndicated talk show host Rush Limbaugh declared that

Jennings had questioned Bush's character; ten thousand angry phone calls and e-mails flooded into ABC.[39]

Aided by a wave of such fervor—and also by the largely inaccurate, administration-fed reports by *New York Times* reporter Judith Miller that Saddam Hussein possessed weapons of mass destruction—the Bush administration launched its invasion.

Waging war was one thing; winning the propaganda war was another. As Frank Rich details in his book *The Greatest Story Ever Sold*, the White House became ever more vigilant (and creative) in controlling its message. The administration even gave its invasion a cinematic title: Shock and Awe. "Onscreen the pyrotechnics of Shock and Awe looked like a distant fireworks display, or perhaps the cool computer graphics of a *Matrix*-inspired video game, rather than the bombing of a large city. None of Baghdad's nearly six million people were visible."[40] Those in charge made the war appear bloodless, justified, and unimpeachable. What was not to like? Networks like CNN, "mindful of the sensibilities of our viewers,"[41] agreed to minimize the blood and guts, and former first lady Barbara Bush applauded. "Why should we hear about body bags and deaths and how many, what day it's gonna happen?" she asked on *Good Morning America*. "It's not relevant. So why should I waste my beautiful mind on something like that?"[42]

The memory hole also devoured recollections of how the first President George Bush had used propaganda and lies to excite the American public to support an earlier war with Iraq. In October 1990, a new entity calling itself the Congressional Human Rights Caucus, but in reality a creation of the public relations powerhouse Hill and Knowlton, held hearings in order to substantiate claims of Iraqi human rights violations.

The committee heard a particularly moving testimony from a fifteen-year-old Kuwaiti girl, Nayirah, who described the horrors she witnessed in a Kuwait City hospital: "While I was there, I saw the Iraqi soldiers come into the hospital with guns, and go into the room where 15 babies were in incubators. They took the babies out of the incubators, took the incubators, and left the babies on the cold floor to die."[43] The media gave the story major play. Poppy used it to help justify the war that would begin three months later. It turned out, however, that the girl was actually a member of the Kuwaiti royal family—the daughter of Saud Nasir al-Sabah, Kuwait's ambassador to the United States. The vice president of Hill and Knowlton had even coached Nayirah, whose entire testimony was eventually deemed false by investigators.[44]

Great Moments in Chutzpah

Once the 2003 invasion had taken place, with the predictable portrayal of a magnificent battle with no blood or human toll, it was time for the next stage of pageantry. Here, the Bush team was able to enjoy the sort of accolades showered upon Margaret Thatcher after the British victory in the tiny Falklands War.

The quick dispatch of Saddam was crowned first with the symbolic toppling of the dictator's statue, followed by an even more stunning photo op: W. appearing to land a fighter jet on board an aircraft carrier that appeared to be at sea somewhere in relation to the war effort. A large banner proclaimed MISSION ACCOMPLISHED. Almost none of it was true. The plane, renamed *Navy One*, was normally used for refueling. The aircraft carrier was not far out at sea and nowhere near the war—it was in fact just off the coast of San Diego, California. And the mission, it goes without saying, was far from accomplished. But it made for good television, and the media at first lapped it up.

As the war dragged on and it became apparent that the main justification—weapons of mass destruction—did not exist, the national mood turned and the media became more skeptical. It grew clear that Iraq and Saddam Hussein had had nothing to do with September 11.

The emergent truth about Saddam's Iraq—that it had not posed a substantial threat to the United States—raised any number of important questions that got little attention in the national discourse. Some of these were strategic:

- If al-Qaeda and Osama bin Laden were the threats, why was Saddam Hussein attacked, removed, and executed instead?
- If Saddam Hussein was the principal threat, why was an enormous and hugely expensive Homeland Security apparatus constructed to defend against an ongoing threat from al-Qaeda?

One question went right to the heart of the American political process:

- If George W. Bush and his team were so egregiously wrong on such a significant decision, and if they had deliberately distorted and exaggerated a virtually nonexistent threat from Saddam, and if American troops and innocent Iraqis had died or been maimed as a result, why were there no consequences for Bush and his team?

But one question touched on personal morality, and therefore had the potential to become a public-opinion-changing lightning rod: What was a guy who had apparently skipped out on military service, and ditched his National Guard service prematurely, doing sending thousands of National Guardsmen into combat in a foreign country for a war initiated through deception?

And why, after so many years, if Bush had fulfilled his military obligation as he was supposed to, was it so incredibly difficult to verify that seemingly simple fact?

The answer to these questions harkens back to the same skillful perception management and psy-ops that enabled the administration to sell the invasion in the first place. It also enabled W. to banish the ghosts of his own less-than-admirable past. The personal, it turned out, was political indeed.

The Guard—Again?

During the 2000 election, W.'s National Guard record did not catch on with the mainstream press despite the *Boston Globe* report that seemed to definitively establish that Bush had failed to show up for a year of service.[45] The Gore campaign did not aggressively question Bush on the matter, perhaps because Gore himself was vulnerable for exaggerating the risks of his own service as a military journalist in Vietnam. Gore's supporters repeatedly tried to raise the issue, but it never gained traction.

Several journalists did pursue the story, including Mary Mapes, a Dallas-based CBS News producer. In 1999, Mapes had to drop her inquiries into W.'s military service because of conflicting assignments. Five years later, however, her dogged pursuit of the Bush Guard story would explode into an enormous scandal that changed the election, traumatized CBS News, and destroyed her career and that of her colleagues, including the anchorman Dan Rather.

Certainly, the Bush forces were keeping a wary eye on the issue, but by 2004 any potential storm seemed to have passed. The further W. got from TV reporter Jim Moore's persistent questions in 1994 about his Guard service, and the more the damage control effort seemed to be working, the more casual he got about his "military problem." In fact he became down-right cocky. While governor, though he stayed away from Camp Mabry, he bragged about flying an F-102 jet while visiting a veterans' cemetery. As president, speaking at a Veterans Day event at Arlington National Cemetery in 2003, Bush declared:

> Every veteran has lived by a strict code of discipline. Every veteran understands the meaning of personal accountability and loyalty, and shared sacrifice. From the moment you repeated the oath to the day of your honorable discharge, your time belonged to America; your country came before all else.[46]

To many listeners, it sounded as though he was talking about himself.

But by 2004, as the president continued to order National Guard troops to Afghanistan and Iraq—men and women who, like himself, had assumed that Guard duty would not involve fighting abroad even in wartime—deep public doubts had set in. The failure to find weapons of mass destruction was becoming a huge problem. Tough questions threatened to dominate the campaign, and W.'s prospects were iffy at best. Moreover, the Democratic field included not one but two highly decorated war veterans, John Kerry and Wesley Clark. It would be a disaster if a majority of Americans were to conclude that Bush was a trigger-happy commander in chief who had plunged the United States into a cataclysmic and unnecessary war—after he himself had shirked his own service.

CHAPTER 22

Deflection for Reelection

F OR A TIME, THE ISSUE OF BUSH's Guard service bubbled along mostly
on the Internet and talk radio. But in January 2004, the filmmaker
Michael Moore—a supporter of General Wesley Clark's candidacy—
called Bush a "deserter" at a rally of more than thousand people outside
Concord, New Hampshire.

On February 1, matters escalated further when the chairman of the Democratic National Committee, Terry McAuliffe, appeared on a Sunday chat
show and accused Bush of being AWOL. His counterpart at the Republican
National Committee, Ed Gillespie, quickly called the comments "slander-
ous" in an interview with the *New York Times*.[1]

> "President Bush served honorably in the National Guard," Mr.
> Gillespie said in a telephone interview. "He was never AWOL. To
> make an accusation like that on national television with no basis in
> fact is despicable."

Soon, the matter had exploded into a full-scale crisis—so grave that
Bush, who hardly ever gave media interviews, went on NBC's *Meet the Press*
to insist again that he had served in Alabama.[2]

> TIM RUSSERT: The *Boston Globe* and the Associated Press have
> gone through some of the records and said there's no evidence
> that you reported to duty in Alabama during the summer and
> fall of 1972.

BUSH: Yeah, they're—they're just wrong. There may be no evidence, but I did report; otherwise, I wouldn't have been honorably discharged. In other words, you don't just say "I did something" without there being verification. Military doesn't work that way. I got an honorable discharge, and I did show up in Alabama.

W.'s service record was a justifiable line of inquiry. He had included it in his campaign biography, and he invoked the military imagery whenever it was opportune. More, he was sending the current generation of Guardsmen off to Iraq, where the risk of injury or death was great. For the Bush forces, exposure was a fundamental threat. Any new revelations regarding the candidate's own record could be devastating, especially in crucial swing states such as Florida, chockablock with military personnel past and present. Bush was counting on those votes in what looked to be another tight election.

And the stakes were higher still: Abandoning military service is a felony with no statute of limitations. Punishment is at the discretion of the soldier's commander, and can range from a mild "rehabilitation" to more severe penalties, especially in wartime.[3]

A Masterpiece of Spin

Anybody who had watched the Bush team in action knew how it would respond: a fierce defense, followed by a rapid reversion to attack mode. It moved quickly to suppress the Guard story, and then to destroy the messengers. Then it seized the offensive and raised doubts about Kerry's service as a soldier in Vietnam. It was a staggering display of chutzpah, and like a refresher course in Psy-Ops 101.

The first part—diverting inquiry into Bush's missing two years of National Guard duty—was particularly challenging. But the Bush team was primed for challenges.

No sooner had McAuliffe fired his "AWOL" salvo than the White House communications apparatus swung into action. It tried to overwhelm the media by dumping large quantities of military records, usually on short notice. Many of these records turned out to be duplicates of previous releases from 2000; sometimes there were multiple copies within a single set. In some cases, journalists were allowed to look at documents but not make copies. The Bush team understood media time pressures and overburdened reporters, and leveraged those liabilities to its advantage.

The White House also depended on friendly journalists to ask safe questions and run out the clock. There was punishment and virtual exile from Republican campaign sources for those who demanded answers.

Meanwhile, stonewalling was the order of the day. Suddenly, military offices of all types, used to routinely responding to reporters' requests, were indicating that their hands were tied. In general, all inquiries to military offices were redirected, without explanation, to the Pentagon, starting in mid-February. "If it has to do with George W. Bush, the Texas Air National Guard or the Vietnam War, I can't talk with you," Charles Gross, chief historian for the National Guard Bureau in Washington, D.C., told reporters from the Spokane, Washington, *Spokesman-Review*.[4]

None of this erased the fundamental dilemma. There were abundant indications that in May 1972, when he abruptly left Houston for Alabama, the future president and commander in chief had simply walked away from his National Guard duty during the Vietnam War. No amount of equivocation could get around that. Neither could an honorable discharge received in 1973 explain why the sole evidence he had actually shown up anywhere after May 1972 was a machine-generated form listing dates and points earned. The fact was, his own officers had not seen him in Texas, and no credible documentation or witnesses emerged in Alabama.

A related issue was his failure to continue piloting a military jet for the full six-year period of his contract. Though he was supposed to serve as a pilot through 1974, Bush's last time in a cockpit was in April 1972. The Bush White House explained that W. had stopped flying because to continue he would have needed to take an annual flight physical. It was almost laughable, but surprisingly effective in obscuring the central point: Bush had simply left his Houston unit without taking the required physical. He just hadn't bothered; and so it was his own action—or rather inaction—that had led to the end of his flying career. On that basis alone, he was essentially AWOL. Bush had made an effort to join a postal unit in the Alabama Guard. When he was rejected as "ineligible," he got permission to join a flying unit in which he would not be required to fly—where, as best as can be determined, he never even bothered to show up.

In short, Bush abruptly stopped flying, walked away from his unit, failed to take a physical, and, all credible evidence indicates, never again put in a day of service. This, as we have seen, became a problem three decades later. In 2003, Bush was ordering thousands of National Guardsmen into battle in Iraq and Afghanistan—including large numbers from Texas. Few of these part-timers had ever expected to see combat abroad, just as W. himself hadn't. Many of them felt poorly prepared.[5] In interviews, they said that they had had only a few weeks of specialized training and that they had begged for more, in vain. In addition, they complained about inadequate equipment and vehicle armor. One Guard soldier described how his unit lacked even a basic handbook on tactical procedures, much less any briefing on the complicated social fabric of Iraq. In other words, they were sitting ducks.

During this period, the published lists of military casualties in Iraq frequently included Guardsmen. And here was evidence that their commander in chief, the one who had ordered them to duty, had apparently skipped out when it had been his turn to serve, even though it was a cushy assignment that involved practically no physical danger.

REGARDING BUSH'S FAILURE to take his flight physical in 1972, his political handlers presented an array of inadequate and conflicting explanations. During the 2000 presidential campaign, a spokesman stated that Bush did not take the exam prior to his birthday in July 1972 as required because he was in Alabama at the time while his personal physician was back in Texas. That answer was misleading at best. Only authorized flight surgeons could perform the physical, and such surgeons were certainly available in Alabama. And if Bush believed that *any* doctor could perform the physical— i.e., not just his personal one—why didn't he simply go to a doctor in Alabama?

By 2004, the Bush team was putting forward a new excuse. White House communications director Dan Bartlett said Bush had failed to take the physical because he knew he would be on nonflying status in Alabama. That was not credible either, since it was not up to Bush to make that decision. Besides, according to regulations, the physical exam was compulsory for all inducted pilots in the Air National Guard, whether or not they were actively flying at the time.

Some reporters tried to dig deeper, but most ended up getting spun. Dan Bartlett worked backward. Bush's honorable discharge, he said, couldn't have come about unless Bush had attained the required number of annual service points—and you couldn't get the required number of service points without showing up. This argument neatly finessed the possibility that high-ranking Guard officials had manufactured an honorable discharge for a favored son of a favorite son. At the time, Richard Nixon was in the White House, Poppy was head of the Republican Party, and the D.C. offices of the National Guard were notoriously politicized. Indeed, the director would later resign in disgrace over favoritism-related charges.

Besides, as everyone knew, if you could get into the Guard through politics, you could get out the same way. The unsubstantiated points sheet of unknown provenance could easily have been manufactured during this period. And even the honorable discharge itself was questionable on its face. W. got it eight months *before* his service obligation ended. It didn't take a cynical opposition researcher to raise an eyebrow.

The main problem for Bush was simply the lack of hard evidence that he had ever set foot on the Montgomery base during his six months in Alabama. Several supposed eyewitnesses did surface to support Bush, but their claims were less than convincing. For example, one member of the Montgomery-based unit in which Bush was supposed to serve did his best to back up the president in an interview with the *Birmingham News*:

> Joe LeFevers, a member of the 187th in 1972, said he remembers seeing Bush in unit offices and being told that Bush was in Montgomery to work on Blount's campaign.
>
> "I was going in the orderly room over there one day, and they said, 'This is Lt. Bush,'" LeFevers said Tuesday. "They pointed him out to me . . . The reason I remember it is because I associate him with Red Blount."[6]

The account is sketchy at best. Yet apparently, reporters never tried to confirm LeFevers's account, nor to ascertain his credibility or possible motivations, which is standard journalistic practice. Instead, Bush's defenders quickly spread the LeFevers story around the Internet and talk circuit.

Another "witness" would make an appearance by the end of this crucial week, in the *Washington Post*:

A Republican close to Bush supplied phone numbers yesterday for
an owner of an insulated-coating business in the Atlanta area, John
B. "Bill" Calhoun, 69, who was an officer with the Alabama Air
National Guard. Calhoun said in an interview that Bush used to sit
in his office and read magazines and flight manuals as he performed weekend duty at Dannelly Field in Montgomery during
1972. Calhoun estimated that he saw Bush sign in at the 187th Tactical Reconnaissance Group eight to 10 times for about eight hours
each from May to October 1972. He said the two occasionally
grabbed a sandwich in the snack bar.[7]

Calhoun, the unit's flight safety officer, told the Associated Press: "I saw
him each drill period. He was very aggressive about doing his duty there . . .
He showed up on time and he left at the end of the day." Inconveniently,
however, even Bush himself would not claim to have done duty in Alabama
during the summer months. Someone had perhaps forgotten to coordinate
the stories. Still, the White House did not disavow Calhoun's claims. Calhoun even came with a sidekick—a doctor friend who claimed that the officer had brought Bush to him for a physical.

But again, there was no documentation that any physical exam had actually been performed. And again, not even Bush was claiming that. It turned
out that the doctor himself wasn't even making the claim. It was the doctor's
son who spoke to a reporter for the Montgomery Advertiser—because, he
said, at age sixty-four, his father could not handle the volume of inquiries.

Meanwhile, NBC News introduced another witness, of sorts:

> CORRESPONDENT DAVID GREGORY: Joe Holcombe, who worked
>   with Mr. Bush on that Alabama Senate campaign, does recall
>   asking why Mr. Bush was absent from a meeting.
> JOE HOLCOMBE: I just innocently asked where George was, since
>   he wasn't there, and then I was told that he was at a National
>   Guard [drill] that weekend.

Holcombe wasn't claiming that he knew Bush was doing Guard training,
or even that Bush had told him so, only that a third party had said that he
was. This did not stop the White House from pointing Holcombe out as an
"eyewitness" of sorts, and reporters began citing him.

On February 12, 2004, things started to get really knotty for Bush. MSNBC's *Hardball* featured Lieutenant Colonel Bill Burkett, the former Texas National Guard consultant who recounted his claim to have personally observed efforts to clean up Bush's records.

> I witnessed the governor's office call to the adjutant general of the Texas National Guard, [giving him] a directive to gather the files. And then the subscript to that was make sure there was nothing there that would embarrass the governor . . .
>
> I witnessed that in fact there was some activity under way with some files of—some personal files of "Bush, George W., First Lieutenant," "1LT" as it was put in handwriting at the top of files within a trash can . . .
>
> The orders came in a telephone call with Mr. Joe Allbaugh, chief of staff of the governor's office. Mr. Dan Bartlett [Bush's communications director] was also on that telephone call.[8]

Bartlett denied the allegations, and Allbaugh called them "hogwash," but they reinforced the sense of sketchiness about the president's version. If he had done his duty, why had so few people actually seen him? The Burkett story soon jumped into the print media, where the *New York Times* noted that Burkett had first made the allegation way back in 1998 in a letter to a Texas state senator. Then the story made the *CBS Evening News*.

A distraction was urgently needed, and the White House dug deep. Within minutes of the Burkett *Hardball* appearance, it came up with a new military record, this one purporting to show that Bush had visited a dentist, Dr. John Andrew Harris, at Dannelly Field Air National Guard Base in Montgomery on January 6, 1973—well after he had finished working on the Alabama campaign and returned to Texas.

The dentist visit became important corroboration—if not that Bush had done his Guard duty in Alabama during the summer and fall of 1972, at least that he had been present on an Alabama base at some point. The following day, building on the dental visit record, Scott McClellan declared that Bush now recalled returning to Alabama for additional Guard service even though he was no longer living there.[9] As reported by the *New York Times*:

Asked about the 16 members of the 187th who do not remember Mr. Bush serving in Alabama, Mr. McClellan responded that Mr. Bush's dental examination "demonstrates that he was serving in Alabama."[10]

A high school reporter might have had some questions. Yet it seemed to satisfy the major media. ABC's *World News Tonight with Peter Jennings* took the new White House bait. Terry Moran reported, "That puts Mr. Bush in Alabama, on duty, and seems to disprove the charge by Democratic Party leader Terry McAuliffe and others that the president was AWOL at that time."[11]

The same night, *NBC Nightly News* reported: "The White House has released a copy of a dental exam from January 1973 that they say confirms President Bush served at an Alabama air base."[12]

But there was more to work with in McClellan's press conference (again, the *New York Times*):

> Mr. McClellan also said that at least two people recalled Mr. Bush serving in Alabama, among them Joe Holcombe, who worked on the Senate campaign with Mr. Bush, and Emily Marks Curtis, who has said she briefly dated Mr. Bush in Alabama.[13]

So now McClellan had folded in Holcombe, despite the gauziness of his claim—and gotten it into the *New York Times*. And now there was a girlfriend too.

At that press conference, McClellan pointed to an article that had just appeared in the *Times Daily*, an Alabama newspaper (and in its sister papers, including the *Tuscaloosa News*). The article quotes Emily Marks Curtis talking about Bush and his Guard service.

The substance of her brief remarks got a vigorous buffing. First, the Alabama newspaper misrepresented what she said. Then McClellan cited that misrepresentation, and finally it was accepted by the *New York Times* and other media organizations.

Here's how the *Tuscaloosa News* opened its story, headlined "Friend: Bush Did Duty in Alabama":

> A friend of President Bush on Wednesday corroborated Bush's contention that he reported for National Guard training in Alabama in 1972, despite the lack of official supporting records.

In fact, the quote from Emily Marks Curtis did not corroborate Bush in any way. Rather, it suggested the need for further inquiry that might have found that Bush had in fact *not* done his Alabama Guard service:

> "The thing I know about George is that after the election was over in November, George left and he said he came back to Montgomery to do his guard duty," Curtis said. She said she and Bush, then a first lieutenant in the Texas Air National Guard, dated briefly.[14]

Her statement actually said that Bush left Alabama as soon as the election was over, then returned *some time later*, at which time he *told* Emily Marks Curtis that he had come back to do his Guard duty. As the Bush-friendly interpretation gained circulation, Emily Marks Curtis would often be characterized as Bush's girlfriend. That seemed to give greater credibility to her ability to vouch for Bush, since, presumably, a girlfriend would know whether he had actually been doing military service. Seven months later, with the 2004 general election nearing, she was still being presented that way.

Here's the *New York Times* on September 20, 2004:

> Ms. Marks, the daughter of an old Montgomery family, was dating George Bush, and she remembers that he was in the Guard but could offer no detailed recollections. "A lot of people were doing Guard duty," she said in an interview.[15]

Yet Emily Marks Curtis had not been Bush's girlfriend. The two had not even dated during the six months they both worked on the Blount campaign. Several campaign staffers, including Devere McLennan, who was friendly with Bush, confirmed that to me. In fact, the only time the two went out was during that brief period when Bush came back to Alabama—in early January 1973.

So here's the full extent of the Emily Marks Curtis–dental connection: When Bush returned briefly to Alabama, he did three things. He called up Emily Marks and asked her out. He told her he was in town for Guard duty. And he went to get a dental checkup.

For the complete story, you'd have to ask Poppy Bush. As noted in chapter 8, the events in this period suggest that it was the father's idea that his son go to Alabama in the first place, and his idea also that his son go *back* to Alabama and have the dental checkup at the military base—along with a "date" with a local girl to confirm his presence in the state.

The Bush camp would insist that the dental visit established Bush's presence on an Alabama base on a single day, and thus somehow supported his claim to have done his Guard service. Despite the meagerness of the evidence, much of the media was apparently persuaded, with the result that the Guard story seemed to gradually die down at that point.

When I talked to people who worked in the dental clinic, they could not remember such a routine exam from decades ago, which was not surprising. However, I did learn that they would have treated *anyone* who walked in wearing a flight jacket (Bush never relinquished his and liked to wear it publicly for many years thereafter). They would not have required him to present evidence that he was serving in an Alabama Guard unit, or even that he had done so in the past.

So the dental exam proved only that W. had a flight jacket and was wearing it on a particular day in Alabama. Yet the media reported the story as though it corroborated Bush's account.

Within a couple of weeks of that media frenzy in February 2004, *Doonesbury* creator Garry Trudeau upped the ante. In his syndicated newspaper comic strip, he offered a ten-thousand-dollar reward to anyone who claimed he or she had "personally witnessed" Bush reporting for drills at Dannelly Air National Guard base in Alabama between May and November 1972. No one did so. (Seven months later, in September 2004, a group called Texans for Truth went further and offered fifty thousand dollars to anyone who could prove President Bush had fulfilled his service requirements, including mandatory duties and drills, in the Alabama Air National Guard in 1972. No one claimed that either. This reward was offered just as Bush traveled to Las Vegas to address the National Guard Association's convention.)

By March 2004, Texas television reporter James Moore published *Bush's War for Reelection: Iraq, the White House and the People*. The new book examined Burkett's allegations and explored in the most detail ever the specific documentation surrounding Bush's service record. Moore, too, concluded that Bush had been AWOL beginning in May 1972.

Eyewitness News

More than anything, Bush needed former members of the Champagne Unit to assert that he had been an exemplary airman until the moment he left for Alabama. This would suggest that there was nothing questionable about his abrupt departure and justify his honorable discharge. For that, he had a core group that he had been cultivating since his early days as governor, through help with legal and personal problems, among other things. Four men would supply most of the quotes on Bush's service.[16] A fifth witness was Jim Bath, Bush's fellow pilot, drinking buddy, and later, business investor, who provided early quotes and then essentially went underground. Unlike the others, Bath was close enough to both George Bushes that he needed no cue cards to know what to say. But Bath had so many liabilities himself that eventually he was removed from the witness list.

Certainly the most interesting of Bush's witnesses were Major Dean Roome and Colonel Maury H. Udell. Together they did much to keep a lid on the Guard story straight through the 2004 election. Roome, who claimed to have been Bush's formation flying partner and roommate during full-time fighter pilot training, provided journalists, including myself, with bland accounts of a fellow who never did anything interesting. "He was very friendly, and outgoing, affable, fun to be around, and, uh, just an overall super good guy," Roome told me.[17]

Roome's sidekick, Maury Udell, had been George Bush's flight instructor at Ellington Field. Bush would devote only a few pages to his Guard service in his autobiography, *A Charge to Keep*, but Udell was singled out for praise. Bush described him as a tough and exacting instructor, a "270-pound black belt in judo" who required "blindfold" position checks for the plane's instruments. While Bush's flattering autobiography was in the works, Udell in turn was ladling out admiring reports on Bush to reporters. "He had his boots shined, his uniform pressed, his hair cut and he said, 'Yes, sir' and 'No, sir,' Udell would recall. "I would rank him in the top 5 percent of pilots I knew. And in the thinking department, he was in the top 1 percent. He was very capable and tough as a boot."[18]

Reporters who quoted Roome, Udell, and Walter "Buck" Staudt, Bush's top commanding officer, did not know that they were not independent witnesses. Besides being avid Bush boosters, Roome and Udell were hoping that Governor Bush would help them address lingering problems with the Texas National Guard, while Staudt was embroiled in his own little scandal.[19]

The three stayed in regular contact with Bush's staff, and reported any and all inquiries from the media. Roome in particular became part of an e-mail chain that served as a nerve center and feedback loop. It included Bush campaign (and later White House) staff as well as top Guard officials. The e-mail chain could give Bush's operatives information on media inquiries and stories in the works, and also receive "talking points" and defensive strategies. The list, with blind copies to recipients, grew to the extent that the talking points were being shared not only with pilots but with many of the country's top conservative talk show hosts as well.

A Roome with a View

The story that became colloquially known as "Memogate" or "Rathergate" is understood by many people as about a news organization that used phony documents to tar President Bush's military service record. It was, in this telling, a prime example of media bias. What actually happened was that an accusation against Bush—probably an accurate one—was used to hang his accusers. It was a brilliant exercise in disinformation; and like so many matters we have encountered, it has "covert operation" written all over it.

It began in March 2004, when, with John Kerry holding an eight-point lead in the polls, W. flew to Houston to reinvigorate his base.[20] The scene was quintessentially Texan: the Houston Livestock Show and Rodeo. "I thought there was a lot of bull in *Washington*," W. chortled, donning the obligatory cowboy hat and gazing admiringly at prize heifers.[21] W. also attended a fund-raiser at a nearby Hilton Hotel. But two events not on the press itinerary were more significant and telling. In a private Hilton suite away from prying eyes, W. held court with some old buddies he hadn't seen in a long while: his former fellow pilots from the Texas National Guard.

Bush flattered, seduced, and wheedled. The country needed to stick together at this difficult time, he said. And, heck, if a president couldn't count on old chums to back him, whom could he trust? To the dozen or so in attendance, the message was clear: you'll be hearing from reporters and dirt-diggers, and we need you to close ranks. "We had the president of the United States give us essentially a national security briefing [on Iraq]," recalled Dean Roome. "I was very thrilled that somebody of his stature would take time out of his day."[22]

The meeting did not come to light until after the election, in an interview between Roome and Corey Pein of the *Columbia Journalism Review*. Roome told Pein that between briefings on Iraq and Afghanistan, "there was a lot of joking around, slapping on the back. Weird to call him Mr. President but we did." He added, "It made you feel pretty important, getting briefed by the president on world affairs." When Pein visited with Roome, a photograph of Roome's meeting with Bush hung on the wall.

While W. was at the livestock show, so too was his nemesis Bill Burkett. The retired officer and rancher was expecting a package. In early March, according to Burkett, he had received a call from a man who instructed him to call a Houston Holiday Inn that night and speak with a guest named Lucy Ramirez. When he got Ramirez on the line, she told him that she was an intermediary whose responsibility was to deliver to him a packet of documents.

During that phone call Ramirez had asked if Burkett would be in Houston anytime soon. He replied that he would be there in two weeks to attend the Houston livestock show, where he displayed and sold his prize Simmenthal cattle and promoted the bull semen that was a source of income for ranchers.

In Houston, Burkett was approached by a man who could have been Hispanic, who handed him a legal-sized envelope—presumably the man associated with "Lucy Ramirez." (A woman in the next booth confirmed to two reporters that a man approached Burkett and gave him an envelope.) That package would turn out to be metaphorical dynamite, and in a few months it would blow up in the faces of quite a few people—including Burkett, Mary Mapes, and the TV correspondent and news anchor Dan Rather.

A Swift Boot

The Bush forces began to regain the campaign offensive in May. That month, a day after John Kerry unveiled a twenty-seven-million-dollar advertising campaign highlighting his Vietnam service, a new group calling itself the Swift Boat Veterans for Truth held its first press conference.

One of Karl Rove's basic tenets is that you attack an opponent at their point of strength. Kerry, oblivious to this, had led with his proverbial chin, and rested his campaign first and foremost upon his status as a decorated veteran of the Vietnam War. That is where the Swift Boat cadre went to work and eventually demolished the most threatening point of comparison between Kerry and Bush.

To be sure, Kerry had invited the venom from some of his fellow Swift Boat officers. He had authorized the historian Douglas Brinkley to write a book about his military service, in which he criticized several fellow officers. One of them was Roy Hoffmann, the former commander who up until then had been friendly to Kerry. It is quite possible that this slight played a role in Kerry's defeat. It did not matter that even John O'Neill, a lead figure in the Swift Boat Veterans for Truth, apparently did not think much of George W. Bush either. "He always referred to him in private as 'an empty suit,'" recalled Bill White, who was a law client of O'Neill's.

The anger these men felt toward Kerry was catnip for the Republican attack operation, and before long, hardened pros were helping spread their anti-Kerry message. George W. Bush's biggest backers footed the lion's share of the bill—even though the anti-Kerry groups supposedly were independent. There were million-dollar-plus infusions from a cast of characters straight out of Dickens. From builders of houses whose roofs routinely caved in to leading emitters of cancer-causing substances, these moneymen were kept way in the background while public relations experts quietly directed grizzled veterans before the cameras.

The Swift Boat vets themselves had plenty of Bush connections. One legal adviser, Benjamin Ginsberg, had been serving as national counsel for W.'s presidential campaign. The vets' advertising production team was the same one that had helped mock Michael Dukakis for Poppy in 1988. And the biggest donor to the Swift Boaters was Texas homebuilder Bob Perry, a longtime friend and associate of Karl Rove.[23] Rove and the White House insisted that they had nothing to do with it. No one could prove otherwise.

To its credit, the mainstream media approached the claims with skepticism. (A study by the organization Media Matters found that only one of the fifteen major newspaper editorial boards gave credence to the charges of the Swift Boat Veterans.[24]) However, on cable TV and in the blogosphere, the accusations raged twenty-four hours a day for weeks. This was especially true after the release in August of the book *Unfit for Command: Swift Boat Veterans Speak Out Against John Kerry*, published by Regnery, which media critic and former conservative journalist David Brock describes as "a right-wing Washington house that filled the best-seller lists in the 1990s with a slew of largely fictional anti-Clinton tracts packaged as nonfiction."[25] The various arms of

Rupert Murdoch's News Corporation—especially Fox News and the *New York Post*—helped push the book into bestseller territory.

This was a serious problem for Kerry. At the 2004 Democratic Convention, noted Frank Rich, he "placed most, if not all, of his chips on presenting himself as a military hero."[26] It was not exactly brilliant strategy. In effect he was making himself the issue, rather than the incumbent Bush. Making matters worse, when the Swift Boaters attacked, Kerry did virtually nothing, thus confirming the popular impression that he was actually a wimp who wouldn't hit back. Instead, he gave news photographers a photo op of himself windsurfing off Nantucket, thus suggesting that he was an elitist wimp to boot. He decided he didn't want to dignify the smear with a response, thus conceding the spin war to the attackers.

Eventually, other Swift boat veterans surfaced to defend Kerry, but the damage had been done. Kerry's service had become the issue, rather than W.'s failure to serve. It was a psy-ops coup, and just a warm-up to what was ahead.

The Chase Is On

After the February scrum, the pack of journalists looking at Bush's service record had quickly diminished. Among the small band who continued was Mary Mapes, the Dallas-based CBS producer who had scored a big success earlier in the year by breaking the story about the Abu Ghraib prisoner abuse. (Despite the CBS scoop, investigative reporter Seymour Hersh and the *New Yorker* now receive, and deserve, the lion's share of the credit for exposing the scandal, because CBS initially bowed to the Pentagon's request not to broadcast the prison abuse photos. The network only went ahead when it learned that Hersh's article was about to run—and only the *New Yorker* ran the pictures.) But now Mapes was back on the Guard story.

As for Bill Burkett, he had hidden away his little care package. But by summer, rumors began circulating about the existence of documents that could explain or corroborate W.'s missing service record. According to Burkett, "Lucy Ramirez" had instructed him to handle the documents in a precise manner, and made him promise that he would do so. He was to copy the documents, and then burn the originals, along with the envelope they had come in.[27] Ramirez made Burkett promise to keep her identity—and her role in providing the documents—a secret.

Burkett claims to have done exactly as he was told. Though Burkett had personal axes to grind with Bush, given his military history and his own fierce sense of honor, many reporters considered his story credible. Burkett said he believed that Ramirez's insistence that he burn the materials was for security reasons—to remove any traces of DNA, which might expose whoever originally obtained them.

As the temperature rose around the story, various reporters from the *New York Times*, *Vanity Fair*, *USA Today*, and other news organizations sought a piece of the action. But *60 Minutes II* had the inside track. What happened next morphed into an epic scandal that would soon overwhelm questions about Bush, and influence media coverage for the rest of the election. There would be many casualties: CBS anchorman Rather, producer Mapes, and three other CBS staffers were fired or dismissed. Bill Burkett would become a pariah, and his life would collapse around him. As such, he became yet another in a long line of people who had stood up to the Bushes and suffered the consequences.

A Texas-based freelance researcher, Mike Smith, on retainer for CBS, had been communicating with Burkett, and as the document rumors grew, he began pressing the former Guard official for concrete evidence. In late August, Burkett agreed to meet with Mapes and Smith. Burkett, accompanied by his wife, brought a huge stack of documents, many of them pertaining to his own history with the Guard, to their rendezvous at a pizza parlor in rural West Texas. The CBS team suffered through Burkett's agonizingly extensive preliminaries and finally pressed him to get to the matter at hand.

Burkett reached into a blue folder and pulled out a sheet of paper, dated August 1, 1972. It appeared to be an order from Bush's superior, Lieutenant Colonel Jerry Killian, suspending Bush both for "failure to meet annual physical examination as ordered" and for "failure to perform to USAF/Tex ANG standards." It said that Bush "has made no attempt to meet his training certification or flight physical" and that he "expresses desire to transfer out of state including assignment to non-flying billets." It also referred to his pilot status as "critical."

Burkett showed Mapes and Smith a second, related document (and three days later would provide another four). Mapes read the two documents with growing excitement, and then focused on the reportorial issue: how to get copies. Burkett, however, was ambivalent. He told Mapes he was worried about the consequences of getting into a renewed dustup with the president of the United States. His wife, Nicki, was even more reticent. After a show of what Mapes took to be great anguish—perhaps it was—Burkett released the documents.

If there was a single moment at which things went off track for Mary Mapes and CBS, this was it. Mapes was elated at the appearance of manna from heaven, as most reporters would be. The documents comported with what she knew of Bush's military service based on years of reporting. Now she had what seemed to be concrete evidence. Her main concern at the moment was to get out of the pizza joint before Burkett changed his mind. Every second seemed like an hour. The group drove to a Kinko's copy center in Abilene, the nearest large town, and her heart beating, Mapes faxed the documents to New York.

Mapes instructed an associate there to begin the crucial process of vetting—to the extent that it is possible to verify such photocopies. The documents were presented to a handful of experts, from a CBS military consultant to independent document examiners around the country. After scrutinizing the materials in New York, and comparing the purported Killian signatures with verified ones found on other official documents, handwriting expert Marcel Matley told Mapes that he felt that, on balance, the memo signatures seemed to be authentic. Colonel David Hackworth, a CBS consultant and the most decorated living soldier in the United States, gave his overview of what the documents suggested to him about Bush: "He was AWOL."[28]

The sentiment was not universal. It was exceedingly difficult to establish with any degree of certainty whether the documents were real. For one thing, Burkett had presented the reporters with copies, not originals. That eliminated telltale signs of authenticity such as age of paper, an ink signature, and evidence of the model of typewriter used. Furthermore, as a copy is further copied, other clues become degraded. With each generation, details such as spacing and even the appearance of letters begin to change subtly.

What Burkett gave to Mapes was at best a copy of an original, and perhaps a copy of a copy. What CBS New York received by fax from Abilene and sent to several document examiners was a generation worse. Then there were issues surrounding the skills required to judge these copies. One needed some kind of expertise in specialized military procedure and jargon from a particular time frame, as well as a detailed knowledge of the history of typography. Could such documents have been produced in 1972? One could not prove them real beyond question, but could they be proven fake? In a somewhat parallel case, the distinguished investigative reporter Seymour Hersh had used what he believed to be letters from Marilyn Monroe to sign a $2.5 million contract with ABC for a new Kennedy documentary.[29] Then someone noticed that the letters contained a five-digit zip code, though those had not yet been invented.[30]

Mapes desperately wanted more time. But CBS executives, under competitive pressures, decided that the story had to air within a few days. Other news organizations were pressing Burkett for the documents, and there were scheduling issues as well. The CBS brass didn't want to be scooped.

The Bloggers Who Ate CBS

60 Minutes II had a monumental broadcast planned for September 8, 2004. In the middle of a tight election, the program was prepared to challenge the veracity of a sitting president's military service. Former Texas lieutenant governor Ben Barnes was ready to tell the story of how he kept W. from getting drafted. And Dan Rather was ready to present the documents that would finally help answer the broadcast's tantalizing question: "So what happened with Mr. Bush, the draft and the National Guard?"[31]

Within 30 seconds of the documents appearing on television screens, one Internet user was already posting his doubts. An active Air Force officer, Paul Boley—who was serving in Montgomery, Alabama, the same place George W. Bush had been in 1972—was the first to weigh in. On the right-wing Web site FreeRepublic.com, using the pseudonymous handle TankerKC, Boley wrote:

> WE NEED TO SEE THOSE MEMOS AGAIN!
> They are not in the style that we used when I came in to the USAF. They looked like the style and format we started using about 12 years ago (1992). Our signature blocks were left justified, now they are rigth [sic] of center . . . like the ones they just showed.
> Can we get a copy of those memos?[32]

Less than four hours after Boley's post came a more "authoritative" statement of doubt from a fellow FreeRepublic.com poster—a group that self-identify as "FReepers"—calling himself "Buckhead."

Every single one of these memos to file is in a proportionally spaced font, probably Palatino or Times New Roman.

In 1972 people used typewriters for this sort of thing, and typewriters used monospaced fonts.

The use of proportionally spaced fonts did not come into common use for office memos until the introduction of laser printers, word processing software, and personal computers. They were not widespread until the mid to late 90's. Before then, you needed typesetting equipment, and that wasn't used for personal memos to file. Even the Wang systems that were dominant in the mid 80's used monospaced fonts.

I am saying these documents are forgeries, run through a copier for 15 generations to make them look old.

This should be pursued aggressively.[33]

And it was. In the wee hours, the discussion began to spread across the blogosphere. First it was picked up by two conservative blogs, Power Line and Little Green Footballs. It went quickly from blogs to online magazines, starting with Rupert Murdoch's conservative opinion publication the *Weekly Standard*, which cited document experts who pronounced the memos probable forgeries.[34] The story didn't linger in the blogosphere or opinion media, but leaped right to the commercial outlets.

Twenty-four hours after the story aired, Buckhead proclaimed triumph back on the FreeRepublic.com message board:

Victory in this case justly has a thousand fathers. Tanker KC first pegged them as fakes by the overall look, and I later noted the font issue. Many other defects have been noted by others. I haven't gotten any work done, but it's been a ton of fun. The most amazing thing is how this thing has exploded across the internet.
Mwuhahahahaha!!![35]

Another commenter chimed in with:

Isn't this cool? It's on the front page of tomorrow's Washington Post! Great work![36]

As one "FReeper" posted:

With all due respect, this event showcases a phenomenon of "new media" power that could only have occurred through a vehicle with the community force multiplying tools of FR [Free Republic].

... No single blog can rally a rapid response over a huge number of vital issues like FR can. This forum is, to use a trite old 90s term, synergy at its most powerful.

Places like FR (in other words FR because it is inimitable) and the blogosphere can work in concert. We're the town square arguing, vetting and digesting, they're the disseminating REPORTERS of valuable insights, leads and other interesting stuff we shake loose.[37]

MEANWHILE, *LOS ANGELES* Times reporter Peter Wallsten did some digging, and unearthed Buckhead's identity.[38] He was Harry MacDougald, an activist Republican lawyer in Atlanta and a member of the Federalist Society, a conservative law group. He played coy with the *Times*, declining to tell the reporter how he was able to create his critique so quickly, and failing to explain the basis for his expertise in the matter.

Another aspect, this one not reported by the *L.A. Times*, was the manner in which MacDougald's critique was amplified. Shortly after he posted under a pseudonym, his wife, posting under her own name, Liz MacDougald, and making no mention of their connection, recommended his post to Power Line, which propelled the story further. Actually, there were two people who did so. The other, Tom Mortensen, was also deeply involved with the Swift Boat group.

Whether the response to the memos was coordinated beyond that is difficult to say. Boley (TankerKC) told me in an interview that he had seen the *60 Minutes* show by accident, as his wife just happened to turn the set on. He could post his suspicions so quickly, he said, because his computer was on and just steps away. He said that as a career Air Force officer, he noticed instantly that the position of the signature block was based on military protocol that existed only since 1992, and that the memo header deviated from standard.

Regardless of the intentions of the posters and the merits of the arguments about the authenticity of the documents, the story of the backstory took on a life of its own. Soon more people were convinced that Dan Rather and Mary Mapes had done something wrong than that Bush had. Lost in all this was the fact that the documents merely confirmed what reporters had already concluded from their own investigative work. Indeed, the *New York Times* had asked CBS if it could co-report the memo content and break the story at the same time. And *USA Today* published the documents the morning after CBS aired its story—though it did not face the firestorm or consequences that CBS did.

USA Today later turned on Burkett and CBS—claiming that, in exchange for providing the documents, Burkett had asked Mapes to put him in touch with the Kerry campaign. Mapes said she merely called the Democrats, with her boss's permission, to check out a claim Burkett had made about how he had offered them advice on responding to the Swift Boat attacks. It was a tempest in a beer can, but again, it became an Internet sensation.[39]

The Independent Panel

Faced with a growing storm, CBS initially stood firm. Two days later, on its Web site, the company declared:

> This report was not based solely on recovered documents, but rather on a preponderance of evidence, including documents that were provided by unimpeachable sources, interviews with former Texas National Guard officials and individuals who worked closely back in the early 1970s with Colonel Jerry Killian and were well acquainted with his procedures, his character and his thinking.

On CBS *Evening News with Dan Rather*, the old warhorse echoed that, and added, "If any definitive evidence to the contrary is found, we will report it." But for the time being, he said, "There is none."

As the criticism mounted, though, CBS News president Andrew Heyward was demanding answers. One of the questions, to Burkett, was about the source of the documents. In the days after Mapes faxed them from Abilene, she had barraged Burkett with demands that he reveal his source. Finally, grudgingly, he had identified George Conn, a friend from the National Guard, who divided his time between Germany and Texas. Mapes had tried repeatedly to reach Conn for confirmation, without success.

But now that the story had exploded, Burkett admitted to Heyward that he had only told Mapes the Conn story to get her off his back, because he had promised not to reveal the involvement of Lucy Ramirez. Now the Ramirez version—supposedly the truthful one—came out.

But was this the real story? As I later learned, there was a Hispanic couple who had worked for the Guard, could have had access to the files of the late Lieutenant Colonel Killian, and were a possible match for the pseudonymous Ramirezes. Their surname was even similar. When I visited their home in Houston, the woman seemed to know exactly why I was there. She cryptically explained that her husband had prohibited her from speaking about the matter. I noticed what seemed to be their recent good fortune: they had apparently just moved into a brand-new house in a brand-new housing development, and had a brand-new car out front. Beyond that, there was little by way of clues, let alone answers.

Meanwhile, CBS's parent company was shifting into damage-control mode. On September 22, two weeks after the program aired, CBS announced plans to convene an "independent review panel" headed by pedigreed outsiders. The two big names on the panel created for this purpose turned out to be former U.S. attorney general Richard Thornburgh and former Associated Press chief Lou Boccardi. Thornburgh was a particularly odd choice, considering that he had been attorney general during Poppy Bush's administration. Thornburgh, who had briefly made headlines back then for ordering the statues of scantily clad females on display in the Justice Department modestly draped on official occasions, was back on the morals beat. During the CBS inquiry, he expressed keen interest in Mapes's use of salty language. "Did you use the word 'horseshit'? Was that really appropriate in a newsroom?"

After retiring from the AP, Boccardi had been retained by the *New York Times* to investigate the fabrications of its reporter Jayson Blair. But he remained almost entirely silent during the closed panel hearings. He only asked two questions, including, "When did you realize the documents had been faked?" When Mike Smith replied that it had not been established that the documents were counterfeit, the panel lawyers laughed at him.

Although Smith had been assured that CBS had his best interests at heart, and that the company would look out for him, it soon became apparent that he was raw meat. To Smith, it felt like a McCarthy hearing. The panelists were concerned that Smith had worked for the late columnist Molly Ivins. They even asked if he had ghostwritten columns for Ivins, which was unlikely, since Ivins had one of the nation's most distinctive—and idiosyncratic—writing styles. There also was a question about a hundred-dollar donation to a fund-raiser for a liver transplant involving a liberal partisan.

Potential bias could have been relevant, but it unquestionably is a secondary consideration behind truth. Nevertheless, the upshot became clear: CBS was going to cover its own behind by portraying its reporters as anti-Bush liberals who didn't deserve the company's support. The network did nothing to defend the principles of journalistic inquiry. Still less did CBS get past the procedural missteps of its employees to resolve the underlying factual issues of the Guard story—as Mary Mapes herself had wanted to do. No formal inquiry by military and document experts was ever convened, and to this day the question of whether the documents are forgeries hasn't been resolved.

CBS-Viacom CEO Sumner Redstone, whose company was facing crucial regulatory decisions by Bush's Federal Communications Commission, admitted his "severe distress" at the Rather report.[40] He noted his belief "that a Republican administration is better for media companies than a Democratic one."[41]

In the end, what mattered most was this: the documents were either real or they were forgeries that closely mirrored the reality of Bush's National Guard experience at that point in time. If the latter, then this could mean that they had been concocted with built-in anomalies to set up CBS and Bush's critics. Might that explain why the bloggers were ready to respond so quickly?

On the other hand, if the forgeries were designed by anti-Bush conspirators to *hurt* the president, it wasn't clear how. The memos didn't add a great deal to what reporters had already established, beyond a kind of black-and-white confirmation—though it was enough of an addition to trigger the CBS report. If anti-Bush forgers were going to go to all that trouble, wouldn't they have added some juicy new meat to the rather skeletal facts that were already known?

Lost in all the commotion about the authenticity of the documents and the ethics of the journalists at CBS was this undeniable fact: The overwhelming evidence, even absent these documents, is that the president of the United States had gone absent without leave from his military unit in 1972 and had never been held accountable for that crime.

But in the court of public opinion, the only jurisdiction that counted in this case, it was a trifecta for the defense: CBS, Bill Burkett, and the entire Guard story had been taken out in one fell swoop.

To this day, most Americans think that it was Dan Rather, and not George W. Bush, who did something wrong related to Bush's National Guard service during the Vietnam War. Whatever the truth about those documents, it must be recalled that the Bush family had long expressed deep animus for Dan Rather, who alone among major television newsmen had dared to talk back to them. In a heated 1988 interview, Rather pressed Poppy for details on the Iran-contra scandal, eventually stating, "You made us hypocrites in the face of the world!"[42] There was certainly an effort to destroy Rather in the aftermath of the report on W. That effort to take down one of the most powerful figures in journalism—among the few relatively independent voices in American television—was one of the most successful attempts to intimidate the media in American history.

After the CBS debacle, no news organization wanted to get near anything about Bush and the Guard or Bush and Iraq. In fact, no news organization really felt like being out front with anything critical of Bush at all. They just wanted the whole thing over with.

In September 2004, after the CBS piece aired, I interviewed Janet Linke, the Florida widow of the man who replaced W. in the Champagne Unit after he left for Alabama in 1972. As noted in chapter 8, she told me how Bush's commanding officer, Lieutenant Colonel Killian, had confided to her and her husband that W. had been having trouble operating his plane, and had intimated that it was some combination of nerves and perhaps substance abuse that had led him to depart his unit.

In the end, it was not reporting or truth that triumphed, but the forces of disinformation. Memogate appears to underline the extent to which the cynical techniques of the spy world have leaped the wall and taken root in the processes of American democracy itself.

This is what people like Karl Rove and his allies effectuate on a daily basis. While the media thinks it is reporting an electoral contest with a Madison Avenue gloss, something deeper and more insidious often is going on, largely unexamined. It is fitting that the Bushes, with their long-standing ties to the covert side of things, have been a vehicle through which the political process has been further subverted and the public sandbagged.

And it has worked, time and again. After Mickey Herskowitz shared with me his account of Bush's admissions—on the Guard and on Iraq—I found editors deeply wary about publishing those revelations. Most told me that CBS's experience made tough stories on related subjects essentially radioactive. Without a tape of Bush himself saying something incriminating, it was too dangerous to touch.

The public would be none the wiser, and Bush slid sideways into another narrow victory and another four years in office.

CHAPTER 23

Domestic Disturbance

AS WE HAVE SEEN, A PERCEPTUAL GAP is at the essence of the Bush enterprise. The actuality has tended toward wars for resources and the preservation of class prerogative, all abetted by secrecy, intimidation, and the dark arts of both psychological and covert ops. The appearance has been of a genial Poppy and a born-again if bumptious George W.

Their campaign themes played off these perceptions: compassionate conservatism and an ability to work with political adversaries; a patrician concern for the environment and a desire to balance stewardship of natural resources with private property rights; a desire to shrink the federal government but only so as to empower people to control their own lives and destinies; an aversion to liberal—and costly—nation-building exercises abroad. These were the polemical packages; and in their different ways, both Poppy and son conveyed a sense of rectitude and traditional values, even as their campaigns were run with the hard and cynical calculus of political hit jobs.

Poppy, as mentioned, was more discreet and could be persuaded to act in a responsible manner. An example was when Richard Darman, his budget director, convinced him to raise taxes to help control the deficit. The right never forgave him, and W. was not about to repeat the mistake.

What Poppy had done quietly, even furtively, W. often did with the swagger of the entitled prince. The result was a government that in essence was not unlike those of third world oligarchs—a vehicle for military dominance and bountiful favors for supporters and friends. The ruler would preside unchallenged. Dissonant truths would be suppressed, and the tellers of them banished.

VIRTUALLY THE FIRST order of business after the 2001 inauguration had been to make sure that no nasty secrets came back to embarrass the new occupant of the White House—or his father. Thus began one of the most extraordinary clampdowns in American history. It culminated in November 2001, when W. took time out of the frenzied response to the 9/11 attacks to issue an executive order declaring that a former president could assert executive privilege over his papers against the will of the incumbent. In doing so, Bush overturned a measure Ronald Reagan had instituted just before he left office. At the same time, Bush's order allows a sitting president to block the release of a predecessor's papers, even if that predecessor had approved the release. The bias was consistently toward secrecy, rather than toward coming clean with the public.

There followed a full-scale assault on open-government laws. Agencies that had once been happy to provide documents turned suspicious and at times hostile. Archives were locked up and the affairs of Bush's father, Donald Rumsfeld, and Dick Cheney in previous administrations were essentially closed to view. Just one example: the administration began dismantling the Environmental Protection Agency's network of technical libraries, which, among other things, made pollution and hazardous substance discharge data available to the public. In 2007, Congress ordered the libraries restored.

For his part, Poppy chose to put his presidential library and papers at Texas A&M University, a hub of military recruitment and one of the few American universities with direct links to the CIA. The head of the library, and later of the university itself, was Robert Gates, who had been CIA director under Poppy. With Gates in charge, the presidential library was built on donations from oil sheikhdoms and U.S. oilmen.[1] No surprise, this. Throughout the administrations of the two George Bushes, and in the period of exile between, we would see the old crew: Rumsfeld, Cheney, Gates, and James A. Baker III. When the Iraq situation grew increasingly untenable and Defense Secretary Rumsfeld had to go, Gates became his successor. When the clamor for an inquiry into 9/11 became too great, Poppy's lieutenant Baker cochaired an investigative panel. In charge of evaluating wiretap requests? Baker's son, James A. Baker IV.[2]

The extended Bush family, which had helped Poppy write history, now was closing ranks to prevent disclosure of what they had done—and were still doing. The term "library" was turned upside down, and became not a way to make information available but rather a way to bury it. It became about disinformation instead of information. It is fitting that such a monument was funded by oil millions from essentially closed, despotic regimes supported by the United States.

In addition, back in Washington there was an unprecedented effort to reclassify thousands of documents and remove them from public view. Other documents simply disappeared. Data were slanted for political ends, often for the convenience of corporations. "Secrecy in the Bush administration is not limited to one or two individuals," Steven Aftergood, director of the nonprofit Project on Government Secrecy, told me in 2002. "It is a guiding philosophy."[3]

Indeed it was. As we have seen in preceding chapters, governance and spycraft merged under the Bushes, with a cynical and Machiavellian edge. Secrecy, destruction of documents, creation of alibis, control of information flow, and the rewriting of history—these were not occasional exercises but rather operating principles.

During W.'s Texas governorship, Alberto Gonzales had instructed staffers to obtain their own private e-mail accounts for in-house communication. The purpose was to keep the public business from the public. Later, during W.'s presidency, it emerged that Karl Rove and other staffers were using accounts at the Republican National Committee, not the White House, to communicate with each other for a similar reason. Later they claimed that most of those e-mails had been accidentally deleted.[4]

As White House counsel, Gonzales told W. himself to stop using e-mail altogether. Shortly after taking office, the president sent off a good-bye message to a select group of "dear friends" and family members, top aides and key supporters. "My lawyers tell me that all correspondence by e-mail is subject to open record requests," Bush wrote. "Since I do not want my private conversations looked at by those out to embarrass, the only course of action is not to correspond in cyberspace. This saddens me. I have enjoyed conversing with each of you."[5]

Dick Cheney was fanatical about secrecy, as noted by the *Washington Post* in its insightful 2007 series on the vice president: "Even talking points for reporters are sometimes stamped *Treated As: Top Secret* . . . Cheney declined to disclose the names or even the size of his staff, generally released no public calendar and ordered the Secret Service to destroy his visitor logs. His general counsel boldly asserted that 'the vice presidency is a unique office that is neither a part of the executive branch nor a part of the legislative branch,' and is therefore exempt from rules governing either."[6]

Signs of Intelligence

This obsession involved a double standard of no small proportions. While the administration sought to protect its own secrets at all costs, it wanted to know everything about everyone else, including ordinary citizens. As the extent of the administration's spying came out, it became clear that the White House had skipped even the modest requirement that a judge be consulted on domestic surveillance cases—modest because over 99 percent of applications submitted for Foreign Intelligence Surveillance Court approval are approved each year.[7] Bush and Cheney didn't like that law, so they just ignored it. Even telecommunications companies had been persuaded—or strong-armed—to turn over private records of their customers.[8]

Anyone who had lived in an authoritarian or totalitarian society might have felt a chill of recognition. Few could feel comfortable knowing that a Karl Rove might have access to their personal data. Reassurances from the White House were not helped by the cavalier leaking of the identity of CIA officer Valerie Plame as retribution when Joseph Wilson, her husband and a former diplomat, blew the whistle on the administration's falsification of the threat posed by Saddam Hussein.[9] The Plame affair showed the administration's willingness to effectively shoot one of its own soldiers to advance strategic ends. The White House even covered up the actual shooting of a soldier—hiding the fact that the heroic professional football player Pat Tillman, who had volunteered for Afghanistan duty after 9/11, died not at the hands of the enemy but by "friendly fire."

Politicization of intelligence was also apparent in W.'s appointments to the President's Foreign Intelligence Advisory Board (PFIAB), a little-known entity with superhigh security clearances. W. initially followed the family course and selected Brent Scowcroft, his father's national security adviser, to be chairman. But he forced out Scowcroft in 2004, after the retired general's criticism of W.'s Iraq occupation began to circulate publicly. The new chairman was James Langdon, the energy lawyer who played a role in W.'s Texas Rangers deal.

It is common for big donors to get places on the PFIAB, but W. went whole hog.[10] Bill Clinton had appointed a former secretary of defense, a former chairman of the Joint Chiefs of Staff, and a former Speaker of the House. W.'s picks included his old oil company rescuer and Rangers baseball partner William DeWitt, and also Ray Hunt, the Dallas oil billionaire who was a major financial backer of W.'s. As a member of the Halliburton board, Hunt had played a major role in determining CEO Dick Cheney's lucrative pay package. The oilman's former top aide James Oberwetter was appointed as W.'s ambassador to Saudi Arabia. Hunt, sitting on a gold mine of secret information at PFIAB, would, coincidentally or not, obtain an exclusive drilling contract in the Kurdish parts of Iraq after the invasion.[11]

The primacy of connections over qualifications was underscored when W. chose his old friend and top fund-raiser Don Evans to join Hunt on the board. After leaving his post as commerce secretary, Evans briefly considered an offer to run a large Russian oil company. In the end, that was deemed too controversial for a Bush lieutenant, and instead Evans became CEO of the Financial Services Forum, an organization representing twenty giant financial institutions from around the world that do business in the United States.

The growing role of the corporate world in spying was underlined in 2007, when the government revealed that 70 percent of its intelligence budget was contracted out to private firms. In essence, the Bush administration was putting the most secretive part of government into outside hands with little oversight.

AUTHORITARIANISM THRIVES IN a climate of fear, and the administration invoked fear continually. Fear justified invading Iraq; fear justified spying on American citizens; fear was the trump card in vanquishing political opposition. In July 2008, the American Civil Liberties Union reported that America's terrorist watch list had hit one million names. One month later, a congressional investigation concluded that a half-billion-dollar emergency program to retool the flawed watch list was "on the brink of collapse."[12]

But when it came to security, there was the usual exemption for large corporate entities. Though grandmothers were strip-searched at airports, the Bush team resisted calls for more stringent security at ports, power and chemical plants, and other vulnerable sites. Otherwise, the tattoo of terror was relentless, especially during the political high season. There was a steady stream of warnings, often in the form of so-called orange alerts, in the months leading up to the 2004 election. Even when other nations found potential terrorists, the administration sought political gains, in one case prompting complaints from the British that the White House was pushing for premature arrests before full intelligence gains had been realized.[13]

The psychology of fear tends to seep outward, and to justify ever greater intrusions. It was a short step from perceived security threats to the political inconvenience of oppositional speech. W. made it a pressing objective to put an ideologue in charge of "reforming" the Public Broadcasting Service—not so much for its purportedly liberal bias, but simply because it exhibited independence.[14] In one of many examples of what certainly looks like harassment of critics, Jim Moore, the journalist who first asked W. about his National Guard record, found himself on a no-fly list.[15] And so he joined a long list of people—from Bill Burkett to Bill White to John Kerry—who had challenged the Bush apparatus and suffered the consequences.

The Hackocracy

Bush and Cheney had campaigned on the conservative principle of limited government. But their actions upon attaining office showed that they weren't interested in limited government, so much as in one that was *theirs*. This was evident in many ways: the intrusions on basic American rights such as voting; the enshrinement of forms of religion as policies of state; the cynical uses of power for political expediency and personal enrichment; the secrecy that withheld the people's business from the people; the cronyism and self-dealing that treated government and its bounty as a personal entitlement and fiefdom.

Republican National Committee chairman Kenneth Mehlman was not subtle about this: "One of the things that can happen in Washington when you work in an agency is that you forget who sent you there. And it's important to remind people—you're George Bush people . . . If there's one empire I want built, it's the George Bush empire."[16] The quaint notion that federal employees are actually responsible to the people who pay their salaries seems to have gone down the drain as well.

To be sure, they continued to invoke the banner hoisted by GOP activist Grover Norquist, who famously declared, "My goal is to cut government in half in twenty-five years, to get it down to the size where we can drown it in the bathtub." But in practice, the only parts that went down the drain were the ones that were distasteful to friends. The Food and Drug Administration, the agency that monitors the safety of what Americans put into their bodies, faced drastic budget cuts and restrictions in its abilities to inspect products before they went to market.[17] At one congressional hearing, former FDA chief counsel Peter Barton Hutt said the agency was "barely hanging on by its fingertips." He begged for more funding and skilled personnel.[18]

Faced with the overwhelming evidence of climate change, the Bush administration seemed content to pass the buck. Though the Supreme Court provided the Environmental Protection Agency with the power to create emissions standards for motor vehicles, EPA administrator Stephen Johnson found that even his agency's modest suggestions fell on deaf White House ears. He had his staff write a draft of new regulations for limiting carbon emissions, but once sent to the White House, it "fell into a black hole."[19]

Nearly every federal agency became politicized. The regulated were controlling the regulators, and cooking the books. A few career employees were willing to speak out. At NASA, leading climate scientist James Hansen revealed how the White House had worked to suppress the truth about climate change.[20] David Kuo, former deputy director of the office of faith-based initiatives, claimed that the White House used taxpayer funds to plan events that recruited evangelical votes for the Republicans.

Government spending mainly took a hit in areas such as food stamps, energy assistance, community development, public housing, and the like. But once the Bush team had inflicted pain on the needy, they opened the public spigot of largesse for their friends. The well-connected benefited from contracts, jobs, and the indulgence of forbearing regulators. Financial institutions were rewarded for recklessness. Just as Poppy Bush had sheltered savings and loan executives from the consequences of their own greed, W. bailed out big investment houses such as Bear Stearns that had rewarded their executives with giant bonuses for taking even bigger—and ultimately dangerous—risks with other people's money. These moves violated the bedrock conservative principle that people must bear the consequences for their own actions. Yet these gamblers were taken care of, and W. himself was never made to answer for the policy. Even a measure presented as in the public interest, like the Medicare prescription benefit plan, was essentially a political play, with a Cinderella's slipper for the pharmaceutical industry thrown in.

In 2007, W. vetoed the State Children's Health Insurance Program (S-CHIP), which would have utilized an increased tobacco tax to provide health coverage to millions of uninsured children. Bush's decision reflected his distaste for anything resembling universal health care. "After all," the president suggested, "you [can] just go to an emergency room."[21] As *Times* columnist Paul Krugman pointed out, the S-CHIP program would have cost less over five years than the country spends on four months in Iraq. So W.'s opposition to the program was philosophical in nature. After all, if the nation were to experience a federal health care program that worked, what would stop people from demanding universal health care?

Krugman saw this as representing a fundamental Bush doctrine:

> He wants the public to believe that government is always the problem, never the solution. But it's hard to convince people that government is always bad when they see it doing good things. So his philosophy says that the government must be prevented from solving problems, even if it can. In fact, the more good a proposed government program would do, the more fiercely it must be opposed.[22]

W.'s crony statism and his contempt for regulation helped plunge the nation into the worst economic crisis since the Great Depression. Even before the crash of 2008, he presided over the poorest job-creation rate in modern history. And according to a series of USA Today–Gallup polls, only once in Bush's eight-year reign did even a slight majority of respondents characterize the economy as "excellent" or "good" rather than "fair" or "poor."[23]

The cronyism was rampant, the corruption rife. The name of the GOP's favorite super-lobbyist and fixer, Jack Abramoff, became a synonym for "business as usual." If one did not believe in government by the people to begin with—as the Bush crew didn't—what difference did such behavior make? How can one degrade that which one already holds in contempt? The result was evident in scandals large and small. Every week came new revelations about no-bid contracts awarded to contributors, loyal functionaries hired despite dubious qualifications, regulations and data skewed on behalf of powerful industries, and on and on.

For the cooperative and the connected, lack of qualifications was no bar. It became so evident that the *New Republic* devoted an entire issue to indexing the Bush "hackocracy."[24] A typical appointment was Julie Myers, head of Immigration and Customs Enforcement at the Homeland Security Department. Ms. Myers is the niece of General Richard Myers, former chairman of the Joint Chiefs of Staff. She had recently married the chief of staff for

Michael Chertoff, who was secretary of Homeland Security. This led Frank Rich to label the appointment a "nepotistic twofer."[25] Even conservative columnist Michelle Malkin noted, "Great contacts, but what exactly are the 36-year-old lawyer's main credentials to solve . . . dire national security problems?" She answered: "Zip, Nada, Nil."[26] Myers's main qualification: working for Kenneth Starr, the man who prosecuted the Monica Lewinsky case.

Regulatory agencies hung out the sign: Foxes, Report to Henhouse Duty. All manner of chemical, nuclear, and coal industry executives and the like rushed in to provide oversight of their former (and future) employers.

Even when the administration seemed to be taking care of ordinary people, there was always a skunk at the picnic's close. The historic overhaul of Medicare was within a few years marred by revelations of fraud and improper payments to medical equipment manufacturers, to the tune of $2.8 billion.[27]

All in the Family

It seemed there was always room at the table for contributors and friends. It wasn't just the occasional Billy Carter or Roger Clinton who regarded the White House as a winning lottery ticket. It was an entire clan that had built its political rhetoric around the need to curb government spending.

The dossier is thick. Back in 1985, while Poppy was vice president, third son Neil Mallon Bush had become a director of the Silverado Savings and Loan. Soon he was embroiled in one of the biggest financial scandals in U.S. history—one that cost taxpayers about one billion dollars.[28] In February 1993, a month after Poppy Bush left office, the World Trade Center was bombed. In the wake of that, an American firm with Kuwaiti backing got a contract to provide security to the buildings, and Poppy's fourth son, Marvin, joined the board, remaining until 2000. W.'s brother Jeb, the one Poppy and Barbara thought would rise highest, set up shop in Miami and established strong ties to the right-wing Cuban exile community. He was quickly brought under the wing of Armando Codina, a real estate developer and longtime political supporter of the family and its staunch backing of the Cuba embargo; Jeb got a 40 percent share of the real estate company's profits without investing in the firm. The duo were bailed out for a loan default with taxpayers footing the bill, in excess of $3 million.[29]

With a Bush back in the White House, the process required a bit more subtlety. Neil Bush, brother of the "education president," backed by money from Kuwait and elsewhere, was busy selling educational software to the Saudis.[30] William "Bucky" Bush, Poppy's younger brother and W.'s uncle, sat on the board of ESSI, a St. Louis–based firm that received multiple no-bid contracts from the Pentagon.[31] One was for equipment to help search for—and protect soldiers from—what turned out to be Iraq's nonexistent store of chemical and biological weapons.[32] Friends of the family also got a piece of the taxpayer's dollar. Ernie Ladd, W.'s faithful buddy since his days supervising Bush's community service at Project PULL in inner-city Houston, started getting military contracts for spray-on plastic coating.[33]

And then of course there was Poppy. After leaving the White House, he began accepting handouts from grateful past beneficiaries of one generation of Bushes and those hopeful for largesse from the next. In 1998, Poppy addressed an audience in Tokyo on behalf of telecom company Global Crossing and accepted stock in the soon-to-go-public corporation in lieu of his normal $100,000 overseas speaking fee. Within a year, that stock was worth $14.4 million.[34]

Poppy also became an adviser to, and speechmaker for, the Carlyle Group, a secretive private equity firm that made its name buying low-valued defense contractors, using connections to secure government contracts, then selling the firms at huge profits. Poppy joined Carlyle in 1995 and earns between $80,000 and $100,000 per speech on its behalf.[35] As a former president with access to CIA briefings, Poppy is an indispensable asset to Carlyle. "Imagine what a global enterprise, that does large amounts of business with arms contractors and foreign governments, could do with weekly CIA briefings," wrote business journalist Dan Briody, author of a book on the Carlyle Group.[36]

Whether or not Carlyle was a direct beneficiary of inside information, the company's investors have made more than $6.6 billion off the Iraq War. Referring to the beginning of the war, Carlyle's chief investment officer said: "It's the best eighteen months we ever had. We made money and we made it fast."[37]

The myriad cozy financial deals involving Bushes and their friends and associates have attracted only sporadic media interest. This is in contrast to the frenzied coverage of Bill and Hillary Clinton's investment in the Arkansas real estate venture Whitewater. The couple actually lost money in the deal, and an independent investigation headed by Clinton nemesis Kenneth Starr found no evidence of illegality. Other Democrats, in particular Barack Obama, saw every aspect of their personal lives scrutinized, often with the most nefarious possible interpretation.

The Bush crew's political operation required exemption from, and therefore control over, the law. Thus the infamous White House crusade to fire uncooperative United States attorneys—the highest prosecutors, each supervising his or her own regional office. Most of the targets, though loyal Republicans, had refused to pursue prosecutions that were overtly political in nature.[38] Even when Attorney General Alberto Gonzales stepped down in the scandal's wake, his nominally independent-minded replacement, Michael Mukasey, declined to pursue charges against the Justice Department. "Not every wrong, or even every violation of the law, is a crime," he said.[39] That same approach helped former Cheney aide I. Lewis "Scooter" Libby, who was pardoned after his conviction for perjury and obstruction of justice in the Valerie Plame case.

In 2005, W. nominated Harriet Miers, his friend and fellow Texan, to replace Sandra Day O'Connor on the U.S. Supreme Court—even though she had never before served as a judge and lacked distinction among her legal peers. Miers's main qualification was that she had handled some of W.'s most delicate matters in the 1990s. In W.'s gubernatorial campaign, Miers "was deemed to be just the right person to inoculate George W. Bush against any further inquiries into his legal and business dealings."[40] As detailed in chapter 18, it was Miers who helped Bush escape scrutiny for his membership in the controversial Rainbo Club. Thus, even the highest court in the land was to house a Bush family enforcer.

Because of their contempt for government, Bush and Cheney ended up flubbing the most essential function of government from a conservative standpoint: security and defense.

The tendentious justification for the invasion of Iraq was only one obvious example. In some ways, an even more striking one was the fiasco of the response to Hurricane Katrina.

The botched handling of Katrina cut deep; and the reason for it was the same as for the other derelictions and misdeeds. Government was to be a honeypot for cronies and supporters, and a grindstone for ideological axes. It did not exist to solve problems—and therefore under Bush it ended up creating more of them.

Partners in Disaster

In late August 2005, what would become one of the deadliest hurricanes in American history—and certainly the most costly—was bearing down on the Gulf Coast and the city of New Orleans. The warnings from the National Weather Service and the National Hurricane Center grew increasingly ominous. In charge of preparing a response to this mounting threat was the Federal Emergency Management Agency (FEMA), which was run by a little-known figure named Michael D. Brown.

As a forewarned nation braced for the worst, and Gulf Coast residents frantically prepared to weather the storm, George Bush and his top aides showed little concern. The president opted not to cut his vacation short. He had finished the photo ops of himself clearing brush in Crawford, Texas, and by then was in California. A day after the hurricane made its second landfall, the news carried another photo op, of the president strumming a guitar. Vice president Dick Cheney had emerged from his often-bunkered lifestyle to enjoy some fly-fishing in Wyoming. As for the country's disaster-management agency, the only FEMA official actually in New Orleans—Marty J. Bahamonde—was there by accident. He had been visiting on business and had tried to leave but could not because of the clogged roads.

FEMA chief Michael Brown made it to Baton Rouge, a city seventy-five miles from New Orleans, but he seemed out of reach. As Hurricane Katrina battered the Gulf states and wiped out one of America's signature cities, stories of incompetence and disorganization began trickling out. FEMA staff couldn't find Brown. Brown wasn't aware of developments familiar to anyone with a television. By the time he was, he couldn't get through to the governor of Louisiana; he couldn't get the president of the United States to pay attention.

Worst of all, there was no evidence of advance planning for a disaster of this magnitude, even though such planning was Brown's primary job. At the peak of the crisis, he was seen working on an organizational chart. As a critical levee collapsed and one of the country's largest port cities started to slip beneath the water, Bahamonde fired off a series of increasingly desperate e-mails. On August 31, he e-mailed Brown directly: "I know you know, the situation is past critical . . . Hotels are kicking people out, thousands gathering in the streets with no food or water." The response came, several hours later. "It is very important that time is allowed for Mr. Brown to eat dinner," it said.[41] Four days after the hurricane hit, Bush arrived to survey the damage and famously proclaimed, "Brownie, you're doing a heckuva job."

But two weeks into the disaster, with the Bush administration facing its worst PR nightmare, Brown was finally replaced as on-site manager by an experienced outsider.

When it was over, the Gulf Coast was devastated, and New Orleans in particular. The city's protective levee system was swamped; 80 percent of the city—along with many of its neighboring areas—was underwater for weeks. Destruction stretched from Louisiana through Mississippi into Alabama. The images of frightened families clinging to rooftops awaiting rescue, of elderly people who died strapped to their beds in retirement homes, of gun-toting vigilantes protecting wealthy areas against looters—these were the legacy of Brownie's heckuva job.

Despite the fact that the warnings had been more than ample, with accurate forecasts and lots of advance notice from the National Weather Service and the National Hurricane Center, more than 1,800 people died, and damage was estimated to exceed $81 billion. The agency that is charged to act, didn't. Brown later blamed state and local officials for the slow response, but it was clear to the nation that he and his agency had fallen down on the job.

THE STATE OF FEMA under George W. Bush stood in stark contrast to its condition under Bill Clinton. The latter had inherited an agency riddled with patronage. For example, Bush Sr. had appointed as director Wallace Stickney, a former neighbor of John Sununu, his chief of staff.[42] Stickney, who lacked crisis management experience, presided over FEMA's inept response to Hurricanes Hugo and Andrew during the first and last years of the elder Bush's term. Many observers believe the administration's handling of these events contributed to Poppy's loss to Clinton in 1992.

Clinton, by contrast, appointed a seasoned pro to head the agency—James Lee Witt, who had been in charge of disaster management in Arkansas. Clinton even gave the FEMA director a seat in his cabinet. Morale soared, and a bipartisan group of senators actually sought to keep Witt on indefinitely, drafting legislation to make the FEMA directorship a longer-term, fixed position. Even George W. Bush praised Witt—and then canned him.

In 2001, W. appointed his longtime enforcer Joe Allbaugh. Allbaugh had almost no relevant experience or qualifications, beyond serving as the governor's liaison to emergency agencies during minor crises in Texas. At FEMA, he would have more than eight thousand employees and a four-billion-dollar budget. Allbaugh was confirmed by the Senate after minimal scrutiny in a 91–0 vote. He became head of FEMA in February 2001.

A true Bush acolyte, Allbaugh took a harshly partisan approach. Anyone Witt had liked, Allbaugh saw as a potential problem. One holdover senior staffer made the mistake of complimenting Allbaugh on his fine performance on *Meet the Press* the previous weekend. "Why would you care?" Allbaugh snapped. "Joe Allbaugh didn't trust many people," Trey Reid, a former senior FEMA official, told me in 2005. "He was very insular, and had a tight circle."[43]

Allbaugh soon embarked on a Nixonian purge and a series of internal investigations into everything undertaken by the Witt administration. Allbaugh's lengthiest inquiry was into a headdress that used to hang on Witt's wall, a token of appreciation from a Native American tribe in recognition of his efforts following the Oklahoma City bombing. Someone said it might contain feathers from the protected bald eagle—a federal offense—but the probe, which even involved the FBI, fizzled when they turned out to be dyed chicken feathers.

Abandoning a tradition of placing civil-service professionals in vital posts, Allbaugh quickly staffed the agency with loyalists, many of them political operatives with no professional experience in emergency disaster management.

Possessing little experience with large-scale disasters, Allbaugh was happy to embrace the administration's view of FEMA as a bloated entitlement program in need of drastic cutbacks. "His position was that the states ought to take a bigger role," said Reid. And that's where the problems in New Orleans partially began. Flood mitigation, a high priority under Witt, received short shrift under Allbaugh. The chief of mitigation, Anthony Lowe, was replaced with a veteran of an insurance industry determined to minimize its own liability to homeowners.[44]

At FEMA, as throughout the administration, the foxes had taken over the henhouse and were partying up. Out the door, one by one, went the experienced disaster-relief managers, and in came the political opportunists and the industry lobbyists. "Many of their skilled management team left," said Steve Kanstoroom, an independent fraud detection expert. "You had a train running down the tracks with nobody driving it."[45]

Cashing In

As Governor Bush's chief of staff and campaign manager, Allbaugh had pushed the antigovernment rhetoric. Yet the moment he left government, he began finding ways for it to spend more, not less, taxpayer money. Following his departure from FEMA, he quickly formed the lobbying firm Allbaugh Company with his wife, Diane, an attorney, to cash in on his years in government. *Newsweek* said Joe Allbaugh has "the hide of a rhino" when it comes to criticism of conflicts of interest, and it showed.

When the Allbaughs first moved to Texas, Diane had signed on as a lobbyist with a number of large corporate clients with pressing business before the state. That was while her husband held a highly visible position as the governor's top aide. When the newspapers reported the story, Governor Bush's office hastened to announce new rules, and Diane declared an end to her Texas lobbying career. However, she was soon ensconced in a "nonlobbying" position with a law firm representing some of the same companies. In Washington, she jumped into the K Street bazaar, becoming "of counsel" to Barbour, Griffith & Rogers, which *Fortune* magazine described at the time as the country's most powerful lobbying firm.[46] The name partner Haley Barbour served as Republican National Committee chairman from 1993 to 1997, the period in which the GOP captured both houses of Congress for the first time since 1954.[47] He was truly wired, and his decision to hire Mrs. Allbaugh was a shrewd one.

While Joe Allbaugh was still at FEMA and serving on Cheney's secretive energy task force, his wife was being paid as a "consultant" by Reliant Energy, Entergy, and Texas Utilities Co. The connection couldn't have hurt Barbour as he pushed the Cheney task force to recommend that the new administration renege on its campaign promise to limit the carbon-dioxide emissions from power plants—the ones that contribute heavily to climate change. Bush, citing the task force findings, complied.

Bad news was good news where Joe Allbaugh was concerned. Cheney's former employer, Halliburton, became one of Allbaugh's biggest lobbying clients. Its then-subsidiary Kellogg, Brown, and Root would get at least sixty-one million dollars' worth of Katrina business from the federal government.[48]

Allbaugh's post-FEMA ventures were not restricted to the domestic disaster business. His departure from government and entrance into defense contracting took place precisely as the invasion of Iraq unfolded. September 11 had not only offered a pretext for invading Iraq; it also set in motion a boom for military contractors, which had been concerned about the diminishing demand for weaponry in a post-Communist era. At the same time it justified the creation of a vast new domestic security industry, another lucrative component of the military-industrial complex. Both the Pentagon and the Department of Homeland Security now had endless programs to fund in the name of a new kind of war—carried out abroad and at home, against an invisible enemy, and with no expiration date. The annual corporate reports of government contractors practically gushed over the new opportunities. "I think our shareholders understand why we're in this business," said Halliburton chief executive David J. Lesar.[49]

With Barbour Griffith and numerous ex-officials of the Reagan and Bush 41 administrations, Allbaugh formed a company called New Bridge Strategies, which moved to secure contracts in Iraq the moment hostilities commenced. He also formed Blackwell Fairbanks, a joint venture with Andrew Lundquist, with whom he had served on Cheney's energy task force. (The name of the company is based on the hometowns of the two principals.) Clients in 2004 included the aerospace giant Lockheed Martin; Blackwell Fairbanks would later report that it had lobbied the offices of both the president and the vice president. Filings for the Allbaugh Company show among its clients Oshkosh Truck, the leading supplier of vehicles to the Pentagon.

A COG in the Big Wheel

Why did Joe Allbaugh even want to run FEMA? In the first days of the Clinton-Bush transition, amid speculation about who might get what post, Allbaugh's name was bandied about in connection with a few positions, among them White House chief of staff. No one mentioned FEMA, but then another factor came into play: Allbaugh's close relationship with Dick Cheney, who saw FEMA's principal role less as helping Americans during an emergency than as maintaining White House control during one.

Few people realize that Joe Allbaugh even played a role in Dick Cheney's advance to the vice presidency. In 2000, while Allbaugh was W.'s presidential campaign manager, Cheney was brought in to help research the backgrounds of prospective running mates. When Cheney concluded that he himself was the ideal choice,[50] the job of vetting Cheney's qualifications went to Allbaugh. He quickly signed off on the former congressman and defense secretary, which cleared Cheney's path to the White House. To be sure, given Cheney's prior security clearances, Allbaugh's scrutiny was probably less than thorough. In any case, the Allbaughs and Cheneys quickly felt at home with each other—literally so. When the Cheneys moved into the vice presidential residence in 2001, the Allbaughs bought Cheney's town house in McLean, Virginia, for $690,000. And Cheney put Allbaugh onto his secretive energy task force.

FEMA had been created in 1979 by President Jimmy Carter through an executive order; before that, emergency and disaster services were scattered among a host of agencies. From the beginning, FEMA was seen as a vehicle of White House command and control, in times of war more than natural disasters. Samuel Huntington, who drafted the presidential memorandum creating the agency, summed up the basic concept in a book, *The Crisis of Democracy*. "A government which lacks authority," he wrote, "will have little ability, short of a cataclysmic crisis, to impose on its people the sacrifices which may be necessary to deal with foreign policy problems and defense."[51] Carter's FEMA director, John Macy, had emphasized that preparation for natural disasters would take a backseat to defense against nuclear, biological, and terror threats.[52] It was principally under Bill Clinton that FEMA focused on disaster relief.

The Bush-Cheney view of FEMA was an almost pure expression of their underlying philosophy. For all their talk of limited government, Bush-Cheney did everything they could to expand the power and reach of the presidency. Often, this took the form of curtailing basic rights long considered the people's last line of defense against tyranny. The suspension of the writ of habeas corpus in the case of detainees, the abrogation of the Geneva Conventions on the rights of combatants, the illegal wiretapping, all supposedly instituted in response to 9/11, had in fact been discussed long before that attack. Natural disasters were a minor concern. They were thinking mainly about a vehicle for White House command and control in case of enemy attack, without the constitutional restraints that they considered outmoded and counterproductive.

When the planes hit on 9/11, FEMA was nominally in charge. But off the national radar, that event also represented the first-ever implementation of a concept known as "continuity of government," or COG. According to a *Washington Post* report, President Bush "dispatched a shadow government of about one hundred senior civilian managers to live and work outside Washington, activating for the first time long-standing plans to ensure survival of federal rule after catastrophic attack."[53] The *Post* story, which expanded on material published in Cleveland's *Plain Dealer* months earlier, asserted that the plan was "deployed 'on the fly' in the first hours of turmoil on Sept. 11."[54]

Actually, the plan went back to Executive Order 12656, issued by President Reagan in 1988, which stipulated that the Constitution could be suspended for any emergency "that seriously degrades or seriously threatens the national security of the United States."[55] In his book *Rumsfeld*, journalist Andrew Cockburn quotes a former Pentagon official who claims that during the 1990s, Cheney and Rumsfeld formed "a secret government-in-waiting."[56]

Most important for the Bush administration, the Cheney-Rumsfeld group had worked for three decades on preparations to control the American population in the event of a disaster. These included the de facto suspension of the Constitution through a number of steps that became more hotly debated as the Bush administration entered its final months. The administration's response to terror went far beyond the legal boundaries and reflected a sense that whatever the president wanted to do, he could do. Cheney backed what author Ron Suskind dubbed the "one percent doctrine," in which if there is even a 1 percent chance of something coming true, it is important to treat it as a certainty.[57]

A key part of continuity of government was control of segments of the population during periods of unrest. In a 1984 "readiness exercise" implemented by Lieutenant Colonel Oliver North, the National Security Council staffer who also coordinated the secret and illegal contra supply effort, FEMA simulated rounding up four hundred thousand "refugees" for detainment. This was cast as preparation for a possible "uncontrolled population movement" from Mexico to the United States. In 2006, the Army Corps of Engineers awarded a $385 million contract to Halliburton subsidiary Kellogg, Brown & Root for building "temporary immigration detention centers."[58]

The implications are obvious. Yet they penetrated only to the furthest edges of popular culture, where paranoia becomes entertainment. In *The X-Files* movie of 1998, Agent Fox Mulder is warned of FEMA's ability to "suspend constitutional government upon declaration of a national emergency." According to a *Washington Post* article written just after the movie's release, officials at FEMA were not amused by what they claimed was an inaccurate portrayal of their mandate. "The history of this thing is serious," said FEMA spokesman Morrie Goodman. "We've tightened security at all our facilities because of this."[59]

It is necessary, of course, for the government to have a contingency plan for worst-case scenarios. But in focusing on an all-out response to a hypothetical aggressor, the "Cheney doctrine" paid little mind to the kinds of emergencies that, based on prior experience and study, were certain to come—such as major hurricanes—and to affect the largest numbers of people.

Preparing the Turkey Shoot

Whatever leading role Joe Allbaugh might have anticipated in this kind of "national security" activity vanished after 9/11, when Congress mandated that FEMA be absorbed into a new Department of Homeland Security. FEMA insiders say that the merger was a principal factor in Allbaugh's decision to leave—and to turn the agency over to Michael Brown.

Allbaugh had initially hired Brown, an old friend from Oklahoma, as FEMA general counsel, presiding over a legal staff of thirty. Allbaugh included him in all key deliberations, and even named him chief operating officer. Brown's influence was apparent to all. Within six months of his arrival, Allbaugh was ready to promote him. First, though, he had to oust his current acting deputy director, John Magaw—a former director of the U.S. Secret Service and the Bureau of Alcohol, Tobacco and Firearms, whom Clinton had placed in charge of coordinating domestic-terrorism efforts for FEMA.

"One day, Mr. Allbaugh came in and said, 'I know you've got these other things to do. I'm going to ask Mr. Brown to be deputy,'" recalled Magaw, who promptly returned to the subordinate position assigned him by Clinton.[60] The timing was remarkable. Just a week before September 11, 2001, Allbaugh replaced a key anti-terrorism official with a crony who had close to zero relevant experience.

Before Brown could take over permanently as deputy director, he had to face the Senate. In June 2002, he presented a résumé that was full of exaggerations about his experience and serious omissions about his financial and legal problems. Nevertheless, as with most presidential nominees, Brown was confirmed without ado.

Later, after the Katrina disaster, Michael Brown's incompetence, and Bush's pronouncement that "Brownie" was doing "a heckuva job," would turn him into a laugh line. By and large, the media treated him that way. We learned of his prior job with the International Arabian Horse Association and that his prime qualification was that he had been Joe Allbaugh's college roommate. *CNN* even handed him its "Political Turkey of the Year" award.[61] Yet as it turned on the hapless Brown, the media got its facts wrong. Brown and Allbaugh were not in fact college roommates, and did not even attend the same university. Instead, Michael Brown's rise to prominence—and therefore the bumbling of the Katrina disaster—tracked back to the Poppy Bush organization.

The Right Stable

Before he joined FEMA, the pinnacle of Brown's professional experience was as an inspector of Arabian-horse judges. His highest governmental executive position had been as an assistant to a city manager in Edmond, Oklahoma, decades before. (Brown had told the Senate that he was an "assistant city manager," responsible for police, fire, and emergency services. In truth, he had been "more like an intern," the town's PR liaison told *Time*.)[62]

After passing the Oklahoma bar in 1982, Brown moved to the oil boomtown of Enid, where he was hired by the law firm of Stephen Jones, the flamboyant, nationally known defense attorney. When the firm broke up, thirty-four staffers found immediate work. Brown was one of two not offered employment by the successor firms. "When I saw Brown up there at FEMA, I had a premonition of bad things to come," Jones recalled when I visited him at his Enid office.[63]

In the ensuing years, Brown would be sued for failing to pay his rent for shared law offices—a piece of civil litigation he neglected to mention in the Senate confirmation process, even though he was required to do so. He would also be accused by his sister-in-law of changing her father's will in a way that benefited Brown and his wife while leaving the sister-in-law a virtual pauper.

Brown found haven in another state, as commissioner of judges and stewards with the International Arabian Horse Association (IAHA), which is based in Colorado. He stayed there for a decade, by far his longest term of employment. His official bio on the FEMA Web site didn't even mention this job, which suggests how irrelevant it was to the responsibilities that had been entrusted to him. Yet it turns out that Brown had his own reasons to be modest about this portion of his career.

Brown supposedly was hired to root out cronyism and corruption in the horse world. Instead, he devoted the bulk of his energies to an Allbaugh-style crusade against the sport's most successful trainer. That was a man named David Boggs, who had angered powerful people with connections at the top of the Republican Party. Karl Hart, a Florida lawyer and longtime IAHA member who headed the group's legal review committee, describes Brown's efforts against Boggs as an "obsessive vendetta." According to Hart and others, the trainer was envied and even hated by several extremely rich Arabian-horse owners—who also happened to be very large Republican donors. These included the late Bob Magness, a founder of the TCI cable giant; David Murdock, the Dole food company billionaire; and the late Alec Courtelis, a Florida developer.[64]

Courtelis had been a good friend of, and top fund-raiser for, Poppy Bush, and Poppy was a frequent guest at Courtelis's horse farm during his presidency. At an April 1990 fund-raising dinner in Florida, Bush introduced Courtelis thus: "Here's a man who breeds racehorses for the same reason he works so hard for the party: only one place will do for Alec—first place."

Indeed. The year after Poppy made these remarks, Michael Brown, whose experience also included work as a lobbyist for an Allbaugh venture called Campground Associates, suddenly emerged as the Inspector Javert of the show horse circuit. A year after Brown was installed at the horse association, Poppy rewarded Allbaugh himself by appointing him to the Arkansas-Oklahoma Arkansas River Compact Commission, a modest but telling acknowledgment of service.

At the IAHA, Brown got special treatment. While other staffers had to report to work each day, Brown, on a full salary, was allowed to work from his sprawling home in Lyons, which was more than an hour's drive north of IAHA's headquarters in Denver. His lifestyle was so pleasant and relaxed that some in Lyons assumed him to be semi-retired. James Van Dyke, chef-owner at Lyons's Gateway Café, said Brown had leisurely lunches there almost daily. "He seemed to have a lot of time on his hands," Van Dyke told me when I visited the village.[65]

Brown's single-minded pursuit of David Boggs contrasted sharply with a pronounced reluctance to pursue another case that seemed to have considerable merit—one involving Murdock's trainer, who was accused of filing false papers for a show horse. Boggs initiated a battery of lawsuits against both the association and Brown, the financial toll of which contributed to the association's near bankruptcy and eventual merger with another group.

Ironically, it would be the GOP titan Murdock himself who would eventually sink Brown, in his zeal to help the horse inspector's cause. One day, Murdock mentioned to Hart that he'd written Brown a fifty-thousand-dollar personal check at Brown's request, ostensibly for a legal-defense fund to deal with the Boggs suits. Hart was surprised, since the association was paying Brown's legal bills already. Hart took Brown aside at an IAHA board meeting and told him what he knew. Brown panicked. "He grabbed me, literally, and pushed me into a closet," said Hart. "He said, 'Is there any way you and I can work this out?'"

There wasn't, and Brown was terminated immediately.

But only a few months later, in February 2001, he resurfaced—first as general counsel and ultimately director at FEMA. While most folks who knew Brown over the years were startled, the IAHA brass was not. As Hart recalled, "Brown had been saying for six months or more that, if Bush was elected, he was going to have a high position in Washington because he was very close to someone who was very active in Bush's campaign."

Like Allbaugh, Brown appeared to have well-connected angels looking after him. His bumpy career was punctuated by timely assists from his self-described "longtime friend and family attorney," Andrew Lester. An Andover prep-school mate of George W.'s brother Marvin, and onetime employee in the Washington office of the Bush-family-connected Dresser Industries, Lester pops up at crucial points in Brown's life. When Brown lost his job with the Jones law firm, Lester brought him in for a brief stint as his law partner. When horse-association problems engulfed Brown, Lester rushed to his defense. And on September 27, 2005, at a House Select Committee hearing investigating the Katrina blunders, there was the pin-striped Lester conspicuously whispering legal advice in Brown's ear.

Lester, a regional director for the Federalist Society, an association of rightward lawyers, represented the Oklahoma Republican Party in a 2002 reapportionment battle. He was also short-listed for a federal judgeship under George W. Bush. Over lunch at an Oklahoma City steak house, Lester told me that his support for Brown arises merely from their friendship. He continued to maintain, even in the wake of the Katrina debacle, that Brown was eminently qualified for FEMA.[66]

AFTER 9/11, WITH pressure building for coordinated antiterror responses, it was evident that FEMA could not remain independent. Bush initially opposed the creation of a Department of Homeland Security, but eventually he caved to congressional demands, and Joe Allbaugh began to look for an exit strategy. The moment Homeland Security swallowed FEMA, Allbaugh departed for the private sector, leaving Brown in charge.

Initially, Brown seemed to be a better FEMA director than Allbaugh. This was because Brown realized that he didn't know much about the job and was smart enough to turn to whatever experts remained on staff. He also was a welcome relief to staffers after the fearsome Allbaugh. "I was pretty impressed with him," said Trey Reid. "He was articulate, bright, a quick study. I didn't have to spend much time going over things with him." In terms of disaster management, there were two possibilities FEMA lifers always worried about: a really big California earthquake and levee breaks in New Orleans. But worrying and fixing were two different things. Brown, on the advice of aides, asked for more money for levee improvements and catastrophic planning, but neither the Republican-controlled Congress nor the White House would agree.

If Allbaugh had been disinclined to press Bush for strong remedial action, the inconsequential Brown lacked even that option. He didn't really have a relationship with the president, his diminutive nickname notwithstanding, and the Department of Homeland Security was focused almost exclusively on terrorism. "I don't think any of the budget requests we submitted went through," said Reid. "Everything went for terrorism."

With the defections of several senior managers and the firing of others, compounded by the denial or reduction of budget requests, FEMA's staff was left paper thin. "At this point, there's only one person in the building who knows how to do certain things," Reid told me in our 2005 interview. "If that person gets sick or dies, you're shit out of luck."

Despite the cuts, however, there was always money for political purposes. Ever mindful of avoiding his father's mistakes—among them the disastrous handling of Hurricane Andrew in 1992—Bush was not about to lose to John Kerry over disaster relief. Under Brown, the response to a series of hurricanes that battered Florida during the 2004 presidential campaign was as choreographed as Bush's landing on the U.S.S. *Abraham Lincoln* the previous year. Agency staffers were everywhere, in FEMA T-shirts, and Brown was especially visible. An investigation by the *South Florida Sun-Sentinel* later found that FEMA had handed out tens of millions of dollars following Hurricane Frances to residents and businesses in the Miami-Dade County area, where no deaths and only mild damage had occurred.

There was much less assistance to areas that were harder hit but less politically crucial.[67]

Contracts

Like most federal agencies under George W., FEMA received little attention until disaster struck, and the attention vanished soon thereafter. But there were warning signs at the agency well before the hurricane. One such example was FEMA's abrupt decision in 2003, not long after Brown had taken over, to award an exclusive contract for emergency water supplies.

Over the years, FEMA had entered into water contracts with a variety of companies. One, not surprisingly, was Nestlé Waters North America, easily the continent's biggest producer. Then, after W.'s inauguration, without explanation, FEMA went sole-source, and picked a little-known, family-run firm called Lipsey Mountain Spring Water. The company, based in Norcross, Georgia, had just fifteen full-time employees, no production capacity, and no distribution network.

"The father and son came in and said, 'We want you to sell us water,'" recalled Kim Jeffery, president and CEO of Nestlé Waters North America. "I said, 'Why would I do that? I have a contract with FEMA.' He said, 'Because we have the contract now.'"[68]

Lipsey trumpeted a sophisticated computer system that supposedly would ensure speedy water deliveries and so justify its exclusive five-year contract. But the system did not work so well during the crisis, according to some in the industry. Joe Doss, president of the trade group for water suppliers, said his members were besieged with reports of delays in water deliveries after the hurricane. Within one twenty-four-hour period they voluntarily trucked in 1.5 million bottles.

Lipsey Mountain Spring Water may have been new to the world of federal water contracts, but its principals were not new to politics. The Lipseys are part of a politically connected family that gives regularly to both political parties and owns one of the country's largest gun wholesalers. The gun lobby is among the nation's most powerful, and a group whose events both Cheney and Allbaugh attended with regularity.

The Pentagon later confirmed that its inspector general was investigating Lipsey in response to complaints from truck drivers, trucking brokers, and ice producers, who did much of the actual work under Lipsey's FEMA contract. These said Lipsey had not paid its bills or even answered its phone calls. (In 2005, following my request for an interview, company president Joe Lipsey III asked to see a list of questions, then never responded.) In 2007, Department of Defense auditors determined that the company owed the government $881,000 in overpayments in cases where the company erroneously received multiple duplicate fees.[69]

BY AUGUST 2005, Brown was already rumored to be preparing his own exit into the private sector. And just as Allbaugh had a reliable understudy in Brown, Brown was readying his own—Patrick Rhode, his chief of staff, whom he elevated to deputy director. Rhode was a former Bush campaign advance man; and while he too lacked experience in emergency management, his PR and media skills had been sharpened as a former television news anchor and reporter. Perhaps they'd been sharpened a bit too much: it was Rhode who, several days into the Katrina disaster, would call FEMA's performance "one of the most efficient and effective responses in the country's history."

CHAPTER 24

Conclusion

ESPITE IT ALL, THERE ARE THINGS for which we can thank George W. Bush. Perhaps most important, he has, inadvertently, invited us to examine anew many things we have long taken for granted. He enabled me, for instance to gain a whole new understanding of how power works in America.

Were it not for W. and his self-dramatizing swagger, his blustery excesses, and his cavalier indifference to the havoc he wrought, I might not have asked myself how such a man came to be president in the first place.

Because I did ask myself that question, I was compelled to study W.'s life carefully. So doing, I discovered the extent to which conventional portraits of him miss the mark. W. was not the dimwit that some writers have claimed. Lazy and incurious, yes. Rigid and unimaginative, yes. But not dumb—and possessed of a kind of shrewdness where his own interests were concerned. Moreover, George W. Bush never was the rebel in chief he sometimes has been made out to be. To the contrary, he and his father were in many respects a team. At times, the son served as enforcer and trusted operative, while the two shared secrets and connections with the powerful.

Once I began focusing on the continuity between father and son, I realized that I had to reexamine Poppy. When I did that, I learned the conventional picture of him too was wrong. And not just wrong; it omitted a major part of the story that lay behind the political rise of the entire Bush clan. Reading the Bush bios I began to feel that I was examining Soviet-era photographs of the politburo, in which disfavored persons were made to vanish, leaving a curious hole in the ensemble. Except in this case, what was missing was not a person but an entire dimension of power in the United States.

I discovered that Poppy was not really the sentimental preppy, the oft-bumbling public servant most of us believed him to be. Poppy had led what amounted to a double life, and the secret portion of that life included participation in an astonishing range of covert operations. As I began to examine Poppy's most improbable statements about himself, I found myself struggling through the miasma surrounding the John F. Kennedy assassination, Watergate, the American relationship with the Saudis, and other chapters of the American experience that have never been properly explained. While I was in my reporting phase and sharing some of my more surprising findings with colleagues, one of them suggested, only half in jest, that the book be called "Everything You Thought You Knew Is Wrong."

If indeed we are so totally in the dark, how come?

Trying to answer that question, I began studying the messengers themselves, and even directly querying those who had participated in the creation of the Bush narrative—and indeed the larger American narrative—as "witnesses" or scribes. What I found was something that the mainstream media in the United States resists. Namely, there have been concerted efforts to control the way in which the big stories are told, and these efforts go deeper into the American establishment—corporate and government both—than most people would like to believe.

Among the themes that emerged:

- Presidents have a lot less power and independence than I had assumed. Party affiliation is not a major factor in this regard.
- Initiating reforms or standing up to powerful interests can invite retribution of a kind I had not imagined. Presidents are subject not only to pressure but also to entrapment, blackmail, and even, in one way or another, removal.
- The constant recourse to the "lone wolf" theory to explain assassinations and comparable national traumas is not only empirically challenged but also represents a kind of large scale cop-out. At what point, I wondered, is it permissible to doubt that the assassinations of both Kennedys and Martin Luther King Jr.—all of whom challenged the status quo in significant ways—were the result of independent actions by three "crazed loners"?

Time and again, there has been a rush to bury inquiries into the most per-plexing events of our time, along with a determination to subject dissenting views to ridicule. And the media weren't just enabling these efforts; they were complicit in them—not least by labeling anyone who dared to subject conventional views to a fresh and quizzical eye as a *conspiracy theorist.*

I'll admit it. Fear of being so labeled has haunted me throughout this work. It's been an internal censor that I've had to resist again and again. And also an external one, as friends within the journalistic establishment reviewed my findings, found them both credible and highly disturbing, and yet urged me to stay away from them for my own good.

I began to realize that I was experiencing the very thing the process is de-signed to induce. The boundaries of permissible thought are staked out and enforced. We accept the conventional narratives because they are repeated and approved, while conflicting ones are scorned. Isn't this how authoritar-ian regimes work? They get inside your mind so that overt repression be-comes less necessary.

Whose interests does this serve? As this book demonstrates, the deck has long been, and continues to be, stacked on behalf of big-money players, es-pecially those in commodities and natural resources—from gold to oil—and those who finance the extraction of these materials. The defense industry, and the aligned growth business of "intelligence," provide muscle. On a lower level is an army of enablers—the campaign functionaries, the PR people, the lawyers. This was the Bush enterprise. The Bushes embod-ied it as a dynasty, but it is larger than them, and will prove more enduring.

DECEPTION RESIDES AT the very center of our national psyche. It affects us in incalculable ways, from decisions in the voting booth to our own life choices.

The solution, clearly, is to pull away the veil.

Now the good news. Telling stories that need to be told is less dependent on the good graces of those with a vested interest in concealment. This book would not have been possible ten years ago, before the Internet's tremen-dous search and storage capabilities, and the new ways it offers to exchange information and ideas with others. Much has been made of the havoc the Internet has wrought with old business models, from publishing to recorded music. Less has been said about emerging opportunities to crack the wall of secrecy and disinformation—not just in authoritarian regimes abroad, but right here at home as well.

Whether professional journalists or concerned citizens, we are all offered a new lease on life with these technologies, provided we neither abuse the privilege nor allow the apparatus itself to fall under the control of those who keep the secrets.

My work, and that of many others, would not be possible without good laws—the First Amendment, the Freedom of Information Act—and the untiring efforts of individuals and groups devoted to transparency in government and in society at large. Also, we must thank the legions of anonymous individuals within both government and private business who try to do the right thing while bringing home the paycheck. They continue to be our best sources of information.

Under the aegis of the Bush enterprise, we have seen constant efforts to circumvent, ignore, and even repeal constitutional protections for free speech and inquiry. I hope this book has helped demonstrate why some people work so hard at such repression—and why we cannot allow them to prevail. It is not simply a matter of arcane legal disputes in Washington, but of the determination of powerful and secretive forces to twist our national story to their own ends.

Author's Note

The research for this book, by definition, is a work in progress. You are invited to visit www.familyofsecrets.com for more detailed background information and for updates.

Acknowledgments

My agent, Andrew Stuart, understood the project and helped find it a great home. My editor, Peter Ginna, publisher and editorial director of Bloomsbury Press, saw the possibilities immediately, and has been unfailingly thoughtful and supportive. Also, thanks to all of the people at Bloomsbury, including managing editor Mike O'Connor, who handled my endless changes to the manuscript with dexterity and grace; Peter Miller and Sabrina Farber, who enthusiastically went forth to sell the book and the ideas in it; Pete Beatty; publicist Gene Taft; counsel Alan Kaufman; and copy editor Maureen Klier, who edited with enthusiasm and offered many good suggestions.

I owe a great deal to my aide-de-camp Akiva Gottlieb, without whose common sense, sharp mind, reliability, efficiency, and amiable disposition I don't think I could have gotten through the final year of this project. Akiva had his hand in everything: research, brainstorming, coordinating fact-checking, editing. Jonathan Rowe, an old friend and one of the more contemplative journalists I know, played a crucial role in helping me work out my thinking on matters large and small, and suggested improvements in how I told this story. Jon devoted hundreds of hours to this, and I am deeply grateful. I also cannot offer enough thanks to Gerald Jonas, who looked at the manuscript through endless iterations over several years, offering superb suggestions for clarifying and styling sprawling, difficult material. Jonathan Z. Larsen, a former editor of mine, provided invaluable guidance, assistance, and material support, and worked with me on research in the early stages of the project.

Charlotte Dennett researched several key topics with enthusiasm, and, with her husband Gerard Colby, offered advice from their years as serious biographers. John Beckham, Eric Stoner, Lyle Deixler, and Mark Levey also did research. Inez Baker uncomplainingly transcribed hundreds of hours of interviews and provided a steady stream of amusing e-mails. Photo researcher Nancy Novick worked quickly and effectively to put together a gallery that does justice to this story. Tanya Elder organized my files and books. Linda Minor offered me her vast knowledge of financial intrigue and Texas history. Joseph Coscarelli, Juliet Linderman, and Susannah Vila were dedicated and professional fact-checkers; Joe also made sure that the footnotes were right. Adam Federman served as a savvy and even-keeled assistant in earlier stages of the book. There are many other people to thank for providing help of all kinds, large and small. With apologies to anyone whom I may have overlooked, my appreciation goes, in no particular order, to: David Callahan, David Margolick, Steve Weinberg, James Rosen, James Moore, Len Colodny, Jonathan Beaty, Jim Hougan, Bill Moyers, Richard Cummings, Jim Baldauf, David Smallman, John Moscow, Sam Smith, David Cay Johnston, Corey Pein, Rex Bradford, John Connolly, Peter Dale Scott, Jo Thomas, Randall Henriksen, Mark Dowie, Anthony Lappé, Jonathan Wimpenny, Nadine Eckhardt, James Huang, Tom Zoellner, John Hawkins, Louis Wolf, John Labbé, Roger Morris, Alice Concari, Tom "Smitty" Smith, Jack Blum, Nicholas von Hoffman, David Armstrong, Harvey Gough, Jonathan Winer, Michael Klare, Victor Navasky, Richard Gooding, Hendrik Hertzberg, Sissy Farenthold, Paul Lukasiak, Bruce Shapiro, Paul Myers, Bob Fertik, David MacMichael, Dan Arshack, Ann Louise Bardach, Dave Block, Neil Reisner, Jim Mulvaney, Ben and Coco van Meerendonk, James Hamilton-Paterson, Roane Carey, Melanie Einzig, Craig McDonald, Herbert Parmet, James Lesar, John McGarvey, Adam Davids, Ron Baker, George Knapp, Hamilton Fish, Mike Hoyt, Wim Dankbaar, Jerry Shinley, Dusty Martin, Frosty Troy, George Shipley, Erika Mayo, Dan Alcorn, Jim Norman, Ron Brynaert, Ryan Wadle, Steve Wasserman, John Fine, Bob Mahlburg, Dan Moldea, Robert Dreyfuss, Ellen Hopkins, Todd Gitlin, Steve Ross, Steve Rose, Bryan Farrell, and Steven Aftergood.

Many archives, libraries, and newsrooms provided access to and copies of articles and files, including the *Palm Beach Post*; Sixth Floor Museum; Richard M. Nixon and George H. W. Bush presidential libraries; National Archives; Texas State Archives; Texas Secretary of State's office; Princeton, Columbia, Stanford, and New York University. Thanks to David Smith of the New York Public Library for helping obtain unusual materials through interlibrary loan. With appreciation to the remarkable Strand Bookstore, which invariably had most of the out-of-print books I needed. I would also like to acknowledge Dragon Naturally Speaking, a voice dictation program that allowed me to continue writing when the endless typing began to take its toll on my hands and elbows.

The opinions in this book are not necessarily shared in whole or in part by anyone on this list, and of course any errors or omissions are mine alone, and unintended.

Finally, special thanks to my family and friends for their support and forbearance.

Notes

Note: For the Mary Ferrell Foundation, visit www.maryferell.org.

2: Poppy's Secret

1. Joseph McBride, *Frank Capra: The Catastrophe of Success* (New York: St. Martin's Griffin, 1992).
2. Joseph McBride, "The Man Who Wasn't There, 'George Bush,' C.I.A. Operative," *Nation*, July 16, 1988.
3. The Rowland Evans and Robert Novak column, appearing January 1, 1976, in the Syracuse *Post-Standard* under the title "CIA: Maxi vs. Mini," in the same month Bush's nomination went to the Senate, quoted one CIA insider as saying: "We have to get rid of those three little letters, C-I-A. Sure, it's a cosmetic change, but the CIA won't ever overcome its unfair stigma as a government-sanctioned international murder organization until it gets a new name."
4. Actually, the memo had been written twenty-five years previous, not twenty-seven.
5. Joseph McBride, "Where Was George?" *Nation*, August 13, 1988.
6. George William Bush's affidavit had been filed as evidence in a suit brought by the nonprofit Assassination Archives and Research Center that sought an emergency injunction compelling, before the 1988 election, release of records on Bush's past (*AARC v. CIA*). Judge Charles Revercomb of the U.S. District Court for the District of Columbia declined the request, and the CIA continued its refusal to confirm or deny a relationship with George Herbert Walker Bush.
7. The Mary Ferrell Foundation, founded in the name of JFK researcher Mary Ferrell, has for the past few years been scanning and making available online documents from her collection and that of the Assassination Archives and Research Center, History Matters, and others, most of them obtained over the years under the Freedom of Information Act. They can be accessed online at www.maryferrell.org. Not insignificantly, the documents regarding the Bush memo were declassified under the Clinton administration in 1997. Few, if any, documents that shed light on these activities were declassified under either George H. W. Bush or George W. Bush.
8. Jim Hougan, *Secret Agenda: Watergate, Deep Throat, and the CIA* (New York: Random House, 1984).
9. An article by Richard Cummings ("An American in Paris," *American Conservative*, February 16, 2004) asserts that *Paris Review* cofounder and editor Peter Matthiessen was a CIA agent whose literary activities served as cover for intelligence work. Also, the *Review*'s longtime editor George Plimpton "was an 'agent of influence' for the CIA . . . invariably paid for [his] services." Also see Hugh Wilford, *The Mighty Wurlitzer: How the CIA Played America* (Cambridge, MA: Harvard University Press, 2008), p. 106; and Frances Stonor Saunders, *Who Paid the Piper? The CIA and the Cultural Cold War* (London: Granta, 1999).

10. Joseph J. Trento, *Prelude to Terror: Edwin P. Wilson and the Legacy of America's Private Intelligence Network* (New York: Carroll & Graf, 2005), p. 16.

11. John A. Kouwenhoven, *Partners in Banking: An Historical Portrait of a Great Private Bank, Brown Brothers Harriman & Co., 1818–1968* (New York: Doubleday & Company, 1983 reprint), p. 189.

12. Kevin Phillips, *American Dynasty: Aristocracy, Fortune, and the Politics of Deceit in the House of Bush* (New York: Penguin Books, 2004), pp. 19–20.

13. Ibid., pp. 38–39.

14. Thomas Petzinger Jr., *Oil & Honor: The Texaco-Pennzoil Wars* (New York: G. P. Putnam's Sons, 1987), p. 93.

15. George H. W. Bush's nickname became a way to distinguish him from his son George W. Bush. But H. W. had long been known as "Poppy" to relatives and close friends. His older brother, Prescott Bush Jr., became known as "Pressy." As the second son, H. W. had been named George Herbert Walker Bush, after his maternal grandfather. Because his Walker uncles called their father "Pop," they decided to call his young namesake grandson "Poppy," and the name stuck. See Peter Schweizer and Rochelle Schweizer, *The Bushes: Portrait of a Dynasty* (New York: Doubleday, 2004), p. 37.

16. Robert B. Stinnett, *George Bush: His World War II Years* (New York: Brassey's, 1992), p. 89.

17. Terence Hunt, Associated Press, "Bush Praised for War Heroism," September 2, 1984.

18. James Bradley, *Flyboys: A True Story of Courage* (New York: Back Bay, 2002), p. 182.

19. George Bush with Doug Wead, *George Bush: Man of Integrity* (Eugene, OR: Harvest House, 1988), pp. 4–5.

20. Associated Press, "Gunner in Squadron Disputes Bush on Downing of Bomber," *New York Times*, August 13, 1988.

21. The closest he came was *Looking Forward: An Autobiography* (New York: Doubleday, 1987), co-written with longtime Washington PR man Victor Gold, which was styled as an autobiography but was notably brief and episodic. It was also full of self-serving inaccuracies.

3: Viva Zapata

1. Kitty Kelley, *The Family: The Real Story of the Bush Dynasty* (New York: Doubleday, 2004), pp. 342–43.

2. Robin Winks, *Cloak and Gown: Scholars in the Secret War, 1939–1961* (New York: William Morrow, 1987), p. 247. According to Winks, both the wartime Office of Strategic Services and its successor, the CIA, wanted "young men with high grades, a sense of grace, with previous knowledge of Europe . . . and ease with themselves, a certain healthy self-respect and independent means . . . Oh yes, and good social connections." That was one reason that the "OSS" was said to stand for "Oh So Social." Winks, himself a former Yale professor, says the university's crew coach even received ten thousand dollars annually from the CIA for his efforts to direct team members to the agency, though by all indications, many recruiters were unpaid.

3. For the job, Pearson tasked Yale graduate Richard W. Cutler. See Richard W. Cutler, *Counterspy: Memoirs of a Counterintelligence Officer in World War II and the Cold War* (Washington, D.C.: Brassey's, 2004).

4. Alexandra Robbins, *Secrets of the Tomb: Skull and Bones, the Ivy League, and the Hidden Paths of Power* (New York: Back Bay, 2002), p. 53.

5. Ibid., p. 187.

6. Besides Bush, two other CIA directors, Porter Goss and R. James Woolsey, are Yale alumni. So are top CIA Operations Division directors Richard M. Bissell Jr. and Tracy Barnes, engineers of the Bay of Pigs invasion, and Walter L. Pforzheimer, who headed several key OSS operations and helped draft the act that created the CIA in 1947.

7. The Edward Wilson character was in reality a loose composite of several CIA figures, in particular the agency's longtime counterintelligence chief James Jesus Angleton, Yale '41.

8. In a November 1, 2005, editorial for the *National Review*, Buckley recounted: "When in 1951 I was inducted into the CIA as a deep cover agent, the procedures for disguising my affiliation and my work were unsmilingly comprehensive. It was three months before I was formally permitted to inform my wife what the real reason was for going to Mexico City to live. If, a year later, I had been apprehended, dosed with sodium pentothal, and forced to give out the names of everyone I knew in the CIA, I could have come up with exactly one name, that of my immediate boss (E. Howard Hunt, as it happened). In the passage of time one can indulge in idle talk on spook life. In 1980 I found myself seated next to the former president of Mexico at a ski-area restaurant. What, he asked amiably, had I done when I lived in Mexico? 'I tried to undermine your regime, Mr. President.' "

   Another graduate, Jack Downey, Yale '51, was convicted of espionage in China a year after graduation, charged with secretly air-dropping supplies and agents in a CIA attempt to foment an uprising. See Jerome Alan Cohen, "Will Jack Make His 25th Reunion," *New York Times*, July 7, 1971.

9. Darwin Payne, *Initiative in Energy: The Story of Dresser Industries* (New York: Simon & Schuster, 1979), p. 114.

10. The stories of characters throughout the Bush saga are full of unexplained, lengthy hiking trips, circumnavigations, and the like, all preceding important new assignments.

11. Randall Rothenberg, "In Search of George Bush," *New York Times*, March 6, 1988.

12. Mallon's brother-in-law Alan Tower Waterman served as the Navy's technology purchasing liaison. Later Waterman became the first head of the National Science Foundation, created by Congress in 1950 to fund basic research with a statutory mandate "to promote the progress of science; to advance the national health, prosperity, and welfare; to secure the national defense" (National Science Foundation Web site, www.nsf.gov/about). Such a mission, paralleling as it does the lofty language of the preamble to the U.S. Constitution, captures the sense of importance that men like Mallon brought to their government service, and which they carried with them into their private business endeavors.

13. Over the years, board members would include the publisher of the *Los Angeles Times*, a former Texas governor, an official of the Massachusetts Institute of Technology, an executive of the predecessor to Citibank, and President Eisenhower's treasury secretary. Several were Bonesmen.

14. Prescott Bush, interview for the Columbia University Oral History Research Project, 1966.

15. Daniel Yergin, *The Prize: The Epic Quest for Oil, Money and Power* (New York: Free Press, 1992), p. 395.

16. Author interview with Valta Ree Casselman, August 14, 2006.

17. George Bush with Victor Gold, *Looking Forward: An Autobiography* (New York: Doubleday, 1987), pp. 49–50.

18. National Security Council policy papers, NSC 18/2, published February 17, 1949; and NSC 18/4, published November 17, 1949 (both declassified October 1, 1987).

19. Joseph J. Trento, *Prelude to Terror: Edwin P. Wilson and the Legacy of America's Private Intelligence Network* (New York: Carroll & Graf, 2005), pp. 13–14.

20. Gerald M. Boyd, "Bush Gets Harsh Reception at Shipyard in Oregon," *New York Times*, September 7, 1988. Bush, confronted by boos and obscenities from shipyard union members critical of

DRIFTWOOD PUBLIC LIBRARY
801 SW HWY. 101
LINCOLN CITY, OREGON 97367

Reagan's economic policies, got out his wallet and had a supporter wave his old union card in front of the crowd. "How many guys running for President of the United States has been a member of the C.I.O. steelworkers?" Bush asked. "You are looking at one."

21. Payne, *Initiative in Energy*, pp. 176–77.

22. Trento, *Prelude to Terror*, p. 13.

23. Bob Woodward and Walter Pincus, "Bush Opened Up to Secret Yale Society, Turning Points in a Life Built on Alliances," *Washington Post*, August 7, 1988.

24. This had been created under the National Security Act of 1947 by President Truman with significant input from his key advisers, Prescott Bush's business partners Averell Harriman and Robert A. Lovett. Its mandate was to help prepare the country for industrial and civilian mobilization in time of war.

25. Prescott Bush, interview for the Columbia University Oral History Research Project, 1966, p. 83.

26. Mallon wrote to Allen Dulles: "What [Slick] really wants is to take Eric Johnston's place as head of the advisory committee for Technical Cooperation Administration or whatever the Point Four program will be called from now on." TCA ostensibly provided "scientific and technical assistance to underdeveloped countries in order to maintain political stability and to further economic and social progress," but it was also a key means of carrying out clandestine intelligence operations.

27. Loren Coleman wrote *Tom Slick and the Search for the Yeti* (Boston: Faber & Faber, 1989) and *Tom Slick: True Life Encounters in Cryptozoology* (Fresno, CA: Linden, 2002).

28. Trento, *Prelude to Terror*, p. 14.

29. Ibid., p. 10.

30. Ibid., pp. 11–12. See also Leonard Mosley, *Dull: A Biography of Eleanor, Allen, and John Foster Dulles and Their Family Network* (London: Hodder & Stoughton, 1978), p. 480, which speaks of Allen Dulles Jr.'s "absolute hatred" of his father.

31. Herbert S. Parmet, *George Bush: The Life of a Lone Star Yankee* (New Brunswick, NJ: Transaction, 2000), p. 68.

32. Even Poppy's paternal grandfather, Samuel Bush, had Rockefeller connections. William Goodsell Rockefeller, John D. Rockefeller's brother, was a major backer of the Milwaukee & St. Paul Railroad, where Samuel Bush worked as a top executive at the turn of the nineteenth century. After that, Samuel began running Buckeye Malleable Iron & Coupler Company, a Columbus, Ohio, company backed by John D. Rockefeller's other brother, Franklin.

33. George Bush, *Looking Forward*.

34. Carl Bernstein, "The CIA and the Media," *Rolling Stone*, October 20, 1977. Bernstein bases his assertion on the following evidence: "Katharine Graham, Philip Graham's widow and the current publisher of the Post, says she has never been informed of any CIA relationships with either Post or Newsweek personnel. In November of 1973, Mrs. Graham called William Colby and asked if any Post stringers or staff members were associated with the CIA. Colby assured her that no staff members were employed by the Agency but refused to discuss the question of stringers."

35. Peter Schweizer and Rochelle Schweizer, *The Bushes: Portrait of a Dynasty* (New York: Doubleday, 2004), p. 127.

36. Zapata Petroleum filed its certificate of incorporation in Delaware on March 27, 1953, and registered to do business in Texas on April 30, 1953.

37. Letter from Neil Mallon to Allen Dulles, April 10, 1953. Allen W. Dulles Papers, 1845–1971. Seeley G. Mudd Manuscript Library, Princeton University. Discovered by independent researcher Bruce Adamson.

DRIFTWOOD PUBLIC LIBRARY
801 SW HWY. 101
LINCOLN CITY, OREGON 97367

38. At the time, U.S. public opinion was very much behind the insurgency of Fidel Castro, which was growing quickly in its struggle against the stunningly corrupt dictator Fulgencio Batista, but corporate interests with large Cuban holdings watched the situation nervously.

39. In an odd twist, Dresser Industries had tried, unsuccessfully, to buy out Hughes's drill bit company years earlier.

40. Michael Drosnin, *Citizen Hughes: The Power, the Money and the Madness* (New York: Holt, Rinehart and Winston, 1985).

41. Trento, *Prelude to Terror*, p. 16.

42. These include Theodore Shackley, E. Howard Hunt, Felix Rodriguez, and Porter Goss.

43. The training base for the Bay of Pigs invasion was the plantation of Roberto Alejos Arzu, a powerful and feared figure who would later run a notorious death squad, La Mano Blanca, and chair the local efforts of several Bush-backed ventures, including AmeriCares, the contra-friendly relief organization founded by yet another of Poppy's college roommates, Connecticut resident Robert Macauley. See Russ Baker, "A Thousand Points of Blight," *Village Voice*, January 8, 1991.

44. John A. Kouwenhoven, *Partners in Banking: An Historical Portrait of a Great Private Bank: Brown Brothers Harriman & Co., 1818–1968* (New York: Doubleday & Co., 1968), pp. 206–7.

45. Conventional historical accounts restrict the causes of the split to disputes between the strong-willed Hugh Liedtke and the equally bullheaded Herbie Walker. But there may have been more to it. If in fact Zapata Offshore, like Mallon's Dresser Industries, was allowing itself to be used as a chess piece in global intrigues, the Liedtkes, who went on to great wealth independent of Bush, may not have been that enthusiastic about sacrificing profits for a "greater cause."

46. Trento, *Prelude to Terror*, p. 17.

47. Jonathan Kwitny, "The Mexican Connection: A Look at an Old George Bush Business Venture," *Barron's*, September 19, 1988. After Kwitny unearthed duplicate copies elsewhere, Bush admitted through a spokesman a brief business relationship with Jorge Diaz Serrano, claiming it lasted just seven months. Yet Kwitny was able to independently locate Zapata SEC filings that made clear that Bush's dealings with the Mexican lasted four years. They also established that the relationship involved both breaking Mexican law and keeping Zapata's own shareholders in the dark about the deal, a violation of U.S. securities law. The principal method of moving funds to Diaz Serrano was to drastically undercharge him for an oil rig. "It was mighty generous of Bush to sell us the rig," Diaz Serrano said. (Kwitny's reporting, which was published less than two months before Bush was elected president in 1988, received little attention or follow-through from other media outlets.)

48. At the time, Diaz Serrano was on his way to Moscow for a stint as Mexico's ambassador to the Soviet Union.

49. Robert H. Gow, *You Can't Direct the Wind; You Can Only Reset the Sails: My First 62 Years* (Houston: Xixim Publishing, 2002), p. 109.

50. Trento, *Prelude to Terror*, p. 21.

51. Joseph J. Trento interview with Vincent Bounds, March 27, 1992. Cited in Trento, *Prelude to Terror*, p. 21.

52. Fitzhugh Green, *George Bush: An Intimate Portrait* (New York: Hippocrene, 1989), pp. 73–74.

53. Farish was sole heir to a family that helped found Humble Oil, which later became part of the Rockefeller's Standard Oil of New Jersey (which is now Exxon). Farish's grandfather, chairman of Standard, found himself, like Prescott Bush, under investigation by the U.S. Senate for his wartime dealings with the Nazis and died of a heart attack shortly afterward. Farish III, who served as an aide to Poppy Bush when he ran for the U.S. Senate in 1964, hardly needed a paycheck. His

avocations included breeding racehorses (even stabling for Queen Elizabeth II, who was a guest at Farish's Lane's End Farm).

54. Gow, *You Can't Direct the Wind*, p. 104.

55. Payne, *Initiative in Energy*, p. 221.

56. Gow, *You Can't Direct the Wind*, pp. 104–24.

4: WHERE WAS POPPY?

1. Kitty Kelley, *The Family: The Real Story of the Bush Dynasty* (New York: Doubleday, 2004), p. 213.

2. Warren Hinckle and William Turner, *Deadly Secrets: The CIA-MAFIA War Against Castro and the Assassination of J.F.K.* (New York: Thunder's Mouth Press, 1992), p. 103. The "something" looks more and more like the assassination of Castro. *Bay of Pigs Declassified: The Secret CIA Report on the Invasion of Cuba* (New York: New Press, 1998), edited by Peter Kornbluh of the non-profit National Security Archive, reports that the CIA's Richard Bissell told Robert F. Kennedy that "the CIA's 'associated planning' for the Bay of Pigs invasion included 'the use of the underworld against Castro'" (p. 10). This suggests that knocking off the leader was an integral part of the original plan.

3. "C.I.A.: Maker of Policy, or Tool," *New York Times*, April 25, 1966.

4. Peter Dale Scott, *Deep Politics and the Death of JFK* (Berkeley: University of California Press, 1993).

5. Michael R. Beschloss, *Taking Charge: The Johnson White House Tapes, 1963–1964* (New York: Simon & Schuster, 1997), p. 72.

6. Statistics on the number of questions, by panel member, can be found in Walt Brown's *The Warren Omission* (Florence, KY: Delmar, 1996), p. 85. There were 2,154 questions by Dulles to Warren's 608, with Ford, Cooper, and McCloy in between. But Warren was present at the most sessions (p. 83), 110 to Dulles's 85, with Ford in between at 95.

7. E. Howard Hunt, *Give Us This Day* (New York: Arlington House, 1973), p. 215.

8. Prescott Bush to Allen Dulles, 1969. Allen W. Dulles Papers, 1845–1971. Seeley G. Mudd Manuscript Library, Princeton University, box 10, folder 11.

9. Herbert S. Parmet, *George Bush: The Life of a Lone Star Yankee* (New Brunswick, NJ: Transaction, reprint 2000), p. 94.

10. George Bush Presidential Library and Museum, College Station, Texas: "Zapata—Business Alpha File, Box 3, World Trip, 1963."

11. The oil depletion allowance sheltered 27.5 percent of oil income as compensation for the "depletion" of finite reserves. As the journalist Robert Bryce noted in *Cronies: Oil, Bushes, and the Rise of Texas, America's Superstate* (New York: PublicAffairs, 2004): "Numerous studies showed that the oilmen were getting a tax break that was unprecedented in American business. While other businessmen had to pay taxes on their income regardless of what they sold, the oilmen got special treatment."

12. The FBI report is available through the Mary Ferrell Foundation Web site (www.maryferell.org): Graham Kitchel report in Warren Commission document 14. This brief report, but not one that described George Bush in more detail and contained other additional information, was apparently received by Warren Commission staff. There is no reason to think that in 1964, staffers would have paid particular attention to this as one of many such tips.

13. Author interview with Leslie Acoca, January 26, 2007.

14. Miguel Acoca, "Documents: Bush Blew Whistle on Rival in JFK Slaying," *San Francisco Examiner*, August 25, 1988.

15. Barbara Bush, *Barbara Bush: A Memoir* (New York: Scribner, 1994), pp. 59–60.

16. Tyler lies about ninety miles to the east of Dallas; its population in 1963 was around thirty-eight thousand.

17. Kelley, *The Family*, p. 212.

18. Author interview with Aubrey Irby, February 1, 2007.

19. Burton Hersh, *The Old Boys: The American Elite and the Origins of the CIA* (St. Petersburg, FL: Tree Farm, 1992); and Peter Grose, *Gentleman Spy: The Life of Allen Dulles* (Boston: Houghton Mifflin, 1994).

20. Hersh, *The Old Boys*, p. 394.

21. Tim Weiner, *Legacy of Ashes: The History of the CIA* (New York: Anchor, 2008), p. 144.

22. Ulmer was running things in Greece during the country's vicious civil war; the Athens CIA station was also in charge of most Middle East operations and anti-Soviet-bloc efforts in Yugoslavia, Albania, and other Balkan countries. Ulmer would go on to a host of key CIA assignments, including running the Paris station and the CIA's Far East division, overseeing operations in Southeast Asia, and an attempted coup against the populist Indonesian president with the typically Indonesian one-word name: Sukarno.

23. Niarchos personally won Dulles over when the director stopped in Athens to visit Ulmer as part of a secret 1956 "world tour" of CIA stations. Dulles was treated to a weekend on Niarchos's 190-foot yacht. Niarchos introduced the bon vivant Dulles to the willful and alluring Queen Frederika of Greece (granddaughter of Kaiser Wilhelm) and made his yacht available to them for their private purposes. See Grose, *Gentleman Spy*, pp. 430, 452.

24. Peter Evans, *Nemesis* (New York: HarperCollins, 2004), p. 140.

25. Grose, *Gentleman Spy*, p. 452.

26. James Presley, *Never in Doubt: A History of Delta Drilling Company* (Houston: Gulf, 1981), pp. 41–45.

27. Author interview with Keating Zeppa, February 3, 2007.

28. The FBI document is available at the Assassination Archives Research Center on page 14 of this longer file: www.aarclibrary.org/notices/Affidavit_of_George_William_Bush_880921.pdf

29. Author interview with Kearney Reynolds, March 4, 2007.

30. This cannot be corroborated, as no relevant Secret Service records have been publicly released.

31. Telephone interview with James Parrott conducted by independent researcher Bruce Campbell Adamson, May 31, 1993.

32. Steve Berg, "Republicans Tear Into Clinton; Family Values Issue Widens Cultural Gap," *Minneapolis Star-Tribune*, August 19, 1992.

5: OSWALD'S FRIEND

1. Letter from de Mohrenschildt to Bush, available through the Mary Ferrell Foundation Web site (www.maryferrell.org). It includes the official routing slip where Bush checks "yes" after "do you know this individual?" (104-10414-10013). Also available is a memorandum from Inspector General John Waller to Bush summarizing what is in the CIA files on de Mohrenschildt (104-10414-10378); and a letter from Bush to de Mohrenschildt (104-10414-10134).

2. Associated Press, "Russian-Born Society Figure Knew Kennedy's Family and His Assassin," *Washington Post*, November 25, 1964.

3. Norman Mailer, *Oswald's Tale* (New York: Random House, 1995), p. 458.

4. George de Mohrenschildt's family were Russian nobility of Swedish and German extraction; de Mohrenschildt de-Germanized his name upon immigrating to the United States.

5. David L. Francis, former mayor of St. Louis and governor of Missouri.

6. Serving with Samuel Bush on the War Industries Board was Robert S. Lovett, president of the Union Pacific Railroad, chief counsel to E. H. Harriman, and executor of Harriman's will. Lovett had been in the Texas law firm of the family of future secretary of state and Middle East envoy James Baker. Lovett's son, Robert A. Lovett, would go on to become an important figure in the Bush saga, as a business partner with Prescott Bush and Averell Harriman, and during World War II, as an aide to Ambassador Harriman in Moscow. Under Harry S Truman, he would be instrumental in the establishment of the Central Intelligence Agency.

7. Mrs. Harriman's late husband was a cousin, major financier, and business associate of E. H. Harriman, whose sons, Averell and Roland Harriman, were Skull and Bones mates and later business partners of Prescott Bush, and employers of Prescott's father-in-law, George Herbert Walker.

8. Steve LeVine, *The Oil and the Glory: The Pursuit of Empire and Fortune on the Caspian Sea* (New York: Random House, 2007), p. 34.

9. Dimitri called himself von Mohrenschildt, while George, who didn't find the German appendage useful in America, went by de Mohrenschildt.

10. Obituary of Edward G. Hooker, *New York Times*, March 30, 1967.

11. From the University of Liège, Belgium, 1938.

12. Long before he headed up the CIA, Dulles had revealed his consummate skill in government service, which included a stint at the U.S. embassy in Istanbul at the time the United States was trying to wedge its way into the now-defeated Ottoman Empire—whose former oil properties in Mesopotamia (Iraq) were the subject of intense international competition following World War I—and in Washington as chief of the Near East desk at the State Department. He would also serve as an adviser on German war reparations. During his trips to Europe as a lawyer, Dulles gathered intelligence on political conditions. Switching between public and private service seemed to come naturally to him, particularly when it involved carrying out intelligence work.

13. Peter Grose, *Gentleman Spy: The Life of Allen Dulles* (Boston: Houghton Mifflin, 1994), p. 147.

14. Serge Obolensky, *One Man in His Time* (London: Hutchinson, 1960).

15. William F. Buckley Sr. had started Pantepec in Mexico in 1914. After he resisted restrictions placed on American oil companies and land ownership by the Mexican Constitution of 1917, Buckley Sr. was expelled in 1921 by Mexican president Álvaro Obregón. The Mexicans suspected Buckley of working with other American corporate figures to topple the government.

16. David A. Andelman, *A Shattered Peace: Versailles 1919 and the Price We Pay Today* (New York: Wiley, 2007).

17. Warren Commission testimony, p. 267.

18. Other members included Clint Murchison (employer of George de Mohrenschildt and friend of J. Edgar Hoover), Fred Florence (executive of the CIA-controlled Republic National Bank), oilman H. L. Hunt (business associate and friend of Murchison and a staunch anti-Communist), Bernard L. Gold (owner of Nardis Sportswear, which employed both Abraham Zapruder and Mrs. George de Mohrenschildt), and R. Gerald Storey (later, chief of the JFK assassination investigation in Texas).

19. Letter from Senator Prescott Bush to Eisenhower national security aide and cold war propaganda expert C. D. Jackson, dated March 26, 1953. Found in a footnote to Warren Hinckle and William W. Turner, *The Fish Is Red: The Story of the Secret War Against Castro* (New York: HarperCollins, 1981).

20. Though the couple divorced in 1973, they remained close until de Mohrenschildt's death in 1977.

21. As a one-paragraph article with a Havana dateline buried in the *New York Times* of June 14, 1954, noted: "Interest in the possibility of petroleum production in Cuba increased here today with the announcement that a group of American oil operators would start a series of wells within ninety days. The announcement said these operators, from Texas and California, had

signed a contract to drill exploratory wells on leases of the Transcuba Oil Company and the Cuban Venezuelan oil voting trust."

Eighteen months later, on January 4, 1956, the *Times* reported:

> Cuba's hopes of taking her place among the oil producing nations of the world are rising slowly. There has been no spectacular strike but the steady increase in production from small wells and the inflow of capital for exploration work is highly encouraging.
>
> Oilmen from Texas, Oklahoma and California in particular are appearing in Cuba in increasing numbers. Various small companies and some with considerable resources have been formed.
>
> Last September the Stanolind Oil and Gas Company (Standard Oil of Indiana) signed a contract with Trans-Cuba Oil Company and the Cuban-Venezuelan Oil Voting Trust in Havana, which have large holdings. The Stanolind will spend $2,000,000 yearly in exploration and drilling during the next five years. It is estimated that investors will have committed $25,000,000 for exploration work during the next two years.

22. Back in the 1930s, Lansky had hit upon the Caribbean as a perfect place to launder illegal profits for mob bosses from the Northeast. He funneled the cash into a wide range of gambling ventures, hotels, and other businesses, as well as the drug trade, and became close to the Cuban authorities. For more, see Alfred McCoy, *The Politics of Heroin: CIA Complicity in the Global Drug Trade* (Chicago: Lawrence Hill, 1991).

23. During the first six months of 1955, Cuba produced 151,122 barrels of oil, three times the production of the previous year. October 1955 saw daily production running more than 50 percent above the average for the first half of the year. "Rise in Domestic Oil Flow Bolsters Cuba; Exploratory Capital Pouring into Island," *New York Times*, January 5, 1956.

24. "Oil Drilling Deal Set," *New York Times*, November 30, 1956.

25. "Cuban-Venezuelan Unit Chooses Trustee," *New York Times*, May 14, 1956.

26. Stephen Birmingham, *Our Crowd: The Great Jewish Families of New York* (New York: Harper and Row, 1967), pp. 409–410.

27. Empire Trust corporate filings with the Texas Secretary of State's Office, as of 1966.

28. Henry Brunie, Empire Trust's president, was a best friend of and served as best man at the wedding of Warren Commission member John J. McCloy.

29. John A. "Jack" Crichton interview, July 6, 2001, Oral History Collection, Sixth Floor Museum, Dallas.

30. The 488th Army Intelligence Detachment.

31. R. Hart Phillips, "Cuba Limits Search for Oil; Nationalization Step Seen," *New York Times*, November 22, 1959.

32. These refineries were not affected, however, since most of the oil they refined came from other countries. Much of it, in fact, came from Venezuela.

33. William A. Doyle, "The Daily Investor," *Portsmouth Herald* (New Hampshire), August 14, 1961.

34. John Kouwenhoven, *Partners in Banking: An Historical Portrait of a Great Private Bank, Brown Brothers, Harriman & Co., 1818–1968* (New York: Doubleday & Company, 1983 reprint), p. 206.

35. Erik Hedegaard, "The Last Confessions of E. Howard Hunt," *Rolling Stone*, April 5, 2007.

36. Fabian Escalante, *The Cuba Project: CIA Covert Operations, 1959–62* (Melbourne and New York: Ocean Press, 2004), p. 44. The book was originally published in Spanish in 1993; the

first English-language version was published in 1995. It should be noted that the book does contain mistakes and exaggerations—for example, Prescott Bush is referred to as "Preston," and he is given almost singular credit for the rise of Eisenhower and Nixon to the presidency. While that was certainly an oversimplification, as we shall see, in fact Prescott Bush and his friends did play a crucial if little-known role in the rise of both men. See also John Newman, *Oswald and the CIA* (New York: Carroll & Graf, 1995), p. 115.

37. As her husband told the Warren Commission, Mrs. de Mohrenschildt managed to clear Mikoyan's extensive security and exchange pleasantries with the Communist official on board his plane before takeoff; she claimed to have told him he would be welcome in the United States at any time.

6: THE HIT

1. Richard Reeves, *President Kennedy: Profile of Power* (New York: Simon & Schuster, 1993), p. 103.
2. George Bush, *Looking Forward* (New York: Doubleday, 1987), p. 87. All he says is, "When President Kennedy came to Dallas on November 22, 1963, it took all his powers of persuasion just to get his Vice President and the Democratic senator from Texas to shake hands."
3. Arthur M. Schlesinger Jr., *Robert Kennedy and His Times* (Boston: Houghton Mifflin, 2002), p. 524.
4. Fletcher Knebel and Charles W. Bailey II, *Seven Days in May* (New York: Harper & Row, 1962).
5. Frankenheimer also directed the film adaptation of *The Manchurian Candidate*, Richard Condon's novel about a brainwashed assassin stalking a president.
6. David Talbot, *Brothers: The Hidden History of the Kennedy Years* (New York: Free Press, 2007), p. 148.
7. Laurence Leamer, *The Kennedy Men: 1901–1963* (New York: HarperCollins, 2002), p. 438.
8. For a full description of how Kennedy's policies aggravated Rockefeller interests in Latin America, see Gerard Colby and Charlotte Dennett, *Thy Will Be Done: The Conquest of the Amazon: Nelson Rockefeller and Evangelism in the Age of Oil* (New York: HarperCollins, 1995), especially chapter 27, "Camelot Versus Pocantico: The Decline and Fall of John F. Kennedy," pp. 396–420.
9. JFK to Walter Heller, September 12, 1963, audiotape 110.3 transcript, Presidential Recordings, John F. Kennedy Presidential Library and Museum, Boston, Massachusetts. Cited in Reeves, *President Kennedy*, p. 622.
10. Many prominent oilmen, including Robert Kerr and D. Harold Byrd, were involved with uranium mining.
11. Peter Dale Scott, *Deep Politics and the Death of JFK* (Berkeley: University of California Press, 1993), p. 160. Scott quotes a Ku Klux Klan organizer saying, in 1961, that "half of the police force in Dallas were members of the KKK."
12. Jack Langguth, "Group of Businessmen Rules Dallas Without a Mandate from the Voters," *New York Times*, January 19, 1964.
13. Burton Hersh, *Bobby and J. Edgar: The Historic Face-Off Between the Kennedys and J. Edgar Hoover That Transformed America* (New York: Carroll & Graf, 2007), pp. 162–64.
14. Kennedy ordered FBI interviews at the offices of several steel executives who, by raising their prices, had gone against a pact with unions to protect workers' job security in return for the unions' not making demands for higher wages. Kennedy asked the steel executives how they could expect workers to forgo raises when the companies were raising prices. The companies quickly repealed their price increases as a result of the intimidation. See Michael O'Brien, *John F. Kennedy: A Biography* (New York: Macmillan, 2004), pp. 643–45.
15. "The New Athenians," *Time*, May 24, 1954.
16. William Denslow, *10,000 Famous Freemasons*, with a foreword by Harry S Truman (Metairie, LA: Cornerstone Book Publishers, reprint 2004).

17. The company's practices would draw public attention years later with the release of the film *Silkwood*, starring Meryl Streep as Karen Silkwood, the factory activist who died in a mysterious car crash on her way to hand a reporter documents about the uranium-related deaths of Kerr-McGee workers.

18. Robert Baker and Larry L. King, *Wheeling and Dealing: Confessions of a Capitol Hill Operator* (New York: W. W. Norton, 1978), pp. 123–26.

19. Robert Dallek, *Lyndon B. Johnson: Portrait of a President* (New York: Oxford University Press, 2004), p. 142.

20. Thomas Petzinger Jr., *Oil & Honor: The Texaco-Pennzoil Wars* (New York: G. P. Putnam's Sons, 1987), p. 38.

21. Oral history interview with George C. McGhee, June 11, 1975, Harry S Truman Library and Museum, Independence, Missouri.

22. Ibid.

23. Schlesinger, *Robert Kennedy and His Times*, p. 438.

24. Adam Bernstein, "George C. McGhee Dies; Oilman, Diplomat," *Washington Post*, July 6, 2005.

25. Bruce Campbell Adamson, *Oswald's Closest Friend: The George de Mohrenschildt Story* (Santa Cruz, CA: privately printed, 1996), vol. 2, p. 6.

26. Scott, *Deep Politics*, p. 249.

27. House Select Committee on Assassinations, vol. 9, pp. 103–115. Available through the Mary Ferrell Foundation.

28. *National Geographic*, May 1956, p. 665.

29. "Memo: Meeting with HSCA Staffers" (NARA record number 104-10066-10201). Available through the Mary Ferrell Foundation.

30. Testimony of George A. Bouhe, Warren Commission Hearings, vol. 8, pp. 369, 374.

31. Photo accompanying a Newspaper Enterprise Association feature story on Lady Bird Johnson, as published August 15, 1963, in the *Evening Tribune* (Albert Lea, MN).

32. Allen W. Dulles Papers: Digital File Series, 1939–77. Seeley G. Mudd Manuscript Library, Princeton University, NJ.

33. Raymond L. Garthoff, *A Journey Through the Cold War: A Memoir of Containment and Coexistence* (Washington, D.C.: Brookings Institution, 2001), p. 193.

34. Scott, *Deep Politics*, p. 31.

35. Warren Commission Hearings, vol. 9, p. 235. Available through the Mary Ferrell Foundation.

36. Dick Russell, *The Man Who Knew Too Much: Hired to Kill Oswald and Prevent the Assassination of JFK* (New York: Carroll & Graf, 2003), p. 168.

37. Edward Jay Epstein, *The Assassination Chronicles: Inquest, Counterplot, and Legend* (New York: Carroll & Graf, 1992), p. 558.

38. "Memo on the Oswald Case," M. D. Stevens of the CIA to Chief/Research Branch/SRS/OS, December 30, 1963, based on Stevens's review of files, including State Department cables (NARA record number: 1993.08.17.09:41:50:590064). In the HSCA Segregated CIA Collection, available through the Mary Ferrell Foundation. The State Department maintained an interest in Marina Oswald, who was a Soviet alien seeking U.S. citizenship.

39. Testimony of George A. Bouhe, Warren Commission Hearings, Vol. 8, p. 371.

40. House Select Committee on Assassinations, FBI file on George de Mohrenschildt, document, section 8, 100-32965-251, pp. 23–25. Found by researcher Bruce Campbell Adamson.

41. Letter from George de Mohrenschildt to John F. Kennedy, February 16, 1963. Found by researcher Bruce Campbell Adamson at John F. Kennedy Presidential Library and Museum, Boston, Massachusetts.

42. The club's members at that time included David Rockefeller and John Hay Whitney, publisher of the *New York Herald Tribune*.

43. Multiple government debriefing documents available through the Mary Ferrell Foundation. See NARA records 104-10436-10014 and 104-10070-10076.

44. HSCA Segregated CIA Collection, box 14, "Contact Report WUBRINY Haitian Operations" (NARA record number 104-10070-10076). Available through the Mary Ferrell Foundation.

45. Though Devine is not identified by name in this document, he is in another CIA document: "Memorandum: MESSRS. George Bush and Thomas J. Devine," January 30, 1968 (NARA record number 104-10310-10271). Available through Mary Ferrell Foundation. That document identifies Devine specifically as working in operation BRINY and claims that he began working in this capacity that June. No documents have surfaced showing anyone else being part of the very small operation WUBRINY. Indeed, all the available evidence indicates that Devine was the main or even only member of WUBRINY, and therefore the person code-named WUBRINY/1, the designated top dog of the operation. If, in fact, Devine and WUBRINY/1 were synonymous, then the CIA memo noting that Devine joined WUBRINY in June was in itself an attempt to hide the involvement of Poppy's business associate in the April meetings with de Mohrenschildt.

46. Author interview with Thomas Devine, September 4, 2008; author interview with Gale Allen, September 15, 2008.

47. When George de Mohrenschildt came to Washington, he was accompanied by his wife Jeanne. LBJ's private secretary at the time of their visit was Marie Fehmer. According to Marie Fehmer's oral history, she was recruited to be Vice President Johnson's secretary in 1962, directly from her college sorority. She claimed not to have known him, to be surprised by the offer, and to be somewhat reluctant to accept it (see Marie Fehmer oral history interview, August 16, 1972, Lyndon Baines Johnson Library and Museum, Austin, Texas). But she was not unconnected herself. Her father, Ray, worked for D. Harold Byrd's military contracting firm LTV. And her mother, Olga, worked at Nardis Sportswear with Jeanne de Mohrenschildt and Abraham Zapruder. After working for LBJ, Marie Fehmer joined the CIA, where she became one of the top female supervisors; see William Marvin Watson with Sherwin Markman, *Chief of Staff: Lyndon Johnson and His Presidency* (New York: Macmillan, 2004), p. 39.

48. Correspondence from Walter Jenkins to George de Mohrenschildt, April 18, 1963, De Mohrenschildt file, Lyndon Baines Johnson Library and Museum, Austin, Texas.

49. Pete Brewton, *The Mafia, CIA & George Bush* (New York: S.P.I., 1992), p. 194.

50. Matlack had been a longtime aide to General Edward Landsdale, a top counterinsurgency figure and intelligence officer deeply involved in anti-Castro operations. (See chapter 16 for more on Lansdale.)

51. Russell, *The Man Who Knew Too Much*, p. 305.

52. Seymour Hersh, "Hunt Tells of Early Work for a CIA Domestic Unit," *New York Times*, December 31, 1974.

53. Warren Commission Hearings, vol. 9, p. 25. Available through the Mary Ferrell Foundation.

54. The motorcade route was designed by Secret Service agents Winston G. Lawson and Forrest V. Sorrels. On November 22, 1963, the *Dallas Morning News* detailed the president's route on its front page, reporting that "the motorcade will move slowly so that crowds can 'get a good view' of President Kennedy and his wife."

55. Warren Commission Executive Session, January 27, 1964, p. 185. Available through the Mary Ferrell Foundation.

56. "17 of Dallas Will Direct CF Chapter," *Dallas Morning News*, September 9, 1962.

57. David Harold Byrd, *I'm an Endangered Species* (Houston: Pacesetter, 1978), pp. 101–2.

58. Testimony of Linnie Mae Randle, Warren Commission, vol. 2, p. 245.

59. Orleans Parish grand jury testimony of Marina Oswald Porter, February 8, 1968. Available through the Mary Ferrell Foundation.

60. Analysis based on cross section of articles and interviews with officials of the Texas School Book Depository company, in which they describe how their operations occupied nearly all of the floors of the building.

61. The Warren Commission Report fails to answer the basic question of who owned the building that the shots were allegedly fired from. See page 664 for a "speculation and finding" where they merely assert that "the TSBD is a private corporation."

62. U.S. Senate, *Final Report of the Select Committee to Study Government Operations with Respect to Intelligence Activities*, S.R. No. 94-755, 94th Congress, 2nd session (Washington, D.C.: GPO, 1976).

63. James T. Carter, "Books and Things," *Victoria Advocate*, March 24, 1963.

64. Michael E. Young, "Perch of JFK Sniper Offered up on eBay," *Dallas Morning News*, February 8, 2007.

65. HSCA Segregated CIA Collection, reel 5, folder M–George de Mohrenschildt, p. 425 (NARA record number: 1994.04.25.14:02:25:940005). Available through the Mary Ferrell Foundation.

66. Review by Maurice Dolbier of New York–based HTNS wire service, as published in *Valley Independent*, October 25, 1963.

67. Kent Biffle, "Allen Dulles Looks Behind Red Moves," *Dallas Morning News*, October 28, 1963.

68. Hunt's presence is disputed. He claimed that he was at home with his family, but his son St. John Hunt told *Rolling Stone* that not only was his father not home on November 22, but his mother also claimed he was on a business trip to Dallas. (Hedegaard, "The Last Confessions of E. Howard Hunt," *Rolling Stone*, April 5, 2007.)

69. George L. Lumpkin obituary, *Dallas Morning News*, July 18, 1994.

70. HSCA staff interview of George L. Lumpkin, November 3, 1977, p. 1.

71. Neely Tucker, "Nov. 22, 1963," *Washington Post*, July 24, 2008.

72. Max Holland, "Private Sources of U.S. Foreign Policy: William Pawley and the 1954 Coup d'Etat in Guatemala," *Journal of Cold War Studies*, Fall 2005, pp. 69–70.

73. Jim Marrs, *Crossfire: The Plot That Killed Kennedy* (New York: Carroll & Graf, 1989), pp. 30–31.

74. Witt worked as an insurance salesman for Rio Grande National Life Insurance in its seventeen-story building on the corner of Elm and Field Streets in downtown Dallas. This building housed the Office of Immigration and Naturalization, with which Oswald communicated about his wife's citizenship status, as well as the offices of the Secret Service. Rio Grande did significant business with the U.S. government, writing insurance policies for the military.

75. Hearings before the Subcommittee on the Assassination of John F. Kennedy of the Select Committee on Assassinations, House of Representatives, vol. 4, p. 431.

76. However, some HSCA members suggested a highly complicated scenario in which the umbrella gesture signaled displeasure with Kennedy's policies. JFK's father, Joseph Kennedy, had served as U.S. ambassador to Britain at the same time that Neville Chamberlain was Britain's prime minister. Chamberlain, who always carried an umbrella, was widely considered to have appeased Hitler, and some wondered whether the umbrella stunt could have been a way of expressing the notion that JFK was appeasing the Communists. If so, it would have been a remarkably oblique way to send a message. See Robert J. Groden's *The Killing of a President: The Complete Photographic Record of the JFK Assassination, the Conspiracy and the Cover-up* (New York: Viking Studio, 1993), for more information on the matter.

77. Hearings before the Subcommittee on the Assassination of John F. Kennedy of the Select Committee on Assassinations, House of Representatives, vol. 4, p. 453.

78. Ruby was a neighbor of de Mohrenschildt's White Russian friend George Bouhe, the first person to squire Oswald in Texas. (Adamson, *Oswald's Closest Friend*, vol. 1, p. 108.)

79. To watch Ruby making this statement, go to http://video.google.com/videoplay?docid=
-177236594543303.

7: After Camelot

1. For a detailed examination of this issue, see Peter Dale Scott, *Deep Politics and the Death of JFK* (Berkeley: University of California Press, 1993).

2. Corporate filings of Dorchester Gas Producing Co., Texas Secretary of State.

3. Paul Harvey, "Dallas' Program Model for Civil Defense Effort," *Dallas Morning News*, September 29, 1960.

4. The first interagency planning meeting for Dallas Civil Defense came in December 1952, shortly after Eisenhower was elected and just as his team, including the Dulles brothers, was preparing to take over (see *Dallas Morning News*, December 10, 1952). The head of Dallas Civil Defense was B. F. McLain, a prominent local furniture dealer who sat on the board of Republic National Bank, and with Neil Mallon and other Republic bank figures, on the board of the Communities Foundation of Texas—whose projects included the Dallas Police Memorial. McLain had long-standing ties to Jack Cason, president of the Texas School Book Depository Company. After World War II, McLain, then president of the Dallas Chamber of Commerce, worked closely with Cason, then head of an important American Legion post in Dallas, to forge a powerful local political force from the ranks of returning veterans (see *Dallas Morning News*, February 1, 1946).

5. *Dallas Times Herald*, March 27, 1962.

6. Larry Hancock, "Mysteries of the 112th Intelligence Corps," *Kennedy Assassination Chronicles* (Winter 2001): 20–27. See also Scott, *Deep Politics*, p. 275.

7. Jack Crichton interview, July 6, 2001, Oral History Collection, Sixth Floor Museum, Dallas.

8. Richard Harwood, "CIA Reported Ending Aid to Some Groups," *Washington Post*, February 22, 1967.

9. Jack Crichton interview, July 6, 2001.

10. Warren Commission, p. x.

11. Meeting of Warren Commission, December 16, 1963.

12. Warren Commission executive session, December 16, 1963, p. 39.

13. Richard Harwood, "Business Leaders Are Tied to CIA's Covert Operations," *Washington Post*, February 18, 1967.

14. Willem Oltmans interview with George de Mohrenschildt, 1969.

15. Tape recording of de Mohrenschildt reading his memoirs to Willem Oltmans, 1969.

16. "Mr. Jenner: Mr. De Mohrenschildt, we have had some discussions off the record, and I had lunch with you a couple of times. Is there anything that we discussed during the course of any off-the-record discussions which I have not already brought out on the record that you think is pertinent and should be brought out?" (De Mohrenschildt said that there was not.) Transcript of the testimony of George S. and Jeanne de Mohrenschildt to Warren Commission, vol. 9, p. 284.

17. Ibid., pp. 166–331.

18. "I'll Be the Boss," *Time*, February 2, 1962.

19. William Proxmire, *Report from Wasteland: America's Military-Industrial Complex* (Westport, CT: Praeger, 1970).

20. Barbara Gamarekian, "Social Scene: For Bushes, Coziness Is in and the Jellybean Out," *New York Times*, November 24, 1988.

21. Peter Paul Gregory was a consulting petroleum engineer who taught Russian part-time. Oswald had purportedly been referred to Gregory as someone who could certify his Russian-language skills.

22. Edward Hooker would explain to FBI agents in 1964, "de Mohrenschildt was a very popular guest in that he was an excellent conversationalist, played fine tennis, and was an expert horseman."

23. Letter provided by Mrs. Auchincloss to the Warren Commission.

24. George de Mohrenschildt, *I Am a Patsy! I Am a Patsy!* (unpublished), p. 226; House Select Committee on Assassinations, vol. II appendix. De Mohrenschildt was in discussions with a Dutch publisher about a possible book deal at the time of his death.

25. Peter Evans, *Nemesis* (New York: HarperCollins, 2004), p. 137. This book, which focuses on the relationship between Aristotle Onassis and the Kennedys, features cameos by many characters from the assassination saga.

26. De Mohrenschildt, *I Am a Patsy!* pp. 225–28; HSCA vol. II appendix.

27. Bush's original lawyer was Patrick Holloway, member of a law firm in the Republic National Bank Building with its offices on the same floor as George de Mohrenschildt's. Holloway's wife Linda would later divorce him and end up marrying Bush's friend and political lieutenant Jimmy Allison. She and Jimmy would end up effectively babysitting George W. Bush in Alabama in 1972 when he got in trouble with his Guard unit.

28. By 1968, that transformation would already be in process, as Richard Nixon only narrowly lost Texas's big chunk of electoral votes to Hubert Humphrey.

29. In compliance with 1964's *Wesberry v. Sanders*, Houston was divided into the Seventh, Eighth, and Ninth Texas Congressional Districts. *Bush v. Martin*, 224 F. Supp. 499 (S.D. Tex. 1963), affirmed, 376 U.S. 222 (1964).

30. "Vietnam—Representative Visit Itinerary and Correspondence, 1967–1968." George Bush Presidential Library, College Station, Texas.

31. "Memorandum: MESSRS. George Bush and Thomas J. Devine," CIA document, January 30, 1968. Available through the Mary Ferrell Foundation (NARA record number 104-10310-10271).

32. Author interview with Pat Holloway, March 11, 2008. Halliburton had merged with Brown and Root in 1962.

33. "Telephone Conversation Between the President and J. Edgar Hoover, 23 Nov 1963." Transcript available through Mary Ferrell Foundation.

34. Produced under Freedom of Information Act request to independent researcher Bruce Campbell Adamson.

35. J. Gilberto Quezada, *Border Boss: Manuel B. Bravo and Zapata County* (College Station: Texas A&M University Press, 1999).

36. Mary Kahl, *Ballot Box 13: How Lyndon Johnson Won His 1948 Senate Race by 87 Contested Votes* (Jefferson, NC: McFarland, 1983).

8: WINGS FOR W.

1. Jacob Weisberg, *The Bush Tragedy* (New York: Random House, 2008), p. 13.

2. Todd S. Purdum, "43+41=84," *Vanity Fair*, September 2006.

3. Alan Bernstein, "Bush: The Houston Years," *Houston Chronicle*, April 11, 1999.

4. Kitty Kelley, *The Family: The Real Story of the Bush Dynasty* (New York: Doubleday, 2004), p. 262.

5. She married a fellow CIA employee and later divorced him; though in 1967 she went by Wolfman, it is no longer her surname.

6. Author interview with Cathryn Wolfman, November 21, 2006. Wolfman recalled that W. rarely displayed any interest in politics. "I thought he'd be a stockbroker," she said. Had the two discussed politics, they might have broken up sooner. Wolfman says she was against the Vietnam War; in 2004 she donated to John Kerry's bid to unseat W.

7. Tina's uncle Igor was prosecuted in this period on tax charges by the crusading attorney general Bobby Kennedy a few months before the JFK assassination—one of numerous Bush family friends to face investigation by the Kennedy White House—and would later write in a book how he planned to "tear the robe of respectability" off RFK. See Igor Cassini, *Pay the Price* (New York: Kensington, 1983).

8. Bill Minutaglio, *First Son: George W. Bush and the Bush Family Dynasty* (New York: Three Rivers Press, 1999), pp. 124–125. This book, published before the 2000 election, provides the most comprehensive study of W.'s rise to power in Texas.

9. Richard Ben Cramer, *What It Takes: The Way to the White House* (New York: Vintage, 1992), p. 419.

10. George Lardner Jr., "Texas Speaker Reportedly Helped Bush Get Into Guard," *Washington Post*, September 21, 1999.

11. Richard A. Serrano, "Bush Received Quick Air Guard Commission," *Los Angeles Times*, July 4, 1999.

12. Author interview with Bill White, July 18, 2004.

13. R. G. Ratcliffe, "Debate Renewed over Military Choices," *Houston Chronicle*, August 19, 1988.

14. Serrano, "Bush Received Quick Air Guard Commission."

15. Elizabeth Mitchell, *W: Revenge of the Bush Dynasty* (New York: Berkley, 2000), pp. 120–121.

16. Honneus was the name from her first marriage, and the name she used at the time. She has since readopted her maiden name.

17. Author interview with Inge Honneus, April 11, 2006.

18. Honneus says that besides Bush, she had no other partners for a considerable period before and after that episode.

19. Ellington Air Force Base press release, March 24, 1970.

20. Kenneth T. Walsh, "From Boys to Men," *U.S. News & World Report*, May 3, 2004.

21. Jo Thomas, "After Yale, Bush Ambled Amiably into His Future," *New York Times*, July 22, 2000.

22. R. W. Apple Jr., "Bush Implies He Has Used No Drugs in Last 25 Years," *New York Times*, August 20, 1999.

23. Kelley, *The Family*, p. 575.

24. Ibid., p. 300.

25. Lowman was her maiden name, and she now uses her married name.

26. Compilation of unpublished reporting by four journalists from separate major news organizations.

27. Author interview with Jo Thomas, Syracuse, New York, August 28, 2004.

28. Author interview with David Klausmeyer, November 14, 2006.

29. Minutaglio, *First Son*, p. 139.

30. Associated Press, "Bush Flew in Training Planes Before Losing Pilot Privileges," September 11, 2004. Also see Susan Cooper Eastman, "Fear of Flying," *Folio Weekly* (Jacksonville, FL), September 23, 2004.

31. Jimmy Allison had been a newspaper publisher in Midland. He left that to run Poppy's congressional campaigns and D.C. congressional office, as well as Edward Gurney's 1968 Florida Senate campaign, with which W. had been involved. The wealthy Blount was seeking political office for the first time, and Allison's job was to get him elected—and importantly to add Alabama's electoral votes to Richard Nixon's landslide.

32. Manuel Roig-Franzia and Lois Romano, "Few Can Offer Confirmation of Bush's Guard Service," *Washington Post*, February 15, 2004.
33. Minutaglio, *First Son*, p. 143; and Kelley, *The Family*, pp. 304–5.
34. Author interview with Linda Allison, July 20, 2004.
35. James Moore, *Bush's War for Reelection: Iraq, the White House, and the People* (Hoboken, NJ: Wiley, 2004), p. 150.
36. In a crisp letter dated May 31, 1972, the director of personnel resources at the Denver headquarters of the Air Reserve Personnel Center noted in his rejection that Bush had a "Military Service Obligation until 26 May 1974"—that is, to do serious and meaningful duty for another two years.
37. Walter V. Robinson, "Questions Remain on Bush's Service as Guard Pilot," *Boston Globe*, October 31, 2000.
38. Much of the Alabama material, reported by the author, appeared in "Why Bush Left Texas," the *Nation*, September 14, 2004.
39. Unpublished 2004 C. Murphy Archibald interview with Alabama freelancer Glynn Wilson.
40. Author interview with Janet Linke, September 29, 2004.
41. Author interview with Dr. Richard Mayo, July 23, 2004.
42. Minutaglio, *First Son*, p. 148.
43. Author interview with Linda Allison, July 20, 2004.
44. Author interview with Dr. John Andrew Harris, the dentist who examined Bush, August 23, 2004, and dental record released by the Bush White House.
45. Tom Wicker, *George Herbert Walker Bush* (New York: Viking, 2004). For the PULL donation story, see Alan Bernstein, "Bush: The Houston Years," *Houston Chronicle*, April 11, 1999.
46. Kenneth T. Walsh, "The Lost Years of Al and Dubya," *U.S. News & World Report*, November 1, 1999.
47. Meg Laughlin, "Former Workers Dispute Bush's Pull in Project P.U.L.L.," Knight-Ridder, October 23, 2004.
48. The effort to tap into state and federal grants would be a precursor to a veritable industry in which Republican-favored, minority-headed charities, often with a "faith-based" component, would garner outsized grants.
49. Author interview with Jack Gazelle, August 2, 2004.
50. Author interview with Jimmy Wynn, July 24, 2004.
51. Moore, *Bush's War for Reelection*, p. 171.
52. Jim Drinkard and Dave Moniz, "Memos Debate Eclipses Content," *USA Today*, September 13, 2004.
53. E-mail to author from Jim Moore, July 22, 2008.
54. Minutaglio, *First Son*, p. 148.

9: THE NIXONIAN BUSHES

1. Robert Dallek, "The Kissinger Presidency," *Vanity Fair*, May 2007.
2. Membership on the House Ways and Means Committee has historically been a stepping-stone to the highest office in American government. Bush joined seven past presidents on that ladder to power.
3. The official Senate history refers to this shameless nepotism in a more flattering light: "Both Nixon and Ford had known Prescott Bush in Washington. Due to his father's prominence and his own well-publicized race for the Senate, George Bush arrived in the House better known than most of the forty-six other freshmen Republicans. As a freshman he won a coveted seat on

the Ways and Means Committee (which put the Bushes on everyone's 'list' of social invitations)." Available on www.senate.gov.

4. Kitty Kelley, *The Family: The Real Story of the Bush Dynasty* (New York: Doubleday, 2004), p. 245.

5. Ibid., p. 246.

6. Ibid., p. 47.

7. Irwin F. Gellman, *The Contender: Richard Nixon, the Congress Years, 1946–1952* (New York: Free Press, 1999), pp. 25–26, 31–32.

8. Although Voorhis was characterized as a leftist, his record was more that of a moderately liberal man with an independent streak. In fact, when the Council of Industrial Organizations rated members of Congress based on their votes on labor issues from 1943 to 1946, Voorhis scored only 84.6, well below the 100 percent awarded Henry M. Jackson of Washington, below the 86.9 awarded Estes Kefauver of Tennessee, and only nominally higher than the conservative Democratic congressman Lyndon Baines Johnson of Texas.

9. Letter from Richard Nixon to Norman Chandler, December 28, 1960, Richard Nixon Presidential Library, Yorba Linda, California.

10. Anthony Summers, *The Arrogance of Power: The Secret World of Richard Nixon* (New York: Penguin Books, 2000), pp. 46–47.

11. Roger Morris, *Richard Milhous Nixon* (New York: Henry Holt, 1990), pp. 257, 261.

12. Jerry Voorhis, *Confessions of a Congressman* (New York: Doubleday, 1970), p. 331.

13. To be sure, Dresser Industries did not want a union-friendly congressman any more than the local businessmen did. With the end of World War II, labor troubles had become endemic in the American economy. Dresser had been racked by union agitation, including work stoppages and strikes.

14. During the 1952 campaign, Nixon had been accused of controlling a secret "slush fund" of contributions from shadowy backers. In response, Nixon went on TV to give his famous "Checkers speech," in which he denied accepting any personal gifts, with one exception: a black-and-white cocker spaniel named Checkers, for his daughter. He emphasized that he was a man of modest means who could not afford a mink coat for his wife, only a "respectable Republican cloth coat."

15. Kelley, *The Family*, p. 162.

16. Daniel Yergin, *The Prize: The Epic Quest for Oil, Money and Power* (New York: Free Press, 1992), p. 753.

17. Yergin, *The Prize*, p. 215.

18. Robert Caro, *The Path to Power: The Years of Lyndon Johnson* (New York: Knopf, 1982).

19. Robert Bryce, *Cronies: Oil, the Bushes, and the Rise of Texas, America's Superstate* (New York: PublicAffairs, 2004), p. 93.

20. As president, Eisenhower stopped a grand jury investigation into the "International Petroleum Cartel" on the basis of "national security." Eisenhower chose Robert B. Anderson, president of the Texas Mid-Continent Oil and Gas Association, as his secretary of the Navy, deputy secretary of defense, and secretary of the treasury.

21. Rick Perlstein, *Before the Storm: Barry Goldwater and the Unmaking of the American Consensus* (New York: Hill and Wang, 2001), p. 196.

22. Ibid., p. 197.

23. Letter from William C. Liedtke Jr. to Richard Nixon, July 16, 1968, Richard Nixon Presidential Library.

24. Bill Clements, who would serve under both Nixon and Ford (where his boss was Donald Rumsfeld), owned the giant offshore drilling equipment and drilling contractor SEDCO, which was

deeply wired into the Bush political machine. During the 1950s, Dresser Industries had recommended SEDCO to the government of Argentine strongman Juan Perón, who was trying to develop Argentina's oil reserves. SEDCO drilled about one thousand wells for Peron, and bought ten million dollars' worth of supplies from Dresser. In 1964, Clements served as statewide campaign finance chair for Poppy's 1964 U.S. Senate bid. When Bush decided to get out of the oil business, as noted in chapter 3, there was discussion about Clements taking over Zapata; instead, the two firms went into a joint venture in the Persian Gulf. Like many of the entities associated with the rise of the Bushes, SEDCO had its share of international crises requiring a friendly ear in Washington: the company was involved in the world's largest oil spill (in the Gulf of Mexico) and later filed suit against the revolutionary Iranian government over the seizure of its rigs. When a *New York Times* reporter tried to interview Clements's son, the company's president, he declined, explaining, "We like to keep a low profile." See William K. Stevens, "SEDCO: Growth in Adversity," *New York Times*, October 20, 1981. In 1984, Clements sold SEDCO to Schlumberger, the firm that had assisted with clandestine operations against Castro and whose head had interacted with George de Mohrenschildt in 1962 and '63. After becoming Texas's first Republican governor since Reconstruction, Clements hired—first as his deputy chief of staff and later as direct mail consultant—the youthful Karl Rove at the request of Poppy Bush, helping the future political superstar get his start.

25. The Federal Power Commission was replaced in 1977 by the Federal Energy Regulatory Commission.

26. The commission allowed Pennzoil to divert natural gas that had been committed for low-priced sale within hard-pressed Louisiana into other markets, where it could charge much more. Louisiana ended up with a severe natural gas shortage. "The health and physical safety of millions of Louisiana's citizens are gravely threatened," a 1972 state announcement warned.

27. In April 1969, shortly after Morton was named Republican National Committee chair, he and Bush called for the IRS to create a division to begin examining nonprofit groups—then a quickly growing sector largely identified with liberal values and criticism of the establishment.

28. Iwan W. Morgan, *Nixon* (London: Hodder Arnold, 2002), p. 125.

29. Stephen E. Ambrose, *Nixon: The Triumph of a Politician, 1962–1972* (New York: Simon & Schuster, 1989), p. 234.

30. For the best account of this, see Robert Dallek, *Nixon and Kissinger: Partners in Power* (New York: HarperCollins, 2007).

31. For detailed accounts of the so-called Moorer-Radford affair, see James Rosen, *The Strong Man: John Mitchell and the Secrets of Watergate* (New York: Doubleday), pp. 165–81; and Len Colodny and Robert Gettlin, *Silent Coup: The Removal of a President* (New York: St. Martin's, 1991), pp. 3–67, 373–403.

32. Herbert S. Parmet, *George Bush: The Life of a Lone Star Yankee* (New Brunswick, NJ: Transaction, 2000), p. 126.

33. The oil industry had actually asked Nixon to simply refrain from doing anything. He was to resist efforts to get him involved in reducing the oil depletion allowance and leave it to industry supporters to bottle up the legislation in Congress.

34. Yergin, *The Prize*, p. 754.

35. Author interview with Jack Gleason, April 2008.

36. Robert Baskin, "Liberals Conclude Nixon Lost to Right," *Dallas Morning News*, July 9, 1969.

37. Rosen, *The Strong Man*, pp. 65–114.

38. Gail Sheehy, *Character: America's Search for Leadership* (New York: William Morrow, 1988), p. 174.

39. Fitzhugh Green, *George Bush: An Intimate Portrait* (New York: Hippocrene Books, 1989), p. 113.

40. Kelley, *The Family*, p. 284.

41. George Bush with Victor Gold, *Looking Forward: An Autobiography* (New York: Doubleday, 1987), p. 102.

42. Parmet, *George Bush*, p. 146.

43. By 1972, the White House would secretly support 42.5 percent of all Democrats running for Congress—so long as their conservative views generally comported with the administration's. See Lowell P. Weicker with Barry Sussman, *Maverick: A Life in Politics* (Boston: Little, Brown, 1995), pp. 79–80.

44. William Safire, *Before the Fall: An Inside Look at the Pre-Watergate White House* (Garden City, NY: Doubleday, 1975), p. 646.

45. Bob Woodward and Walter Pincus, "Presidential Posts and Dashed Hopes; Appointive Jobs Were Turning Point," *Washington Post*, August 9, 1988.

46. Parmet, *George Bush*, p. 147.

47. Ibid., p. 148.

48. Dallek, "The Kissinger Presidency."

49. Parmet, *George Bush*, p. 148.

10: DOWNING NIXON, PART I: THE SETUP

1. Richard M. Nixon, *RN: The Memoirs of Richard Nixon* (New York: Grosset & Dunlap), pp. 626–29.

2. H. R. Haldeman, *The Haldeman Diaries: Inside the Nixon White House* (New York: G. P. Putnam's Sons, 1994), p. 31.

3. Howard Hunt, *Give Us This Day* (New Rochelle, NY: Arlington House, 1973), p. 40.

4. Rhodri Jeffreys-Jones, *The CIA and American Democracy* (New Haven, CT: Yale University Press, 2003), p. 99.

5. *The Haldeman Diaries*, p. 26.

6. Deposition of Richard Helms, in *Hunt v. Weberman*. See A. J. Weberman, Coup dEtat in America Data Base, www.ajweberman.com/nodules2/nodulec24.htm.

7. H. R. Haldeman, *The Ends of Power* (New York: Times Books, 1978), pp. 37–38.

8. Carl Freund, "Nixon Predicts JFK May Drop Johnson," *Dallas Morning News* (early edition), November 22, 1963.

9. Stephen Ambrose, *Nixon: The Triumph of a Politician, 1962–1972* (New York: Simon & Schuster, 1989), p. 32.

10. Jules Witcover, *The Resurrection of Richard Nixon* (New York: Putnam, 1970), p. 61.

11. Author interview with Donald Kendall, September 12, 2008.

12. "Nixon to Robert Humphreys, 11/7/63," Nixon vice presidential papers (Laguna Niguel, California), quoted in Ambrose, *Nixon, 1962–72*, p. 31.

13. February 1, 1966, call from President Lyndon Johnson to Senator Eugene McCarthy, cited by James Rosen, "What's Hidden in the LBJ Tapes," *Weekly Standard*, September 29, 2003.

14. Rudy Rochelle, "Little Relief Seen for Sugar Problem," *Dallas Morning News*, November 22, 1963.

15. Haldeman's notes were first published in James Rosen's "An Insider's Notes from the Oval Office," *Newsday*, April 25, 1994.

16. Years later, Kendall became a member of the International Council at Harvard's Belfer Center for Science and International Affairs, at the John F. Kennedy School of Government.

17. FBI JFK Assassination File 62-109060. Available through the Mary Ferrell Foundation.

18. Jack Langguth, "Group of Businessmen Rules Dallas Without a Mandate from the Voters," *New York Times*, January 19, 1964.

19. Robert Dallek, *Partners in Power: Nixon and Kissinger* (New York: HarperCollins, 2007), p. 434.

20. George Bush, *All the Best, George Bush: My Life in Letters and Other Writing* (New York: Scribner, 1999), p. 191.

21. *The Haldeman Diaries*, December 16, 1969, pp. 115–16.

22. Author interview with Jack Gleason, April 6, 2008.

23. *The Haldeman Diaries*, December 11, 1969, p. 114.

24. Prior to a new stricter law that went into effect in April 1972, the then-governing Federal Corrupt Practices Act of 1925 required campaign contributions over one hundred dollars to be reported by a candidate's election committee. Each committee was to have a formal chairman and treasurer who did the reporting. The national committees of political parties were then supposed to file postelection reports regarding their contributions to individual candidates. Up until 1970, this law was rarely followed, let alone enforced by the Justice Department. But in 1970, a new public interest group called Common Cause, heavily financed by Rockefeller interests—whose philanthropy has certainly mitigated to some extent the methods of an earlier generation—sued both the Republican and Democratic Parties for violating the Corrupt Practices Act, triggering a public clamor for election reform. The public, quite simply, was disgusted over influence-buying of politicians by large donors. It was in this milieu that the Townhouse Operation warily functioned. See Herbert E. Alexander, ed., *Campaign Money: Reform and Reality in the States* (New York: Macmillan, 1976), pp. vii–ix.

25. Such efforts in secrecy were ultimately defeated. By 1972, Common Cause's lawsuit against the Committee to Re-elect the President (CREEP) bore substantial results: through the discovery process, its lawyers were able to identify the major donors to Townhouse. "Among the gifts disclosed," wrote Herbert Alexander in *Campaign Money*, "were funds that financed some of the most unsavory episodes of Watergate." Ibid., p. viii.

26. Author interview with Jack Gleason, April 21, 2008.

27. Jeff Gerth with Robert Pear, "Files Detail Aid to Bush by Nixon White House," *New York Times*, June 11, 1992.

28. Memorandum from Charles Ruff, Assistant Special Prosecutor, to Leon Jaworski, Special Prosecutor, August 19, 1974. National Archives and Records Administration.

29. Department of Justice interview with Charles Colson, Febrary 2, 1972, Townhouse files, National Archives and Records Administration.

30. Department of Justice interview with John Mitchell, December 19, 1973, Townhouse files, National Archives and Records Administration.

31. When I called Kalmbach in 2008, he declined to discuss the subject, citing his age—eighty-seven—and attorney-client privilege, "and all that." He told prosecutors that he sat in on Townhouse planning meetings and solicited funds from large contributors (though these were to go to the campaign in general, he stated, rather than to specific candidates), and insisted that he never gave cash to any *specific* candidates. (Department of Justice interview with Herbert Kalmbach, October 11, 1973, Townhouse files, National Archives and Records Administration.) On June 29, 1972, White House counsel John Dean met with Kalmbach on a bench in Lafayette Park across from the White House. "We would like you to raise funds for the burglars," Dean told Kalmbach, whereupon Nixon's attorney, believing the president was in full approval, agreed. See also Len Colodny and Robert Gettlin, *Silent Coup: The Removal of a President* (New York: St. Martin's Press, 1991), p. 212.

32. Colodny and Gettlin, *Silent Coup*, p. 96.

33. Colson recalled that delivery to Dean would entitle them to certain legal privileges, presumably against disclosure. Department of Justice interview with Charles Colson.

34. Dean would later turn over some of those notebooks and documents to the Senate Watergate

Committee as evidence against Nixon. One document that apparently was not contained in the prosecutors' files was the letter Gleason requested assuring him of no illegalities in the Townhouse Operation. Author interview with Jack Gleason, April 6, 2008.

35. Joseph J. Trento and Jacquie Powers, "Was Howard Hunt in Dallas the Day JFK Died?" *Wilmington* (Del.) *Sunday News Journal*, August 20, 1978. The article described a secret 1966 CIA memo, initialed by both counterintelligence chief James Angleton and director Richard Helms, that cited E. Howard Hunt's presence in Dallas on November 22, 1963. The memo reportedly noted that a cover story providing him with an alibi for being somewhere else "ought to be considered." Trento had learned about the memo directly from Angleton. "In 1978, Angleton called and asked me to come down for lunch at the Army-Navy Club," Trento recalled in an interview with the author Dick Russell. "He said he wanted to talk to me about something. This was as the House Committee's investigation was winding up, and he told me a number of things concerning the Kennedy assassination and its aftermath. Then he explained some very complicated counter intelligence operations. 'Did you know Howard Hunt was in Dallas on the day of the assassination? . . . What I'm trying to tell you is, some very odd things were going on that were out of our control.' Then he added the possibility that Hunt was there on orders from a high-level KGB mole inside the agency—and that this should have been looked into at the time." Trento said Angleton also informed the House Assassinations Committee. "I later came to conclude that the mole-sent-Hunt idea was, to use his phrase, disinformation; that Angleton was trying to protect his own connections to Hunt's being in Dallas." See Dick Russell, *The Man Who Knew Too Much* (New York: Carroll & Graf, 1992), pp. 306–7.

36. Various sources, including: the House Select Committee on Assassinations; Jim Hougan, *Secret Agenda: Watergate, Deep Throat and the CIA* (New York: Random House, 1984); Tad Szulc, "Cuba on Our Minds," *Esquire*, January 1974; and James Rosen, *The Strong Man: John Mitchell and the Secrets of Watergate* (New York: Doubleday, 2008).

37. Charles Wendell Colson Papers, Billy Graham Center, Wheaton, Illinois. The late Howard Liebengood, who served as deputy minority counsel to the Senate Watergate Committee, has verified the factual accuracy of this material.

38. Hougan, *Secret Agenda*, pp. 27–29.

39. Ibid., p. 119.

40. The Pentagon Papers consisted of a multivolume report detailing top-secret planning and policy regarding United States involvement in Southeast Asia and the Vietnam War. These papers were leaked to the *New York Times* by Daniel Ellsberg, a former military analyst. They proved that Johnson routinely lied about what was going on in the war to cover up that the situation was much worse than the administration had claimed; the Pentagon was furious. The president, however, initially seemed indifferent, especially since it was LBJ's administration, not his, that was being embarrassed. According to Ehrlichman, "He was really cranked up pretty hard by Henry [Kissinger] on those." (Interview by author Len Colodny of John Ehrlichman, April 29, 1986.) Kissinger, who had known Ellsberg for years, sought to convince Nixon that Ellsberg was "the most dangerous man in America today."

41. Charles Wendell Colson Papers, Billy Graham Center, Wheaton, Illinois. Verified by Senate Watergate Committee staffer Howard Liebengood.

42. John Dean, *Blind Ambition: The White House Years* (New York: Simon & Schuster, 1976), pp. 256–57.

43. Renata Adler, *Canaries in the Mines: Essays on Politics and Media* (New York: Macmillan, 2001), p. 82.

44. The so-called Moorer-Radford affair has been documented in several books, notably *Silent Coup* by Len Colodny and Robert Gettlin.

45. Rosen, *The Strong Man*, p. 295, citing a June 15, 1987, interview of John Mitchell by Len Colodny.

46. This was the kind of top-level job that few college graduates ever dreamed of, and according to military writer and Green Beret veteran Shelby Stanton, "It sounds like Woodward was being groomed. They would not have assigned just anybody to that ship." For a detailed description of Woodward's background, see Adrian Havill, *Deep Truth: The Lives of Bob Woodward and Carl Bernstein* (New York: Birch Lane Press, 1993).

47. Author interview with Bob Woodward, September 5, 2008. To listen to Colodny's tapes, go to www.watergate.com. Interview with Admiral Thomas H. Moorer, by Robert Gettlin, October 4, 1989; interview of Al Woodward, by Robert Gettlin, August 29, 1989; interview of Melvin Laird, by Robert Gettlin, September 6, 1990; interview with Jerry Friedheim, by Robert Gettlin, September 25, 1990.

48. Brendan McGarry, "Uncovering History: Editor Looks Back at Breaking the Watergate Story," *Saratogian* (Saratoga Springs, NY), August 1, 2004.

49. Author interview with Harry Rosenfeld and Paul R. Ignatius, September 14, 2008.

50. Bradlee served in naval intelligence during World War II. *Post* publisher Katharine Graham's deceased father had been a great fan of the intelligence services, a close friend of CIA wunderkind Frank Wisner and of Prescott Bush—and a generous ground-floor investor in Poppy Bush's first, fledgling Midland business, the landman firm of Bush-Overbey. See Deborah Davis, *Katharine the Great: Katharine Graham and the Washington Post* (Bethesda, MD: National Press, 1979).

51. James M. Perry, "Watergate," in Tom Rosenstiel and Amy S. Mitchell, eds., *Thinking Clearly: Cases in Journalistic Decision-Making* (New York: Columbia University Press, 2003), p. 149.

52. Charles Wendell Colson Papers, Billy Graham Center, Wheaton, Illinois. Verified by Senate Watergate Committee staffer Howard Liebengood.

53. Eric Boehlert, "Team Bush Declares War on the New York Times," *Guardian* (U.K.), October 19, 2004.

54. Richard Harwood, "O What a Tangled Web the CIA Wove," *Washington Post*, February 26, 1967. Harwood's series built on work by *Ramparts* magazine, regarding the funding and control of the National Student Association and other supposedly independent domestic groups over many years. The *New York Times* followed up with a series of articles that would expand considerably our understanding of CIA involvement on U.S. college campuses. This included the manipulation of student groups and the use of academics as authors of propaganda materials to be distributed abroad. As a result of this coverage, President Johnson announced a halt to such funding.

55. Carl Bernstein, "The CIA and the Media," *Rolling Stone*, October 20, 1977.

56. Perry, "Watergate," pp. 148–49.

57. On the twenty-fifth anniversary of the Watergate break-in, *Washington Post* editor Sussman wrote that he never knew the identity of Deep Throat—a rare situation, he said, because reporters usually revealed their sources to their editors. Several months after the break-in, Sussman recalled, Woodward approached him with a "minor story" and made "an unusual request: He said he could tell me who the source was if I really wanted to know, but that in this instance he would rather not. I had no problem in acceding." But on later reflection, it struck him that *Post* editor Ben Bradlee "wasn't concerned enough to ask about Deep Throat's identity" until it was revealed to him after Nixon's resignation in 1975, or, for that matter, that Bradlee even kept Deep Throat's identity as secret. As Sussman wryly noted, "This is one of the few secrets Bradlee ever kept." His final thoughts on the matter are not

complimentary toward his own reporters: "The logic of the Deep Throat myth is confounding. On the one hand, *Post* reporters Bob Woodward and Carl Bernstein deserve credit for helping uncover the Watergate scandal. On the other hand, the basic legend is that one of them, Woodward, did little more than show up with a bread basket that Deep Throat filled with goodies." In other words, "it can't work both ways. The greater the importance of Deep Throat the less the achievement of the two reporters." Sussman's account can be found on www.watergate.info.

58. Colodny and Gettlin, *Silent Coup*, p. 284.

59. Ibid., p. 234.

60. Author interview with Pierre Ausloos, April 22, 2008.

61. The important fact that Poppy had hired Lias out of his office supervising Townhouse appears to have been obscured by Barbara Bush in an error she introduced into her book *Barbara Bush: A Memoir*—in almost exactly the manner she had used with the letters she wrote about November 22, 1963. "There were 11 floors of State Department people at the US mission—for the most part, very able and dedicated people," wrote Barbara. "George brought Tom Lias, Jane Kenny, and Aleene Smith with him from his congressional office." *Barbara Bush: A Memoir* (New York: Scribner, 1994), p. 90.

62. Author interview with John Dean, September 12, 2008; John Dean's phone logs, National Archives.

63. Sam Ervin, Democrat of North Carolina, headed up the committee. The other Democrats were Herman Talmadge of Georgia, Daniel Inouye of Hawaii, and Joseph Montoya of New Mexico. The Republicans were Minority Leader Howard Baker of Tennessee, Edward Gurney of Florida, and Lowell Weicker of Connecticut.

64. Lowell P. Weicker Jr., with Barry Sussman, *Maverick: A Life in Politics* (New York: Little, Brown and Company, 1995), pp. 27–28.

65. In 1988, Weicker decided to support George H. W. Bush, not Robert J. Dole, in the GOP presidential primaries, in part because of Bush's ties to Connecticut. "For me and all other Republican candidates in Connecticut, there was more to gain with Bush at the top of the ticket. I supported Bush and he supported me. If that seems cold and calculated, so be it." (Weicker, *Maverick*, p. 179.)

66. Author interview with Jack Gleason, April 6, 2008. Round Hill is both an exclusive part of Greenwich and a golf club there.

67. Weicker, *Maverick*, p. 46.

68. The six defendants were Bernard Baker, Virgilio Gonzalez, Howard Hunt, Gordon Liddy, Eugenio Martinez, and Frank Sturgis. James McCord would be sentenced at a later date.

69. John M. Crewdson, "Nixon Suggests High Court Ruling on Refusing Data," *New York Times*, March 16, 1973.

70. The Bull Elephant Club was composed of male assistants to GOP House members.

71. Stanley I. Kutler, *Abuse of Power: The New Nixon Tapes* (New York: Free Press, 1997), pp. 241–42.

72. John Ehrlichman, *Witness to Power: The Nixon Years* (New York: Simon & Schuster, 1982), p. 369.

73. Kutler, *Abuse of Power*, p. 242.

74. "Telephone conversation, the President and John Dean, March 20, 1973, 7:29–7:43 P.M.," *The White House Transcripts* (New York: Viking Press, 1974), p. 128.

75. Ibid., pp. 130–31.

76. Author interview with Stanley Kutler, July 17, 2008. See also John H. Taylor, "Cutting the Nixon Tapes," *American Spectator*, March 1998.

77. Transcript prepared by the Impeachment Inquiry Staff for the House Judiciary Committee of a recording of a meeting on March 13, 1973, from 12:42 P.M. to 2:00 P.M.

78. Gordon Strachan, testimony to Senate Watergate Committee, book six.

79. Transcript of recording of a meeting between the president and John Dean in the Oval Office on March 17, 1973, from 1:25 P.M. to 2:10 P.M. (H. R. Haldeman was present for only a portion of the meeting.)

11: Downing Nixon, Part II: The Execution

1. Lowell P. Weicker Jr. with Barry Sussman, *Maverick: A Life in Politics* (Boston, Little, Brown, 1995), pp. 54, 59–60.

2. According to a February 16, 1972, memo from Gordon Strachan to H. R. Haldeman: "The registration drive (Target '72) begins in Florida and Texas in January and will continue through the spring. Ed DeBolt at the RNC is the man responsible to register 1½ million Republicans by May 15 and 8 million by October 1972." Cited in House Judiciary Report, 1974.

3. Author interview with Ed DeBolt, August 30, 2008.

4. Richard J. McGowan, "Watergate Revisited," *Barnes Review*, March 2003.

5. Gerald Ford was then House minority leader; in October 1973, Republican leaders would compel Nixon to make Ford his vice president with the resignation of Spiro Agnew over tax evasion and money-laundering charges. Bryce Harlow was a top Washington lobbyist and close friend of Ford's who had advised every president of both parties since Eisenhower.

6. Weicker, *Maverick*, p. 63. Back in 1970, according to Gleason, when he had tried to deliver the cash to Weicker, he had not been able to make it all the way to Connecticut that day. Instead, he had made the delivery to Weicker's campaign committee in Washington, D.C. As Weicker explained to me in a 2008 interview, "Jack didn't have the time, and I didn't have the time to meet him, to receive the money personally. And therefore, probably by luck, I escaped the violation of the law. Had I received it, instead of my campaign manager [who duly reported the donation], that would have been something different."

7. See, for example, Dean's post-Watergate books, *Worse Than Watergate: The Secret Presidency of George W. Bush* (New York: Little, Brown and Co., 2004) and *Conservatives Without Conscience* (New York: Viking, 2008).

8. As noted in chapter 6, Kerr also was the staunchest congressional defender of the oil depletion allowance.

9. "How John Dean Came Center Stage," *Time*, June 25, 1973.

10. Kleindienst was director of field operations for Goldwater in 1964.

11. Memorandum from Bud Krogh to Trudy Brown, March 2, 1970; memorandum from Bud Krogh to H. R. Haldeman, March 24, 1970. Both available through Nixon Project, National Archives.

12. Unpublished interview by Len Colodny of John Ehrlichman, April 29, 1986.

13. Unpublished letter from Charles W. Colson to Len Colodny, July 1, 1993.

14. Unpublished memorandum from Charles W. Colson to Len Colodny, June 23, 1993.

15. For more on Prosterman's programs, see Mark Dowie, "Behind the Myth of Land Reform," *Mother Jones*, June 1981.

16. For more on Krogh, Prosterman, and Vietnam, see, generally: Egil "Bud" Krogh with Matthew Krogh, *Integrity: Good People, Bad Choices and Life Lessons from the White House* (New York: PublicAffairs, 2007).

17. Maureen Dean with Hays Gorey, *"Mo": A Woman's View of Watergate* (New York: Simon & Schuster, 1975), p. 50.

18. Len Colodny and Robert Gettlin, *Silent Coup: The Removal of a President* (New York: St. Martin's Press, 1991), p. 106.

19. Transcript of "cancer on the presidency" discussion, March 21, 1973, in Stanley I. Kutler, *Abuse of Power: The New Nixon Tapes* (New York: Free Press, 1997), pp. 247–57.

20. G. Gordon Liddy, *Will: The Autobiography of G. Gordon Liddy* (New York: Macmillan, 1991), pp. 251–52.

21. Jim Hougan, *Secret Agenda: Watergate, Deep Throat and the CIA* (New York: Random House, 1984), pp. 106–7.

22. Caulfield worked for Dean throughout 1971, as "Dean's appetite for political intelligence continued to increase." Colodny and Gettlin, *Silent Coup*, p. 106.

23. Liddy, *Will*. E. Howard Hunt would later confirm Liddy's version, reporting that Liddy explained, "Dean tells me there's plenty of money available—half a million." See Colodny and Gettlin, *Silent Coup*, pp. 116–17. See also James Rosen, *The Strong Man: John Mitchell and the Secrets of Watergate* (New York: Doubleday, 2008), pp. 258–75.

24. G. Gordon Liddy, *Will*.

25. Colodny and Gettlin, *Silent Coup*, pp. 124–25. Magruder has provided varying and inconsistent accounts over the years. For more on this, see Rosen, *The Strong Man*, pp. 293–95.

26. For an account of this from Robert Bennett, see the three-hour documentary *John Ehrlichman: In the Eye of the Storm* (American International Television, 1997), hosted by the author Tom Clancy.

27. Meeting between President Nixon and H. R. Haldeman in the Oval Office, June 23, 1972, 10:04–11:39 A.M., Richard M. Nixon Presidential Library, College Park, Maryland. (The main Nixon library is located in Yorba Linda, California.)

28. L. Patrick Gray III, with Ed Gray, *In Nixon's Web: A Year in the Crosshairs of Watergate* (New York: Times Books, 2008), pp. 64–69.

29. J. Anthony Lukas, "Good Man's Bad Book, Bad Man's Good Book," *New York Times Book Review*, October 31, 1976.

30. Weicker, *Maverick*, p. 65.

31. Ibid., p. x.

32. Jeff Gerth with Robert Pear, "Files Detail Aid to Bush by Nixon White House," *New York Times*, June 11, 1992.

33. Bill Choyke, "Is Fensterwald a CIA Plant?" *Washington Star*, October 4, 1976.

34. Philip Agee and Louis Wolf, *Dirty Work: The CIA in Western Europe* (New York: Lyle Stuart, 1978), p. 133.

35. John Stauber and Sheldon Rampton, *Toxic Sludge Is Good for You: Lies, Damn Lies and the Public Relations Industry* (Monroe, ME: Common Courage Press, 1995), pp. 152–53.

36. Hays Gorey, "John Dean Warns: A Mile to Go," *Time*, June 4, 1973.

37. John Dean, *Blind Ambition: The White House Years* (New York: Simon & Schuster, 1976), pp. 314–15.

38. Ibid., p. 317.

39. Gleason recalled the origin of Bush's call this way: Some time in the early spring of 1973, he found some receipts related to the Townhouse Operation and brought them over to Bush at the RNC. "I made a decision with my lawyer that I would take Bush a list of the guys who received the cash, just so somebody could alert the members—the few who had gotten elected," Gleason told me. "Their names were going into the special prosecutor's hopper. I went down and saw Bush and Tom Lias."

40. Weicker, *Maverick*, p. 83.

41. "Lowell Weicker Gets Mad," *Time*, July 9, 1973.

42. Ibid.

43. Weicker, *Maverick*, p. 76.

44. Author interview with Lowell Weicker, March 31, 2008.

45. Colodny and Gettlin, *Silent Coup*, pp. 325–27.

46. Kutler, *Abuse of Power*, p. 638.

47. A. Robert Smith, "The Butterfield Exchange," *New York Times*, July 20, 1975.

48. Colodny and Gettlin, *Silent Coup*, p. 323.

49. As Sam Dash, chief counsel to the committee, put it, "The White House knew that Carmine Bellino, a wizard at reconstructing the receipts and expenditures of funds despite laundering techniques . . . was hot on the trail of Nixon's closest money men, Herbert Kalmbach and Bebe Rebozo." Samuel Dash, *Chief Counsel: Inside the Ervin Committee—The Untold Story of Watergate* (New York: Random House, 1976), p. 192.

50. Douglas E. Kneel, "Watergate Panel Begins an Inquiry into Charges Against Its Chief Investigator," *New York Times*, August 4, 1973. Joseph Shimon, a retired investigator and former captain of the Washington, D.C., police, claimed in an affidavit that another investigator, Oliver Angelone, had asked him to help in bugging the hotel room of unidentified Republicans. Shimon said the other investigator had said the request originated with Bellino. Angelone called Shimon's claim "absolutely untrue."

51. Bellino had been close to the Kennedy family and admitted that he had sought to investigate the source of anti-Catholic literature in the 1960 campaign. But he would heatedly deny engaging in anything like illegal wiretapping or bugging.

52. Webster G. Tarpley and Anton Chaitkin, *George Bush: The Unauthorized Biography* (Washington, D.C.: Executive Intelligence Review, 1992), p. 259.

53. See, generally, Ken Gormley and Elliot Richardson, *Archibald Cox: Conscience of a Nation* (Cambridge, MA: DaCapo Press, 1999); see also Colodny and Gettlin, *Silent Coup*, chapter 21.

54. Leon Jaworski with Mickey Herskowitz, *Confession and Avoidance: A Memoir* (Garden City, NY: Anchor, 1979), p. 183. (Herskowitz would be George W. Bush's temporary ghostwriter twenty years later. See chapter 20.)

55. Jaworski, *Confession and Avoidance*, pp. 183, 195.

56. See Seymour M. Hersh, *The Price of Power: Kissinger in the Nixon White House* (New York: Summit, 1984).

57. Bernard A. Weisberger, *Cold War, Cold Peace: The United States and Russia Since 1945* (Boston: Houghton Mifflin, 1984), p. 295.

58. Joseph A. Califano Jr., *Inside: A Public and Private Life* (New York: PublicAffairs, 2004), pp. 216–17.

59. George Bush, *All the Best: My Life in Letters and Other Writings* (New York: Scribner, 1999), p. 186.

60. Ibid., p. 186.

61. "Reagan Seeks Leon Jaworski's Backing," *Newsweek*, September 29, 1980.

62. "Business Leaders Are Tied to CIA's Covert Operations," *Washington Post*, February 18, 1967.

63. Memorandum from Charles Ruff, Assistant Special Prosecutor, to Leon Jaworski, Special Prosecutor, August 19, 1974. National Archives.

64. Jaworski was not the only Texas Democrat who was cozy with Poppy in this period. Poppy would lunch weekly during his tenure as RNC chairman with his Democratic National Committee counterpart, Robert Strauss of Dallas, a conservative oil-industry lawyer. In his book *All the Best*, Poppy calls him "a great friend to this day." As president, Poppy appointed Strauss ambassador to the USSR. The relationship underlines a longtime fact about Texas politics whose significance cannot be underlined too strongly. There were two types of Democrats in that

state: the populists and the royalists, with the latter being Democrats more for historical and tribal reasons than ideological ones.

65. Gray, *In Nixon's Web*, p. 100.

66. The five Democrats on the committee who voted against investigating seem to have had a range of motives, not the least of which was they were not inclined to support a controversial action close to election day. "House Panel Bars Pre-Nov. 7 Inquiry into Bugging Case," *New York Times*, October 4, 1972.

67. Richard Harwood, "CIA Reported Ending Aid to Some Groups," *Washington Post*, February 22, 1967.

68. Philip Agee and Louis Wolf, *Dirty Work: The CIA in Western Europe* (New York: Lyle Stuart, 1978), p. 133.

69. Nicholas D. Kristof, "The Success of the President's Men," *New York Times*, June 13, 1986.

70. From 2000 to 2002, Pulitzer Prize–winning reporter William Gaines and his journalism students at the University of Illinois attempted to uncover the identity of Deep Throat. At some point, according to the students' Web site, John Dean "learned of the student project and helped with valuable first-person knowledge of the White House staff."

From an article about a Watergate documentary: "Dean says a younger generation has to be reminded of Watergate's lessons—and that even those who remember the Watergate hearings need reminding exactly what happened. That's why he was happy, he says, to be interviewed for 'Watergate Plus 30.' . . . In the documentary, Dean says, 'Unfortunately, I think the lesson of Watergate is "Don't get caught." ' " Jonathan Curiel, "From Break-in to Murder: The Watergate Plot Thickens in 'Plus 30,' " *San Francisco Chronicle*, July 30, 2003.

71. Anne E. Kornblut, "Mystery Solved: The Sleuths," *New York Times*, June 2, 2005.

72. Ibid.

73. *Daily Oklahoman*, June 17, 1992 (also distributed by the Associated Press).

74. Gray, *In Nixon's Web*, pp. 291–300. Woodward and Bernstein's archival papers were purchased by the University of Texas for $5 million and are now housed at the university's Austin campus.

75. Gerald S. Strober and Deborah Hart Strober, *Nixon: An Oral History of His Presidency* (New York: HarperCollins, 1994), p. 528.

76. Ibid., 519.

77. H. R. Haldeman, *The Haldeman Diaries: Inside the Nixon White House* (New York: G. P. Putnam's Sons, 1994), p. 472.

78. For McCord testimony on this, see U.S. Congress, Senate Select Committee on Presidential Campaign Activities, *Presidential Campaign Activities of 1972, Senate Resolution 60: Watergate and Related Activities: Hearings*, 93rd Cong. 1st [2nd] sess. (Washington, D.C.: Government Printing Office, 1973), p. 205.

79. Herbert S. Parmet, *George Bush, The Life of the Lone Star Yankee* (New Brunswick, NJ: Transaction, 2001), p. 166.

80. George Bush, *All the Best*, pp. 188–91.

81. "The Sun Is Shining Again," *Newsweek*, August 26, 1974: "Behind the scenes, NEWSWEEK learned, Republican National Chairman George Bush, the other heavy favorite, had slipped badly because of alleged irregularities in the financing of his 1970 Senate race in Texas . . . Bush's youthful, middle-ground image was clearly appealing. But White House sources told NEWSWEEK there was potential embarrassment and reports that the Nixon White House funneled about $100,000 from a secret fund called the 'townhouse operation' into Bush's losing Senate campaign against Lloyd Bentsen four years ago. There were indications that $40,000 of the money may not have been properly reported as required by election law."

82. Verbatim from a memorandum of conversation between Gerald Ford and George H. W. Bush, declassified in 1992. Gerald R. Ford Presidential Library, Ann Arbor, Michigan.

83. "He was an embarrassment," recalled Sydney M. "Terry" Cone III, a member of the heavily Rockefeller-dominated Council on Foreign Relations. "The man knew nothing. Absolutely nothing. It was my opinion that he had no concept of the world; no understanding of foreign policy. He was obviously a political appointee that Nixon had to do something for . . . George was only a meeter and a greeter." Kelley, *The Family*, p. 287.

84. Walter Pincus and Bob Woodward, "Presidential Posts and Dashed Hopes," *Washington Post*, August 9, 1988.

85. George Bush with Victor Gold, *Looking Forward* (New York: Doubleday, 1987), p. 130.

12: In from the Cold

1. Karen DeYoung and Walter Pincus, "CIA to Air Decades of Its Dirty Laundry," *Washington Post*, June 22, 2007.

2. As a member of the Warren Commission, Gerald Ford made numerous handwritten edits to the draft report. The original text on page 5 read, "A bullet had entered his back at a point slightly above the shoulder to the right of the spine." Ford changed that sentence to read, "A bullet had entered the back of his neck at a point slightly to the right of the spine." That change suggested a different trajectory from the initial description of the bullet wound in Kennedy's back to an entry point higher up in his body. See the document reproduced at JFK Lancer, www .jfklancer.com/docs.maps/ford1.gif.

3. Several weeks after the *New York Times* published Seymour Hersh's expose of the "family jewels," President Ford invited the *Times'* editorial board to an "off the record" White House lunch to discuss CIA abuses. Ford broached the subject of the agency's role in foreign assassinations and then attempted to retract his comment on the subject, which the Ford administration had not wanted the Rockefeller Commission to touch. *Time* magazine observed, the commission "final report pleads—not too convincingly—that there was not enough time to examine the subject fully." See "Lunch with the President," *Time*, June 23, 1975.

4. Author interview with William G. Ronan, June 12, 2007.

5. December 1954 to December 1955.

6. The full declassified report available at the National Security Archive, George Washington University, Web site, www.gwu.edu/~nsarchiv/NSAEBB/NSAEBB222/index.htm.

7. It was, in fact, the Senate Intelligence Committee chaired by Senator Frank Church that the Rockefeller Commission had been set up to preempt, if not to convince Congress that its own investigation was not needed.

8. Together, the Church Committee's reports have been said to constitute the most extensive review of intelligence activities ever made available to the public. Much of the contents were classified, but more than fifty thousand pages have since been declassified under the 1992 JFK Assassination Records Collection Act, and most are available online at the National Security Archive at George Washington University, www.gwu.edu/~nsarchiv.

9. Among the matters investigated were CIA attempts to assassinate foreign leaders in the Congo, the Dominican Republic, Vietnam, and Chile, as well as the agency's having withheld from the Warren Commission information on the CIA's efforts to use the Mafia to kill Fidel Castro. The Church Committee also discovered a host of domestic programs aimed at American citizens: COINTELPRO, Operation Chaos, and other related domestic political operations. The committee found that the CIA, in tandem with the FBI, the NSA, and other military intelligence agencies,

ran a clandestine and highly illegal surveillance operation called Project MINARET. Americans deemed "subversive" were placed on "watch lists" for electronic surveillance. The watch lists were populated by civil rights and antiwar leaders like Dr. Martin Luther King Jr., Malcolm X, Dr. Benjamin Spock, and Joan Baez.

10. "Assassination Ban and E.O. 12333: A Brief Summary," available at the Federation of American Scientists Web site www.fas.org/irp/crs/RS21037.pdf.

11. "Of Moles and Molehunters: Spy Stories," Center for the Study of Intelligence, October 1993.

12. Final Report of the Assassination Records Review Board, chapter 1.

13. Henry Kissinger, *Years of Upheaval* (Boston: Little, Brown & Co., 1982), p. 153.

14. When the original text of "Family Jewels" was finally declassified in 2007, the *Washington Post* reported, "Only a few officials had previously been privy to the scope of its illegal activities. Schlesinger collected the reports, some of which dated to the 1950s, in a folder that was inherited by his successor, Colby, in September of that year. But it was not until Hersh's article that Colby took the file to the White House." DeYoung and Pincus, "CIA to Air Decades of Its Dirty Laundry." Also see Thomas Powers, "Inside the Department of Dirty Tricks," *Atlantic Monthly*, August 1979.

15. James M. Naughton, "Sweeping Change: Cheney Is White House Staff Chief—General Is Security Adviser," *New York Times*, November 4, 1975.

16. "A Breezy Head of the C.I.A.," *New York Times*, November 4, 1975.

17. "Bush Explains Decision," *New York Times*, November 4, 1975.

18. *Houston Post*, November 8, 1975. See Tarpley, p. 293, footnote 4; found in Philip Buchen Files, Box 24, Gerald R. Ford Presidential Library, Ann Arbor, Michigan.

19. Bill Peterson, "Bush Says He Reported 1970 'Townhouse' Donation," *Washington Post*, February 8, 1980.

20. Nicholas M. Horrock, "Mr. Bush Does Not Fit the Top-Spy Mold," *New York Times*, November 9, 1975.

21. U.S. Senate Committee on Armed Services, *Nomination of George Bush to Be Director of Central Intelligence*, December 15–16, 1975, p. 10.

22. Walter Pincus and Bob Woodward, "Presidential Posts and Dashed Hopes; Appointive Jobs Were Turning Point," *Washington Post*, August 9, 1988.

23. "George Bush: Hot Property in Presidential Politics," *Washington Post*, January 27, 1980.

24. Count de Marenches and David A. Andelman, *The Fourth World War: Diplomacy and Espionage in the Age of Terrorism* (New York: William Morrow and Company, 1992), pp. 248–49.

25. John Ranelagh, *The Agency: The Rise and Decline of the CIA* (New York: Simon & Schuster, 1986), p. 576. Also see Tim Weiner, *Legacy of Ashes* (New York: Doubleday, 2007), p. 324.

26. Loch K. Johnson, *A Season of Inquiry: The Senate Intelligence Investigation* (Lexington: University Press of Kentucky, 1985), pp. 108–9.

27. Letter from Richard M. Nixon to George Bush, November 12, 1975, Richard Nixon Presidential Library, Yorba Linda, California.

28. Letter from George Bush to Richard M. Nixon, December 4, 1975, Richard Nixon Presidential Library.

29. De Marenches and Andelman, *The Fourth World War*, p. 247.

30. Nicholas M. Horrock, untitled article, *New York Times*, February 18, 1976.

31. Fareed Zakaria, "Exaggerating the Threats," *Newsweek*, June 16, 2003.

32. John Dinges, *The Condor Years: How Pinochet and His Allies Brought Terrorism to Three Continents* (New York: New Press, 2004); Dinges was the *Washington Post*'s South America correspondent from 1975 to 1983. Also see Saul Landau, *Assassination on Embassy Row* (New York: Pantheon, 1980).

33. Though no longer the powerhouse that it once was, *Reader's Digest* has remained a "reliable" publication. When George W. Bush became president, he would install a top *Reader's Digest* executive, Kenneth Tomlinson, to lead the Corporation for Public Broadcasting, with the mandate to exorcise a perceived liberal slant, particularly at PBS.

34. Fulton Oursler worked closely with Hoover and later, as a senior editor at *Reader's Digest*, with FBI assistant director Louis B. Nichols. See Curt Gentry, *J. Edgar Hoover: The Man and the Secrets* (New York: W. W. Norton & Company, 1991).

35. Epstein himself admitted that Angleton was a key source, two years after the counterintelligence chief's death. See Edward J. Epstein, *Deception: The Invisible War Between the KGB and the CIA* (New York: Simon & Schuster, 1989).

36. The House Select Committee on Assassinations would issue its final report in 1979.

37. Poppy Bush's assertion that he was out of touch with de Mohrenschildt in the years surrounding the Kennedy assassination are further cast in doubt by an interoffice memo to Poppy from his employee R. C. Mosby, dated March 30, 1965, which cites a bevy of men tied to de Mohrenschildt through business and friendship:

> You have asked that we prepare a list of individuals to be invited to a small gathering next Monday. The following is a list of contract drilling people and construction people who would be interested in having equipment built in the Niarchos facilities in Greece.

> Among the names are "G. B. Kitchel, Vice President, Kerr-McGee Oil Industries, Inc.," with the notation that the letter to him should be addressed to "George"; "Mr. George Brown, Brown and Root"; "Mr. John Mecom"; and, added in pencil beside a notation for "Mr. Carnes Weaver, Worldover Drilling Company," "Mr. W. C. Savage (for Mr. Weaver)." Internal correspondence from Zapata Offshore, on company letterhead, dated March 30, 1965, found in the files of the George H. W. Bush Library, College Station, Texas. (Handwritten notes show that at least Kitchel and Savage had RSVP'd affirmatively.) Interestingly, Kitchel, Brown, Mecom, and Savage were all close with de Mohrenschildt—and the above-mentioned Greek, Stavros Niarchos, was a longtime CIA asset.

38. See independent researcher Bruce Campbell Adamson's work available at www.ciajfk.com/images/l-319b.jpg.

39. According to handwritten notes provided by Adamson available at www.ciajfk.com/images/Bush-7a.jpg and www.ciajfk.com/images/Bush-8.jpg.

40. George and Jeanne de Mohrenschildt were divorced in 1974 but had three little chihuahuas they shared. He lived in an apartment at Bishop College, in Texas, and she lived alone in Dallas. While he was committed to the mental hospital, she moved to California. After he was released, he lived alone in Dallas.

41. Kurtz, who has been studying the assassination for decades, does not cite the dates of his conversations with these sources, which apparently occurred years ago. In an interview with me on August 2, 2008, he said he recalled that the three CIA veterans had actually called *him*, in part, he believes, because they appreciated his conclusion that the agency was *not* involved with the assassination. As he recalled, their knowing Mrs. de Mohrenschildt came up during the conversation but was not the central topic. Michael Kurtz, *The JFK Assassination Debates: Lone Gunman Versus Conspiracy* (Lawrence: University Press of Kansas, 2006), pp. 149–51.

42. Jim Marrs, "Widow Disputes Suicide," *Fort Worth Evening Star-Telegram*, May 11, 1978.

43. De Marenches and Andelman, *The Fourth World War*, pp. 22–23.

44. HSCA transcript, p. 21.

45. De Mohrenschildt's first wife, Dorothy Pierson, had been just eighteen when she became pregnant with Alexandra. Dorothy abandoned her daughter, who was raised by Dorothy's cousin Nancy Pierson. The relationship between Nancy Pierson and de Mohrenschildt was often strained.

46. Rangely Field, Colorado.

47. Savage interview with independent researcher Bruce Campbell Adamson.

48. The two were Hoyt S. Taylor and Harry Wayne Dean.

49. Bruce Campbell Adamson interview with George B. Kitchel.

50. Ibid.

51. Combined Warren Commission testimonies of George and Jeanne de Mohrenschildt.

52. The Palm Beach County Sheriff's Death Investigation Report is available at http://mcadams.posc .mu.edu/death2.txt.

53. Marrs, "Widow Disputes Suicide."

54. Michael Canfield interview with Paul Raigorodsky, November 22, 1976.

13: POPPY'S PROXY AND THE SAUDIS

1. That Bath opened his plane brokerage in 1976 was asserted in Jonathan Beaty and S. C. Gwynne, "A Mysterious Mover of Money and Planes," *Time*, October 28, 1991.

2. Craig Unger, *House of Bush, House of Saud: The Secret Relationship Between the World's Two Most Powerful Dynasties* (New York: Scribner, 2004), p. 20.

3. Roughly a dozen brothers manage the Bin Laden Brothers for Contracting and Industry—one of the largest construction firms in the Middle East. For more information on its origins, see Steve Coll, *The Bin Ladens: An Arabian Family in the American Century* (New York: Penguin Press, 2008), pp. 176–79.

4. There are varying accounts as to Mohammed's date of death. Some sources say 1967, others say 1968.

5. By 1991, as Osama's radicalism threatened the security of Saudi Arabia itself, the family would completely disown him. Steve Coll, *Ghost Wars* (New York: Penguin, 2004), p. 231.

6. A passenger manifest, made public by Senator Frank Lautenberg (D-NJ), shows that at least thirteen relatives of Osama bin Laden, accompanied by bodyguards and associates, were allowed to leave the United States on a chartered flight eight days after the September 11, 2001, terrorist attacks. The manifest, which Lautenberg obtained from officials of Boston's Logan International Airport, was released on July 21, 2004.

7. Author interviews with multiple Bath associates.

8. Christopher Robbins, *Air America: The Story of the CIA's Secret Airline* (New York: Avon, 1985), p. 21.

9. Author interview with Dr. Richard Mayo, July 23, 2004.

10. Atlantic Aviation's chairman was Edward B. Du Pont. One board member, Edward Du Pont's cousin Richard C. Du Pont Jr., owned the CIA-connected Summit Aviation, which was active during both Vietnam and later Iran-contra. (For background on Summit, see Jeff Gerth, "Ex-U.S. Intelligence and Military Personnel Supply Anti-Nicaragua Rebels," *New York Times*, November 8, 1983.) Another Du Pont relative, Samuel H. Du Pont Jr., headed the Civil Air Patrol nationally circa 1970. Bath's employment as a VP of Atlantic Aviation is referenced by Alexander Cockburn and Jeffrey St. Clair, *Imperial Crusades: Iraq, Afghanistan and Yugoslavia* (New York: Verso, 2004), p. 125.

11. Timothy Noah, "Found Object: Bush's Early Discharge," *Slate*, November 11, 2003.

12. National Guard Bureau, Aeronautical Order, no. 87, September 29, 1972.

13. Craig Unger, "Mystery Man," Salon.com, April 27, 2004.

14. Author interview with General Belisario Flores (Ret.), August 30, 2004.

15. Unger, "Mystery Man."

16. Unger, *House of Bush, House of Saud*, p. 34.

17. E-mail to author from Bill White, May 17, 2008.

18. Daniel Yergin, *The Prize: The Epic Quest for Oil, Money and Power* (New York: Free Press, 1992), p. 393.

19. That same year, in Washington, the son of Abdul Aziz's adviser St. John Philby, Kim Philby, a high-ranking British intelligence officer, met with Lieutenant Commander William Conkling Ladd of the Office of Naval Intelligence. The meeting was an important one to discuss collaboration between Britain and the United States on intelligence concerning Russia and Communism. The meeting represented the formal launching of postwar intelligence cooperation and would lead to the founding of an American civilian intelligence service, the Central Intelligence Agency. Philby was the official representative of British intelligence in Washington, and in the ensuing years he would often dine with Allen Dulles. Kim Philby would later be unmasked as a notorious Soviet double agent. Lieutenant Commander Ladd's daughter, Olivia, would marry a Wall Street operator named Marion Gilliam. Marion Gilliam would end up involved in a little-known company called Lucky Chance Mining, one of whose directors would be George W. Bush.

20. Michael Klare, *Blood and Oil* (New York: Henry Holt, 2004), p. 41.

21. Ibid., p. 41.

22. The Saudis had become alarmed over Egypt's relentless bombardments of Yemen, just south of Saudi Arabia, using Soviet-supplied weapons. Worried that Egyptian nationalist president Nasser would extend his influence into southern Arabia, the Saudis decided to beef up their own defenses.

23. That was the same plane George W. Bush was flying, and at the same exact time. Bandar, who had a very real reason for developing military skills as a guardian of his family's sometimes-threatened hold on power, would fly for seventeen years, while Bush would quit after two.

24. The interest on the part of privileged and connected Saudis in coming to the United States to learn to fly made the practice seem routine by the time some nonroyal Saudis began arriving in the United States to do the same—the men who became the pilots of the hijacked craft on 9/11. There are no known connections between the royal pilots and the terrorists—indeed, the 9/11 pilots are dedicated to bringing down the Saudi royal family. Nevertheless, the general U.S. effort to accommodate Saudis wishing to learn to fly is believed by some to have lowered security standards in general in a way that may have inadvertently made it easier for the hijackers to gain visas.

25. Bandar's rise to prominence had begun in 1981, when he came to the United States to argue before Congress for the sale of AWACs (airborne control and warning systems) and F-15 equipment to the Saudis. Part of his strategy was to carry around with him a photo of his grandfather Abdul Aziz ibn Saud, who had negotiated the original concession with the United States in 1933 and had developed a particularly warm friendship with Franklin Delano Roosevelt during World War II. Ever since then, Saudi princes had toured the United States, studied in its colleges, trained in its military bases, and received overall red carpet treatment. But this visit by Prince Bandar was particularly noteworthy. For now, the Saudis were seriously trying to counterbalance the influence of the pro-Israel lobby in Congress. By engaging in an intensive lobbying campaign coordinated by Bandar, they won Senate approval of the AWAC sale, 52–48. It was a milestone in Saudi-U.S. relations.

26. A significant if little-discussed by-product of the embargo was the extent to which American oil companies themselves reaped the profits of quadrupled oil prices. By 1974, Exxon overtook General Motors as the biggest American corporation in gross revenues, with its competitors following closely behind.

27. "Annual Oil Market Chronology Energy Data, Statistics and Analysis," available through the Energy Information Administration at www.eia.doe.gov.

28. In March 1973, an American firm, Vinnell Corporation, was hired by the Department of Defense to "modernize" the Saudi National Guard, and has ever since played a major role in the kingdom's internal security. Vinnell had a long history of association with U.S. intelligence and had been involved in arming and supplying Chinese anti-Communist forces in the 1940s. See also: Matt Gaul, "Regulating the New Privateers: Private Military Service Contracting and the Modern Marque and Reprisal Clause," *Loyola of Los Angeles Law Review*, June 1998; Dan Briody, *The Iron Triangle: Inside the Secret World of the Carlyle Group* (Hoboken, NJ: Wiley, 2003).

    In 1992, Vinnell along with its parent company, BDM, were acquired by the Carlyle Group. Frank C. Carlucci, a former secretary of defense under President Reagan, was chairman of BDM for most of the 1990s. Carlucci also served as Reagan's national security adviser and a deputy director of the CIA from 1978 to '81; he headed the Carlyle Group from 1992 until 2003.

29. John Perkins, *Confessions of an Economic Hit Man* (San Francisco: Berrett-Kohler, 2004), p. 12.

30. For more on the symbiotic relationship between American big oil and its even bigger Saudi brethren, and those who serve them, see, generally, John MacArthur, "The Vast Power of the Saudi Lobby," *Harper's*, April 17, 2007; and Unger, *House of Bush, House of Saud*.

31. Steven Emerson, *The American House of Saud* (New York: Franklin Watts, 1985), pp. 112–13.

32. Nixon had labeled as priorities the deregulation of natural gas, development of nuclear energy, and faster exploitation of offshore oil and gas deposits.

33. Dr. Pinkney C. Walker was dean of the University of Missouri school of business administration. A leading Democrat had criticized Walker's appointment, complaining that he was too close to the power industry. See Robert Bryce, *Pipe Dreams: Greed, Ego, and the Death of Enron* (New York: Public Affairs, 2004) for more on Walker's own relationship with George W.

34. Lay's boss was Under Secretary Rogers C. B. Morton, who was pushing for deregulation of natural gas prices.

35. Beaty and Gwynne, "A Mysterious Mover of Money and Planes."

36. Pharaon's Houston-based mini-conglomerate, Arabian Services Corporation, had a majority stake in the Sam P. Wallace Company, a Dallas-based mechanical contracting concern that in 1983 pleaded guilty to paying bribes of nearly $1.4 million to a government official in Trinidad and Tobago and was fined $530,000. See: *U.S. v. Sam P. Wallace Company, Inc.* (Cr. No. 83-0034) (PG), D.P.R., 1983; also see the *Annual Report of the Security and Exchange Commission*, 1981, SEC, available at www.sec.gov/about/annual_report/1981.pdf.

37. Jonathan Beaty and S.C. Gwynne, *The Outlaw Bank: A Wild Ride into the Secret Heart of BCCI* (New York: Random House, 1993), p. 274. Beaty and Gwynne call this statement a certifiable lie. As the BCCI scandal broke, Beaty and Gwynne, then *Time* magazine correspondents, quote another *Time* reporter covering the story as writing, "There is a feeling that someone in Washington is trying to cut a deal on BCCI; that they don't really want the U.S. Attorney's offices to return indictments because that would muck up their ability to do some sort of overall package deal."

38. The nephew who killed King Faisal, Faisal bin Musa'id, studied at several American universities, including UC Berkeley, and was described as having drug problems and having undergone

psychiatric treatments. In both Saudi Arabia and the Arab world in general, popular belief holds that Faisal bin Musa'id was some kind of a pawn in a Western conspiracy.

39. Anthony Cave Brown, *Oil, God and Gold: The Story of Aramco and the Saudi Kings* (Boston: Houghton Mifflin, 1999), p. 306.

40. Walters does not say what he was doing in that period. His memoirs end at the moment he leaves the CIA. He does not say where he went next. See Vernon A. Walters, *Silent Missions* (Garden City, NY: Doubleday, 1978). Walters was an aide to Averell Harriman during the early days of the cold war.

41. This figure is highly imprecise and does not include untold private transactions, of which there have clearly been many. It comes from Unger's *House of Bush, House of Saud.* In an appendix, Unger totals up $1.4 billion worth of publicly identifiable business transacted between the Saudi royal family and businesses tied in various ways—some closer than others—to the Bush family and its associates. These include dealings with Dick Cheney's old firm Halliburton, donations to Bush senior's presidential library, and investments in the Carlyle Group. Poppy Bush has served as a senior adviser to Carlyle, and James Baker, his former secretary of state, has been a Carlyle senior partner, while Baker's law firm defended the House of Saud in a lawsuit brought by relatives of victims of September 11.

42. CBC interview with Bill White by Bob McKeown, *The Fifth Estate,* aired October 29, 2003.

43. Ibid.

44. Ibid.

45. Ibid.

46. Unger, *House of Bush, House of Saud,* p. 23.

47. JB&A was incorporated in Texas in 1976.

48. In sworn depositions taken during a legal dispute, Bath admitted that he served as a trustee for the bin Laden family and fronted for three other wealthy Saudi businessmen. He also admitted that he received a 5 percent personal ownership interest, in lieu of immediate cash compensation, in the businesses he purchased on behalf of the Saudis: "The investments were sometimes in my name as trustee, sometimes offshore corporations and sometimes in the name of a law firm," he said. "It would vary."

49. Vinson & Elkins would later defend Enron and provide major "bundled" donations to W.'s presidential campaign.

50. CBC interview with Bill White.

14: POPPY'S WEB

1. Cited on George W. Bush's application for Air Force flight training, AF 65, May 28, 1968.

2. Funds from those accounts would find their way to support two of the 9/11 hijackers, and Riggs secretly handled the ill-gotten gains of Augusto Pinochet, Chile's brutal military dictator. Riggs began a relationship with Poppy's brother Jonathan Bush in 1970, when his company began offering Riggs money-management advice. In 1997, Riggs bought out Jonathan's firm, and in 2000, while serving as a major fund-raiser for George W. Bush's presidential campaign, he was appointed the head of Riggs Investment Management Co. Riggs finally closed its doors in 2005 after being fined twenty-five million dollars for violation of money-laundering laws.

3. Jonathan Beaty and S. C. Gwynne, *The Outlaw Bank: A Wild Ride into the Secret Heart of BCCI* (New York: Random House, 1993), p. 250.

4. Casey died two years before the initial raid on BCCI, which occurred in 1988.
    The 1992 Senate "Kerry" Committee report states in its introduction:

Outside the documentary record provided to the Subcommittee by the CIA, there is additional material, consisting of BCCI documents, testimony from BCCI officials and insiders, and extrinsic, circumstantial and historic information describing other substantial contacts between BCCI and the intelligence community. These include contacts between BCCI and: former U.S. intelligence officials, including a former head of the CIA; former and current foreign intelligence officials; and individuals engaged in covert operations on behalf of the United States government, including in the Iran/Contra affair. In addition, the Subcommittee has received allegations of meetings between former CIA director William Casey and BCCI's head, Agha Hasan Abedi.

5. Connally ended up ninety-three million dollars in debt and declared bankruptcy; see "Real Estate Woes Force Connally Bankruptcy," *New York Times*, August 1, 1987.

6. Craig Unger, *House of Bush, House of Saud: The Secret Relationship Between the World's Two Most Powerful Dynasties* (New York: Scribner, 2004), p. 34.

7. Lance effectively became an employee of FGB's controlling shareholder, a fellow named George Olmsted. A retired Army general who had headed up the China section of the OSS (predecessor to the CIA), during World War II, Olmsted went on to serve as a top Pentagon official involved with supplying materiel to allied Asian countries in the cold war. In 1948, along with Allen Dulles and former secretary of state Edward Stettinius, Olmsted helped create a curious shipping venture called International Registries Incorporated (IRI). In 1976, when Poppy Bush was CIA director, IRI/Liberian Services moved its headquarters to Reston, Virginia. Long rumored to be a CIA front, it registered ships owned by the Greek shipping tycoon Stavros Niarchos (who had been close to Poppy Bush's friends Al Ulmer and Allen Dulles) and even brokered deals for Zapata Offshore.

Olmsted was a founder of the powerful defense-contractor-backed anti-Communist group Committee on the Present Danger. In 1953, at the same time that Allen Dulles took over the CIA, Olmsted left the military and began assembling a financial empire, including insurance companies and banks. In retrospect, this entity looks a lot like an apparatus for managing the enormous sums required for an intelligence agency, or at least the off-the-books aspects of one. In that sense, it may have been a precursor to BCCI and other such financial institutions.

8. Count de Marenches and David A. Andelman, *The Fourth World War: Diplomacy and Espionage in the Age of Terrorism* (New York: William Morrow and Company, 1992), pp. 248–49.

9. Abboud, who is Lebanese American, was forced out in 1980 after five years as head of First National Bank of Chicago, which was ultimately acquired by Chase Bank. In 1991, after three years of large losses, Houston's First City Bank Corp. of Texas replaced him. Thomas C. Hayes, "Abboud Out as Chief at Houston's First City," *New York Times*, March 28, 1991.

10. "The Sharpening Battle Over Bert Lance," *Time*, August 1, 1977. Abboud would also show up on the board of the National Bank of Washington, where Poppy's national security adviser and close friend Brent Scowcroft was heavily invested. (Jeff Gerth, "Scowcroft Sold Military Holdings Months Before Persian Gulf War," *New York Times*, June 18, 1991.) Abboud would later appear as a savior of Harken Energy, an oil company that had George W. Bush on its board.

11. James Ring Adams and Douglas Frantz, *A Full Service Bank: How BCCI Stole Billions Around the World* (New York: Pocket, 1992), pp. 32–33.

12. Abedi in particular could not acquire the National Bank of Georgia because it was a national

bank, regulated by the Office of the Comptroller of the Currency—and the then-comptroller, John Heiman, a former superintendent of New York State Banking, knew enough about Abedi to keep him out of the country.

13. "Lance's Mysterious Rescuer," *Time*, January 9, 1978.

14. Beaty and Gwynne, *The Outlaw Bank*, p. 22.

15. Ibid., pp. 195–96.

16. George Lardner Jr., "Carter Criticized on Billy," *Washington Post*, September 30, 1980.

17. E-mail from Bill White to the author, May 7, 2008.

18. Zbigniew Brzezinski, *Power and Principle: Memoirs of the National Security Adviser, 1977–1981* (New York: Farrar, Straus & Giroux, 1983), pp. 473–74; James A. Bill, *The Eagle and the Lion: The Tragedy of American-Iranian Relations* (New Haven, CT: Yale University Press, 1988), p. 331; Charlotte Dennett, "Suffering in Silence," *Nation*, December 12, 1980; Peter Dale Scott, *The Road to 9/11: Wealth, Empire, and the Future of America* (Berkeley: University of California Press, 2007), pp. 80–92.

19. Raymond Bonner, *Waltzing with a Dictator: The Marcoses and the Making of American Policy* (New York: Times Books, 1987), p. 335.

20. Gary Sick, *October Surprise: America's Hostages in Iran and the Election of Ronald Reagan* (New York: Three Rivers, 1991), p. 12.

21. Robert Parry, "Original October Surprise (Part 3)," *Consortium News*, October 19, 2006.

22. CBC interview with Bill White by Bob McKeown, *The Fifth Estate*, aired October 29, 2003.

23. Per court documents, after Salem bin Laden died in a plane crash in 1988, Mahfouz took over his airport interests.

24. Thomas B. Edsall and Ted Gup, "The Lake Resources Inc. Account," *Washington Post*, March 7, 1987.

25. David Johnston, "North's Notebook Is Played Down," *New York Times*, May 10, 1990.

26. CBC interview with Bill White.

27. According to campaign-finance disclosure reports.

28. In order to deal with the disruption to his business and personal life caused by the onslaught of civil litigation and criminal charges, White had to take a leave of absence from the Naval Reserves at a time when he needed only four more years to qualify for his retirement. When the litigation was finally over and he applied for reinstatement to complete the remaining four years of reserve duty, he was advised that the Navy would not let him back in because he had been passed over for promotion. This occurred because he was not actively attending drills at the time that the promotion board met. The Navy's policy is "up or out": anyone not making rank is discharged from the service.

29. CBC interview with Bill White.

30. Jerry Urban, "Feds Investigate Entrepreneur Allegedly Tied to Saudis," *Houston Chronicle*, June 4, 1992.

31. Jerry Urban, "Banking Scandal Figure Seeks to Claim Airport Contract," *Houston Chronicle*, September 10, 1994.

32. Author interview with Bill White, November 14, 2006.

15: THE HANDOFF

1. Author interview with Neil Bergt, April 16, 2008.

2. Jo Thomas, "The Missing Chapter in the Bush Bio: A Modest Summer in Alaska," *New York Times*, October 21, 2000.

3. Ibid.

4. Author interview with Bill White, November 14, 2006.

5. When I called the O'Neills, Mrs. O'Neill asked if the White House had authorized them to speak to me.

6. George Lardner Jr. and Lois Romano, "At Height of Vietnam, Bush Picks Guard," *Washington Post*, July 28, 1999.

7. At the time, Bath was chairman of the aviation committee for the Houston Chamber of Commerce, and in that position he frequently chose the speakers who addressed chamber luncheons. The big oil companies and the larger independents had their own corporate aviation departments, so Jim Bath's position on the chamber's aviation committee gave him real clout.

8. CBC interview with Bill White.

9. E-mail to the author from Bill White, August 3, 2008.

10. Antonia Felix, *Laura: America's First Lady, First Mother* (Avon, MA: Adams, 2002), p. 67.

11. Bill Minutaglio, *First Son: George W. Bush and the Bush Family Dynasty* (New York: Three Rivers Press, 1999). p. 184.

12. Nicholas D. Kristof, "Learning How to Run: A West Texas Stumble," *New York Times*, July 27, 2000.

13. Hance went on to serve six years, and when Bush became governor, Hance even became a Bush enthusiast, switching to the Republican Party.

14. Kelley, *The Family*, p. 424.

15. Author interview with Wright Ohrstrom, August 3, 2006.

16. Kevin Sack, "George Bush the Son Finds That Oil and Blood Do Mix," *New York Times*, May 8, 1999.

17. Author interview with James Lee Brown, June 24, 2006.

18. CBC interview with Bill White.

19. Jonathan Beaty and S. C. Gwynne "A Mysterious Mover of Money and Planes," *Time*, October 28, 1991.

20. About $150,000 in today's dollars.

21. The DeWitts became a prominent Cincinnati family, along with Bush family friends the Tafts (founders of Skull and Bones and descendants of a president) and the Mallons (Neil Mallon ran Dresser Industries). Over the years, DeWitt and broadcasting executive Dudley Taft have been part of a small circle that co-invested in many ventures; both DeWitt and Dudley Taft graduated from Yale in the early '60s.

22. Reinsurance is a little-known specialty, but can be extraordinarily profitable. Companies get a portion of the premiums paid by insurance customers in return for agreeing to cover any extraordinary losses. Because reinsurance is handled offshore, it is virtually tax-free. There is even a provision that permits some companies to register as nonprofits and invest unlimited amounts of money in the reinsurance company, collecting tax-free profits that can run into the hundreds of millions of dollars.

23. The company was founded by a DeWitt-Reynolds vice president named J. Thomas Markham, with DeWitt and Reynolds as major shareholders.

24. Author interview with Marion Gilliam, May 18, 2007. Gilliam was well connected to the British royal family. His mother-in-law, Marie-Antoinette Ladd, had been tutor to Queen Elizabeth and her sister when they were young, and her son had become the queen's art curator. Gilliam's father-in-law, William C. Ladd, had been a major figure in the intelligence community—and had for a time been the principal American contact with the British intelligence official Kim Philby, who would later and sensationally be unmasked as a double agent when he defected to the Soviet Union. His family's history in America went back to the mid-1600s; they were good

friends of the Kentucky Mortons—Senator Thruston B. Morton, Yale '29 (whose son Thruston Jr. is Skull and Bones '54). Morton Sr. was chairman of the RNC from 1959 to '61 and close to both Prescott Bush and Richard Nixon. His brother, Maryland representative Rogers C. B. Morton (Yale, RNC chairman under Nixon from 1969 to '71, and secretary of the interior and commerce), was close with Poppy Bush.

25. Allen Dulles also served as a member of Schroder's board of directors. Several Schroder's officials played important roles in wartime intelligence activities. See Richard Roberts, *Schroders: Merchants and Bankers* (London: Macmillan, 1992), p. 295. According to *Forbes*, Gilliam was subject to a three-year FBI probe for alleged stock manipulation and wire fraud, though he was never charged.

26. Gilliam also brought in Raffie Aryeh, who was from one of the wealthiest families in Iran—a family that had literally financed the shah in exile, shortly before the CIA brought him back in the 1953 coup against the democratically elected president Mohammad Mossadegh. According to Klausmeyer, through Schroder the immediate family of the shah may have also been involved with Lucky Chance. "One of their clients was the shah of Iran," Klausmeyer said. "And he wanted to buy some gold mines in the United States."

27. E-mail from David Klausmeyer to the author, May 22, 2007.

28. The firm brought in Daniel Lezak, an accountant and reorganization specialist with his own checkered past and future. Lezak, working with Poppy Bush's ex-lieutenant Gow in another corporate reorganization, was compelled to sign a consent decree with the Securities and Exchange Commission over failure to make proper disclosures to shareholders. (By the millennium, regulators had become totally fed up with Lezak and barred him from securities practice altogether.) "Lezak sometimes was called 'Sleazak,'" former Lucky Chance board chairman Ernest Lambert told me with a chuckle.

29. Marting's father, Walter Marting Sr., ran the Ohio-based Hanna Mining Company, which was founded by Mark Hanna, who was William McKinley's political mentor and considered a role model for Karl Rove.

30. Around the time of the Lucky Chance takeover, Gow and Klausmeyer had dined with Jerome Schneider, author of *How to Profit and Avoid Taxes by Organizing Your Own Private Bank* and *Complete Guide to Offshore Money Havens*. In 2004, Schneider would plead guilty to conspiring to help his clients evade tax laws, and be sentenced to twenty-four months in federal prison. See David Cay Johnston, "Pioneer of Sham Tax Havens Sits Down for a Pre-Jail Chat," *New York Times*, November 18, 2004; and Robert Gow's *You Can't Direct the Wind, You Can Only Reset the Sails: My First 62 Years* (Houston, Xixim Publishing, 2002).

31. Author interview with Ernest Lambert, May 17, 2007. Americans are generally taxed on their worldwide income; any reported income, even that collected in Bermuda, would be taxable.

16: THE QUACKING DUCK

1. This included more than $600,000 in stock and options—and a consulting contract eventually worth about $220,000 a year in today's dollars.

2. Richard Behar, "The Wackiest Rig in Texas," *Time*, October 28, 1991.

3. Its proprietor, Phil Kendrick, had grown up working in his family's oil company, left to become a stockbroker, and returned to try his own hand at the game. The company, then known as Harken Oil and Gas Inc., started doing well enough for itself—by 1980 *Inc.* magazine listed it as among the "100 Fastest Growing Companies in America"—but by 1983 it was reeling from the industry-wide price collapse and looking to merge or get bought out.

4. Americans steeped in intelligence work and covert operations have flocked to the Philippines

to hunt, literally, for treasure. Among these are General John Singlaub, who became a star figure in the Iran-contra scandal. One venture ostensibly set up for treasure hunting was a corporation founded by Singlaub, whose days in intelligence go back to the wartime OSS and who served as chairman for one of the principal cold war organs, the World Anti-Communist League. His gold-hunting company cofounder was Major General Robert Schweitzer, who had been deputy director of the National Security Council under the Reagan-Bush administration.

5. According to the Securities and Exchange Commission (SEC), "A reverse stock split reduces the number of shares and increases the share price proportionately. For example, if you own 10,000 shares of a company and it declares a one for ten reverse split, you will own a total of 1,000 shares after the split. A reverse stock split has no affect on the value of what shareholders own. Companies often split their stock when they believe the price of their stock is too low to attract investors to buy their stock. Some reverse stock splits cause small shareholders to be 'cashed out' so that they no longer own the company's shares."

6. According to the SEC filing "Nar Group Ltd, et al. • SC 13D/A • Harken Energy Corp," SEC File 5-31404, January 30, 1995. Available online at www.secinfo.com/dsvr4.a44.c.htm.

7. What in the world was Soros, of all people, doing in this mess? In 2002, the *Nation*'s David Corn attended the opening of Soros's Open Society offices in D.C., and sought to find out. David Corn, "Bush and the Billionaire: How Insider Capitalism Benefited W.," *Nation*, July 17, 2002.

> While chatting with one of his employees, I said to her, "One day, you should ask Soros what he knew about the Harken deal and why his company took on Bush." She blanched and mumbled that she could never raise that with Soros.
>
> Later, when I saw the billionaire almost alone, I sidled up to him. "Nice offices," I said. "But can I ask you about some ancient history?" Sure, he said, with a good-natured smile. What was the deal with Harken buying up Spectrum 7? I inquired. Did Soros know Bush back then?
>
> "I didn't know him," Soros replied. "He was supposed to bring in the Gulf connection. But it didn't come to anything. We were buying political influence. That was it. He was not much of a businessman."

8. The conservative pantheon would almost universally revile Soros, with one Fox News wag referring to him as "the Dr. Evil of the whole world of left-wing foundations." Transcript from *The O'Reilly Factor*, Fox, April 23, 2007.

9. Harvard currently manages a thirty-five-billion-dollar endowment with a 13.3 percent annual growth rate—the largest in higher education. In a 2008 *New York Times* op-ed, alumna Carroll Bogert marveled that the university "can cover next year's entire undergraduate financial aid budget with what it earns in the market in eight and a half days." Carroll Bogert, "Enjoy the Reunion. Skip the Check," *New York Times*, May 25, 2008.

10. As Bogert points out, Harvard, unlike Gates, is not required to pay taxes or spend 5 percent of its income per year. "Nor is it bound by most of the strictures of financial reporting that make spending at Gates transparent and publicly accountable." (See ibid.) Lawmakers are catching on: in 2008, the *Wall Street Journal* reported that Massachusetts legislators are considering plans to levy a 2.5 percent yearly tax on college endowments exceeding one billion dollars. John Hechinger, "College Endowment Tax Is Studied," *Wall Street Journal*, May 9, 2008.

11. Alexander J. Blenkinsopp, "Harvard Stock Under Scrutiny," *Harvard Crimson*, July 19, 2002.

12. Ibid.

13. Beth Healy and Michael Kranish, "Harvard Invested Heavily in Harken," *Boston Globe*, October 30, 2002. As the *Globe* wrote:

> It was a moment of deep embarrassment in 1991 when Harvard University's prestigious endowment fund admitted it had just experienced its worst loss ever. Jack Meyer, Harvard Management Co. president, said at the time he hoped the fund would never again take such a big hit, a $200 million write-down.
>
> Back then there was relatively little focus on one major reason for the loss: Harvard Management's large and ill-timed bet on little-known Harken Energy Co., whose board included George W. Bush, then the son of the US president and now the president himself. Even as losses mounted, Harvard Management bailed out the troubled company, first by splitting up Harken and then by sheltering Harken's liabilities in a partnership.
>
> Indeed, even as Bush was dumping the bulk of his Harken holdings—about $848,000 in stock sold to a buyer whose name has never been disclosed—Harvard Management plowed millions more into the firm . . .
>
> . . . The Texas-based energy company was, in 1990, the seventh-largest stock holding in Harvard's portfolio, bigger even than the university's stake in Exxon Corp. In all, Harvard Management risked 1 percent of the university's endowment in the small, struggling company, a surprisingly large bet by any measure, but particularly given Harken's dismal prospects . . .
>
> The Globe review also found no evidence to support the contention by some critics of Harvard Management and some adversaries of Bush that its deep involvement in Harken was a political favor to the Bush family.

14. Ibid.
15. Ibid.
16. In 1989, following Poppy's inauguration as president, and while Harvard was deeply involved with Harken and George W., Robert G. Stone was elected to the board of a large, private, Greenwich-based financial services executive recruiting firm called Russell Reynolds Associates. Another board member was W.'s uncle Jonathan Bush. And another was Landon Hilliard, a partner in Brown Brothers Harriman. Both Russell Reynolds and Jonathan Bush had been lead fundraisers for Poppy Bush's presidential campaign. Russell Reynolds Associates is not only private, but it is also unusual in the way it operates: although executive recruiting firms by definition seek to bring experienced personnel from one firm to another, and though most of its competitors seek to lure recruiters from each other, Reynolds is distinguished by its preference to recruit and train its own personnel while they are still green. One might call it a kind of Poppy Bush approach.
17. Stone's grandfather Galen L. Stone had cofounded the investment firm Hayden, Stone (which later became part of the giant, oft-renamed brokerage firm Shearson Lehman). In 1919 Galen Stone had hired a young fellow named Joseph P. Kennedy, giving him a start on his way to the riches that would, paradoxically, finance the political career of another, more liberal Harvard alumnus, John F. Kennedy. (A World War II Liberty ship, the S.S. *Galen L. Stone*, was named in honor of the banker.)

Robert G. Stone Jr. interrupted his Harvard studies to serve in World War II, and after the war married Marian Rockefeller, daughter of Godfrey Rockefeller. (Godfrey was the grandson of John D. Rockefeller's brother William, who had been a major investor in the railroad that had employed George W. Bush's great-grandfather Samuel Bush early in his career.) Godfrey, Andover class of 1942, was a trustee of the Fairfield Foundation, which provided funds to a British publication later financed by the CIA. In addition, Fairfield financed the Congress for Cultural Freedom, also exposed as a CIA front. Prescott and Dorothy Bush were not only good friends with Godfrey and Marian Rockefeller; more important, they had been instrumental in introducing Godfrey to his future wife, who knew Dorothy from St. Louis. It was truly all in the family.

18. Marcella Bombardieri, "Robert G. Stone Jr., a Fund-raising Stalwart for Harvard; at 83," *Boston Globe*, April 25, 2006.

19. Healy and Kranish, "Harvard Invested Heavily in Harken."

20. Stone's father-in-law, Godfrey Rockefeller, identified in 1970s congressional inquiries as having been involved with CIA-fund-disbursing private foundations, sat on the Freeport board for a remarkable *fifty years*.

21. John Newman, *Oswald and the CIA* (New York: Carroll & Graf, 1995), pp. 123–24.

22. Many Americans came to the Philippines to make their fortune. One of them was Henry Crown, who would go on to be the controlling shareholder of the giant military contractor General Dynamics, and in effect the boss of Albert Jenner, the Warren Commission counsel who so ineffectively interrogated George de Mohrenschildt.

23. Allin's wartime job was to inspect and secure military ports over a third of the world, including the strategic oil reserve of Iran. (Allin is an enormously important if little-remembered figure. From 1919 to 1931 he was director and chief engineer of the Port of Houston, helping this landlocked city become the fifth biggest port in the United States, while in the process helping to reshape the modern oil industry.) Benjamin Casey Allin III, *Reaching for the Sea* (Boston: Meador, 1956), p. 19.

24. Peter Schweizer and Rochelle Schweizer, *The Bushes: Portrait of a Dynasty* (New York: Doubleday, 2004), p. 76.

25. Rudy Abramson, *Spanning the Century: The Life of W. Averell Harriman, 1891–1986* (New York: William Morrow and Company, 1992), p. 451.

26. Douglas MacArthur and his milieu showed up in myriad ways. After Kennedy sacked Allen Dulles over the Bay of Pigs affair, he turned to MacArthur, who warned him that he had unleashed powerful forces. "The chickens are coming home to roost," MacArthur told Kennedy, according to presidential aide Theodore Sorensen, "and you happen to just have moved into the chicken house." Meanwhile, General Charles Willoughby, a pronounced racist and anti-Semite who had been MacArthur's chief of intelligence in the Pacific, had joined forces with H. L. Hunt, the leader of the anti-Kennedy group in Dallas at the time of the assassination.

27. A 1939 Manila directory lists Whitney as president of Casamac Inc.; VP of Southern Cross Mining Corp.; president of Abra Mining Co.; chairman of the board of Consolidated Mines; and department commander of the American Legion.

28. After a period, Quasha became the deputy administrator.

29. Sterling Seagrave and Peggy Seagrave's decades-long investigations of the Yamashita gold saga have been criticized for minor historical and linguistic inaccuracies, but their book *Gold Warriors: The Covert History of Yamashita's Gold—How Washington Secretly Recovered It to Set Up Giant Cold War Slush Funds and Manipulate Foreign Governments* (Bowstring Books, 2002) has a CD-ROM appendix containing over nine hundred megabytes of documentary evidence. *Booklist* noted, "The Seagraves, reputable authors of East Asian histories, advance considerable sourcing for their claims, some of which, however, rely precariously on the word of single individuals, while others are anonymous." Writing in the *London Review of Books*,

the author and historian Chalmers Johnson noted the Seagraves' stylistic shortcomings, while still calling *Gold Warriors* "easily the best guide available to the scandal of 'Yamashita's gold.' "

30. Seagrave and Seagrave, *Gold Warriors*, p. 4. McCloy, a member of the Warren Commission, was a longtime deputy to the Rockefeller family. Stimson was a Skull and Bones alumnus and good friend of Prescott Bush. Lovett, too, was Skull and Bones as well as a friend—and business partner—to Prescott. Anderson, a Texas native and treasury secretary during Eisenhower's second term, served on the board of the Bush family's Dresser Industries.

31. Tim Weiner, *Legacy of Ashes: The History of the CIA* (New York: Doubleday, 2007), p. 182.

32. Charles Maechling, "Camelot, Robert Kennedy, and Counter-Insurgency: A Memoir," *Virginia Quarterly Review*, Summer 1999, pp. 438–58.

33. Evan Thomas, *The Very Best Men* (New York: Simon & Schuster, 1995), p. 271.

34. For a thorough account of the U.S.-Marcos relationship, see Raymond Bonner, *Waltzing with a Dictator: The Marcoses and the Making of American Policy* (New York: Times Books, 1987).

35. James Hamilton-Paterson, *America's Boy: The Marcoses and the Philippines* (London: Granta Books, 1999), p. 147.

   According to the Seagraves, Marcos's close associate Amelito Mutuc had claimed that Marcos had recovered fourteen billion dollars' worth, principally from a single site, although the Seagraves assert that was just part of the Japanese war loot Marcos acquired. As noted in *Gold Warriors*, some believe that the Japanese treasure story is untrue, but utilized by the Marcoses themselves as a way of explaining Ferdinand's vast private wealth, "which in fact came from far more disreputable dealings, cheatings and carpetbaggings in the aftermath of the war." The accepted importance of the Philippines as a strategic location does not by itself seem to adequately explain the American intelligence apparatus's apparent obsession with both the islands and with gold.

36. During the 1960s and part of the '70s, the Philippines was the free world's second-largest producer of gold after South Africa—with half a dozen major mines and output exceeding even that of the United States and Canada. For many years, the gold was sent abroad for refining. But in 1975, a world-class domestic refinery was built. The Briton James Hamilton-Paterson, who has lived in the Philippines on and off since 1979 and authored *America's Boy*, a biography of Marcos, asserts that this was not only so the Philippines could finally refine its own domestic production, but also "so that bars of Japanese and other gold could be re-smelted into untraceable bullion before being spirited away to Swiss banks." He quotes an unnamed figure from the Philippines gold industry: "By law the gold had to be sold to the Central Bank. Theoretically, between about 1977 and 1982 Marcos was in a position to 'buy' all the gold mined and refined in the Philippines at a discount. Practically, he could steal the lot." On page 341 of *Gold Warriors*, the Seagraves quote a Marcos crony asserting that in 1973, the first full year of martial law, Marcos was able to steal as much gold as he wanted; and that proof of this was that in that year, Manila's gold reserves dropped by 45 percent (or twenty-five tons).

37. It is unknown how much gold Marcos sold to the Central Bank. But, according to the Seagraves' *Gold Warriors*, "Most of his gold was already refined, and once in the Central Bank could be moved directly into the international market—if a way could be found to disguise it from the inevitable statisticians, a question of complicating the paper chase." Based on what they were told by gold industry officials, the Seagraves go on to explain that Marcos began a program to lease quantities of dormant bullion to banks—and that this was actually cover for Marcos to move large quantities of "black gold" (i.e., gold unacknowledged by world markets) out of the Philippines. They also cite eyewitness accounts of Marcos's personal plane ferrying

gold to a Zurich bank, and waybills that they say document the use of commercial planes for that purpose as well.

38. "Together Again," *Time*, July 13, 1981.

39. Jeffrey Toobin, "The Dirty Trickster," *New Yorker*, June 2, 2008.

40. Ed Rollins with Tom DeFrank, *Bare Knuckles and Back Rooms: My Life in American Politics* (New York: Broadway, 1996), pp. 214–15.

41. In later years, Poppy would serve on the advisory board of Barrick Gold Company, which mines for strategic metals in Central Africa.

42. As strange as a "Communist Takeover Fund" sounds, NATO actually created stay-behind networks all over Europe after World War II. One example is a secret paramilitary force called Operation Gladio, which was originally set up to resist a potential Communist takeover in Italy. See Daniel Williams, "Italy Was Warned of Iraq Attack; Report of Threats to Nasiriyah Base Were Disregarded," *Washington Post*, December 8, 2003. It then helped spark right-wing military coups in Greece and Turkey on NATO's behalf. See Craig Unger, "The War They Wanted, the Lies They Needed," *Vanity Fair*, July 2006.

43. Russ Baker and Adam Federman with response by Alan G. Quasha and Terence R. McAuliffe, "Hillary's Mystery Money Men," *Nation*, November 5, 2007.

44. Nugan Hand had been involved in drug-trafficking operations that originated in Southeast Asia during the Vietnam War. When the bank got into trouble in the Philippines, its operatives turned to Quasha for legal help. According to one Nugan Hand salesman, Quasha gave them atypical legal advice—urging them to flee the country. "He said, 'You could wind up in jail.'" See Jonathan Kwitny, *The Crimes of Patriots: A True Tale of Dope, Dirty Money, and the CIA* (New York: W. W. Norton and Company), p. 36.

45. Steve Dvin, "Homer Williams Develops Opportunity with Wits, Charm," *Oregonian* (Portland, Oregon), July 5, 1998.

46. Ibid.

47. Jeff Gerth, "Marcos U.S. Bank Dealings Modest," *New York Times*, March 22, 1986.

48. William Glaberson, "The Marcos Verdict; The 'Wrong' Court," *New York Times*, July 3, 1990.

49. Robert Trigaux, "Bush Built Success on Harken Sale," *St. Petersburg Times*, July 21, 2002.

50. According to SEC filing "Axp Selected Series Inc N-30D," SEC File 811-04132, March 31, 2003. Available online at www.secinfo.com/dsvr4.a44.c.htm.

51. L. J. Davis, "Where Are You Al?" *Mother Jones*, November–December 1993.

52. Most of the Harken shares handled by UBS were snapped up by Abdullah Bakhsh, a Saudi real estate magnate, who bought the stock through a Netherlands Antilles shell company. Though he became Harken's third-largest stockholder, with a 17.6 percent stake, he rarely met with company officials, instead sending a representative to sit on the Harken board. Back in Saudi Arabia, Bakhsh was a business partner of Ghaith Pharaon, the fellow who had partnered with Jim Bath in Main Bank, and whom the Federal Reserve had labeled a "frontman" for BCCI. (Harken filings from the 1990s, though enormously complicated, seem to show additional UBS involvement with the company through partnerships with affiliated Harken entities.)

53. In an interview, Senn said: " 'Petty apartheid,' the physical separation of the races, is about to disappear. The grand scheme of apartheid, a wholesale democratic solution including 'one man–one vote' will, however, take time . . . 'One man–one vote' to me is not a world religion." *Khulumani et al. v. Barclays National Bank et al.* brief, available at www.kosa.org/documents/Swiss_campaign_amici_curiae.pdf

54. Alexander L. Taylor III, "Swiss Secrets Are Put to a Vote," *Time*, May 28, 1984.

55. www.kosa.org/documents/Swiss_campaign_amici_curiae.pdf

56. Anton Rupert also launched Quadrant Management Inc., a corporate takeover and reorganization firm that principally manages the U.S. assets of a company called North American Resources, a company that is a joint venture between the Quasha family and Financière Richemont SA, a Swiss tobacco and luxury goods company that had just formed, and whose board Quasha joined. Financial interests were held by a Bermuda-based trust controlled by his mother. Thus, Quasha was deeply involved with a network of Swiss, Luxembourg, American, and offshore entities centered on this relationship. The main function of the consortium appeared to be twofold: controlling natural resources (timber, etc.) and assembling baubles for the rich under one corporate roof.

57. Amoco had already advanced in talks with Bahrain and had an inside track. The tiny emirate, strongly allied with Saudi Arabia, hadn't hit paydirt since 1932, but seismic surveys showed a large undersea geological formation—potentially worth billions.

58. Quasha insisted that the deal had nothing to do with the Bush connection. Yet Harken's exploration chief, Monte Swetnam, recalled to the *Wall Street Journal* mentioning names of company directors to the Bahrainis, including invoking W.'s name at least twice. See Thomas Petzinger Jr., Peter Truell, and Jill Abramson "Family Ties: How Oil Firm Linked to a Son of Bush Won Bahrain Drilling Pact," *Wall Street Journal*, December 6, 1991. Whatever role the Bush connection played during the negotiations, it seems likely that it was the basis for Harken's entry into those negotiations in the first place.

59. The official story of how Bahrain found Harken is as follows: The Bahraini oil minister contacted a longtime friend, a Houston oil consultant with Mideast experience named Michael Ameen. For a previous employer, Ameen had dealt closely with the Saudi royal family, including Kamal Adham, the former chief of Saudi intelligence and a key BCCI figure. Ameen was also close to Ghaith Pharaon's family and had been a friend of Abdullah Bakhsh, the big Harken shareholder, for twenty-five years. Ameen says that ten minutes after he got the oil minister's call for his advice on which of hundreds of oil companies should get the Bahrain contract, and while pondering this deeply, his phone happened to ring. On the other end was a Harken investment banker at Stephens Inc. in Little Rock. Soon Ameen, who would later receive a $100,000 fee from Harken, was escorting Harken delegations to London and Bahrain.

60. An unnamed institutional client "offered" to take W.'s shares off his hands. Bush is said to have initially declined, but to have told the stockbroker on the deal, Ralph Smith at the Los Angeles–based Sutro & Co., to check back in two weeks. Meanwhile, Harken's lawyers issued a memo to Harken staffers warning against selling stock based on insider information. One week passed, and Bush called Smith back. Despite the apparent warning not to do so, he went ahead and sold 212,140 Harken shares for $4 per share, netting $848,560.

61. Author interview with Steve Rose, September 27, 2006.

62. Documents from the Securities and Exchange Commission and elsewhere, gathered by HarvardWatch, a student and alumni group, and the nonpartisan Center for Public Integrity.

63. Cited by the Center for Public Integrity. It's worth noting that Harken itself did business with Enron, as confirmed by a 1990 letter of credit between the two firms.

64. "President Urges Congress to Support Nation's Priorities," George W. Bush press conference, July 8, 2002.

65. R. G. Ratcliffe, "Business Associates Profit During Bush's Term as Governor," *Houston Chronicle*, August 16, 1998.

66. Alan Quasha's ties to Hillary Clinton's presidential campaign were detailed in Baker and Federman, "Hillary's Mystery Money Men."

67. Eamon Javers, "Is Obama Good for Business?" *BusinessWeek*, February 13, 2008.

17: Playing Hardball

1. Prescott Bush was captain of the varsity baseball team at Yale, where he played first base. George H. W. Bush lacked his father's physical prowess, and batted near the bottom of the lineup, but he too eventually served as Yale team captain. W. "played sparingly" for the Yale freshman team. For more, see Peter Schweizer and Rochelle Schweizer, *The Bushes: Portrait of a Dynasty* (New York: Doubleday, 2004), p. 90. Prescott, Poppy, and W. were all members of the Yale cheerleading squad. See Simone Berkower, "Cheerleading of the '20s: Epitome of Masculinity," *Yale Daily News*, January 28, 2008.

2. James Moore and Wayne Slater, *Bush's Brain: How Karl Rove Made George W. Bush Presidential* (Hoboken, NJ: John Wiley & Sons, 2003), p. 152.

3. For Barbara's public comments, see Bill Minutaglio, *First Son: George W. Bush and the Bush Family Dynasty* (New York: Three Rivers, 1999), p. 243. The concern that it would be seen as a referendum was expressed by several sources interviewed by the author.

4. Author interview with Doug Wead, December 14, 2006.

5. Kevin Sack, "George Bush the Son Finds That Oil and Blood Do Mix," *New York Times*, May 8, 1999.

6. Author interview with Comer Cottrell, June 20, 2006.

7. Because shares were bought from various owners over time, there is some disagreement on the total amount paid.

8. W. served on the board of Carlyle subsidiary CaterAir. Carlyle Group's advisers and board members have included Poppy Bush, James Baker, Clinton chief of staff Mack McLarty, former British prime minister John Major, and former Philippine president Fidel Ramos.

9. Author interview with Glenn Sodd, June 9, 2006.

10. Jim Landers, "Lawyer Represented Bush on Harken," *Dallas Morning News*, September 19, 2004.

11. Elisabeth Bumiller, "For President and Close Friend, Forget the Politics," *New York Times*, January 14, 2005.

12. Betts's father, Allan W. Betts, had, after Yale, been a partner at G. H. Walker and Company, the company run by Poppy Bush's favorite uncle, Herbie—himself one of the principal owners of a baseball team, the New York Mets. And Allan Betts and his wife had a home in the exclusive enclave of Hobe Sound, Florida, as did the Bushes and many in their intelligence-finance circle. Allan Betts was also for many years director of the Astor Foundation and co-executor of the Vincent Astor estate. Astor not only ran intelligence in the New York area circa World War II, but he also started *Newsweek*, which was known to have strong ties to intelligence circles in its early days. (Vincent Astor bought *Newsweek* with Mary Harriman Rumsey, the sister of Averell and Roland Harriman.) Even Betts's mother had a spy background, having worked in Washington for the OSS during World War II. For the latter point, see the *New York Times'* wedding announcement for Allan Whitney Betts and Evelyn Ohman, April 21, 1945.

13. Author interview with Comer Cottrell.

14. Attorney Glenn Sodd, who represented plaintiffs in the suit against the Rangers' owners, said that he had been led to believe that Eisner may have been one of the investors in W.'s owner group.

15. "Yale Corporation Members," *Yale Herald*, October 5, 2001, www.yaleherald.com/archive/xxxii/10.05.01/news/p3yalecorp.html.

16. David Cay Johnston, *Free Lunch: How the Wealthiest Americans Enrich Themselves at Government Expense (and Stick You with the Bill)* (New York: Portfolio, 2007), p. 79.

17. Molly Ivins and Lou Dubose, *Shrub: The Short but Happy Political Life of George W. Bush* (New York: Random House, 2000), p. 38.

18. Johnston, *Free Lunch*, p. 80.

19. "Best and Worst Legislators Since 1973," *Texas Monthly*, www.texasmonthly.com/bestworst.

20. James Langdon's father had been a member of the all-powerful Texas Railroad Commission, the misleadingly named entity that regulates oil production in the state, during the agency's primacy in the 1960s and '70s.

21. Nicholas D. Kristof, "Breaking Into Baseball; Road to Politics Ran Through a Texas Ballpark," *New York Times*, September 24, 2000.

22. Greene was also president of the SavingsBanc, an Arlington thrift that lost $41.1 million and was taken over by the federal government. Greene admitted no wrongdoing, and said he was "not unlike literally hundreds of people in the state of Texas and thousands nationwide that were caught up in the disastrous takeover of the S&Ls by the federal government." See Laura Vozzella, "Many Texas Officials Starred in S&L Scandals," *Fort Worth Star-Telegram*, January 1, 1996.

23. U.S. Environmental Protection Agency, "Richard E. Greene Appointed EPA Region 6 Administrator," March 17, 2003, yosemite.epa.gov/opa/admpress.nsf/e8f4ff7f7970934e85257359004 00c2e/a0386518e18d1d88852570d6005e7e41!OpenDocument

24. Johnston, *Free Lunch*, p. 82.

25. Kristof, "Breaking Into Baseball."

26. Author interview with Jim Runzheimer, June 20, 2006.

27. Johnston, *Free Lunch*, pp. 77–78.

28. Bill Minutaglio, *The President's Counselor: The Rise to Power of Alberto Gonzales* (New York: HarperCollins, 2006), p. 99.

29. Author interview with David Rosen, Midland, Texas, June 24, 2006.

30. Clayton Williams commented that poor weather is just like rape—"if it's inevitable, just relax and enjoy it." "Texas Primary; Higher Aspirations from Low Campaign," *New York Times*, April 15, 1990.

18: MEET THE HELP

1. Tucker Carlson, *Inside Politics*, CNN, October 4, 2000. Also see Eric Alterman, *What Liberal Media?: The Truth About Bias and the News* (New York: Basic, 2003), p. 156.

2. Eric Boehlert, "The Press vs. Al Gore," *Rolling Stone*, November 26, 2001.

3. Lou Dubose, Jan Reid, and Carl M. Cannon, *Boy Genius: Karl Rove, the Brains Behind the Remarkable Political Triumph of George W. Bush* (New York: PublicAffairs, 2003), p. 12.

4. Nicholas Lemann, "The Controller," *New Yorker*, May 12, 2003.

5. Atwater, who built his arsenal based on weapons he and Rove first developed in the College Republicans, was a notoriously brash dirty trickster and claimed to think of politics as war. He spearheaded a smear on behalf of Poppy's campaign that sought to exploit Dukakis's liberal political stances on such topics as gun control, environmental policy, mandatory pledge of allegiance in schools, and the death penalty, among others. Atwater's most famous attempt to "strip the bark off the little bastard" was an attack-ad project that employed the image of convicted murderer William R. Horton, who was furloughed under a program begun by a Republican governor but supported by Dukakis. Horton kidnapped a couple, torturing the man and raping his girlfriend. Although Horton went by "William," Atwater rebranded him "Willie" for the television ads. See Tim Hope and Richard Sparks, editors, *Crime, Risk and Insecurity* (New York: Routledge, 2000), p. 266.

6. Author interview with John Taliaferro, July 11, 2006.

7. In the same period, Taliaferro's partner, publisher Chris Hearne, remembers going to the P.O. box and finding that someone had mailed in *bricks*—postage due.

8. James Moore and Wayne Slater, *Bush's Brain* (Hoboken, NJ: John Wiley & Sons, 2003), p. 38.

9. Ibid., p. 40. The statement was attributed to speechwriter Matt Lyon, now deceased, by a friend, Patricia Tierney Alofsin, a longtime fixture in Austin governmental circles.

10. Author interview with Royal Masset, May 27, 2004.

11. Psy-ops, or psychological operations, are sophisticated propaganda techniques meant to influence the behavior and state of mind of a targeted person or group. The U.S. military includes special units devoted to psy-ops.

12. Rove made much of bringing the FBI into the bugging affair; the agent on the case went on to investigate nearly every statewide Democratic officeholder in Texas during Rove's tenure in Austin. See Moore and Slater, *Bush's Brain*, p. 34.

13. Miriam Rozen, "The Nerd Behind the Throne," *Dallas Observer*, May 13, 1999.

14. David Frum, "Justice Miers?" David Frum's Diary, September 29, 2005. Former White House speechwriter David Frum's online diary is available through the *National Review* online at http://frum.nationalreview.com.

15. Author interview with Brian Berry, October 11, 2005.

16. Author interview with Gypsy Hogan, October 6, 2005. Allbaugh also borrowed money from an elderly widow and faithful GOP donor, but never paid her back.

17. In September 1990, Allbaugh left the job with Stephens for reasons unknown. His résumé suggests that he was then unemployed until February 1991, when he reappeared back on the other side of the customer-service counter, this time as deputy secretary of transportation under Democratic governor David Walters. (A grand jury later issued eight felony indictments against Walters, who pled guilty to one misdemeanor charge of violating state campaign-contribution laws.)

18. Author interview with Wayne Slater, October 11, 2005.

19. Debra Dickerson, "The Real Bush Drug Scandal," Salon.com, September 14, 1999.

20. *National Law Journal*, January 21, 1988.

21. Mimi Swartz, "Hurt? Injured? Need a Lawyer? Too Bad!" *Texas Monthly*, November 2005.

22. Phillip Rawls, "Karl Rove Built Reputation in Alabama Court Races," Associated Press, October 28, 2005.

23. R. G. Ratcliffe, "Secrecy Cloaks $1.7 Billion in UT Investments," *Houston Chronicle*, March 21, 1999.

24. "The company claims that the demonstrations, which go under the name Rally for America, reflect the initiative of individual stations, but this is unlikely. According to Eric Boehlert, who has written revelatory articles about Clear Channel for Salon.com, the company is notorious—and widely hated—for its iron-fisted centralized control." See Paul Krugman, "Channels of Influence," *New York Times*, March 25, 2003.

25. Raymond Hernandez and Andrea Elliott, "Antiwar Group Says Its Ad Is Rejected," *New York Times*, July 12, 2004.

26. Author interview with Doug Wead, December 14, 2006.

27. In the summer of 2008, with former Karl Rove aides holding top positions in John McCain's presidential campaign, McCain began appropriating the leftover Teddy Roosevelt comparison, in a Sunday front-page article. Adam Nagourney and Michael Cooper, "McCain's Conservative Model? Roosevelt (Theodore, That Is)," *New York Times*, July 13, 2008.

28. Author interview with Lewis L. Gould, July 12, 2006.

29. Alicia Montgomery, "School's Out for Bush 'Miracle,'" Salon.com, October 24, 2000.

30. "The 'Texas Miracle,'" *60 Minutes II*, CBS, August 25, 2004.

31. Robert H. Gow, *You Can't Direct the Wind; You Can Only Reset the Sails: My First 62 Years* (Houston: Xixim Publishing, 2002), p. 108.

32. Jonathan Tilove, "Dynamic Duo Assures Event's Diversity," *San Francisco Chronicle*, January 21, 2001.

33. Carl Redman, "Bush-Foster Fund-Raiser Big on Praise, Cash," *The Advocate* (Baton Rouge, Louisiana), August 19, 1999.

34. Mike Allen, "With Eye on Transition, Bush Confers with Powell," *Washington Post*, December 1, 2000.

35. Noam Scheiber, "Public Schooling: Rod Paige Learns the Hard Way," *New Republic*, July 2, 2001.

36. Carol D. Leonnig, "HUD Chief Inattentive to Crisis, Critics Say," *Washington Post*, April 13, 2008.

37. Ibid.

38. David Broder, "Jesse Helms, White Racist," *Washington Post*, August 28, 2001.

39. Holli Chmela, "Ex-Bush Aide Admits Shoplifting and Is Fined," *New York Times*, August 5, 2006.

19: THE CONVERSION

1. George W. Bush, *A Charge to Keep* (New York: William Morrow, 1999), pp. 136–37. Throughout the writings of Poppy, W., and Barbara Bush, a pattern emerges regarding the selective inclusion of names. Wherever a person is likely to provide reporters with a favorable story, that person's name is included—no matter how gratuitous their mention or how obscure they may be. By contrast, the names of many important figures in their lives appear to have been excised.

2. Ibid., pp. 19, 86.

3. Elizabeth Mitchell, *W.: Revenge of the Bush Dynasty* (New York: Berkley Publishing, 2003), p. 220.

4. As president, Poppy appointed Teeley ambassador to Canada—a particularly nice perk for a former press secretary.

5. Jodi Kantor and David D. Kirkpatrick, "Pulpit Was the Springboard for Huckabee's Rise," *New York Times*, December 6, 2007.

6. Garry Wills, *Under God: Religion and American Politics* (New York: Simon & Schuster, 2007), p. 120.

7. Eric Pooley with S. C. Gwynne, "How George Got His Groove," *Time*, June 21, 1999.

8. Doug Wead, *All the President's Children: Triumph and Tragedy in the Lives of America's First Families* (New York: Simon & Schuster, 2004).

9. Jacob Weisberg, *The Bush Tragedy* (New York: Random House, 2008), p. 78.

10. Arthur Blessitt, "Praying with George W. Bush," www.blessitt.com/?q=praying_with_george_w _bush.

11. Graham also played to his friends' prejudices, telling Nixon, who periodically complained about Jews, that he believed they had a "stranglehold" on the media. See "Graham Regrets Jewish Slur," BBC News, March 2, 2002.

12. Terry M. Neal, "Nominees Make Final Forays to Tossup States," *Washington Post*, November 6, 2000.

13. Weisberg, *The Bush Tragedy*, p. 77.

14. Lois Romano and George Lardner Jr., "1986: A Life-Changing Year; Epiphany Fueled Candidate's Climb," *Washington Post*, July 25, 1999.

15. David Maraniss, "The Bush Bunch," *Washington Post*, January 22, 1989.

16. Author interview with Doug Wead, May 27, 2008.

17. Scott McClellan, *What Happened: Inside the Bush White House and Washington's Culture of Deception* (New York: PublicAffairs, 2008), pp. 48–49.

18. "Author: I Should Give Tapes to Bush," CNN.com, February 21, 2005.

20: THE SKELETON IN W.'S CLOSET

1. Moore knew something about this issue. Unlike Bush, he had actively opposed the Vietnam War, but he had been unable to gain a pilot slot in the National Guard of his home state of Michigan. "I was told that there was a five-year waiting list for anyone interested in flying,

whether as a pilot or as a navigator or whatever, and I was told that there was a minimum three-year list to get in as a soldier," Moore recalled.

2. Moore, with Wayne Slater, later wrote a book about Karl Rove, called *Bush's Brain: How Karl Rove Made George W. Bush Presidential* (Hoboken, NJ: John Wiley & Sons, 2003).

3. Eric Boehlert, "Unwitting Drudge Indicts Bush," Salon.com, September 14, 2004.

4. James Moore, *Bush's War for Reelection: Iraq, the White House and the People* (New York: John Wiley & Sons, 2004), p. 222.

5. Burkett and his team of strategic planners calculated the "ghost" element of the Texas National Guard to be on the order of 7.8 percent. That turned out to be conservative. Several years later, *USA Today* would run a story largely based on Burkett's research. In checking the figures, the newspaper came up with a higher figure: 11 percent ghost soldiers. Dave Moniz, " 'Ghost Soldiers' Inflate Guard Numbers," December 18, 2001.

6. Author interview with Bill Burkett, September 4, 2004.

7. Author interview with Bill Burkett, July 7, 2004.

8. Author interview with Bill Burkett, July 31, 2008.

9. In a 1998 letter to Texas state senator Gonzalo Barrientos, Burkett complained that he had not received adequate medical care when he became seriously ill after returning from the mission to Panama. Michael Rezendes, "Doubts Raised on Bush Accuser," *Boston Globe*, February 13, 2004.

10. There were additional factors in their firing, also related to allegations of Guard corruption.

11. These were led by an Iowa farmer and railroad brakeman named Marty Heldt, who made the first information requests; Bob Fertik, a Queens, New York, Internet political consultant who obtained a second batch; and Paul Lukasiak, a Philadelphia caterer who scrutinized arcane regulations.

12. Author interview with Albert Lloyd, July 23, 2004.

13. George W. Bush, *A Charge to Keep* (New York: William Morrow, 1999), p. 54.

14. There was no Officer Effectiveness Rating form for his final year; there was no Leave and Earnings Statement. And when Bush was suspended from flight status, there should have been a Board of Inquiry Report. Finally, a complete set of pay records with accumulated totals was never produced. Moore, *Bush's War for Reelection*, pp. 174–75.

15. Undated anonymous letter to U.S. Attorney Dan Mills, obtained in discovery process for a lawsuit by Larry Littwin against the GTech Corporation.

16. In 2005, James Moore wrote on the Huffington Post: "The same month that Lottery Commission Chair Harriet Miers was instructing staff to prepare to re-bid the G-Tech contract, Barnes and the company had informed the Texas lottery commission that he had agreed to a 23 million dollar settlement to buy out his contract. G-Tech had decided Barnes had become a 'lightning rod,' in part because he was included in a federal grand jury investigation in New Jersey, which accused Barnes of kicking back a share of his monthly retainer to G-Tech's president. Barnes was not charged in connection with the G-Tech investigation." James Moore, "Bush, Miers, the Guard, and the Texas Lottery: A Reprise," Huffington Post, October 9, 2005.

17. Harriet Miers may not have been informed that a "Barnes problem" existed, but others on the staff seem to have known. As early as March 1996, Allbaugh had been making inquiries about the lottery contract, though perhaps that was only because it was identified with Democrats. Miers, appointed to the chair by Bush, had sent Allbaugh notebooks of lottery meetings and details on the operator's contract, according to a note from her to Allbaugh dated March 7, 1996.

18. Littwin made the same allegation of a Barnes-Bush deal in court pleadings during his suit alleging wrongful termination.

19. Pete Slover and George Kuempel, "Adviser Asked Barnes to Recall Guard Details Before Bush Joined Race," *Dallas Morning News*, September 26, 1999.

20. Thomas B. Edsall and Mike Allen, "Bush 'Bundlers' Take Fundraising to New Level," *Washington Post*, July 14, 2003.

21. Association records show Spellings as a lobbyist in 1999; five years later he was president of the association.

22. The No Child Left Behind Act is a federal law with a budget of over fifty billion dollars aimed at reforming various areas of U.S. primary and secondary schooling with a focus on outcome-based education such as standardized testing. The act also requires schools to release the names, addresses, and phone numbers of every enrolled student to military recruiters unless the student specifically opts out.

23. Ron Suskind, *The One Percent Doctrine: Deep Inside America's Pursuit of Its Enemies* (New York: Simon & Schuster, 2006), p. 2.

24. A colleague who had accompanied me to Spellings's office spoke to him by phone the next day. In that subsequent conversation, Spellings confirmed that he knew George W. Bush in 1968, when he worked for Barnes.

25. Bill Minutaglio, *First Son: George W. Bush and the Bush Family Dynasty* (New York: Three Rivers Press, 1999), pp. 175–76.

26. Laurence I. Barrett, "Junior Is His Own Bush Now," *Time*, July 31, 1989.

21: SHOCK AND . . . OIL?

1. David Brooks, "Obama Admires Bush," *New York Times*, May 16, 2008.

2. David Nyhan, "A Bush Slip-Up at the End," *Boston Globe*, December 3, 1999.

3. Few families were more involved in the military economy than the Bushes. Munitions had long been part of the family business, starting with W.'s great-grandfather Samuel Bush, who served as point man for American small arms manufacturing in World War I and also played a crucial role in the nation's oldest continually operating gun company, Remington Arms. Dresser Industries, with Prescott Bush on its board, had expanded greatly during World War II, thanks to defense contracts. Poppy served as a senior adviser to the Carlyle Group, which, until just after September 11, enjoyed substantial investments from Saudi Arabia's bin Laden family and specialized in buying and selling defense companies that did business with the government.

4. Naomi Klein, *The Shock Doctrine: The Rise of Disaster Capitalism* (New York: Metropolitan, 2007), p. 380.

5. Project for the New American Century, *Rebuilding America's Defenses: Strategy, Forces and Resources for a New Century*, September 2000, p. 51.

6. Klein, *Shock Doctrine*, p. 441.

7. Stephen J. Glain, "Halliburton Says Employees Got Kickbacks on Iraq Work," *Boston Globe*, January 24, 2004.

8. Don Van Natta Jr., "High Payments to Halliburton for Fuel in Iraq," *New York Times*, December 10, 2003. Also Joel Brinkley and Eric Schmitt, "Halliburton Will Repay U.S. Excess Charges for Troops' Meals," *New York Times*, February 3, 2004.

9. James Risen, "Electrical Risks at Iraq Bases Are Worse Than Said," *New York Times*, July 18, 2008.

10. Lou Dubose and Jake Bernstein, *Vice: Dick Cheney and the Hijacking of the American Presidency* (New York: Random House, 2006), pp. ix–x.

11. Barton Gellman and Jo Becker, " 'A Different Understanding with the President,' " *Washington Post*, June 24, 2007.

12. Dana Milbank and Justin Blum, "Document Says Oil Chiefs Met with Energy Task Force," *Washington Post*, November 16, 2005.

13. Judicial Watch, "Cheney Energy Task Force Documents Feature Map of Iraqi Oilfields," July 17, 2003, www.judicialwatch.org/iraqi=oilfield=pr.shtml.

14. Author interview with Royal Masset, May 27, 2004.

15. For an excellent account of the U.S. role in propping up and arming Saddam Hussein, see Alan Friedman, *Spider's Web: The Secret History of How the White House Illegally Armed Iraq* (New York: Bantam, 1993).

16. Andrew Cockburn, *Rumsfeld: His Rise, Fall, and Catastrophic Legacy* (New York: Scribner, 2007), pp. 76–77.

17. Richard Sale, "Saddam Key in Early CIA Plot," United Press International, April 11, 2003.

18. Tom Barry, *Central America Inside Out: The Essential Guide to Its Societies, Politics, and Economics* (New York: Grove, 1994), p. 470.

19. At the same time, Noriega authorized intelligence-gathering flights by U.S. Lockheed Martin SR-71 "Blackbird" high-altitude reconnaissance aircraft over Nicaragua and El Salvador in order for the CIA to supply intelligence data to the contras and the Salvadoran government forces fighting the leftist and FLMN guerrillas.

20. Author interview with Larry Birns, August 15, 2008.

21. Count de Marenches and David A. Andelman, *The Fourth World War: Diplomacy and Espionage in the Age of Terrorism* (New York: William Morrow, 1992), p. 254.

22. In an interview with Paris's *Le Nouvel Observateur* in January 1998, Brzezinski was asked, "Do you regret having supported the Islamic [integrisme], having given arms and advice to future terrorists?" He answered: "What is most important to the history of the world? The Taliban or the collapse of the Soviet empire? Some stirred-up Moslems or the liberation of Central Europe and the end of the cold war?"

23. See among others Cockburn, *Rumsfeld*, pp. 1–10; and Gail Sheehy, "Who's in Charge Here," *Mother Jones*, July 22, 2004, http://motherjones.com/news/update/2004/07/07_400.html.

24. *Late Edition with Wolf Blitzer*, CNN, September 8, 2002.

25. In 2004, Secretary-General Kofi Annan would denounce the invasion in blunt terms: "It was illegal." See "Iraq War Illegal, Says Annan," BBC News, September 16, 2004.

26. Kevin Phillips, *American Dynasty: Aristocracy, Fortune, and the Politics of Deceit in the House of Bush* (New York: Viking, 2004), pp. 18–19.

27. Simon Pia, "Scotsman Diary: Oiling the Wheels," *Scotsman*, September 15, 2000.

28. Heather Connon, "Cairn Builder Reaches Peak," *Observer*, January 25, 2004.

29. Author interview with Mark Vozar, November 12, 2006.

30. As noted in chapter 15, when George W. Bush's Arbusto received an infusion of more than a million dollars from Moran Exploration, Moran staffers in Midland expressed misgivings about the deal to their bosses. Years later, Dick Moran said that he did not recall putting the money into Bush's company. It is worth noting that about the time of Moran's bet on Bush's risky deal, Moran itself was benefiting from a twenty-million-dollar infusion from London American Energy (LAE), a U.K.-financed enterprise. LAE's board members included John Mackin, a Scottish American who chaired Zapata Offshore, and London American chairman Sir Alastair Down, a former head of BP who had spearheaded drilling in Alaska and who was in 1982 serving as a director of the Scottish American Investment Trust. (At least two of the companies funded by LAE, Moran and Adobe Oil and Gas, were drilling heavily off Scotland at the time.)

31. Nicholas Christian, "Bush Not Sheepish About Trick," *Scotsman*, February 20, 2005.

32. White House press release, "Interview of the President by the Times of London," June 30, 2005. Available at www.whitehouse.gov.

33. In 1998, Gammell's Cairn Energy, together with Brown and Root (then part of the Dick Cheney–run Halliburton), signed a deal to build a gas pipeline from Burma to the Indian state of Orissa with the Indian government's Oil and Natural Gas Corporation. But when India exploded its first nuclear bomb the following month, the Clinton administration imposed sanctions, which nixed the deal (and the enormous income promised by Halliburton to the brutal Burmese military regime). Still, Cairn persevered, despite conventional wisdom about India's lack of oil. A report in the *New Zealand Herald* (Paran Balakrishnan, "Proving the Critics Wrong," July 17, 2007) highlighted the improbability of Cairn's making a profit: "Ask any oilman and he will probably tell you that India is rated fairly low in the oil industry." In 1999, Cairn ended up striking oil off the west coast of India in the Gulf of Cambay—a lucrative addition to the company's already sizable natural gas interests in Bangladesh and oil wells on the Indian mainland. Enron began expanding its operations to India and was already running a privatized electrical-distribution system in Bombay. President George W. Bush took a different tack to India than Clinton, granting it a special exemption to the Nuclear Nonproliferation Treaty. By 2006, Cairn was so focused on India that Gammell became chairman of the firm's Indian subsidiary, which was listed on the Mumbai/Bombay Stock Exchange and made $1.4 billion on the market. Now, Cairn has almost 90 percent of its assets in India and Bangladesh.

34. Kevin Maguire, "Among Friends at 'Blair Petroleum,'" *Guardian*, November 9, 2001.

35. Andrew Grice, "Blair Confidante Quits Downing Street to Join BP," *Independent* (London), November 9, 2001.

36. David Rose, "Bush and Blair Made Secret Pact for Iraq War," *Observer* (London), April 4, 2004.

37. Heraldo Muñoz, *A Solitary War: A Diplomat's Chronicle of the Iraq War and Its Lessons* (Golden, CO: Fulcrum, 2008).

38. Frank Rich, *The Greatest Story Ever Sold: The Decline and Fall of Truth from 9/11 to Katrina* (New York: Penguin, 2006), p. 30.

39. Howard Kurtz, "Peter Jennings, in the News for What He Didn't Say," *Washington Post*, September 24, 2001.

40. Rich, *The Greatest Story Ever Sold*, p. 75.

41. Ibid., p. 77.

42. Ibid., p. 76.

43. John R. MacArthur, *Second Front: Censorship and Propaganda in the Gulf War* (Berkeley: University of California Press, 1992), p. 58.

44. "To Sell a War," *The Fifth Estate*, Canadian Broadcasting Corporation, January 1992.

45. Walter V. Robinson, "1-year Gap in Bush's Guard Duty," *Boston Globe*, May 23, 2000.

46. White House press release, "President Honors America's Veterans," November 11, 2003. Available at www.whitehouse.gov/news/releases/2003/11/20031111-8.html.

22: DEFLECTION FOR REELECTION

1. Katharine Q. Seelye, "Democratic Chief Says 'AWOL' Bush Will Be an Issue After a Nominee Emerges," *New York Times*, February 1, 2004.

2. George W. Bush interview with Tim Russert, *Meet the Press*, NBC, February 8, 2004.

3. United States Statutes (1971), Title 10: Armed Forces, 10 USC 843, art. 43 states, "A person charged with desertion or absence without leave in time of war, or with aiding the enemy, mutiny, or murder, may be tried and punished at any time without limitation." Failure to perform military obligations or to report for regular duty can be construed either as being AWOL or a deserter; the distinction is a technical one, made more complex by the part-time nature of National Guard service. Desertion is taken seriously by the military. Between 1998

and 2007 alone, 670 people were prosecuted for desertion. There is no statute of limitations, and deserters from the Vietnam era are still occasionally picked up and arrested. Commanders are given wide discretion on how to handle deserters, and punishment ranges all the way from counseling and pay forfeiture to—in cases of desertion in wartime—the death penalty, though no such punishment has been meted out in recent memory. The separate and distinct charge under the Uniform Code of Military Justice (UCMJ) for desertion is violation of Article 85, Desertion, UCMJ. The last service member executed for desertion was Private Eddie Slovik, shot by a firing squad in France on January 31, 1945, following his conviction for desertion under fire.

4. Bill Morlin and Karen Dorn Steele, "Bush's Partial History: Stringent Military Screening Program May Explain Gaps on President's Record," *Spokesman-Review*, March 14, 2004.

5. Based on unpublished reporting by the author and Stefanie Von Brochowski.

6. Mary Orndorff and Brett J. Blackledge, "Bush Met Military Obligation," *Birmingham News*, February 11, 2004.

7. Mike Allen and Lois Romano, "Aides Study President's Service Records; White House Won't Release More Documents Now but Is Awaiting Another Batch," *Washington Post*, February 13, 2004.

8. *Hardball with Chris Matthews*, MSNBC, February 12, 2004.

9. In 2008, Scott McClellan published his memoirs of his time working for Bush. Although he gave media interviews for his book, he did not respond to an e-mail requesting an interview for this one.

10. David Barstow, "Seeking Memories of Bush at an Alabama Air Base," *New York Times*, February 13, 2004.

11. *World News Tonight with Peter Jennings*, ABC, February 12, 2004.

12. *NBC Nightly News*, February 12, 2004.

13. Barstow, "Seeking Memories of Bush."

14. Dana Beyerle, "Friend: Bush Did Duty in Alabama," *Tuscaloosa News*, February 12, 2004.

15. Sara Rimer, Ralph Blumenthal, and Raymond Bonner, "Portrait of George Bush in '72: Unanchored in Turbulent Time," *New York Times*, September 20, 2004.

16. Retired general Walter ("Buck") Staudt, the profane, cigar-chewing commander of 147th Fighter Group; Major Dean Roome, a fellow pilot who had been Bush's roommate off base, and was now an antiques dealer; Colonel Maurice Udell, the man who taught Bush how to fly an F-102; and Colonel Albert Lloyd Jr., who had been the personnel director at Ellington and would go on the Bush campaign's payroll in mid-1999 to try to explain away the anomalies and deficiencies in Bush's records.

17. Author interview with Dean Roome, July 19, 2004.

18. Walter V. Robinson, "1-year Gap in Bush's Guard Duty," *Boston Globe*, May 23, 2000.

19. Roome and Udell had been involuntarily discharged from the Guard in the eighties, and their joint petitions for redress would eventually find their way to the commander in chief of the Texas Air National Guard, Governor George W. Bush. Udell had been thrown out of the Guard and was seeking redress in the same petition that Roome had before Governor Bush's office. At some point in the eighties Udell had been named as commander of the 147th Flight Interceptor Group, taking Buck Staudt's old job. Udell had been in the job but a short while before he was accused of harassment and impropriety by a group of officers and an enlisted NCO. Although ensuing investigations did not establish wrongdoing (per Dean Roome's letter to Governor Bush), Udell had nonetheless left the Guard involuntarily. As for Staudt, in the spring of 1972, at the precise time W. was vanishing from his Houston Guard unit, Staudt and his superior Ross Ayers were taken to task by columnist Jack Anderson for outfitting a huge Boeing KC-135 Stratotanker according to specifications supplied by Ayers's wife, so that the couple could fly off in style on a twenty-five-thousand-dollar junket to visit their daughter in Germany.

Enlisted men had carried out the refurbishment of the plane, which included a stateroom, using tax dollars to pay for it. Ayers and Staudt were also using Texas Air National Guard planes to fly businessmen and politicians to Las Vegas. Finally, Staudt, then still a colonel, had also been caught wearing the plumage of a brigadier general. After retirement, Staudt became a member of the committee that controlled the leasing of commercial space at Ellington Field, where Jim Bath had a lease and where Air Force One landed.

20. "Wolf Blitzer Reports," CNN, March 8, 2004.
21. Ken Herman, "Bush Takes Aim at Kerry During Texas Campaign Stops," *Austin American-Statesman*, March 9, 2004.
22. Author interview with Dean Roome, June 9, 2006.
23. Kate Zernike and Jim Rutenberg, "Friendly Fire: The Birth of an Attack on John Kerry," *New York Times*, August 20, 2004.
24. Media Matters for America survey, August 25, 2004, http://mediamatters.org/items/200408250006.
25. David Brock, *The Republican Noise Machine: Right-Wing Media and How It Corrupts Democracy* (New York: Crown, 2004), p. 110.
26. Frank Rich, *The Greatest Story Ever Sold: The Decline and Fall of Truth in Bush's America* (New York: Penguin, 2007), p. 137.
27. Mary Mapes, *Truth and Duty: The Press, the President, and the Privilege of Power* (New York: St. Martin's, 2005), pp. 212–15.
28. Mapes, *Truth and Duty*, p. 169.
29. David Rubien, "Seymour Hersh," Salon.com, January 18, 2000.
30. John Carlin, "What the Movie Star Did Not Say to the President," *Independent* (London), October 19, 1997.
31. "New Questions on Bush Guard Duty," *CBS News*, September 20, 2004.
32. Message board post by "TankerKC," FreeRepublic.com, September 8, 2004, 17:19:00 PDT.
33. Message board post by "Buckhead," FreeRepublic.com, September 8, 2004, 23:59:43 EDT.
34. Stephen F. Hayes, "Is It a Hoax?" *Weekly Standard*, September 9, 2004.
35. Message board post by "Buckhead," FreeRepublic.com, September 9, 2004, 22:51:04 EDT.
36. Message board post by "NYCVirago," FreeRepublic.com, September 9, 2004, 23:02:27 EDT.
37. Message board post by "Barlowmaker," FreeRepublic.com, September 9, 2004, 23:06:26 EDT.
38. Peter Wallsten, "GOP Activist Made Allegations on CBS Memos," *Los Angeles Times*, September 18, 2004.
39. Mapes, *Truth and Duty*, pp. 237–40.
40. There was even a historic Bush connection. Bush family investment bank Brown Brothers Harriman had played a key role in helping CBS chief executive William Paley expand the network, and Paley's good friend Prescott Bush had sat on the CBS board for two decades.
41. Neil Gough, "10 Questions for Sumner Redstone," *Time*, September 26, 2004.
42. George H. W. Bush interview with Dan Rather, *CBS Evening News*, January 25, 1988.

23: DOMESTIC DISTURBANCE

1. These included Kuwait and Saudi Arabia, along with funds from Texas oil baron Edwin L. Cox Sr. and other tycoons. See Michael Weisskopf, "A Pardon, a Presidential Library, a Big Donation," *Time*, March 6, 2001. The Texas A&M Foundation has also taken in excess of one million dollars from the ExxonMobil Foundation. See Texas A&M Newswire, "ExxonMobil Foundation Presents $1 Million to Texas A&M Foundation," press release, June 26, 2008.
2. Baker IV was counsel for the Justice Department's Office of Intelligence Policy and Review.

3. Author interview with Steven Aftergood, February 2002.

4. Michael Abramowitz, "Rove E-Mail Sought by Congress May Be Missing," *Washington Post*, April 13, 2007.

5. Richard L. Berke, "The Last (E-Mail) Goodbye, from 'gwb' to His 42 Buddies," *New York Times*, March 17, 2001.

6. Barton Gellman and Jo Becker, "Angler: The Cheney Vice Presidency," *Washington Post*, June 24, 2007.

7. Foreign Intelligence Surveillance Act (FISA) annual reports to Congress, available through the Federation of American Scientists, www.fas.org/irp/agency/doj/fisa/#rept.

8. In 2001, the USA Patriot Act expanded FISA, allowing the government access to personal records of all Americans from Internet service providers and libraries. Meanwhile, the National Security Agency was authorized by W. to eavesdrop domestically on both phone calls and e-mails without a warrant, even forgoing the prior setup's allowance of a seventy-two-hour window for a Foreign Intelligence Surveillance Court to approve the wiretapping retroactively. Now the NSA did not need to provide any form of evidence, as the 2007 Protect America Act (PAA) granted even more expansive surveillance powers to W.'s administration. When the Democratic-controlled Congress allowed the PAA to expire in February 2007, Republicans reproached the Democrats as being soft on terrorism, leading to the passing of a new FISA bill in 2008. The Democrats, sensing that their only chance at regaining power lay in showing their "security credentials," still were reluctant to take the issue on, even with Bush an unpopular lame duck. In July 2008, Congress voted to expand the government's surveillance powers and give immunity to telecommunications companies that cooperated with President Bush's illegal snooping. In May 2008, the *Los Angeles Times* would report on the sizable gap between the administration's efforts and its results. One study found that terrorism and national security cases initiated by the Justice Department were down 19 percent from 2006. At the same time, the number of warrants requested for eavesdropping on suspected terrorists had risen by 9 percent. The article described this as "further evidence that the government has compromised the privacy rights of ordinary citizens without much to show for it." Richard B. Schmitt, "Spying Up, but Terror Cases Drop," *Los Angeles Times*, May 12, 2008.

9. Wilson had been deputy chief of mission in Iraq during the first Gulf War under Poppy Bush and had been sent to Niger under W. to investigate claims that Saddam had sought so-called yellowcake uranium.

10. Robert Bryce, "Top-Secret Cronies," Salon.com, November 17, 2005.

11. By summer 2008, reports were emerging that some State Department officials had objected to the contract because it undermined the authority of the Iraqi government, while others in the administration appeared to have given Hunt the go-ahead. A *New York Times* article mentioned in passing that Hunt had notified fellow members of the PFIAB of its drilling plans, though the article does not explore why Hunt was on that board or what exactly the board's role is in the intersection between business and intelligence. James Glanz and Richard A. Oppel Jr., "Panel Questions State Dept. Role in Iraq Oil Deal," *New York Times*, July 3, 2008.

12. Editorial, "That Troubled Terrorism List," *New York Times*, August 24, 2008.

13. After British police uncovered a possible transatlantic attack plot in August 2006 and sought to conduct further surveillance in hopes of bagging a larger network, the Bush administration demanded an immediate raid and high-profile arrests. Thus, W. was able to cite the operation in his weekly radio address, just three months before the midterm elections. He admonished Americans that "we must never make the mistake of thinking the danger of terrorism has passed" (office of the Press Secretary, President's Radio Address, August 12, 2006, http://www .whitehouse.gov/news/releases/2006/08/20060812.html). Aram Roston, Lisa Myers, and the

NBC News Investigative Unit, "U.S., U.K. at Odds over Timing of Arrests," *NBC Nightly News,* August 14, 2006.

14. Karl Rove's friend Ken Tomlinson, formerly of *Reader's Digest,* was appointed to head the Corporation for Public Broadcasting (CPB), where he hired a crony to "investigate" programs, such as *Now with Bill Moyers,* that he thought reflected a liberal bias. Tomlinson was brought in to supervise broadcasting following a career spent almost entirely working his way to the helm at the politically conservative magazine *Reader's Digest,* where among other things, he served in the propaganda post of "Vietnam correspondent." Tomlinson resigned from the *Digest* in 1996 to work on the presidential campaign of Steve Forbes, whose philosophy centered on the inherent pride in inheriting wealth. His eventual rise to U.S. broadcasting czar was undoubtedly smoothed back in 1995 when PBS agreed to accept seventy-five million dollars in *Reader's Digest*–developed programming, part of a desperate effort by the network to replace dwindling federal contributions. Tomlinson's inquiry into the Moyers program included a $14,170 study that subjectively classified guests as "liberal" or "conservative" and gave segments labels like "anti-Bush," "anti-DeLay," and "anti-corporation." Tom DeLay was at the time the highly partisan and outspoken House majority leader, dubbed "the Hammer" for his fierce approach to dealing with opponents. Meanwhile, Tomlinson raised five million dollars to air *The Journal Editorial Report,* a program that showcased unfailingly pro-Bush, pro-DeLay, pro-corporation *Wall Street Journal* editorial board figures. (The show soon jumped to the more ideologically resonant Fox News Channel.) Tomlinson would later be forced to resign from the CPB. Like Michael Brown at FEMA, Tomlinson also had some problems over horses. Investigators say that while heading the Broadcasting Board of Governors, the outfit that oversees U.S. foreign broadcasting, including the Voice of America, Tomlinson ran a "horseracing operation." He seems to have been using his office to oversee a stable of horses he named after Afghan leaders who fought the Taliban and the Russians.

15. Drew Griffin and Kathleen Johnston, "Political Author's Name Matches Name on Terrorist Watch List," CNN.com, http://www.cnn.com/2008/SHOWBIZ/books/08/14/author.terror.list/index.html.

16. Tom Hamburger and Peter Wallsten, *One Party Country: The Republican Plan for Dominance in the 21st Century* (Hoboken, NJ: Wiley, 2006), p. 102.

17. William Hubbard, "The Overwhelmed FDA," *Boston Globe,* June 3, 2007.

18. Editorial, "The F.D.A. in Crisis: It Needs More Money and Talent," *New York Times,* February 3, 2008.

19. Editorial, "More Flimflam on Warming," *New York Times,* March 29, 2008.

20. Andrew C. Revkin, "Climate Expert Says NASA Tried to Silence Him," *New York Times,* January 29, 2006.

21. Office of the Press Secretary, "President Bush Visits Cleveland, Ohio," White House press release, July 10, 2007, www.whitehouse.gov/news/releases/2007/07/20070710-6.html.

22. Paul Krugman, "An Immoral Philosophy," *New York Times,* July 30, 2007.

23. Paul Krugman, "The Anxiety Election," *New York Times,* March 7, 2008.

24. "Welcome to the Hackocracy," *New Republic,* October 17, 2005.

25. Frank Rich, "Bring Back Warren Harding," *New York Times,* September 26, 2005.

26. Michelle Malkin, "Not Another Homeland Security Hack," September 21, 2005.

27. Charles Duhigg, "Report Rejects Medicare Boast of Paring Fraud," *New York Times,* August 20, 2008.

28. Silverado was finally shut down the day after Poppy's election as president, which hints at backdoor political maneuvering to delay a major Bush scandal. At one press conference, Neil stood defiant, repeating over and over that there had been no conflict of interest, despite his loan of

over a hundred million dollars to business partners who also invested in his oil ventures. "Even in the face of irrefutable evidence that everyone but he seemed to understand," wrote financial reporter Steven Wilmsen, "he seemed to believe it was his birthright to profit at the nation's expense." Steven Wilmsen, "The Corruption of Neil Bush," *Playboy*, June 1, 1991.

29. Kevin Phillips, *American Dynasty: Aristocracy, Fortune and the Politics of Deceit in the House of Bush* (New York: Penguin, 2004), p. 130.

30. "No Bush Left Behind," *BusinessWeek*, October 16, 2006.

31. Rupert Cornwell, "President's Uncle Bucky Emerges as a Big Winner from Iraq War," *Independent*, February 24, 2005. The Pentagon's inspector general announced a review of $158 million worth of contracts to ESSI, for suspected "anomalies," referring specifically to questionable "relationships and the sole source nature" of the deal. (Letter from Henry A. Waxman to Donald Rumsfeld, April 5, 2006.) Meanwhile, Uncle Bucky claimed to have never used his family to help his company win contracts, stating, "I don't make any calls to the 202 area code." Bucky Bush served as Missouri state chairman for W.'s 2004 reelection campaign.

32. Walter F. Roche Jr., "Company's Work in Iraq Profited Bush's Uncle," *Los Angeles Times*, February 23, 2005. The company later faced inquiries into how it had acquired its government business. Bucky Bush sold his options in January 2005 for around $450,000, just as the shares hit a record $60.39 per share.

33. Ladd was made a partner in the Monroe, Louisiana–based Pro Set Inc., which makes spray-on plastic coating, or polyurea. Up until a certain point, Pro Set was a pretty obscure operation. Its projects included working on the roof of the Louisiana Baptist Children's Home and getting rid of the odor from the bathrooms of a minor league baseball team. Then, in late 2000, as the presidential general election approached and George Bush was locked in a close race with Al Gore, Pro Set began getting work from military contractors. Soon, naval research offices were reporting that in tests, hardened polyurea coating had been found to stop large-caliber bullets and protect a dummy driver when a Humvee gets bombed. After 9/11, Pro Set also began stressing the value of its product in reducing federal bomb-proofing requirements.

34. "Trade-off for Speech Fee Pays Off for Bush," *Los Angeles Times*, March 20, 1999.

35. Leslie Wayne, "Elder Bush in Big G.O.P. Cast Toiling for Top Equity Firm," *New York Times*, March 5, 2001.

36. Dan Briody, *The Iron Triangle: Inside the Secret World of the Carlyle Group* (Hoboken, NJ: Wiley, 2003), p. 120.

37. Naomi Klein, *The Shock Doctrine: The Rise of Disaster Capitalism* (New York: Metropolitan, 2007), pp. 400–401.

38. The administration wanted its attorneys to concentrate on voter fraud, an issue that can disenfranchise the poor, the elderly, and recent immigrants—all groups that tend to vote Democrat.

39. Eric Lichtblau, "Mukasey Won't Pursue Charges in Hiring Inquiry," *New York Times*, August 12, 2008.

40. Bill Minutaglio, *The President's Counselor: The Rise to Power of Alberto Gonzales* (New York: HarperCollins, 2006), p. 105. Heavy criticism from both conservatives and liberals over an array of concerns forced Miers to withdraw her name from contention for a spot on the high court.

41. Eric Lipton, "Worker Tells of Response by FEMA," *New York Times*, October 21, 2005.

42. Stickney had been had been an engineer in the Environmental Protection Agency and later headed New Hampshire's Department of Transportation.

43. Author interview with Trey Reid, September 8, 2005.

44. Steve Kanstoroom, an independent fraud-detection and pattern-recognition expert with twenty-two years' experience, found that FEMA was allowing insurance adjusters to use software that

set artificially low settlement amounts for flood victims, and that the claims-assessment process was deeply compromised by involvement from insurance-industry figures.

45. Author interview with Steve Kanstoroom, September 8, 2005.

46. In 2002, when an ice storm hit Allbaugh's native Kay County, Oklahoma, Joe Allbaugh arranged a conference call with county officials, who ended up choosing the Florida-based environmental services firm AshBritt Inc. over other firms with much lower competing bids. Later, AshBritt hired Barbour Griffith—and was awarded a $568 million contract by the Army Corps of Engineers to help lead the Katrina cleanup effort. The months after the hurricane saw numerous articles in local media raising questions about AshBritt's operations, its candor, and its spectacular growth during the Bush years—all through its lucrative subcontracts to other firms that do most of the actual cleanup work.

    On August 15, 2005, with hurricane season getting under way, Joe and Diane's Allbaugh Company registered as a lobbyist for Shaw Group, a Baton Rouge engineering and construction firm, which began advertising for workers to man its rebuilding projects before Katrina even struck. After the levees broke, Shaw, which had not been a FEMA contractor during the Clinton years, received two separate hundred-million-dollar federal cleanup contracts and saw its stock price shoot up 50 percent in a few weeks. (After Brown departed FEMA, the agency announced it would rebid some contracts that were given on a noncompetitive basis, including Shaw's. Allbaugh continued to be well rewarded: according to federal lobbyist registrations, the Shaw group paid Allbaugh Company three hundred thousand dollars in the first six months of 2007 alone.)

47. Barbour was elected governor of Mississippi in 2004, which put him in the limelight as he led Hurricane Katrina recovery efforts in his devastated state.

48. Lolita C. Baldor, "Halliburton Subsidiary Taps Contract for Repairs," *Washington Post*, September 5, 2005.

49. Simon Romero, "Halliburton, in Iraq for the Long Haul, Recruits Employees Eager for Work," *New York Times*, April 24, 2004.

50. Barton Gellman, *Angler: The Cheney Vice Presidency* (New York: Penguin Press, 2008).

51. Michel Crozier, Samuel Huntington, and Joji Watanuki, *The Crisis of Democracy* (New York: New York University Press, 1975), p. 105. Also noted in Peter Dale Scott, *The Road to 9/11* (Berkeley: University of California Press, 2007), p. 69.

52. Tim London, "Emergency Management in the Twenty-first Century," www.homestead.com/emergencymanagement/files/21STCEN2.htm.

53. Barton Gellman and Susan Schmidt, "Shadow Government Is at Work in Secret," *Washington Post*, March 1, 2002.

54. Sabrina Eaton, "Interior Officials Join Cheney in Mountain Hideaways," *Cleveland Plain Dealer*, October 7, 2001.

55. Executive Order 12656, "Assignment of Emergency Preparedness Responsibilities," National Archives, www.archives.gov/federal-register/codification/executive-order/12656.html.

56. Andrew Cockburn, *Rumsfeld: His Rise, Fall, and Catastrophic Legacy* (New York: Scribner, 2007), p. 88.

57. Ron Suskind, *The One Percent Doctrine: Deep Inside America's Pursuit of Its Enemies Since 9/11* (New York: Simon & Schuster, 2006).

58. Rachel L. Swarns, "Halliburton Subsidiary Gets Contract to Add Temporary Immigration Detention Centers," *New York Times*, February 4, 2006.

59. Al Kamen, "At FEMA, 'X' Is for Exasperation," *Washington Post*, June 24, 1998.

60. In December, with the country focused on terrorism and on preventing any more attacks, Magaw left FEMA altogether, at the White House's request, to help start the Transportation Security Administration.

61. *CNN Sunday Morning*, November 27, 2005.

62. Brown moved quickly after his arrival in Edmond into a job with the state legislature, where he helped draft legislation creating the Oklahoma Municipal Power Authority (OMPA), a little-known public-power entity that he would later chair. The attraction of the unpaid OMPA position was that it allowed him to interact with major bond-underwriting firms, all clamoring for the group's lucrative business. When Brown was forced to relinquish his seat on the utility board because he had moved from Edmond, he found his way back by persuading the town of Goltry, Oklahoma, with a population of eight hundred and one stoplight, to join the energy consortium and make him its representative.

63. Author interview with Stephen Jones, October 2, 2005.

64. Author interview with Karl Hart, October 10, 2005.

65. Author interview with James Van Dyke, October 7, 2005.

66. Author interview with Andrew Lester, October 4, 2005.

67. Sally Kestin and Megan O'Matz, "FEMA Gave $21 Million in Miami-Dade, Where Storms Were 'Like a Severe Thunderstorm,'" *South Florida Sun-Sentinel*, October 10, 2004.

68. Author interview with Kim Jeffery, October 12, 2005.

69. Julia Malone, "Bill for FEMA water disputed; Norcross business may be ordered to refund $881,000," *Atlanta Journal-Constitution*, July 25, 2007.

Index

A Note on the Author

Award-winning investigative journalist Russ Baker has written for the *New Yorker*, *Vanity Fair*, the *New York Times*, the *Nation*, the *Los Angeles Times*, the *Washington Post*, and *Esquire*, and served as contributing editor for *Columbia Journalism Review*. In 2005, he founded the Real News Project, a nonprofit investigative news organization. His exclusive reporting on George W. Bush's military record received a 2005 Deadline Club award.